Applying Big Data Analytics in Bioinformatics and Medicine

Miltiadis D. Lytras
Deree – The American College of Greece, Greece

Paraskevi Papadopoulou
Deree – The American College of Greece, Greece

A volume in the Advances in Bioinformatics and
Biomedical Engineering (ABBE) Book Series

Published in the United States of America by
    IGI Global
    Medical Information Science Reference (an imprint of IGI Global)
    701 E. Chocolate Avenue
    Hershey PA, USA 17033
    Tel: 717-533-8845
    Fax: 717-533-8661
    E-mail: cust@igi-global.com
    Web site: http://www.igi-global.com

Library of Congress Cataloging-in-Publication Data

Names: Lytras, Miltiadis D., 1973- editor. | Papadopoulou, Paraskevi, 1961-
  editor.
Title: Applying big data analytics in bioinformatics and medicine / Miltiadis
  D. Lytras and Paraskevi Papadopoulou, editors.
Description: Hershey PA : Medical Information Science Reference, [2018] |
  Includes bibliographical references and index.
Identifiers: LCCN 2017006764| ISBN 9781522526070 (hardcover) | ISBN
  9781522526087 (ebook)
Subjects: | MESH: Databases, Factual | Computational Biology | Medical
  Records Systems, Computerized | Organizational Culture
Classification: LCC QH324.2 | NLM W 26.55.I4 | DDC 570.285--dc23 LC record available at https://lccn.loc.
gov/2017006764

This book is published in the IGI Global book series Advances in Bioinformatics and Biomedical Engineering (ABBE) (ISSN: 2327-7033; eISSN: 2327-7041)

British Cataloguing in Publication Data
A Cataloguing in Publication record for this book is available from the British Library.

All work contributed to this book is new, previously-unpublished material. The views expressed in this book are those of the authors, but not necessarily of the publisher.

For electronic access to this publication, please contact: eresources@igi-global.com.

Advances in Bioinformatics and Biomedical Engineering (ABBE) Book Series

Ahmad Taher Azar
Benha University, Egypt

ISSN:2327-7033
EISSN:2327-7041

MISSION

The fields of biology and medicine are constantly changing as research evolves and novel engineering applications and methods of data analysis are developed. Continued research in the areas of bioinformatics and biomedical engineering is essential to continuing to advance the available knowledge and tools available to medical and healthcare professionals.

The **Advances in Bioinformatics and Biomedical Engineering (ABBE) Book Series** publishes research on all areas of bioinformatics and bioengineering including the development and testing of new computational methods, the management and analysis of biological data, and the implementation of novel engineering applications in all areas of medicine and biology. Through showcasing the latest in bioinformatics and biomedical engineering research, ABBE aims to be an essential resource for healthcare and medical professionals.

COVERAGE

- Data Analysis
- Genetics
- Protein Structure
- Orthopedic Bioengineering
- Genetic Engineering
- Finite Elements
- Biomedical Sensors
- Structural Biology
- Prosthetic Limbs
- Tissue Engineering

IGI Global is currently accepting manuscripts for publication within this series. To submit a proposal for a volume in this series, please contact our Acquisition Editors at Acquisitions@igi-global.com or visit: http://www.igi-global.com/publish/.

Titles in this Series

For a list of additional titles in this series, please visit: www.igi-global.com/book-series

Comparative Approaches to Biotechnology Development and Use in Developed and Emerging Nations
Tomas Gabriel Bas (University of Talca, Chile) and Jingyuan Zhao (University of Toronto, Canada)
Medical Information Science Reference ● copyright 2017 ● 592pp ● H/C (ISBN: 9781522510406) ● US $205.00
(our price)

Computational Tools and Techniques for Biomedical Signal Processing
Butta Singh (Guru Nanak Dev University, India)
Medical Information Science Reference ● copyright 2017 ● 415pp ● H/C (ISBN: 9781522506607) ● US $225.00
(our price)

Handbook of Research on Computational Intelligence Applications in Bioinformatics
Sujata Dash (North Orissa University, India) and Bidyadhar Subudhi (National Institute of Technology, India)
Medical Information Science Reference ● copyright 2016 ● 514pp ● H/C (ISBN: 9781522504276) ● US $230.00
(our price)

Applying Business Intelligence to Clinical and Healthcare Organizations
José Machado (University of Minho, Portugal) and António Abelha (University of Minho, Portugal)
Medical Information Science Reference ● copyright 2016 ● 347pp ● H/C (ISBN: 9781466698826) ● US $165.00
(our price)

Biomedical Image Analysis and Mining Techniques for Improved Health Outcomes
Wahiba Ben Abdessalem Karâa (Taif University, Saudi Arabia & RIADI-GDL Laboratory, ENSI, Tunisia) and
Nilanjan Dey (Department of Information Technology, Techno India College of Technology, Kolkata, India)
Medical Information Science Reference ● copyright 2016 ● 414pp ● H/C (ISBN: 9781466688117) ● US $225.00
(our price)

Big Data Analytics in Bioinformatics and Healthcare
Baoying Wang (Waynesburg University, USA) Ruowang Li (Pennsylvania State University, USA) and William
Perrizo (North Dakota State University, USA)
Medical Information Science Reference ● copyright 2015 ● 528pp ● H/C (ISBN: 9781466666115) ● US $255.00
(our price)

701 East Chocolate Avenue, Hershey, PA 17033, USA
Tel: 717-533-8845 x100 ● Fax: 717-533-8661
E-Mail: cust@igi-global.com ● www.igi-global.com

Table of Contents

Section 1
Introduction to Bioinformatics in Medicine and Medical Systems

Detailed Table of Contents

Section 1
Introduction to Bioinformatics in Medicine and Medical Systems

This section covers topics related to inferring gene function from expression data, genome sequence data, integrating expression data with other genome-wide data for functional annotation, functional study of specific molecular and pathway analysis, genome annotation and comparative genomics bioinformatics algorithm and tool development, RNAseq and microarray gene expression data analysis, gene regulatory network construction and Next-Generation Sequencing (NGS) analysis. Furthermore, this section covers topics related to translational bioinformatics, protein sequencing and classification, protein structure prediction, protein function analysis, protein interactions, protein subcellular localization prediction.

The emerging advances of Bioinformatics have already contributed toward the establishment of better next generation medicine and medical systems by putting emphasis on improvement of prognosis, diagnosis and therapy of diseases including better management of medical systems. The purpose of this chapter is to explore ways by which the use of Bioinformatics and Smart Data Analysis will provide an overview and solutions to challenges in the fields of genomics, medicine and Health Informatics. The focus of this chapter would be on Smart Data Analysis and ways needed to filter out the noise. The chapter addresses challenges researchers and data analysts are facing in terms of the developed computational methods used to extract insights from NGS and high-throughput screening data. In this chapter the concept "Wise Data" is proposed reflecting the distinction between individual health and wellness on the one hand, and social improvement, cohesion and sustainability on the other, leading to more effective medical systems, healthier individuals and more socially cohesive societies.

This chapter describes the overview of bioinformatics; bioinformatics, data mining, and data visualization; bioinformatics and secretome analysis; bioinformatics, mass spectrometry, and chemical cross-linking reagents; bioinformatics and Software Product Line (SPL); bioinformatics and protein kinase; bioinformatics and MicroRNAs (miRNAs); and clinical bioinformatics and cancer. Bioinformatics is the application of computer technology to the management and analysis of biological data. Bioinformatics is an interdisciplinary research area that is the interface between biology and computer science. The primary goal of bioinformatics is to reveal the wealth of biological information hidden in the large amounts of data and obtain a clearer insight into the fundamental biology of organisms. Bioinformatics entails the creation and advancement of databases, algorithms, computational and statistical techniques, and theory to solve the formal and practical problems arising from the management and analysis of biological data.

The great disagreement between the number of known protein sequences and the number of experimentally determined protein structures indicate an enormous necessity of rapid and accurate protein structure prediction methods. Computational techniques such as comparative modeling, threading and *ab initio* modelling allow swift protein structure prediction with sufficient accuracy. The three phases of computational protein structure prediction comprise: the pre-modelling analysis phase, model construction and post-modelling refinement. Protein modelling is primarily comparative or *ab initio*. Comparative or template-based methods such as homology and threading-based modelling require structural templates for constructing the structure of a target sequence. The *ab initio* is a template-free modelling approach which proceeds by satisfying various physics-based and knowledge-based parameters. The chapter will elaborate on the three phases of modelling, the programs available for performing each, issues, possible solutions and future research areas.

Chapter 4

The idea of personalized medicine system is an evolution of holistic approach of treatment and in more evidence based manner. The chapter begins with an introduction of how body system works naturally and impact of modern medicine on overall health, followed by a historical background and brief review of literature providing the description that the concept of personalized medicine is not new but a very old ideology which stayed neglected until the development in the field of medical genetics, followed by the role of omics in modern medicine, the comparison of modern medicine and personalized medicine, medical concepts relevant to proteomics in personalized medicine, impact of proteomics in drug development and clinical safety and finally closing the chapter with future prospects and challenges of proteomics in personalized medicine.

Chapter 5

Sushma Munugala, Charles Sturt University, Australia

Gagandeep K. Brar, Charles Sturt University, Australia

Ali Syed, Charles Sturt University, Australia

Azeem Mohammad, Charles Sturt University, Australia

Malka N. Halgamuge, Charles Sturt University, Australia

Cloud computing has shifted our old documents up into the clouds, with the advancement of technology. Fast-growing virtual document storage platforms provide amenities with minimal expense in the corporate society. Despite living in the 20th century, even the first world countries have issues with the maintenance of document storage. Cloud computing resolves this issue for business and clinic owners as it banishes the requirement of planning, provisioning, and allows corporations to advance their filling system according to service demands. Medical practices heavily, rely on document storage as; almost all information contained in medical files is stored in a printed format. Medical practices urgently need to revolutionize their storage standards, to keep up with the growing population. The traditional method of paper storage in medical practice has completely been obsolete and needs to improve in order to assist patients with faster diagnosis in critical situations. Obtaining Knowledge and sharing it is an important part of medical practice, so it needs immediate attention to reach its full service potential. This chapter has analyzed content from literature that highlights issues regarding data storage and recommends solution. This inquiry has found a useful tool that can be beneficial for the development of this problem which is, 'data mining' as it gives the option of predictive, and preventative health care options, when medical data is searched. The functionality and worthiness of each algorithm and methods are also determined in this study. By using cloud and big data services to improve the analysis of medical data in network of regional health information system, has huge advancements that assure convenient management, easy extension, flexible investment, and low requirements for low technical based private medical units.

Section 2
Bioinformatics in the Fields of Genomics and Proteomics as Applied to Medicine, Health Issues, and Medical Systems

This section covers topics related to computational systems biology, machine learning in protein fold recognition, integrative data analysis, structural class prediction of protein, functional study of specific molecular and pathway analysis, data mining in proteomics, homology detection and sequence alignment methods, protein expression analysis, protein sequencing and classification, molecular dynamics simulation, protein docking and drug design, homology detection and sequence alignment methods, multiscale network construction. Environment and health issues as related to integration of big data analytics with bioinformatics, integrated exposure modelling assimilation of exposure measurements and human biomonitoring, data statistics and big data analytics for exposome-wide association studies.

Chapter 6

Dimosthenis A. Sarigiannis, Aristotle University of Thessaloniki, Greece

Spyros P. Karakitsios, Aristotle University of Thessaloniki, Greece

Evangelos Handakas, Aristotle University of Thessaloniki, Greece

Krystalia Papadaki, Aristotle University of Thessaloniki, Greece

Dimitris Chapizanis, Aristotle University of Thessaloniki, Greece

Alberto Gotti, Aristotle University of Thessaloniki, Greece

This chapter provides a comprehensive overview of the state of the art and beyond regarding modelling and data analytics towards refined external and internal exposure assessment, for elucidating the human exposome. This includes methods for more accurate measurement of personal exposure (using wearable sensors) and for extrapolation to larger population groups (agent-based modelling). A key component in the modern risk and health impact assessment is the translation of external exposure into internal exposure metrics, accounting for age, gender, genetic and route of exposure dependent differences. The applicability of biokinetics covering a large chemical space is enhanced using quantitative structure activity relationships, especially when the latter are estimated using machine learning tools. Finally, comprehensive biomonitoring data interpretation and assimilation are supported by exposure reconstruction algorithms coupled with biokinetics

Chapter 7

Dimosthenis A. Sarigiannis, Aristotle University of Thessaloniki, Greece
Alberto Gotti, Aristotle University of Thessaloniki, Greece
Evangelos Handakas, Aristotle University of Thessaloniki, Greece
Spyros P. Karakitsios, Aristotle University of Thessaloniki, Greece

This chapter aims at outlining the current state of science in the field of computational exposure biology and in particular at demonstrating how the bioinformatics techniques and algorithms can be used to support the association between environmental exposures and human health and the deciphering of the molecular and metabolic pathways of induced toxicity related to environmental chemical stressors. Examples of the integrated bioinformatics analyses outlined herein are given concerning exposure to airborne chemical mixtures, to organic compounds frequently found in consumer goods, and to mixtures of organic chemicals and metals through multiple exposure pathways. Advanced bioinformatics are coupled with big data analytics to perform studies of exposome-wide associations with putative adverse health outcomes. In conclusion, the chapter gives the reader an outline of the available computational tools and paves the way towards the development of future comprehensive applications that are expected to support efficiently exposome research in the 21st century.

Chapter 8

Ankush Bansal, Jaypee University of Information Technology, India
Pulkit Anupam Srivastava, Jaypee University of Information Technology, India

A lot of omics data is generated in a recent decade which flooded the internet with transcriptomic, genomics, proteomics and metabolomics data. A number of software, tools, and web-servers have developed to analyze the big data omics. This review integrates the various methods that have been employed over the years to interpret the gene regulatory and metabolic networks. It illustrates random networks, scale-free networks, small world network, bipartite networks and other topological analysis which fits in biological networks. Transcriptome to metabolome network is of interest because of key enzymes identification and regulatory hub genes prediction. It also provides an insight into the understanding of omics technologies, generation of data and impact of in-silico analysis on the scientific community.

    Aditi Gangopadhyay, Jhargram Raj College, India
    Hirak Jyoti Chakraborty, Central Inland Fisheries Research Institute, India
    Abhijit Datta, Department of Botany, Jhargram Raj College, India

Protein docking is integral to structure-based drug design and molecular biology. The recent surge of big data in biology, the demand for personalised medicines, evolving pathogens and increasing lifestyle-associated risks, asks for smart, robust, low-cost and high-throughput drug design. Computer-aided drug design techniques allow rapid screening of ultra-large chemical libraries within minutes. This is immensely necessary to the drug discovery pipeline, which is presently burdened with high attrition rates, failures, huge capital and time investment. With increasing drug resistance and difficult druggable targets, there is a growing need for novel drug scaffolds which is partly satisfied by fragment based drug design and *de novo* methods. The chapter discusses various aspects of protein docking and emphasises on its application in drug design.

Section 3
Big Data Analytics for Medical and Health informatics

This section covers topics related to health analytics and informatics, medical and health informatics by using "-omics" data, system biology, disease control, predictive model of disease state, translational medicine, drug design, combinatorial drug discovery, proteomics in personalized medicine, image processing including medical imaging, healthcare and healthcare delivery, healthcare policy research, healthcare outcomes research, monitoring and evaluation, hospital information system, Electronic Medical Record and Electronic Health Record, population health management, decision support systems, telemedicine, Human-Machine Interfaces, ICT, Ageing and Disability, Mobile technologies for Healthcare applications (m-Health), Evaluation and use of Healthcare IT, Health Knowledge Management, Healthcare Management and Information Systems, Software Systems in Medicine, Data Mining and Visualization, Virtual Healthcare Teams, e-Health for Public Health integrating genetics with e-health.

    Marco Spruit, Utrecht University, The Netherlands
    Max Lammertink, Utrecht University, The Netherlands

This research focuses on the design process of an effective and efficient dashboard which displays management information for an Electronic Health Record (EHR) in Dutch long-term and chronic healthcare. It presents the actual design and realization of a management dashboard for the YBoard 2.0 system, which is a popular solution on the Dutch market. The design decisions in this investigation were based on human perception and computer interaction theory, in particular Gestalt theory. The empirical interviews with medical professionals supplemented valuable additional insights into what the users wanted to see most of all in a dashboard in their daily practices. This study successfully shows how effective and efficient dashboard design can benefit from theoretical insights related to human perception and computer interaction such as Gestalt theory, in combination with integrated end user requirements from daily practices.

Chapter 11

M. Saqib Nawaz, Peking University, China
Raza Ul Mustafa, COMSATS Institute of IT, Sahiwal, Pakistan
M. Ikram Ullah Lali, University of Sargodha, Pakistan

Search engines and social media are two different online data sources where search engines can provide health related queries logs and Internet users' discuss their diseases, symptoms, causes, preventions and even suggest treatment by sharing their views, experiences and opinions on social media. This chapter hypothesizes that online data from Google and Twitter can provide vital first-hand healthcare information. An approach is provided for collecting twitter data by exploring contextual information gleaned from Google search queries logs. Furthermore, it is investigated that whether it is possible to use tweets to track, monitor and predict diseases, especially Influenza epidemics. Obtained results show that healthcare institutes and professional's uses social media to provide up-to date health related information and interact with public. Moreover, proposed approach is beneficial for extracting useful information regarding disease symptoms, side effects, medications and to track geographical location of epidemics affected area.

Chapter 12

Nesma Settouti, Tlemcen University, Algeria
Mostafa El Habib Daho, Tlemcen University, Algeria
Mohammed El Amine Bechar, Tlemcen University, Algeria
Mohammed Amine Chikh, Tlemcen University, Algeria

The semi-supervised learning is one of the most interesting fields for research developments in the machine learning domain beyond the scope of supervised learning from data. Medical diagnostic process works mostly in supervised mode, but in reality, we are in the presence of a large amount of unlabeled samples and a small set of labeled examples characterized by thousands of features. This problem is known under the term "the curse of dimensionality". In this study, we propose, as solution, a new approach in semi-supervised learning that we would call Optim Co-forest. The Optim Co-forest algorithm combines the re-sampling data approach with two selection strategies. The first one involves selecting random subset of parameters to construct the ensemble of classifiers following the principle of Co-forest. The second strategy is an extension of the importance measure of Random Forest (RF). Experiments on high dimensional datasets confirm the power of the adopted selection strategies in the scalability of our method.

    Jesús Manuel Puentes Gutiérrez, Universidad de Alcalá, Spain
    Salvador Sánchez-Alonso, Universidad de Alcalá, Spain
    Miguel-Angel Sicilia, University of Alcalá, Spain
    Elena García Barriocanal, Universidad de Alcalá, Spain

Predicting patterns to extract knowledge can be a tough task but it is worth. When you want to accomplish that task you have to take your time analysing all the data you have and you have to adapt it to the algorithms and technologies you are going to use after analysing. So you need to know the type of data that you own. When you have finished making the analysis, you also need to know what you want to find out and, therefore, which methodologies you are going to use to accomplish your objectives. At the end of this chapter you can see a real case making all that process. In particular, a Classification problem is shown as an example when using machine learning methodologies to find out if a hospital patient should be admitted or not in Cardiology department.

    Prativa Agarwalla, Heritage Institute of Technology, India
    Sumitra Mukhopadhyay, Institute of Radiophysics and Electronics, India

Pathway information for cancer detection helps to find co-regulated gene groups whose collective expression is strongly associated with cancer development. In this paper, a collaborative multi-swarm binary particle swarm optimization (MS-BPSO) based gene selection technique is proposed that outperforms to identify the pathway marker genes. We have compared our proposed method with various statistical and pathway based gene selection techniques for different popular cancer datasets as well as a detailed comparative study is illustrated using different meta-heuristic algorithms like binary coded particle swarm optimization (BPSO), binary coded differential evolution (BDE), binary coded artificial bee colony (BABC) and genetic algorithm (GA). Experimental results show that the proposed MS-BPSO based method performs significantly better and the improved multi swarm concept generates a good subset of pathway markers which provides more effective insight to the gene-disease association with high accuracy and reliability.

    Placido Rogerio Pinheiro, University of Fortaleza, Brazil
    Mirian Caliope Dantas Pinheiro, University of Fortaleza, Brazil
    Victor Câmera Damasceno, University of Fortaleza, Brazil
    Marley Costa Marques, University of Fortaleza, Brazil
    Raquel Souza Bino Araújo, University of Fortaleza, Brazil
    Layane Mayara Gomes Castelo Branco, University of Fortaleza, Brazil

The diseases and health problems are concerns of managers of the Unified Health System has costs in more sophisticated care sector are high. The World Health Organization focused on prevention of chronic diseases to prevent millions of premature deaths in the coming years, bringing substantial gains in economic growth by improving the quality of life. Few countries appear to be aimed at prevention, if not note the available knowledge and control of chronic diseases and may represent an unnecessary risk to future generations. Early diagnosis of these diseases is the first step to successful treatment in any age group. The objective is to build a model, from the establishment of a Bayesian network, for the early diagnosis of nursing to identify eating disorders bulimia and anorexia nervosa in adolescents, from the characteristics of the DSM-IV and Nursing Diagnoses The need for greater investment in technology in public health actions aims to increase the knowledge of health professionals, especially nurses, contributing to prevention, decision making and early treatment of problems.

Chapter 16

Medical diagnosis has been gaining importance in everyday life. The diseases and their symptoms are highly varying and there is always a need for a continuous update of knowledge needed for the doctors. The diseases fall into different categories and a small variation of symptoms may leave to different categories of diseases. This is further supplemented by the medical analysts for a continuous treatment process. The treatment generally starts with a diagnosis and further goes through a set of procedures including X-ray, CT-scans, ultrasound imaging for qualitative analysis and diagnosis by doctors. A small level of error in disease identification introduces overhead in diagnosis and difficult in treatment. In such cases, an automated system that could retrieve medical images based on user's interest. This chapter deals with various techniques, methodologies that correspond to the classification problem in data analysis process and its methodological impacts to big data.

Preface

The emerging advances of Bioinformatics and the need to improve Healthcare and the Management of Medical Systems has promoted research collaborations among researchers from the field of Bioinformatics and Health Informatics together with administrators, clinicians and data scientists. There is increased need to improve target drug therapy, personalized medicine and the way clinical decisions are made for the welfare of patients and on the management of medical systems. These needs demand Big Data Analytics incorporating the latest computational intelligence and statistical methodologies together with Data Mining and Machine Learning Methodologies. Big Data aspects such as data volume, data velocity, data veracity and data value are considered and examined in terms of usefulness and importance as to which is the most decisive criterion turning data from big to smart as a real time assistance for the improvement of living conditions. The increased need to improve healthcare and the welfare of patients and people in general, requires that we fast improve prognosis, diagnosis and therapies in order to advance personalized medicine and targeted drug/gene therapy (Alyass, et al., 2016; Chen et al., 2013; Tenenbaum, 2016; Greene et al., 2013).

The overall scope and main objective of the book is to expose the reader to the latest developments in Bioinformatics and Health Informatics but to also put emphasis on increasing awareness of all stakeholders of the importance to move from a data management organizational culture to a learning organization culture. We believe that the carefully chosen individual chapters address effective ways of communication and dissemination of the biological relevance of genomic and proteomic discoveries and related specific gene expression to realizing the clinical potential to make possible targeted therapy, personalized medicine and enhancement of human wellness and social cohesion. The recent advances in Bioinformatics and in Healthcare Informatics for next generation medical research are examined with the goal to improve medical practices and the management of Medical Systems both at the national and global level. The book includes chapters on innovation of advanced methods and techniques from medicine bioinformatics/ health informatics as also from computer science, statistics, and information theory which infer the relationships and dynamics among genes and their products. Both the genes and their products could be targets for treatment but also help propose predictive models which will enable the industry to develop an array of algorithms and software and overall accurate and intelligent computational systems for next generation medicine and medical systems.

THE CHALLENGES

The rapid development of biomedical research has given rise to an increasing demand of various computational and mathematical approaches to analyze and integrate the resulting large-scale data with the molecular and bioinformatics basis of clinical science. The new approaches will provide useful therapeutic targets to improve diagnosis, therapies and prognosis of diseases but to also help toward the establishment of better and more efficient next generation medicine and medical systems.

Declines in the cost of generating genomic and proteomic data have made the approaches to DNA sequencing, RNA- sequencing, and high-throughput screening and protein analysis more efficient and effective to analyze data but also have created new challenges in data analysis. Researchers, such as data analysts, specialize in developing computational methods for extracting insights from next-generation sequencing and high-throughput screening data with the goal to find the most efficient and effective ways to analyze data and generate insights of the function of biological systems. The emerging field of Systems Biology with its recent technical breakthroughs in next generation sequencing (NGS) technology with advanced gene and protein bioinformatics analysis, provides formal approaches to modeling and simulating regulatory processes in biological systems and has accelerated the convergence of discovery science with clinical medicine and improvement of medical systems (He et al., 2013; Hirak, et al., 2014; Huang et al., 2013; Lewis et al., 2012; Lin et al., 2015; Luo et al., 2016; Margolis et al., 2014; Ng et al., 2014; Niemenmaa et al., 2012).

One very big challenge in the healthcare system is how to connect it to basic research and its applications together with the technical and structural problems encountered. In addition to powerful computational tools that need to be developed, many practical problems exist as far as the proper training and handling and analysis of big data is concerned and in the development of a common technical language and terms so that meta-data is aligned and clinical data is properly analyzed and shared. There have been a number of international efforts to develop global and local frameworks via global and local associations and alliances which take into consideration ethical and regulatory challenges and address privacy and security issues via secure electronic methods (European Bioinformatics Institute (EBI), 2016; Global Alliance for Genomics and Health (GA4GH) 2016; The Precision Medicine Initiative® (PMI) Cohort Program, 2016; The Phenotype-Genotype Integrator (PheGenI), 2016; The International Medical Informatics Association (IMIA), 2016; United Nations (UN), 2016; World Health Organization (WHO), 2016). Academics, commercial groups, and industry in general must come together and through good team work decide on what is best for an individual's well-being and health and also psychological and social needs. Improved synergies and good team work of talented and well trained people could help improve personalized medicine and possibly precision medicine.

SEARCHING FOR SOLUTIONS

Researchers, clinicians and administrators continue looking for solutions to the many challenges of Big Data Analytics in the field of Health Informatics in relation to its applications and implications. For example, by translating information from cancer genomics into diagnostics and therapeutics will revolutionize cancer treatment and management as they develop next generation sequencing (NGS) and advanced bioinformatics-based non-invasive cancer management systems that may provide a better way to monitor and diagnose cancer recurrence and therapy effectiveness. Identification of genomic and protein alterations that lead to health problems enhances our understanding and classification of human diseases and accelerates the discovery of new approaches for clinical diagnosis, outcome prediction and risk stratification. Emphasis nowadays is put on the importance of establishing the biological relevance of genomic discoveries and related specific gene expression to realizing the clinical potential to make possible targeted therapy, personalized medicine and effective medical management systems.

RECOMMENDATIONS

At present time, within the field of Bioinformatics, massive amounts of biological information becomes available, such as genome sequences, gene expression data, protein sequences, protein interaction data etc. and therefore, there is high need for more efficient, sensitive, and specific big data analytic technology in Bioinformatics. For example, in biological and biomedical imaging process and analysis, large volumes of data are generated. As a consequence the research community faces many challenges mainly those that have to do with storage, indexing, managing, mining, and visualizing big data. The field of Bioinformatics enhances therefore, the development of databases, algorithms, computational and statistical techniques and tools to solve a variety of practical problems, and abstract biological data by mainly analyzing and correlating genomic and proteomic information (Greene et al., 2013; He et al., 2013; Hirak, et al., 2014; Huang et al., 2013; Lewis et al., 2012; Lin et al., 2015; Luo et al., 2016; Margolis et al., 2014; Ng et al., 2014; Niemenmaa et al., 2012).

Similarly in Health Informatics, healthcare organizations and companies are trying to digitize, store as well as manipulate medical data efficiently and cost effectively. We recommend that more serious efforts should be made to use predictive analytic models and apply risk adjustment methodologies embedded within data analysis platforms and thus allowing the healthcare organizations to make predictions for the cost and help develop strategies on population health management. In addition with Big Data Analytics, healthcare organizations can be helped to perform risk assessments and adjustments so the action plans fall within the budget and at the same time be helped to develop better treatment guidelines, plan care management strategies, measure physician performance, and also work closely with insurance companies (European Bioinformatics Institute (EBI), 2016; Global Alliance for Genomics and Health (GA4GH) 2016; The Precision Medicine Initiative® (PMI) Cohort Program, 2016; The Phenotype-Genotype Integrator (PheGenI), 2016;The International Medical Informatics Association (IMIA), 2016; United Nations (UN), 2016; World Health Organization (WHO), 2016).

The Bioinformatics discipline together with that of Health Informatics should facilitate the development of big data analytic technology as in the case of the integration of genetic test results, patient-specific sequencing, expression profiling, tissue image data and overall clinical data in patients' medical records. This fusion will provide opportunities for personalized medicine, targeted drug research and therapy but also, create new challenges for big data analytics from database design, data mining, data knowledge representation, to data analytics, and clinical decisions.

The target audience of this book would be undergraduate and graduate students, practitioners, researchers, clinicians, and data scientists in the area of Bioinformatics and Health Informatics who would be exposed to the latest findings in the field, and would be helped to explore the intersections between Bioinformatics and Health Informatics as well as the new research areas brought by advancement in big data analytics, data mining, machine learning and statistical learning.

The book can also serve as a guide for professionals, researchers, clinicians, and data scientists on ways of communication and how to share opinions and exchange ideas, so as to facilitate a better fusion of Bioinformatics and Health Informatics, academic and industry research, and the improvement in the quality of people's daily health and life activities. Big data analytics will therefore support and promote such research activities.

The potential benefits to individual and the society can be great if the efforts to transform Big Data into Smart Data and from that to Wise Data, as we propose, are successful. This transformation can be achieved when the motivation of people to participate and the rewards of collaboration are high and are based on mutual respect of all stakeholders. This we think, is not an unachievable goal and all stakeholders should be working toward that direction. The fact that a good number of associations, organizations and world alliances are working toward establishing policies, regulations, and safety measures including risk analysis studies, is a very positive step.

In our mind, it is clear that genomics and health informatics data can be useful in selection of therapies and prevention. We must not forget however, that each one and each society has different value priorities, different understanding of health and quality of life.

In July 2016, an international team published a map of the human brain's cerebral cortex (Glasser et al., 2016). Despite the highest resolution ever achieved in human brain-brain connectivity map (1 cubic millimeter spatial resolution), each voxel contains tens of thousands of neurons but still it is not comparable to the mapped at single-cell resolution in the fruit fly. Neuroscientists however have started sharing and integrating big brain data following a team approach which is not easy. Using multi-modal magnetic resonance images from the Human Connectome Project (HCP) and semi-automated neuroanatomical approach for example, they have made accurate real maps of cortical architecture, function and connectivity (Glasser et al., 2016). Despite the advances in bioinformatics and the revolution that swept the genomics field decades ago, in neurobiology where big data is truly big and a single neuroimaging data measures in terabytes the challenges are many. Brain mappers face richer sets of imaging and electrophysiological data which goes without saying that a concentrated effort is needed to produce accurate real brain maps (Glasser et al., 2016). A culture shift will be required so that scientists not only develop new computational tools but to also share and visualize the resulting data, so that we expand the limits of what is possible. Mapping the Human brain will be indeed one of the greatest future challenges that scientists will be facing which however will greatly advance our understanding of ourselves as a *Home sapiens* species, the wise one.

We, as editors of this book but also as co-authors of one of its chapters we hold the belief that "Making big data smart implies ability to technically connect relevant data to identify patterns. Turning smart data to wise implies the integral consideration of social, cultural and political considerations to ensure the holistic wellbeing of the individual, but also a community that promotes health, wellness and spiritual integrity above anything else".

ORGANIZATION OF THE BOOK

The book is organized into 16 chapters. A brief description of each of the chapters follows:

Chapter 1 reviews the emerging advances of Bioinformatics which have already contributed toward the establishment of better next generation medicine and medical systems by putting emphasis on improvement of prognosis, diagnosis and therapy of diseases including better management of medical systems. The authors of this chapter explore ways by which the use of Bioinformatics and Smart Data Analysis offer solutions to challenges in the fields of genomics, medicine and Health Informatics. They focus on Smart Data Analysis and ways needed to filter out the noise. The chapter addresses challenges researchers and data analysts are facing in terms of the developed computational methods used to extract insights from NGS and high-throughput screening data. The authors propose the concept "Wise Data" reflecting the distinction between individual health and wellness on the one hand, and social improvement, cohesion and sustainability on the other, leading to more effective medical systems, healthier individuals and more socially cohesive societies.

Chapter 2 is an overview of Bioinformatics in relation to data mining, data visualization, secretome analysis, mass spectrometry, chemical cross-linking reagents, Software Product Line (SPL), protein kinase, microRNAs (miRNAs, clinical bioinformatics and cancer. The author focuses on how bioinformatics helps reveal the wealth of biological information hidden in the large amounts of data and obtain a clearer insight into the fundamental biology of organisms. The author finally points to the need of the creation and advancement of databases, algorithms, computational and statistical techniques, and theory to solve the formal and practical problems arising from the management and analysis of biological data.

Chapter 3 identifies the existing challenges in the management of computational techniques in protein structure prediction such as comparative modeling, threading and ab initio modelling. In this chapter the authors elaborate on the three phases of modelling (the pre-modelling analysis phase, model construction and post-modelling refinement phases), the programs available for performing each, issues, possible solutions and future research areas.

Chapter 4 examines the idea of personalized medicine system as an evolution of holistic approach of treatment and in more evidence based manner. The authors begin the chapter with an introduction of how body systems work naturally and examine the impact of modern medicine on overall health, followed by a historical background and brief review of literature providing the description that the concept of personalized medicine is not new but a very old ideology which stayed neglected until the development in the field of medical genetics, followed by the role of omics in modern medicine, the comparison of modern medicine and personalized medicine, medical concepts relevant to proteomics in personalized medicine, impact of proteomics in drug development and clinical safety and finally closing the chapter with future prospects and challenges of proteomics in personalized medicine.

Chapter 5 presents an analysis of issues and concerns in managing cloud computing and have examined virtual document storage platforms as providers of amenities with minimal expense in the corporate society. The authors discuss how cloud computing is appeasing to owners of clinics and businesses as it banishes the requirement of planning, provisioning, and allows corporations to advance their filling systems according to service demand. The authors identify the importance that Medical practices urgently need to revolutionize their storage standards, to keep up with the growing population.

Chapter 6 examines how Informatics and Data Analytics supports Exposome-based discovery Part I. The totality of exposures from conception onwards, simultaneously identifying, characterizing and quantifying the exogenous and endogenous exposures and modifiable risk factors that predispose to and predict diseases throughout a person's life span are discusses. The authors discuss how the unravelling of the exposome implies that both environmental exposures and genetic variation can reliably be measured simultaneously. To achieve this, they claim, we need to bring together a comprehensive array of novel technologies, data analysis and modelling tools that support efficient design and execution of exposome studies. This requires an innovative approach bringing together and organizing environmental, socioeconomic, exposure, biomarker and health effect data; in addition, this effort includes all the procedures and computational sequences necessary for applying advanced bioinformatics coupling advanced data mining, biological and exposure modelling so as to ensure that environmental exposure-health associations are studied comprehensively. The authors explore the type of novel tools exposome studies will require to address the complexity of emerging environmental health issues. Critical for success will be the ability to bring together existing geospatial, environmental, health and socioeconomic data, and to collect new high resolution data using innovative environmental micro-sensors, remote sensing or other community and omics/systems biology based approaches to describe the exposome for e.g. endocrine disruption-related syndromes and sex-related changes (menopause), neurodegenerative or respiratory diseases.

Chapter 7 examines how Informatics and Data Analytics supports Exposome-based discovery Part II. The authors outline the connectivity-based methodology and introduce a new exposome-based paradigm for interdisciplinary scientific work in the area of environment and health. It is an approach that builds on the exploration of the interconnections between the co-existence of multiple stressors and the different scales of biological organization that together produce the final adverse health effect. The authors state that their approach marks a clear departure from the conventional paradigm, which seeks to shed light on the identification of singular cause-effect relationships between stressors and health outcomes. It entails creating a new way of combining health-relevant information coming from different disciplines, including (but not limited to) environmental science, epidemiology, toxicology, physiology, molecular biology, biochemistry, mathematics and computer science. According to the connectivity approach, all factors affecting the internal and external exposome are treated as co-variates, rather than just as confounders. The functional integration of these different information classes into a unique framework results in understanding the complex interaction between the genome and exposure to environmental factors that determines physiological response to environmental insults and, ultimately, the onset or exacerbation of adverse health outcomes.

Chapter 8 presents an analysis of issues and concerns in managing the big omics data generated in the recent decade which flooded the internet with transcriptomic, genomics, proteomics and metabolomics data. The authors refer to a number of software, tools, and web-servers that have developed to analyze the big data omics. In this review, the authors integrate the various methods that have been employed over the years to interpret the gene regulatory and metabolic networks. They illustrate random networks, scale-free networks, small world network, bipartite networks and other topological analysis which fits in biological networks. They point to the fact that transcriptome to metabolome network is of interest because of key enzymes identification and regulatory hub genes prediction. This chapter also provides an insight into the understanding of omics technologies, generation of data and impact of in-silico analysis on the scientific community.

Chapter 9 focuses on protein docking as an integral part to structure-based drug design and molecular biology. The authors argue that the recent surge of big data in biology, the demand for personalised medicines, evolving pathogens and increasing lifestyle-associated risks, asks for smart, robust, low-cost and high-throughput drug design. Computer-aided drug design techniques allow rapid screening of ultra-large chemical libraries within minutes. This the authors think is immensely necessary to the drug discovery pipeline, which is presently burdened with high attrition rates, failures, huge capital and time investment. With increasing drug resistance and difficult druggable targets, there is a growing need for novel drug scaffolds which is partly satisfied by fragment based drug design and de novo methods. This chapter discusses various aspects of protein docking and emphasises on its application in drug design.

Chapter 10 focuses on the design process of an effective and efficient dashboard which displays management information for an Electronic Health Record (EHR) in Dutch long-term and chronic healthcare. The authors presents the actual design and realization of a management dashboard for the YBoard 2.0 system, which is a popular solution on the Dutch market. The authors based their design decisions in this investigation on human perception and computer interaction theory, in particular Gestalt theory. The empirical interviews with medical professionals supplemented valuable additional insights into what the users wanted to see most of all in a dashboard in their daily practices. This study successfully shows how effective and efficient dashboard design can benefit from theoretical insights related to human perception and computer interaction such as Gestalt theory, in combination with integrated end user requirements from daily practices.

Chapter 11 analyses and compares how search engines and social media are two different online data sources where search engines can provide health related queries logs and Internet users' discuss their diseases, symptoms, causes, preventions and even suggest treatment by sharing their views, experiences and opinions on social media. This chapter hypothesizes that online data from Google and Twitter can provide vital first-hand healthcare information. An approach is provided for collecting twitter data by exploring contextual information gleaned from Google search queries logs. Furthermore, the authors investigated whether it is possible to use tweets to track, monitor and predict diseases, especially Influenza epidemics. The authors argue that their obtained results show that healthcare institutes and professional uses of social media helps provide up-to date health related information and interact with public. Moreover, the proposed approach is beneficial for extracting useful information regarding disease symptoms, side effects, medications and to track geographical location of epidemics affected area.

Chapter 12 addresses the issue of how the semi-supervised learning has become one of the most interesting fields for research developments in the machine learning domain beyond the scope of supervised learning from data. Medical diagnostic process works mostly in supervised mode, but in reality, we are in the presence of a large amount of unlabeled samples and a small set of labeled examples characterized by thousands of features. This problem is known under the term "the curse of dimensionality". In this chapter, the authors propose, as solution, a new approach in semi-supervised learning that they call Optim Co-forest. The Optim Co-forest algorithm combines the re-sampling data approach with two selection strategies. The first one involves selecting random subset of parameters to construct the ensemble of classifiers following the principle of Co-forest. The second strategy is an extension of the importance measure of Random Forest (RF). Experiments on high dimensional datasets confirm the power of the adopted selection strategies in the scalability of their method.

Chapter 13 focuses on how Medical Diagnosis has been gaining significance in everyday life and the need for good medical analysts. The diseases and their symptoms are highly varying and there is always a need for a continuous update of knowledge needed for the doctors and the associated stakeholders' i.e. medical analyst. The diseases fall into different categories and a small variation of symptoms may leave to different categories of diseases. This is further supplemented by the medical analysts for a continuous treatment process. A small level of error in disease identification introduces overhead in diagnosis and further consequences in treatment.

Chapter 14 explores pathway information for cancer detection which helps to find co-regulated gene groups whose collective expression is strongly associated with cancer development. In this chapter the authors propose a collaborative multi-swarm binary particle swarm optimization (MS-BPSO) based gene selection technique that outperforms to identify the pathway marker genes. The authors have compared their proposed method with various statistical and pathway based gene selection techniques for different popular cancer datasets as well as a detailed comparative study is illustrated using different meta-heuristic algorithms like binary coded particle swarm optimization (BPSO), binary coded differential evolution (BDE), binary coded artificial bee colony (BABC) and genetic algorithm (GA). Experimental results show that the proposed MS-BPSO based method performs significantly better and the improved multi swarm concept generates a good subset of pathway markers which provides more effective insight to the gene-disease association with high accuracy and reliability.

Chapter 15 identifies the existing challenges and concerns in the management of the diseases and health problems managers of the Unified Health System face and the high costs. The World Health Organization focused on prevention of chronic diseases to prevent millions of premature deaths in the coming years, bringing substantial gains in economic growth by improving the quality of life. Few countries appear to be aimed at prevention, if not note the available knowledge and control of chronic diseases and may represent an unnecessary risk to future generations. The authors support the idea that early diagnosis of these diseases is the first step to successful treatment in any age group. Their objective is to build a model, from the establishment of a Bayesian network, for the early diagnosis of nursing to identify eating disorders bulimia and anorexia nervosa in adolescents, from the characteristics of the DSM-IV and Nursing Diagnoses. The need for greater investment in technology in public health actions aims to increase the knowledge of health professionals, especially nurses, contributing to prevention, decision making and early treatment of problems.

Chapter 16 explores how predicting patterns to extract knowledge can be worth the efforts despite the difficulties. The authors argue that in order to accomplish a task good knowledge of the type of data is needed together with adequate time for analysis and also adapt it to the algorithms and technologies used together with the appropriate methodologies. In this chapter a real case is examined following all this process. In particular, a classification problem is shown as an example of using machine learning methodologies to find out whether a hospital patient should be admitted or not in Cardiology department.

Miltiades D. Lytras
Deree – The American College of Greece, Greece

Paraskevi Papadopoulou
Deree – The American College of Greece, Greece

REFERENCES

Alyass, A., Turcotte, M., & Meyre, D. (2016). From Big Data analysis to personalized medicine for all: Challenges and opportunities. *BMC Medical Genomics*, 8(33). PMID:26112054

Chen J, Qian F, Yan W. (2013). Translational biomedical informatics in the cloud: present and future. *Biomed Res Int*. 658925.

European Bioinformatics Institute (EBI). (2016). Retrieved November 21, 2016, from http://www.ebi.ac.uk/

Glasser, M. F., Coalson, T. S., Robinson, E. C., Hacker, C. D., Harwell, J., Yacoub, E., & Van Essen, D. C. et al. (2016). A multi-modal parcellation of human cerebral cortex. *Nature*, 536(7615), 171–178. doi:10.1038/nature18933 PMID:27437579

Global Alliance for Genomics and Health (GA4GH). (2016). Retrieved November 21, 2016, from http://www.ebi.ac.uk/about/news/press-releases/ewan-birney-leads-global-alliance-genomics-and-health

Greene, A. C., Giffin, K. A., Greene, C. S. & Moore, J. H. (2015). Adapting bioinformatics curricula for Big Data. *Briefings in Bioinformatics-Bioinformatics Curricula, 1-8.*

He, C., Fan, X., & Li, Y. (2013). Toward ubiquitous healthcare services with a novel efficient cloud platform. *IEEE Transactions on Bio-Medical Engineering, 60*(1), 230–234. doi:10.1109/TBME.2012.2222404 PMID:23060318

Hirak, K., Hasin, A. A., Nazrul, H., Swarup, R. & Dhruba, K. B. (2014). Big Data Analytics in Bioinformatics: A Machine Learning Perspective. *Journal of Latex Class Files, 13*(9), 1-20.

Huang, H., Tata, S., & Prill, R. J. (2013). BlueSNP: R package for highly scalable genome-wide association studies using Hadoop clusters. *Bioinformatics (Oxford, England), 29*(1), 135–136. doi:10.1093/bioinformatics/bts647 PMID:23202745

Lewis, S., Csordas, A., Killcoyne, S., Hermjakob, H., Hoopmann, M. R., Moritz, R. L., & Boyle, J. et al. (2012). Hydra: A scalable proteomic search engine which utilizes the Hadoop distributed computing framework. *BMC Bioinformatics, 13*(1), 324. doi:10.1186/1471-2105-13-324 PMID:23216909

Lin, W., Dou, W., Zhou, Z., & Liu, C. (2015). A cloud-based framework for home-diagnosis service over big medical data. *Journal of Systems and Software, 102*, 192–206. doi:10.1016/j.jss.2014.05.068

Luo, J., Wu, M., Gopukumar, D., & Zhao, Y. (2016). Big Data Application in Biomedical Research and Health Care: A Literature Review. *Biomedical Informatics Insights, 8*, 1–10. doi:10.4137/BII.S31559 PMID:26843812

Margolis, R., Derr, L., Dunn, M., Huerta, M., Larkin, J., Sheehan, J., & Green, E. D. et al. (2014). The National Institutes of Healths Big Data to Knowledge (BD2 K) initiative: Capitalizing on biomedical Big Data. *Journal of the American Medical Informatics Association, 21*(6), 957–958. doi:10.1136/amiajnl-2014-002974 PMID:25008006

Ng, K., Ghoting, A., Steinhubl, S. R., Stewart, W. F., Malin, B., & Sun, J. (2014). PARAMO: A PARAllel predictive MOdeling platform for healthcare analytic research using electronic health records. *Journal of Biomedical Informatics, 48*, 160–170. doi:10.1016/j.jbi.2013.12.012 PMID:24370496

Niemenmaa, M., Kallio, A., Schumacher, A., Klemela, P., Korpelainen, E., & Heljanko, K. (2012). Hadoop-BAM: Directly manipulating next generation sequencing data in the cloud. *Bioinformatics (Oxford, England), 28*(6), 876–877. doi:10.1093/bioinformatics/bts054 PMID:22302568

Tenenbaum, J. D. (2016). Translational Bioinformatics: Past, Present, and Future. *Genomics, Proteomics & Bioinformatics, 14*(1), 31–41. doi:10.1016/j.gpb.2016.01.003 PMID:26876718

The International Medical Informatics Association (IMIA). (2016). Retrieved November 21, 2016, from http://imia-medinfo.org/wp/welcome-to-imia-2/

The Phenotype-Genotype Integrator (PheGenI). (2016). Retrieved November 21, 2016, from https://www.ncbi.nlm.nih.gov/gap/phegeni

The Precision Medicine Initiative® (PMI) Cohort Program. (2016). Retrieved November 21, 2016, from https://www.nih.gov/precision-medicine-initiative-cohort-program

United Nations (UN). (2016). *Sustainable Development Goals. 17 Goals to Transform the World.* Retrieved November 21, 2016, from http://www.un.org/sustainabledevelopment/sustainable-development-goals/

World Health Organization (WHO). (2016) Retrieved November 21, 2016, from http://www.who.int/en/

Acknowledgment

The editors would like to acknowledge the help of all the people involved in this project and, more specifically, the authors who contributed their time and expertise to this book and the reviewers for their valuable contributions regarding the improvement of quality, coherence, and content presentation of chapters.

Miltiades D. Lytras
Deree – The American College of Greece, Greece

Paraskevi Papadopoulou
Deree – The American College of Greece, Greece

Section 1
Introduction to Bioinformatics in Medicine and Medical Systems

This section covers topics related to inferring gene function from expression data, genome sequence data, integrating expression data with other genome-wide data for functional annotation, functional study of specific molecular and pathway analysis, genome annotation and comparative genomics bioinformatics algorithm and tool development, RNAseq and microarray gene expression data analysis, gene regulatory network construction and Next-Generation Sequencing (NGS) analysis. Furthermore, this section covers topics related to translational bioinformatics, protein sequencing and classification, protein structure prediction, protein function analysis, protein interactions, protein subcellular localization prediction.

Chapter 1
Bioinformatics as Applied to Medicine:
Challenges Faced Moving from Big Data to Smart Data to Wise Data

Paraskevi Papadopoulou
Deree – The American College of Greece, Greece

Miltiadis Lytras
Deree – The American College of Greece, Greece

Christina Marouli
Deree – The American College of Greece, Greece

ABSTRACT

The emerging advances of Bioinformatics have already contributed toward the establishment of better next generation medicine and medical systems by putting emphasis on improvement of prognosis, diagnosis and therapy of diseases including better management of medical systems. The purpose of this chapter is to explore ways by which the use of Bioinformatics and Smart Data Analysis will provide an overview and solutions to challenges in the fields of genomics, medicine and Health Informatics. The focus of this chapter would be on Smart Data Analysis and ways needed to filter out the noise. The chapter addresses challenges researchers and data analysts are facing in terms of the developed computational methods used to extract insights from NGS and high-throughput screening data. In this chapter the concept "Wise Data" is proposed reflecting the distinction between individual health and wellness on the one hand, and social improvement, cohesion and sustainability on the other, leading to more effective medical systems, healthier individuals and more socially cohesive societies.

DOI: 10.4018/978-1-5225-2607-0.ch001

INTRODUCTION

Nowadays, there is an increased need to improve healthcare and the way clinical decisions are made for the welfare of patients by improving diagnosis, therapies and prognosis of diseases so as to advance personalized medicine and targeted drug/gene therapy. The demands of Big Data analytics incorporating the latest computational intelligence and statistical methodologies together with data mining and machine learning methodologies are high and quite challenging. Especially due to the rapid developments of biomedical research, there seems to be an ever-increasing demand of various computational and mathematical approaches to analyze and integrate the resulting large-scale data with the molecular and bioinformatics basis of clinical science. In fact, the latest developments in Bioinformatics require that we move from a data management organizational culture to a learning organization culture. This perspective requires better and more effective collaboration among various stakeholders with the researchers who should be able to solve problems in an effective and flexible manner by efficiently collecting and analyzing data to meaningfully optimize and automate solutions. Big Data as a concept needs to be communicated to a wider community of stakeholders. Big Data is usually defined around four aspects: data volume, data velocity, data veracity and data value. Veracity and value aspects of Big Data deal with the quality and the usefulness of Big Data. Those two aspects make management a major challenge for most enterprises in terms of quality. The decisive criterion here isn't necessarily the amount of (big) data, but its valuable content (smart) see Figure 1. Turning this data from big to smart is the challenge that needs to be addressed today in order to lead to real time assistance hoping to improve medicine and provide better more personalized treatment.

The main focus of this chapter will be on Smart Data Analysis (focusing on veracity and value) and the various ways needed to filter out the noise and hold the valuable data. That way, one can expect that problems would be solved more effectively ranging from business problems to the improvement of healthcare operations. Smart Data Analysis will open new avenues to optimize computing capacities, explore molecular biology, genomics and proteomics and Health Informatics applications and implications. Smart Data Analysis combined with declines in the cost of generating genomic and proteomic data have made the approaches to DNA sequencing, RNA- sequencing, and high-throughput screening and protein analysis more efficient and effective in terms of analyzing data but also have created new challenges in data analysis. Formal approaches to modeling and simulating regulatory processes in biological systems are supported by the emerging field of Systems Biology which has accelerated the convergence of discovery science with clinical medicine and their connection to improvement of medical systems. The chapter addresses these challenges researchers and data analysts are facing in terms of the developed computational methods they use to extract insights from next-generation sequencing (NGS) and high-throughput screening data. However, a great challenge remains: how to apply Smart Data in ways that lead to wise decisions concerning individual wellness and social welfare, and not focused on market imperatives. This leads to a critical perspective on Smart Data. As a consequence, in this chapter a new concept is proposed (i.e. "Wise Data") see Figure 1, which aside of the focus of Smart Data on veracity and value also reflects the distinction between individual health and wellness on the one hand, and social improvement, cohesion and longevity on the other, leading to more efficient medical systems, healthier individuals and more socially cohesive societies. Therefore, the overall objective of the chapter is to help communicate and disseminate the importance of establishing the biological relevance of genomic and proteomic discoveries and related specific gene expression to realizing the clinical potential to make possible targeted therapy, personalized medicine and enhancement of human wellness

Figure 1. Going from big data to smart data to wise data

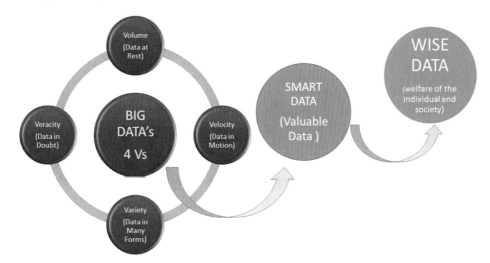

and social cohesion. The recent advances therefore, in Bioinformatics and in Healthcare Informatics for next generation medical research are examined with the goal to improve medical practices and the management of Medical Systems both at the national and global level.

BACKGROUND

Bioinformatics and Health Informatics

Bioinformatics was coined as a term in 1970 by Paulien Hogeweg and Ben Hesper and it was defined as the study of information processes in biotic systems. As a field, it was placed mainly next to biophysics which focuses on the physical processes in biological systems as compared to biochemistry which focused on the chemical processes in biological systems (Hesper, B. et al., 1970). Nowadays, Bioinformatics is the name given mainly to developments that require mathematical and computing approaches that have been used in genomic, proteomic and molecular biology research. Over the past few decades the vast amount of information produced has led to new developments in information technologies such as advancement of new theories and algorithms, computational and statistical techniques, pattern recognition, data mining, machine learning algorithms, and visualization creation of databases, and ways of management and analysis of big biological data.

Major research efforts in the field include sequence alignment, gene finding, genome assembly, drug design, drug discovery, protein structure alignment, protein structure prediction, prediction of gene expression and protein–protein interactions, genome-wide association studies, the modeling of evolution.

Bioinformatics is a distinct field in comparison to biological computation which uses bioengineering and biology to build biological computers and computational biology which builds theoretical models of biological systems. Bioinformatics uses computation to understand, organize and analyze and interpret biological data. Common activities in bioinformatics especially deriving from experimental molecular biology and genetics include image and signal processing, mapping and analyzing of DNA and proteins sequences, aligning DNA and protein sequences to compare them, sequencing and annotating genomes and their observed mutations, gene finding, genome assembly, drug design, drug discovery, creating and viewing 3-D protein models protein structure alignment, protein structure prediction etc. Bioinformatics has helped to greatly advance the analysis of gene and protein expression and regulation including the studies on protein to protein interactions genome-wide association studies, the modeling of evolution and has also contributed significantly toward an integrative analysis and cataloguing biological pathways and networks. Structural Biology and Systems Biology as disciplines in fact, have benefited greatly from the bioinformatics aid in the simulation of DNA, RNA, Proteins and other biomolecular interactions (Hesper et al., 1970; Alyass et al., 2015).

As the primary goal of bioinformatics is to increase the understanding of biological processes, bioinformaticians work toward developing and applying computationally intensive techniques to achieve this goal. In addition, this requires development of new algorithms, computational and statistical techniques, and theory that assess relationships among members of large data sets. The algorithms they develop depend on theoretical foundations such as discrete mathematics, control theory, system theory, information theory, and statistics. Those techniques enable efficient access to, use and management of, various types of information and Big Data and new applications and implications became possible.

Health informatics is one of many other related terms which apply to available health resources, medical data generation and acquisition, storage and retrieval of data plus the various devices used in medicine and in health. It is an interdisciplinary field of study which combines knowledge from biology, medicine, and health for the design, development and adoption of various health care services by utilizing mostly IT-based innovations and applications for the better management of Medical Systems and improvement of Human Health. All around the world there are serious efforts for better management of medical systems focusing on higher quality and higher efficiency of data handling in order to improve the overall effectiveness of patient care delivery (Alyass et al., 2015; Luo, 2016; Chen et al., 2013).

BIOINFORMATICS AS APPLIED TO MEDICINE

Bioinformatics and Health Informatics Main Challenges

Bioinformatics has a strong interdisciplinary and transdisciplinary nature and together with the exponential expansion of biological data and other related types of data numerous difficulties are encountered in storage and analysis of these vast amounts of data. The gap between sequencing throughput and computer capabilities in dealing with such big biological data is growing despite the advances in high-throughput experimental technologies. Especially when it comes to handling the volume of data which grows exponentially in the biomedical informatics fields, the challenge is to properly collect, analyze, process and manage data coming for example from GenomicsDB, ProteomicsDB, MetabolomicsDB, to protein interactions and Phenomics together with appropriately processing electronic health records, (EHRs) currently available with the goal to move towards Smart Data. Faster speeds are required for the production of data such as for the production of billions of DNA sequence data and the New Generation Technologies (NGTs) already allow that. Big data technologies and time-saving tools need to be tailored to match the high speed data production. In clinical settings, data from millions of patients has already been collected and the big challenge is how this accumulated data could be used to enhance health-care services but also help improve research toward new types of investigation and personalized medicine (Alyass et al., 2015; Luo, 2016; Chen et al., 2013).

As a way to cope with not only the volume of Big Data but also features such as variety and veracity in addition to the value of data, a good number of national and global associations and organizations have as their primary mission and goal to help align the various research groups in related bioinformatics centers and institutions into working together to create a common framework in a responsible, voluntary, and secure manner of sharing genomic, proteomic and clinical data (see table 1). At the same time various IT software and tools and the application of information science and technology in the fields of healthcare and research in medical, health and bio-informatics are examined so as to ensure a common basic approach to dealing with the challenges of Big Data moving toward Smart Data.

To start getting an idea of the ongoing massive data production, storage and analysis, it is useful to refer to the European Bioinformatics Institute (EBI) in Hinxton, UK together with the US National Center for Biotechnology Information in Bethesda, Maryland which currently store many petabytes (1 petabyte is 10^{15} bytes) of genomic, proteomic and small molecule data as data repositories. CERN, Europe's particle-physics laboratory in Geneva, Switzerland generates around 15 petabytes every year. Data sharing and analysis have therefore become a great challenge, especially nowadays where small laboratories become Big Data generators but also Big Data users by accessing data at least in the range of terabytes (10^{12} bytes) (Marx, V. 2013). Extremely powerful computers are needed to handle large data sets and at the same time handle bottlenecks due to data explosion and wide use of Big Data. A promising solution is Cloud Computing (see Figure 2 below), which exploits the use of multiple computers operating at the same time and storage allocated in virtual resources via Web Application Programming Interfaces. Cloud Computing can be a public utility for both data storage and computing (Dai et al., 2012; Luo et al., 2016; Angiuoli et al., 2011; Deb et al., 2011).

It has become evident that parallel computing as a fundamental infrastructure would offer a solution to managing Big Data. The main feature of parallel computing is that algorithms are executed simultaneously on a cluster of machines or supercomputers. An open cloud resource MapReduce package is what is called the Apache Hadoop software library. Hadoop is a framework which allows for the distributed

Figure 2. Features of cloud computing

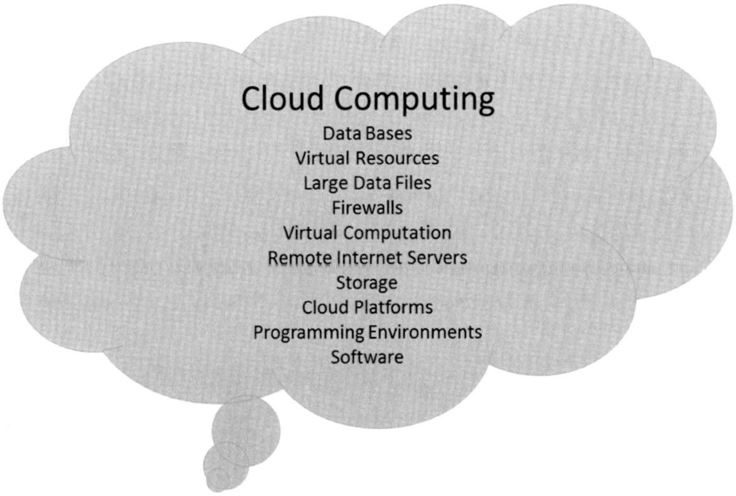

Cloud Computing
Data Bases
Virtual Resources
Large Data Files
Firewalls
Virtual Computation
Remote Internet Servers
Storage
Cloud Platforms
Programming Environments
Software

processing of large data sets across clusters of computers using simple programming models. (http://hadoop.apache.org) (Dai et al., 2012; Luo et al., 2016; Huang, 2012, 2013; Jourden, 2012; Lewis et al., 2012; Lin, 2015; Niemenmaa et al., 2012). The MapReduce and Hadoop Distributed File System (HDFS) have been proposed by Google as novel parallel computing models (Markonis et al., 2012). The project includes these modules. (http://hadoop.apache.org)

- **Hadoop Common:** The common utilities that support the other Hadoop modules.
- **Hadoop Distributed File System (HDFS™):** A distributed file system that provides high-throughput access to application data.
- **Hadoop YARN:** A framework for job scheduling and cluster resource management.
- **Hadoop MapReduce:** A YARN-based system for parallel processing of large data sets.

Hadoop balances load among multiple nodes and allows distributed processing of large datasets by utilizing multiple computer nodes, supports Big Data scaling and also detects node failures that are re-executed on any node (Dai et al., 2012; Luo et al., 2016; Deligiannis et al., 2012; He et al., 2013; Hirak et al., 2014). Thus, according to Dai et al. (2012) and a number of cloud-based resources and studies, Hadoop meets the needs of bioinformatics.

The Amazon Elastic Compute Cloud (EC2) and the IBM/Google Cloud Computing University Initiative launched by Google and IBM are large utility-computing services from the commercial sector (Chen et al., 2013). Other examples of cloud computing include the EasyGenomics cloud in Beijing Genomics Institute (BGI), and "Embassy" clouds as part of ELIXIR project (Alyass et al., 2015). In addition, Graphic Processing Units (GPUs) recently provide faster computations than Central Processing Units (CPUs). Novel tools are publicly available such as Bioconductor and CytoScape and offer free storage and computing platforms for exchange of data and algorithms (see footnote for related links) (Alyass et al., 2015).[1]

Moreover, mathematicians and statisticians have to also cope with the issue of high-dimensionality when deciphering omics data. The multi-level ontology analyses (MONA) is such a method that integrates multiple omics information and uses the expectation propagating algorithm to cope with redundancies related to multiple testing problems by approximating probabilities (Saas et al., 2013) (Alyass et al., 2015). Statistical good methods are also needed to minimize errors and be able to distinguish between random error and true interaction signals, sample swapping and improper data entry. Alyas et al. (2015) mention in their paper some new methodologies for assessing data quality such as Multi-Omics Data Matcher (MODMatcher) and the growing need for metadata 'data about data'. Such software that integrate and interpret omics data are currently being developed such as Anaxomics and LifeMap (Alyass et al., 2015).

Noise (due to mainly measurement errors and sampling variability) and true heterogeneity (due to dynamic biological nature and multi-factorial complexity) within complex systems are other challenges for integrating omics data via standardizations and calibrations in deriving meaningful correlations as between transcriptomics and proteomics profiles, see figure 5 in Alyass et al., 2015. This will require improvements in networks analysis to account for such complex interactions and to be able to integrate various types of omics data.

Moreover, the advances in high-throughput technologies have led to the emergence of *Systems Biology* as a holistic science which will help toward the establishment of personalized medicine. Even though the *Omics* facilities and advanced health systems seem to currently be restricted to developed countries there is a growing need to narrow the gap between developed and less developed countries. Major investments will be needed in the bioinformatics field together with new generations of multi-talented scientists, bio-mathematicians and biostatisticians who will make best use of high- throughput technologies. This will require hybrid education and multidisciplinary teams who will be trained to best generate and analyze Big Data in a cost-effective way, appropriately store, process, integrate and interpret Big Data with the forward strategy to smoothly transition to personalized medicine.

At the level of undergraduate and graduate training in bioinformatics curricula should be updated on an annual or biennial basis. Educators should be regularly trained but also have frequent meetings amongst themselves and the students. Course evaluations should be a common practice during and after the class ends. Challenges such as data collection, data unification, data wrangling, data normalization, bias and confounding in the data, multiple hypothesis testing, data storage, computational limitations, network cost etc. need to be addressed by all stakeholders (Greene et al., 2015; Robinson et all, 2011). It appears that in many countries of the world significant resources have been allocated to research and training in bioinformatics. Reference is made to the US governmental *Big Data Initiative* and the NIH *Big Data to Knowledge (BD2K)* initiative (Greene et al., 2015). Another example comes from the UK where the *Medical Research Council* supports the Big Data challenges with a 90 million pound initiative (Greene et al., 2015). At least in the developed countries a number of universities have received grants from private foundations and governmental resources ensuring proper student training in extracting smart information found in Big Data (Greene et al., 2015).

It is therefore, very important that young people are educated and trained in the field of bioinformatics and its applications in medicine. The present day curricula should focus on biological problems in bioinformatics and delve more into computational, mathematical and statistical sciences for proper statistical analysis, data visualization, machine learning and data management (Greene et al., 2015). One should not only be familiar with ICT tools and mathematical/statistical tools but also be trained in biological sciences and be exposed to all those research groups and centers connected to bioinformatics. S/he should also be aware of the numerous tools that exist and their applications, including the role major continental and global institutes and associations play in the dissemination of knowledge and bioinformatics applications, the ethical issues involved, privacy, safety and security matters as well. For this reason, as this chapter introduces the reader to the challenges we face on Big Data Analysis as applied to Medicine, an indicative list of research groups and centers is listed together with some common bioinformatics/health informatics tools including related global alliances, associations, organizations and institutes (see next section).

Global Associations and Organizations Related to Health Informatics

A number of international-global, non-profit associations, organizations or alliances have formed to help to create a common framework of standards in relation to secure sharing of genomic, proteomic and clinical data and to enhance the potential of genomic medicine to advance related research, human health, healthcare, disease control and patient advocacy.

Starting from the *United Nations (UN)* declaration on Sustainable Development Goals "17 Goals to Transform Our World", one can see that at least on paper a very optimistic Goal 3 has been declared and that is to ensure healthy lives and promote well-being for all at all ages (United Nations, 2016). Healthy lives and the well-being of humans is connected to sustainable development. United Nations officials state that significant strides have been made as spelled out in goal 3 in terms of disease prevention and mortality rates. They nevertheless recognize the need to increase efforts in order to fully eradicate diseases and improve access to clean water and sanitation (United Nations, 2016).

At the same time that the 17 Sustainable Development Goals have been declared by UN, 6.67 billion people live with excessive air pollution. See excerpt from the UN report below:

Vast majority of world – 6.76 billion people out of 7.35 billion – living with excessive air pollution – UN report... 27 September 2016 – With some 6.5 million people dying annually from air pollution and 92 per cent of the world's population living in places where levels exceed recommended limits, the United Nations today rolled out its most detailed profile of the scourge ever in a bid to slash the deadly toll. (United Nations, 2016)

Fast action to tackle air pollution can't come soon enough, top UN World Health Organization (WHO) environmental official Maria Neira said of the new air quality model, which includes interactive maps that highlight areas within countries exceeding WHO limits (WHO, 2016).

UN and the WHO are nevertheless optimistic that the goals related to public Health will be met, as stated by Dr. Neira *Solutions exist with sustainable transport in cities, solid waste management, access to clean household fuels and cook-stoves, as well as renewable energies and industrial emissions reductions* (United Nations, 2016, WHO, 2016). Both UN and WHO officials seem to agree that all people of the world must breathe clean air so they be healthy. The next decades will be very challenging for the entire world and all the issues addressed in the 17 UN delegations together with climate change challenges and overpopulation concerns will test our willingness as humans to meet and confront those problems or fail Humanity all together.

In 1967, a technical committee of the International Federation for Information Processing (IFIP) was established named the International Medical Informatics Association (IMIA) which became independed in 1987 and was established under Swiss law in 1989. It is the world body for health and biomedical informatics. It is considered as an 'association of associations.' *Its role is to bring together, from a global perspective, scientists, researchers, users, vendors, developers, consultants and suppliers in an environment of cooperation and sharing. IMIA plays a major global role in the application of information science and technology in the fields of healthcare and research in medical, health and bio-informatics* (IMIA, 2016). For more information on the basic goals and objectives of the association and its function as a bridge organization one can visit the site (IMIA, 2016). It is obvious that IMIA's vision is that there should be a *world-wide systems approach for healthcare* supported by informatics tools, processes and behaviors to properly improve health care for all. Best practices are used for the promotion of research, clinical care and public health in support of the organizations of the world.

Along the same line of thought comes also Ewan Birney who presently leads the global Alliance for Genomics and Health since November 1, 2016. Ewan Birney, currently Director of EMBL-EBI and nonexecutive Director of Genomics England, has been asked to lead the consortium's efforts to accelerate medical and research advancements through the responsible sharing of genomic and clinical data. *The Global Alliance for Genomics and Health (GA4GH) was formed to help accelerate the potential of genomic medicine to advance human health* (GA4GH, 2016). Learn more at: http://genomicsandhealth.org

The diverse members of the Global Alliance are working together to create interoperable approaches to catalyze projects that will help unlock the great potential of genomic data. Table 1 provides a list of such global associations and organizations and their related site (s).

Table 1. Global associations and organizations related to health informatics

Organization	Web Link	Related Sites
United Nations (UN)	http://www.un.org/ sustainabledevelopment/ sustainable-development-goals/	
World Health Organization (WHO)	http://www.who.int/en/	
the International Medical Informatics Association (IMIA)	http://imia-medinfo.org/wp/ welcome-to-imia-2/	
The Global Alliance for Genomics and Health (GA4GH)	http://genomicsandhealth.org, http://www.ebi.ac.uk/about/ news/press-releases/ewan-birney-leads-global-alliance-genomics-and-health	https://genomicsandhealth.org/working-groups/data-working-group https://genomicsandhealth.org/files/public/CWG-poster-2015-04%20 %281%29.pdf hhttps://genomicsandhealth.org/files/public/GlobalAlliancePoster-version6.pdfhttps://genomicsandhealth.org/files/public/DWG_poster_rf.pdf https://genomicsandhealth.org/files/public/SWG_poster_rf.pdf https://genomicsandhealth.org/working-groups/our-work http://www.ebi.ac.uk/about/news/press-releases/genomics-api https://genomicsandhealth.org/work-products-demonstration-projects/matchmaker-exchange-0 http://imia-medinfo.org/wp/

Bioinformatics Research Organizations, Groups and Centers

A short description for Bioinformatics Research Organizations, Institutes, Groups and Centers from all around the word is provided below to assist the reader in developing a better understanding of the current status of bioinformatics, its applications and implications. Many are multinational or international companies with global operations.

http://www.bioinformatics.org/groups/list.php

From: https://www.dmoz.org/Science/Biology/Bioinformatics/Research_Groups_and_Centers/

The European Bioinformatics Institute (EBI), Genome Campus in Hinxton, Cambridge, UK. is a good example of such institutes in addition to many others from all over the world (European Bioinformatics Institute, 2016). EMBL-EBI is international and interdisciplinary. At EMBL-EBI, public biological data is freely available to the scientific community and they provide a range of services and tools, basic research and professional training in bioinformatics.

Another example is BGI which was founded in 1999 as a nonprofit research organization. BGI is a multinational organization with significant global operations. Their focus is on improving human health and empowering large-scale human, plant, and animal genomics research (BGI, 2016).

Indicative List of Bioinformatics Tools

There are numerous bioinformatics tools as open or not source which focus on genomic and proteomic analyses, protein structure prediction and biocomputing. These tools focus on data-driven knowledge acquisition in computational molecular biology from diverse, distributed, biological data sets with applications in genetic network inference and macromolecular structure-function characterization. Others focus on developing algorithms and applications in the field of gene ontology, phenotypic analysis, machine learning and modeling of biological networks. Mathematical and statistical analysis is accomplished with the use of tools based on linear algebra and graph theory.[2] A very good indicative list of Bioinformatics Tools can be found at https://www.ncbi.nlm.nih.gov/home/analyze.shtml.

Health Informatics in the World

Soon after the establishment of top research centers and groups, Bioinformatics became an important key driver to advancement of many other areas of biology including medicine and healthcare which are presently undergoing profound changes. Automation and miniaturization accompanied with technological innovations such as whole-genome sequencing, DNA arrays and other high-throughput technologies including advancements in high-resolution imaging technologies, genomic medicine, wide range of mobile health applications and sensors, connected devices, and many more, triggered an explosion in Big Data production. Even though the potential of Big Data exploitation for improving health is enormous, the technical, legal, ethical and political challenges cannot easily be overcome worldwide.

Health informatics (also called health care informatics, healthcare informatics, medical informatics, nursing informatics, clinical informatics, or biomedical informatics) is a multidisciplinary field that uses pattern recognition, data mining, machine learning algorithms, and visualization via various health information technologies (HIT) to improve health care. This requires the synergies of clinicians, and researchers together with laypersons. Transparency, legitimacy, knowledge of process and use of data must be built upon trustful and honest relationships in order to improve the retrieval methods, develop new tools, and receive appropriate training to generate, analyze, and query data effectively and efficiently.

Examining, for example, the role Health Informatics has played on the management of Medical Systems in various parts of the world is quite challenging. In continents such as Europe where cultural and economic diversity is high, plus the European health systems and databases are diverse and fragmented, it is hard to find a common ground. Medical systems in Europe seem to lack compatibility in terms of data formats, processing, analysis, and data transfer. It is nevertheless interesting to see that despite the lack of harmony, legal frameworks for data sharing are already established and are evolving.

Europeans are in the process of addressing barriers to a common way of medical system management and improvement of health of the citizens, hoping that these efforts will contribute to creating the European Single Market for health, which will improve healthcare for all Europeans. The European Federation for Medical Informatics Association (EFMI) represents 32 countries and it acts as a nonprofit organization in medical informatics in Europe concerned with the theory and practice of Information Science and Technology within Health and Health Science in a European context (EFMI, 2016). See in Table 2 the site and some recent conferences and workshops organized by EFMI.

The objectives of EFMI when founded in 1976 were:

- To advance international co-operation and dissemination of information in Medical Informatics on a European basis;
- To promote high standards in the application of medical informatics;
- To promote research and development in medical informatics;
- To encourage high standards in education in medical informatics;
- To function as the autonomous European Regional Council of IMIA.

Soon it became imperative for Europeans to develop high quality Electronic Health Record Systems (HERs) an effort that has brought together scientists, politicians, representatives from the industry and developers (Ng et al., 2014). See mission in Table 2 under http://www.eurorec.org/

A number of annual conferences and congress meetings are presently devoted to Informatics for Free/Libre Health and Hospital Information System in Europe. Representatives from key sectors such as politics, science, users and industry participate. See Table 2.

Furthermore, projects have been developed such as 'ARGOS' see link. http://www.isi.edu/~argos/

The main goal of the ARGOS project was to contribute to creating:

A Transatlantic Observatory for Meeting Global Health Policy Challenges through ICT-Enabled Solutions and to allow promotion of Common Methods for Responding to Global eHealth Challenges in the EU and the US. The results are used to provide various users recommendations in sustaining coordinated actions. It is important to both Europe and America of United States because:

1. *There is a barrier in fostering healthcare globally as citizens travel and migrate*
2. *It will help improve their products to better promote themselves in global markets*
3. *The global experiences will become important information for both Europe and America.*

Similarly, across the Atlantic from the European Continent, US has undertaken some very interesting initiatives toward improving Health and Managing Health Systems more effectively as one can see if the links in Table 2 are explored. The situation is similar in Canada, Japan, Australia and even China and India. However, there are so many other factors that influence the use and development of Health Informatics in the different parts of the world, including level of economic development, which has made the establishment of relevant World Organizations necessary in order to promote equity among poor and rich countries. See Table 2.

An important initiative to enhance innovation in biomedical research with the ultimate goal of moving the U.S. into an era where medical treatment can be tailored to each patient is called Precision Medicine Initiative (PMI, 2016).

Precision medicine is an approach to disease treatment and prevention that seeks to maximize effectiveness by taking into account individual variability in genes, environment, and lifestyle. Precision medicine seeks to redefine our understanding of disease onset and progression, treatment response, and health outcomes through the more precise measurement of molecular, environmental, and behavioral factors that contribute to health and disease. This understanding will lead to more accurate diagnoses, more rational disease prevention strategies, better treatment selection, and the development of novel therapies. In March of 2015, NIH Director Dr. Francis Collins formed the PMI Working Group of the Advisory Committee to the Director to develop a plan for creating and managing such a research cohort. (PMI, 2016)[3]

Health Informatics in Japan, China, N. and S. America, Australia, Africa and other parts of the World have followed similar support and promotion from nonprofit organizations which represent the interests of a broad range of clinical and non-clinical professionals. The list of such organizations in Table 2, even though not exhaustive, is nevertheless indicative of the current state of Health Informatics and policy initiatives worldwide.

Table 2. Medical and health informatics in the world

	Main Associations/ Organizations	**Conferences/Workshops in Bioinformatics and Health Informatics**
Health Informatics in Europe	*The European Federation for Medical Informatics Association (EFMI)* https://www.efmi.org/about/mission-and-history *The EUROREC Institute (EuroRec)* http://www.eurorec.org/ The EUROREC Institute (EuroRec) is an independent not-for-profit organisation, promoting in Europe the use of high quality Electronic Health Record systems (EHRs). One of its main missions is to support, as the European authorised certification body, EHRs certification development, testing and assessment by defining functional and other criteria."	***Conferences*** *Global Healthcare Management Conferences* http://healthinformatics.conferenceseries.com/ GNU Health Con is an annual conference that brings together enthusiasts and developers of the Free/Libre Health & Hospital Information System. http://gnuhealthcon.org/2016-las_palmas/ The Congress will bring together: Europe's leading conference, Medical Informatics Europe (MIE2017) from the European Federation for Medical Informatics (EFMI – www.efmi.org) and The Farr Institute International Conference 2017 (www.farrinstitute.org). http://informaticsforhealth.org/ Medical Informatics Europe (MIE2017) from the European Federation for Medical Informatics (EFMI – www.efmi.org) and The Farr Institute International Conference 2017 (www.farrinstitute.org). Predictive modeling in healthcare – from prediction to prevention http://www.ehealthsummit.at/ehome/ehsat16/english/ ***Workshops*** http://bigdata2015.uni.lu/eng/European-Commission-satellite-workshop
Health Informatics in the USA	*National Academy of Sciences (NAS)* http://www.nasonline.org/ *National Academy of Medicine (NAM)* https://nam.edu/initiatives/ *Centers for Diseases Control* https://www.cdc.gov/ *National Institutes of Health* https://www.nih.gov/ https://www.nih.gov/health-information *The Precision Medicine Initiative® (PMI) Cohort Program* https://www.nih.gov/precision-medicine-initiative-cohort-program *All of Us^{SM} Research Program* https://www.nih.gov/AllofUs-Research-Program *The National Center for Biotechnology Information* https://www.ncbi.nlm.nih.gov/ *NCBI data analysis tools* https://www.ncbi.nlm.nih.gov/home/analyze.shtml *The Phenotype-Genotype Integrator (PheGenI)* https://www.ncbi.nlm.nih.gov/gap/phegeni *Health Insurance Portability and Accountability Act of 1996 (HIPAA)* *Omics International* http://research.omicsgroup.org/index.php/Main_Page http://research.omicsgroup.org/index.php/National_Center_for_Biotechnology_Information	***Conferences*** *Global Healthcare Management Conferences* http://healthinformatics.conferenceseries.com/ *4th International Conference on Biomedical and Health Informatics May 25-26, 2017 Chicago, USA* http://healthinformatics.conferenceseries.com/
Health Informatics in Australia	*Asia-Pacific Association of Medical Informatics* http://www.apami.org/ *The Australasian College of Health Informatics* http://www.achi.org.au/	

continued on next page

Table 2. Continued

	Main Associations/ Organizations	Conferences/Workshops in Bioinformatics and Health Informatics
Health Informatics in China	China Medical Information Association (CMIA) http://www.cmia.info/cn/index.asp *National and Health Planning Commission in China* http://www.moh.gov.cn/public/open.aspx?n id=9787&seq=0 www.moh.gov.cn/ uploadfile/200406/2004629144259379.doc	
Health Informatics in Japan	*JAPAN: Center for Public Health Informatics* https://www.niph.go.jp/soshiki/12kenkyuu/ index_en.html *Japan Association of Medical Informatics* https://www.jami.jp/english/index.php	
Health Informatics in India	*National Health Portal India* http://www.nhp.gov.in/health-informatics_pg *Bioinformatics Institute of India Medical and Healthcare Informatics* http://www.bii.in/programs/distancelearning/ healthcare.html#	
Health Informatics in Canada	*Canada's Health Informatics Association* http://coachorgnew.com/ *eHealthOntario* http://www.ehealthontario.on.ca/en/	
Health Informatics in Africa	*The Pan African Health Informatics Association* http://www.helina-online.org/	
Health Informatics in South America	*The International Medical Informatics Association for Latin America and the Caribbean (IMIA-LAC)* http://www.uia.org/s/or/en/1100037886 *Brazilian Society of Health Informatics* http://www.sbis.org.br/	
Health Informatics in Saudi Arabia	*Saudi Association for Health Informatics* http://www.ksau-hs.edu.sa/English/ KnowledgeCenter/ScientificAssociation/Pages/ HealthInformatics.aspx	

GOING FROM BIG DATA TO SMART DATA TO WISE DATA

Data Collection, Analysis and ICT Considerations

Data collection and analysis require that innovative methods and technologies are explored for data acquisition and management. Investment on research initiatives in the field of Big Data analysis and integration has become a necessity. Major investments are needed on Omics data and on fields of bioinformatics, biomathematics, and biostatistics as such data is a mixture of meaning full signals, noise and errors.

Analyses of omics data and best use of high-throughput technologies can be achieved by multi-talented scientists and multidisciplinary research teams. Such teams will be examining high-value variables in their biologic investigations analyses and identification data from electronic health records EHRs.

Furthermore, health insurance organizations and participant surveys will greatly benefit from mHealth technologies.

Data Structure and Management

When it comes to actual data structure and management a research team should ensure the following:

- Sensitivity of the data,
- Need for committees,
- Use of a common data model to organize data similarly,
- Careful early selection of commonly used Health technologies,
- Proper integration,
- Careful analysis of data,
- Visualization,
- Maintain data security and privacy.

In Figure 3, one can see features of Big Data which need to be considered as Big Data is collected, stored and integrated often, the truth is, without the consent of the patient. This needs to change and engage patients in the process. At the same time where as volume, velocity and variety of data encountered are technical problems and with innovative computing methods and tools could be managed, for veracity to be achieved and obtain smart data value for better predictions and therapies, new investments are required so as to make wise decisions concerning Health matters.

Figure 3. Features of big data and smart data toward becoming wise data

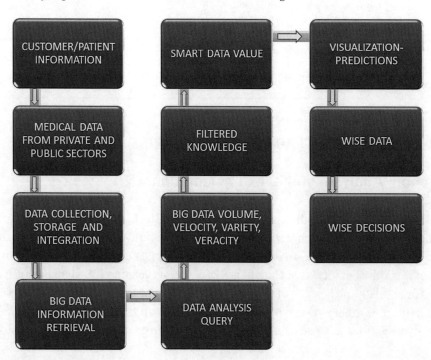

Data Access, Data Normalization, and Participant Engagement

When it comes to data access and data normalization, stakeholders should ensure the following, see Figure 3:

- Not for profit collaborations,
- Appropriate participant communication,
- Careful coordination of data,
- Appropriate biospecimens collection and storage,
- Use of Biobanking when needed,
- Hybrid data and analytics architecture,
- Ensure smooth transition from Big Data to Smart Data to Wise Data.

In order to ensure sufficient access to needed data and data normalization so that Health Informatics are effective, the engagement of patients / users of the Health Systems is important. No Health System can function without legitimacy; thus, the perceptions and trust of the users are significant. Patients should also consent to the use of their data in the context of these informatics; security and privacy issues and relevant cultural values are important concerns. Thus, participant's engagement will not only facilitate Health Informatics but it can better guarantee the "good" use of these data, which leads us to the next point.

Governance and Social Cohesion

In order to ensure a sustainable health system both in terms of cohesion and longevity, care must be taken through appropriate services and governance structure to not only achieve better health but also social improvement. This requires investment on health infrastructure and adequate health resources that demand good and effective leadership and institutional authority based on professional expertise. It also requires effective social control and participation mechanisms that can ensure the use of data for the public good. Often a good number of steering and executive committees should be put together in order to have a smooth operation and management of Big Data from individuals but also Big Data related to medical systems operations as a whole. Figure 4 below schematically shows the processes and cooperation that are needed for effective and socially useful Health Informatics.

Both Figures 4 and 5 outline a generic framework of Health Informatics governance for individual wellness and social welfare. In this framework, the individual is prioritized, the interests of the medical centers, data providers and analyzers and the health industry are considered so that eventually healthy and satisfied people live in sustainable smart communities. This of course can be achieved if data curation privacy and security is ensured through open or shared repositories. These kind of operations would be a result of careful planning from the part of associations, organizations, administrators and clinicians who should look into allocating resources appropriately and into using the right health applications and software tools for health monitoring, filtering out the wise data for an overall wellness determination.

Figure 4. From the individual to clinicians to governance to social cohesion

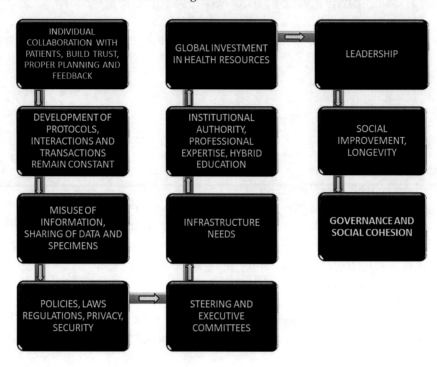

Figure 5. Framework of health informatics governance- Policies and regulations for all stakeholders

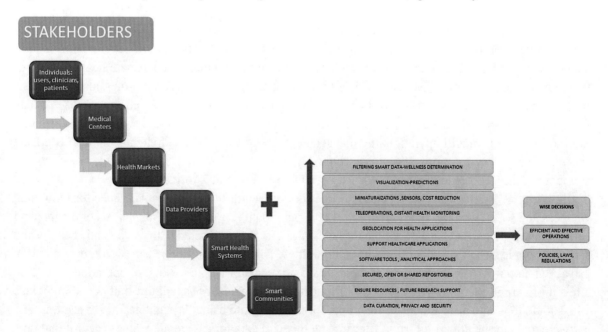

Policy, Laws and Regulations Considerations

As a number of these issues require that privacy and security matters are carefully considered, it is of high importance that the process is guided by strict and clear policies, laws and regulations when handling and sharing, for example, data and specimens. Appropriate biospecimens collection should follow strict agreed protocols and regulations that will not create problems in handling and storage of materials and specimens, nor when use of Biobanking is needed. In a similar way, all kinds of miniaturizations, monitors and sensors should follow strict restrictions and standards in their making and also maintain low cost without sacrificing quality of accessibility.

Participants-Stakeholders-Patient Engagement

This integration and interoperation of omics data comes as an important limiting factor in the transition to personalized medicine. Trust needs to build up with the patients and achieve collaborations which will allow interactions and transactions to remain constant. This can be relatively easily achieved if there is development of protocols that lead to proper personal information handling. Prevention also requires changes in our culture and institutions / structures that support preventive approaches (e.g. medical exams for prevention preferred and supported in the health system). This kind of patient engagement, transparency and legitimacy is what is required for effective prevention, diagnosis and treatment strategies to be established. Only in this way, one can expect effective personalized medicine to become a common practice.

Large omics (genomics, transcriptomics, proteomics, epigenomics, metagenomics, metabolomics, nutriomics, etc.) data has certainly revolutionized biology and has led to the emergence of systems biology for a better understanding of biological mechanisms. Systems biology relies on experimental and computational approaches in order to provide mechanistic insights to an endpoint. So all these omics approaches are becoming less and less about data generation and more and more about data management, integration, analysis, and interpretation.

1. **Translational Bioinformatics:** A relatively new term used referring to the collection of vast amounts of health related biomedical and genomic data and its translation into individual tailored clinical entities as an effort to narrow the growing gaps in the socioeconomic and scientific progress toward personalized medicine (Tenenbaum, 2016). There are four themes categorized under this field.
2. **Clinical Big Data:** A collection of electronic health records used for innovations (Marr, 2016)
3. **Genomics in Clinical Care Genomic Data:** Gene involvement in unknown or rare conditions/ syndromes (Tenenbaum, 2016)
4. **Omics for Drugs Discovery and Repurposing:** An already approved drug by FDA could be used for treatment of another disease/condition (Tenenbaum, 2016)
5. **Personalized Genomic Testing:** Direct- to-consumer (DTC) genetic testing (Tenenbaum, 2016)

According to Chen J. et al. 2013, another similar way of categorizing translational bioinformatics is the following four subdisciplines:

(1) bioinformatics (molecules and cells); (2) imaging informatics (tissues and organs); (3) clinical informatics (individuals); and (4) public health informatics (populations). In their table 1 there is good reference to a wide spectrum of translational bioinformatics activities along several dimensions, including (1) areas of research purpose;(2) data types;(3) informatics tools to support practice.

As these activities span a wide spectrum of translational bioinformatics it is easier for personalized medicine to meet the four p's depicted in Figure 6 i.e. be effectively preventive, predictable, participatory and personalized. For personalized medicine to be considered preventive, effective methods and tools should exist for early intervention and prognosis and these should be supported (e.g. financially too) by health institutions (like insurance companies). This immediately could enhance disease risk analysis as scientists and clinicians will be able to predict the outcome of disease. At the same time, trust is built as a firm and honest relationship amongst all stakeholders if the patient is expected to become involved in the treatment and decision making.

Finally, one indeed easily comes to understand that conventional medicine, although it is still the mainstream approach to treating diseases especially in urgent medical cases, often fails to provide personalized treatment and cure as it targets branches of diseases, while multiple medications exist that do not necessarily fit well with the specific problem. Personalized medicine was the next goal to be targeted by a number of medical systems, private and public, and has improved treatments and therapies in some parts of the world as it tries to tailor each person's unique genetic makeup. But only very recently as seen in the US precision medicine initiative, serious efforts have been made to take into account the individual variability in genes, the environment one lives and the life style (see Figure 7). This is in fact, it is hoped to be the best possible outcome with minimum side effects and that many other countries will follow the example of US.

Figure 6. Framework of personalized medicine

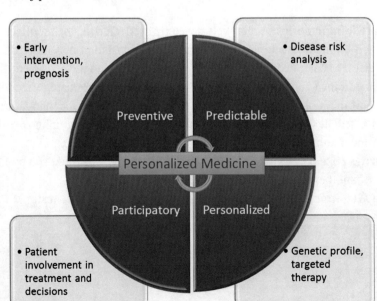

Figure 7. Moving from conventional medicine to individualized medicine to precision medicine

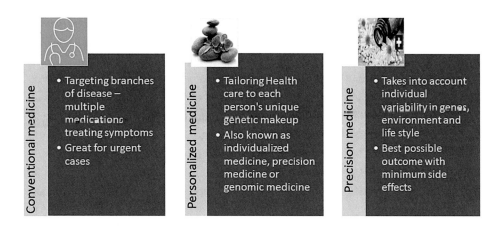

SOLUTIONS AND RECOMMENDATIONS

Healthcare bioinformatics will generate many challenges, as it is a very complex issue at the same time that it holds significant promise. In fact, it can allow a more integrative approach to health – a serious shortcoming of western medicine – and support a turn to prevention and conception of health as a holistic state of wellness. However, for this to happen, appropriate scientific and technological advances are not adequate; social, political, cultural and ethical considerations should be carefully thought of and guide the application of health bioinformatics.

In the near future, healthcare bioinformatics will change the collection of patient data concerning molecular measurements, DNA, RNA, protein and metabolite data and along with traditional medicine practices, a more comprehensive and routine collection will be in place to provide relevant information in assessing more appropriately the individuals' health state and needs. A good example is The Phenotype-Genotype Integrator (PheGenI) which merges NHGRI genome-wide association study (GWAS) catalog data with several databases housed at the National Center for Biotechnology Information (NCBI), including Gene, dbGaP, OMIM, GTEx and dbSNP. This type of data is intended for clinicians and epidemiologists who can search based on chromosomal location, gene, SNP, or phenotype and view and download results including annotated tables of Single Nucleotide Polymorphisms (SNPs), genes and association results, a dynamic genomic sequence viewer, and gene expression data (PheGenI, 2016; Zhang, 2011; Schuster, 2007; Schultz, 2013; Wang, 2014; Lin et al., 2015). Patients should be actively engaged in the whole process of health care, from its design to its evaluation, with the aim being a high degree of trust, the securing of public health as a public good and the protection of privacy. The health care system should be structured to reflect widely open public deliberations regarding its mission, aims and priorities. This requires careful and collective discussions and decision making processes that can generate common social visions for a health care system and the aim of Health Informatics (e.g. not only lengthening human life but also improving the quality of life but within the limits of nature). Regular monitoring and evaluation of health care institutions and the applications of Health Informatics by all stakeholders (i.e. patients / users, doctors and administrative staff) should also be included as integral parts of the health system and should aim to provide valuable information for subsequent enhancements as needed. Information and Communication Technologies can facilitate such open processes of deliberation, monitoring and evaluation.

Future societies will increase their capacity to improve their health status if they invest on advances in genomic technologies, data collection and storage, computational analysis, and various electronic and mobile health applications. Knowledge of the genetic factors contributing to diseases together with epigenetic modifications resulting from gene and environment interactions along with being in the position to identify single nucleotide polymorphisms will lead to better prognosis, diagnosis and treatment. The discovery of biomarkers is helpful in the identification of people with increased or decreased risk of developing certain diseases. This will lead to empowerment of patients as they will be in the position to not only be better informed about their health problem but to also make wiser decisions about their therapy plan and improvement of health. Such information may also be used by people themselves to organize their lives in ways that promote their well being and prevention of diseases – based on their strengths and genetic predispositions to disease. This presupposes the advancement of our knowledge on preventative medicine and wellness practices in parallel with Health Informatics; the two bodies of knowledge and practice – on the one hand, alternative medical practices aiming to strengthen healthy organisms and maintain health and therapeutic practices and Health Informatics on the other – should be used in a complementary manner.

In addition, gathering and analyzing human genome related data and large metabolomics data is expected to transform basic and applied scientific research as well. Despite the fact that most of molecular biology research data is open, repurposing healthcare data for research will not be a very smooth transition as its use is regulated by national legislation and policies that vary in terms of societal norms, culture and language. The present constraints for access should change toward making healthcare data available to all stakeholders involved if it will help to bring forward better solutions even when reference to research is not made. However, this should be done with careful consideration of all possibilities and the concurrent installation of safety measures that would protect individuals and communities from malignant practices that can increase social inequalities and exclusion, or even more collective forms of discrimination.

Basic research nevertheless needs to be connected to healthcare, as there are many practical problems to be resolved where research holds solutions. If healthcare is to leverage the fields of Omics, then powerful computational tools must be developed together with the appropriate training in the handling and analysis of data on massive scales. A number of technical and structural problems must be resolved and common technical language and terms be used so that meta-data is aligned and clinical data is properly analyzed and shared. This will certainly require development of global frameworks which take into consideration ethical and regulatory challenges. Security issues must be carefully coordinated so as to allow data accessibility and visualization via secure electronic methods. Given the close interrelation between an individual's wellbeing and health on the one hand and psychological and social needs and parameters on the other, the balance between security of private data and private life and access to health information that can inform better decisions on and approaches to health concerns should be carefully considered.

Academic and commercial groups and industry in general need to be coordinated better and this can be achieved if common global frameworks exist to which there is agreement from all parties involved. A good number of teams need to coordinate their work in terms of technical, meta-data, ethical, regulatory and security work and no longer work in isolation. It seems that global associations and alliances could help improve such synergies. Good teamwork together with enabling talented people to deliver their expertise could greatly shrink the time needed to improve personalized medicine and why not precision medicine.

Making big data smart implies ability to technically connect relevant data to identify patterns. Turning smart data to wise implies the integral consideration of social, cultural and political considerations to ensure the holistic wellbeing of the individual, but also a community that promotes health, wellness and spiritual integrity above anything else.

The potential benefits to society and the individual then are great if such efforts to transform Big Data into Smart Data and from that to Wise Data are successful. This transformation can be achieved when the motivation of people to participate and the rewards of collaboration are high. This is not an unachievable goal and all stakeholders should be working toward that direction.

It is clear that genomics & health informatics data can be useful in selection of therapies and prevention. We must not forget however, that each one and each society has different value priorities, different understanding of health and quality of life. Maybe genomics / healthcare informatics call us to rethink what we consider good quality of life and thus, what the health care system should be doing.

Although the connection between health care information and research – via bio/health informatics – is very promising, opening unimaginable new ways for health care enhancement and even prevention, significant issues relating to privacy of health data, security issues of ICTs, the reconception of the health system as something promoting wellness and prevention for all and the organization of the health care system based on transparency and trust should be addressed first. The future societies should move away from the current view of health, therapies or the health care system as commodities to be purchased and sold. A good suggestion is that the promotion of Bioinformatics / Health Informatics, precision medicine etc. should be done by interdisciplinary groups that involve health and social experts, clinicians and researchers alike, in a system that aims to systemic biology and medicine (looking at the individual as an integrated system). Furthermore, their use and applications should be regulated with the guidance of international health organizations, while organized and administered with control and decision making at the local level with the active involvement of social groups at all levels. High level leadership with clear vision and goals is incredibly important but even more important is to find people with the right expertise, motivation and skills together with the will to contribute toward the direction set forward. Talented people need to be given the space and also be allowed to creatively form the conditions and manifestations of intelligent and wise delivery.

CONCLUSION

As authors of this paper, we are convinced that the time is right to mount an ambitious effort worldwide to transform the understanding of factors contributing to individual health and wellness, with the conviction that success in this effort will advance human societies. Individuals will be healthier if they live in a World where the patients are engaged participants in full trust and belief that medical systems and clinicians will closely collaborate in improving their health and where maintaining a healthy balance in individual human organisms is a priority before treatment of disease. To move toward sustainable societies with healthy individuals being its members, we need to facilitate data access, and storage, data normalization and data management as well as an inseparable connection of data management with ethical considerations. This can be accomplished with the right type of education and training of individuals and the establishment of systems for the maintenance of healthy individuals and societies, but also by taking into consideration the health resources that need to be allocated in Medicine and Medical Systems including the development of powerful computational tools and methods. Policy considerations and governance then become a number one priority for all societies both at local and global level but also the individual engagement to this vision of improving human health and condition of all people. This then will be the time where Big Data not only will have passed successfully through the Smart Data stage but also will have managed to be viewed as Wise Data. After all, for individuals to achieve satisfaction in their life, body and mind should coexist in harmony and in health.

REFERENCES

Alyass, A., Turcotte, M., & Meyre, D. (2015). From Big Data analysis to personalized medicine for all: Challenges and opportunities. *BMC Medical Genomics*, *8*(33). PMID:26112054

Angiuoli, S. V., Matalka, M., Gussman, A., Galens, K., Vangala, M., Riley, D. R., & Fricke, W. F. et al. (2011). CloVR: A virtual machine for automated and portable sequence analysis from the desktop using cloud computing. *BMC Bioinformatics*, *12*(1), 356. doi:10.1186/1471-2105-12-356 PMID:21878105

BGI. (2016) Retrieved from http://www.bgi.com/

Chen, C.-C., Chang, Y.-J., Chung, W.-C., Lee, D.-T., & Ho, J.-M. (2013). CloudRS: an error correction algorithm of high-throughput sequencing data based on scalable framework. *Proceedings of the IEEE International Conference on Big Data*, Santa Clara, California (pp. 717–722). doi:10.1109/Big-Data.2013.6691642

Chen J, Qian F, Yan W, et al. (2013). Translational biomedical informatics in the cloud: present and future. *Biomed Res Int*.

Deb, B., & Srirama, S. N. (2013). Social networks for eHealth solutions on cloud. *Frontiers in Genetics*, *4*, 171. doi:10.3389/fgene.2013.00171 PMID:24027578

Deligiannis, P., Loidl, H.-W., & Kouidi, E. (2012). Improving the diagnosis of mild hypertrophic cardiomyopathy with MapReduce. *Proceedings of Third International Workshop on MapReduce and its Applications Date*, Delft, Netherlands (pp. 41–48). ACM. doi:10.1145/2287016.2287025

European Bioinformatics Institute (EBI). (2016) Retrieved from http://www.ebi.ac.uk/

Global Alliance for Genomics and Health. (GA4GH). (2016). Retrieved from http://genomicsandhealth.org

Greene, A. C., Giffin, K. A., Greene, C. S. & Moore, J. H. (2015). Adapting bioinformatics curricula for Big Data. *Briefings in Bioinformatics-Bioinformatics Curricula*.

He, C., Fan, X., & Li, Y. (2013). Toward ubiquitous healthcare services with a novel efficient cloud platform. *IEEE Transactions on Bio-Medical Engineering*, *60*(1), 230–234. doi:10.1109/TBME.2012.2222404 PMID:23060318

Hesper, B., ... (1970). Bioinformatica: een werkconcept (In Dutch.). Kameleon. 1(6), 28–29.

Hirak, K., Hasin, A. A., Nazrul, H., Swarup, R. & Dhruba, K. B. (2014). Big Data Analytics in Bioinformatics: A Machine Learning Perspective. *Journal of Latex class files, 13*(9), 1-20.

Huang, H., Tata, S., & Prill, R. J. (2013). BlueSNP: R package for highly scalable genome-wide association studies using Hadoop clusters. *Bioinformatics (Oxford, England), 29*(1), 135–136. doi:10.1093/bioinformatics/bts647 PMID:23202745

Huang, W., Li, L., Myers, J. R., & Marth, G. T. (2012). ART: A next-generation sequencing read simulator. *Bioinformatics (Oxford, England), 28*(4), 593–594. doi:10.1093/bioinformatics/btr708 PMID:22199392

Jourdren, L., Bernard, M., Dillies, M.-A., & Le Crom, S. (2012). A cloud computing-based framework facilitating high throughput sequencing analyses. *Bioinformatics (Oxford, England), 28*(11), 1542–1543. doi:10.1093/bioinformatics/bts165 PMID:22492314

Lewis, S., Csordas, A., Killcoyne, S., Hermjakob, H., Hoopmann, M. R., Moritz, R. L., & Boyle, J. et al. (2012). Hydra: A scalable proteomic search engine which utilizes the Hadoop distributed computing framework. *BMC Bioinformatics, 13*(1), 324. doi:10.1186/1471-2105-13-324 PMID:23216909

Lin, W., Dou, W., Zhou, Z., & Liu, C. (2015). A cloud-based framework for home-diagnosis service over big medical data. *Journal of Systems and Software, 102*, 192–206. doi:10.1016/j.jss.2014.05.068

Luo, J., Wu, M., Gopukumar, D., & Zhao, Y. (2016). Big Data Application in Biomedical Research and Health Care: A Literature Review. *Biomedical Informatics Insights, 8*, 1–10. doi:10.4137/BII.S31559 PMID:26843812

Margolis, R., Derr, L., Dunn, M., Huerta, M., Larkin, J., Sheehan, J., & Green, E. D. et al. (2014). The National Institutes of Healths Big Data to Knowledge (BD2 K) initiative: Capitalizing on biomedical Big Data. *Journal of the American Medical Informatics Association, 21*(6), 957–958. doi:10.1136/amiajnl-2014-002974 PMID:25008006

Markonis, D., Schaer, R., Eggel, I., ….. (2012). Using MapReduce for large-scale medical image analysis. *Proceedings of the 2012 IEEE Second International Conference on Healthcare Informatics, Imaging and Systems Biology (HISB)*, La Jolla, California. IEEE. doi:10.1109/HISB.2012.8

Nagasaki, H., Mochizuki, T., Kodama, Y., Saruhashi, S., Morizaki, S., Sugawara, H., & Nakamura, Y. et al. (2013). DDBJ read annotation pipeline: A cloud computing-based pipeline for high-throughput analysis of next-generation sequencing data. *DNA Research, 20*(4), 383–390. doi:10.1093/dnares/dst017 PMID:23657089

Ng, K., Ghoting, A., Steinhubl, S. R., Stewart, W. F., Malin, B., & Sun, J. (2014). PARAMO: A PARAllel predictive MOdeling platform for healthcare analytic research using electronic health records. *Journal of Biomedical Informatics, 48*, 160–170. doi:10.1016/j.jbi.2013.12.012 PMID:24370496

Niemenmaa, M., Kallio, A., Schumacher, A., Klemela, P., Korpelainen, E., & Heljanko, K. (2012). Hadoop-BAM: Directly manipulating next generation sequencing data in the cloud. *Bioinformatics (Oxford, England), 28*(6), 876–877. doi:10.1093/bioinformatics/bts054 PMID:22302568

NIH. (2016). The Precision Medicine Initiative (PMI) Cohort Program. Retrieved from https://www.nih.gov/precision-medicine-initiative-cohort-program

Robinson, T., Killcoyne, S., Bressler, R., & Boyle, J. (2011). SAMQA: Error classification and validation of high-throughput sequenced read data. *BMC Genomics*, *12*(1), 419. doi:10.1186/1471-2164-12-419 PMID:21851633

Salzberg, S. L., Phillippy, A. M., Zimin, A., Puiu, D., Magoc, T., Koren, S., & Yorke, J. A. et al. (2012). A critical evaluation of genome assemblies and assembly algorithms. *Genome Research*, *22*(3), 557–567. doi:10.1101/gr.131383.111 PMID:22147368

Schultz, T. (2013). Turning healthcare challenges into Big Data opportunities: A use-case review across the pharmaceutical development lifecycle. Bulletin of the Association for Information Science and Technology, *39*(5), 34–40. doi:10.1002/bult.2013.1720390508

Schumacher, A., Pireddu, L., Niemenmaa, M., Kallio, A., Korpelainen, E., Zanetti, G., & Heljanko, K. (2014). SeqPig: Simple and scalable scripting for large sequencing data sets in Hadoop. *Bioinformatics (Oxford, England)*, *30*(1), 119–120. doi:10.1093/bioinformatics/btt601 PMID:24149054

Schuster, S. C. (2007). Next-generation sequencing transforms today's biology. *Nature*, *200*(8), 16–18. PMID:18165802

Tenenbaum, J. D. (2016). Translational Bioinformatics: Past, Present, and Future. *Genomics, Proteomics & Bioinformatics*, *14*(1), 31–41. doi:10.1016/j.gpb.2016.01.003 PMID:26876718

The International Medical Informatics Association (IMIA). (2016). Retrieved from http://imia-medinfo.org/wp/welcome-to-imia-2/

The Phenotype-Genotype Integrator (PheGenI). (2016). Retrieved from https://www.ncbi.nlm.nih.gov/gap/phegeni

United Nations (UN). (2016). *Sustainable Development Goals. 17 Goals to Transform the World.* Retrieved from http://www.un.org/sustainabledevelopment/sustainable-development-goals/

United Nations (UN). (2016). *Vast majority of world – 6.76 billion people – living with excessive air pollution – UN report.* Retrieved from http://www.un.org/apps/news/story.asp?NewsID=55138#.WD-NFVH2K_NI

Wang, W., & Krishnan, E. (2014). Big Data and clinicians: A review on the state of the science. *JMIR Med Inform.*, *2*(1), e1. doi:10.2196/medinform.2913 PMID:25600256

Wiewiórka, M. S., Messina, A., Pacholewska, A., Maffioletti, S., Gawrysiak, P., & Okoniewski, M. J. (2014). SparkSeq: Fast, scalable, cloud-ready tool for the interactive genomic data analysis with nucleotide precision. *Bioinformatics (Oxford, England)*, *30*(18), 2652–2653. doi:10.1093/bioinformatics/btu343 PMID:24845651

World Health Organization (WHO). (2016) Retrieved from http://www.who.int/en/

Zhang, J., Chiodini, R., Badr, A., & Zhang, G. (2011). The impact of next-generation sequencing on genomics. *Journal of Genetics and Genomics = Yi Chuan Xue Bao*, *38*(3), 95–109. doi:10.1016/j.jgg.2011.02.003 PMID:21477781

ENDNOTES

[1] Other examples of cloud computing include:
The Amazon Elastic Compute Cloud (EC2) http://aws.amazon.com/ec2/ (Chen. J. et al., 2013)
IBM/Google Cloud https://cloud.google.com/products/#big-data (Chen et al., 2013)
the *EasyGenomics cloud* www.easygenomics.com (Alyass et al., 2015)
in *Beijing Genomics Institute (BGI),* http://www.genomics.cn/en/navigation/show_navigation?nid=64 (Alyass et al., 2015)
and *"Embassy" clouds as part of ELIXIR project* https://www.elixir-europe.org/platforms/compute (Alyass et al., 2015)
Graphic Processing Units (GPUs) http://toolshed.g2.bx.p-su.edu Alyass et al., 2015)
Bioconductor https://www.bioconductor.org/ (Alyass et al., 2015)
CytoScape http://www.cytoscape.org/ (Alyass et al., 2015).

[2] Major categories of Bioinformatics Tools:
https://www.quora.com/What-are-commonly-used-bioinformatics-tools
There are both standard and customized products to meet the requirements of particular projects. There are data-mining software that retrieve data from genomic sequence databases and also visualization tools to analyze and retrieve information from proteomic databases. These can be classified as homology and similarity tools, protein functional analysis tools, sequence analysis tools and miscellaneous tools."
https://en.wikipedia.org/wiki/List_of_open-source_bioinformatics_software
https://en.wikipedia.org/wiki/List_of_open-source_health_software
https://toolkit.tuebingen.mpg.de/
https://genomicsandhealth.org/
https://en.wikipedia.org/wiki/List_of_open-source_bioinformatics_software
https://en.wikipedia.org/wiki/List_of_open-source_health_software
https://toolkit.tuebingen.mpg.de/
https://genomicsandhealth.org/

[3] For more information on PMI and the working groups' report check the link in Table 2 and also see the report https://www.nih.gov/sites/default/files/research-training/initiatives/pmi/pmi-working-group-report-20150917-2.pdf

Chapter 2
Bioinformatics:
Applications and Implications

Kijpokin Kasemsap
Suan Sunandha Rajabhat University, Thailand

ABSTRACT

This chapter describes the overview of bioinformatics; bioinformatics, data mining, and data visualization; bioinformatics and secretome analysis; bioinformatics, mass spectrometry, and chemical cross-linking reagents; bioinformatics and Software Product Line (SPL); bioinformatics and protein kinase; bioinformatics and MicroRNAs (miRNAs); and clinical bioinformatics and cancer. Bioinformatics is the application of computer technology to the management and analysis of biological data. Bioinformatics is an interdisciplinary research area that is the interface between biology and computer science. The primary goal of bioinformatics is to reveal the wealth of biological information hidden in the large amounts of data and obtain a clearer insight into the fundamental biology of organisms. Bioinformatics entails the creation and advancement of databases, algorithms, computational and statistical techniques, and theory to solve the formal and practical problems arising from the management and analysis of biological data.

INTRODUCTION

Bioinformatics involves algorithms to represent, store, and analyze the biological data (Li, 2015), including DNA (deoxyribosenucleic acid) sequence, RNA (ribosenucleic acid) expression, protein, and small-molecule abundance within cells (Altman, 2012). Bioinformatics is an interdisciplinary approach utilizing both data collection and information modeling to organize, analyze, and visualize the biological data (Al-Ageel, Al-Wabil, Badr, & AlOmar, 2015) based on the optimal use of big data gathered in genomics, proteomics, and functional genomics research (Song, Kim, Zhang, Ding, & Chambers, 2014).

Big data contains the very large sets of data that are produced by people using the Internet, and that can only be stored, understood, and utilized with the help of special tools and methods (Kasemsap, 2016a). Big data can enhance the significant value by making information transparent and usable at much higher frequency in modern operations (Kasemsap, 2017a). The important goal of bioinformatics is to

DOI: 10.4018/978-1-5225-2607-0.ch002

facilitate the management, analysis, and interpretation of biological data from biological experiments and observational studies (Moore, 2007).

With the increasingly accumulated data from high-throughput technologies, study on biomolecular networks has become one of the most important perspectives in systems biology and bioinformatics (Zhang, Jin, Zhang, & Chen, 2007). Many bioinformatics tools developed for DNA microarrays can be reused in proteomics, however, the uniquely quantitative nature of proteomics data also offers the novel analysis possibilities, which directly enhance the biological mechanisms (Kumar & Mann, 2009). DNA microarray enables investigators to simultaneously study the gene expression profile and gene activation of thousands of genes and sequences (Chen, Weixing, Sheng, & Zhilong, 2013). Health care-related bioinformatics databases are increasingly offering the possibility to maintain, organize, and distribute the DNA data (Dalpé & Joly, 2014).

Recently, the interests in proteomics have been increased, and the proteomic methods have been widely applied to many problems in cell biology (Haga & Wu, 2014). Proteomics is the large-scale study of proteins, particularly their structures and functions (Anderson & Anderson, 1998), and has become one of the most important approaches to analyzing and understanding biological systems (Oveland et al., 2015). Protein-protein interactions have been at the focus of computational biology in recent years (Hooda & Kim, 2012). Solving the problem of predicting protein interactions from the genome sequence leads to the obvious understanding of complex networks, evolution, and human disease (Reimand, Hui, Jain, Law, & Bader, 2012). Nibbe et al. (2011) stated that protein interaction databases play an increasingly important role in systems biology approaches to the study of disease.

Bioinformatics tools for proteomics, also known as proteome informatics tools, span a large panel of very diverse applications, ranging from simple tools to compare protein amino acid compositions to sophisticated software for the large-scale protein structure determination (Palagi, Hernandez, Walther, & Appel, 2006), and deal with the analysis of protein sequences (one dimensional pattern) and structures (three-dimensional pattern) (Mardia, 2013). Courcelles et al. (2011) indicated that the novel and improved computational tools are required to transform large-scale proteomics data into valuable information of biological relevance.

This chapter is based on a literature review of bioinformatics. The extensive literature of bioinformatics provides a contribution to practitioners and researchers by describing the applications and implications of bioinformatics in order to maximize the scientific impact of bioinformatics in the fields of biology and computer science.

BACKGROUND

In recent years, there has been an explosion of biological data stored in the central databases, tools to handle the data, and educational programs to train scientists in utilizing bioinformatics resources (Shachak, 2006). Bioinformatics is a significant discipline that performs the analysis, modeling, and simulation of complex biological systems by using computer science approach, dealing with large amounts of biological data (Merelli, Pérez-Sánchez, Gesing, & D'Agostino, 2014). Bioinformatics enables biomedical investigators to exploit the existing and emerging computational technologies to effectively store, mine, retrieve, and analyze the biological data from genomics and proteomics technologies (Fenstermacher, 2005). Modern technologies have rapidly transformed biology into a data-intensive discipline (Strizh, 2006).

Regarding bioinformatics, differential gene expression analysis and proteomics have exerted the significant impact on the illustration of cellular processes, as the simultaneous measurement of hundreds to thousands of individual objects on the level of RNA and protein ensembles became technically feasible (Perco et al., 2006). RNA molecules are the key building blocks, sensors, and regulators of modern cells (Dieterich & Stadler, 2013). MicroRNAs (miRNAs) are the endogenous single-stranded, 22-nt (nucleotide) RNAs which complement mRNA to initiate post-transcriptional regulation (Gana, Victoriano, & Okamoto, 2012). miRNAs are a large family of endogenous small RNAs derived from the non-protein coding genes (Singh, Srivastava, & Sharma, 2016), and are the primary regulators of fundamental biological processes including cellular differentiation, proliferation, apoptosis, as well as synaptic plasticity (Carroll, Goodall, & Liu, 2014). miRNAs belong to the family of noncoding RNAs (ncRNAs) and have gained importance due to its role in the complex biochemical approaches (Omer, Singh, Yadav, & Singh, 2015).

High-throughput sequencing technologies generate millions of sequence reads from DNA/RNA molecules rapidly and cost-effectively, enabling single investigator laboratories to address a wide variety of "omics" questions in nonmodel organisms, fundamentally changing the way genomic approaches are used to advance biological research (Zhou & Rokas, 2014). Understanding complex biological systems requires the extensive support of computational tools (Ghosh, Matsuoka, Asai, Hsin, & Kitano, 2013). The huge increase in data being produced in the genomic era has produced a need to incorporate computers into the research process (Badotti et al., 2014). To execute the genomic data and understand the embedded information significantly demands the complex computational analysis in a field known as bioinformatics (Fu & Fu, 2015).

SIGNIFICANT PERSPECTIVES ON BIOINFORMATICS

This section provides the overview of bioinformatics; bioinformatics, data mining, and data visualization; bioinformatics and secretome analysis; bioinformatics, mass spectrometry, and chemical cross-linking reagents; bioinformatics and software product line (SPL); bioinformatics and protein kinase; bioinformatics and miRNAs; and clinical bioinformatics and cancer.

Overview of Bioinformatics

Bioinformatics approaches have been found useful in several research areas which include disease detection, control and diagnosis, drug discovery and development, genome informatics, epidemiology, biomedical imaging, and ecosystems modeling (Ojo & Omabe, 2011). The choice of technology and bioinformatics approach is critical in obtaining the accurate information from the next-generation sequencing (NGS) experiments (Nevado & Perez-Enciso, 2015). NGS technologies have produced a substantial decrease in the cost and the complexity of generating sequence data and are allowing researchers to tackle questions that were not previously possible (Belcaid & Toonen, 2015). Orobitg et al. (2015) indicated that the multiple sequence alignment (MSA) plays a key role in many domains in bioinformatics and can be in a wide range of applications, such as phylogenetic analysis, and homology detection.

Proteins are the principal element of the organization of the cell architecture (Garcia-Garcia et al., 2012). Proteins are the important cellular molecules, and the interacting protein pairs provide the biologically important information, such as functional relationships (Mamitsuka, 2012). Complexes of physically interacting proteins constitute the fundamental functional units responsible for driving biological processes within cells (Srihari, Yong, Patil, & Wong, 2015). Many bioinformatics programs have been developed to indicate the functional positions from the sequence alignments of protein families (Tungtur, Parente, & Swint-Kruse, 2011).

Advances in bioinformatics help biomedical research community obtain the deeper insights into the fundamentals of biology through modern technologies, such as high-throughput genomic sequencing and its data analysis, as well as mathematical modeling of biological processes (Karikari & Aleksic, 2015). High-throughput genomic technologies (e.g., DNA microarray) generate large amounts of data, establishing an interest in data mining and modeling (Fu & Fu, 2015), causes a paradigm shift in the life sciences (Hack & Kendall, 2005), and detect hundreds of candidate disease genes (Doncheva, Kacprowski, & Albrecht, 2012). One of the most common goals of DNA microarray experiments is to identify the genes related to biological processes (Bair, 2013). DNA metabarcoding, which couples the principles of DNA barcoding with NGS technologies, provides an opportunity to easily produce large amounts of data on biodiversity (Coissac, Riaz, & Puillandre, 2012).

The main result of a great deal of the proteomics studies is a list of identified proteins, which requires to be interpreted concerning research question and existing knowledge (Laukens, Naulaerts, & Berghe, 2015). Proteomics offers the most direct approach to understanding disease and its molecular biomarkers (Brusic, Marina, Wu, & Reinherz, 2007). Biomarkers denote the biological states of tissues, cells, or body fluids that are useful for disease detection and classification. Clinical proteomics is used for early disease detection, molecular diagnosis of disease, identification and formulation of therapies, and disease monitoring and prognostics. Focusing on the use of informatics tools (e.g., Lima & Garcês, 2006; Smith, M'ikanatha, & Read, 2015), bioinformatics employs novel informatics techniques to organize and analyze biological data (Shachak & Fine, 2008). Bioinformatics tools are essential for converting raw proteomics data into knowledge and subsequently into useful applications (Brusic et al., 2007).

Although bioinformatics usually requires less infrastructural investments compared to bench science-intensive disciplines, essential resources (e.g., powerful computer systems, reliable high-speed Internet, access to essential databases, software programs, and reliable electricity supply) are necessary (Ojo & Omabe, 2011). Graphical bioinformatics is the branch of bioinformatics that initiates analysis of DNA, RNA, and proteins by considering various graphical representations of these sequences (Randic, Novic, & Plavsic, 2013). There are numerous examples of the application of evolutionary algorithms (EAs) in bioinformatics (Fogel & Corne, 2003). Many problems in bioinformatics deal with complex optimization tasks (Pinho, Sobral, & Rocha, 2013). EAs are the computational methods that can solve the bioinformatics-related problems based on the analogies with the process of evolution through natural selection (Holland, 1975).

Bioinformatics and genome science (BGS) are the new disciplines, gaining importance across the biomedical research, health care, and agriculture sectors due to their importance in helping to improve the timeliness and accuracy of disease diagnosis, prognosis and treatment, as well as enhancing crop yield (Machuka, 2004). While the scientifically advanced countries in North America and Europe have been the major leaders in BGS, many developing countries have made important achievements in applying genomics technologies to enhance biomedical research, health care, and agriculture (Machuka, 2004).

In the past decades, with the rapid development of high-throughput technologies, biology research has generated an unprecedented amount of data (Zhou, Liao, & Guan, 2013). In order to store and process such a great amount of data, cloud computing is applied to many fields of bioinformatics (Zhou et al., 2013). Cloud computing is a new style of computing in which virtualized resources are provided as the services over the Internet (Kasemsap, 2015a). In addition, cloud computing deployment can enable supply chain organizations to explore the new graphic territories and reach out to more customers, toward gaining the effective utilization of resources, expansion of business, and the higher revenues in global supply chain (Kasemsap, 2015b).

Regarding bioinformatics perspectives, acquiring sequence data is followed by the large-scale computational analysis in order to execute the data, validate experiment results, and provide scientific insights (Liu et al., 2014). Investment in the sequencing instrument should be accompanied by substantial investment in computer hardware, skilled informatics support, and bioinformaticians who are competent in configuring and utilizing specific software to analyze the data (Krampis et al., 2012). Most research institutes significantly implement their bioinformatics applications on the laboratory-hosted servers (Rosenthal et al., 2010), and as data volume greatly varies, the capabilities in storing and analyzing genome data are not enough to fulfill the dynamic requirements of different workflows.

Bioinformatics, Data Mining, and Data Visualization

Data mining is the computational procedure of pioneering schemes in the large data sets regarding methods at the integration of artificial intelligence, machine learning, statistics, and database systems (Kasemsap, 2015c). Artificial intelligence is the branch of computer science that develops intelligent machines and software (Kasemsap, 2017b). Data mining is profitably utilized to discover patterns and relationships in the data in order to help make better business decisions (Kasemsap, 2016b). Data mining is increasingly used in the analysis of data generated in life sciences, including biological data produced in several disciplines, such as genomics and proteomics, medical data produced in clinical practice, and administrative data produced in health care (Cannataro, Guzzi, & Sarica, 2013).

Human factors significantly contribute to the information visualization-related design considerations and usability evaluation process, and play an important role in the design, development, and quality assurance of bioinformatics tools (Al-Ageel et al., 2015). Despite the technological advances in bioinformatics computational methods, humans are an essential part of the data mining and decision-making process (Al-Ageel et al., 2015). With the increased reliance on web-based systems in bioinformatics research and the rapid developments in biological databases, the human factors in designing interactive bioinformatics systems continues to be an important issue (Mirel, 2009).

The revolutionary nature of bioinformatics domain and the increased volume of data available in biological data sets contribute to increasing the number of applications that serve the bioinformatics community (Mao & McEnhimer, 2010). Classification techniques are important in bioinformatics analysis as they can separate various bioinformatics data into distinct groups (Guan, Yuan, Ma, & Lee, 2014). Accessing, examining, analyzing and publishing biological data are the frequent activities of biologists (Douglas, Goulding, Farris, & Atkinson-grosjean, 2011). Bioinformatics specialists and scientists utilize the biological data obtained from the web-based bioinformatics systems to conduct the experimental studies and answer the research questions (Mirel, 2007). The major responsibility of software engineers who develop bioinformatics tools is to measure the usability of their computational systems by utilizing the reliable metrics that reflect the accuracy of the retrieved data and usefulness of these systems (Al-Ageel et al., 2015).

Data visualization plays an essential role in the high-throughput biology and is the method to explore, understand, and communicate the data in a way descriptive statistical properties can hardly compete with (Gatto, Breckels, Naake, & Gibb, 2015). Information visualization can provide valuable assistance for data analysis in bioinformatics by visually depicting sequences, genomes, alignments, and macromolecular structures. Information visualization and the interaction modalities of bioinformatics tools affect the efficiency of decision-making tasks in the applied bioinformatics computing (Al-Ageel et al., 2015).

Data mining and machine learning techniques (Alpaydin, 2010) have become a need in many bioinformatics applications (Bacardit, Widera, Lazzarini, & Krasnogor, 2014). The applications of data mining and machine learning techniques to biological and biomedicine data continue to be the ubiquitous research themes in current bioinformatics (Triguero et al., 2015) and effectively enhance the extraction of useful information from data in a wide variety of biological problems, such as genomics, proteomics, and microarrays (Larraaga et al., 2006).

Bioinformatics and Secretome Analysis

The analyses of secretomes (i.e., complete sets of secreted proteins) have been reported in various organisms, cell types, and pathologies (Caccia, Dugo, Callari, & Bongarzone, 2013). The term secretome refers to a set of proteins that includes extracellular matrix (ECM) proteins, which are proteins shed from the cell membrane, and vesicle proteins (e.g., from exosomes and microsomal vesicles) (Makridakis & Vlahou, 2010). An interesting fraction of secreted factors comprise cell surface receptor ligands, such as hormones, growth factors, and cytokines with the regulatory functions in the biological processes (Walsh, 2009).

While the earliest secretome analyses were performed in bacteria and fungi (Antelmann et al., 2001), there have been many investigations into the mammalian secretome. The majority of secretome studies are conducted in vitro utilizing cell culture methods in which secreted proteins are obtained from conditioned media of serum-starved cell lines (Blanco et al., 2012). These studies employ the high-resolution separation techniques (e.g., two-dimensional gel electrophoresis and liquid chromatography) in combination with advanced mass spectrometric methods for the unequivocal identification of peptides and proteins in samples (Peterson, Grinyer, & Nevalainen, 2011).

Many bioinformatics tools can be utilized to predict prokaryotic and eukaryotic secreted proteins from genomic/transcriptomic annotations (Shah et al., 2009). Such predictions are available because of the particular conserved features of secreted proteins. In eukaryotes, classical secreted proteins can be indicated by the presence of an N-terminal cleavable signal peptide (SP) that is 15–30 amino acids long (Caccia et al., 2013). Signal peptides do not exhibit the high sequence homology, but they share the same structural composition: a hydrophobic core established by hydrophilic N- and C-terminal regions, with conserved amino acids at the -3 and -1 positions related to the cleavage site (von Heijne, 1985). Proteins that are secreted through alternative pathways can be indicated by various signal peptides, such as the twin-arginine translocation (TAT) signal in prokaryotes and plants and the lipobox signal in bacteria (Lee, Tullman-Ercek, & Georgiou, 2006). The class of secretory proteins recognized as leaderless proteins is exported from the cell without signal sequences, through non-classical secretion pathways, such as cell surface shedding and inclusion in exosomes and other secretory vesicles (Raimondo, Morosi, Chinello, Magni, & Pitto, 2011).

Bioinformatics, Mass Spectrometry, and Chemical Cross-Linking Reagents

Mass spectrometry proteomics data significantly contain much information about cell functions and disease conditions (Cannataro & Veltri, 2007). The discovery of such information is enabled by the combined utilization of modern bioinformatics tools and data mining techniques requiring the integration of large data sources and the composition of different software tools (Cannataro & Veltri, 2007). For the analysis of protein-protein interactions and protein conformations, cross-linking coupled with mass spectrometry has become an important tool in recent years (Tran, Goodlett, & Goo, 2016). A variety of cross-linking reagents are utilized to link the interacting amino acids to indicate the protein-binding partners.

Bioinformatics promoting the detection of cross-link peptides has been limited to a small number of protein sequence database and often utilized for the targeted analysis in considering cross-linked sites with prior knowledge about what protein complexes are interacting (Tran et al., 2016). To enhance the mass spectrometry detection, cross-linked peptides may incorporate the functional labeling groups that produce a mass difference between heavy- and light-stable isotope patterns (Krauth, Ihling, Ruttinger, & Sinz, 2009), toward facilitating effective detection (Muller, Dreiocker, Ihling, Schafer, & Sinz, 2010). The tools that can detect the cross-links from the complex samples using the larger protein databases by either use of isotopically tagged cross-linkers or cleavable cross-linkers have demonstrated the feasibility of high-throughput identification of cross-link sites and peptides (Panchaud, Singh, Shaffer, & Goodlett, 2010).

Bioinformatics and Software Product Line

Most scientists that utilize bioinformatics applications do not have appropriate training on software development (Costa, Braga, David, & Campos, 2015). Software product line (SPL) employs the concept of reutilization and is viewed as a set of systems that are developed from a common set of base artifacts (Costa et al., 2015). Clements and Northrop (2002) considered SPL as a set of software-intensive systems sharing a common set of features which are managed to satisfy the particular needs of the specific market segment and that are developed from a common set of core assets in an effective manner.

SPL engineering can help understand the software being developed because scientists can follow the scientific model that indicates the product line and make decisions according to their needs, for each point of variation of this model (Remmel, Paech, Engwer, & Bastian, 2011). In SPL context for the scientific domain, analyzing the difficulties when indicating scientific experiments and recognizing the possibility of scientific applications composition, there is a need for a more suitable semantic support for the domain analysis phase (Costa et al., 2015).

The application of scientific workflows (van der Linden, Schmid, & Rommes, 2007) in the SPL with the support of the feature model (Czarnecki, Kim, & Kalleberg, 2006), related to ontologies (Gruber, 1995), can enable the development of scientific experiments. The development process of a family of programs is divided into two phases: domain engineering and application engineering (Yu & Smith, 2009). The development of core artifacts or the domain engineering phase is related to the development of reusable components from the domain analysis of SPL. Application engineering is responsible for analyzing the requirement of scientific application to be generated (Costa et al., 2015).

Bioinformatics and Protein Kinase

Protein kinases have been implicated in a number of diseases, where kinases participate many aspects that control cell growth, movement, and death (Chen, Luo, Zhang, & Chen, 2015). Protein kinases are considered as the second most important group of drug targets after G-protein-coupled receptors (Cohen, 2002). Deciphering protein structure and protein-protein interactions has provided the insight into protein conformation and has led to the characterization of unknown protein functions (Tran et al., 2016). When proteins interact, conformational changes lead to the formation of transient or stable protein complexes that control various cellular processes (Tran et al., 2016).

Bioinformatics (Hunter, 1993) involving the aspects of computer science, mathematics, and molecular biology has become integral to the perspectives of protein kinases. Bioinformatics has been widely applied to investigate the regulatory mechanisms of protein kinase, including their structural and functional features (Chen & Chen, 2006). The study of in-depth knowledge of kinase pathways and possible role to disease state is a big challenge (Kitano, 2007). There are many studies that combine the molecular biology, biochemistry, genetics, and bioinformatics for modern drug development (Chen & Chen, 2006).

Bioinformatics analysis can be used to study large protein superfamilies and to predict the structural changes which can increase enzyme stability (Suplatov, Voevodin, & Švedas, 2015). There are several groups of protein kinases, and each group can be categorized into families and subfamilies (Hanks & Hunter, 1995). Nearly 400 human diseases have been reported to be connected to protein kinases, such as cancer (Song et al., 2010), cardiovascular (Rose, Force, & Wang, 2010), neurological disorders (Guo, Kozlov, Lavin, Person, & Paull, 2010), diabetes (Sengupta, Peterson, & Sabatini, 2010), rheumatoid arthritis (Shao, Goronzy, & Weyand, 2010), and asthma (Verdino, Witherden, Havran, & Wilson, 2010). Kinase activity is highly regulated by phosphorylation, by combining activator proteins or inhibitor proteins (Noble, Endicott, & Johnson, 2004), or by changing their cellular location.

Bioinformatics and MicroRNAs

MicroRNAs (miRNAs) are involved in many biological processes (Yin, Shen, Xie, Cheng, & Zhu, 2016). miRNA regulates the gene expression at the post-transcriptional level and plays an important role in plant development (Singh et al., 2016). Bioinformatics approaches can improve the functional characterization of cardiovascular miRNAs and optimize the identification of miRNA candidate selection for testing (Kunz et al., 2015). Several online bioinformatics tools can predict miRNA targets, such as PicTar, miRanda, TargetScan and RNAhybrid (Witkos, Koscianska, & Krzyzosiak, 2011).

As mammalian miRNAs reduce protein output predominantly by the destabilization of the target mRNAs (Guo, Ingolia, Weissman, & Bartel, 2010), the inverse correlation between the expression levels of miRNA and targeted mRNA should reflect their functional interaction. Large numbers of plant genes with the perspectives of development, progression, and root development (Wang et al., 2005), leaf organ morphogenesis and polarity (Mallory, Dugas, Bartel, & Bartel, 2004), environmental stresses (Stief et al., 2014) are regulated by miRNAs. Bioinformatics screening is utilized to indicate which of those throughput sequences are miRNAs (Prakash, Ghosliya, & Gupta, 2014).

Clinical Bioinformatics and Cancer

Clinical bioinformatics as a new way to combine clinical measurements and signs with human tissue-generated bioinformatics is crucial to translate biomarkers into clinical application, validate the disease specificity, and understand the role of biomarkers in clinical settings. Bioinformatics provides an important platform to assist biologists in developing the minimally invasive biomarkers to detect cancer, and in designing effective personalized therapies to treat cancer patients (Banwait & Bastola, 2015). The small non-coding RNAs including miRNAs have shown the potential to act as the biomarkers for cancer diagnosis as well as therapeutic agents to cure cancer (Iorio & Croce, 2012).

Scientists have been trying to decipher the molecular mechanism of cancer cell formation and the role of oncogene (i.e., a kind of abnormal gene that predisposes cells to develop into cancers.) and tumor suppressor gene (i.e., a kind of gene that protects a cell from one step on the path to cancer) in cancer development (Abba, Mudduluru, & Allgayer, 2012). The discovery of various oncogenes and tumor suppressor genes has provided the insight into the biology of cancer and the development of drugs to combat these potential targets (Broderick & Zamore, 2011). Integrating gene and miRNA expression data with computational analysis tools has helped to identify the role of miRNAs in cancer progression and metastasis and their potential role in acting as therapeutic agents in the treatment and cure for cancer (Edelman, Eddy, & Price, 2010).

FUTURE RESEARCH DIRECTIONS

The classification of the extensive literature in the domains of bioinformatics will provide the potential opportunities for future research. Bioinformatics is an interdisciplinary field that develops and improves on methods for storing, retrieving, organizing, and analyzing the biological data. A major activity in bioinformatics is to develop software tools to generate the useful biological knowledge. Bioinformatics is being used in the establishment of global databases in microbiology to build an accumulative knowledge repository that captures the reams of experimental data and meta-data about microorganisms and to develop general data mining tools for knowledge discovery within this data-rich environment.

Proteogenomics is a research area that combines areas as proteomics and genomics in a multi-omics setup using both mass spectrometry and high-throughput sequencing technologies. Cheminformatics evolves from a field of study associated with drug discovery into the major discipline that embraces the distribution, management, access, and sharing of chemical data. Information retrieval is the process of obtaining relevant information from a collection of informational resources (Kasemsap, 2017c). Through text mining, information can be extracted to derive summaries for the words contained in the document or to compute summaries for the document based on the words contained in them (Kasemsap, 2017d). An examination of linkages among bioinformatics, proteogenomics, cheminformatics, information retrieval, and text mining would seem to be viable for future research efforts.

CONCLUSION

This chapter explained the overview of bioinformatics; bioinformatics, data mining, and data visualization; bioinformatics and secretome analysis; bioinformatics, mass spectrometry, and chemical cross-linking reagents; bioinformatics and SPL; bioinformatics and protein kinase; bioinformatics and miRNAs; and clinical bioinformatics and cancer. Bioinformatics is the application of computer technology to the management and analysis of biological data. Bioinformatics is an interdisciplinary research area that is the interface between biology and computer science. The primary goal of bioinformatics is to reveal the wealth of biological information hidden in the large amounts of data and obtain a clearer insight into the fundamental biology of organisms. Bioinformatics entails the creation and advancement of databases, algorithms, computational and statistical techniques, and theory to solve the formal and practical problems arising from the management and analysis of biological data.

In experimental molecular biology, bioinformatics techniques (e.g., image and signal processing) allow the extraction of useful results from large amounts of raw data. In the field of genetics and genomics, bioinformatics aids in sequencing and annotating genomes and their observed mutations. Bioinformatics plays an important role in the textual mining of biological literature and the development of biological and gene ontologies to organize the biological data. Bioinformatics plays a crucial role in the analysis of gene and protein expression. Bioinformatics helps analyze and categorize the biological pathways and networks that are an important part of systems biology. In structural biology, bioinformatics aids in the simulation and modeling of DNA, RNA, and protein structures as well as molecular interactions.

REFERENCES

Abba, M., Mudduluru, G., & Allgayer, H. (2012). MicroRNAs in cancer: Small molecules, big chances. *Anti-cancer Agents in Medicinal Chemistry*, *12*(7), 733–743. doi:10.2174/187152012802650273 PMID:22292749

Al-Ageel, N., Al-Wabil, A., Badr, G., & AlOmar, N. (2015). Human factors in the design and evaluation of bioinformatics tools. *Procedia Manufacturing*, *3*, 2003–2010. doi:10.1016/j.promfg.2015.07.247

Alpaydin, E. (2010). *Introduction to machine learning*. Cambridge, MA: MIT Press.

Altman, R. B. (2012). Translational bioinformatics: Linking the molecular world to the clinical world. *Clinical Pharmacology and Therapeutics*, *91*(6), 994–1000. doi:10.1038/clpt.2012.49 PMID:22549287

Anderson, N. L., & Anderson, N. G. (1998). Proteome and proteomics: New technologies, new concepts, and new words. *Electrophoresis*, *19*(11), 1853–1861. doi:10.1002/elps.1150191103 PMID:9740045

Antelmann, H. (2001, September 1). A proteomic view on genome-based signal peptide predictions. *Genome Research*, *11*(9), 1484–1502. doi:10.1101/gr.182801 PMID:11544192

Bacardit, J., Widera, P., Lazzarini, N., & Krasnogor, N. (2014). Hard data analytics problems make for better data analysis algorithms: Bioinformatics as an example. *Big Data*, *2*(3), 164–176. doi:10.1089/big.2014.0023 PMID:25276500

Badotti, F., Barbosa, A. S., Reis, A. L. M., do Valle, Í. F., Ambrósio, L., & Bitar, M. (2014). Comparative modeling of proteins: A method for engaging students interest in bioinformatics tools. *Biochemistry and Molecular Biology Education*, *42*(1), 68–78. doi:10.1002/bmb.20721 PMID:24167006

Bair, E. (2013). Identification of significant features in DNA microarray data. *Wiley Interdisciplinary Reviews: Computational Statistics*, *5*(4), 309–325. doi:10.1002/wics.1260 PMID:24244802

Banwait, J. K., & Bastola, D. R. (2015). Contribution of bioinformatics prediction in microRNA-based cancer therapeutics. *Advanced Drug Delivery Reviews*, *81*, 94–103. doi:10.1016/j.addr.2014.10.030 PMID:25450261

Belcaid, M., & Toonen, R. J. (2015). Demystifying computer science for molecular ecologists. *Molecular Ecology*, *24*(11), 2619–2640. doi:10.1111/mec.13175 PMID:25824671

Blanco, M. A., Leroy, G., Khan, Z., Aleckovic, M., Zee, B. M., Garcia, B. A., & Kang, Y. (2012). Global secretome analysis identifies novel mediators of bone metastasis. *Cell Research*, *22*(9), 1339–1355. doi:10.1038/cr.2012.89 PMID:22688892

Broderick, J. A., & Zamore, P. D. (2011). MicroRNA therapeutics. *Gene Therapy*, *18*(12), 1104–1110. doi:10.1038/gt.2011.50 PMID:21525952

Brusic, V., Marina, O., Wu, C. J., & Reinherz, E. L. (2007). Proteome informatics for cancer research: From molecules to clinic. *Proteomics*, *7*(6), 976–991. doi:10.1002/pmic.200600965 PMID:17370257

Caccia, D., Dugo, M., Callari, M., & Bongarzone, I. (2013). Bioinformatics tools for secretome analysis. *Biochimica et Biophysica Acta (BBA). Proteins and Proteomics*, *1834*(11), 2442–2453. doi:10.1016/j.bbapap.2013.01.039

Cannataro, M., Guzzi, P. H., & Sarica, A. (2013). Data mining and life sciences applications on the grid. *Data Mining and Knowledge Discovery*, *3*(3), 216–238.

Cannataro, M., & Veltri, P. (2007). MS-Analyzer: Preprocessing and data mining services for proteomics applications on the Grid. *Concurrency and Computation*, *19*(15), 2047–2066. doi:10.1002/cpe.1144

Carroll, A. P., Goodall, G. J., & Liu, B. (2014). Understanding principles of miRNA target recognition and function through integrated biological and bioinformatics approaches. *Wiley Interdisciplinary Reviews: RNA*, *5*(3), 361–379. doi:10.1002/wrna.1217 PMID:24459110

Chen, L., Weixing, S., Sheng, S., & Zhilong, A. (2013). Gene expression patterns combined with bioinformatics analysis identify genes associated with cholangiocarcinoma. *Computational Biology and Chemistry*, *47*, 192–197. doi:10.1016/j.compbiolchem.2013.08.010 PMID:24140882

Chen, Q., Luo, H., Zhang, C., & Chen, Y. P. P. (2015). Bioinformatics in protein kinases regulatory network and drug discovery. *Mathematical Biosciences*, *262*, 147–156. doi:10.1016/j.mbs.2015.01.010 PMID:25656386

Chen, Q. F., & Chen, Y. P. P. (2006). Mining frequent patterns for AMP-activated protein regulation on skeletal muscle. *BMC Bioinformatics*, *7*(394), 1–14. PMID:16939655

Clements, P., & Northrop, L. (2002). *Software product lines: Practices and patterns*. Boston, MA: Addison–Wesley.

Cohen, P. (2002). Protein kinases: The major drug targets of the twenty-first century? *Nature Reviews. Drug Discovery*, *1*(4), 309–315. doi:10.1038/nrd773 PMID:12120282

Coissac, E., Riaz, T., & Puillandre, N. (2012). Bioinformatic challenges for DNA metabarcoding of plants and animals. *Molecular Ecology*, *21*(8), 1834–1847. doi:10.1111/j.1365-294X.2012.05550.x PMID:22486822

Costa, G. C. B., Braga, R., David, J. M. N., & Campos, F. (2015). A scientific software product line for the bioinformatics domain. *Journal of Biomedical Informatics*, *56*, 239–264. doi:10.1016/j.jbi.2015.05.014 PMID:26079262

Courcelles, M., Lemieux, S., Voisin, L., Meloche, S., & Thibault, P. (2011). ProteoConnections: A bioinformatics platform to facilitate proteome and phosphoproteome analyses. *Proteomics*, *11*(13), 2654–2671. doi:10.1002/pmic.201000776 PMID:21630457

Czarnecki, K., Kim, C. H. P., & Kalleberg, K. T. (2006). *Feature models are views on ontologies.* Paper presented at the 10th International on Software Product Line Conference (SPLC 2006), Washington, DC. doi:10.1109/SPLINE.2006.1691576

Dalpé, G., & Joly, Y. (2014). Opportunities and challenges provided by cloud repositories for bioinformatics-enabled drug discovery. *Drug Development Research*, *75*(6), 393–401. doi:10.1002/ddr.21211 PMID:25195583

Dieterich, C., & Stadler, P. F. (2013). Computational biology of RNA interactions. *Wiley Interdisciplinary Reviews: RNA*, *4*(1), 107–120. doi:10.1002/wrna.1147 PMID:23139167

Doncheva, N. T., Kacprowski, T., & Albrecht, M. (2012). Recent approaches to the prioritization of candidate disease genes. *Wiley Interdisciplinary Reviews: Systems Biology and Medicine*, *4*(5), 429–442. PMID:22689539

Douglas, C., Goulding, R., Farris, L., & Atkinson-grosjean, J. (2011). Socio-cultural characteristics of usability of bioinformatics databases and tools. *Interdisciplinary Science Reviews*, *36*(1), 55–71. doi:1 0.1179/030801811X12941390545726

Edelman, L. B., Eddy, J. A., & Price, N. D. (2010). In Silico models of cancer. Wiley Interdisciplinary Reviews: Systems Biology and Medicine, 2(4), 438–459. doi:10.1002/wsbm.75

Fenstermacher, D. (2005). Introduction to bioinformatics. *Journal of the American Society for Information Science and Technology*, *56*(5), 440–446. doi:10.1002/asi.20133

Fogel, G., & Corne, D. W. (2003). *Evolutionary computation in bioinformatics.* San Francisco, CA: Morgan Kaufmann Publishers.

Fu, L. M., & Fu, K. A. (2015). Analysis of Parkinson's disease pathophysiology using an integrated genomics-bioinformatics approach. *Pathophysiology*, *22*(1), 15–29. doi:10.1016/j.pathophys.2014.10.002 PMID:25466606

Gana, N. H. T., Victoriano, A. F. B., & Okamoto, T. (2012). Evaluation of online miRNA resources for biomedical applications. *Genes to Cells*, *17*(1), 11–27. doi:10.1111/j.1365-2443.2011.01564.x PMID:22077698

Garcia-Garcia, J., Bonet, J., Guney, E., Fornes, O., Planas, J., & Oliva, B. (2012). Networks of protein–protein interactions: From uncertainty to molecular details. *Molecular Informatics*, *31*(5), 342–362. doi:10.1002/minf.201200005 PMID:27477264

Gatto, L., Breckels, L. M., Naake, T., & Gibb, S. (2015). Visualization of proteomics data using R and Bioconductor. *Proteomics*, *15*(8), 1375–1389. doi:10.1002/pmic.201400392 PMID:25690415

Ghosh, S., Matsuoka, Y., Asai, Y., Hsin, K. Y., & Kitano, H. (2013). Toward an integrated software platform for systems pharmacology. *Biopharmaceutics & Drug Disposition*, *34*(9), 508–526. doi:10.1002/bdd.1875 PMID:24150748

Gruber, T. R. (1995). Toward principles for the design of ontologies used for knowledge sharing. *International Journal of Human-Computer Studies*, *43*(5/6), 907–928. doi:10.1006/ijhc.1995.1081

Guan, D., Yuan, W., Ma, T., & Lee, S. (2014). Detecting potential labeling errors for bioinformatics by multiple voting. *Knowledge-Based Systems*, *66*, 28–35. doi:10.1016/j.knosys.2014.04.013

Guo, H., Ingolia, N. T., Weissman, J. S., & Bartel, D. P. (2010). Mammalian microRNAs predominantly act to decrease target mRNA levels. *Nature*, *466*(7308), 835–840. doi:10.1038/nature09267 PMID:20703300

Guo, Z., Kozlov, S., Lavin, M. F., Person, M. D., & Paull, T. T. (2010). ATM activation by oxidative stress. *Science*, *330*(6003), 517–521. doi:10.1126/science.1192912 PMID:20966255

Hack, C., & Kendall, G. (2005). Bioinformatics: Current practice and future challenges for life science education. *Biochemistry and Molecular Biology Education*, *33*(2), 82–85. doi:10.1002/bmb.2005.494033022424 PMID:21638550

Haga, S. W., & Wu, H. F. (2014). Overview of software options for processing, analysis and interpretation of mass spectrometric proteomic data. *Journal of Mass Spectrometry*, *49*(10), 959–969. doi:10.1002/jms.3414 PMID:25303385

Hanks, S. K., & Hunter, T. (1995). Protein kinases 6. The eukaryotic protein kinase superfamily: Kinase (catalytic) domain structure and classification. *The FASEB Journal*, *9*(8), 576–596. PMID:7768349

Holland, J. H. (1975). *Adaptation in natural and artificial systems*. Ann Arbor, MI: University of Michigan Press.

Hooda, Y., & Kim, P. M. (2012). Computational structural analysis of protein interactions and networks. *Proteomics*, *12*(10), 1697–1705. doi:10.1002/pmic.201100597 PMID:22593000

Hunter, L. (1993). *Artificial intelligence and molecular biology*. Cambridge, MA: MIT Press.

Iorio, M. V., & Croce, C. M. (2012). MicroRNA dysregulation in cancer: Diagnostics, monitoring and therapeutics. A comprehensive review. *EMBO Molecular Medicine*, *4*(3), 143–159. doi:10.1002/emmm.201100209 PMID:22351564

Karikari, T. K., & Aleksic, J. (2015). Neurogenomics: An opportunity to integrate neuroscience, genomics and bioinformatics research in Africa. *Applied & Translational Genomics*, *5*, 3–10. doi:10.1016/j.atg.2015.06.004 PMID:26937352

Kasemsap, K. (2015a). The role of cloud computing adoption in global business. In V. Chang, R. Walters, & G. Wills (Eds.), *Delivery and adoption of cloud computing services in contemporary organizations* (pp. 26–55). Hershey, PA: IGI Global. doi:10.4018/978-1-4666-8210-8.ch002

Kasemsap, K. (2015b). Adopting cloud computing in global supply chain: A literature review. *International Journal of Social and Organizational Dynamics in IT*, *4*(2), 49–62. doi:10.4018/IJSODIT.2015070105

Kasemsap, K. (2015c). The role of data mining for business intelligence in knowledge management. In A. Azevedo & M. Santos (Eds.), *Integration of data mining in business intelligence systems* (pp. 12–33). Hershey, PA: IGI Global. doi:10.4018/978-1-4666-6477-7.ch002

Kasemsap, K. (2016a). Mastering big data in the digital age. In M. Singh & D. G. (Eds.), Effective big data management and opportunities for implementation (pp. 104–129). Hershey, PA: IGI Global. doi:10.4018/978-1-5225-0182-4.ch008

Kasemsap, K. (2016b). Multifaceted applications of data mining, business intelligence, and knowledge management. *International Journal of Social and Organizational Dynamics in IT, 5*(1), 57–69. doi:10.4018/IJSODIT.2016010104

Kasemsap, K. (2017a). Software as a service, Semantic Web, and big data: Theories and applications. In A. Turuk, B. Sahoo, & S. Addya (Eds.), *Resource management and efficiency in cloud computing environments* (pp. 264–285). Hershey, PA: IGI Global. doi:10.4018/978-1-5225-1721-4.ch011

Kasemsap, K. (2017b). Mastering intelligent decision support systems in enterprise information management. In G. Sreedhar (Ed.), *Web data mining and the development of knowledge-based decision support systems* (pp. 35–56). Hershey, PA: IGI Global. doi:10.4018/978-1-5225-1877-8.ch004

Kasemsap, K. (2017c). Mastering web mining and information retrieval in the digital age. In A. Kumar (Ed.), *Web usage mining techniques and applications across industries* (pp. 1–28). Hershey, PA: IGI Global. doi:10.4018/978-1-5225-0613-3.ch001

Kasemsap, K. (2017d). Text mining: Current trends and applications. In G. Sreedhar (Ed.), *Web data mining and the development of knowledge-based decision support systems* (pp. 338–358). Hershey, PA: IGI Global. doi:10.4018/978-1-5225-1877-8.ch017

Kitano, H. (2007). A robustness-based approach to systems-oriented drug design. *Nature Reviews. Drug Discovery, 6*(3), 202–210. doi:10.1038/nrd2195 PMID:17318209

Krampis, K., Booth, T., Chapman, B., Tiwari, B., Bicak, M., Field, D., & Nelson, K. E. (2012). Cloud BioLinux: Pre-configured and on-demand bioinformatics computing for the genomics community. *BMC Bioinformatics, 13*(42), 3448–3449. PMID:22429538

Krauth, F., Ihling, C. H., Ruttinger, H. H., & Sinz, A. (2009). Heterobifunctional isotope-labeled amine-reactive photo-cross-linker for structural investigation of proteins by matrix-assisted laser desorption/ionization tandem time-of-flight and electrospray ionization LTQ-Orbitrap mass spectrometry. *Rapid Communications in Mass Spectrometry, 23*(17), 2811–2818. doi:10.1002/rcm.4188 PMID:19653199

Kumar, C., & Mann, M. (2009). Bioinformatics analysis of mass spectrometry-based proteomics data sets. *FEBS Letters, 583*(11), 1703–1712. doi:10.1016/j.febslet.2009.03.035 PMID:19306877

Kunz, M., Xiao, K., Liang, C., Viereck, J., Pachel, C., Frantz, S., & Dandekar, T. et al. (2015). Bioinformatics of cardiovascular miRNA biology. *Journal of Molecular and Cellular Cardiology, 89*, 3–10. doi:10.1016/j.yjmcc.2014.11.027 PMID:25486579

Larraaga, P., Calvo, B., Santana, R., Bielza, C., Galdiano, J., & Inza, I., & Robles, V. et al. (2006). Machine learning in bioinformatics. *Briefings in Bioinformatics, 7*(1), 86–112. doi:10.1093/bib/bbk007 PMID:16761367

Laukens, K., Naulaerts, S., & Berghe, W. V. (2015). Bioinformatics approaches for the functional interpretation of protein lists: From ontology term enrichment to network analysis. *Proteomics*, *15*(5/6), 981–996. doi:10.1002/pmic.201400296 PMID:25430566

Lee, P. A., Tullman-Ercek, D., & Georgiou, G. (2006). The bacterial twin-arginine translocation pathway. *Annual Review of Microbiology*, *60*(1), 373–395. doi:10.1146/annurev.micro.60.080805.142212 PMID:16756481

Li, L. (2015). The potential of translational bioinformatics approaches for pharmacology research. *British Journal of Clinical Pharmacology*, *80*(4), 862–867. doi:10.1111/bcp.12622 PMID:25753093

Lima, A. O. S., & Garcês, S. P. S. (2006). Intrageneric primer design: Bringing bioinformatics tools to the class. *Biochemistry and Molecular Biology Education*, *34*(5), 332–337. doi:10.1002/bmb.2006.494034052641 PMID:21638710

Liu, B., Madduri, R. K., Sotomayor, B., Chard, K., Lacinski, L., Dave, U. J., & Foster, I. T. et al. (2014). Cloud-based bioinformatics workflow platform for large-scale next-generation sequencing analyses. *Journal of Biomedical Informatics*, *49*, 119–133. doi:10.1016/j.jbi.2014.01.005 PMID:24462600

Machuka, J. (2004). Agricultural genomics and sustainable development: Perspectives and prospects for Africa. *African Journal of Biotechnology*, *3*(2), 127–135.

Makridakis, M., & Vlahou, A. (2010). Secretome proteomics for discovery of cancer biomarkers. *Journal of Proteomics*, *73*(12), 2291–2305. doi:10.1016/j.jprot.2010.07.001 PMID:20637910

Mallory, A. C., Dugas, D. V., Bartel, D. P., & Bartel, B. (2004). MicroRNA regulation of NAC-domain targets is required for proper formation and separation of adjacent embryonic, vegetative, and floral organs. *Current Biology*, *14*(12), 1035–1046. doi:10.1016/j.cub.2004.06.022 PMID:15202996

Mamitsuka, H. (2012). Mining from protein–protein interactions. *Wiley Interdisciplinary Reviews: Data Mining and Knowledge Discovery*, *2*(5), 400–410. doi:10.1002/widm.1065

Mao, W., & McEnhimer, S. (2010). *Survey: The application of GMOD in bioinformatics research.* Paper presented at the 4th International Conference on Bioinformatics and Biomedical Engineering (iCBBE 2010), Chengdu, China. doi:10.1109/ICBBE.2010.5516243

Mardia, K. V. (2013). Statistical approaches to three key challenges in protein structural bioinformatics. *Journal of the Royal Statistical Society. Series C, Applied Statistics*, *62*(3), 487–514. doi:10.1111/rssc.12003

Merelli, I., Pérez-Sánchez, H., Gesing, S., & D'Agostino, D. (2014). Latest advances in distributed, parallel, and graphic processing unit accelerated approaches to computational biology. *Concurrency and Computation*, *26*(10), 1699–1704. doi:10.1002/cpe.3111

Mirel, B. (2007). *Usability and usefulness in bioinformatics: Evaluating a tool for querying and analyzing protein interactions based on scientists' actual research questions.* Paper presented at 2007 IEEE International Professional Communication Conference (IPCC 2007), Seattle, WA. doi:10.1109/IPCC.2007.4464064

Mirel, B. (2009). Supporting cognition in systems biology analysis: Findings on users' processes and design implications. *Journal of Biomedical Discovery and Collaboration, 4*(2), 1–17. PMID:19216777

Moore, J. H. (2007). Bioinformatics. *Journal of Cellular Physiology, 213*(2), 365–369. doi:10.1002/jcp.21218 PMID:17654500

Muller, M. Q., Dreiocker, F., Ihling, C. H., Schafer, M., & Sinz, A. (2010). Fragmentation behavior of a thiourea-based reagent for protein structure analysis by collision-induced dissociative chemical cross-linking. *Journal of Mass Spectrometry, 45*(8), 880–891. doi:10.1002/jms.1775 PMID:20607845

Nevado, B., & Perez-Enciso, M. (2015). Pipeliner: Software to evaluate the performance of bioinformatics pipelines for next-generation resequencing. *Molecular Ecology Resources, 15*(1), 99–106. doi:10.1111/1755-0998.12286 PMID:24890372

Nibbe, R. K., Chowdhury, S. A., Koyutürk, M., Ewing, R., & Chance, M. R. (2011). Protein–protein interaction networks and subnetworks in the biology of disease. Wiley Interdisciplinary Reviews: Systems Biology and Medicine, 3(3), 357–367. doi:10.1002/wsbm.121

Noble, M. E., Endicott, J. A., & Johnson, L. N. (2004). Protein kinase inhibitors: Insights into drug design from structure. *Science, 303*(5665), 1800–1805. doi:10.1126/science.1095920 PMID:15031492

Ojo, O. O., & Omabe, M. (2011). Incorporating bioinformatics into biological science education in Nigeria: Prospects and challenges. *Infection, Genetics and Evolution, 11*(4), 784–787. doi:10.1016/j.meegid.2010.11.015 PMID:21145989

Omer, A., Singh, P., Yadav, N. K., & Singh, R. K. (2015). microRNAs: Role in leukemia and their computational perspective. Wiley Interdisciplinary Reviews: RNA, 6(1), 65–78. PubMed 10.1002/wrna.1256

Orobitg, M., Guirado, F., Cores, F., Llados, J., & Notredame, C. (2015). High performance computing improvements on bioinformatics consistency-based multiple sequence alignment tools. *Parallel Computing, 42*, 18–34. doi:10.1016/j.parco.2014.09.010

Oveland, E., Muth, T., Rapp, E., Martens, L., Berven, F. S., & Barsnes, H. (2015). Viewing the proteome: How to visualize proteomics data? *Proteomics, 15*(8), 1341–1355. doi:10.1002/pmic.201400412 PMID:25504833

Palagi, P. M., Hernandez, P., Walther, D., & Appel, R. D. (2006). Proteome informatics I: Bioinformatics tools for processing experimental data. *Proteomics, 6*(20), 5435–5444. doi:10.1002/pmic.200600273 PMID:16991191

Panchaud, A., Singh, P., Shaffer, S. A., & Goodlett, D. R. (2010). xComb: A cross-linked peptide database approach to protein-protein interaction analysis. *Journal of Proteome Research, 9*(5), 2508–2515. doi:10.1021/pr9011816 PMID:20302351

Perco, P., Rapberger, R., Siehs, C., Lukas, A., Oberbauer, R., Mayer, G., & Mayer, B. (2006). Transforming omics data into context: Bioinformatics on genomics and proteomics raw data. *Electrophoresis, 27*(13), 2659–2675. doi:10.1002/elps.200600064 PMID:16739231

Peterson, R., Grinyer, J., & Nevalainen, H. (2011). Secretome of the coprophilous fungus Doratomyces stemonitis C8, isolated from koala feces. *Applied and Environmental Microbiology, 77*(11), 3793–3801. doi:10.1128/AEM.00252-11 PMID:21498763

Pinho, J., Sobral, J. L., & Rocha, M. (2013). Parallel evolutionary computation in bioinformatics applications. *Computer Methods and Programs in Biomedicine, 110*(2), 183–191. doi:10.1016/j.cmpb.2012.10.001 PMID:23127284

Prakash, P., Ghosliya, D., & Gupta, V. (2014). Identification of conserved and novel microRNAs in *Catharanthus roseus* by deep sequencing and computational prediction of their potential targets. *Gene, 554*(2), 181–195. doi:10.1016/j.gene.2014.10.046 PMID:25445288

Raimondo, F., Morosi, L., Chinello, C., Magni, F., & Pitto, M. (2011). Advances in membranous vesicle and exosome proteomics improving biological understanding and biomarker discovery. *Proteomics, 11*(4), 709–720. doi:10.1002/pmic.201000422 PMID:21241021

Randic, M., Novic, M., & Plavsic, D. (2013). Milestones in graphical bioinformatics. *International Journal of Quantum Chemistry, 113*(22), 2413–2446.

Reimand, J., Hui, S., Jain, S., Law, B., & Bader, G. D. (2012). Domain-mediated protein interaction prediction: From genome to network. *FEBS Letters, 586*(17), 2751–2763. doi:10.1016/j.febslet.2012.04.027 PMID:22561014

Remmel, H., Paech, B., Engwer, C., & Bastian, P. (2011). *Supporting the testing of scientific frameworks with software product line engineering: A proposed approach.* Paper presented at the 4th International Workshop on Software Engineering for Computational Science and Engineering (SE–CSE 2011), Waikiki, HI. doi:10.1145/1985782.1985785

Rose, B. A., Force, T., & Wang, Y. (2010). Mitogen-activated protein kinase signaling in the heart: Angels versus demons in a heart-breaking tale. *Physiological Reviews, 90*(4), 1507–1546. doi:10.1152/physrev.00054.2009 PMID:20959622

Rosenthal, A., Mork, P., Li, M. H., Stanford, J., Koester, D., & Reynolds, P. (2010). Cloud computing: A new business paradigm for biomedical information sharing. *Journal of Biomedical Informatics, 43*(2), 342–353. doi:10.1016/j.jbi.2009.08.014 PMID:19715773

Sengupta, S., Peterson, T. R., & Sabatini, D. M. (2010). Regulation of the mTOR complex 1 pathway by nutrients, growth factors, and stress. *Molecular Cell, 40*(2), 310–322. doi:10.1016/j.molcel.2010.09.026 PMID:20965424

Shachak, A. (2006). Diffusion pattern of the use of genomic databases and analysis of biological sequences from 1970–2003: Bibliographic record analysis of 12 journals. *Journal of the American Society for Information Science and Technology, 57*(1), 44–50. doi:10.1002/asi.20251

Shachak, A., & Fine, S. (2008). The effect of training on biologists acceptance of bioinformatics tools: A field experiment. *Journal of the American Society for Information Science and Technology, 59*(5), 719–730. doi:10.1002/asi.20772

Shah, R., Lu, Y., Hinkle, C. C., McGillicuddy, F. C., Kim, R., Hannenhalli, S., & Reilly, M. P. et al. (2009). Gene profiling of human adipose tissue during evoked inflammation in vivo. *Diabetes, 58*(10), 2211–2219. doi:10.2337/db09-0256 PMID:19581417

Shao, L., Goronzy, J. J., & Weyand, C. M. (2010). DNA-dependent protein kinase catalytic sub-unit mediates T-cell loss in rheumatoid arthritis. *EMBO Molecular Medicine, 2*(10), 415–427. doi:10.1002/emmm.201000096 PMID:20878914

Singh, N., Srivastava, S., & Sharma, A. (2016). Identification and analysis of miRNAs and their targets in ginger using bioinformatics approach. *Gene, 575*(2), 570–576. doi:10.1016/j.gene.2015.09.036 PMID:26392033

Smith, R. A., M'ikanatha, N. M., & Read, A. F. (2015). Antibiotic resistance: A primer and call to action. *Health Communication, 30*(3), 309–314. doi:10.1080/10410236.2014.943634 PMID:25121990

Song, G., Zeng, H., Li, J., Xiao, L., He, Y., Tang, Y., & Li, Y. (2010). miR-199a regulates the tumor suppressor mitogen-activated protein kinase kinase kinase 11 in gastric cancer. *Biological & Pharmaceutical Bulletin, 33*(11), 1822–1827. doi:10.1248/bpb.33.1822 PMID:21048306

Song, M., Kim, S., Zhang, G., Ding, Y., & Chambers, T. (2014). Productivity and influence in bioinformatics: A bibliometric analysis using PubMed central. *Journal of the Association for Information Science and Technology, 65*(2), 352–371. doi:10.1002/asi.22970

Srihari, S., Yong, C. H., Patil, A., & Wong, L. (2015). Methods for protein complex prediction and their contributions towards understanding the organisation, function and dynamics of complexes. *FEBS Letters, 589*(19 Part A), 2590–2602. doi:10.1016/j.febslet.2015.04.026 PMID:25913176

Stief, A., Altmann, S., Hoffmann, K., Pant, B. D., Scheible, W. R., & Baurle, I. (2014). Arabidopsis miR156 regulates tolerance to recurring environmental stress through SPL transcription factors. *The Plant Cell, 26*(4), 1792–1807. doi:10.1105/tpc.114.123851 PMID:24769482

Strizh, I. G. (2006). Ontologies for data and knowledge sharing in biology: Plant ROS signaling as a case study. *BioEssays, 28*(2), 199–210. doi:10.1002/bies.20368 PMID:16435295

Suplatov, D., Voevodin, V., & Švedas, V. (2015). Robust enzyme design: Bioinformatic tools for improved protein stability. *Biotechnology Journal, 10*(3), 344–355. doi:10.1002/biot.201400150 PMID:25524647

Tran, B. Q., Goodlett, D. R., & Goo, Y. A. (2016). Advances in protein complex analysis by chemical cross-linking coupled with mass spectrometry (CXMS) and bioinformatics. *Biochimica et Biophysica Acta (BBA). Proteins and Proteomics, 1864*(1), 123–129. doi:10.1016/j.bbapap.2015.05.015

Triguero, I., del Rio, S., Lopez, V., Bacardit, J., Benitez, J. M., & Herrera, F. (2015). ROSEFW-RF: The winner algorithm for the ECBDL'14 big data competition: An extremely imbalanced big data bioinformatics problem. *Knowledge-Based Systems, 87*, 69–79. doi:10.1016/j.knosys.2015.05.027

Tungtur, S., Parente, D. J., & Swint-Kruse, L. (2011). Functionally important positions can comprise the majority of a protein's architecture. *Proteins: Structure, Function, and Bioinformatics, 79*(5), 1589–1608. doi:10.1002/prot.22985 PMID:21374721 van der Linden, F. J., Schmid, K., & Rommes, E. (2007). *Software product lines in action: The best industrial practice in product line engineering.* Berlin, Germany: Springer–Verlag. doi:10.1007/978-3-540-71437-8

Verdino, P., Witherden, D. A., Havran, W. L., & Wilson, I. A. (2010). The molecular interaction of CAR and JAML recruits the central cell signal transducer PI3K. *Science, 329*(5996), 1210–1214. doi:10.1126/science.1187996 PMID:20813955

von Heijne, G. (1985). Signal sequences: The limits of variation. *Journal of Molecular Biology, 184*(1), 99–105. doi:10.1016/0022-2836(85)90046-4 PMID:4032478

Walsh, K. (2009). Adipokines, myokines and cardiovascular disease. *Circulation Journal, 73*(1), 13–18. doi:10.1253/circj.CJ-08-0961 PMID:19043226

Wang, J. W., Wang, L. J., Mao, Y. B., Cai, W. J., Xue, H. W., & Chen, X. Y. (2005). Control of root cap formation by microRNA-targeted auxin response factors in Arabidopsis. *The Plant Cell, 17*(8), 2204–2216. doi:10.1105/tpc.105.033076 PMID:16006581

Witkos, T. M., Koscianska, E., & Krzyzosiak, W. J. (2011). Practical aspects of microRNA target prediction. *Current Molecular Medicine, 11*(2), 93–109. doi:10.2174/156652411794859250 PMID:21342132

Yin, Y., Shen, C., Xie, P., Cheng, Z., & Zhu, Q. (2016). Construction of an initial microRNA regulation network in breast invasive carcinoma by bioinformatics analysis. *The Breast, 26*, 1–10. doi:10.1016/j.breast.2015.11.008 PMID:27017236

Yu, W., & Smith, S. (2009). *Reusability of FEA software: A program family approach.* Paper presented at the 2nd International Workshop on Software Engineering for Computational Science and Engineering (SE–CSE 2009), Vancouver, Canada. doi:10.1109/SECSE.2009.5069161

Zhang, S., Jin, G., Zhang, X. S., & Chen, L. (2007). Discovering functions and revealing mechanisms at molecular level from biological networks. *Proteomics, 7*(16), 2856–2869. doi:10.1002/pmic.200700095 PMID:17703505

Zhou, S., Liao, R., & Guan, J. (2013). When cloud computing meets bioinformatics: A review. *Journal of Bioinformatics and Computational Biology, 11*(5), 1330002. doi:10.1142/S0219720013300025 PMID:24131049

Zhou, X., & Rokas, A. (2014). Prevention, diagnosis and treatment of high-throughput sequencing data pathologies. *Molecular Ecology, 23*(7), 1679–1700. doi:10.1111/mec.12680 PMID:24471475

ADDITIONAL READING

Banerjee, P. M. (2012). From information technology to bioinformatics: Evolution of technological capabilities in India. *Technological Forecasting and Social Change, 79*(4), 665–675. doi:10.1016/j.techfore.2011.08.002

Butte, A. J., & Ito, S. (2012). Translational bioinformatics: Data-driven drug discovery and development. *Clinical Pharmacology and Therapeutics*, *91*(6), 949–952. doi:10.1038/clpt.2012.55 PMID:22609903

Byrnes, A. E., Wu, M. C., Wright, F. A., Li, M., & Li, Y. (2013). The value of statistical or bioinformatics annotation for rare variant association with quantitative trait. *Genetic Epidemiology*, *37*(7), 666–674. doi:10.1002/gepi.21747 PMID:23836599

Chan, L. L., & Jiang, P. (2015). Bioinformatics analysis of circulating cell-free DNA sequencing data. *Clinical Biochemistry*, *48*(15), 962–975. doi:10.1016/j.clinbiochem.2015.04.022 PMID:25966961

Chen, H., Zhu, Z., Zhu, Y., Wang, J., Mei, Y., & Cheng, Y. (2015). Pathway mapping and development of disease-specific biomarkers: Protein-based network biomarkers. *Journal of Cellular and Molecular Medicine*, *19*(2), 297–314. doi:10.1111/jcmm.12447 PMID:25560835

Fober, T., Mernberger, M., Klebe, G., & Hüllermeier, E. (2013). Graph-based methods for protein structure comparison. *Wiley Interdisciplinary Reviews: Data Mining and Knowledge Discovery*, *3*(5), 307–320. doi:10.1002/widm.1099

Goh, W. W. B., Lee, Y. H., Chung, M., & Wong, L. (2012). How advancement in biological network analysis methods empowers proteomics. *Proteomics*, *12*(4/5), 550–563. doi:10.1002/pmic.201100321 PMID:22247042

Helmberg, W. (2012). Bioinformatic databases and resources in the public domain to aid HLA research. *Tissue Antigens*, *80*(4), 295–304. doi:10.1111/tan.12000 PMID:22994154

Karikari, T. K., Quansah, E., & Mohamed, W. M. Y. (2015). Widening participation would be key in enhancing bioinformatics and genomics research in Africa. *Applied & Translational Genomics*, *6*, 35–41. doi:10.1016/j.atg.2015.09.001 PMID:26767163

Kumar, S. S., Shantkriti, S., Muruganandham, T., Murugesh, E., Rane, N., & Govindwar, S. P. (2016). Bioinformatics aided microbial approach for bioremediation of wastewater containing textile dyes. *Ecological Informatics*, *31*, 112–121. doi:10.1016/j.ecoinf.2015.12.001

Lanc, I., Bui, P., Thain, D., & Emrich, S. (2014). Adapting bioinformatics applications for heterogeneous systems: A case study. *Concurrency and Computation*, *26*(4), 866–877. doi:10.1002/cpe.2927

Leman, J. K., Ulmschneider, M. B., & Gray, J. J. (2015). Computational modeling of membrane proteins. *Proteins: Structure, Function, and Bioinformatics*, *83*(1), 1–24. doi:10.1002/prot.24703 PMID:25355688

Li, J., Fan, S., Han, D., Xie, J., Kuang, H., & Ge, P. (2014). Microarray gene expression profiling and bioinformatics analysis of premature ovarian failure in a rat model. *Experimental and Molecular Pathology*, *97*(3), 535–541. doi:10.1016/j.yexmp.2014.10.015 PMID:25445499

Liu, L. Z., Wu, F. X., & Zhang, W. J. (2012). Reverse engineering of gene regulatory networks from biological data. *Wiley Interdisciplinary Reviews: Data Mining and Knowledge Discovery*, *2*(5), 365–385. doi:10.1002/widm.1068

McArthur, A. G., & Wright, G. D. (2015). Bioinformatics of antimicrobial resistance in the age of molecular epidemiology. *Current Opinion in Microbiology*, *27*, 45–50. doi:10.1016/j.mib.2015.07.004 PMID:26241506

Monger, C., Kelly, P. S., Gallagher, C., Clynes, M., Barron, N., & Clarke, C. (2015). Towards next generation CHO cell biology: Bioinformatics methods for RNA-Seq-based expression profiling. *Biotechnology Journal*, *10*(7), 950–966. doi:10.1002/biot.201500107 PMID:26058739

Nevado, B., Ramos-Onsins, S. E., & Perez-Enciso, M. (2014). Resequencing studies of nonmodel organisms using closely related reference genomes: Optimal experimental designs and bioinformatics approaches for population genomics. *Molecular Ecology*, *23*(7), 1764–1779. doi:10.1111/mec.12693 PMID:24795998

Ophir, R. (2013). Bioinformatics tools for marker discovery in plant breeding. *Israel Journal of Chemistry*, *53*(3/4), 173–179. doi:10.1002/ijch.201200090

Ray, S. S., & Maiti, S. (2015). Noncoding RNAs and their annotation using metagenomics algorithms. *Wiley Interdisciplinary Reviews: Data Mining and Knowledge Discovery*, *5*(1), 1–20. doi:10.1002/widm.1142

Spampinato, C., Kavasidis, I., Aldinucci, M., Pino, C., Giordano, D., & Faro, A. (2014). Discovering biological knowledge by integrating high-throughput data and scientific literature on the cloud. *Concurrency and Computation*, *26*(10), 1771–1786. doi:10.1002/cpe.3130

Washietl, S., Will, S., Hendrix, D. A., Goff, L. A., Rinn, J. L., Berger, B., & Kellis, M. (2012). Computational analysis of noncoding RNAs. Wiley Interdisciplinary Reviews RNA, 3(6), 759–778. 10.1002/wrna.1134

Wei, G. (2015). Bioinformatics analysis of microRNA comprehensive regulatory network in congenital microtia. *International Journal of Pediatric Otorhinolaryngology*, *79*(10), 1727–1731. doi:10.1016/j.ijporl.2015.07.036 PMID:26282502

Wierschin, T., Wang, K., Welter, M., Waack, S., & Stanke, M. (2015). Combining features in a graphical model to predict protein binding sites. *Proteins: Structure, Function, and Bioinformatics*, *83*(5), 844–852. doi:10.1002/prot.24775 PMID:25663045

Xiong, D., Zeng, J., & Gong, H. (2015). RBRIdent: An algorithm for improved identification of RNA-binding residues in proteins from primary sequences. *Proteins: Structure, Function, and Bioinformatics*, *83*(6), 1068–1077. doi:10.1002/prot.24806 PMID:25846271

Zaki, N., Berengueres, J., & Efimov, D. (2012). Detection of protein complexes using a protein ranking algorithm. *Proteins: Structure, Function, and Bioinformatics*, *80*(10), 2459–2468. doi:10.1002/prot.24130 PMID:22685080

Zhou, D., & Dai, X. (2015). Integrating granular computing and bioinformatics technology for typical process routes elicitation: A process knowledge acquisition approach. *Engineering Applications of Artificial Intelligence*, *45*, 46–56. doi:10.1016/j.engappai.2015.06.014

Zou, Q., Zeng, J., Cao, L., & Ji, R. (2016). A novel features ranking metric with application to scalable visual and bioinformatics data classification. *Neurocomputing*, *173*, 346–354. doi:10.1016/j.neucom.2014.12.123

KEY TERMS AND DEFINITIONS

Bioinformatics: The modern application of storing, analyzing, and visualizing the biological data.

Biology: The scientific study of the natural processes of the living things.

Computer Science: The study of computing, programming, and computation in correspondence with computer systems.

Data Mining: The process of finding anomalies, patterns, and correlations within large data sets to predict outcomes.

Data Visualization: The presentation of data in a graphical format.

Gene: The unit on a chromosome that determines a specific trait in an organism.

Genomics: The study of the genomes of the living things.

Machine Learning: The ability of a machine to improve its own performance through the use of a software that employs the artificial intelligence techniques to imitate the ways by which humans seem to learn, such as repetition and experience.

MicroRNAs: The small RNA (ribosenucleic acid) molecules encoded in the genomes of plants and animals.

Chapter 3
Protein Structure Prediction

Hirak Jyoti Chakraborty
Central Inland Fisheries Research Institute, India

Sayak Ganguli
Amplicon Institute of Interdisciplinary Science and Technology, India

Aditi Gangopadhyay
Jhargram Raj College, India

Abhijit Datta
Jhargram Raj College, India

ABSTRACT

The great disagreement between the number of known protein sequences and the number of experimentally determined protein structures indicate an enormous necessity of rapid and accurate protein structure prediction methods. Computational techniques such as comparative modeling, threading and ab initio *modelling allow swift protein structure prediction with sufficient accuracy. The three phases of computational protein structure prediction comprise: the pre-modelling analysis phase, model construction and post-modelling refinement. Protein modelling is primarily comparative or* ab initio. *Comparative or template-based methods such as homology and threading-based modelling require structural templates for constructing the structure of a target sequence. The* ab initio *is a template-free modelling approach which proceeds by satisfying various physics-based and knowledge-based parameters. The chapter will elaborate on the three phases of modelling, the programs available for performing each, issues, possible solutions and future research areas.*

INTRODUCTION: THE PROTEIN FOLDING PROBLEM

The protein folding problem is one of the top 125 problems in science (Dill, Ozkan, Shell, & Weikl, 2008). It is both bewildering and beautiful how cells have been structuring amino acid strings into their precise folds through millions of years of evolution. It is one of the supreme mysteries of Nature that man is striving to understand. So how old is this folding problem? It began quite harmlessly in the 1960s when mankind first set eyes on the atomic structure of the protein. Back then, he expected to see more regular structures, instead of the irregularly packed globin. It was then that he set his foot on "How do

DOI: 10.4018/978-1-5225-2607-0.ch003

proteins fold?"and has been on the journey ever since. The folding problem has three facets: the folding code, the structure prediction and the folding process (Dill et al., 2008). The folding code problem deals with the system thermodynamics that determine the fold the protein is adopting. Structure prediction concerns itself with predicting the structures of proteins from amino acid sequences with computational power. The question of the protein folding process tries to find answers to the routes that proteins follow to achieve a particular structure. This chapter deals with the second facet of the folding problem: the computational approach to predicting protein structures.

BACKGROUND: MAKING PROTEINS WITH MACHINES

The wide disparity between the number of experimentally derived protein structures and the number of protein sequences in databases clearly indicates that experimental structure prediction methods are lagging behind the sequencers. Less than 1/500th of protein sequences have corresponding experimentally available structures (Moult, Fidelis, Kryshtafovych, Schwede, & Tramontano, 2016). However, the structure of a protein is a mandatory requirement for several applications in biology and medicine such as evolution, interactome study, drug design, protein function, enzymology or molecular biology. Experimental techniques such as NMR, crystallography or cryo electron microscopy are used to determine accurate structures of proteins and biomolecules. Some proteins pose a challenge during crystallisation, such as the membrane proteins, which owing to partial hydrophobicity and instability are difficult to purify (Carpenter, Beis, Cameron, & Iwata, 2008; White, 2004). Structural information of these proteins may be vital for drug design, as in the very case of membrane proteins, which make up more than 40% of drug targets (Overington, Al-Lazikani, & Hopkins, 2006). Also, experimental techniques for protein structure determination are hugely time consuming. In situations like these, protein structure prediction asks for computational techniques with the ability to provide rapid and reliable structures of proteins (Al-Lazikani, Jung, Xiang, & Honig, 2001; Dorn, E Silva, Buriol, & Lamb, 2014; Hardin, Pogorelov, & Luthey-Schulten, 2002). It is necessary to note that since comparative computational protein structure prediction is dependent on existing experimental structures, the accuracy and reliability in such cases heavily relies on the robustness of template selection and alignment.

PHASES OF PREDICTION

Protein modelling can be generally categorised into three phases: pre-modelling analyses, modelling and post-modelling refinement (Figure 1).

Figure 1. Phases of protein modelling: pre modelling analyses, modelling and post-modelling refinement

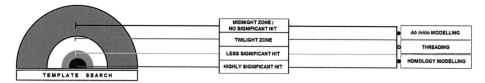

1. PRE-MODELLING ANALYSES: GROUNDWORK IS IMPORTANT

In computational protein structure prediction the amino acid sequence of the protein is moulded into the tertiary structure. The primary and sole information available to *in silico* protein modelling is the amino acid sequence of the protein to be modelled. The structural information stored in the sequence is extracted to identify any structural signatures of the protein such as conserved domains, motifs, secondary structures, hydrophobic regions, post-translational modifications, location of signal peptides and so on.

Protein domains are independent functional units, generally conserved within protein families. The identification of conserved domains helps in template identification by analysing target-template domain agreement. With secondary structure prediction the alpha helices and beta sheets are identified which are applied to analyse the agreement of the secondary structure assessment in the modelled protein. This sequence-structure agreement is also true for hydrophobic and hydrophilic regions of the protein. There are several methods for secondary structure prediction, such as Chou-Fasman, GOR (Garnier-Osguthorpe-Robson), use of Hidden Markov Models (HMMs), neural networks (NN), as well as knowledge-based processes. The location of transmembrane regions is necessary for membrane protein modelling and is achieved through the use of HMMs, NNs or SVMs (support vector machines). Intrinsically disordered proteins contain disordered stretches of amino acids which do not take up any particular structural motif, and this disorder is necessary for protein function. It is necessary to identify the location of such disordered residues prior to predicting the structures of such proteins. Protein structures often undergo post translation chemical modifications, such as glycosylations, phosphorylations, myristoylations and others, which are sometimes necessary for protein function. Glycosylations for instance act as binding sites for other receptors or other proteins. Protein signal peptides serve the purpose of intracellular translocation and are generally cleave off post translocation and are not structurally involved with the mature protein. Table 1 provides a list of the different kinds of tools available for deriving sequence-based information extracted during pre-modelling analyses.

2. MODELLING: THE ART AND SCIENCE OF THE CRAFT

The modelling task can be categorised broadly into comparative and *ab initio* methods. Comparative methods include homology modelling and threading-based methods for fold recognition. The *ab initio* is a template-free approach which considers various physics-based or knowledge-based parameters for computational protein structure prediction. The protein modelling method applied depends on the template-target alignment. While homology modelling is used for template-target alignments which are above the twilight zone, proteins with alignments close to or in the twilight zone are subjected to threading methods. Proteins in the midnight zone or without experimental structures of homologous proteins are modelled with *ab initio* methods [Figure 2].

a. Homology Modelling: Homologues Come to Help

Homology or homologue-based modelling uses a pre-existing protein structure homologue as a template to construct the structure of a target sequence. The selected template homologue serves as comparative guide for constructing the structure of the target protein (Andras Fiser, 2010). Among the three approaches for computational protein structure prediction, structures predicted with homology modelling

Table 1. Programs for different kinds of pre-modelling analyses

Applied in Prediction of	Program (Server*/ Standalone°)	Available at	Reference
Secondary structure	CFSSP*	http://www.biogem.org/tool/chou-fasman/	(Chou & Fasman, 1974)
Coiled coil regions	COILS*	http://embnet.vital-it.ch/software/COILS_form.html	(Lupas, Van Dyke, & Stock, 1991)
Secondary structure	PHD*	https://npsa-prabi.ibcp.fr/cgi-bin/npsa_automat.pl?page=/NPSA/npsa_phd.html	(Burkhard Rost & Sander, 1993)
Location and oreintation of transmembrane regions	TMpred*	http://www.ch.embnet.org/software/TMPRED_form.html	(Hofmann & Stoffel, 1993)
Secondary structure	GOR IV*	https://npsa-prabi.ibcp.fr/cgi-bin/npsa_automat.pl?page=/NPSA/npsa_gor4.html	(Garnier, Gibrat, & Robson, 1996)
Coiled coil residues	MultiCoil* °	http://groups.csail.mit.edu/cb/multicoil/cgi-bin/multicoil.cgi	(Wolf, Kim, & Berger, 1997)
Bonding state of cysteines	CysPred *	http://gpcr.biocomp.unibo.it/cgi/predictors/cyspred/pred_cyspredcgi.cgi	(Fariselli, Riccobelli, & Casadio, 1999)
Secondary structure, fold recognition, TM helix topology, disorder prediction	PSIPRED * °	http://bioinf.cs.ucl.ac.uk/psipred/?disopred=1	(L J McGuffin, Bryson, & Jones, 2000)
TM helices, topology	HMMTOP 2.0 * °	http://www.enzim.hu/hmmtop/	(Tusnády & Simon, 2001)
TM topology	TMHMM* °	http://www.cbs.dtu.dk/services/TMHMM/	(Krogh, Larsson, von Heijne, & Sonnhammer, 2001)
Location of TM region	DAS-TMFilter*	http://www.enzim.hu/DAS/DAS.html	(Cserzö, Eisenhaber, Eisenhaber, & Simon, 2002)
Coiled coil domains	MARCOIL* °	bcf.isb-sib.ch/webmarcoil/webmarcoilC1.html	(Delorenzi & Speed, 2002)
Globularity, domain and disorder prediction	GlobPlot* °	http://globplot.embl.de/	(Linding, Russell, Neduva, & Gibson, 2003)

continued on next page

Table 1. Continued

Applied in Prediction of	Program (Server*/ Standalone°)	Available at	Reference
Intrinsic protein disorder	DisEMBL * °	http://dis.embl.de/	(Linding, Jensen, et al., 2003)
Predicts transmembrane region	SVMtm*	http://ccb.imb.uq.edu.au/svmtm/svmtm_predictor.shtml	(Yuan, Mattick, & Teasdale, 2004)
Secondary structure	PORTER* °	http://distill.ucd.ie/porter/	(Pollastri & McLysaght, 2005)
Transmembrane region prediction	TMMOD*	http://liao.cis.udel.edu/website/servers/TMMOD/scripts/frame.php?p=submit	(Kahsay, Gao, & Liao, 2005)
Intrinsic unstructure	IUPred * °	http://iupred.enzim.hu/	(Dosztanyi, Csizmok, Tompa, & Simon, 2005)
Disulphide bond prediction	DIpro 2.0 * °	http://download.igb.uci.edu/bridge.html	(Jianlin Cheng, Saigo, & Baldi, 2005)
Disulphide bond connectivity	DiANNA*	http://clavius.bc.edu/~clotelab/DiANNA/	(Ferrè& Clote, 2005)
Solvent accessibility, secondary structure, TM alpha helices and beta barrels, disorder, contact maps, contact number, solubility propensity, antigenicity	SCRATCH* °	http://scratch.proteomics.ics.uci.edu/	(J Cheng, Randall, Sweredoski, & Baldi, 2005)
Parallel coiled coils	PairCoil2* °	http://groups.csail.mit.edu/cb/paircoil2/	(McDonnell, Jiang, Keating, & Berger, 2006)
Disulfide bond state and cysteine connectivity	DISULFIND *	http://disulfind.dsi.unifi.it/	(Ceroni, Passerini, Vullo, & Frasconi, 2006)
Intrinsic disorder	VSL2 * °	http://www.dabi.temple.edu/disprot/Predictors.html	(Peng, Radivojac, Vucetic, Dunker, & Obradovic, 2006)

continued on next page

Table 1. Continued

Applied in Prediction of	Program (Server*/ Standalone°)	Available at	Reference
Protein disorder	PrDOS *	http://prdos.hgc.jp/cgi-bin/top.cgi	(Ishida & Kinoshita, 2007)
Rotational orientation of TM helices	HTMSRAP (Helical TransMembrane Segment Rotational Angle Prediction) *	http://pbiotechnology.tbzmed.ac.ir/sequence_analysis.aspx	(Dastmalchi, Beheshti, Morris, & Bret Church, 2007)
Protein disorder	OnD-CRF*	http://babel.ucmp.umu.se/ond-crf/	(L. Wang & Sauer, 2008)
Predicts if a protein is a Knottin	KNOTER1D *	http://knottin.cbs.cnrs.fr/Tools_1D.php	(Gracy et al., 2008)
Domain linker prediction	DLP-SVM *	http://domserv.lab.tuat.ac.jp/dlpsvm.html	(Ebina, Toh, & Kuroda, 2009)
Transition from disorder to order upon binding to other proteins	ANCHOR * °	http://anchor.enzim.hu/	(Mészáros et al., 2009)
Secondary structure and surface accessibility	NetSurfP* °	http://www.cbs.dtu.dk/services/NetSurfP/	(Petersen et al., 2009)
Coiled coils	CCHMM_ PROF*	http://gpcr.biocomp.unibo.it/cgi/predictors/cchmmprof/pred_cchmmprof.cgi	(Bartoli, Fariselli, Krogh, & Casadio, 2009)
Disorder prediction	PreDisorder*	http://sysbio.rnet.missouri.edu/predisorder.html	(Deng et al., 2009)
Beta-turn regions	NetTurnP* °	http://www.cbs.dtu.dk/services/NetTurnP/	(Petersen et al., 2010)
Intrinsic disorder prediction meta-server	MetaDisorder*	http://iimcb.genesilico.pl/metadisorder/predict_protein_disorder_by_ metadisorder.html	(Kozlowski et al., 2012)
Molecular Recognition Features (MoRF) for disorder to order transition	MoRFPred *	http://biomine-ws.ece.ualberta.ca/MoRFpred/index.html	(Disfani et al., 2012)
Disulphide bonds	DinoSolve *	http://hpcr.cs.odu.edu/dinosolve/	(Yaseen & Li, 2013)
Disulfide Connectivity Pattern	x3CysBridges *	http://m24.giga.ulg.ac.be/x3CysBridges/	(Becker et al., 2013)

continued on next page

Table 1. Continued

Applied in Prediction of	Program (Server*/ Standalone°)	Available at	Reference
Predicts amylogenicity of sequences	MetAmyl *	http://metamyl.genouest.org/e107_plugins/metamyl_aggregation/db_prediction_meta.php	(Emily et al., 2013)
Disorder prediction	disCoP*	http://biomine-ws.ece.ualberta.ca/disCoP/	(Fan & Kurgan, 2014)
Regular and non-regular secondary structures, solvent accessibility, TM helices and beta barrels, coiled coils, low complexity regions, disulphide bridges, residue mobility, disorder, protein-protein and protein-polynucleotide binding sites, effect of point mutations on protein function	PredictProtein*	https://www.predictprotein.org/	(Yachdav et al., 2014)
Secondary structure prediction	JPred4*	http://www.compbio.dundee.ac.uk/jpred/	(Drozdetskiy, Cole, Procter, & Barton, 2015)
Disulphide connectivity	Cyscon *	http://www.csbio.sjtu.edu.cn/bioinf/Cyscon/	(Jing Yang, He, Jang, Zhang, & Shen, 2015)
TM topology prediction	CCTOP (Constrained Consensus TOPology) * °	http://cctop.enzim.ttk.mta.hu/	(Dobson, Reményi, & Tusnády, 2015)
Proteome-level disorder prediction	AUCpreD *	http://raptorx2.uchicago.edu/StructurePropertyPred/predict/	(S. Wang, Ma, & Xu, 2016)
Disordered flexible linker regions	DFLpred*	http://biomine-ws.ece.ualberta.ca/DFLpred/index.php	(Meng & Kurgan, 2016)
MoRF identification in proteins	MoRFchibi SYSTEM* °	http://www.chibi.ubc.ca/faculty/joerg-gsponer/gsponer-lab/software/morf_chibi/	(Malhis, Jacobson, & Gsponer, 2016)

Figure 2. Protein modelling categories on the basis of target alignment with structure hits

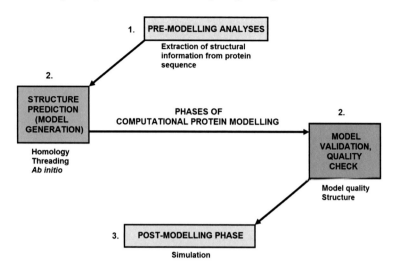

are the most biologically accurate (Moult et al., 2016). However, since homology modelling relies on template structure information, the generation of the complete structure of the protein may not always be possible in cases where partial information is available [Figure 3]. *Ab initio* methods, on the other hand, can generate complete protein models. Hybrid modelling methods are applied in such cases.

The basic steps of the homology modelling technique are:

- Template identification
- Template-target alignment
- Model generation
- Structural refinement

Figure 3. Comparison of biological accuracy and coverage of protein models across different categories of modelling methods. Coverage refers to the length of sequence that is covered by the model structure. Since homology methods rely on template structures, homology models may not always cover the entire target sequence. Ab initio *models on the other hand cover the entire query sequence.*

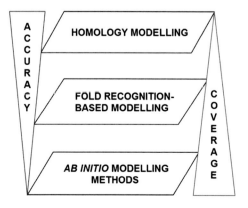

- Validation

i. Template Identification

This is one of the most vital stages of comparative modelling, since the structure that is going to be constructed relies largely on the structure of the template. Structure homologues of a given target are identified with a structure BLAST against a protein structure database, such as the Protein Data Bank (PDB). Parameters such as the e-value, query coverage, identity, similarity and the protein biology are considered during template selection. The e-value or expect value is probability value that denotes the probability of a random alignment that one can expect (Mount, 2004). The e-value is so designed that "significant" alignments have lower e-values. The closer the e-value is to zero, the more significant an alignment is expected to be. Since the calculation of the e-value considers the sequence length, sometimes short sequences can assume higher values, indicating a random alignment even when the sequences are quite similar. Therefore, the e-value must be analysed carefully before selecting a template.

The query coverage of a structure alignment implies the stretch of target sequence that has a structure homologue. In the alignment, the number of amino acids of the target sequence that are "equal to" the amino acids in the structure hit gives the sequence identity. An identity exceeding 40% is said to be "high" and homology modelling can be performed without difficulty (B Rost, 1999). However, when the identity drops and ranges between 20-35%, the alignment is said to fall within the "twilight zone"(B Rost, 1999). The twilight zone is an uncertain region where an alignment could highly be a false negative. Sequence alignment studies with over a million alignments show that when the identity is above 30%, the chance of identifying a homologue is as high as 90%. As the identity falls below 25%, the chance of detecting a homologue is even below 10% (B Rost, 1999). The similarity of an alignment is sometimes more suited to diminish false positive homologues.

ii. Template-Target Alignment

Template-target alignment in homology modelling is a sequence-structure alignment, which can be achieved with dynamic programming. Here, as the target sequence is aligned with the template, the structural information from the template is also incorporated. Since target structure prediction directly derives information from the template, correct alignment of the target sequence to appropriate regions in the template is vital to the procedure.

iii. Model Generation

Given a structural template, a target-template alignment and a target sequence, homology modelling can initiate the process of target structure generation. The general scheme of model generation involves determining the structural restraints on the target due to the target-template alignment. This is followed by generation of target coordinates for those regions which have aligned with the template. The coordinates of the remaining unaligned target portions are derived from a topology library. The approximate initial model thus generated is next subjected to randomisation and optimisation to generate models satisfying stereochemical, dihedral, distance and other structural restraints. In the final step, the models are refined and minimised. The final models are assessed with various model validation parameters such as DOPE, GA341 or SOAP. There are several tools available for constructing a homology model, some of which use combine homology methods with fold recognition or *ab initio* techniques [Table 2].

Table 2. Some programs for homology modelling

Program (Server*/ Standalone°)	Application	Available at	Reference
ICM-Pro *	Homology modelling	http://www.molsoft.com/ icm_pro.html	(Abagyan, Totrov, & Kuznetsov, 1994)
ESyPred3D*	Automated homology modelling	http://www.unamur.be/sciences/ biologie/urbm/bioinfo/esypred/	(Lambert, Léonard, De Bolle, & Depiereux, 2002)
Geno3D *	Automated homology modelling	https://geno3d-prabi.ibcp.fr/cgi-bin/geno3d_automat.pl?page=/ GENO3D/geno3d_home.html	(Combet, Jambon, Deléage, & Geourjon, 2002)
MODWEB*	Homology modelling using MODELLER	https://modbase.compbio.ucsf. edu/modweb/	(Eswar et al., 2003)
MODLOOP*	Loop modelling using MODELLER	https://modbase.compbio.ucsf. edu/modloop/	(András Fiser & Sali, 2003)
MODPIPE°	Automated homology modelling with MODELLER for a large number of sequences	https://salilab.org/modpipe/	(Eswar et al., 2003)
Prime °	Homology modelling and fold recognition	https://www.schrodinger.com/ prime	(Jacobson et al., 2004)
HHPred *°	Homology modelling using HMM for template identification	https://toolkit.tuebingen.mpg. de/hhpred	(Soding, 2005)
Robetta*	Comparative and *ab initio* modelling	http://robetta.bakerlab.org/	(Raman et al., 2009)
Rosetta Antibody *	Homology modelling of antibody proteins	http://antibody.graylab.jhu.edu/ antibody	(Lyskov et al., 2013; Sivasubramanian, Sircar, Chaudhury, & Gray, 2009)
CPHModels3 * °	Homology modelling	http://www.cbs.dtu.dk/services/ CPHmodels/	(Nielsen, Lundegaard, & Lund, 2010)
BioSerf *	Automated and homology modelling	http://bioinf.cs.ucl.ac.uk/ psipred/	(Buchan et al., 2010)
GalaxyTBM *	Template-based modelling and refinement	http://galaxy.seoklab.org/cgi-bin/submit.cgi?type=TBM	(Ko et al., 2012)
BBSP °	Template-based modelling	http://www.acbrc.org/tools.html	(Gullotto, Nolassi, Bernini, Spiga, & Niccolai, 2013)
SWISS-MODEL *	Homology modelling		(Biasini, Bienert, & Waterhouse, 2014)
Modeller °	Homology modelling	https://salilab.org/modeller/	(Webb, Sali, Webb, & Sali, 2014)
RaptorX*	Template-based modelling	http://raptorx.uchicago.edu/ StructurePrediction/predict/	(Källberg, Margaryan, Wang, Ma, & Xu, 2014)
Phyre2*	Fold recognition based homology modelling	http://www.sbg.bio.ic.ac. uk/~phyre2/html/page. cgi?id=index	(Kelley, Mezulis, Yates, Wass, & Sternberg, 2015)

iv. Refinement, Validation

The protein structure thus generated must be validated for structural conformity. Structural validation generally involves analyses of the Ramachandran plot, analyses of stereochemical or geometric deviations such as bond angle, distance and planarity distortions [Table 3]. The models can be scored by a standard scoring function such as the QMean or PROSA Z-score.

Table 3. Tools for model validation

Program	Validation Parameters	Available at	References
Procheck	Ramachandran plot Most favoured regions Additionally allowed regions Generously allowed regions Disallowed regions Stereochemical deviations Geometric distortions	http://www.ebi.ac.uk/thornton-srv/software/PROCHECK/; http://services.mbi.ucla.edu/PROCHECK/; http://swissmodel.expasy.org/workspace/?func=tools_structureassessment1	(Laskowski, MacArthur, Moss, Thornton, & IUCr, 1993)
Verify3D	Raw-score for global quality Z-score for global quality Compatibility of structure with the sequence composition	http://services.mbi.ucla.edu/Verify_3D/	(Eisenberg, Lüthy, & Bowie, 1997)
VADAR (Volume Area Dihedral Angle Reporter)	Ramachandran plot Steric quality Packing quality Fold quality	http://vadar.wishartlab.com/	(Willard et al., 2003)
ProQ	Uses neural network to predict: LG score (-log of P-value) MaxSub score	http://www.sbc.su.se/~bjornw/ProQ/ProQ.html	(Wallner & Elofsson, 2003)
HARMONY server	Sequence-structure compatibility HARMONY propensity score HARMONY substitution score	http://caps.ncbs.res.in/harmony/	(Pugalenthi, Shameer, Srinivasan, & Sowdhamini, 2006)
NQ-Flipper	Validation and correction of asparagine and glutamine amide rotamers	https://flipper.services.came.sbg.ac.at/cgi-bin/flipper.php	(Weichenberger & Sippl, 2006)
Protein Structure Validation Suite (PSVS)	Validation meta-server including: ProCheck MolProbity Verify3D Prosa II PDB Validation	http://psvs-1_5-dev.nesg.org/	(A. Bhattacharya, Tejero, & Montelione, 2006)
Ramachandran plot 2.0	Ramachandran plot	http://dicsoft1.physics.iisc.ernet.in/rp/	(Gopalakrishnan, Sowmiya, Sheik, & Sekar, 2007)
ProSA	PROSA Z-score for global model quality Local model quality Comparison of model quality with NMR or X-ray structures	https://prosa.services.came.sbg.ac.at/prosa.php	(Wiederstein & Sippl, 2007)
QMEAN	• QMEAN-score • QMEAN Z-score for absolute model quality estimation • Residue error plot	https://swissmodel.expasy.org/qmean/cgi/index.cgi	(Benkert, Tosatto, & Schomburg, 2008)
MolProbity	• Ramachandran plot	http://molprobity.biochem.duke.edu/	(Chen et al., 2010)

continued on next page

Table 3. Continued

Program	Validation Parameters	Available at	References
ModFOLD	• Confidence and P-value • Global model quality score • Residue error plot	http://www.reading.ac.uk/bioinf/ModFOLD/	(Liam J McGuffin, Buenavista, & Roche, 2013)
SAVES	Meta server incorporates: • PROCHECK • WHAT_CHECK • Verify3D • PROVE • Ramachandran plot	http://services.mbi.ucla.edu/SAVES/	(Eisenberg et al., 1997; Hooft, Vriend, Sander, & Abola, 1996; Laskowski et al., 1993; Pontius, Richelle, & Wodak, 1996)
ProtSAV	ProtSAV normalised Z-score calculated with Inputs from different validation servers: DFire Errat NAccess Prosa ProCheck Verify3D MolProbity D2N ProQ PSN-QA	http://www.scfbio-iitd.res.in/software/proteomics/protsav.jsp	(Singh, Kaushik, Mishra, Shanker, & Jayaram, 2016)

Following protein structure generation, it is necessary to refine and minimise the protein model before it can be utilised for study. Minimisation approaches such as steepest descent or conjugate gradients aim to shift the protein structure towards a lower energy state. Methods such as side-chain, backbone, hydrogen-bond network refinement; use of Support Vector Machines; simulation, energy minimisation are commonly to refine protein structures [Table 4].

v. Types of Homology Modelling

- Basic Homology Modelling: When Templates Favour

The task of homology modelling can be basic or advanced, depending on the nature of the alignment with the structural template. Basic homology modelling techniques are employed when the alignment with a structural hit is "significant", with alignment identities well above the twilight zone.

- Advanced homology modelling: When Templates Trouble

Advanced homology modelling methods come to aid when the template structure alignment is close to, but not below the twilight zone. In these cases, the information from the template needs to be supported by other structural information to generate the protein model. When the information from one template is not enough, multiple templates are employed to the task, as in *multiple template based homology modelling*. In this method, the target sequence is aligned to multiple templates and structural information for the aligned regions are obtained from different templates to construct the protein. Gaps in the template-target alignment can subjected to loop modelling or loop refinement that optimise loop

Table 4. Tools for protein refinement and minimisation

Program (Server*/ Standalone°)	Application	Available at	Reference
Swiss Pdb-Viewer°	Minimisation	http://spdbv.vital-it.ch/	(Guex & Peitsch, 1997)
Chimera°	Energy minimisation	https://www.cgl.ucsf.edu/chimera/	(Pettersen et al., 2004)
NOMAD-Ref*	Refinement based on all-atom normal mode analysis	http://lorentz.immstr.pasteur.fr/ nomad-ref.php	(Lindahl, Azuara, Koehl, & Delarue, 2006)
YASARA*	Energy minimisation	http://www.yasara.org/ minimizationserver.htm	(Krieger et al., 2009)
REMO*°	Protein refinement of backbone hydrogen bonding networks	http://zhanglab.ccmb.med.umich.edu/ REMO/	(Li & Zhang, 2009)
FG-MD*	Fragment-guided Molecular dynamics	http://zhanglab.ccmb.med.umich.edu/ FG-MD/	(Zhang, Liang, & Zhang, 2011)
ModRefiner*°	Atomic-level energy minimisaition	http://zhanglab.ccmb.med.umich.edu/ ModRefiner/	(Dong Xu & Zhang, 2011)
KoBaMIN*	Knowledge-based energy minimisation	http://csb.stanford.edu/kobamin/	(Rodrigues, Levitt, & Chopra, 2012)
GalaxyRefine*°	Refinement by side-chain repacking	http://galaxy.seoklab.org/cgi-bin/ submit.cgi?type=REFINE	(Heo, Park, & Seok, 2013)
Princeton_TIGRESS*	Protein refinement with SVM and simulation	http://atlas.engr.tamu.edu/refinement/	(Khoury et al., 2014)
3DRefine*	Protein refinement	http://sysbio.rnet.missouri. edu/3Drefine/	(Bhattacharya, Nowotny, Cao, & Cheng, 2016)

regions by an initial randomisation followed by optimisation of loop regions. When structural information about a protein-protein interface is not available, the application of advanced techniques like multi-chain modelling can produce erroneous results. Such cases require structural restraints or homologous complexes as inputs for generating reliable quaternary structures. Similarly, symmetry restraints are used for the construction of symmetrical protein complexes.

b. Threading-Based Modelling: Finding the Fold

Since homology techniques require a significant homologue hit for structure prediction, it starts to face difficulties as alignment identities approach the twilight zone. In the darkness of twilight, the technique of protein threading arrives to throw light on template selection via fold recognition. The threading method is somewhat like drawing a thread or string with a needle to create a stitched pattern or motif. In protein threading, the thread is a string of amino acids that is drawn through a library of protein folds to identify the pattern in which the thread is most comfortable. In other words, threading aims to find the protein fold which best suits a target sequence (Godzik, 2003). Threading is also a comparative method; however, unlike classical homology modelling which selects templates on the basis of sequence alignments, threading employs structural information to select templates via fold recognition. For alignments in the twilight zone, threading-based fold recognition is employed together with homology modelling to construct protein structures. A structure database such as the PDB is used to identify the best suitable fold or motif. Profile-profile sequence and sequence-structure alignments, secondary structure alignments, residue-residue contacts are scored to identify the template with the most appropriate fold for a target (Khor et al., 2015).

c. *Ab Initio* Modelling: Doing It *De Novo* When We Don't Know

When the identity of a target-structure alignment falls even below 20%, it gets even darker. This zone of sequence identity between 8-10% is the "midnight zone" which is sometimes observed between structurally homologous proteins that might have attained low sequence similarity due to convergence or divergence during their evolutionary timeline (Doolittle, 1994; B Rost, 1999). Sometimes target sequences can have no structural homologues at all in the structure databases. In these cases when the target-structure alignment is in poor twilight or below twilight or has no homologues in structure databases, *ab initio* modelling is used (Khor et al., 2015). Here, the tertiary structure of a protein is predicted from its sequence by scanning the energy landscape. The idea is to find the biologically relevant *optimum conformation* that the protein assumes in real life. However, the energy landscape can have a number of low energy conformations, and the biologically appropriate optimum structure of the protein may not necessarily correspond to the lowest energy conformation. The energy of the optimum conformation can be higher than the lowest energy conformation. *Ab initio* methods scan the protein energy landscape for the optimum conformation using energy functions and search algorithms. *Ab initio* modelling employs physics-based and knowledge-based scoring functions. In physics-based scoring, the interaction energy between atoms is calculated for evaluating the energy. Knowledge-based scoring utilises pre-calculated empirical energies from existing experimental structures to determine the energy of the protein. Knowledge-based scoring in combination with fragment assembly has been successful in many cases (Lee, Wu, & Zhang, 2009). For midnight zone proteins, *ab initio* methods are sometimes combined with threading-based fold recognition to predict protein structures [Table 5].

Table 5. Threading-based, ab initio and hybrid protein structure prediction tools

Program (Server*/ Standalone°)	Application	Available at	Reference
GenTHREADER *	Fold recognition	http://bioinf.cs.ucl.ac.uk/psipred/	(Jones, 1999)
PROSPECT °	Threading-based protein modelling	http://compbio.ornl.gov/structure/prospect/	(Y. Xu & Xu, 2000)
Bhageerath *	Energy-based *ab initio* modelling	http://www.scfbio-iitd.res.in/bhageerath/index.jsp	(Jayaram et al., 2006)
LOMETS *°	Protein threading meta-server	http://zhanglab.ccmb.med.umich.edu/LOMETS/	(S Wu & Zhang, 2007)
MUSTER *	Protein threading and modelling	http://zhanglab.ccmb.med.umich.edu/MUSTER/	(S Wu & Zhang, 2008)
ANGLOR *°	*Ab initio* prediction of protein backbone torsion angles	http://zhanglab.ccmb.med.umich.edu/ANGLOR/	(Sitao Wu et al., 2008)
pGenTHREADER *°	Profile-based fold recognition	http://bioinf.cs.ucl.ac.uk/psipred/	(Lobley, Sadowski, & Jones, 2009)
pDomTHREADER *°	Fold domain recognition	http://bioinf.cs.ucl.ac.uk/psipred/	(Lobley et al., 2009)

continued on next page

Table 5. Continued

Program (Server*/ Standalone°)	Application	Available at	Reference
DescFold	Fold recognition	http://202.112.170.199/DescFold/index.html	(Yan et al., 2009)
SEGMER *°	Segmental threading server	http://zhanglab.ccmb.med.umich.edu/SEGMER/	(Sitao Wu & Zhang, 2010)
COTH *	Protein complex structure prediction with multimeric threading	http://zhanglab.ccmb.med.umich.edu/COTH/	(Mukherjee & Zhang, 2011)
EVFold*	Modelling based on residue contacts	http://evfold.org/evfold-web/newprediction.do	(Morcos et al., 2011)
SPARKS-X *°	Fold recognition	http://sparks-lab.org/yueyang/server/SPARKS-X/	(Y. Yang, Faraggi, Zhao, & Zhou, 2011)
SAXTER *	Combines small-angle x-ray scattering (SAXS) data with threading for protein structure determination	http://zhanglab.ccmb.med.umich.edu/SAXSTER/	(dos Reis, Aparicio, & Zhang, 2011)
QUARK *	*Ab initio* modelling	http://zhanglab.ccmb.med.umich.edu/QUARK/	(D Xu & Zhang, 2012)
ThreaDom *	Threading-based protein domain prediction	http://zhanglab.ccmb.med.umich.edu/ThreaDom/	(Xue, Xu, Wang, & Zhang, 2013)
SPRING *	Modelling protein-protein structures using threading-based template selection	http://zhanglab.ccmb.med.umich.edu/spring/	(Guerler, Govindarajoo, & Zhang, 2013)
CABS-fold *	*De novo* and consensus modelling	http://biocomp.chem.uw.edu.pl/CABSfold/	(Blaszczyk, Jamroz, Kmiecik, & Kolinski, 2013)
PEP-FOLD *	*De novo* protein structure prediction	http://bioserv.rpbs.univ-paris-diderot.fr/services/PEP-FOLD3/	(Shen, Maupetit, Derreumaux, & Tufféry, 2014)
FFAS-3D *°	Fold recognition	http://ffas.sanfordburnham.org/ffas-cgi/cgi/ffas.pl	(D. Xu, Jaroszewski, Li, & Godzik, 2014)
GalaxyLoop*	Loop modelling	http://galaxy.seoklab.org/loop	(Park et al., 2014)
I-TASSER *°	Threading and *ab initio* modelling	http://zhanglab.ccmb.med.umich.edu/I-TASSER/	(Jianyi Yang et al., 2015)
GPCR-I-TASSER	Threading and *ab initio* modelling of GPCRs	http://zhanglab.ccmb.med.umich.edu/GPCR-I-TASSER/	(Zhang, Yang, Jang, & Zhang, 2015)
FALCON@home*	Template-based and *ab initio* modelling	http://protein.ict.ac.cn/FALCON/	(C. Wang et al., 2016)
RCD+ *	*Ab initio* loop modelling	http://rcd.chaconlab.org/	(López-Blanco, Canosa-Valls, Li, & Chacón, 2016)

Genetic algorithms or simulation methods such as the Monte Carlo, simulated annealing, molecular dynamics offer conformational search strategies across the energy landscape. Selection of the final model is based on the energy, the compatibility of the sequence with the structure or use of structural clustering to identify the lowest energy of the most populated clusters(Lee et al., 2009).

3. POST-MODELLING PHASE: THE FINAL TOUCH

Once a refined protein structure has been obtained, it is necessary to study the stability of the structure that has been generated. Proteins also contain dynamics loops and flexible linker residues which play important roles in protein function. The very function of a protein depends on its structural dynamicity. Protein flexibility is responsible for ligand binding, denoted by the induced fit and conformation selection models of protein-ligand interactions. Sometimes it is necessary to study the disorder-to-order transition of proteins or the dynamics of unstructured regions. A NMR or crystal structure is a snapshot of a protein at a certain moment of time. Sometimes it becomes necessary to investigate the structural dynamicity involved in the folding or unfolding of protein structures, the flexibility of loops, linkers, unstructured regions or binding sites. In such cases simulation techniques are used to provide insights on protein flexibility and stability.

With simulation, a certain biological phenomenon is mimicked and the observations are recorded for a certain period of time. The time of simulation (t) depends on the biological behaviour that is being studied. For instance, if a protein takes 100 ns (nanoseconds) to fold, the simulation time must be set slightly larger than 100 ns, so that the simulation can record all observations related to protein folding. The idea is to ensure that the simulation frame can capture the biological behaviour in its entirety. In protein simulation, the biological system is placed in a simulated biological environment, such as a solvent or a membrane. A perturbation is applied to the system and the behavior of the system is recorded at certain time intervals (Δt) for a certain period of time (t). Molecular dynamics, Monte Carlo methods are applied to simulate biological systems. Molecular dynamics simulations generally include feeding the typology and parameters, solvation, minimisation, equilibration, production and trajectory analysis (Figure 4).

The simulation engine needs to be fed with different kinds of information such as the number and type of atoms, bonds, dihedral angles and other structural parameters about the biological system. The information is generally contained in the topology and parameter files. In molecules, the atoms are connected by bonds, which stretch and become shorter. Angular motions between bonds and planes which contribute to angle bending and torsional motions. These movements are represented as the simple harmonic motion of a spring, where the spring constant represents the ease with which a movement can occur. Various attractive and repulsive interactions take place between the atoms of the system. The most common non-bonded interaction between atoms is the van der Waals. The van der Waals is a weak interaction, which is repulsive when the atoms are closer, but attractive when the atoms are at long distance. The van der Waals can be calculated by several functions such as the Lennard-Jones potential, which is very commonly used. The Lennard-Jones contains attractive and repulsive terms and is represented as:

$$U\left(r\right) = \varepsilon_{ij}\left[\left(\frac{R_{ij}}{r_{ij}}\right)^{12} - 2\left(\frac{R_{ij}}{r_{ij}}\right)^{6}\right]$$

Figure 4. Flowchart of molecular dynamics simulations

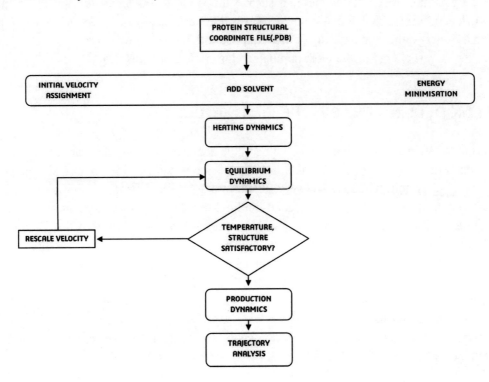

Where, R_{ij} = sum of van der Waals radii of two atoms;

r_{ij} = distance between the two atoms;

ε = the depth of the potential energy well .

For atoms with partial charges, electrostatics contribute to the attraction and repulsion between atoms. Electrostatic interactions between atoms follow the inverse square law and is calculated as:

$$F = k_c \frac{q_1 q_2}{r^2}$$

Where, k_c = Coulomb's constant;

$q1$ = Charge on particle (atom) 1;

$q2$ = Charge on particle (atom) 2;

r = Distance between the particles.

Non-bonded (e.g. van der Waals, electrostatics) and bonded terms (bond stretching, angle bending, torsions) contribute to the design of the potential energy function, which calculates the potential energy of the system at each time interval Δt. Several other contributions can be included in the potential energy function.

Classical molecular dynamics uses Newtonian mechanics to calculate the acceleration (and thus velocity) acting on each atom of the system at Δt. According to Newtonian mechanics, the force (P) acting on a system is a product of mass (m) and acceleration (f), given as $P = mf$. Since the acceleration is the rate of change of velocity, the velocity (v) of each atom at each interval Δt can be calculated from $f = v / \Delta t$. The position and velocity of each atom at Δt is calculated and recorded. The process is repeated for time t. Once the simulation is complete, the trajectory of the run is analysed over time t. Regions of abrupt fluctuations in the system behaviour are easily visible from the trajectory, which require the system to be visualised and quantified for any interesting molecular changes.

In Langevin dynamics, additional friction terms and random noise contributions are included in the Newtonian equations.

PRESENT STATUS OF PROTEIN STRUCTURE PREDICTION: CASP STUDIES

The Critical Assessment of protein Structure Prediction (CASP) is a community-wide experiment to assess protein structure prediction methods, in order to detect the progress in the field and underline

Table 6. Commonly used tools for protein simulation

Program (Server*/ Standalone°)	Application	Available at	Reference
CHARMM °	Macromolecular simulation	www.charmm.org	(B. R. Brooks et al., 2009; Bernard R. Brooks et al., 1983)
AMBER °	Biomolecular simulation	http://ambermd.org/	(Pearlman et al., 1995)
GROMACS °	Molecular dynamics simulation	http://www.gromacs.org/	(Berendsen, van der Spoel, & van Drunen, 1995)
GROMOS °	Biomolecular simulation	www.gromos.net	(Walter R. P. Scott et al., 1999)
NAMD°	Scalable molecular dynamics	http://www.ks.uiuc.edu/ Research/namd/	(Phillips et al., 2005)
Desmond °	High performance molecular dynamics simulations	https://www.schrodinger.com/ desmond; https://www.deshawresearch. com/resources_desmond.html	(Bowers et al., 2006)
CHARMMing *	Web portal for CHARMM	https://www.charmming.org/ charmming/	(Miller et al., 2008)
MDWeb*	Web-based molecular dynamics	http://mmb.irbbarcelona.org/ MDWeb/	(Hospital et al., 2012)
CABS-Flex *	Rapid simulation of protein fluctuations	http://biocomp.chem.uw.edu.pl/ CABSflex/	(Jamroz, Kolinski, & Kmiecik, 2013)
QwikMD*	Molecular dynamics simulations for novices and experts	http://www.ks.uiuc.edu/ Research/vmd/plugins/qwikmd/	(Ribeiro et al., 2016)

areas for future improvement. The experiment is generally conducted once every two years; however, from 2011, an all-year-round rolling CASP has been initiated for *ab initio* modelling. The results of the latest CASP experiment reveals that template-based modelling is still the most accurate modelling technique (Moult et al., 2016). Experimental information such as NMR constraints and chemical cross-linking data directs the modelling towards more reliable structure generation. A recent thrill in protein modelling methods in the success of residue-residue contact information derived from evolutionary data for predicting near-accurate protein models (Monastyrskyy, D'Andrea, Fidelis, Tramontano, & Kryshtafovych, 2016). Residue contact-based model prediction, stereo-chemical quality, refinement, model assessment and non-template protein modelling are presently the areas of principal growth in protein structure prediction (Moult et al., 2016).

ISSUES, PROBLEMS, RECOMMENDATIONS, SOLUTIONS

The gap between the number of known protein sequences and experimentally determined protein structures is very wide. Experimental techniques such as NMR or crystallography that provide accurate protein models are time consuming and difficult to apply for some proteins. In these cases computational protein structure prediction provides a more rapid alternative, however, the biological exactness of computationally-determined models need to improve. Modifications in template identification methods and application of modified algorithms can improve comparative protein structure prediction. Identifying the right template and striking the optimum template-target alignment remain the most crucial steps of template-dependent modelling. Some of the ways to ensure proper template selection include SMART BLAST, profile comparison, fold recognition, use of evolutionary information. For proteins that do not have homologues in structure databases, template-free modelling is the only alternative. The success of *ab initio* methods are more pronounced for smaller proteins with less than 100 amino acids, but the accuracy falls with larger proteins. The successful *ab initio* model will be able to answer the protein folding problem, and is aptly called the "holy grail" of structure prediction. Residue contact-based modelling has been recently successful in larger proteins, and can be applied to model accurate structures. The use of consensus force fields might be able to provide more accurate information on protein stability. However, such computations would require supercomputing technologies, cloud computing or use of computer clusters.

FUTURE RESEARCH DIRECTIONS

Biology is yet to understand how proteins fold. Once there is an answer to the protein folding question, computational methods can apply the required parameters to generate more accurate and reliable models, even for proteins with no experimentally determined structures of homologues. However, in the mean time, computational structure prediction needs to rely on structural templates or scanning the energy landscape. The flawless *ab initio* modelling is rightly called the "holy grail" of structure prediction. *Ab initio* methods have always been more successful for shorter proteins (less than 100 amino acid residues). However, in a recent CASP ROLL experiment, the *ab initio* method exhibited successful improvement in the prediction of larger protein domains (Kinch, Li, Monastyrskyy, Kryshtafovych, & Grishin, 2016). Although residue contact-based structure prediction has been successful, the method would face difficulties for proteins that have structure-function variation within the same family, requiring the development of substitute approaches such as the use of alternative or multiple templates (Källberg et al., 2012; Moult et al., 2016). Several authors rightly argue that the real trial of a protein model lies not in how structurally close it is to the experimental model, but more so in how well it can help solve a biological query (Moult et al., 2016).

The optimum biologically correct computational structure prediction method, when invented, will not be an answer to protein structure prediction, but will be *the* answer to protein structure prediction. The discovery of such a method would replace experimental structure prediction methods, and will throw light on the protein folding problem.

CONCLUSION

The craft of protein structure prediction extends beyond Science. It is also a work of Art to be able to construct the perfectly crafted protein, taking into account each delicate detail of evolution, thermo-dynamics, function and structure. The protein model should be a representative of all that the protein is (structure), has been through (evolution) and is able to do (function). Since template-based methods rely on homology, protein evolution is a vital aspect. The history of evolution of each protein is a very individual and personal story: proteins face individual triggers in their own microcosms, causing them to gain, lose or rearrange domains on the way, and there are hundreds of domains to choose from. Protein sequences change over time, their structures and functions need to comply with diverse temporal stresses of Nature. Proteins once widely apart can come closer due to convergent evolution. Those once close can become distant due to divergence. Sometimes proteins with very unlike sequences can have very similar folds, in contrast to Anfinsen's principle. Proteins carry stories of changing climates, of love and hatred for domains, of desperation that asks for new functions, passed on for generations from parent to offspring over millions of years - from the primordial soup to the golden age of biology. Proteins behave variably in the presence of other cellular individuals and mingle with other proteins to create new skills, employed by cells for communicating with one another or passing down signals. Proteins can be unruly and unstructured, and the very lack of structural discipline can enable them to accomplish multiple functions. So when all of these are put together, it is understandable that the protein is like any other life form, and listening to its story is vital for its construction. The subject of protein modelling is thus not restricted to Science alone: there is an unspoken Art to the Science of crafting proteins.

REFERENCES

Abagyan, R., Totrov, M., & Kuznetsov, D. (1994). ICM - A new method for protein modeling and design: Applications to docking and structure prediction from the distorted native conformation. *Journal of Computational Chemistry*, 15(5), 488–506. doi:10.1002/jcc.540150503

Al-Lazikani, B., Jung, J., Xiang, Z., & Honig, B. (2001). Protein structure prediction. *Current Opinion in Chemical Biology*. doi:10.1016/S1367-5931(00)00164-2

Bartoli, L., Fariselli, P., Krogh, A., & Casadio, R. (2009). CCHMM_PROF: A HMM-based coiled-coil predictor with evolutionary information. *Bioinformatics (Oxford, England), 25*(21), 2757–2763. doi:10.1093/bioinformatics/btp539 PMID:19744995

Becker, J., Maes, F., Wehenkel, L., Anfinsen, C., Matsumura, M., & Signor, G., ... Frasconi, P. (2013). On the Relevance of Sophisticated Structural Annotations for Disulfide Connectivity Pattern Prediction. *PLoS ONE, 8*(2). doi:10.1371/journal.pone.0056621

Benkert, P., Tosatto, S. C. E., & Schomburg, D. (2008). QMEAN: A comprehensive scoring function for model quality assessment. *Proteins: Structure, Function, and Bioinformatics, 71*(1), 261–277. doi:10.1002/prot.21715

Berendsen, H. J. C., van der Spoel, D., & van Drunen, R. (1995). GROMACS: A message-passing parallel molecular dynamics implementation. *Computer Physics Communications, 91*(1), 43–56. doi:10.1016/0010-4655(95)00042-E

Bhattacharya, A., Tejero, R., & Montelione, G. T. (2006). Evaluating protein structures determined by structural genomics consortia. *Proteins: Structure, Function, and Bioinformatics, 66*(4), 778–795. doi:10.1002/prot.21165

Bhattacharya, D., Nowotny, J., Cao, R., & Cheng, J. (2016). 3Drefine: An interactive web server for efficient protein structure refinement. *Nucleic Acids Research, 44*(W1), W406–W409. doi:10.1093/nar/gkw336 PMID:27131371

Biasini, M., Bienert, S., & Waterhouse, A. (2014). SWISS-MODEL: modelling protein tertiary and quaternary structure using evolutionary information. *Nucleic Acids.* Retrieved from http://nar.oxford-journals.org/content/early/2014/04/29/nar.gku340.short

Blaszczyk, M., Jamroz, M., Kmiecik, S., & Kolinski, A. (2013). CABS-fold: Server for the de novo and consensus-based prediction of protein structure. *Nucleic Acids Research, 41*(W1), W406–W411. doi:10.1093/nar/gkt462 PMID:23748950

Bowers, K., Chow, E., Xu, H., Dror, R., Eastwood, M., & Gregersen, B. ... Shaw, D. (2006). Scalable Algorithms for Molecular Dynamics Simulations on Commodity Clusters. *Proceedings of ACM/IEEE SC 2006 Conference (SC'06)* (pp. 43–43). IEEE. doi:10.1109/SC.2006.54

Brooks, B. R., Brooks, C. L., Mackerell, A. D., Nilsson, L., Petrella, R. J., & Roux, B. ... Karplus, M. (2009). CHARMM: The biomolecular simulation program. *Journal of Computational Chemistry, 30*(10), 1545–1614. doi:10.1002/jcc.21287

Brooks, B. R., Bruccoleri, R. E., Olafson, B. D., States, D. J., Swaminathan, S., & Karplus, M. (1983). CHARMM: A program for macromolecular energy, minimization, and dynamics calculations. *Journal of Computational Chemistry, 4*(2), 187–217. doi:10.1002/jcc.540040211

Buchan, D. W. A., Ward, S. M., Lobley, A. E., Nugent, T. C. O., Bryson, K., & Jones, D. T. (2010). Protein annotation and modelling servers at University College London. *Nucleic Acids Research, 38*(Web Server issue), W563-8. doi:10.1093/nar/gkq427

Carpenter, E. P., Beis, K., Cameron, A. D., & Iwata, S. (2008). Overcoming the challenges of membrane protein crystallography. *Current Opinion in Structural Biology.* doi:10.1016/j.sbi.2008.07.001

Ceroni, A., Passerini, A., Vullo, A., & Frasconi, P. (2006). DISULFIND: a disulfide bonding state and cysteine connectivity prediction server. *Nucleic Acids Research, 34*(Web Server issue), W177-81. doi:10.1093/nar/gkl266

Chen, V. B., Arendall, W. B., Headd, J. J., Keedy, D. A., Immormino, R. M., & Kapral, G. J. ... Richardson, D. C. (2010). MolProbity: All-atom structure validation for macromolecular crystallography. *Acta Crystallographica Section D: Biological Crystallography, 66*(1), 12–21. doi:10.1107/S0907444909042073

Cheng, J., Randall, A. Z., Sweredoski, M. J., & Baldi, P. (2005). SCRATCH: a protein structure and structural feature prediction server. *Nucleic Acids Research, 33*(Web Server issue), W72-6. doi:10.1093/nar/gki396

Cheng, J., Saigo, H., & Baldi, P. (2005). Large-scale prediction of disulphide bridges using kernel methods, two-dimensional recursive neural networks, and weighted graph matching. *Proteins: Structure, Function, and Bioinformatics, 62*(3), 617–629. https://doi.org/10.1002/prot.20787

Chou, P. Y., & Fasman, G. D. (1974). Prediction of protein conformation. *Biochemistry, 13*(2), 222–245. doi:10.1021/bi00699a002 PMID:4358940

Combet, C., Jambon, M., Deléage, G., & Geourjon, C. (2002). Geno3D: Automatic comparative molecular modelling of protein. *Bioinformatics (Oxford, England), 18*(1), 213–214. doi:10.1093/bioinformatics/18.1.213 PMID:11836238

Cserzö, M., Eisenhaber, F., Eisenhaber, B., & Simon, I. (2002). On filtering false positive transmembrane protein predictions. *Protein Engineering, 15*(9), 745–752. doi:10.1093/protein/15.9.745 PMID:12456873

Dastmalchi, S., Beheshti, S., Morris, M. B., & Bret Church, W. (2007). Prediction of rotational orientation of transmembrane helical segments of integral membrane proteins using new environment-based propensities for amino acids derived from structural analyses. *The FEBS Journal, 274*(10), 2653–2660. doi:10.1111/j.1742-4658.2007.05800.x PMID:17451441

Delorenzi, M., & Speed, T. (2002). An HMM model for coiled-coil domains and a comparison with PSSM-based predictions. *Bioinformatics (Oxford, England), 18*(4), 617–625. Retrieved from http://www.ncbi.nlm.nih.gov/pubmed/12016059 doi:10.1093/bioinformatics/18.4.617 PMID:12016059

Deng, X., Eickholt, J., Cheng, J., Tompa, P., Receveur-Bréchot, V., & Bourhis, J. ... McGuffin, L. (2009). PreDisorder: ab initio sequence-based prediction of protein disordered regions. *BMC Bioinformatics, 10*(1), 436. doi:10.1186/1471-2105-10-436

Dill, K. A., Ozkan, S. B., Shell, M. S., & Weikl, T. R. (2008). The protein folding problem. *Annual Review of Biophysics, 37*(1), 289–316. doi:10.1146/annurev.biophys.37.092707.153558 PMID:18573083

Disfani, F. M., Hsu, W.-L., Mizianty, M. J., Oldfield, C. J., Xue, B., & Dunker, A. K. ... Kurgan, L. (2012). MoRFpred, a computational tool for sequence-based prediction and characterization of short disorder-to-order transitioning binding regions in proteins. *Bioinformatics (Oxford, England), 28*(12), i75-83. doi:10.1093/bioinformatics/bts209

Dobson, L., Reményi, I., & Tusnády, G. E. (2015). CCTOP: A Consensus Constrained TOPology prediction web server. *Nucleic Acids Research*, *43*(W1), W408–W412. doi:10.1093/nar/gkv451 PMID:25943549

Doolittle, R. F. (1994). Convergent evolution: The need to be explicit. *Trends in Biochemical Sciences*, *19*(1), 15–18. Retrieved from http://www.ncbi.nlm.nih.gov/pubmed/8140615 doi:10.1016/0968-0004(94)90167-8 PMID:8140615

Dorn, M. E., Silva, M. B., Buriol, L. S., & Lamb, L. C. (2014). Three-dimensional protein structure prediction: Methods and computational strategies. *Computational Biology and Chemistry*. doi:10.1016/j.compbiolchem.2014.10.001

dos Reis, M. A., Aparicio, R., & Zhang, Y. (2011). Improving Protein Template Recognition by Using Small-Angle X-Ray Scattering Profiles. *Biophysical Journal*, *101*(11), 2770–2781. doi:10.1016/j.bpj.2011.10.046 PMID:22261066

Dosztanyi, Z., Csizmok, V., Tompa, P., & Simon, I. (2005). IUPred: Web server for the prediction of intrinsically unstructured regions of proteins based on estimated energy content. *Bioinformatics (Oxford, England)*, *21*(16), 3433–3434. doi:10.1093/bioinformatics/bti541 PMID:15955779

Drozdetskiy, A., Cole, C., Procter, J., & Barton, G. J. (2015). JPred4: A protein secondary structure prediction server. *Nucleic Acids Research*, *43*(W1), W389-94. doi:10.1093/nar/gkv332 PMID:25883141

Ebina, T., Toh, H., & Kuroda, Y. (2009). Loop-length-dependent SVM prediction of domain linkers for high-throughput structural proteomics. *Biopolymers*, *92*(1), 1–8. doi:10.1002/bip.21105 PMID:18844295

Eisenberg, D., Lüthy, R., & Bowie, J. U. (1997). VERIFY3D: Assessment of protein models with three-dimensional profiles. *Methods in Enzymology*, *277*, 396–404. Retrieved from doi:10.1016/S0076-6879(97)77022-8 PMID:9379925

Emily, M., Talvas, A., Delamarche, C., Jiménez, J., Guijarro, J., & Orlova, E. …Chiti, F. (2013). MetAmyl: A META-Predictor for AMYLoid Proteins. *PLoS ONE, 8*(11). doi:10.1371/journal.pone.0079722

Eswar, N., John, B., Mirkovic, N., Fiser, A., Ilyin, V. A., & Pieper, U. … Sali, A. (2003). Tools for comparative protein structure modeling and analysis. *Nucleic Acids Research, 31*(13), 3375–80. doi:10.1093/NAR/GKG543

Fan, X., & Kurgan, L. (2014). Accurate prediction of disorder in protein chains with a comprehensive and empirically designed consensus. *Journal of Biomolecular Structure and Dynamics*. Retrieved from http://www.tandfonline.com/doi/abs/10.1080/07391102.2013.775969

Fariselli, P., Riccobelli, P., & Casadio, R. (1999). Role of evolutionary information in predicting the disulfide-bonding state of cysteine in proteins. *Proteins*, *36*(3), 340–346. Retrieved from http://www.ncbi.nlm.nih.gov/pubmed/10409827 doi:10.1002/(SICI)1097-0134(19990815)36:3<340::AID-PROT8>3.0.CO;2-D PMID:10409827

Ferrè, F., & Clote, P. (2005). DiANNA: a web server for disulfide connectivity prediction. *Nucleic Acids Research, 33*(Web Server issue), W230-2. doi.org/10.1093/nar/gki412

Fiser, A. (2010). Template-based protein structure modeling. *Methods in Molecular Biology (Clifton, N.J.)*, *673*, 73–94. doi:10.1007/978-1-60761-842-3_6 PMID:20835794

Fiser, A., & Sali, A. (2003). ModLoop: Automated modeling of loops in protein structures. *Bioinformatics (Oxford, England)*, *19*(18), 2500–2501. Retrieved from http://www.ncbi.nlm.nih.gov/pubmed/14668246 doi:10.1093/bioinformatics/btg362 PMID:14668246

Garnier, J., Gibrat, J. F., & Robson, B. (1996). GOR method for predicting protein secondary structure from amino acid sequence. *Methods in Enzymology*, *266*, 540–553. Retrieved from http://www.ncbi.nlm.nih.gov/pubmed/8743705 doi:10.1016/S0076-6879(96)66034-0 PMID:8743705

Godzik, A. (2003). Fold recognition methods. *Methods of Biochemical Analysis*, *44*, 525–546. Retrieved from http://www.ncbi.nlm.nih.gov/pubmed/12647403 PMID:12647403

Gopalakrishnan, K., Sowmiya, G., Sheik, S. S., & Sekar, K. (2007). Ramachandran plot on the web (2.0). *Protein and Peptide Letters*, *14*(7), 669–671. Retrieved from http://www.ncbi.nlm.nih.gov/pubmed/17897092 doi:10.2174/092986607781483912 PMID:17897092

Gracy, J., Le-Nguyen, D., Gelly, J.-C., Kaas, Q., Heitz, A., & Chiche, L. (2008). KNOTTIN: The knottin or inhibitor cystine knot scaffold in 2007. *Nucleic Acids Research*, *36*(Database issue), D314–D319. doi:10.1093/nar/gkm939 PMID:18025039

Guerler, A., Govindarajoo, B., & Zhang, Y. (2013). Mapping Monomeric Threading to Protein–Protein Structure Prediction. *Journal of Chemical Information and Modeling*, *53*(3), 717–725. https://doi.org/10.1021/ci300579r doi:10.1021/ci300579r PMID:23413988

Guex, N., & Peitsch, M. (1997). SWISS-MODEL and the Swiss-Pdb Viewer: an environment for comparative protein modeling. *Electrophoresis*. Retrieved from http://onlinelibrary.wiley.com/doi/10.1002/elps.1150181505/full

Gullotto, D., Nolassi, M. S., Bernini, A., Spiga, O., & Niccolai, N. (2013). Probing the protein space for extending the detection of weak homology folds. *Journal of Theoretical Biology*, *320*, 152–158. doi:10.1016/j.jtbi.2012.12.005 PMID:23261396

Hardin, C., Pogorelov, T. V., & Luthey-Schulten, Z. (2002). Ab initio protein structure prediction. [pii]. *Current Opinion in Structural Biology*, *12*(2), 176–181. doi:10.1016/S0959-440X(02)00306-8 PMID:11959494

Heo, L., Park, H., & Seok, C. (2013). GalaxyRefine: Protein structure refinement driven by side-chain repacking. *Nucleic Acids Research*, *41*(W1), W384–W388. doi:10.1093/nar/gkt458 PMID:23737448

Hofmann, K., & Stoffel, W. (1993). TMbase-A database of membrane spanning protein segments. Retrieved from http://en.journals.sid.ir/ViewPaper.aspx?ID=118765

Hooft, R., Vriend, G., Sander, C., & Abola, E. (1996). Errors in protein structures. *Nature*. Retrieved from http://www.cheric.org/research/tech/periodicals/view.php?seq=221219

Hospital, A., Andrio, P., Fenollosa, C., Cicin-Sain, D., Orozco, M., & Gelpí, J. L. (2012). MDWeb and MDMoby: An integrated web-based platform for molecular dynamics simulations. *Bioinformatics (Oxford, England)*, *28*(9), 1278–1279. doi:10.1093/bioinformatics/bts139 PMID:22437851

Ishida, T., & Kinoshita, K. (2007). PrDOS: prediction of disordered protein regions from amino acid sequence. *Nucleic Acids Research, 35*(Web Server), W460–W464. doi:10.1093/nar/gkm363

Jacobson, M. P., Pincus, D. L., Rapp, C. S., Day, T. J. F., Honig, B., Shaw, D. E., & Friesner, R. A. (2004). A hierarchical approach to all-atom protein loop prediction. *Proteins: Structure, Function, and Bioinformatics, 55*(2), 351–367. doi.org/10.1002/prot.10613

Jamroz, M., Kolinski, A., & Kmiecik, S. (2013). CABS-flex: Server for fast simulation of protein structure fluctuations. *Nucleic Acids Research, 41*(Web Server issue), W427-31. https://doi.org/10.1093/nar/gkt332

Jayaram, B., Bhushan, K., Shenoy, S. R., Narang, P., Bose, S., & Agrawal, P. … Pandey, V. (2006). Bhageerath: an energy based web enabled computer software suite for limiting the search space of tertiary structures of small globular proteins. *Nucleic Acids Research, 34*(21), 6195–204. doi:10.1093/nar/gkl789

Jones, D. T. (1999). GenTHREADER: An efficient and reliable protein fold recognition method for genomic sequences. *Journal of Molecular Biology, 287*(4), 797–815. doi:10.1006/jmbi.1999.2583 PMID:10191147

Kahsay, R. Y., Gao, G., & Liao, L. (2005). An improved hidden Markov model for transmembrane protein detection and topology prediction and its applications to complete genomes. *Bioinformatics (Oxford, England), 21*(9), 1853–1858. doi:10.1093/bioinformatics/bti303 PMID:15691854

Källberg, M., Margaryan, G., Wang, S., Ma, J., & Xu, J. (2014). *RaptorX server: A Resource for Template-Based Protein Structure Modeling.* doi:10.1007/978-1-4939-0366-5_2

Källberg, M., Wang, H., Wang, S., Peng, J., Wang, Z., Lu, H., & Xu, J. (2012). Template-based protein structure modeling using the RaptorX web server. *Nature Protocols, 7*(8), 1511–1522. doi:10.1038/nprot.2012.085 PMID:22814390

Kelley, L. A., Mezulis, S., Yates, C. M., Wass, M. N., & Sternberg, M. J. E. (2015). The Phyre2 web portal for protein modeling, prediction and analysis. *Nature Protocols, 10*(6), 845–858. doi:10.1038/nprot.2015.053 PMID:25950237

Khor, B. Y., Tye, G. J., Lim, T. S., Choong, Y. S., Wu, S., & Zhang, Y. … Zhang, Y. (2015). General overview on structure prediction of twilight-zone proteins. *Theoretical Biology and Medical Modelling, 12*(1), 15. doi:10.1186/s12976-015-0014-1

Khoury, G. A., Tamamis, P., Pinnaduwage, N., Smadbeck, J., Kieslich, C. A., & Floudas, C. A. (2014). Princeton_TIGRESS: Protein geometry refinement using simulations and support vector machines. *Proteins: Structure, Function, and Bioinformatics, 82*(5), 794–814. doi:10.1002/prot.24459

Kinch, L. N., Li, W., Monastyrskyy, B., Kryshtafovych, A., & Grishin, N. V. (2016). Evaluation of free modeling targets in CASP11 and ROLL. *Proteins: Structure, Function, and Bioinformatics, 84*, 51–66. doi:10.1002/prot.24973

Ko, J., Park, H., Seok, C., Zhang, Y., Marti-Renom, M., & Stuart, A. … Zhou, Y. (2012). GalaxyTBM: template-based modeling by building a reliable core and refining unreliable local regions. *BMC Bioinformatics, 13*(1), 198. doi:10.1186/1471-2105-13-198

Kozlowski, L. P., Bujnicki, J. M., Dunker, A., Oldfield, C., Meng, J., & Romero, P. … Dunker, A. (2012). MetaDisorder: a meta-server for the prediction of intrinsic disorder in proteins. *BMC Bioinformatics, 13*(1), 111. doi:10.1186/1471-2105-13-111

Krieger, E., Joo, K., Lee, J., Lee, J., Raman, S., & Thompson, J. ... Karplus, K. (2009). Improving physical realism, stereochemistry, and side-chain accuracy in homology modeling: Four approaches that performed well in CASP8. *Proteins: Structure, Function, and Bioinformatics, 77*(S9), 114–122. doi:10.1002/prot.22570

Krogh, A., Larsson, B., von Heijne, G., & Sonnhammer, E. L. (2001). Predicting transmembrane protein topology with a hidden markov model: application to complete genomes11Edited by F. Cohen. *Journal of Molecular Biology, 305*(3), 567–580. doi:10.1006/jmbi.2000.4315

Lambert, C., Léonard, N., De Bolle, X., & Depiereux, E. (2002). ESyPred3D: Prediction of proteins 3D structures. *Bioinformatics (Oxford, England), 18*(9), 1250–1256. doi:10.1093/bioinformatics/18.9 1250 PMID:12217917

Laskowski, R. A., MacArthur, M. W., Moss, D. S., Thornton, J. M., & Cr, I. U. (1993). PROCHECK: A program to check the stereochemical quality of protein structures. *Journal of Applied Crystallography, 26*(2), 283–291. doi:10.1107/S0021889892009944

Lee, J., Wu, S., & Zhang, Y. (2009). Ab Initio Protein Structure Prediction. In *From Protein Structure to Function with Bioinformatics* (pp. 3–25). Dordrecht: Springer Netherlands. doi:10.1007/978-1-4020-9058-5_1

Li, Y., & Zhang, Y. (2009). REMO: A new protocol to refine full atomic protein models from C-alpha traces by optimizing hydrogen-bonding networks. *Proteins: Structure, Function, and Bioinformatics, 76*(3), 665–676. doi:10.1002/prot.22380

Lindahl, E., Azuara, C., Koehl, P., & Delarue, M. (2006). NOMAD-Ref: visualization, deformation and refinement of macromolecular structures based on all-atom normal mode analysis. *Nucleic Acids Research, 34*(Web Server issue), W52-6. doi:10.1093/nar/gkl082

Linding, R., Jensen, L. J., Diella, F., Bork, P., Gibson, T. J., & Russell, R. B. (2003). Protein disorder prediction: implications for structural proteomics. *Structure, 11*(11), 1453–9. Retrieved from http://www.ncbi.nlm.nih.gov/pubmed/14604535

Linding, R., Russell, R. B., Neduva, V., & Gibson, T. J. (2003). GlobPlot: Exploring protein sequences for globularity and disorder. *Nucleic Acids Research, 31*(13), 3701–3708. doi:10.1093/nar/gkg519 PMID:12824398

Lobley, A., Sadowski, M. I., & Jones, D. T. (2009). pGenTHREADER and pDomTHREADER: New methods for improved protein fold recognition and superfamily discrimination. *Bioinformatics (Oxford, England), 25*(14), 1761–1767. doi:10.1093/bioinformatics/btp302 PMID:19429599

López-Blanco, J. R., Canosa-Valls, A. J., Li, Y., & Chacón, P. (2016). RCD+: Fast loop modeling server. *Nucleic Acids Research, 44*(W1), W395-400. doi:10.1093/nar/gkw395 PMID:27151199

Lupas, A., Van Dyke, M., & Stock, J. (1991). Predicting coiled coils from protein sequences. *Science, 252*(5009), 1162–1164. doi:10.1126/science.252.5009.1162 PMID:2031185

Lyskov, S., Chou, F.-C., Conchúir, S. Ó., Der, B. S., Drew, K., & Kuroda, D. ... Meiler, J. (2013). Serverification of Molecular Modeling Applications: The Rosetta Online Server That Includes Everyone (ROSIE). *PLoS ONE, 8*(5), e63906. doi:10.1371/journal.pone.0063906

Malhis, N., Jacobson, M., & Gsponer, J. (2016). MoRFchibi SYSTEM: Software tools for the identification of MoRFs in protein sequences. *Nucleic Acids Research, 44*(W1), W488-93. doi:10.1093/nar/gkw409 PMID:27174932

McDonnell, A. V., Jiang, T., Keating, A. E., & Berger, B. (2006). Paircoil2: Improved prediction of coiled coils from sequence. *Bioinformatics (Oxford, England), 22*(3), 356–358. doi:10.1093/bioinformatics/bti797 PMID:16317077

McGuffin, L. J., Bryson, K., & Jones, D. T. (2000). The PSIPRED protein structure prediction server. *Bioinformatics (Oxford, England), 16*(4), 404–405. doi:10.1093/bioinformatics/16.4.404 PMID:10869041

McGuffin, L. J., Buenavista, M. T., & Roche, D. B. (2013). The ModFOLD4 server for the quality assessment of 3D protein models. *Nucleic Acids Research, 41*(Web Server issue), W368-72. doi:10.1093/nar/gkt294

Meng, F., & Kurgan, L. (2016). DFLpred: High-throughput prediction of disordered flexible linker regions in protein sequences. *Bioinformatics (Oxford, England), 32*(12), i341–i350. doi:10.1093/bioinformatics/btw280 PMID:27307636

Mészáros, B., Simon, I., Dosztányi, Z., Wright, P., Dyson, H., & Dyson, H. ...Pliska, V. (2009). Prediction of Protein Binding Regions in Disordered Proteins. *PLoS Computational Biology, 5*(5), e1000376. doi:10.1371/journal.pcbi.1000376

Miller, B. T., Singh, R. P., Klauda, J. B., Hodoscek, M., Brooks, B. R., Woodcock, H. L., & III. (2008). CHARMMing: a new, flexible web portal for CHARMM. *Journal of Chemical Information and Modeling, 48*(9), 1920–9. doi:10.1021/ci800133b

Monastyrskyy, B., D'Andrea, D., Fidelis, K., Tramontano, A., & Kryshtafovych, A. (2016). New encouraging developments in contact prediction: Assessment of the CASP11 results. *Proteins: Structure, Function, and Bioinformatics, 84*(S1), 131–144. doi:10.1002/prot.24943

Morcos, F., Pagnani, A., Lunt, B., Bertolino, A., Marks, D. S., & Sander, C. ...Weigt, M. (2011). Direct-coupling analysis of residue coevolution captures native contacts across many protein families. *Proceedings of the National Academy of Sciences of the United States of America, 108*(49), E1293-301. doi:10.1073/pnas.1111471108

Moult, J., Fidelis, K., Kryshtafovych, A., Schwede, T., & Tramontano, A. (2016). Critical assessment of methods of protein structure prediction: Progress and new directions in round XI. *Proteins: Structure, Function, and Bioinformatics, 84*(S1), 4–14. doi:10.1002/prot.25064

Mount, D. W. (2004). *Bioinformatics: sequence and genome analysis*. Cold Spring Harbor Laboratory Press.

Mukherjee, S., & Zhang, Y. (2011). Protein-Protein Complex Structure Predictions by Multimeric Threading and Template Recombination. *Structure (London, England), 19*(7), 955–966. doi:10.1016/j. str.2011.04.006 PMID:21742262

Nielsen, M., Lundegaard, C., & Lund, O. (2010). CPHmodels-3.0—remote homology modeling using structure-guided sequence profiles. *Nucleic Acids*. Retrieved from http://nar.oxfordjournals.org/content/ early/2010/06/11/nar.gkq535.short

Overington, J. P., Al-Lazikani, B., & Hopkins, A. L. (2006). How many drug targets are there? *Nature Reviews. Drug Discovery, 5*(12), 993–996. doi:10.1038/nrd2199 PMID:17139284

Park, H., Lee, G. R., Heo, L., Seok, C., Fiser, A., & Do, R. … Dill, K. (2014). Protein Loop Modeling Using a New Hybrid Energy Function and Its Application to Modeling in Inaccurate Structural Environments. *PLoS ONE, 9*(11), e113811. doi:10.1371/journal.pone.0113811

Pearlman, D. A., Case, D. A., Caldwell, J. W., Ross, W. S., Cheatham, T. E., & DeBolt, S. … Kollman, P. (1995). AMBER, a package of computer programs for applying molecular mechanics, normal mode analysis, molecular dynamics and free energy calculations to simulate the structural and energetic properties of molecules. *Computer Physics Communications, 91*(1), 1–41. doi:10.1016/0010-4655(95)00041-D

Peng, K., Radivojac, P., Vucetic, S., Dunker, A. K., & Obradovic, Z. (2006). Length-dependent prediction of protein intrinsic disorder. *BMC Bioinformatics, 7*(1), 208. doi:10.1186/1471-2105-7-208 PMID:16618368

Petersen, B., Lundegaard, C., & Petersen, T. N. GD, G. R., Smith, J., Milner-White, E. J., … Ho, T. (2010). NetTurnP – Neural Network Prediction of Beta-turns by Use of Evolutionary Information and Predicted Protein Sequence Features. *PLoS ONE, 5*(11), e15079. doi:10.1371/journal.pone.0015079

Petersen, B., Petersen, T., Andersen, P., Nielsen, M., Lundegaard, C., & Lundegaard, C. … Sander, C. (2009). A generic method for assignment of reliability scores applied to solvent accessibility predictions. *BMC Structural Biology, 9*(1), 51. doi:10.1186/1472-6807-9-51

Pettersen, E. F., Goddard, T. D., Huang, C. C., Couch, G. S., Greenblatt, D. M., Meng, E. C., & Ferrin, T. E. (2004). UCSF Chimera - A visualization system for exploratory research and analysis. *Journal of Computational Chemistry, 25*(13), 1605–1612. doi:10.1002/jcc.20084 PMID:15264254

Phillips, J. C., Braun, R., Wang, W., Gumbart, J., Tajkhorshid, E., & Villa, E. … Schulten, K. (2005). Scalable molecular dynamics with NAMD. *Journal of Computational Chemistry, 26*(16), 1781–1802. doi:10.1002/jcc.20289

Pollastri, G., & McLysaght, A. (2005). Porter: A new, accurate server for protein secondary structure prediction. *Bioinformatics (Oxford, England), 21*(8), 1719–1720. doi:10.1093/bioinformatics/bti203 PMID:15585524

Pontius, J., Richelle, J., & Wodak, S. J. (1996). Deviations from Standard Atomic Volumes as a Quality Measure for Protein Crystal Structures. *Journal of Molecular Biology, 264*(1), 121–136. doi:10.1006/ jmbi.1996.0628 PMID:8950272

Pugalenthi, G., Shameer, K., Srinivasan, N., & Sowdhamini, R. (2006). HARMONY: a server for the assessment of protein structures. *Nucleic Acids Research, 34*(Web Server), W231–W234. https://doi. org/10.1093/nar/gkl314

Raman, S., Vernon, R., Thompson, J., Tyka, M., Sadreyev, R., & Pei, J. … Baker, D. (2009). Structure prediction for CASP8 with all-atom refinement using Rosetta. *Proteins, 77*(Suppl. 9), 89–99. doi:10.1002/prot.22540

Ribeiro, J. V., Bernardi, R. C., Rudack, T., Stone, J. E., Phillips, J. C., & Freddolino, P. L. … Schulten, K. (2016). QwikMD—Integrative Molecular Dynamics Toolkit for Novices and Experts. *Scientific Reports, 6*, 26536. doi:10.1038/srep26536

Rodrigues, J. P. G. L. M., Levitt, M., & Chopra, G. (2012). KoBaMIN: A knowledge-based minimization web server for protein structure refinement. *Nucleic Acids Research, 40*(W1), W323–W328. doi:10.1093/nar/gks376 PMID:22564897

Rost, B. (1999). Twilight zone of protein sequence alignments. *Protein Engineering, 12*(2), 85–94. doi:10.1093/protein/12.2.85 PMID:10195279

Rost, B., & Sander, C. (1993). Prediction of Protein Secondary Structure at Better than 70% Accuracy. *Journal of Molecular Biology, 232*(2), 584–599. doi:10.1006/jmbi.1993.1413 PMID:8345525

Shen, Y., Maupetit, J., Derreumaux, P., & Tufféry, P. (2014). Improved PEP-FOLD Approach for Peptide and Miniprotein Structure Prediction. *Journal of Chemical Theory and Computation, 10*(10), 4745–4758. doi:10.1021/ct500592m PMID:26588162

Singh, A., Kaushik, R., Mishra, A., Shanker, A., & Jayaram, B. (2016). ProTSAV: A protein tertiary structure analysis and validation server. *Biochimica et Biophysica Acta (BBA) - Proteins and Proteomics, 1864*(1), 11–19. doi:10.1016/j.bbapap.2015.10.004

Sivasubramanian, A., Sircar, A., Chaudhury, S., & Gray, J. J. (2009). Toward high-resolution homology modeling of antibody Fv regions and application to antibody-antigen docking. *Proteins: Structure, Function, and Bioinformatics, 74*(2), 497–514. doi:10.1002/prot.22309

Soding, J. (2005). Protein homology detection by HMM-HMM comparison. *Bioinformatics (Oxford, England), 21*(7), 951–960. doi:10.1093/bioinformatics/bti125 PMID:15531603

Tusnády, G. E., & Simon, I. (2001). The HMMTOP transmembrane topology prediction server. *Bioinformatics (Oxford, England), 17*(9), 849–850. Retrieved from http://www.ncbi.nlm.nih.gov/pubmed/11590105 doi:10.1093/bioinformatics/17.9.849 PMID:11590105

Wallner, B., & Elofsson, A. (2003). Can correct protein models be identified? *Protein Science : A Publication of the Protein Society, 12*(5), 1073–86. doi:10.1110/ps.0236803

Walter, R. P. Scott, Philippe H. Hünenberger, Ilario G. Tironi, Alan E. Mark, Salomon R. Billeter, Jens Fennen, … Gunsteren. (1999). The GROMOS Biomolecular Simulation Program Package. doi:10.1021/JP984217F

Wang, C., Zhang, H., Zheng, W.-M., Xu, D., Zhu, J., & Wang, B. … Bu, D. (2016). FALCON@home: a high-throughput protein structure prediction server based on remote homologue recognition. *Bioinformatics (Oxford, England), 32*(3), 462–4. doi;10.1093/bioinformatics/btv581

Wang, L., & Sauer, U. H. (2008). OnD-CRF: Predicting order and disorder in proteins using [corrected] conditional random fields. *Bioinformatics (Oxford, England), 24*(11), 1401–1402. doi:10.1093/bioinformatics/btn132 PMID:18430742

Wang, S., Ma, J., & Xu, J. (2016). AUCpreD: Proteome-level protein disorder prediction by AUC-maximized deep convolutional neural fields. *Bioinformatics (Oxford, England), 32*(17), i672–i679. doi:10.1093/bioinformatics/btw446 PMID:27587688

Webb, B., Sali, A., Webb, B., & Sali, A. (2014). Comparative Protein Structure Modeling Using MODELLER. In *Current Protocols in Bioinformatics* (p. 5.6.1-5.6.32). Hoboken, NJ, USA: John Wiley & Sons, Inc. doi:10.1002/0471250953.bi0506s47

Weichenberger, C. X., & Sippl, M. J. (2006). NQ-Flipper: Validation and correction of asparagine/glutamine amide rotamers in protein crystal structures. *Bioinformatics (Oxford, England), 22*(11), 1397–1398. doi:10.1093/bioinformatics/btl128 PMID:16595557

White, S. H. (2004). The progress of membrane protein structure determination. *Protein Science : A Publication of the Protein Society, 13*(7), 1948–9. doi:10.1110/ps.04712004

Wiederstein, M., & Sippl, M. J. (2007). ProSA-web: interactive web service for the recognition of errors in three-dimensional structures of proteins. *Nucleic Acids Research, 35*(Web Server issue), W407-10. doi:10.1093/nar/gkm290

Willard, L., Ranjan, A., Zhang, H., Monzavi, H., Boyko, R. F., Sykes, B. D., & Wishart, D. S. (2003). VADAR: A web server for quantitative evaluation of protein structure quality. *Nucleic Acids Research, 31*(13), 3316–3319. doi:10.1093/nar/gkg565 PMID:12824316

Wolf, E., Kim, P. S., & Berger, B. (1997). MultiCoil: A program for predicting two-and three-stranded coiled coils. *Protein Science, 6*(6), 1179–1189. doi:10.1002/pro.5560060606 PMID:9194178

Wu, S., & Zhang, Y. (2007). LOMETS: a local meta-threading-server for protein structure prediction. *Nucleic Acids Research*. Retrieved from http://nar.oxfordjournals.org/content/35/10/3375.short

Wu, S., & Zhang, Y. (2008). MUSTER: improving protein sequence profile–profile alignments by using multiple sources of structure information. *Proteins: Structure, Function, and.* Retrieved from http://onlinelibrary.wiley.com/doi/10.1002/prot.21945/full

Wu, S., & Zhang, Y. (2010). Recognizing Protein Substructure Similarity Using Segmental Threading. *Structure (London, England), 18*(7), 858–867. doi:10.1016/j.str.2010.04.007 PMID:20637422

Wu, S., Zhang, Y., Neal, S., Berjanskii, M., Zhang, H., & Wishart, D. … Zhang, Y. (2008). ANGLOR: A Composite Machine-Learning Algorithm for Protein Backbone Torsion Angle Prediction. *PLoS ONE, 3*(10), e3400. doi:10.1371/journal.pone.0003400

Xu, D., Jaroszewski, L., Li, Z., & Godzik, A. (2014). FFAS-3D: Improving fold recognition by including optimized structural features and template re-ranking. *Bioinformatics (Oxford, England), 30*(5), 660–667. doi:10.1093/bioinformatics/btt578 PMID:24130308

Xu, D., & Zhang, Y. (2011). Improving the Physical Realism and Structural Accuracy of Protein Models by a Two-Step Atomic-Level Energy Minimization. *Biophysical Journal, 101*(10), 2525–2534. doi:10.1016/j.bpj.2011.10.024 PMID:22098752

Xu, D., & Zhang, Y. (2012). Ab initio protein structure assembly using continuous structure fragments and optimized knowledge-based force field. *Proteins: Structure, Function, and.* Retrieved from http://onlinelibrary.wiley.com/doi/10.1002/prot.24065/full

Xu, Y., & Xu, D. (2000). Protein threading using PROSPECT: Design and evaluation. *Proteins, 40*(3), 343–354. doi:10.1002/1097-0134(20000815)40:3<343::AID-PROT10>3.0.CO;2-S PMID:10861926

Xue, Z., Xu, D., Wang, Y., & Zhang, Y. (2013). ThreaDom: Extracting protein domain boundary information from multiple threading alignments. *Bioinformatics (Oxford, England), 29*(13), i247–i256. doi:10.1093/bioinformatics/btt209 PMID:23812990

Yachdav, G., Kloppmann, E., Kajan, L., Hecht, M., Goldberg, T., & Hamp, T. … Rost, B. (2014). PredictProtein--an open resource for online prediction of protein structural and functional features. *Nucleic Acids Research, 42*(W1), W337–W343. doi:10.1093/nar/gku366

Yan, R.-X., Si, J.-N., Wang, C., Zhang, Z., Petrey, D., & Honig, B. … Bourne, P. (2009). DescFold: A web server for protein fold recognition. *BMC Bioinformatics, 10*(1), 416. doi:10.1186/1471-2105-10-416

Yang, J., He, B.-J., Jang, R., Zhang, Y., & Shen, H.-B. (2015). Accurate disulfide-bonding network predictions improve ab initio structure prediction of cysteine-rich proteins. *Bioinformatics (Oxford, England), 31*(23), 3773–3781. doi:10.1093/bioinformatics/btv459 PMID:26254435

Yang, J., Yan, R., Roy, A., Xu, D., Poisson, J., & Zhang, Y. (2015). The I-TASSER Suite: Protein structure and function prediction. *Nature Methods, 12*(1), 7–8. doi:10.1038/nmeth.3213 PMID:25549265

Yang, Y., Faraggi, E., Zhao, H., & Zhou, Y. (2011). Improving protein fold recognition and template-based modeling by employing probabilistic-based matching between predicted one-dimensional structural properties of query and corresponding native properties of templates. *Bioinformatics (Oxford, England), 27*(15), 2076–2082. doi:10.1093/bioinformatics/btr350 PMID:21666270

Yaseen, A., & Li, Y. (2013). Dinosolve: A protein disulfide bonding prediction server using context-based features to enhance prediction accuracy. *BMC Bioinformatics, S9*(Suppl. 13). https://doi.org/10.1186/1471-2105-14-S13-S9 PMID:24267383

Yuan, Z., Mattick, J. S., & Teasdale, R. D. (2004). SVMtm: Support vector machines to predict transmembrane segments. *Journal of Computational Chemistry, 25*(5), 632–636. doi:10.1002/jcc.10411 PMID:14978706

Zhang, J., Liang, Y., & Zhang, Y. (2011). Atomic-Level Protein Structure Refinement Using Fragment-Guided Molecular Dynamics Conformation Sampling. *Structure (London, England), 19*(12), 1784–1795. doi:10.1016/j.str.2011.09.022 PMID:22153501

Zhang, J., Yang, J., Jang, R., & Zhang, Y. (2015). GPCR-I-TASSER: A Hybrid Approach to G Protein-Coupled Receptor Structure Modeling and the Application to the Human Genome. *Structure (London, England), 23*(8), 1538–1549. doi:10.1016/j.str.2015.06.007 PMID:26190572

KEY TERMS AND DEFINITIONS

Ab Initio **Modelling:** Template-free *de novo* protein modelling. It selects the optimum energy conformation from the protein's energy landscape.

Homology Modelling: Computational protein structure prediction based on the experimental structure of a homologous protein.

Minimisation: Computational approach to search the protein energy landscape for finding lower energy states of the protein.

Target: The protein sequence to be modelled.

Template: An experimentally derived protein structure from which structural information is derived to construct a protein from its sequence. Applied in homology modelling.

Threading: Computational protein fold recognition where an amino acid sequence string is passed through several protein folds in a fold library.

Validation: Macromolecular structure evaluation for structural and biological reliability.

Chapter 4
Proteomics in Personalized Medicine:
An Evolution Not a Revolution

Srijan Goswami
Institute of Genetic Engineering, Badu, India

ABSTRACT

The idea of personalized medicine system is an evolution of holistic approach of treatment and in more evidence based manner. The chapter begins with an introduction of how body system works naturally and impact of modern medicine on overall health, followed by a historical background and brief review of literature providing the description that the concept of personalized medicine is not new but a very old ideology which stayed neglected until the development in the field of medical genetics, followed by the role of omics in modern medicine, the comparison of modern medicine and personalized medicine, medical concepts relevant to proteomics in personalized medicine, impact of proteomics in drug development and clinical safety and finally closing the chapter with future prospects and challenges of proteomics in personalized medicine.

INTRODUCTION

Human body is a complex combination of various extremely specialized systems. All these specialized system functions in two major ways. First each and every system performs their functions at individual level and second, they work together with other systems of the body thus making the life possible. The ultimate goal of these specialized systems is to maintain the Homeostasis of the body. As it is known that Homeostasis is the maintenance of nearly constant condition in the internal environment of the body. Disturbance of any form caused to the homeostasis of the body leads to disease. Thus a Disease can be interpreted as the dynamic destruction of the homeostasis of the body. There are several complex biochemical reactions working together as a chain system in the body for maintaining the constant condition of the internal environment. One component from a biochemical pathway is related to some other biochemical pathway and so on. So fault in a single component of a biochemical pathway may

DOI: 10.4018/978-1-5225-2607-0.ch004

lead to the collapse of the entire system. There are various control systems in our body that are the contributing factor(s) in the maintenance of homeostasis. Genetic Control System is the most intricate one. It operates in each and every cell in the body for controlling intracellular as well as extracellular functions. Every individual possess a wide range of genes in their body that determines their genotype. But mere presence of the gene in an individual does not mean all those characters will be expressed in that person's lifetime. It is the gene products or Proteins that determines the phenotype of an individual. Expression of a certain gene and production of the functional gene product is broadly dependent on the surrounding environment and lifestyle of that individual. So genotype of individuals may be same but every individual becomes unique at Proteomic level. Proteome is defined as the set of all the gene products/proteins present in an individual. Variation in composition of the protein i.e. Proteome is a key factor that determines an individual's susceptibility to a disease and their response to a particular drug.

Modern Medicine is the dominant form of medicine in the world today and portrays that it is the only system of medicine that actually restores the health of an individual, even though it works by suppression of normal physiological and immunological response to stress or by palliating the complaints of the patient ultimately converting a disease from superficial state to a much deeper state where the patient have either one of the following two choices:

1.   Becoming dependent on more and more variety of drugs to keep their systems running till the rest of their life.
2.   In cases where modern medicine no longer can manage through palliative and suppressive treatments, they look forward to surgery.

According to World Health Organization the definition of HEALTH is and the author quotes "Health is a state of complete physical, mental and social well-being and not merely the absence of the disease or infirmity".

If the definition of health proposed by W.H.O is compared with the way of treatment followed by the modern system of medicine, it will be clear that it does not restore the health of the patient at all. Instead it only make the body system dependent on more and more drugs, which in long term resulting in dependency of that particular medicine(s) to survive. Deposition of these drug substances in the blood stream and body cells leads to deterioration of mental health which ultimately cripples the patient's social well-being.

There are many factors that contributes to effectivity of modern medicines. Among the many factors the 5 major reasons behind the loop holes of the modern medicine are as follows:

1.   Medicines used in Conventional System are first tested on animals or model organisms followed by controlled human trials. The medicines may have worked perfectly on those selected and standardized situation(s) but it doesn't mean that it will have same effect on each and every individual in the world.
2.   They does not consider the various systems of the body as a functional whole. They applies the medicine as if all the systems are isolated and discrete units.
3.   The medicines used in Conventional System acts at systemic level, so their actions are either suppressive or palliative or both.

4.   Since every individual is different at proteomic level, so one drug will have different effects on different individuals. It will produce side effects. And to suppress those side effects other medicines will be prescribed that will have side effects too.

5.   It does not takes into consideration the reaction of the body to the prescribed drug in long term.

The solution to the above issues can be achieved through Personalized Medicine System. Medicine that are compatible to one's genetic makeup and gene products in their system. This system have the potential to reduce the drawbacks faced by modern medicines.

HISTORICAL BACKGROUND AND REVIEW OF LITERATURE

The first concept of individualization in healthcare was provided by the philosophies of Ayurveda, the ancient Indian medicine system in 4000-500 BC. In 3000 BC Chinese medicine and acupuncture techniques were introduced. During 510 BC, Pythagoras documented that some individual developed a potentially lethal reaction after consuming fava beans, which on today's date known as deficiency of G6PD. During sixteen to eighteenth century important discoveries took place in the domain of anatomy and physiology but no relevant progress took place in the field of pharmacology. In the year 1789 Dr. Samuel Hahnemann, a German physician of Conventional System of Medicine founded Homeopathic System of Medicine based on the concept of like cures like. Homeopathic treatment is highly personalized to a person's constitutional picture, both inherited and acquired rather than being specific to diseases. Since it is kind of personalized form of treatment it does not possess side effects and treated conditions that conventional medicine failed to cure. Nineteenth and late nineteenth century Claude Bernard's introduction of scientific methods into medicine founded by experimentation and observation on controlled test subjects, started to endanger the personalized aspect of treatment. Most of the advances in medicine occurred in 20th Century including imaging techniques, laboratory diagnostic techniques, and modern surgical techniques, molecular diagnostics, genetic engineering techniques etc. Introduction of the terms genotype and phenotype by Wilhelm Johannsen in 1908. Between the years 1920 to 1950 development of scientific basis of pharmacology took place. In 1931, Garrod published a book suggesting that individual differences in response to drugs should be anticipated because of the marked individual differences in each person's genetic constitution. James Watson and Francis Crick in the year 1953 discovered double stranded structure of DNA. In 1955, Butler et al. observed and documented high incidence of hemolysis on exposure to antimalarial drugs among individuals with G6PD deficiency. Kalow in the year 1956 and Motulsky in the year 1957, reported the adverse reaction to drugs can be caused by genetically determined variations in enzyme activity that led to the concept of Pharmacogenetics. In the year 1959, Vogel introduced the term Pharmacogenetics converging the techniques and concepts of pharmacology and genetics. In 1968, Wilson and Jungner developed the principles of population screening, which later became the basis for application of genetics for population screening. Application of molecular biology on pharmacological studies took place during 1980 to 1990. In the year 1986, Mullis et al. introduced the principles and applications of Polymerase Chain Reaction (PCR). Kuska, 1998 reported that the term Genomics was introduced by Roderick as the title of the journal which started publication in 1987. The year 1990 to 2000 is termed as the genomic decade because human genome sequencing, implementation of sequencing in drug discovery, pharmacogenomics and cell and gene therapy became popular. Fahy in 1993 provided the concept of implementation of molecular nanotechnology to base medical therapy on the biochemical individuality of specific patients. Wilkins et al. 1995 coined the term proteomics. The first monograph with the title Personalized Medicine and Pharmacogenetics, Jain 1998, published by Decision Resources Inc. In 2000 human genome sequencing was completed. The year 2001 to 2010 is termed as post genomic era. Impact of genomics combined with proteomics in drug discovery and development. Development of personalized medicine and integration of diagnosis with therapy in healthcare.

The term Personalized Medicine is new to the world but the underlying concepts is not new to the history of medical sciences. The review of the history of medicine shows that the development of personalized medicine will be an evolution and not a revolution in medicine. The concept of one drug fits all was first questioned and proved wrong by a German physician, Sir Christian Fredrick Samuel Hahnemann. Dr. Hahnemann was an M.D in Conventional System of Medicine. Based on his lifelong study and practice of conventional system of medicine, he found out that the medicines and treatment procedures implemented by the conventional system does not actually cures the underlying cause of the disease. It only palliates and suppresses the normal physiological, immunological and psychological response to the underlying cause. Thus providing an instant relief to the patient, creating an illusion that it has cured the underlying cause of the disease. But in reality all it does is suppress the body's normal reaction to the root cause of the disease. As long as the signs and symptoms stays suppressed the patient thinks that his or her disease is cured. But instead the root cause of the disease resides in the body and resurfaces again when the medication is stopped. Dr. Hahnemann also pointed out that medicine and treatment procedures followed by conventional system acts by violating the body's Natural Laws of Cure, and thus resulting in complete deterioration of the homeostasis or normal functioning mechanism of the body. This is the reason Dr. Hahnemann called the conventional system of medicine, Allopathy. Conventional system of medicine follows the principle Contraria Contrariis Curentur for treating diseases. He documented and published all his research findings in his scholarly work, Organon of Medicine. To overcome the flaws of systemic approach of treatment, he implemented the holistic approach in which Dr. Hahnemann considered that each and every component of a body is structurally and functionally interdependent on each other. Holistic approach viewed the body as a complex combination of extremely specialized systems functioning as a whole making the life possible. The ultimate goal of these specialized systems is to maintain the homeostasis of the body. As long as the normal homeostasis of the body is maintained the body is protected from diseases. So in case of a particular disease the efforts were made to identify the root cause that actually disturbed the homeostasis and resulted in the disease under consideration. Treatment procedures and medications were performed keeping in mind that to cure the disease the root cause must be identified and eliminated. It was also kept under consideration that the treatment and medication procedure must not cause any kind of disturbance in homeostasis. Dr. Hahnemann lived in a time before the concepts of germ theory of infectious disease, antibiotics, genetics and molecular biology came into existence. During the time Dr. Hahnemann did not have specialized technologies or equipments to perform his research and convert his findings into modern day Evidence Based format. A personalized form of medicine system termed as Homoeopathy thus came to existence that cured various critical diseases that even conventional medical science failed to cure, and that even without any side effects and at a cheaper cost. It actually cured disease conditions in a permanent manner and no side effects of the treatment were documented at that time. This phenomenal breakthrough in medical science research resulted in tremendous blow to the Conventional System of Medicine both economically and intellectually. Practitioners of conventional medicine and with the help of political and industrial support, demoralized the homoeopathic practitioners and prohibited the practice and research on this holistic approach of treatment known as Homeopathy, and calling it a pseudo-science. They portrayed to the world that Homeopathy or the holistic system of treatment is a belief that were wrongly presented as science. They used the ignorance of the common people to their own advantage and made them believe that holistic approach like that of Homoeopathy are not effective for treating any condition. This is one of the biggest conspiracy in the history of medical sciences and research. Where a promising System of Curing disease was restricted and regulated in a way that it does not takes over Conventional System of Treatment. Conventional System of medicine thus prevailed as the most dominant form of medicine system. According to Ayurveda, Unani, Chinese System of Medicine and other Complementary System of medicine more or less followed the holistic approach of treatment like that of Homoeopathic System of Medicine. All these medicine systems which in today's date collectively termed as Alternative or Complementary Systems of Medicine by the practitioners of Modern or Conventional System of Medicine, takes into consideration the medically proven disease triangle while treating a patient. Considering and implementing the underlying principles of disease triangle the Alternative or Complementary System of Medicine follows the personalized or individualized format of treatment. Until in recent years with the exponential growth of research and development in the field of Human Genetics, Medical Genetics, Molecular Biology and Genetic Engineering techniques and their implementation in modern medicine and pharmacological studies it became evident that medicines and treatment procedures implemented by conventional system of medicine does have adverse consequences.

PERSONALIZED MEDICINE AND RELEVANT MEDICAL CONCEPTS

The Trio of Medical Philosophies

Systemic Approach

In this system of treatment every organ or components of a body are regarded or viewed as discrete units working in isolation to other organs or components of that body. So when a particular organ gets affected, the treatment procedures are performed and medications are prescribed with intention of providing relief to the particular organ under consideration. What are the effects and consequences of treatment and medication imposes on the other components of the body and overall health of an individual is beyond the scope of this treatment. Thus systemic approach aims in restoration and preservation of the organ under consideration. It does not deals with the consequences it imposes on other organs and overall homeostasis of the body. Conventional or Modern System of Medicine follows the Systemic approach for treating disease. This is why conventional medicine have specializations like cardiology, pulmonology, nephrology, neurology etc. and every physician is concerned strictly with one specialized organ and their issues.

Holistic Approach

In this system of treatment each and every component of the body are regarded as functional whole. They are functionally and structurally intertwined with each other at biochemical level. In this approach a body is considered as complex combinations of various specialized systems functioning at multiple levels. These systems performs their individual functions and also works in concert with the other systems of the body thus making the life possible. The ultimate goal of these systems are to maintain the homeostasis of the body. As long as the homeostasis is maintained the body is protected from diseases. So in case of a particular disease the efforts are made to identify the root cause that actually disturbed the homeostasis and resulted in the disease under consideration. Treatment procedures and medications are performed keeping in mind that to cure a disease the root cause must be identified and eliminated. And it is also kept under consideration that medication and treatment procedure must not cause disturbance in homeostasis and must never violate the Natural Laws of Cure.

Personalized Approach

In this system of treatment, it is considered that each and every individual is unique at biochemical or molecular level. Every individual possesses a wide range of genes present in their body that determines their genotype. But mere presence of the gene in an individual does not mean that all those characteristics will be expressed in that person's lifetime. It is the gene products or proteins that determines the phenotype of an individual. Expression of a certain gene and production of the functional gene product is broadly dependent on the surrounding environment and lifestyle of that individual. So, genotype of individuals may be same but every individual becomes unique at proteomic level. Proteome is defined as the set of all the gene products or proteins present in an individual. Variation in the composition of the protein i.e. proteome is a key factor that determines an individual's susceptibility to a disease and their response to a particular drug. In case of particular disease, the efforts are made to determine the underlying genetic defect(s). Treatment procedures and medications are prescribed that are compatible to one's genetic makeup. This system aids in selection of appropriate remedy and without any side effects. The personalized approach are also known as personalized medicine system.

THE NATURAL LAWS OF CURE

The first major problem with the Conventional or Systemic Approach of treatment is that it acts by going against the natural laws of cure of the disease. As it is evident from their philosophy Contraria Contrariis Curentur, i.e., fighting disease by using remedies which produces effects or symptoms exactly opposite to the effects or symptoms produced by the disease under consideration.

Symptoms are actually the body's response to certain stress. They are normal physiological responses that the body naturally meant to exert to evade the agent causing the stress and also provide protection to the body from further damage. Sometimes there comes a situation where those normal physiological responses need to be regulated so that it does not cause any harm to the patient. The best way to deal with the situation is to investigate and point out the reason(s) which triggered the symptom. If the physician can identify the body's need, deficiency of which resulted in the stress and if that particular component is administered to the patient in adequate potency, will restore the normal functioning of the components of the body. As soon as the deficiency of the component is replenished the body starts recovering and symptoms are cured. But instead what conventional or modern medicine does is prescribe drugs that acts by suppressing the symptoms or body's response to stress and thus providing palliation to the patient. They point out the symptoms and charges medicines that will by all means block the signal transduction pathways that is triggering the stress response instead of identifying and filling up the deficiency that lead the body to trigger the stress call. As long as the drug substance is active in the patient's blood stream, that particular stress response system stays inactivated, and during that point of time if a disease causing agent enters the patient's body, then there will be no active stress response system to protect the body.

The Natural Laws of Cure was postulated by a Great German Doctor, Constantine Hering, known to the world as the Father of American Homoeopathy in 1830s. The laws are termed as Hering's Laws of the Direction of Cure, which are actually the systematic and logical explanation of how a body responds and tries to eliminate the disease-causing agent from the system. Based on his lifelong research and practice of medicine he observed and documented certain specific patterns followed by the body's defense mechanism for curing and healing certain disease. In a patient who have received the appropriate remedy for certain chronic case, during the period of healing the old symptoms that have been suppressed as a result of faulty medications reappears, though in an attenuated form and shows a tendency to disappear of their own accord. According to Dr. Hering, as he observed based on his studies, no true cure ever took place which does not followed the laws of cure. Dr. Hering published all this research findings on his scholarity works. According to the studies performed by Dr. Hering, the cure takes place only if the symptoms disappear from:

1. Above to downwards.
2. Inside to outwards.
3. Centre to periphery.
4. From more vital organs to organs of less priority.
5. In the reverse order of their appearance.

THE DISEASE TRIANGLE: IT'S IMPORTANCE WHILE TREATING A PATIENT

The disease triangle is a concept that illustrates the importance of host, pathogen and environmental conditions, as the critical factors necessary for a disease to develop. According to Karen et al. 2007, the disease triangle can be implemented for predicting epidemiological outcomes in public health. The disease triangle demonstrates the following facts about a disease:

1. Three major factors are taken into consideration namely the host, the environment and the pathogen. The host represents the organism in which certain disease takes place. The environment represents both the internal environment of the host's body as well as the external environment in which the host lives and interacts with. The pathogen represents the agent that causes disease when it enters host's body.
2. The disease cannot occur in the condition where the host is present, the environment is present but the pathogen is absent.
3. The disease cannot occur in the condition where the host is present, the pathogen is present but the environment is absent.
4. The disease cannot occur in the condition where the host is absent but the pathogen and the environment are present.
5. For a disease to occur it is necessary for all the three factors to be present at the same time. So a disease can only occur if host is present, the pathogen is present and the favorable environment is also present.

All these facts are scientifically proven by several researchers around the world independently and are accepted as an evidence based fact. Now the question arises that the practitioners of modern medicine specially the physicians, when they generally record a case from a patient they only consider the pathogen factor while treating a patient and believes that the pathogen is responsible for the disease of the patient and prescribes the medicine that will somehow act on the pathogen factor under consideration. The two other factors i.e. the host and the environment were totally ignored. So how the physicians of modern or conventional medicine concludes that the pathogen is the main and the only cause, when it is proven and accepted that for a disease to take place all the three factors must be present or else if a single factor is missing then disease cannot occur. How can one claims to cure a disease by fixing only one of the factor and totally excluding the other two, i.e. by rejecting the host factor and the environment factor how can the physician of conventional medicine claims to cure a disease completely? And most importantly when the conventional medicine follows the systemic approach, where they view each and every component of the body as discrete systems.

Figure 1 represents the idea of disease triangle.

OMICS IN PERSONALIZED MEDICINE

The term "OMICS" refers to wide array of technologies, which are relevant to personalized medicine. According to Sherry et al. 2014, these technologies have been employed to explore the roles, relationships and actions of the various types of molecules that makes up the cells of an organism. The following are some of the current omics based technologies that possess the capability of transforming the way medical sciences are practiced and applied:

1.   **Genomics:** The World Health Organization defined genomics as the study of genes and their functions and related techniques. It addresses all genes and their interrelationships in order to identify

Figure 1.

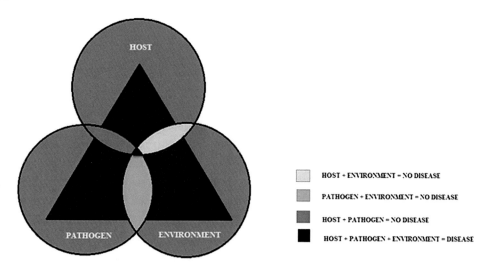

their combined influence on the growth and development of the organism. The following are some of the branches of genomics;

a. **Structural Genomics:** It deals with DNA sequencing, sequence assembly, sequence organization and management. The complete DNA sequence of an organism is its ultimate physical map. Due to rapid advancement in DNA technology and completion of several genome sequencing projects for the last few years, the concept of structural genomics has come to a stage of transition.

b. **Functional Genomic:** Based on the information of structural genomics the next step is to reconstruct genome sequences and to find out the function that the genes do. This information also lends support to design experiment to find out the functions that specific genome does. The strategy of functional genomics has widened the scope of biological investigations. This strategy is based on systematic study of single gene/ protein to all genes/proteins. Therefore, the large scale experimental methodologies (along with statistically analysed/computed results) characterise the functional genomics. Hence, the functional genomics provide the novel information about the genome.

2. **Proteomics:** According to Hans et al. 2001, Proteomics can be defined as the systematic analysis and documentation of proteins in biological samples. It is a branch of science that has a major impact on modern day medical sciences. It can be seen as mass screening approach to molecular biology, which aims to document the overall distribution of proteins in cells, identify and characterize individual proteins of interest and ultimately to elucidate their relationships and functional roles. Such direct, protein level analysis has become necessary because the study of genes, by genomics cannot adequately predict the structure or dynamics of proteins, since it is at the protein level that most regulatory processes takes place, where disease processes primarily occurs and where the most drug targets are to be found. There is a strong relationship between proteomics and genomics as the two disciplines investigates the molecular organization of cells at complementary levels and each domain provides information that increases the effectiveness of other.

3. **Metabolomics:** Roessner et al. 2009, the rapidly emerging field of metabolomics combines strategies to identify and quantify cellular metabolites using sophisticated analytical technologies with the application of statistical and multi-variant methods for information extraction and data interpretation. In the last two decades, huge progress was made in the sequencing of a number of different organisms. Simultaneously, large investments were made to develop analytical approaches to analyze the different cell products, such as those from gene expression (transcripts), proteins, and metabolites. All of these so-called 'omics approaches, including genomics, transcriptomics, proteomics, and metabolomics, are considered important tools to be applied and utilized to understand the biology of an organism and its response to environmental stimuli or genetic perturbation.

According to Hofmann et al. 2006 and Gieger et al. 2008, Metabolites are considered to "act as spoken language, broadcasting signals from the genetic architecture and the environment", and therefore, metabolomics is considered to provide a direct "functional readout of the physiological state" of an organism. A range of analytical technologies has been employed to analyze metabolites in different organisms, tissues, or fluids. Mass spectrometry coupled to different chromatographic separation techniques, such as liquid or gas chromatography or NMR, are the major tools to analyze a large number of metabolites simultaneously. Although the technology is highly sophisticated and sensitive, there are still a few bottlenecks in metabolomics. Due to the huge diversity of chemical structures and the large differences in abundance, there is no single technology available to analyze the entire metabolome. Therefore, a number of complementary approaches have to be established for extraction, detection, quantification, and identification of as many metabolites as possible as reported by Beckles et al. 2009 and Nielsen et al. 2007

Another challenge in metabolomics is to extract the information and interpret it in a biological context from the vast amount of data produced by high-throughput analyzers. The application of sophisticated statistical and multi-variant data analysis tools, including cluster analysis, pathway mapping, comparative overlays, and heat maps, has not only been an exciting and steep learning process for biochemists, but has also demonstrated that current thinking needs to change to deal with large data sets and distinguish between noise and real sample-related information.

As we have described in this paper, metabolomics aims ideally at the analysis of all small molecules in a cell. This is only a portion of the cellular products within a cell. For a systems biology approach, metabolomics only provides the measurement of a portion of all elements in a biological system. Yet, systems biology comprises not only the ability to measure all elements of a system, such as DNA, mRNA, proteins, metabolites, and structural elements such as cell walls and membranes, but also to determine the relationship of those elements to one another as part of the system's response to environmental or genetic perturbation. After integrating all of the different levels of information, the intention is to model the behavior of the system using computational methods that may allow the description of the behavior of the system under any kind of perturbation. A systems biology approach requires biologists, physicists, computer scientists, engineers, chemists, and mathematicians to learn a common language that allows them to communicate with each other. Another important requirement for a successful systems biology approach is creating an environment that provides access to all of the high-throughput platforms needed to obtain and measure the properties and elements of the system of interest. Also, an effective systems biology approach must offer the opportunity and scale for fast development and employment of new global technologies and powerful computational tools that allow gathering, classifying, analyzing, integrating, and ultimately, modeling of biological information.

Systems approaches to human diseases, such as cancer, cardiovascular disease, and obesity, will give the opportunity to greatly facilitate the success of selecting a novel target for treatments and drug development. In the future, systems biology may enable us to develop new approaches in medicine that will be predictive, preventative, and personalized. The aim would be to achieve the ability to determine a probabilistic health history for each individual, and within that framework, systems biology will be a strategy for the discovery and development of new therapeutic as well as preventative drugs.

In summary, studying the response of various organisms to different stresses and environments at the genetic, transcript, protein, and metabolite levels using different methods and comparing these results with those of other organisms will strengthen their integration into a systems biology framework. As the framework develops, the greater synergy between organisms will provide a much clearer picture of the function of cells, organs, and organisms, bringing us closer to understanding their roles in nature.

4. **Transcriptomics:** Transcriptomics is the study of the transcriptome—the complete set of RNA transcripts that are produced by the genome, under specific circumstances or in a specific cell—using high-throughput methods, such as microarray analysis. Comparison of transcriptomes allows the identification of genes that are differentially expressed in distinct cell populations, or in response to different treatments.

5. **Glycomics:** Glycomics is a subset of the field of glycobiology that aims to identify the structure and function of the complete set of glycans (the glycome) produced in a given cell or organism and identify all the genes that encode glycoproteins.
6. Lipomics.

MOLECULAR BIOLOGICAL BASIS OF PERSONALIZED MEDICINES

According to researchers at National Human Genome Research Institute (NHGRI) all the instructions needed for development and performing generalized or specialized cellular activities are stored in DNA or Deoxyribonucleic Acid. Genes are units of DNA that possesses instructions for a specific protein or a set of proteins. Genome is referred to as complete set of DNA present in an organism.

Located on 23 pairs of chromosomes packed into the nucleus of a human cell, genes directs the production of proteins with the assistance of enzymes and messenger molecules. An enzyme copies the information in a gene's DNA into a molecule called messenger ribonucleic acid (mRNA). The mRNA travels out of the nucleus and into the cell's cytoplasm, where the mRNA is read by ribosome, and the information is used to link together small molecules called amino acids in the right order to form a specific protein. Proteins make up the body structures like organs and tissues as well as control chemical reactions and carry signals between cells. If a cell's DNA is mutated, an abnormal protein is produced, which can disrupt body's usual processes and lead to disease.

The Human Genome Project, which was led at the National Institutes of Health (NIH) by the National Human Genome Research Institute, produced a very high-quality version of the human genome sequence that is freely available in public databases. That international project was successfully completed in April 2003, under budget and more than two years ahead of schedule.

The sequence is not that of one person, but is a composite derived from several individuals. Therefore, it is a "representative" or generic sequence. To ensure anonymity of the DNA donors, more blood samples (nearly 100) were collected from volunteers than were used, and no names were attached to the samples that were analyzed. Thus, not even the donors knew whether their samples were actually used.

The Human Genome Project was designed to generate a resource that could be used for a broad range of biomedical studies. One such use is to look for the genetic variations that increase risk of specific diseases, such as cancer, or to look for the type of genetic mutations frequently seen in cancerous cells. More research can then be done to fully understand how the genome functions and to discover the genetic basis for health and disease. Virtually every human ailment has some basis in our genes. Until recently, doctors were able to take the study of genes, or genetics, into consideration only in cases of birth defects and a limited set of other diseases. These were conditions, such as sickle cell anemia, which have very simple, predictable inheritance patterns because each is caused by a change in a single gene.

With the vast trove of data about human DNA generated by the Human Genome Project and other genomic research, scientists and clinicians have more powerful tools to study the role that multiple genetic factors acting together and with the environment play in much more complex diseases. These diseases, such as cancer, diabetes, and cardiovascular disease constitute the majority of health problems. Genome-based research is already enabling medical researchers to develop improved diagnostics, more effective therapeutic strategies, evidence-based approaches for demonstrating clinical efficacy, and better decision-making tools for patients and providers. Ultimately, it appears inevitable that treatments will be tailored to a patient's particular genomic makeup. Thus, the role of genetics in health care is starting to change profoundly and the first examples of the era of genomic medicine are upon us. Clearly, genetics remains just one of several factors that contribute to people's risk of developing most common diseases. Diet, lifestyle, and environmental exposures also come into play for many conditions, including many types of cancer. Still, a deeper understanding of genetics will shed light on more than just hereditary risks by revealing the basic components of cells and, ultimately, explaining how all the various elements work together to affect the human body in both health and disease.

GENETIC VARIATION IN THE GENOME

Single Nucleotide Polymorphisms

Nature Education reported that a single nucleotide polymorphism, or SNP (pronounced "snip"), is a variation at a single position in a DNA sequence among individuals. Recall that the DNA sequence is formed from a chain of four nucleotide bases: A, C, G, and T. If more than 1% of a population does not carry the same nucleotide at a specific position in the DNA sequence, then this variation can be classified as a SNP. If a SNP occurs within a gene, then the gene is described as having more than one allele. In these cases, SNPs may lead to variations in the amino acid sequence. SNPs, however, are not just associated with genes; they can also occur in noncoding regions of DNA. Although a particular SNP may not cause a disorder, some SNPs are associated with certain diseases. These associations allow scientists to look for SNPs in order to evaluate an individual's genetic predisposition to develop a disease. In addition, if certain SNPs are known to be associated with a trait, then scientists may examine stretches of DNA near these SNPs in an attempt to identify the gene or genes responsible for the trait.

Copy Number Variations

Copy number variation (CNVs) is a relatively new field in genomics and it is defined as a phenomenon in which sections of the genome are repeated and the number of repeats in the genome varies between individuals in the human population reports Mccarroll et al. 2007.Sharp et al. 2005 reported that Copy number variation is a type of structural variation, specifically, it is a type of duplication or deletion event that affects a considerable number of base pairs. Pollock et al. 2011 reported that approximately two thirds of the entire human genome is composed of repeats and 4.8-9.5% of the human genome can be classified as copy number variations. Maccarroll et al. 2004 also reports that in mammals, copy number variations play an important role in generating necessary variation in the population as well as disease phenotype.

Copy number variations can be generally categorized into two main groups: short repeats and long repeats. However, there are no clear boundaries between the two groups and the classification depends on the nature of the loci of interest. Short repeats include mainly bi-nucleotide repeats (two repeating nucleotides e.g. A-B-A-B-A-B...) and tri-nucleotide repeats. Long repeats include repeats of entire genes. This classification based on size of the repeat is the most obvious type of classification as size is an important factor in examining the types of mechanisms that most likely gave rise to the repeats,[6] hence the likely effects of these repeats on phenotype.

INDELs

INDEL is a molecular biology term for the insertion or the deletion of bases in the DNA of an organism. It has slightly different definitions between its use in evolutionary studies and its use in germ-line and somatic mutation studies. In evolutionary studies, indel is used to mean an insertion or a deletion as reported by Kondrashov et al, 2004 and indels simply refers to the mutation class that includes both insertions, deletions, and the combination thereof as reported by Hill et al. 2001, Miller et al.2002, Gregory et al 2004, including insertion and deletion events that may be separated by many years, and may not be related to each other in any way as reported by Rubio et al. 2004. Based on research performed by Gonzales et al. 2004, in germline and somatic mutation studies, indel describes a special mutation class, defined as a mutation resulting in both an insertion of nucleotides and a deletion of nucleotides which results in a net change in the total number of nucleotides, where both changes are nearby on the DNA. A microindel is defined as an indel that results in a net change of 1 to 50 nucleotides. Johannsen et al. and Erixon et al. in 2008 defined "Indels," as either an insertion or deletion, can be used as genetic markers in natural populations, especially in phylogenetic studies.

MODERN MEDICINE AND PERSONALIZED MEDICINE

The working mechanism of modern medicine is that it acts by suppressing the body's natural physiological response to the stress causing the disease. Since it solely functions by temporary suppression of physiological symptoms, one drug fits all theory is being implemented by modern medicine. The adverse effects that the modern medicine imparts on a patient's health and proposed that every patient should be treated in an individualized manner was documented in the book named Organon of Medicine or The Organon of the Healing Art by Dr. Samuel Hahnemann in the year 1810, based on his lifelong practice and research on modern or conventional medicine. In his scholarity work he explained in detail the lack of efficacy and adverse effects of modern medicine and also advised the ways these issues could be regulated to an extent. But the theories and proving documented by Dr. Hahnemann was labeled as pseudo-science since His research were not presented as modern day evidence based format. The very fact was ignored that the theories, doctrines and technologies on which modern day medicine relies came to existence several years after the death of Dr. Hahnemann. Despite of lacking powerful modern day technologies he pointed out that One Drug Fits All approach is faulty and does more harm than good, and for actually curing a patient more individualized approach should be implemented. Until recently with the development in the field of medical genetics, Pharmacogenetics, pharmacogenomics, Pharmacoproteomics the drawbacks of One Drug Fits All ideology was proven and documented which Dr. Hahnemann tried to explain to the world several years ago in his Scholarity work Organon of Medicine. The drawbacks of modern medicine are as follows:

1. Genetic variations among individuals leads to difference in response to drugs.
2. High percentage of lack of efficacy with certain medicines.
3. High incidence of adverse effects to drugs.
4. Conventional or Modern or Allopathic supports a standardized application of therapy that does not take into account variations of response in individual patients.

5. Clinical trials are performed and documented around considering statistical information about the general population of patient and applying it to the individual.

According to Goldberger and Buxton, 2013, development of evidence based guidelines based on relatively broad enrolment criteria inhibits the subsequent development of personalized medicine within the enrolment criteria.

Personalized approach of treating and managing diseases possesses the capability to overcome the drawbacks faced by modern system of medicines. But the incorporation of Conventional System of Therapy with Personalized System of therapy is extremely difficult because both the ideologies are exactly opposite of each other because Conventional System of Medicine follows the ideology of One Drug Fits All while Personalized system of medicine proved that One Drug Fits All approach does not holds true. But a pattern of similarity can be observed in the ideology of holistic approach of treatment followed by practitioners of Alternative or Complementary System of Medicine with the ideology of personalized approach of treatment followed by Personalized System of Medicine, both believes that every individual is unique and so is their response to diseases as well as their remedies. Thus, the term Personalized Medicine which the practitioners of modern medicine claims to be a revolution in the field of medical sciences is actually the evolution of holistic approach of treatment followed by the practitioners of alternative medicine, as evident from the history of medical sciences. So, the author infers that the convergence of the ideology of holistic approach of treatment and extensive research and development in the field of medical genetics led to the evolution of the old concepts into what is now termed as Personalized Medicine System.

ROLE OF PROTEOMICS IN PERSONALIZED MEDICINE

The term proteomics refers to the set of proteins expressed by one's genome and is the systemic analysis of protein profiles of a cell or tissues. There is an increasing importance in proteomic technologies at present because DNA sequence information only provides a static idea of various ways in which the cell might use its proteins whereas the life of cell is a dynamic process. Jain 2004, reported the role of proteomics in drug discovery and development is termed as Pharmacoproteomics and is a more functional representation of patient to patient variation than that provided by genotyping, which indicates its important role in development of personalized medicine. Jain 2015, reported that proteomics based characterization of multifactorial diseases may help to match a particular target based therapy to a particular biomarker in a subgroup of patient. By classifying patients as responders and non-responders, this approach may accelerate the drug development process. Because it includes the effects of post translational modification, Pharmacoproteomics connects the genotype with phenotype, a connection that is not always predicted by genotyping alone. For example, a silent SNP can give rise to two or more variants of mRNAs that do not produce an altered amino acid sequence in the proteins that are encoded, but it can alter phenotype by inducing change in mRNA folding. An understanding of mRNA conformational changes could lead to new drug targets such as allele specific targets. Individualized therapy may be based on differential protein expression rather than genetic polymorphism. Proteomics based molecular diagnostics will have an important role in the diagnosis of certain condition and proteomics based medicines would be integrated in the total healthcare of the patient. Proteins that are disturbed by disease and gene regulatory networks differ from their normal counterpart and these differences may be detected by multiparameter measurement of blood. This will have a major role in creating a predictive, personalized, preventive and participatory approach to medicine. Jain 2015, also reported that most human diseases are multifactorial and their complexity needs to be understood at molecular level. Genomic sequencing and mRNA based analysis of gene expression have provided important information but purely gene based expression data is not adequate for the dissection of the disease phenotype at molecular. There is no strict correlation between the gene and actual protein expression. Therefore the cell's full proteome cannot be deciphered by the analysis at genetic level alone. It is necessary to look at the proteins directly to understand the disease at a molecular level. Aberrations in the interactions of proteins with one another are at the heart of molecular basis of many diseases. The proteome is dynamic and reflects the conditions, such as disease to which a cell is exposed. Combining genomics and proteomics will reveal more dynamic picture of the disease process.

PROTEOMICS IN DRUG DISCOVERY

Jain et al. reported that owing to the complexity of intracellular metabolic pathways, the understanding of intercellular pathways has been lagging behind the advances in gene expression. Thus extensive research and development in the domain of single cell based proteomic technologies will prove to be a breakthrough for the molecular diagnosis of disease and development of personalized medicines

Taking on the right shape is vital to a protein's action. To help make sure these happens correctly cells contains chaperone proteins devoted to helping newly made proteins fold. Other proteins, the ubiquitins, bind to the proteins that have failed the shape test and mark them for destruction. Incorrectly folded proteins are root of several disorders. For example, disturbance of protein folding system results in spinocerebellar ataxia, a fatal pediatric disorder. The gene mutation responsible for this disease is SCA1, which codes for a protein ataxin1. Mutation in the gene creates an enlarged portion of ataxin1 containing multiple copies of amino acid glutamine. This stops protein from folding them normally, causing them to clump together and form toxic deposits in neurons. The disease can also arise if neurons make too much of the normal protein pushing the protein folding capacity of chaperones beyond their normal limits. In many cases the mutation is not so severe to render the protein inactive biologically. A number of low molecular weight compounds all of which are known to stabilize proteins in their native form are effective in rescuing the folding or processing defects associated with different mutation that often lead to disease. Page 164 proteomic technologies are now being integrated into the drug discovery process as complementary to genomic approaches. This offers scientists the ability to integrate information from the genome, expressed mRNAs, and their proteins and subcellular localization. By focusing on protein activity levels or expression level the researchers are able to learn more about the role of proteins play in causing and treating diseases. Proteomics also aids in deciphering the mechanisms of diseases and increasing both the opportunity to develop drugs with reduced side effects and an increased probability of clinical trial success. Proteomics has the potential to increase substantially the number of drug targets and thereby the number of new drugs. Automation of proteomics on a scale similar to that used for genome sequencing may be needed and this is feasible by adapting the many tools already developed for genomics for application to proteomic technologies. Application of proteomic technologies has enabled the prediction of all possible protein coding regions and to choose the best candidates among novel drug targets. Proteomics technologies are useful for drug discovery. By helping to elucidate the pathomechanism of diseases, proteomics will help the discovery of rational medications that will fit in with the future concept personalized medicines.

Pharmacoproteomics helps to determine the mechanisms of action of bioactive molecules in a systems pharmacology context. In contrast to traditional drug discovery, Pharmacoproteomics integrates the mechanism if a drug's action, its side effects including toxicity and the discovery of new drug targets in a single approach as reported by Hess et al, 2003. This approach facilitates personalized drug discovery.

PROTEOMICS IN CLINICAL DRUG SAFETY

Drug induced damage to tissues are the most common type of toxicity that results in a treatment being withdrawn from clinical trials. Cardiotoxicity is a frequent occurrence in patient undergoing chemotherapy for cancers. The currently available biomarkers for these common types of drug induced toxicities have limited sensitivity or predictive value. The proteomic tools available today are enabling us to tap into the wealth of genome sequence information to discover and carefully investigate associations of thousands of proteins with drug induced toxicity that are now not easily monitored.

Proteomics can increase the speed and sensitivity of toxicological screening by identifying protein markers of toxicity. Proteomics studies have already provided insight into the mechanism of action of a wide range of substances, from metals to peroxisome proliferators. Current limitations involving speed of throughput are being overcome by increasing automation and development of new techniques. According to Jain et al. (2014), the isotope coded affinity tag (ICAT) method appears particularly promising. Toxicoproteomics involves the evaluation of protein expression for the understanding of toxic events. Transcriptional profiling and proteomics are used to compile toxicology predictors.

FUTURE PROSPECTS AND CHALLENGES

With the convergence of disciplines like genomics, proteomics, metabolomics in drug discovery and drug safety issues will be able to overcome the drawbacks faced by modern medicine to a great extent. The following are few of the reasons supporting the issue:

1. Pharmacoproteomics is the more functional representation of patient to patient variation than that provided by genotyping.
2. Because it includes the effects of post translational modification, Pharmacoproteomics connects the genotype with phenotype.
3. By classifying the patients as responders and non-responders, this approach may accelerate personalized drug development.
4. Protein biomarkers facilitate integration of diagnostics with therapeutics from development stages to translation into clinical applications.
5. Global development of personalized medicine would benefit from Pharmacoproteomics technologies and the ways in which they are being applied in extensive research.

The major problem of these approach is appropriately qualified medical personnel having the knowledge of proteomic technologies. Another major issue is the infrastructure and amount of funding required to perform the research and development in the domain.

REFERENCES

Beutler, E., Dern, R. J., & Alving, A. S. (1955). The hemolytic effect of premaquine. VI. An invitro test for sensitivity of erythrocytes to premaquine. *The Journal of Laboratory and Clinical Medicine, 45*, 40–50. PMID:13233626

Börner, J., Buchinger, S., & Schomburg, D. (2007). A high-throughput method for microbial metabolome analysis using gas chromatography/mass spectrometry. *Analytical Biochemistry, 367*(2), 143–151. doi:10.1016/j.ab.2007.04.036 PMID:17585867

Buettner, V. L., Hill, K. A., Halangoda, A., & Sommer, S. S. (1999). Tandem-based mutations occur in mouse liver and adipose tissue preferentially as G:C to T: A transversions and accumulate with age. *Environmental and Molecular Mutagenesis, 33*(4), 320–324. doi:10.1002/(SICI)1098-2280(1999)33:4<320::AID-EM9>3.0.CO;2-S PMID:10398380

de Koning, A.P., Gu, W., Castoe, T.A., Bazter, M.A., & Pollock, D. D. (2011). Repetitive Elements May Comprise Over Two-Thirds of the Human Genome. *PLOS Genetics, 7*(12). doi:10.1371/journal.pgen.1002384

Durbin, R.M., Abecasis, G.R., Altshuler, D.L., Auton, A., Brooks, L.D., …, McVean, G.A. (2010). A map of human genome variation from population-scale sequencing. *Nature, 467*(7319), 1061–1073. doi:10.1038/nature09534

Erixon, P., & Oxelman, B. (2008). Whole-gene positive selection, elevated synonymous substitution rates, duplication, and indel evolution of the chloroplast clpP1 gene. PLoS ONE, 3(1). doi:10.1371/journal.pone.0001386

Fiehn, O. (2002). Metabolomics–the link between genotypes and phenotypes. *Plant Molecular Biology, 48*(1/2), 155–171. doi:10.1023/A:1013713905833 PMID:11860207

Gelbart, W. M., Lewontin, R. C., Griffiths, A. J. F., & Miller, J. H. (2002). *Modern genetic analysis: integrating genes and genomes*. New York: W.H. Freeman and CO.

Gieger, C., Geistlinger, L., Altmaier, E., Hrabé de Angelis, M., Kronenberg, F., Meitinger, T., & Wichmann, H.-E. et al. (2008). Genetics meets metabolomics: A genome-wide association study of metabolite profiles in human serum. *PLOS Genetics, 4*(11), e1000282. doi:10.1371/journal.pgen.1000282 PMID:19043545

Gonzalez, K. D., Hill, K. A., Li, K., Li, W., Scaringe, W. A., Wang, J.-C., & Sommer, S. S. et al. (2007, January). Somatic microindels: Analysis in mouse soma and comparison with the human germline. *Human Mutation, 28*(1), 69–80. doi:10.1002/humu.20416 PMID:16977595

Gregory, T. R. (2004, January). Insertion-deletion biases and the evolution of genome size. *Gene, 324*, 15–34. doi:10.1016/j.gene.2003.09.030 PMID:14693368

Halangoda, A., Still, J. G., Hill, K. A., & Sommer, S. S. (2001). Spontaneous microdeletions and microinsertions in a transgenic mouse mutation detection system: Analysis of age, tissue, and sequence specificity. *Environmental and Molecular Mutagenesis, 37*(4), 311–323. doi:10.1002/em.1038 PMID:11424181

Hastings, P. J.; Lupski, J. R.; Roseberg, S. M.; Ira, G. (2009). Mechanisms of change in gene copy number. *Nature Reviews Genetics. 10*, 551–564. doi:10.1038/nrg2593

Hess, S. (2013). The emerging field of chemo- and Pharmacoproteomics. *Proteomics. Clinical Applications, 7*(1-2), 171–180. doi:10.1002/prca.201200091 PMID:23184895

Hill, K. A., Wang, J., Farwell, K. D., & Sommer, S. S. (2003, January). Spontaneous tandem-base mutations (TBM) show dramatic tissue, age, pattern and spectrum specificity. *Mutation Research, 534*(1–2), 173–186. doi:10.1016/S1383-5718(02)00277-2 PMID:12504766

Jain, K. K. (2004). Role of Pharmacoproteomics in the development of Personalized medicine. *Pharmacogenomics, 5*(3), 331–336. doi:10.1517/phgs.5.3.331.29830 PMID:15102547

Jain, K. K. (2015). *Proteomics: technologies, markets and companies*. Basel: Jain PharmaBiotech.

Jewett, M. C., Hofmann, G., & Nielsen, J. (2006). Fungal metabolite analysis in genomics and phenomics. *Current Opinion in Biotechnology, 17*(2), 191–197. doi:10.1016/j.copbio.2006.02.001 PMID:16488600

Kaneko, T., Tahara, S., & Matsuo, M. (1996, May). Non-linear accumulation of 8-hydroxy-2-deoxyguanosine, a marker of oxidized DNA damage, during aging. *Mutation Research, 316*(5–6), 277–285. doi:10.1016/S0921-8734(96)90010-7 PMID:8649461

Kim, J. K., Bamba, T., Harada, K., Fukusaki, E., & Kobayashi, A. (2007). Time-course metabolic profiling in *Arabidopsis thaliana* cell cultures after salt stress treatment. *Journal of Experimental Botany, 58*(3), 415–424. doi:10.1093/jxb/erl216 PMID:17118972

Kind, T., Tolstikov, V. V., Fiehn, O., & Weiss, R. H. (2007). A comprehensive urinary metabolomic approach for identifying kidney cancer. *Analytical Biochemistry, 363*(2), 185–195. doi:10.1016/j.ab.2007.01.028 PMID:17316536

Kondrashov, A. S., & Rogozin, I. B. (2004, February). Context of deletions and insertions in human coding sequences. *Human Mutation, 23*(2), 177–185. doi:10.1002/humu.10312 PMID:14722921

Macdonald, M., Ambrose, C. M., Duyao, M. P., Myers, R. H., Lin, C., Srinidhi, L., & Groot, N. et al. (1993). A novel gene containing a trinucleotide repeat that is expanded and unstable on Huntington's disease chromosomes. *Cell, 72*(6), 971–983. doi:10.1016/0092-8674(93)90585-E PMID:8458085

Mank, R., Wilson, M. D., Rubio, J. M., & Post, R. J. (2004, March). A molecular marker for the identification of Simulium squamosum (Diptera: Simuliidae). *Ann. Trop. Med. Parasitol., 98*(2), 197–208. doi:10.1179/000349804225003118

Mccarroll, S. A., & Altshuler, D. M. (2007). Copy-number variation and association studies of human diseases. *Nature Genetics, 39*(7s), 37–42. doi:10.1038/ng2080 PMID:17597780

Nakamura, H., Muro, T., Imamura, S., & Yuasa, I. (2009, March). Forensic species identification based on size variation of mitochondrial DNA hypervariable regions. *International Journal of Legal Medicine, 123*(2), 177–184. doi:10.1007/s00414-008-0306-7 PMID:19052767

Ogurtsov, A.Y., Sunyaev, S., & Kondrashov, A.S. (2004, August). Indel-based evolutionary distance and mouse-human divergence. *Genome Res., 14*(8), 1610–1616. doi:10.1101/gr.2450504

Parveen, I., Moorby, J. M., Fraser, M. D., Allison, G. G., & Kopka, J. (2007). Application of gas chromatography-mass spectrometry metabolite profiling techniques to the analysis of heathland plant diets of sheep. *Journal of Agricultural and Food Chemistry*, *55*(4), 1129–1138. doi:10.1021/jf062995w PMID:17249687

Pereira, F., Carneiro, J., Matthiesen, R., van Asch, B., Pinto, N., Gusmao, L., & Amorim, A. (2010, October 4). Identification of species by multiplex analysis of variable-length sequences. *Nucleic Acids Research*, *38*(22), e203–e203. doi:10.1093/nar/gkq865 PMID:20923781

Pietra, F. (2002). Evolution of the secondary metabolite versus evolution of the species. *Pure and Applied Chemistry*, *74*(11), 2207–2211. doi:10.1351/pac200274112207

Reddy, P. J., Jain, R., & Paik, Y. K. et al.. (2011). Personalized medicine in the age of Pharmacoproteomics: A close up on India and need for social science engagement for responsible innovation in post proteomic biology. *Curr. Pharm. Pers. Med.*, *9*, 67–75. PMID:22279515

Roessner, U., & Beckles, D. M. (2009). Metabolite measurements. In J. Schwender (Ed.), *Plant Metabolic Networks*. NY: Springer. doi:10.1007/978-0-387-78745-9_3

Scholthof, K. B. G. (2007). The disease triangle: Pathogens, the environment and society. *Nature Reviews. Microbiology*, *5*(2), 152–156.

Sharp, A.J., Locke, D.P., Mcgrath, S.D., Cheng, Z., Bailey, J.A., …, Segraves, R. (2005). Segmental Duplications and Copy-Number Variation in the Human Genome. *The American Journal of Human Genetics*, *77*(1), 78–88. doi:10.1086/431652

Taberlet, P., Coissac, E., Pompanon, F., Gielly, L., Miquel, C., Valentini, A., & Willerslev, E. et al. (2007, January 26). Power and limitations of the chloroplast trnL (UAA) intron for plant DNA barcoding. *Nucleic Acids Research*, *35*(3), e14–e14. doi:10.1093/nar/gkl938 PMID:17169982

Taniguchi, Y., Choi, P. J., Li, J. W., Chen, H., Babu, M., Hearn, J., & Xie, X. S. et al. (2010). Quantifying E. coli Proteome and Transcriptome with Single-Molecule Sensitivity in Single Cells. *Science*, *329*(5991), 533–538. doi:10.1126/science.1188308 PMID:20671182

Väli, U., Brandström, M., Johansson, M., & Ellegren, H. (2008). Insertion-deletion polymorphisms (indels) as genetic markers in natural populations. *BMC Genetic*, *9*(8). doi:10.1186/1471-2156-9-8

Villas-Bôas, S. G., Roessner, U., Hansen, M., Smedsgaard, J., & Nielsen, J. (2007). *Metabolome Analysis: An Introduction*. Hoboken, NJ: John Wiley & Sons, Inc. doi:10.1002/0470105518

WHA 57.13: Genomics and World Health, Fifty Seventh World Health Assembly Resolution. (2004, May 22).

WHO. (2002). Genomics and World Health: Report of the Advisory Committee on Health research.

Zarrei, M., Macdonald, J. R., Merico, D., & Scherer, S. W. (2015). A copy number variation map of the human genome. *Nature Reviews. Genetics*, *16*(3), 172–183. doi:10.1038/nrg3871 PMID:25645873

Chapter 5
The Much Needed Security and Data Reforms of Cloud Computing in Medical Data Storage

Sushma Munugala
Charles Sturt University, Australia

Ali Syed
Charles Sturt University, Australia

Gagandeep K. Brar
Charles Sturt University, Australia

Azeem Mohammad
Charles Sturt University, Australia

Malka N. Halgamuge
Charles Sturt University, Australia

ABSTRACT

Cloud computing has shifted our old documents up into the clouds, with the advancement of technology. Fast-growing virtual document storage platforms provide amenities with minimal expense in the corporate society. Despite living in the 20th century, even the first world countries have issues with the maintenance of document storage. Cloud computing resolves this issue for business and clinic owners as it banishes the requirement of planning, provisioning, and allows corporations to advance their filling system according to service demands. Medical practices heavily, rely on document storage as; almost all information contained in medical files is stored in a printed format. Medical practices urgently need to revolutionize their storage standards, to keep up with the growing population. The traditional method of paper storage in medical practice has completely been obsolete and needs to improve in order to assist patients with faster diagnosis in critical situations. Obtaining Knowledge and sharing it is an important part of medical practice, so it needs immediate attention to reach its full service potential. This chapter has analyzed content from literature that highlights issues regarding data storage and recommends solution. This inquiry has found a useful tool that can be beneficial for the development of this problem which is, 'data mining' as it gives the option of predictive, and preventative health care options, when medical data is searched. The functionality and worthiness of each algorithm and methods are also determined in this study. By using cloud and big data services to improve the analysis of medical data in network of regional health information system, has huge advancements that assure convenient management, easy extension, flexible investment, and low requirements for low technical based private medical units.

DOI: 10.4018/978-1-5225-2607-0.ch005

INTRODUCTION

Cloud computing has become one of the fastest emerging techniques in the area of information technology. Information technology has started to gain interest due to population increase and virtualization of documents in a business environment, as it gives possible solutions to this rising problems. Organizations need a sustainable filing system that copes with current demands to solve this issue, in order to serve their clients better and faster. The technology of cloud computing provides a few number of benefits. Firstly, it is convenient, with a common shared infrastructure that provides servers with storage disks, networking components with wires, switches, hubs, and routers. Secondly, the implantation of cloud allows medical related information to be available over the Internet; thereby rendering this information to make it accessible is evolutionary. A huge number of people who use the Internet inspire to reach this ultimate goal. Storage of data, with secure confidentiality, and analysis of the stored data has three important aspects that make cloud computing easy to manage.

Firstly, the information collected in the medical field is referred to as "raw data". This data is stored in the data warehouse for future use or analysis. This Data Warehouse is a collection of databases where volumes of data are stored, then used when needed. Here, the collected data can be stored both in structured and unstructured format. To convert the unstructured data into a structured format, the data needs to be clustered. In addition to the k-means cluster algorithm for clustering the unstructured data into some structured format is also revolutionary. Once the data is clustered, then we will get various patterns that are then subjected to analysis. This enhances the analysis phase by allowing various interesting patterns to rise, and consequently data is abstracted. The aforementioned Fuzzy logic technique is one of the most common methods used for the decision-making process during the analysis.

Additionally, in cloud computing, one of the major issues is security and confidentially of sensitive data. To overcome the security problems of data storage in cloud is to use an encrypted format that makes it hard for hackers to interrupt, and understand. Next, we reviewed the studies in related area about big-data clustering and analyzed cloud computing techniques in relevant medical decision-makings situations. Considering a vast amount of medical data that has been available on the Internet, the easy retrieval of data is helpful to health service providers, and particularly for specialists who need to identify diseases in depth in a limited timeframe.

Once medically relevant data has been collected from networks, it then needs to be stored in a database to precede data analysis (i.e. clustering approach) this process allows users to obtain required information. The current system allows medical organizations to share their confidential information through the Internet, and causes leaks of confidential data. The current system also does not provide sufficient techniques or functions to secure confidential data while transmitting it through the Internet. In lieu of health service providing, organizations that have faced problems when analyzing the required information about a particular medicine or disease through the Internet will also benefit from this function. To avoid these issues in the "medical data security" field, this chapter proposes a technique that will help to organize collected information from the Internet securely. This highlighted method would help these advanced algorithms to share information with others while sustaining confidentiality. Furthermore, K-means technique is used to cluster big data from the database to retrieve required medical information. Some of the necessary steps involved in Parallel clustering algorithms are based on k-means in big data; this is displayed as follows: (i) Centroid-based clustering, (ii) Density-based clustering (iii) Connectivity-based clustering, (iv) High-dimensional clustering, (v) Similarity-based clustering, and (vi) Co-clustering.

Implementing 'decision making' with cloud computing technologies in medical fields is one of the hardest parts of this process. It challenges various traditional approaches when applying design, and management of medical files in an organization or medical data centers, particularly if there are issues with security portability and interoperability. Some decision-making algorithms have been available on networks that use fuzzy logic technique in decision-making, which helps to identify the possible information about various medical data, nevertheless they have been unsuccessful. The decision-making is done based on health service providers' requirements.

The fuzzy logic concept is examined by different researchers and was suggested to make decisions as it provides better results when compared with other algorithms. Another reason for using fuzzy logic is that it is convenient because it explains the decision clearly, and it is process that can be implemented easily. One of the main challenges in ensuring "medical data security" for big data is to come up with a balanced approach towards regulation and analytics of this approach. It shows how various organizations carry out useful analytics to secure the privacy of patients. There are number of techniques available for privacy and preservation of data mining, as privacy-preserving data integration, and privacy preserving information retrieval from big data have been developed with the assurance of security. In the past few years, many organizations started to use cloud computing to store their data for this reason. Companies store confidential and sensitive data in public cloud confidently, as most organization around the world use Big Data for the purpose of decision support, and to get cloud services offered by third parties. There are many benefits of increasing the security usage of cloud computing in business. Some of the advantages are as follows; parallel computing, scalability, elasticity and inexpensive.

This study has used published articles and has compared and contracted studies to analyze highlighted trends of big data. This paper has used content analysis method to draw data from various methods in order to understand multiple aspect of the trends. The comparisons and contrasts of published scholarly articles have used different algorithms and methods that highlighted these trends. The purpose is to evaluate functionality and worthiness of each algorithm method and determined and explained possible issues and ways to overcome them.

The main issues that rises from this content analysis is the fact that, the implementation of cloud computing has various possible ways, to overcome the adverse effects of unstructured data by using cloud computing is effecatious. This chapter has used specific methods to identify trends of algorithms that compares and contrasts data by using specific tools from each research article. The aim of this chapter is to give a better comprehension of cloud computing on medical data and to identify issues that are important for future research directions. . This study has used tools to measure information sourced from articles, for example, "K-means clustering algorithm" to structure data, and encryption algorithms to specifically secure medical data.

CLOUD COMPUTING DATA SECURITY

Data security in cloud computing is massive as it gives a futuristic solution to an existing problem getting bigger day by day because of data breaches on cloud. The protection of users' privacy is the biggest challenge for cloud because it contains vast amount of information from all over the globe. Cloud provides various benefits to the organizations such as low cost security, easy access of data and less management; nonetheless it is risky to upload sensitive data on cloud which can be stolen, modified and deleted by the attackers (Svantesson, 2010). This paper presents security steps which helps an organization to secure their information, and get facilities from service providers, who are aware about some rights and policies etc., (Zhang, 2016). This study will show some basic security steps to protect cloud data as a solution.

Cloud computing provides a set of resources on the internet for user conveniences. For example, a user can store, manage and process data on cloud rather than on local server or a hard disk. Cloud computing or internet computing has also big data centers all over the world, accessible anytime, anywhere, to connect you to your business by using web-enabled devices such as smartphones, tablets and laptops. This gives users big benefits to organize and move their data on cloud because they do not need to purchase big data storage devices to store their data (Pandith, 2014). They can easily store information on cloud and authorize employees to access data by using their username and password even by sitting at home, this is called virtual office. However, to transfer data on cloud is also very risky too. This is because personal information can be stolen and used in an unethical manner (Pitchai, 2016). There have been numerous accounts of news on cloud data breaches of how hackers hack personal accounts and get sensitive data. There are number issues on cloud because of financial data, personal information, and medical data breaches that can have detrimental effect on clients/patients. Without appropriate measures to establish safety set up, and information storage it becomes defenseless against leaks and, conducive to security ruptures and assaults (Mandal, 2013).

How Data Breaches Can Happen

1. **Failure of Authentication and Authorization:** As cloud data can be accessed by anyone from anywhere if the authorization and authentication process is not strong, then data breaches can be happening.
2. **Account Hijacking:** This can be done by expert hackers who can modify data and manipulate transactions.
3. **Dos Attacks:** Denial of service attacks that slows the system or simply time out where you can just sit and wait.
4. **Exfiltration:** If the cybercriminal gets into one computer in a company then the entire medical data can be extracted (Chen, 2009).

This shows that medical data security is a significant concern in cloud environment when it guarantees approved access. Information security manages information assurance and security as this includes protection of information from being lost or decimated, tainted or altered. Rather than putting away the information locally, clients store it in cloud. This way, rightness and accessibility of information must be guaranteed. The essential worry in distributed computing is security of client information which is the biggest concern of all (Waseem, 2016).

There are many methods to secure "medical data" in cloud computing such as Encryption, digital signature, secure authorization, nonetheless, these methods have some limitations which are shown below. The best solution for storing medical data security on cloud is stated according to findings of this study that can be a "powerful solution of keeping medical data in cloud, as it is a combination of three things: Data lockdown, Access policies and security intelligence" (Kumar, 2016).

Basic security methods can be given by:

- **Encryption:** According to this study, utilizing an algorithmic plan to change plain content (data) into a non-meaningful structure is called cipher-text. The opposite procedure is decryption which decodes the data from its encoded structure back to a plain content. To avert unapproved access to plain content information, the numerical calculation requires a secret value, known as key, with a specific end goal to scramble or decode the information appropriately. Cloud encryption is utilized to safe personal data saved and handled through networks, the web, tablets and remote gadgets (Chaves, 2011).
- **Limitation:** As mentioned above the information security models need few perspectives to satisfy the assessment criteria of security systems. Also, a coordinated methodology utilizing diverse strategies for verification, security and information integrity also needs to be exploited to illuminate the pitfalls of existing frameworks.
- **Digital Signatures:** Author said it is based on asymmetric cryptography, as RSA algorithm helps to generate a private and public key which is linked together mathematically. Then this is used to private key to encrypt the hash (Kaur, 2013). Limitation- Digital signatures are products with short life nonetheless it allows to get the software verification, as the sender and receiver does not have to pay any costs.
- **Secure Authorization:** In this security step, there should be a limited number of users and all the users have to have different names and passwords to access the authorized data. These passwords should be strong and secure to avoid breaches (Hagos, 2016).
- **Limitation:** The hacker can guess or break the passwords and access sensitive data.

According to the first key-point the data should not be in readable format which provides a strong key-management, and it should be done by incremental encryption. Incremental encryption use "Collision free hashing" and "Digital signatures". Secondly, after implementing access policies, only the authorized person can get access to sensitive information. The root users or Privileged users also cannot explore sensitive data after implementing these policies. Last but not least, the security intelligence will be incorporated to produce log information of users in cloud. This helps to check the behavior of users and generate alerts against hackers.

RESEARCH ISSUES

Issues and limitations related to big data medical health organizations are described in this section: 1. online information reliability. 2. Big data management and analytics. 3. Improving data analytic techniques. 4. Integrating big data with cloud computing. 5. Security and privacy challenges in cloud computing system. 6. Query and runtime optimizing for iterative and distributed programs.7 Declarative specifications and optimizes asynchronous computations 8. Data protection 9. Administrative rights.

Onllne Information Reliability

Retrieving medically relevant information from the Internet is one of the hardest processes, because many people around the world use their native language to communicate. This creates some difficulty for researchers or for people in the system that retrieves data from these networks. Medical data will be extracted from different resources with different qualities. However, identifying which information source is more reliable than others is impossible and is not a natural process (Hannan 2014).

Identifying the trustworthiness of the data taken from online sources is one of the most important aspects of online research. Due to living in a knowledge-based society surrounded by high-tech gadgets, people have access to various online medical details that help online users to search and identify information about a particular medicine or disease. The drawback of this is the fact that there needs to be increased levels of privacy to assure "medical data security" for confidentiality. The growth of social media, computer technology, medical and other data sets on the Internet, basically heightens the need for a secure storage system than ever. Additionally, data mining also handles the flow of data properly and the prediction of existing relational database, considering other data mining techniques that are insufficient compared to retrieving data from the Internet.

Big Data Management and Analytics

Big data management and analytics are critical in the proposed system, because big data helps to store all information that is collected from the Internet. One of the main issues is implementing infrastructure and high-performance computing techniques for storage of big data. Managing retrieved data from multiple sources and securing access to big data is crucial and hard. There needs to be more concentration on data analytics techniques that will help to manipulate and analyze big data to extract small chunks of information (Thuraisingham, 2015).

Wang (2009) proposed a technique, which helps to increase security of Big Data that not only stores cloud nonetheless also validates the required data to perform some analytical processes. This method contributes to increase the number of cloud users, and allows them to retrieve required medical information quickly from the Internet. The author proposed a technique that helps to identify the frequently searched information from the Internet as well, and also provides natural methods to analyze medical information.

Improving Data Analytic Techniques

Data plays a vital role in the proposed system; here we use k-means algorithms to require data from big data. Using the advanced k-means algorithm can easily improve data analytics. However, developing the data analytic techniques in the proposed system provides more benefits in collecting and analyzing relevant medical data. Cloud environment provides various techniques and methods to maximize the analytics of data (P.R, 2012).

To show the exact value from the database or cloud data analysis methods or tools, there needs to be an inspection system in place or to transform the auditing progress. Author (HAN HU, 2014) states that the proposed concept to improve data analytic techniques, is as follows:

- Searching with keyword that matches several native language codes that helps to increase the search information.
- Application fields leverage opportunities presented by generous data and proposed technique which will retrieve domain-specific analytical methods to derive the intended issues.
- Using the proposed techniques in data analytics will also provide many benefits (Campos, 2010).

Integrating Big Data with Cloud Computing

"ConPaaS" provides an integrated cloud environment for big data, as it helps to minimize the complexity of cloud computing. It also offers two services in Big-data such as MapReduce and Task Farming. This tool will be very helpful for integrating both big-data and cloud (Madden, 2012). Big data mainly concentrates on achieving deep business value from various deployments of advanced analytics and trustworthy data on Internet scales in medical fields. By categorizing and accessing the application loads can be beneficial as it will inadvertently help to improve big data integration with cloud computing, as this will be ideal (Changqing 2012).

The author Chandrashekar, (2015) proposed a novel technique to integrate both cloud computing and big data, He explained how this method helps to minimize the cost, and overhead, as it also triggers rapid provisioning that gives time to market with flexibility and scalability.

Security and Privacy Challenge in Cloud Computing

Collecting data from "Internet storage manipulation" and controlling the medical data security in cloud computing environment is one of the hardest processes that results in security and privacy considerations as mentioned before. However, different methods and techniques have been proposed to handle big data in cloud computing system, as this technology provides high security for data that is stored in cloud computing (Thuraisingham, 2015).

Query and Runtime Optimization for Iterative and Distributed Programs

Runtime optimization is one of the most important processes in the proposed system as it needs to analyze the data sets that are relevant to medical data. Many operations can easily be handled with the help of proposed algorithms. K-means algorithm provides a separate way to cluster information from Big Data to allow it to configure programs that match keywords. The easiest process in this algorithm is one that can easily integrate this approach in the proposed system (Baek 2015).

First of all, the proposal of big data query, and runtime is to measure, evaluate, and compare big data systems and its architecture. To retrieve required information from the Internet is one of the hardest parts that need an algorithm query processer, which matches the information retrieved from the Internet. Wang, (2014) proposed a benchmarking method to process the query, which helps people to retrieve required information from the Internet. This method contributes to minimize security issues as well as contribute to increase the query runtime of the process in the proposed system.

Declarative Specifications and Optimization for Asynchronous Computations

Big data provides room for researchers, to retract data for their research topics in their areas. Declarative specifications which play a vital role in the proposed system gives space to concentrate more on the optimizer for asynchronous computations that leads to high success factor in retrieving relevant medical data from big-data storage (Dean, 2013).

Data Protection

To improve data efficiency many cloud environments such as Hadoop stores data without encryption or any other security methods. If any unauthorized user or hackers accesses a set of machines, then there is no way to stop them from stealing critical medical data stored in machines (Ren, 2012).

The need for an advanced technique to provide data protection in both Big Data and cloud computing seems to be the resolution. Zhang, (2010) Proposed a quick grid method to secure medical data as he developed a framework to maximize the security level of data in Big Data and Cloud computing that helps secure customers medical details as well as healthcare information. At the same time, the development of a security framework that consists of four main parts such as security governance, security management, security maintenance and security technology is still much needed. Furthermore, numerous security solutions have been proposed by researchers and developers to protect users, specifically, medically relevant information in both Big Data and Cloud Computing. Many of these researchers have proposed an identity-based encryption and proxy re-encryption schemes that helps to improve security for communication services in particular processes. Some of the existing techniques and methods that contribute to secure the system are as follows; white hat security, proof point, DocTrackr, Cipher Cloud, Vaultive and SilverSky (Agrawal, 2016).

Administrative Rights

Administrative rights are the most important aspects of the aforementioned systems because they will control all activities that flow in the system. The administrator provides access controls of users, as this method also provides a particular kind of security for both the cloud computing operations as well as data (F.C.P, Oct 6-9, 2013).

Most organizations around the world are unaware of the fact that, employees have administrative rights. The administration has access to critical information that poses a risk, and to permit employees to access sensitive documents that can lead to data theft in organizations leaving them with consequences. Employees or intruders can easily upload viruses or warm codes in the organization to steal confidential information. Therefore, providing administrative rights to particular employees to access sensitive files in an organization is one of the most crucial aspects of secure storage (Perry, 2012).

OVERVIEW OF EXISTING SOLUTIONS RELATED TO ISSUES

Computing information is also another significant aspect in the concept of storage and analysis of data. Only storing medical data securely is not enough, it also needs to be easily retrieved. So it is necessary to turn raw data into some structured format so that it will be easy to retrieve, otherwise it defeats the purpose. Brett and Hannan (2014) have used information fusion algorithm to structure raw data that is collected. They collated similar patterns that are formed by joining existing patterns and leaving out the unnecessary information behind unnoticed. This chapter demonstrates that the use of k-means clustering algorithm is needed to convert raw data into structured one, by clustering them into various patterns, can

Table 1. Comparison of research issues in big data medical health organization

Security Issues and Challenges	Concerns	Analysis and Findings	Limitation	Authors
Privacy of data transmission, data breaches. Confidentiality of data	Sensitive data expose or access while transmission	Multi-layered security where the authors compared 'CCAF multi-layered security with a single-layered approach by performing experiments. It takes more than 50 hours to secure all 2 PB information and above 125 hours to raise a caution to take control of the circumstance in the ULCC Data Centre	Time consuming and expensive process	Chang & Ramachandran (2016)
Accounts hijacking	Authorization and authentication of data	Proposed data security model	In this model all the layers have to interact with each other before starting any process.	Pitchai, & Jayashri (2016)
APIs	Management on cloud	Signals self-collected from good subjects are utilized as health information. All information is changed into binary format based on a particular quantization determination	Actions are performed on each and every layer	Bechtel (2016)
Security and privacy challenge in cloud computing	Collecting data from computer storage, manipulation and controlling of data in the cloud is difficult	Encryption Algorithms, e.g. DET Algorithms differ from one organization to other depend on security challenge. These algorithms facilitate data to be secured		Thuraisingham et al. (2015)
Data is being accessed by the unauthorized users	Certificate management, authentication breakage	Comparison between the old traditional system and three level authentication mechanisms	Three level authentication mechanisms to get higher level of cloud data security.	Sirohi & Aggarwal (2015)
Healthcare - Electronic healthcare records	Privacy sensitive health records are released to the third party in cloud	Used Anonymization With MapReduce method and anonymize health care data via generalization using two-phase clustering approach	A third party in cloud has access to healthcare records	Zhang et al. (2015) [
Healthcare - All digital healthcare industry	Regional secure data process	Raspberry Pi is a pocket-sized computer used in forensic medicine, forensic etymology	collect limit issues in future health care	Feng et al. (2015)
Malicious attacks Monitoring, management	Risk for healthcare applications	Data partitioning and scrambling - ECG signals from MIT- BIH arrhythmia database and ECG	It requires all the TCP-IP layer management and different security	Wang & Yang (2015)
Data loss, sensitive data breaches	Confidentiality, integrity and availability of data	Access control, Encryption. Cloud hosted data remains secret via encrypted transmission of data and encrypted storage of data	Account hijacking, exposer of cloud hosted data. If the private key expose, then whole data will be lost.	Devi & Ganesan (2015)
Hijacking of accounts	Cyber-attacks. Account Credential performs, Preventing Phishing attacks	Both reaction as well as preventive measures in consistence with best industry practices and international standards	This is a kind of research, analysis and prevention plan of account hijacking not a particular solution of that	Tirumala et al. (2015)

continued on next page

Table 1. Continued

Security Issues and Challenges	Concerns	Analysis and Findings	Limitation	Authors
Risk of data exposure, Security of data	Untrusted third party attacks	Holomorphic encryption, the pain-text encryption done by using Holomorphic encryption before sending	Complicated algorithms used	Jain & Madan(2015)
Attacks done by malware Integrity of data, availability of data,	Limited data availability, updating of data without authority	Email-filter set up at high mode - from email setting the filter mode changed to high mode	Not applicable on vast data. Just suitable for email security	Sharif & Cooney (2015)
No authorization, No encryption	Increasing Data breaches	User errors: Methodology Encryption by complex algorithms	Training about new software, and data security by using Complex algorithm	Asaduzzaman & Jain (2015)
Password recovery, Data location, Confidentiality, Data concealment	Performance issues with cipher-text	Dynamic virtualization of software, hardware	Time consuming	Pandith (2014)
Confidentiality, authentication	Control over Information leakage. User errors	Training methods - Proper training session to train employee about new software or techniques		Gong (2014)
Authorization, authentication	Control over un-authorized access	Malicious attacks, Signatures signed on paper and scanned to save in computer then cropped to create a picture	Less effective	Kaaniche & Laurent (2014)
Improving data analytic techniques	Data plays a vital role in the proposed system. So there is a need to develop techniques used for data analysis	K-means algorithm	To cluster require data from big data	Hu et al. (2014)
Query and runtime optimizers for iterative and distributed programs.	Runtime optimization is most important and critical process that was difficult to achieve	Benchmarking Method	To minimize security issues as well as it helps to increase the query and runtime of the process in the proposed study	Wang et al. (2014)
Online information security	The identifying truthfulness of data that is shared online	Map-reduce Algorithm	To analyze various clusters and recommend services used by other users or researchers for the same type of work	Ramamoorthy et al. (2013)
Data exposure, sensitive information leakage	Difficult to stop data exposure and leakage	Phishing attacks, Digital signatures. Less effective for huge amount of data security	Signatures signed on paper and scanned to save in computer then cropped to create a picture	Sirohi & Agarwal (2013)
Data confidentiality: Challenging multitenant environment	Remote server attaches	Virtual infrastructure provided to host services to client for its usage and management of stored data in cloud servers	Public key based framework	Barbori (2012)

continued on next page

Table 1. Continued

Security Issues and Challenges	Concerns	Analysis and Findings	Limitation	Authors
Administrative Rights	They play a major role as they control all activities and flow in the system		Access permissions should be provided to particular employees to access confidential files helps to improve security level for data as well as organization benefits	Perry, (2012)
Healthcare - Covers the person suffering from Alzheimer's Disease	Current system to diagnose the patient has slight range and is not secure	A new method proposed with the long-range outdoor environment with GPS and fine-grained distributed data access control. Using location tracking technology, telediagnosis, Access using PKC	Part of data is not secure	Pramila et al. (2012)
Integrating big data with Cloud computing	The complexity of cloud increases, as there is no integration of big data with the cloud	MapReduce and Task Farming	These are used to integrate Big data and cloud, which reduces cost, overhead	Madden et al. (2012)
Healthcare	Privacy preserving for healthcare data.	Changing the data values by using noise perturbation, data aggregation, and data swapping. Spent $39.4 billion in 2008	Data masking	Motiwalla et al. (2010)
Data protection	Unauthorized users or hackers access critical data	Smart Grid Method	To maximize security level of data that helps to secure customer's personal data as well as health care information	Zhang, (2010)
Big data management and analytics	Implementing infrastructure and high-performance computing technique for storage of big data	Attribute-based Encryption	Increase security for Big data that is stored in the cloud.	Wang et al. (2009)

give a clear image in the data because of its patterns, and its eases retrieval. During the retrieval section of various algorithms that are used in general, here we use the fuzzy logic algorithm in the knowledge retrieval process, simply because the data is stored in a data warehouse so that is not called education. The data is converted into knowledge only if it is retrieved properly. By using the fuzzy logic techniques, the retrieval of data information is done in an efficient manner.

Up until now, this study has looked at, medical data storing and retrieval of stored data. The next section will talk about the importance of data transportation. The primary concern with data transportation is the tedious security requirements. The security issue is one of the threatening factors in cloud computing. There are enormous advantages in the field of cloud computing, and its main drawback is security issues. Blanke et al (2015) describes the usage of artificial intelligence to resolve security issues during the data transformation process. Using artificial intelligence, the author found that whether the medical data is transferred to the correct destination or not detecting injections or hackings during the transformation is important. On top of this, investigating various security features (Pham, 2010a, 2010b, 2011) to avoid hacking so that the system could be an interesting avenue to explore in the future to protect BigData.

Implementing artificial intelligence will be a cost consuming process, so to secure the data simply by a data encryption as well as decryption methods. DES encryption algorithm is a method used for the encryption and decryption of the medical data. Therefore, the data information stored in cloud will be retained only in the encrypted format and the encrypted data will be sent during data transfer. Even if there is a hack in between, the hacker may not find anything useful with the data retrieved, as it will not be in an understandable format because it is encrypted.

DISCUSSION

This chapter has mainly focused on exploring data storage systems from various regional health organizations. It also accomplished the exchange and sharing of medical information between different medical institutions of certain areas that have been studied after a critiquing analysis. Consequently, this chapter proposed a new framework to share medical information across the medical organizations.

At present, the information system that is used in regional health organization is still at its initial stage, and their needs to be more development to eliminate possible security and data privacy breaches. Private experts of medical information suggested that the core of regional health information is to acknowledging the importance of shared electronic health records, and electronic transmission. The accessible medical records will create a potential growth in the medical field, however, it is important to develop a sharing framework that gives attention to the security of personal details. Medical organizations share confidential information about the different diseases and patients, so in that situations, they need to enable high security for particular data transmission in a network. As a result, the emergence of cloud computing technology will bring a brand-new understanding for the development of medical information to store and retrieve confidential data.

The proposed system in this study has found that, Big Data may have many benefits to the medical organization to collect and store information about medical details of clients. Using big data and cloud computing services will significantly help to increase the assistances of decision making in the management of medical organization.

CONCLUSION

Cloud computing provides gigantic advantages, and also increases the security levels of medical data. However, there are some difficulties that still exist even after the adaptation and promotion of cloud computing. There is a strong need for an advanced higher functioning tools and approaches to secure confidentiality requirements of an industry that is growing rapidly. This research has established that Cloud computing and big data provides heightened benefits to the consumers when they adopt to improve their working process in an organization. Additionally, this study has found that, the use of cloud and Big Data services also improves the analysis of medically relevant data in the network and the regional health information systems which is based on cloud computing that has benefits such as, convenient management, easy extension, flexible investment and low requirements for low technical based personal medical units. This study recommends that the above proposed suggestions have been found by this content that will help to increase the quality of medical reports and enhance health information system and inadvertently leverage their storage systems. The extraction, containment and confidentiality of medical records need to be sustained in order to compete with the growing challenges and demands.

REFERENCES

Agrawal, V. (Accessed 2016) Securing Big Data On Cloud – Tools and Measures. Retrieved from http://www.exeideas.com/2015/09/securing-big-data-on-cloud.html

Blanke, C. A. (2015). The (Big) Data-security assemblage: Knowledge and critique. *Big Data & Society*.

Brett Hannan, X. Z. (2014, August 11-14). iHANDs: Intelligent Health Advising and Decision-Support Agent. *Proceedings of the 2014 IEEE/WIC/ACM International Joint Conferences on Web Intelligence (WI) and Intelligent Agent Technologies (IAT)* (Vol. 3, pp. 294 – 301).

Campos, L. M. (2010). Combining content-based and collaborative recommendations: A hybrid approach based on Bayesian networks. *International Journal of Approximate Reasoning, 51*(7), 785–799. doi:10.1016/j.ijar.2010.04.001

Chandrashekar, R. M. K. (2015). Integration of Big Data in Cloud computing environments for enhanced data processing capabilities. *International Journal of Engineering Research and General Science, 3*(3 Part 2), 2091–2730.

Changqing Ji, Y. L. (2012). Big Data Processing in Cloud Computing Environments. *Proceedings of the 2012 International Symposium on Pervasive Systems, Algorithms and Networks*.

Chaves, S. (2011). The Risks Issue in Cloud Computing. doi:10.2139/ssrn.1991156

Chen, Q., & Deng, Q. (2009). Cloud computing and its key techniques. *Journal of Computer Applications, 29*(9), 2562–2567. doi:10.3724/SP.J.1087.2009.02562

Dean, J. G. C. (2013). Large Scale Distributed Deep Networks. *Advances in Neural Information Processing Systems*.

Feng, J. X., Onafeso, B., & Liu, E. (2016). *Computer and Information Technology; Ubiquitous Computing and Communications; Dependable, Autonomic and Secure Computing*. Pervasive Intelligence and Computing.

Hagos, D. (2016). Software-Defined Networking for Scalable Cloud-based Services to Improve System Performance of Hadoop-based Big Data Applications. *International Journal of Grid and High Performance Computing, 8*(2), 1–22. doi:10.4018/IJGHPC.2016040101

Hu, H., Wen, Y., Chua, T. S., & Li, X. (2014). Toward Scalable Systems for Big Data Analytics: A Technology Tutorial.

Joonsang B., Q. H. (2015, April/June). A Secure Cloud Computing Based Framework for Big Data Information Management of Smart Grid. *IEEE Transactions On Cloud Computing*, *3*(2).

Kaur, M., & Singh, R. (2013). Implementing Encryption Algorithms to Enhance Data Security of Cloud in Cloud Computing. *International Journal of Computers and Applications*, *70*(18), 16–21. doi:10.5120/12167-8127

Madden, S. (2012, May). From Databases to Big Data. *IEEE Internet Computing*, *16*(3), 4–6. Retrieved from http://ieeexplore.ieee.org/lpdocs/epic03/wrapper.htm?arnumber=6188576 doi:10.1109/MIC.2012.50

Mandal, S. (2013). Enhanced Security Framework to Ensure Data Security in Cloud using Security Blanket Algorithm. *International Journal of Research in Engineering and Technology*, *2*(10), 225–229. doi:10.15623/ijret.2013.0210033

Motiwalla, L. (2010). Value Added Privacy Services for Healthcare Data.

Muhtaroglu, F. C. P., Demir, S., Obali, M., & Girgin, C. (2013, October 6-9). Business model canvas perspective on big data applications. *Proceedings of the 2013 IEEE International Conference on Big Data*, Silicon Valley, CA (pp. 32 – 37).

Pandith, M. (2014). Data Security and Privacy Concerns in Cloud Computing. *IOTCC*, *2*(2), 6. doi:10.11648/j.iotcc.20140202.11

Perry, D. (2012). Most organizations unaware of employees with admin rights. Retrieved from http://www.tomsitpro.com/articles/administrator_rights-admin_rights-malware-IT_security_professionals,1-353.html

Pham, D. V., Syed, A., & Halgamuge, M. N. (2011). Universal serial bus based software attacks and protection solutions. *Digital Investigation*, *7*(3), 172–184. doi:10.1016/j.diin.2011.02.001

Pham, D. V., Syed, A., Mohammad, A., & Halgamuge, M. N. (2010, June 14-16). Threat Analysis of Portable Hack Tools from USB Storage Devices and Protection Solutions. *Proceedings of the International Conference on Information and Emerging Technologies*, Karachi, Pakistan. doi:10.1109/ICIET.2010.5625728

Pham, D. V., Halgamuge, M. N., Syed, A., & Mendis, P. (2010). Optimizing windows security features to block malware and hack tools on USB storage devices. Proceedings of Progress in electromagnetics research symposium (pp. 350-355).

Pitchai, R., Jayashri, S., & Raja, J. (2016). Searchable Encrypted Data File Sharing Method Using Public Cloud Service for Secure Storage in Cloud Computing. *Wireless Personal Communications*, *90*(2), 947–960. doi:10.1007/s11277-016-3273-1

P.R. (2012). Third Party Data Protection Applied To Cloud and Xacml Implementation in the Hadoop Environment With Sparql.

Ramamoorthy, S. (2013). Optimized Data Analysis in Cloud using BigData Analytics Techniques. Proceedings of 4th ICCCNT.

Rathod, K. R. (2016). Cloud Computing - Key Pillar for Digital India. *International Journal of Information*, *6*(1/2), 27–33.

Ren, Y. a. (2012, October 30-November 1). A Service Integrity Assurance Framework For Cloud Computing Based On Mapreduce. *Proceedings of IEEE CCIS'12*, Hangzhou (pp. 240 –244).

Suji Pramila, R., Shajin Nargunam, A., & Affairs, A. (2010). A study on data confidentiality in early detection of Alzheimer's disease. Proceedings of the 2012 International Conference on Computing, Electronics and Electrical Technologies (ICCEET) (pp. 1004-1008).

Svantesson, D., & Clarke, R. (2010). Privacy and consumer risks in cloud computing. *Computer Law & Security Report*, *26*(4), 391–397. doi:10.1016/j.clsr.2010.05.005

Thuraisingham, D. B. (2015). Big data security and privacy. *Proceedings of the 5th ACM Conference on Data and Application Security and Privacy CODASPY '15* (pp. 279-280).

Thuraisingham, D. B. (2015). *Big Data Security and Privacy. National Science Foundation.*

Wang, L. J. Z. (2014). *BigData Bench: a Big Data Benchmark Suite from Internet Services. State Key Laboratory of Computer Architecture.* Institute of Computing Technology, Chinese Academy of Sciences.

Wang, Q. C. W. (2009). *Enabling Public Verifiability and Data Dynamics for Storage Security in Cloud Computing.* ESORICS. doi:10.1007/978-3-642-04444-1_22

Waseem, M., Lakhan, A., & Jamali, I. (2016). Data Security of Mobile Cloud Computing on Cloud Server. *OALib*, *3*(4), 1–11. doi:10.4236/oalib.1102377

Zhang, T. (2010). The design of information security protection framework to support Smart Grid. *Proceedings of the 2010 International Conference on Power System Technology (POWERCON)* (pp. 1-5).

Zhang, W., Han, S., He, H., & Chen, H. (2016). Network-aware virtual machine migration in an over-committed cloud. *Future Generation Computer Systems.* doi:10.1016/j.future.2016.03.009

Zhang, X., Dou, W., Pei, J., Nepal, S., Yang, C., Liu, C., & Chen, J. (2015). *Proximity-Aware Local-Recoding Anonymization with MapReduce for Scalable Big Data Privacy Preservation in Cloud. IEEE transactions on computers, 64(8), 2293–2307.*

Section 2

Bioinformatics in the Fields of Genomics and Proteomics as Applied to Medicine, Health Issues, and Medical Systems

This section covers topics related to computational systems biology, machine learning in protein fold recognition, integrative data analysis, structural class prediction of protein, functional study of specific molecular and pathway analysis, data mining in proteomics, homology detection and sequence alignment methods, protein expression analysis, protein sequencing and classification, molecular dynamics simulation, protein docking and drug design, homology detection and sequence alignment methods, multiscale network construction. Environment and health issues as related to *integration of big data analytics with bioinformatics, integrated exposure modelling assimilation of exposure measurements and human biomonitoring, data statistics and big data analytics for exposome-wide association studies.*

Chapter 6
Informatics and Data Analytics to Support Exposome-Based Discovery:
Part 1 – Assessment of External and Internal Exposure

Dimosthenis A. Sarigiannis
Aristotle University of Thessaloniki, Greece

Krystalia Papadaki
Aristotle University of Thessaloniki, Greece

Spyros P. Karakitsios
Aristotle University of Thessaloniki, Greece

Dimitris Chapizanis
Aristotle University of Thessaloniki, Greece

Evangelos Handakas
Aristotle University of Thessaloniki, Greece

Alberto Gotti
Aristotle University of Thessaloniki, Greece

ABSTRACT

This chapter provides a comprehensive overview of the state of the art and beyond regarding modelling and data analytics towards refined external and internal exposure assessment, for elucidating the human exposome. This includes methods for more accurate measurement of personal exposure (using wearable sensors) and for extrapolation to larger population groups (agent-based modelling). A key component in the modern risk and health impact assessment is the translation of external exposure into internal exposure metrics, accounting for age, gender, genetic and route of exposure dependent differences. The applicability of biokinetics covering a large chemical space is enhanced using quantitative structure activity relationships, especially when the latter are estimated using machine learning tools. Finally, comprehensive biomonitoring data interpretation and assimilation are supported by exposure reconstruction algorithms coupled with biokinetics

DOI: 10.4018/978-1-5225-2607-0.ch006

INTRODUCTION

The exposome (Wild, 2005) represents the totality of exposures from conception onwards, simultaneously identifying, characterizing and quantifying the exogenous and endogenous exposures and modifiable risk factors that predispose to and predict diseases throughout a person's life span. Unravelling the exposome implies that both environmental exposures and genetic variation are reliably measured simultaneously. To achieve this, we need to bring together a comprehensive array of novel technologies, data analysis and modelling tools that support efficient design and execution of exposome studies. This requires an innovative approach bringing together and organizing environmental, socio-economic, exposure, biomarker and health effect data; in addition, this effort includes all the procedures and computational sequences necessary for applying advanced bioinformatics coupling advanced data mining, biological and exposure modelling so as to ensure that environmental exposure-health associations are studied comprehensively.

Deciphering the human exposome is expected to open new avenues of biomedical discovery and environmental innovation since currently the largest part of the total burden of disease is deemed to be attributable to environmental stressors in the large sense. Exposome-based discovery may overhaul the way environmental chemical risk is assessed to date. The current paradigm in this field deals with chemicals one at a time, not considering vulnerability time windows of exposure. Even when co-exposure to multiple stressors is taken into account, neither the spatio-temporal sequence of exposures nor exposure modifiers are usually considered in risk assessment done for regulatory or scientific reasons. This chapter aims at illustrating new data analytics and advanced computational modelling techniques and how they can be integrated to support exposome discovery and, finally assessment of environmental health risk. It gives an overview of how various state-of-the-art computational tools facilitate the elucidation of exposome as it pertains to external and internal exposure assessment. Overall, the objective is to inform the reader about the integration of different type of data that may originally seem disconnected (e.g. personal wearable sensors for tracking activity and biomonitoring) through the use of data analytics and bioinformatics tools and how the different pieces of information are combined towards the discovery of mechanistic links between environmental exposures and human health.

Background

Exposome studies will require novel tools to address the complexity of emerging environmental health issues. Critical for success will be the ability to bring together existing geospatial, environmental, health and socioeconomic data, and to collect new high resolution data using innovative environmental microsensors, remote sensing or other community and omics/systems biology based approaches to describe the exposome for e.g. endocrine disruption-related syndromes and sex-related changes (menopause), neurodegenerative or respiratory diseases. While an individual's genome is a static sequence of four nucleic acid bases, exposome data have several notable differences: (1) measurement heterogeneity (e.g., biomarkers, external sensors) and type (e.g., continuous, categorical), (2) a denser correlation structure, (3) time-dependence, and (4) spatial dependence (Ioannidis et al., 2009; Patel & Manrai, 2015; Patel & Ioannidis, 2014).

The human exposome data structure is a high-dimensional collection of highly heterogeneous exposure variables that may change upon repeated samplings during an individual's lifetime (e.g. Athersuch, 2012). Time-dependent and high-throughput genome-scaled data types such as gene expression or metabolomics data are similar in structure. For example, to measure gene expression, an array of gene probes indicates the amount of mRNA expressed in a tissue or cell. Similarly, an exposome "array" would measure the amount of a multitude of time-varying external and internal exposures. However, we have yet to have a unified assay to ascertain the exposome array. To this end, the exposome community needs to identify 'omics technologies (e.g., metabolomics and sensor-based technologies) that allow for agnostic and high-throughput ascertainment of the personal exposome in humans. An outline of such technologies is given in this section and the corresponding data structure is explained.

UNRAVELING THE EXPOSOME

Issues, Controversies, Problems

The weakest link in the health risk assessment chain is exposure assessment since we have reliable exposure information only for ca. 4% of manufactured chemicals used to date worldwide. Exposure assessment is hampered by the relative paucity of environmental monitoring data, which although regularly monitored at variable temporal and spatial scales present significant gaps and quality Fusion of environmental data to fill gaps in current environmental monitoring data needs to recognise the fact that all environmental data sources carry residual error, albeit variable. Thus, the task of environmental data characterization is transformed into a quest towards efficient data fusion, which can be obtained through a number of different methods such as the following:

- Kalman filters,
- Information and decision theory approaches,
- Decision trees,
- Artificial intelligence algorithms – Kohonen maps, artificial neural networks.

Current external exposure assessment methodologies lack detailed resolution in time and space and generally omit consideration of the whole life-course of individuals. In addition, large-scale exposure assessments of the European population to environmental stressors rarely exist. Functional integration of the existing dataset and filling data gaps are needed in order to unravel the external exposome of individuals and population subgroups to multiple stressors via different pathways. Data are mined from different information sources including past and ongoing research and survey projects both at National and European level and EU-wide monitoring systems. In this regard a critical step is the harmonization of this data to ensure that, for example, PMx data is directly comparable across Europe.

SOLUTIONS AND RECOMMENDATIONS

Data Fusion, Probabilistic and Agent-Based Modelling for Comprehensive External Exposure Assessment

Environmental data, combined with exposure models, provide the basis for the development of a methodological and computational framework for estimating the external exposures of selected population groups to multiple stressors via different exposure routes (i.e. inhalation, ingestion and dermal). Depending on data availability, geospatial analysis and multimedia modelling may be used to estimate concentrations of the analysed toxic substances in 'microenvironments' and food. Methods for data integration as well as for handling missing data are exploited by using data fusion techniques aiming at maximizing the information available through "intelligent" merging of the disparate environmental data available and the agent-based and other exposure modelling techniques such as personal sensor technologies. Probabilistic exposure modelling methodologies based on Markov-Chain Monte Carlo techniques may be used to estimate external exposure for selected population groups across time and space and to integrate uncertainty associated with the measurement and modelling of the various agent-specific (individual) exposure doses. Thus, based on "individual" exposure estimates, estimations for wider and coherent population subgroups will be derived.

Due to the substantial technical and ethical hurdles involved in collecting real individual space-time movement data for whole populations, we propose simulating movement and interaction behaviour using agent-based models (ABM) informed by sensor technologies. ABM aim to simulate and organise social behaviours in order to understand the dynamics of real-world systems. A style of computational modelling, ABM, focuses on simulating individuals (agents) and their interactions with other agents and their environments, as part of a larger complex system. The use of ABM will enable us to better understand the behaviour of individuals and populations in social and evolutionary settings, and to 'fill-in' the gaps in the exposome currently not available from real-world monitoring and sensor data.

Using data fusion techniques, health and exposure data derived from fixed monitoring networks may be supplemented by a range of emerging novel techniques and technologies such as agent-based modellin, mobile phone apps, environmental sensor-webs, micro-sensors and satellite remote sensing. The information from the coupled use of agent-based models and sensor webs improves exposure modelling using deterministic and/or probabilistic approaches, and supports the application of new epidemiological and biostatistical methods to relate modeled exposure to health outcomes. The input to agent-based models consists of data relating to an individual's behavior within his/her environment (such as movement data within specific micro-environments) and between individuals exploring interactions around health-related behaviors and key risk determinants such as low socio-economic status. Using these parameters and the evolution of the virtual agents, simulations produce detailed information relating to the overall societal systems and populations considered. The estimated values produced can be used to fill the gaps of traditional datasets. This holistic approach is highly novel, taking the best from existing monitoring and sensor technology, but supplementing it with computational modelling. It is of particular relevance where real-world data are unavailable at the spatial and temporal scales that modelling complex exposures at the individual or population subgroup level requires. Although commonly used elsewhere, agent-based models and fusion methods have not been regularly applied in exposure assessment yet. This array of novel technologies, coupled with state-of-the-art fate modelling of chemicals will provide a complete and dynamic picture of external exposure to environmental chemicals in the near future supporting comprehensive, yet refined exposure and health risk assessment.

Improving Assessmicrosoftent of Activity Patterns: Use of Personal Sensors

Technological advances in recent years have produced sophisticated monitoring devices which can be carried or worn by a person during his/her regular daily routine, allowing for personal exposure to be monitored explicitly. Smartphone apps, wireless devices and the downsizing of monitoring technologies and costs make it possible for various environmental stressors and exposure factors to be measured more easily and frequently, thus providing a more reliable "time–geography of exposure" shifting the current paradigm from population to individual level exposure.

Direct reading monitors help us to identify whether peak exposures are more important than average exposure values, identify specific exposure pathways that dominate in critical time windows over an individual's lifetime, and finally build individual exposure profiles. The advent of multiple sensor classes makes the use of sophisticated data and model fusion schemes necessary if the full potential of remote and personal sensing is to be harvested for improved cumulative exposure assessment. Such algorithmic schemes include the use of advanced statistical models such as random forest optimization, artificial intelligence techniques such as back-propagation artificial neural networks or data clustering techniques such as fuzzy set modelling.

Combining information on individual position with spatially resolved pollution levels allows assignment of pollutant concentrations to persons as they move through different microenvironments. Moreover, information on individual physical activity as tracked by personal sensors supports the estimation of breathing rates during different activities, which, in turn, translate into inhaled dose. The possibility to use personal sensors able to provide real-time data on air pollution exposure (CO_2, CO, NO_2, O_3, PM_x of different size fractions) has been explored by several investigators (de Nazelle et al., 2013; Snyder et al., 2013). If proven to be reliable, these sensors will constitute an added value to the array of remote sensing instrumentation building the sensor web of exposome related studies (Nieuwenhuijsen, Donaire-Gonzalez, Foraster, Martinez, & Cisneros, 2014; Sarigiannis & Gotti, 2014).

An indicative framework for sensors used in exposome studies is graphically illustrated in Figure 1, where a set of sensors is worn for the assessment of location, activity and exposure to multiple compounds.

A major challenge regarding the use of activity and location sensors is the disengagement from the commonly used paper-logs and mainly to inform advanced exposure models. The capability of predicting location from sensors data could be greatly facilitated by Artificial Neural Network (ANN). A neural network consists of a number of interconnected processing elements, commonly referred to as neurons. The neurons are logically arranged into two or more layers and interact with each other via weighted

Figure 1. An overview of the personal sensors worn by participants in exposome studies

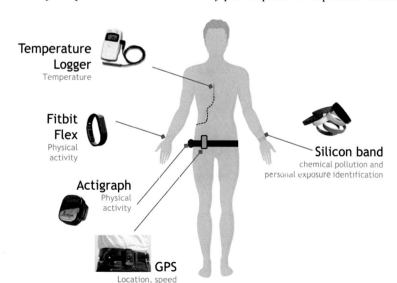

connections (Figure 2). These scalar weights determine the nature and strength of the influence between the interconnected neurons. Each neuron is connected to all the neurons in the next layer. There is an input layer where data are presented to the neural network, and an output layer that holds the response of the network to the input. It is the intermediate layers, also known as hidden layers that enable these networks to represent and compute complicated associations between patterns. Neural networks essentially learn through the adaptation of their connection weights.

Agent Based Modelling

A model that advances our understanding is one that represents what are considered, in a particular context, to be the key features of a system and thus enables us to improve our understanding of how that system works. Any gain in understanding of the system resulting from the modelling process derives from our ability to analyse the model and experiment with it. Complex phenomena are best understood through consideration of the behaviour of all interacting parts since macroscopic events emerge through microscopic actions and interactions. Agent-Based Modelling (ABM) helps to understand and explore this kind of phenomena, such as nonlinear systems, where typically independent and autonomous entities interact together to form a new emergent whole. While direct representation of the behaviours of individuals is organisationally difficult, ABM simplifies this process by managing information at the individual level. An example of such a system is the flocking behaviour of birds (Levy, 1993). Although each bird is independent, somehow they interact together to form a flock, and seemingly without any leading entity, manage to stay in tight formations. With this in mind, simulations using ABM attempt to discover the rules embedded in these individual entities that could lead to the emergent behaviour and eventually attempt to make interpretations about future states of these systems. It is, therefore, a simulation technique, capable of representing the kinds of systems where one level of abstraction (individual agents) can generate a new level of abstraction through the interactions that occur in the system, such as how individual birds form a flock.

Figure 2. Feed Forward Artificial Neural Network

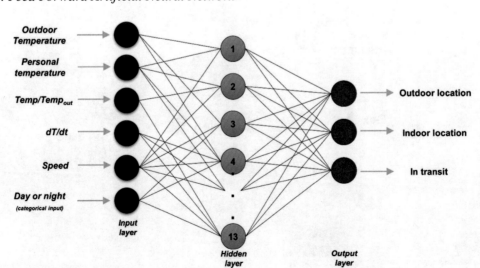

By simulating the actions and interactions of autonomous software objects, the "agents", at an individual level, the full effects of the diversity that exists among agents in their attributes and behaviours can be observed as rise is given to the behaviour of the system as a whole. Patterns, structures, and behaviours that were not explicitly programmed into the model, arise through the agent interactions enabling therefore the prediction and examination of expected and unexpected emerged behaviours.

The agents (which can be people, vehicles, roads, cities, animals, products, etc.) are programmed as autonomous decision-makers to react and act in their environment and to have goals that they aim to satisfy, according to a set of rules. In practice, agent actions in models revolve around exercising choice among available options in order to achieve defined goals. The outcome of an agent making a particular choice is translated as a difference in either the location of the agent (i.e. the agent moves) or in the environment. Depending on the model context, this may involve: (a) the agent exploiting resources at its current location (there will be therefore a shift regarding the supply of those resources at that location), (b) altering the state of the location (e.g. changing the land use), (c) acquiring the land at its present location; or, perhaps simply updating its current 'map' of the environment. In each case, there may be an accompanying change in the state of the agent itself, such as when resource exploitation increases the agent's wealth or energy resources.

In most cases ABMs are a relatively late arrival in a field where there is considerable previous experience with styles of model that adopt a more aggregated approach, and these aggregated models continue to be widely used. The increasing ease with which ABMs can be developed, coupled with their representational approach, in which each software agent represents an "actor" (whether an individual or a group of individuals), is the main reason why this modelling approach became more popular during the recent years. The appeal lies on the fact that individual-level decision-making is the fundamental driver of social systems.

The process of building an agent-based model begins with a conceptual model, where basic questions or goals, elements of the system (e.g. agent attributes, rules of agent interaction and behaviour, the model environment, etc.), and the measurable outcomes of interest are identified (Brown, 2006). According to Couclelis (2001), agents and their environment can either be (a) designed (i.e. explanatory) or (b) analysed (i.e. predictive – empirically grounded). Designed agents are endowed with attributes and behaviours that represent (often simplified) conditions for testing specific hypotheses about general cases. Analysed agents are intended to accurately mimic real-world entities, based on empirical data or ad hoc values that are realistic substitutes for observed processes. Similarly, the environment that agents are situated within can be (a) designed (i.e. provided with characteristics that are simplified to focus on specific agent attributes), or (b) analysed (i.e. represent a real-world location). Once a model has been conceptualised, it must be formalised into a specification which can be developed into a computer programme. The process of formalisation involves being precise about what an identified theory relating to a phenomenon of interest means.

In general, two types of simulation/modelling systems are available to develop ABMs: toolkits or software. Toolkits are simulation systems that provide a conceptual framework for organising and designing ABMs. They provide appropriate libraries of software functionality that include pre-defined routines/functions specifically designed for ABM. However, the object-oriented paradigm allows the integration of additional functionality from libraries not provided by the simulation toolkit, extending the capabilities of these toolkits. The idea of object-oriented programming (OOP) is crucial to ABM, which is why almost all related software packages are built using an OOP language, such as Java, C++, or Visual Basic. A program developed in an OOP language typically consists of a collection of objects.

An object is able to store data in its own attributes, and has methods that determine how it processes these data and interacts with other objects. When using OOP to design an ABM, one creates a class for each type of agent, provides attributes that retain the agents' past current state (memory), and adds suitable methods that observe the agents' environment (perception) and carry out agent actions (performance) according to some rules (policy). In addition, one needs to program a scheduler that instantiates the required number of agents at the beginning of the simulation and gives each of them a turn to act.

During the last years, of particular interest is the integration of functionality from geographic information systems (GIS) software libraries (e.g. ESRI's ArcGIS), which provide ABM toolkits with greater data management and spatial analytical capabilities required for geospatial modelling.

In a spatial ABM:

- Agents may be mobile, it is however important that each agent has a different relationship with the spatial environment, most simply in terms of a location in the environment. If all agents have the same spatial relationship with the environment (if, for example, every agent sees and responds to an aggregate 'average' of the environment), then it makes little sense to formulate the model as an agent model;
- Agents may change their spatial relationship with the environment over time, which may be by moving, or it may be by alteration, acquisition or disposal of locations; and
- Agents are able to evaluate spatial configurations. This ability may be as simple as determining that the availability of some resource at the current location is sufficient for some purpose, or is greater than at neighbouring locations. Alternatively, it may involve a complicated evaluation of the spatial distribution of resources with respect to the current location, relative to a number of alternative locations.

This framework for thinking about agents in a spatial ABM, may be illuminated by considering the example (see also Figure 3) of pedestrians or other mobile agents in a model of an urban streetscape.

The primary choice made by such agents is to determine, with respect to their intended destinations, which - among the possible next locations - they should move to. In most models of this kind, the location of other agents is an important element in the choice, but the decision will also be affected by the agents' local physical environments (e.g. building geometries, road capacity). Decisions are usually made by agents over some timeframe of interest, which may in turn imply a relevant spatial grain. In the pedestrian model this timeframe might be minute-by-minute, as pedestrians adjust their course to avoid obstacles (including other agents). In this specific example, each pedestrian agent is a significant element in the local environment of many other agents, and decisions made by one agent immediately alter the local decision-making environment of nearby agents. Generally, mobile agents (whether human or some other animal) will be making decisions at time scales dictated by their mobility on the one hand and their perception of the nature of the spatial distribution of resources on the other. The decision-making timeframe combined with the speed of movement of the agents then effectively frames a sensible spatial grain for a model of this type.

Decision making is the engine of many ABMs, particularly those involving human actors, and in turn it has many ties to complexity. It has long been a core concern of many fields, including geography, economics, management, and psychology. ABMs have helped draw out the similarities and differences among different decision-making theories by emphasizing the importance of developing basic rules for agents to follow, leading to research focused on how such rules embody their decision-making strategies.

Figure 3. Schematic illustration of possible choices facing agents in different types of models

Agents in an ABM usually pursue certain goals set by the modeller with given resources and constraints. For example, commuters want to minimize their commuting time. The ability of ABMs to describe the behaviour and interactions of a system allows for system dynamics to be directly incorporated into the model. This represents a movement away from the static nature of earlier styles of urban and regional modelling.

An ABM requires many simulations to evaluate any particular situation as it is based upon an underlying stochastic model. Randomness is applied to many involved processes; accordingly, two model runs will not result in exactly the same result. It is also worth noting that the resulting model is often one where a full explanation of the model behaviour calls for a chronological interpretation of the events in the model. Describing and understanding the model specific agent-agent interactions will matter, and a detailed account of the model "history" may be necessary for a complete understanding of any particular model run. The difference from the real world target system we seek to understand, is that a model allows repeated runs and enables a probabilistic or general account of the system behaviours and tendencies to be developed.

Overall, ABM simulations should be viewed as a research tool capable of providing insight into the real system and identifying what needs to be understood about the real system in order to develop a theory of the system itself (Bankes, 2002). When agents' preferences and (spatial) situations differ widely, and when agents' decisions substantially alter the decision-making contexts for other agents, then this is most probably a good case for exploring the usefulness of an ABM approach. This argument focuses attention on three model features: (a) heterogeneity of the decision-making context of agents, (b) the importance of interaction effects, and (c) the overall size and organization of the system. All these criteria favouring the adoption of ABM, call for considerable prior knowledge and insight about system characteristics on the part of those developing models.

A major objective of exposome is to integrate existing datasets and to fill data gaps in order to unravel the external exposome of individuals and population subgroups to multiple stressors via different pathways. Towards this aim, as already mentioned in previous sections, an extensive data collection / data mining scheme is being employed. Using data fusion techniques, traditional health and exposure data derived from fixed monitoring networks are being supplemented by a range of emerging techniques and technologies such as mobile phone apps, environmental sensor-webs, micro-sensors, satellite remote sensing and ABM. In this case, the use of ABM enables us to better understand the behaviour of individuals and populations in social and evolutionary settings, and to 'fill-in' the gaps in the exposome currently not available from real-world monitoring and sensor data.

Innovations in sensor technology create possibilities to collect environmental data at unprecedented depth and breadth. With the advent of GIS, GPS to track individuals, and personal environmental monitoring, undertaking such analyses throughout an individual's routine, or even lifetime, is now possible. Finding the right balance between limited amounts of high quality data from standardized environmental monitoring campaigns and large amounts of moderate quality data by sensor networks can transform the way we understand and interact with our environment. Due to the substantial technical and ethical hurdles involved in collecting real individual space-time movement data for whole populations, a decision has been made to simulate movement and interaction behaviour using ABM, informed by sensor technologies. Measuring personal exposure directly requires a large number of people and therefore is often not feasible due to time and financial constraints, thus in exposome studies such as HEALS, we take advantage of ABM to allow us to extrapolate the sample data from selected cities, to the larger populations of these regions.

There are at least three challenges in the efforts to model human behaviour in agent based systems: (a) understanding humans, (b) data, and (c) validation and verification. Research communities develop data on how people behave under certain circumstances and this is replacing the poor default of assuming that human behaviour is random and unknowable. In the HEALS case, observations and distributions derived from the WP9 sensors campaign are transformed into coding lines that define and shape the agents world. Moreover data on lifestyle/behaviour patterns (e.g.: timetables for various activities per gender and age group) and SES data (e.g.: information on educational level, income, occupational status) derived from EU scale or regional studies and surveys are also implemented in a human agents population. Survey outputs are associated with human agent behavioural rules, with the aim to model representative to real world conditions.

Particular emphasis is given in the case of in-model incorporation of SES data. SES variables can explain differences in external exposure because of different prevalence of specific preferences and decision-making (behaviours) in some groups, e.g. differences in diet between SES groups. Different human agents based on different age, sex or income will follow different rules, will express different behaviours (for example they will choose different means of transportation to reach their destination, they will purchase different consumer products, follow different diet patterns) and this would lead to a different exposure profile. Moreover, knowledge of human agent characteristics by other human agents provide a signal that acts to enable or prevent interaction from occurring.

Towards this aim, the GAMA agent-based simulation platform (Grignard et al., 2013) can be used. This platform offers a complete modelling and simulation development environment for building spatially explicit multi-agent simulations. GAMA provides a rich modelling language based on Java, GAML, which allows to define complex models integrating at the same time, entities of different scales and geographical vector data. It provides a true geometry to all situated agents. This geometry, which is based on vector representation, can be simple (point, polyline or polygon) or complex (composed of several sub-geometries). The agents' geometry can be defined by the modeller (a list of points) or directly loaded from a shapefile. In the context of simulation, the advantage of geographical data agentification is to give the possibility to manage geographical objects (buildings, roads) exactly like other agents (people) in the simulation: you can give them an internal state and a behaviour. It is possible to initialize the virtual work to a present arrangement and then let the model run and observe its behaviour. Agent states of various sub-populations can be measured and aggregated across many simulation runs at each point in time in the simulation.

The developed ABM model is being informed by data related to:

1. An individual's behaviour within his/her environment (such as movement data within specific micro-environments, food consumption, use of consumer products, etc.), derived by WP9 campaigns data that were then analysed and extrapolated to a representative population
2. The interaction between individuals, exploring associated behaviours based on literature, and
3. Risk determinants, such as socio-economic status (SES) data. Using existing national population censuses and surveys, we apply geospatial analysis methods to distribute estimates across all sectors of society at a local neighbourhood scale.

Using these parameters and taking into account the evolution of agents, our simulations can produce detailed information relating to the emulated system, producing data that can be used to fill in the gaps that exist in traditional datasets.

Figure 4. Human agents' behaviour impact on their personal exposure

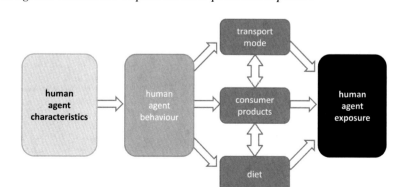

By importing a series of GIS files in the GAMA platform, we are able to project a city's map with its road and buildings network as well as information on land use. Every entity taking part in this system is agentified, it is therefore considered as an individual agent (the system is composed of road, building, vehicle and human agents).

Road and building shapefiles of a building block resolution are imported in GAMA containing spatial information such as the capacity of a street and land use characteristics respectively. Tables with population data with information on sex, gender coming from surveys and censuses are transformed into moving human agents inside the ABM platform. Moreover, national or regional studies usually provide SES information such as occupational status, educational level and ethnicity per postal code (e.g. education level per postal code). In cases where this kind of data is available, human agents will acquire these characteristics, following a distribution among the population of the smaller region for which specific information exists.

When the model is initialized, human agents are clustered in age groups, depending on their age and are randomly allocated to a residential place which will serve as their house for the whole simulation. Human agents' characteristics provide capabilities or constraints on the agents' behavioural rules (the reference point could be, for example, age or income that influence their preferences and decision-making). Based on their age and SES characteristics, and of course based on the distance between point of departure and their targeted destination, human agents will choose different means of transportation. In the same way different human agents will follow a different sequence and types of activities. For example, children and adults are programmed to move from a household to an assigned school or office whereas human agents that belong to the elderly will follow a different sequence of activities.

At the end of a run (a single run corresponds to a typical day), human agents' trajectories, derived by the coded routine, are captured as points (1 point captured per simulation step) and are exported as a GIS shapefile together with a database that contains their coordinates and activities in time through different locations/microenvironments.

The ABM exported GIS layer containing human agents' trajectories can then be superposed onto high spatial resolution urban air quality modelled maps (for the same region) of hourly concentration of

Figure 5. ABM model overview

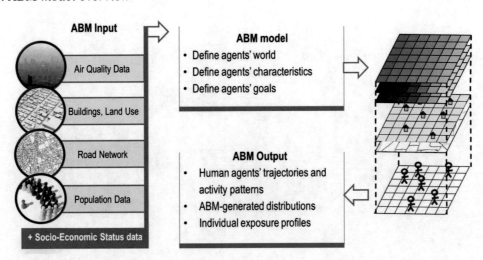

pollutants (such as PM10, PM2.5, NOx). Personal exposure, expressed as inhalation-adjusted exposure to air pollutants can then be evaluated by assigning pollutant concentrations to a human agent based on his/her coordinates, activities and the corresponding inhalation rate.

Such a model can be useful for assessing exposure of specific vulnerable subgroups, such as children, the elderly and people with low socioeconomic status, taking into account their different activity patterns, consumer behaviours and other lifestyles.

Assimilation of Exposure Measurements and Human Biomonitoring Data

Physiology Based Biokinetic Modelling

PBBK models are continuously gaining ground in regulatory toxicology, describing in quantitative terms the absorption, metabolism, distribution and elimination processes in the human body, with a focus on the effective dose at the expected target site (Bois, Jamei, & Clewell, 2010). This trend is further amplified by the continuously increasing scientific and regulatory interest about aggregate and cumulative exposure; PBBK models translate external exposures from multiple routes (Yang, Xu, & Georgopoulos, 2010) into internal exposure metrics, addressing the effects of exposure route in the overall bioavailability (Sarigiannis & Karakitsios, 2011; Valcke & Krishnan, 2011) or the dependence on critical developmental windows of susceptibility, such as pregnancy (Beaudouin, Micallef, & Brochot, 2010), lactation (Verner, Charbonneau, Lopez-Carrillo, & Haddad, 2008) and infancy (Edginton & Ritter, 2009). With regard to cumulative exposure, PBBK models offer the advantage of calculating the effect of the interactions among the mixture compounds at the level of metabolism, however due to the inherent difficulties arising, the existing applications are currently limited mainly to VOCs (Haddad, Charest-Tardif, & Krishnan, 2000; Sarigiannis & Gotti, 2008) and metals (Sasso, Isukapalli, & Georgopoulos, 2010). Recently, efforts have shifted towards the integration of whole-body physiology, disease biology, and molecular reaction networks (Eissing et al., 2011), as well as integration of cellular metabolism into multi-scale whole-body models (Krauss et al., 2012).

Figure 6. Right: ABM model running over a neighbourhood with building, roads and moving people being agentified. Left: At the end of the ABM run, trajectories of specific human agents over the period of a typical day (together with information on their activities over this period of time) can be exported.

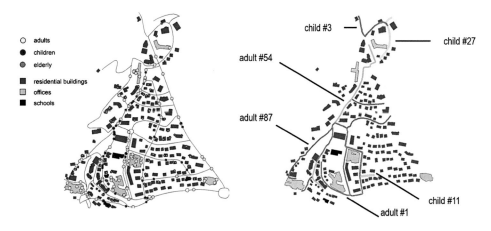

The use of internal dose modelling aims at integrating exposure data and modelling output with human biomonitoring data. Its goals are to (a) provide the time history of the exposure profile, focusing on susceptible developmental stages; (b) assimilate the biomonitoring data related to the cohorts to estimate the individual exposome in quantitative terms; and (c) derive reliable biologically effective dose values for the compounds of interest so that they can be associated to observed health outcomes. The key component of the above is the development of a lifetime (including gestation and breastfeeding) generic PBBK model (Sarigiannis & Karakitsios, 2012) incorporating mixtures interaction (Sarigiannis & Gotti, 2008) and a framework for biomonitoring data assimilation (Georgopoulos et al., 2009). Aiming to expand the applicability of the generic PBBK model to cover the chemical space as much as possible, parameterization of the model for known and new chemicals with limited information is done through the development of QSAR models. The generic PBBK model will also be used to reconstruct exposure from human biomonitoring data (Andra, Charisiadis, Karakitsios, Sarigiannis, & Makris, 2015). A tiered approach will be followed as a function of data availability (periodicity and size of sampling, specimen type) and requirements of the exposure reconstruction analysis (temporal analysis of exposure, contribution from different routes), ranging from Exposure Conversion Factors (Tan et al., 2006), up to Markov Chain Monte Carlo analysis. Inputs involve spatial and temporal information on micro-environmental media concentrations of xenobiotics and corresponding information on human activities, food intake patterns or consumer product use that results in intakes; outputs are the observed biomarkers; and the error metric can be defined in terms of population variation (the latter has to be lower than the intra-individual variation, which may be associated with measurement or other random error source). On the individual level, PBBK will be combined with multimedia models and survey questionnaires to identify exposure sources. PBBK modelling will also be used to estimate the internal doses of xenobiotics that exceed levels associated with biological pathway alterations (Judson et al., 2011) and, eventually, health risk. The latter can involve the use of specific omics results (e.g., metabolomics analysis) and associations of biologically effective doses to early biological responses. In addition, biologically effective doses would be used to quantify the effect of compound-induced extracellular perturbations on metabolic states, so as to directly couple the PBBK model with metabolic regulatory networks. Direct coupling defines a feedback loop that connects clearance and metabolite production rates to metabolism regulation (Eissing et al., 2011) via dynamic flux balance analysis (Krauss et al., 2012). Considering the opportunities offered by the use of PBBK models in exposure/risk characterization, several research groups are developing generic PBBK models, either as stand-alone models such as PK-Sim (Willmann et al., 2003) and Indus-Chem (Jongeneelen & Berge, 2011), or incorporated within integrated computational platforms for exposure assessment such as INTERA (Sarigiannis, Gotti, & Karakitsios, 2011) and MENTOR (Georgopoulos et al., 2008). The development of generic PBBK models is substantiated by the recent advances in quantitative structure–activity relationships (QSARs) and quantitative structure–property relationships (QSPRs) (Peyret & Krishnan, 2011; Price & Krishnan, 2011), providing the basis for development of relevant PBBK models for data-poor or new chemicals. The INTEGRA methodology (Sarigiannis et al., 2016) is advancing the existing state of the art by integrating all of the above elements, with a generic lifetime including pregnancy (Sarigiannis & Karakitsios, 2012) multi-route PBBK model. The integration of this generic PBBK model into a wider modelling framework allows forward (internal exposure) or reverse calculations (exposure reconstruction) so as to provide the link among exposure components and biomonitoring data.

Internal Dosimetry Models

PBBK models are tools that describe the mechanisms of absorption, distribution, metabolism and elimination of chemicals in the body resulting from acute and/or chronic exposure regimes. They are independent structural models, comprising the tissues and organs of the body with each perfused by, and connected via, the blood circulatory system. In PBBK models the organism is frequently represented as a network of tissue compartments (e.g., liver, fat, slowly perfused tissues, and richly perfused tissues) interconnected by systemic circulation. A generic PBBK model, reflects the incorporation of basic physiology and anatomy. The compartments actually correspond to anatomic entities such as liver, lung, etc., and the blood circulation conforms to the basic mammalian physiology. The primary means of transport for xenobiotic chemicals that enter the body through one or more of these routes is via blood, the main vehicle for nutrient supply and waste removal from tissues. In the basic PBPK model, transport of chemicals between blood and tissues is assumed to be flow-limited, which implies that the transport barriers between the free molecules of chemical in blood and tissue are negligible, and equilibration between free and bound fractions in blood and tissue is rapid. Concentrations of chemical in venous blood exiting a tissue, and tissue concentrations are assumed to be at equilibrium, and the tissue is assumed to be homogeneous with respect to the concentration of the chemical. The flow-limited assumption is usually appropriate for lipophilic or low molecular weight compounds, which easily partition or diffuse through cell membranes. Every PBBK model requires several parameters that are critical determinants of chemical uptake and disposition. These determinants can be classified into three main categories, namely, anatomical/physiological, physicochemical, and biochemical. A partial list of anatomical/physiological parameters includes cardiac output, tissue blood flow rate, organ and tissue weight and volumes. In addition to physiological/anatomical data, PBBK models require information on the ability of the body to metabolize chemicals – these are known as biochemical parameters. Typical biochemical parameters include the maximal velocity for metabolism (V_{max}), binding association constant (Kb) and Michaelis affinity constant (K_m). The third type of data required by these models is the solubility of pollutants in the organs and tissues of the body. These are physicochemical data known as partition coefficients (P). Partition coefficients are experimentally determined parameters that give an indication of the distribution of a chemical between two different phases, e.g. air and blood, blood and liver, blood and muscle, blood and fat, etc. The fundamentals of PBBK modelling are to identify the principal organs or tissues involved in the disposition of the chemical of interest and to correlate the chemical absorption, distribution, metabolism, and excretion within and among these organs and tissues in an integrated and biologically plausible manner.

A scheme is usually formed where the normal physiology is followed in a graphical manner. Within the boundary of the identified compartment (e.g., an organ or tissue or a group of organs or tissues), whatever inflows must be accounted for via whatever outflows or whatever is transformed into something else. This mass balance is expressed as a mathematical equation with appropriate parameters carrying biological significance. A generic equation, for any tissue or organ, is:

$$V_i \frac{dC_{ij}}{dt} = Q_i \left(CA_j - CV_{ij} \right) - Metab_{ij} - Elim_{ij} + Absorp_{ij} - PrBinding_{ij}$$

where V_i represents the volume of tissue group i, Q_i is the blood flow rate to tissue group i, CA_j is the concentration of chemical j in arterial blood, and C_{ij} and CV_{ij} are the concentrations of chemical j in tissue group i and in the effluent venous blood from tissue i, respectively. $Metab_{ij}$ is the rate of metabolism for chemical j in tissue group i; liver, is the principal organ for metabolism and, with some exceptions, $Metab_{ij}$ is usually equal to zero in other tissue groups. $Elim_{ij}$ represents the rate of elimination from tissue group i (e.g., biliary excretion from the liver), $Absorp_{ij}$ represents uptake of the chemical from dosing (e.g., oral dosing), and $PrBinding_{ij}$ represents protein binding of the chemical in the tissue. All these terms are zero unless there is definitive knowledge that the particular organ and tissue of interest has such processes.

A series of similar mass balance differential equations representing all of the interlinked compartments are formulated to express a mathematical representation, or model, of the biological system. This model can then be used for computer simulation to predict the time course behavior of any given parameter in the model.

The generic model developed in INTEGRA is designed to describe as closely as possible the actual absorption, distribution, metabolism and elimination processes occurring in the human body, so that it can be easily applicable for a broad variety of chemicals assuming proper parameterization. The model includes the parent compounds and at least three potential metabolites for each of the compounds in the mixture. For each compound/metabolite all major organs are included and the link among the com-

Figure 7. Conceptual representation of the mother-fetus PBBK model

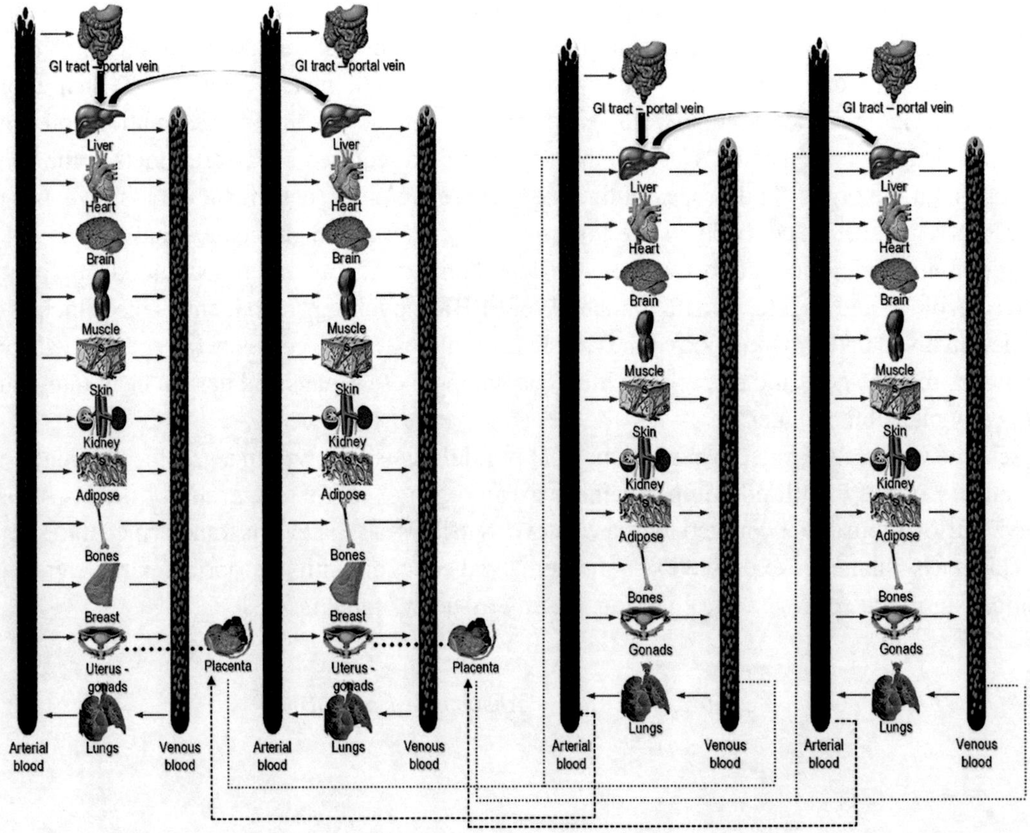

pounds and the metabolites is through the metabolizing tissues. This is mainly the liver, but also other sites of metabolism (e.g., gut, skin) might be considered based on the presence of the enzymes involved in the metabolism of the compound of interest. To capture in utero exposure, the model is replicated to describe the functional interaction of the mother and the developing fetus through the placenta (Figure 7). The anthropometric parameters of both the mother and the fetus models are age-dependent, so as to provide a life stage-dependent internal dose assessment.

Expanding the Chemical Space to Assess Internal Dose for Multiple Chemicals

A critical limiting factor in describing ADME processes accurately for a large chemical space is the proper parameterization of PBBK models for "data poor" compounds. Advanced Quantitative Structure-Activity Relationships (QSARs) can be used to predict input parameters for these models allowing PBBK models to cover a large number, and several classes, of chemicals. In silico approaches, including QSARs, are widely used for the estimation of physicochemical and biochemical properties and predicting how they might lead to biological responses (Puzyn, Leszczynski, & Cronin, 2010). QSARs are described as regression or classification models, which form a relationship between the biological effects and chemistry of each chemical compound (Puzyn et al., 2010). Significant progress in expanding the chemical space for industrial chemicals has been made by the INTEGRA project, where parameterization of essential parameters such as blood:tissue partition coefficients for several tissues, maximum initial velocity of the enzyme catalysed reaction (V_{max}) and the substrate concentration that gives half maximal velocity of an enzymatic reaction (K_m or Michaelis-Menden constant) has been carried out for a large number of chemicals. The mathematical formulation coupled Abraham's solvation equation with Artificial Neural Networks of variable geometry in order to optimize the performance of the model. Abraham's solvation equation (Linear Free Energy Relationship) describes the process of the transfer of chemicals from the liquid phase to a large number of solvents or other condensed phases, including biophases. The descriptors, which characterize these physicochemical and biochemical phenomena, are combined into the following equation:

$$\log SP = c + e \cdot E + s \cdot S + a \cdot A + b \cdot B + v \cdot V$$

where *SP* is a biological property for a set of chemicals in a given system. The independent descriptors are the properties of the examined chemicals, *E* is the excess molar refractivity of the chemical, *S* is the chemical's dipolarity/polarizability, *A* and *B* are the chemical's effective or summation hydrogen bond acidity and basicity, respectively, and *V* is the McGowan characteristic volume of the chemical (Abraham, 1993; Payne & Kenny, 2002). The coefficients *c*, *e*, *s*, *a*, *b* and *v* reflect the properties of chemicals, so *e* corresponds to the tendency of the chemical to interact with solute π- and n- electrons, *s* corresponds to the chemical's dipolarity/polarizability, *a* and *b* correspond to the chemical's hydrogen bond basicity and acidity, respectively, and *v* is a measure of the chemical's lipophilicity. Artificial Neural Networks were used to develop a non-linear model based on Abraham's solvation equation.

The calculated values of metabolic constants using the statistical method described above (Abraham's solvation equation coupled with Artificial Neural Networks) were compared to experimental values and the results obtained by Price and Krishnan (2011) in Figure 8. The methodology followed by Price and Krishnan (2011) was based on the group contribution method, implying that each fragment

Figure 8. Predicted vs. experimental values of normalized maximal velocity and Michaelis – Menten constant under Abraham's equation (orange dots) and a group contribution method (literature data; blue dots)

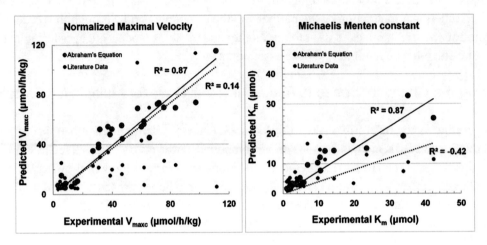

in the molecular structure contributes to the metabolic parameters, depending on its frequency of occurrence in the given molecule (Gao, Goind, & Tabak, 1992). In previous studies, the parameters used to describe the interactions between chemicals and tissues were mainly related to chemical structure or tissue composition in water, proteins and lipids (Price & Krishnan, 2011; Zhang, 2004). In the present example, Abraham's equation descriptors are not linked directly with tissue composition. They encode specific chemical information regarding the size, polarizability and hydrogen bonding of the examined chemicals and each term can reveal the factors that influence a particular interaction. The modelling results indicate that the molecular descriptors of the equation can be suitable for the estimation of the parameters that characterize relevant physicochemical and biochemical phenomena. The improved performance of Abraham's equation compared to the group contribution method can be attributed to its capacity to represent the complex interactions of the micro-processes of chemicals' distribution and metabolism into several tissues.

Overview of Biomonitoring

The main achievement of human biomonitoring is that it provides an integrated overview of the pollutant load to which an individual is exposed, and hence serves as an excellent approximation of aggregate exposure including all pathways, mechanisms and routes of exposure. The internal dose of a chemical, following aggregate exposure has a much greater value for environmental health impact assessment as the internal body concentration is much more relevant to the impact on human health than mere exposure data. However, it needs to be stressed that HBM in itself cannot replace environmental monitoring and modelling data. At the same time, mathematical approaches to describe the pharmacokinetic and toxicokinetic behavior of environmental agents – (PBBK models) offer a more mechanistic insight into the behavior and fate of environmental agents following exposure. As biomarker data also reflect individual ADME characteristics of chemicals, HBM data offer an excellent opportunity to validate PBBK models.

Ultimately, coupling both lines of evidence to assess exposure proves to be the optimal solution towards relating complex exposure to environmental stressors to potential adverse health effects assessment.

There are three approaches for linking biomonitoring data to health outcomes: direct comparison to toxicity values, forward dosimetry, and reverse dosimetry. Biomonitoring data can be directly compared to toxicity values when the relationship of the biomarker to the health effect of concern has been characterized in the human. In forward dosimetry, pharmacokinetic data in the experimental animal can be used to support a direct comparison of internal exposure in humans derived through the application of PBBK models, providing an estimate of the Margin of Safety in humans. It is possible to determine the relationship between biomarker concentration and effects observed in animal studies. An evolution of this concept is the biomonitoring equivalents. Alternatively, reverse dosimetry can be performed to estimate the external exposure that is consistent with the measured biomonitoring data through the backward application of PBBK models. In a more elaborate scheme, the reconstructed exposure, could be used to run the PBBK model in forward mode, so as to estimate the biologically effective dose at the target tissue.

Exposure Reconstruction in Practice

Human biomonitoring typically is an integrative measure of different exposure episodes along various routes and over different time scales; thus, it is often difficult to reconstruct the primary exposure routes from human biomonitoring data alone. This uncertainty limits the interpretative value of biomarker data. However, several mathematical approaches have been developed to reconstruct exposures related to population biomonitoring studies, and can be subdivided into a number of different approaches. Exposure reconstruction techniques combined with PBBK models can be divided into Bayesian and non-Bayesian approaches (Georgopoulos et al., 2009). Moreover, computational inversion techniques (and exposure reconstruction techniques as well), can be classified as deterministic or stochastic (Moles, Mendes, & Banga, 2003) based on the identification of a global minimum of the error metric, the input parameters and the model setup.

The deterministic methods aim to achieve convergence on a global minimum. The problem is solved using an "objective function" based on biomarkers. Additionally, constraints in the form of bounds, equalities and inequalities are incorporated. Deterministic models have been used in several biological applications using different methods. Muzic Jr and Christian (2006) have applied a regression technique to estimate pharmacokinetic parameters. A gradient method has been used by Isukapalli et al. (2000) to calculate the uncertainty in PBBK models. A maximum likelihood method has been carried out for short- and long-term exposure reconstruction using a PBBK model for chloroform (Roy, Weisel, Gallo, & Georgopoulos, 1996).

In contrast, stochastic methods aim to provide a reasonable solution, not a mathematically optimal one. A probabilistic framework for the inverse computation problem is the Bayesian approach, which is based on Bayes' theorem. According to the methodology developed in the frame of the INTEGRA project, the analysis of exposure reconstruction problems based on the Markov Chain Monte Carlo and Differential Evolution Markov Chain technique is realized according to the following steps:

1. The process starts from exposure related data which are fed into the INTEGRA exposure model;
2. This in turn provides input to the PBBK model, taking into account the duration and the magnitude of exposure from all exposure routes (inhalation, skin and oral route);

Figure 9. Exposure reconstruction flowchart

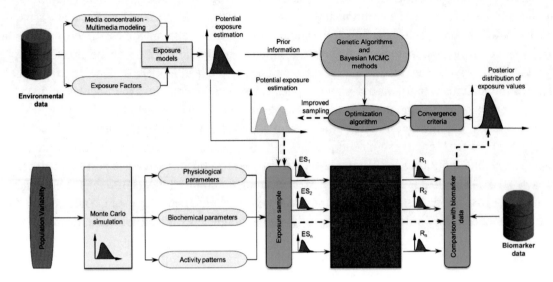

3.   The result of the PBBK model simulation (also taking into account the distribution of PBBK parameters, e.g., inter-individual variability in clearance), is then evaluated against the human biomonitoring data distributions. Based on the outcome of the comparison, the optimization algorithm changes the exposure model input parameters after each iteration, so as to achieve convergence to biomonitoring data;

4.   More detailed information on exposure parameters reduces uncertainty in back-calculating doses from biomarker information, resulting in faster and more efficient convergence;

5.   Several iterations are repeated, until the error between the predicted and the actual biomonitored data is minimized.

The Bayesian Markov Chain Monte Carlo technique described above simulates and calculates the investigated exposure conditions. The sampling scheme is set appropriately according to the problem and to the available data for the proposed function. The flowchart of the overall process is shown in Figure 9.

FUTURE RESEARCH DIRECTIONS

Dynamic External Exposure Assessment

Informatics and data analytics provide unique opportunities in supporting exposome-based discovery, mainly through refining individualized exposure assessment. One of the key aims of exposome deployment is the better integration and interpretation of the vast amount of data provided by personal sensors, towards the development of real-life data for informing agent based models. This will allow the in depth understanding of the effect of sociodemographic factors on individual time-space lines, that will determine societal and consumer behavior. This will allow the simultaneous estimation of (a) how the individual affects the quality of the living environment and (b) estimate the individual exposure in the given environment

This type of approach was explored in the frame of the largest exposome project in EU (project HEALS). For the needs of the study, a multi-layer perceptron network was utilized, which is a feed-forward artificial neural network model that maps sets of input data onto a set of appropriate output. It is a modification of the standard linear perceptron in that it uses three or more layers of neurons (nodes) with nonlinear activation functions, and is more powerful than the perceptron in that it can distinguish data that is not linearly separable, or separable by a hyperplane. Location, motion and intensity of activity data were used as input to an ANN model, aiming at deriving a time-location model based *solely* on sensor data. The independent variables that were fed to the ANN input layer consisted of a) the differential of personal temperature, dT/dt, derived from the wearable temperature sensor, b) the observed outdoor temperature, T_{out}, derived from a central meteorological station of Athens and Thessaloniki respectively, c) the ratio T/T_{out}, d) the rate of change of personal sensor temperature dT/dt and e) personal speed, derived from the GPS devices wore by the participants. Moreover, information on day light was also included as an input variable, transformed into a categorical element (day *or* night).

MATLAB scripts were used in order to combine data from all different sensors which were then merged into a single database with a time step of one minute. The training set was based on data collected during the first four consecutive days of the week (Monday to Thursday) as well as data from day 6 (Saturday) so that different patterns that usually occur on a weekend day are also captured. The data used for training were further divided into an internal training and testing set (85% and 15% of the total record entries, respectively) and the models developed were tested against the independent validation set. Following the same approach, the validation set was based on data from the fifth day of the week (Friday) as well as day 7 (Sunday). The performance of the proposed methodology was evaluated using various training algorithms on different network architectures, such as Bayesian regularization (Dan Foresee & Hagan, 1997), Resilient Backpropagation (Riedmiller & Braun, 1993), Scaled Conjugate Gradient (Møller, 1993), as well as the Broyden, Fletcher, Goldfarb and Shanno (Dennis & Schnabel, 1996) and the Levenberg-Marquardt (Hagan & Menhaj, 1994) algorithms. Different unit numbers in the hidden layer were tested, using 1 or 2 hidden layers with 6 up to 30 hidden neurons. From the obtained results, it was found that Bayesian regularization is constantly among the best results while the use of 1 hidden layer with 13 neurons can model successfully the problem under study. Thus, the proposed ANN model uses three layers as shown in Fig. 2. The first (input) layer consists of 6 neurons, one for each input parameter. The second (hidden) layer consists of 13 neurons that implement the hyperbolic tangent sigmoid transfer function. Finally, the third (output) layer consists of three categorical outputs that correspond to one of the predicted location. Network training was performed using the Bayesian regularisation algorithm. A detailed analysis of the equations constructing the ANN model is described elsewhere (Sarigiannis et al., 2009). Networks were evaluated using Root Mean Square Error (RMSE), Mean Square Error (MSE), R^2 and via cross validation using the following metrics: accuracy, sensitivity, specificity and cross entropy.

Among the several networks tested, the highest performance was achieved by a MLP 7-13-3 network. A visual comparison between the real location data and the ANN predicted ones is showcased in Figure 10. The results illustrate that the ANN performs very well in predicting the various locations, especially the indoor ones. The latter represent the vast majority of entries in the training set, since most of the time of the daily activity is spent in indoor locations. The identification of outdoor locations is not so efficient, since many of these entries are not differentiated from the in-transit mode.

The prediction accuracy for the various locations (for both Athens and Thessaloniki) is demonstrated in Table 1, while the cross-validation metrics are presented in Table 2.

Figure 10. Showcase of the location prediction of a week day of a typical individual in Athens and Thessaloniki respectively

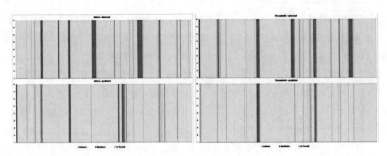

Table 1. Accuracy of location prediction using the ANN in Athens and Thessaloniki

	Overall Accuracy	**Outdoors**	**Indoors**	**In Transit**
Athens	83.7%	15.0%	94.7%	49.8%
Thessaloniki	87.6%	27.4%	98.4%	45.7%

Table 2. Cross validation metrics (accuracy, sensitivity, specificity and cross entropy)

	Overall Accuracy	**Sensitivity %**	**Specificity %**	**Accuracy %**	**Cross-Entropy**
Athens	83.7%	97.2	76.7	95.1	0.1
Thessaloniki	87.6%	97.9	77.4	95.9	0.1

With regard to ABM, the city of Thessaloniki has been chosen as case study to test the aforementioned methodology. In Thessaloniki, SES details are only provided at municipality level (an area with a population ranging from 6000 to 360,000). On average each designated area in the ABM had a population of 1000. This is a useful analysis because population data available to us for other cities may be at different resolutions so the two examples provide an insight to what is possible with the data we may be able to access for other cities. The conceptual model to account for SES in exposure modelling forms a suitable methodology for what we want to achieve in exposome studies such as HEALS and can be applied to real city examples. Thus, the method is easy to implement even in other settings beyond the one tested herein. An example of the input for the model can be understood easily if we look at means of transportation. In this case, the overall population would originally be distributed to use a certain transport mode; for example, 60% will use the car, 25% will walk, 10% cycle, and 5% will use public transport.

However, this will change with each agent depending on sociodemographic characteristics and distance to their destination and infrastructure. This leads to many 'rules' which are applied and thus alter the distribution; so if for example, an agent is male, employed, and belongs to a high income group, the agent will have a higher probability of using the car to travel to work and be in the car for longer, than a woman, who is a homemaker, with children. The output provides us with information regarding the distribution of transport mode choice throughout the day and we can focus on certain time windows within a day for more detail. This is an example where we can achieve a deeper and more precise un-

Figure 11. GIS layers: exposure assessment using Agent Based Modelling in Thessaloniki

derstanding of the underlying phenomena and how they affect overall human exposure. ABM-generated distributions can also work as input for probabilistic exposure assessment modelling.

Biokinetics and Biomonitoring Data Assimilation

Integration of biokinetics in exposure assessment is the missing link for translating exposure and environmental dynamics into biologically effective dose that will eventually result in biological perturbations. Thus, methods that will allow the applicability of internal dosimetry for a larger number of compounds such as QSARs, deserve increased scientific interest. Further development and validation of generic PBBK models is a sine qua non for widespread industrial and regulatory use of advanced biokinetics in health risk management when it comes to industrial and environmental chemicals and pharmaceuticals. In addition, considering the continuously growing body of biomonitoring data, exposure reconstruction algorithms able to quantify more accurately previous exposure regimes will be of major importance. A comprehensive example of exposure reconstruction, is given below regarding the estimation of triclosan exposure levels during teeth brushing. Seven volunteers logged in a time-activity diary the time of teeth brushing and the amount of toothpaste used, while all-day urinary voids were collected and analyzed.

Based on the urinary concentrations of triclosan and knowing the timing that exposure events occurred, the amount of triclosan taken in per each individual brushing event was successfully estimated. The results of the simulation for a typical individual are illustrated in Figure 12. Starting from the measured urinary triclosan (black dots) and knowing the time in the day the individual was exposed to triclosan, the dose received with each brushing was estimated (green dots). The accurate prediction of the dose is shown by the very good fit of the measured urinary concentrations against the ones predicted by the model. This further allows us to estimate the actual internal dose, i.e. the concentration of triclosan in blood (red line) and eventually to potential target tissues.

Figure 12. Measured (black dots) and modelled (grey line) urinary triclosan levels, modelled levels in blood (red line) and predicted dose

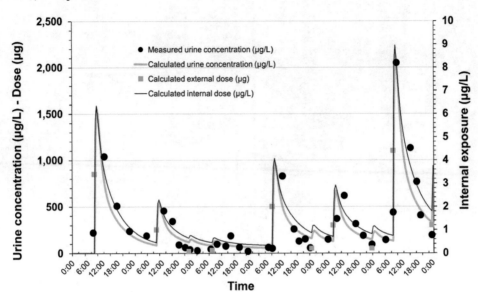

CONCLUSION

The exposome represents the totality of exposure during lifespan, aiming at providing more accurate and comprehensive exposure estimates, towards a better understanding of the respective biological responses that will eventually end up into clinical phenotypes. Major challenges regarding the unravelling of the exposome comprise the following:

- The totality of exposures relates to combined exposure to multiple compounds, thus methods that will allow the realistic estimation (modelled or measured) of personal exposure or media contamination to multiple compounds play a key role in deciphering the human exposome.
- The accurate assessment of contamination of the media that people come into contact; these include outdoor and indoor air, drinking water, food items, soil and settled dust. In addition, consumer product affect human exposome either directly (e.g. clothes and personal care product), or indirectly (e.g. cleaning products and indoor air).
- The accurate assessment of the time people come into contact with the various media (e.g. time spent driving) and the exposure conditions (e.g. intensity of activity). Sensor technologies and the algorithms for interpreting the big data collected by these sensors, are expected to provide the missing pieces for complementing individual exposome.
- Although the exposome is oriented towards assessing individual exposure, accurate extrapolation to population groups is equally important for large population studies; the extrapolation process should not be based only on probabilistic techniques, but also on the dynamic interactions among the members of the study population capturing individual behaviours, affecting both space-time trajectories and consumer choice. As a result, sociodemographic parameters should be explicitly

addressed. In addition, the effect of this behaviour on the environmental quality itself is something that has to be accounted for.

- Another key component of the exposome is the internal exposome. People that are exposed to similar levels of environmental exposure, might be internally exposed to completely different levels to toxicants, as a result of genetic factors, differentiated dietary patterns and health status (e.g. pre-existing disease hampering or modulating the metabolism of xenobiotics). In addition, internal dosimetry, allows the proper integration of uptake from different routes and within variant exposure regimes.

- In addition to the above, the use of biomonitoring data for understanding human exposure bears major advantages compared to bottom up approaches. However, this requires a proper computational framework and a valid biokinetics modelling platform that can cover a large part of the currently existing chemical space. The exposure reconstruction algorithm presented herein, provides unique opportunities for human biomonitoring data assimilation and it is expected to be extensively used in the European Human Biomonitoring Initiative (HBM4EU, 2017-2021). The development of such computationally and biostatistically advanced tools may overhaul the current practice in the use of human biomonitoring (HBM) data for chemical risk assessment. To date, HBM data are used readily as direct proxies of human exposure. This, however, is a gross approximation that does not support the more stringent requirements of internal exposome analysis. In that context, we need to properly translate HBM data into actual external exposure profiles for the study population, expressed in terms of patterns of dose and time profile of delivery.

- Considering the need for better internal dosimetry metrics and biomonitoring data assimilation of a vast number of compounds, computational methods that allow to expand the applicability domain of biokinetic models are of major importance as well.

REFERENCES

Abraham, M. H. (1993). Application of solvation equations to chemical and biochemical processes. *Pure and Applied Chemistry*, *65*(12), 2503–2512. doi:10.1351/pac199365122503

Andra, S. S., Charisiadis, P., Karakitsios, S., Sarigiannis, D. A., & Makris, K. C. (2015). Passive exposures of children to volatile trihalomethanes during domestic cleaning activities of their parents. *Environmental Research*, *136*(0), 187–195. doi:10.1016/j.envres.2014.10.018 PMID:25460636

Bankes, S. C. (2002). Agent-based modeling: A revolution? *Paper presented at the National Academy of Sciences of the United States of America.*

Beaudouin, R., Micallef, S., & Brochot, C. (2010). A stochastic whole-body physiologically based pharmacokinetic model to assess the impact of inter-individual variability on tissue dosimetry over the human lifespan. *Regulatory Toxicology and Pharmacology*, *57*(1), 103–116. doi:10.1016/j.yrtph.2010.01.005 PMID:20122977

Bois, F. Y., Jamei, M., & Clewell, H. J. (2010). PBPK modelling of inter-individual variability in the pharmacokinetics of environmental chemicals. *Toxicology, 278*(3), 256–267. doi:10.1016/j.tox.2010.06.007 PMID:20600548

Brown, D. G. (2006). In H. Geist (Ed.), *The Earth's changing land: An encyclopaedia of land-use and land-cover change Agent-based models* (pp. 7–13). Greenwood Publishing Group.

Couclelis, H. (2001). Why I no longer work with agents: A challenge for ABMs of human-environment interactions. *Paper presented at the Proceeding of Special Workshop on Land-Use/Land-Cover Change*.

Dan Foresee, F., & Hagan, M. T. (1997, June 9-12). Gauss-Newton approximation to Bayesian learning. *Paper presented at the International Conference on Neural Networks*.

de Nazelle, A., Seto, E., Donaire-Gonzalez, D., Mendez, M., Matamala, J., Nieuwenhuijsen, M. J., & Jerrett, M. (2013). Improving estimates of air pollution exposure through ubiquitous sensing technologies. *Environmental Pollution, 176*, 92–99. doi:10.1016/j.envpol.2012.12.032 PMID:23416743

Dennis, J. E. J., & Schnabel, R. B. (1996). *Numerical Methods for Unconstrained Optimization and Nonlinear Equations*: Soc for Industrial &. *Applications of Mathematics*.

Edginton, A. N., & Ritter, L. (2009). Predicting plasma concentrations of bisphenol A in children younger than 2 years of age after typical feeding schedules, using a physiologically based toxicokinetic model. *Environmental Health Perspectives, 117*(4), 645–652. doi:10.1289/ehp.0800073 PMID:19440506

Eissing, T., Kuepfer, L., Becker, C., Block, M., Coboeken, K., Gaub, T., . . . Lippert, J. (2011). A computational systems biology software platform for multiscale modeling and simulation: Integrating whole-body physiology, disease biology, and molecular reaction networks. *Frontiers in Physiology, FEB*.

Gao, C., Goind, R., & Tabak, H. H. (1992). Application of the group contribution method for predicting the toxicity of organic chemicals. *Environmental Toxicology and Chemistry, 11*(5), 631–636. doi:10.1002/etc.5620110506

Georgopoulos, P. G., Sasso, A. F., Isukapalli, S. S., Lioy, P. J., Vallero, D. A., Okino, M., & Reiter, L. (2009). Reconstructing population exposures to environmental chemicals from biomarkers: Challenges and opportunities. *Journal of Exposure Science & Environmental Epidemiology, 19*(2), 149–171. doi:10.1038/jes.2008.9 PMID:18368010

Georgopoulos, P. G., Wang, S. W., Yang, Y. C., Xue, J., Zartarian, V. G., McCurdy, T., & Ozkaynak, H. (2008). Biologically based modeling of multimedia, multipathway, multiroute population exposures to arsenic. *Journal of Exposure Science & Environmental Epidemiology, 18*(5), 462–476. doi:10.1038/sj.jes.7500637 PMID:18073786

Grignard, A., Taillandier, P., Gaudou, B., Vo, D., Huynh, N., & Drogoul, A. (2013). GAMA 1.6: Advancing the Art of Complex Agent-Based Modeling and Simulation. In G. Boella, E. Elkind, B. Savarimuthu, F. Dignum, & M. Purvis (Eds.), *PRIMA 2013: Principles and Practice of Multi-Agent Systems, LNCS* (Vol. 8291, pp. 117–131). Berlin, Heidelberg: Springer. doi:10.1007/978-3-642-44927-7_9

Haddad, S., Charest-Tardif, G., & Krishnan, K. (2000). Physiologically based modeling of the maximal effect of metabolic interactions on the kinetics of components of complex chemical mixtures. *Journal of Toxicology and Environmental Health. Part A.*, *61*(3), 209–223. doi:10.1080/00984100050131350 PMID:11036509

Hagan, M. T., & Menhaj, M. B. (1994). Training feedforward networks with the Marquardt algorithm. *IEEE Transactions on Neural Networks*, *5*(6), 989–993. doi:10.1109/72.329697 PMID:18267874

Ioannidis, J. P., Loy, E. Y., Poulton, R., & Chia, K. S. (2009). Researching genetic versus nongenetic determinants of disease: A comparison and proposed unification. *Science Translational Medicine*, *1*(7), 7ps8. doi:10.1126/scitranslmed.3000247 PMID:20368180

Isukapalli, S., Roy, A., & Georgopoulos, P. (2000). Efficient sensitivity/uncertainty analysis using the combined stochastic response surface method and automated differentiation: Application to environmental and biological systems. *Risk Analysis*, *20*(5), 591–602. doi:10.1111/0272-4332.205054 PMID:11110207

Jongeneelen, F. J., & Berge, W. F. T. (2011). A generic, cross-chemical predictive PBTK model with multiple entry routes running as application in MS Excel; design of the model and comparison of predictions with experimental results. *The Annals of Occupational Hygiene*, *55*(8), 841–864. PMID:21998005

Judson, R. S., Kavlock, R. J., Setzer, R. W., Cohen Hubal, E. A., Martin, M. T., Knudsen, T. B., & Dix, D. J. et al. (2011). Estimating toxicity-related biological pathway altering doses for high-throughput chemical risk assessment. *Chemical Research in Toxicology*, *24*(4), 451–462. doi:10.1021/tx100428e PMID:21384849

Krauss, M., Schaller, S., Borchers, S., Findeisen, R., Lippert, J., & Kuepfer, L. (2012). Integrating Cellular Metabolism into a Multiscale Whole-Body Model. *PLoS Computational Biology*, *8*(10), e1002750. doi:10.1371/journal.pcbi.1002750 PMID:23133351

Levy, S. (1993). *Artificial Life: A Report from the Frontier Where Computers Meet Biology*. Random House Inc.

Moles, C. G., Mendes, P., & Banga, J. R. (2003). Parameter estimation in biochemical pathways: A comparison of global optimization methods. *Genome Research*, *13*(11), 2467–2474. doi:10.1101/gr.1262503 PMID:14559783

Møller, M. F. (1993). A scaled conjugate gradient algorithm for fast supervised learning. *Neural Networks*, *6*(4), 525–533. doi:10.1016/S0893-6080(05)80056-5

Muzic, R. F. Jr, & Christian, B. T. (2006). Evaluation of objective functions for estimation of kinetic parameters. *Medical Physics*, *33*(2), 342–353. doi:10.1118/1.2135907 PMID:16532939

Nieuwenhuijsen, M. J., Donaire-Gonzalez, D., Foraster, M., Martinez, D., & Cisneros, A. (2014). Using Personal Sensors to Assess the Exposome and Acute Health Effects. *International Journal of Environmental Research and Public Health*, *11*(8), 7805–7819. doi:10.3390/ijerph110807805 PMID:25101766

Patel, C., & Manrai, A. K. (2015). Development of exposome correlation globes to map out environment-wide associations. *Paper presented at the Pac Symp Biocomput.*

Patel, C. J., & Ioannidis, J. P. (2014). Placing epidemiological results in the context of multiplicity and typical correlations of exposures. *Journal of Epidemiology and Community Health, 68*(11), 1096–1100. doi:10.1136/jech-2014-204195 PMID:24923805

Payne, M. P., & Kenny, L. C. (2002). Comparison of models for the estimation of biological partition coefficients. *Journal of Toxicology and Environmental Health. Part A., 65*(13), 897–931. doi:10.1080/00984100290071171 PMID:12133236

Peyret, T., & Krishnan, K. (2011). QSARs for PBPK modelling of environmental contaminants. *SAR and QSAR in Environmental Research, 22*(1-2), 129–169. doi:10.1080/1062936X.2010.548351 PMID:21391145

Price, K., & Krishnan, K. (2011). An integrated QSAR-PBPK modelling approach for predicting the inhalation toxicokinetics of mixtures of volatile organic chemicals in the rat. *SAR and QSAR in Environmental Research, 22*(1-2), 107–128. doi:10.1080/1062936X.2010.548350 PMID:21391144

Puzyn, T., Leszczynski, J., & Cronin, M. T. D. (2010). Recent Advances in QSAR Studies. New York: Springer Science+Business Media. doi:10.1007/978-1-4020-9783-6

Riedmiller, M., & Braun, H. (1993). A direct adaptive method for faster backpropagation learning: the RPROP algorithm. *Paper presented at the IEEE International Conference on Neural Networks.*

Roy, A., Weisel, C. P., Gallo, M., & Georgopoulos, P. (1996). Studies of multiroute exposure/dose reconstruction using physiologically based pharmacokinetic models. *Journal of Clean Technology. Environmental Toxicology and Occupational Medicine, 5*(4), 285–295.

Sarigiannis, D., Gotti, A., & Karakitsios, S. (2011). A Computational Framework for Aggregate and Cumulative Exposure Assessment. *Epidemiology (Cambridge, Mass.), 22*(1), S96–S97. doi:10.1097/01. ede.0000391962.03834.66

Sarigiannis, D., & Karakitsios, S. (2011). Perinatal Exposure to Bisphenol A: The Route of Administration Makes the Dose. *Epidemiology (Cambridge, Mass.), 22*(1), S172. doi:10.1097/01.ede.0000392202.15822. bf

Sarigiannis, D., Karakitsios, S., Handakas, E., Simou, K., Solomou, E., & Gotti, A. (2016). Integrated exposure and risk characterization of bisphenol-A in Europe. *Food and Chemical Toxicology, 98*(Part B), 134-147. doi:10.1016/j.fct.2016.10.017

Sarigiannis, D. A., & Gotti, A. (2008). Biology-based dose-response models for health risk assessment of chemical mixtures. *Fresenius Environmental Bulletin, 17*(9 B), 1439-1451.

Sarigiannis, D. A., & Gotti, A. (2014). New methods for personal monitoring of air pollution through the use of passive sensors during childhood. *Pneumologia Pediatrica, 54*, 37–43.

Sarigiannis, D. A., & Karakitsios, S. P. (2012, October 28 - November 2). A dynamic physiology based pharmacokinetic model for assessing lifelong internal dose. *Paper presented at the AICHE '12*, Pittsburgh, PA.

Sarigiannis, D. A., Karakitsios, S. P., Gotti, A., Papaloukas, C. L., Kassomenos, P. A., & Pilidis, G. A. (2009). Bayesian algorithm implementation in a real time exposure assessment model on benzene with calculation of associated cancer risks. *Sensors (Basel, Switzerland)*, *9*(2), 731–755. doi:10.3390/ s90200731 PMID:22399936

Sasso, A. F., Isukapalli, S. S., & Georgopoulos, P. G. (2010). A generalized physiologically-based toxicokinetic modeling system for chemical mixtures containing metals. *Theoretical Biology & Medical Modelling*, *7*(1), 17. doi:10.1186/1742-4682-7-17 PMID:20525215

Snyder, E. G., Watkins, T. H., Solomon, P. A., Thoma, E. D., Williams, R. W., Hagler, G. S., & Preuss, P. W. et al. (2013). The changing paradigm of air pollution monitoring. *Environmental Science & Technology*, *47*(20), 11369–11377. doi:10.1021/es4022602 PMID:23980922

Tan, Y. M., Liao, K., Conolly, R., Blount, B., Mason, A., & Clewell, H. (2006). Use of a physiologically based pharmacokinetic model to identify exposures consistent with human biomonitoring data for chloroform. *Journal of Toxicology and Environmental Health - Part A: Current Issues*, *69*(18), 1727–1756. doi:10.1080/15287390600631367 PMID:16864423

Valcke, M., & Krishnan, K. (2011). Evaluation of the impact of the exposure route on the human kinetic adjustment factor. *Regulatory Toxicology and Pharmacology*, *59*(2), 258–269. doi:10.1016/j. yrtph.2010.10.008 PMID:20969910

Verner, M. A., Charbonneau, M., Lopez-Carrillo, L., & Haddad, S. (2008). Physiologically based pharmacokinetic modeling of persistent organic pollutants for lifetime exposure assessment: A new tool in breast cancer epidemiologic studies. *Environmental Health Perspectives*, *116*(7), 886–892. doi:10.1289/ ehp.10917 PMID:18629310

Wild, C. P. (2005). Complementing the genome with an exposome: The outstanding challenge of environmental exposure measurement in molecular epidemiology. *Cancer Epidemiology, Biomarkers & Prevention*, *14*(8), 1847–1850. doi:10.1158/1055-9965.EPI-05-0456 PMID:16103423

Willmann, S., Lippert, J., Sevestre, M., Solodenko, J., Fois, F., & Schmitt, W. (2003). PK-Sim: A physiologically based pharmacokinetic 'whole-body' model. *Drug Discovery Today: BIOSILICO*, *1*(4), 121–124.

Yang, Y., Xu, X., & Georgopoulos, P. G. (2010). A Bayesian population PBPK model for multiroute chloroform exposure. *Journal of Exposure Science & Environmental Epidemiology*, *20*(4), 326–341. doi:10.1038/jes.2009.29 PMID:19471319

Zhang, H. (2004). A new nonlinear equation for the tissue/blood partition coefficients of neutral compounds. *Journal of Pharmaceutical Sciences*, *93*(6), 1595–1604. doi:10.1002/jps.20084 PMID:15124216

KEY TERMS AND DEFINITIONS

Agent Based Modelling: Models that account for the behaviour of all interacting parts (agents), where macroscopic events emerge through microscopic actions and interactions.

Artificial Neural Networks: A data processing (expert system) algorithm inspired by biological nervous systems, information, in a computing system made up of interconnected processing elements.

Exposure Reconstruction: Estimation of previous exposure regimes starting from biomonitoring data.

Exposure: Contact with chemical, physical, or biological agents occurring in the environment.

Personal Sensor: A wearable device for the acquisition and measurement of data/information on some property(ies) of a phenomenon, object, or material by a recording device in situ.

Physiology Based Biokinetic Models: Models that describe the processes of administration, distribution, metabolism and elimination of xenobiotics entering human body.

QSARs: Models that describe the physicochemical properties of chemical compounds and their interaction with human biological systems accounting for compound structural properties.

Chapter 7

Informatics and Data Analytics to Support Exposome- Based Discovery:
Part 2 – Computational Exposure Biology

Dimosthenis A. Sarigiannis
Aristotle University of Thessaloniki, Greece

Evangelos Handakas
Aristotle University of Thessaloniki, Greece

Alberto Gotti
Aristotle University of Thessaloniki, Greece

Spyros P. Karakitsios
Aristotle University of Thessaloniki, Greece

ABSTRACT

This chapter aims at outlining the current state of science in the field of computational exposure biology and in particular at demonstrating how the bioinformatics techniques and algorithms can be used to support the association between environmental exposures and human health and the deciphering of the molecular and metabolic pathways of induced toxicity related to environmental chemical stressors. Examples of the integrated bioinformatics analyses outlined herein are given concerning exposure to airborne chemical mixtures, to organic compounds frequently found in consumer goods, and to mixtures of organic chemicals and metals through multiple exposure pathways. Advanced bioinformatics are coupled with big data analytics to perform studies of exposome-wide associations with putative adverse health outcomes. In conclusion, the chapter gives the reader an outline of the available computational tools and paves the way towards the development of future comprehensive applications that are expected to support efficiently exposome research in the 21st century.

INTRODUCTION

The advent of new high throughput analytical and multi-sensing methods supports current advances in life and environmental sciences supporting their coming together in the quest to create the premise for delivering precision medicine. Even though this is a true revolution for the promotion of good health and cost-effective healthcare on the individual level, public health promotion warrants paying equal attention

DOI: 10.4018/978-1-5225-2607-0.ch007

to prevention and avoidance/reduction of human exposure to the stressors that contribute to ill health. The exposome, the totality of exposures over one's lifetime, and the genome are the two main determinants of human health. Effectively coupling genetic information with environmental and exposure-related data, as well as capturing epigenetic perturbations and linking them with mechanisms of toxicity and adverse outcome pathways maybe the solution towards the development of efficient environmental policies that protect both the quality of the environment, ecosystem function and human health. Thus, the term exposure biology is introduced to denote the system view of exposure to health stressors considering not only environmental and behavioral dimensions but rather capturing the whole network of interactions between environment and human biology and the corresponding dynamics. Development of exposure biology requires the use of a large array of analytical, biological and computational tools that are put together seamlessly to permit the representation of the complexity of interactions and its interpretation.

This chapter gives a comprehensive overview of the computational tools required focusing on their utility in articulating the mechanistic pathways that link environmental exposures to adverse health outcomes on the individual and population level. Such tools comprise data analytics and machine learning methods for pattern recognition and identification of the most important biological pathways perturbed from human exposure to putative health stressors from the molecular to the metabolic level. They also include advanced statistical bioinformatics algorithms used to explore the association space between the exposome and human health precluding any bias and discarding the use of the term confounders. Unlike the traditional environmental epidemiology paradigm, computational exposure biology and exposome-wide association studies embrace all factors that determine or modulate human health and its interaction with the exposome. Thus, issues such as pre-existing health conditions, prior exposures or deleterious habits such as smoking, but also age, gender, socio-economic status are considered part of an individual's exposome. As such they are included in the high-dimension analysis of multiple –omics data derived from human sampling and phenotypic data stemming from clinical examination or biochemical markers.

Background

The scope of the currently available statistical methods is to understand biological functions comprising toxicity pathways and their interactions in relation to external/internal exposure, to confirm the causative effect between exposure and disease endpoint through theoretical (computational) models, to combine mixed data, resulted from various sources, through the utilization of advanced data mining analysis techniques, to provide the methodological tools for integrating multiple biomarkers into a mechanistic description and to derive the systems biology exposome model.

Gene expression data can be a valuable tool for understanding gene regulation, biological networks, and cellular states. One goal in analyzing expression data is to try to determine how the expression of any particular gene might affect the expression of other genes; the genes involved in this case could belong to the same gene network. By a gene network, we mean a set of genes being expressed together in a non-random pattern. Another goal of expression data analysis is to try to determine what genes are expressed as a result of certain cellular conditions, e.g. what genes are expressed in diseased cells that are not expressed in healthy cells. While early experiments using microarrays profiled only a few samples, more recent experiments profile on the order of dozens or even hundreds of samples, allowing for a more robust statistical analysis of the data. In the near future, data sets containing thousands of samples should become available. As gene expression data sets become larger and larger, spreadsheets will become less and less of an adequate tool for performing transcriptomics data analysis and data mining techniques using large databases should find more and more use in analyzing expression data. In the analysis of gene expression data, the items in an association rule can represent genes that are strongly expressed or repressed, as well as relevant facts describing the cellular environment of the genes (e.g. a diagnosis for a tumor sample that was profiled, or a drug treatment given to cells in the sample before profiling). An example of an association rule mined from expression data might be [cancer] => gene A↑, gene B↓, gene C↑}, meaning that, for the data set that was mined, in most profile experiments where the cells used were cancerous, gene A was measured as being up (i.e. highly expressed), gene B was down (i.e. highly repressed), and gene C was up, altogether. Hence scope is to interpret gene expression technology results via integration of gene expression profiles with corresponding biological knowledge (gene annotations, literature, etc.) extracted from biological databases. Consequently, the key task in the interpretation step is to detect the present co-expressed (sharing similar expression profiles) and co-annotated (sharing the same properties such as function, regulatory mechanism, etc.) gene group. Several approaches dealing with the interpretation problem have recently been reported. These approaches can be classified in three axes (Chang, 2002; Martinez, 2007): expression-based approaches, knowledge-based approaches and co-clustering approaches. The most currently used interpretation axis is the expression-based axis that gives more weight to gene expression profiles. However, it presents many well-known drawbacks. First, these approaches cluster genes by similarity in expression profiles across all biological conditions. However, gene groups involved in a biological process might be only co-expressed in a small subset of conditions (Altman & Raychaudhuri, 2001) Second, many genes have different biological roles in the cell, they may be conditionally co-expressed with different groups of genes. Since almost all clustering methods used place each gene in a single cluster, that is a single group of genes, relationships with different groups of conditionally regulated genes may remain undiscovered (Gasch, 2002). Third, discovering biological relationships among co-expressed genes is not a trivial task and requires a lot of additional work, even when similar gene expression profiles are related to similar biological roles (Shatkay, 2000).

In a wider exposomics analysis, bioinformatics techniques should be applied and enhanced to select the most relevant omics data and derive specific data profiles for given exposure/disease pathways. Predictive biomarkers could be determined, based on heterogeneous datasets, resulting from human biomonitoring, omics and epigenetics analyses and PBBK modelling. This would require, firstly the pre-processing of the data produced, secondly the discovery of specific data patterns and/or clusters, thirdly the creation of data models based on training sets and, finally, the evaluation of the models regarding their validity and prediction capacity based on the test data. Results would be systematically assessed and the model that best describes exposome data would be employed on population survey datasets. Multiple omics biomarkers could also be integrated to a mechanistic description of toxicity pathway interactions, in relation to external/internal exposure, achieved by developing systems biology pathway models and using the predictive bioinformatics approaches.

Data preprocessing is necessary before applying unsupervised learning algorithms to exposome data. This includes:

- Technology specific data pre-processing (e.g. spectra de-convolution).
- Noise removal, to ensure the consistency and high quality of our data from possible outliers or discrepancies in the measurements.
- Data transformation, to normalize the values in our dataset and increase their generalization.
- Data reduction, to decrease both the apparent complexity in our data, through subset representations, and the dimensionality of the derived models.

- Discretization, to scale the data and prepare them for further analysis by means of clustering and pattern extraction.

After pre-processing, training and testing of the various datasets could follow the learning process. This is required to depict relations among the observed variables, to recognize complex patterns and to extract rules. Lastly, since the number of states required to be recognized may be much larger than the available dataset; a representative training data set will be selected to generalize to the entire data set.

BIG DATA ANALYTICS IN SUPPORT OF EXPOSURE BIOLOGY

Data Mining

Data mining (Fayyad, 1996) systems combine techniques from many research areas, e.g., statistics or computer science (database systems and machine learning). The systems can be categorized per the task they solve. There are, e.g., classification, regression, clustering, or descriptive systems. In addition data mining systems can be also characterized by the type of knowledge they produce. In this regard, there are connectionistic (artificial neural networks), statistics (Naïve Bayes classifier), or logic (decision trees or classification rules) systems. Some algorithms combine several methods such as Domingos' RISE algorithm (Dong, 1999) which integrates instance-based and rule-based learning. Lastly, data complexity criteria separate data mining systems into two groups: propositional and relational systems. Although statistics or connectionist systems have achieved good results in text mining, i.e., text classification and categorization, they may not be suitable for mining knowledge intended for further analysis. Nevertheless, it may be very difficult to process a complex dataset, such as data describing chemical molecules (structure of organic molecules) and biological (strings of DNA) data. Following the axiom that "a data mining algorithm is a well-defined procedure that takes data as input and produces output in the form of models or patterns", the data mining algorithms can be classified in accordance to Figure 1.

Accordingly, model structures are categorized per prediction type (incl. linear regression, piecewise linear, nonparametric regression and classification), the probability distributions (incl. parametric models, mixtures of parametric models, graphical Markov models) and structured types (incl. time series, Markov

Figure 1. Model classification scheme

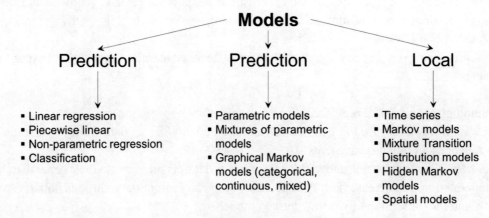

models, mixture transition distribution models, hidden Markov models). In this chapter mining algorithms will be categorized in two clusters: (a) descriptive; and (b) predictive. The former describe the dataset in a concise and brief manner and present general data properties. The latter performs inference on the available dataset and predicts the outcome of the new datasets via the generation of one or more models.

Descriptive Data Mining

A descriptive data mining approach presents the main features, where data are randomly generated from a "good" descriptive model that has the same characteristics as the 'real' data. In the descriptive data mining approach, patterns are evaluated either globally or locally, in accordance to the classification presented in Figure 2. Global patterns include clustering methods via portioning, hierarchical clustering and mixture modelling and local patterns including outlier detection, changepoint detection pattern, 'bump' hunting, scan statistics and association rules.

Predictive Data Mining

Predictive data mining can be used to forecast explicit values, based on patterns determined from known results. Several techniques can be used for that purpose, ranging from typical approaches based on decision trees or k-nearest neighbors to more sophisticated ones that employ Artificial Neural Networks (ANNs), Support Vector Machines (SVMs) or Bayesian Networks (BNs). Hence it is possible to perform inference on the available dataset, to perform a mere classification and to study and unravel the feature attributes concealed in data (e.g. exposome). Various computational techniques, especially machine learning algorithms (Larranaga, 2003), are applied, to select genes or proteins associated with the trait of interest and to classify different types of samples in gene expression of microarrays data (Allison, Cui, Page, & Sabripour, 2006) or Mass Spectrometry (MS)-based proteomics data (Aebersold, 2003), to identify disease associated genes, gene-gene interactions, and gene-environmental interactions from Genome Wide Association (GWA) studies (Hirschhorn & Daly, 2005), to recognize the regulatory elements in DNA or protein sequences (Zeng, Zhu, & Yan, 2009), to identify protein-protein interactions (Valencia & Pazos, 2002), or to predict protein structure (Jones, 2001). The aim of designing/using ensemble methods (Breiman, 1996, 2001; Freund, 1996) is to achieve more accurate classification (on training data) as well as better generalization (on unseen data). However, this is often achieved at the expense of increased model complexity (i.e. decreased model interpretability) (Kuncheva, 2004). A better generalization property of the ensemble approach is often explained using the classic bias-variance

Figure 2. Classifications in the descriptive data mining approach

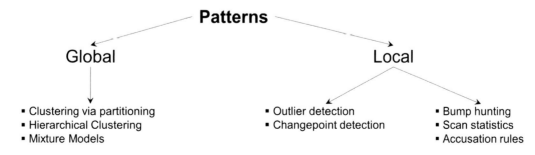

decomposition analysis (Webb, 2004). Specifically, previous studies pointed out methods like bagging (Fig. 8(a)) that improve generalization by decreasing variance (Breiman, 1998) while methods similar to boosting (Figure 3(b)) achieve this by decreasing bias (Schapire, 1998).

Data Mining Algorithms

Clustering

DNA microarray technology has made it possible to simultaneously monitor the expression levels of thousands of genes during important biological processes and across collections of related samples. Elucidating the patterns hidden in gene expression data offers a tremendous opportunity for enhanced understanding of functional genomics. However, the large number of genes and the complexity of biological networks greatly increase the challenges of comprehending and interpreting the resulting mass of data, which often consists of millions of measurements. In this regard, clustering techniques can be utilized to reveal the natural structures and identify the patterns in the underlying data. Specifically, cluster analysis seeks to partition a given data set into groups based on specified features so that the data points within a group are more similar to each other than the points in different groups. Many conventional clustering algorithms are available to be adapted or directly applied to the gene expression data. Assuming that a 2-D matrix of the gene expression is available, the row will represent the genes and the columns will represent different experiments. This representation corresponds to a gene expression profile, available for clustering. Figure 4 illustrates such an example, where rows represent the different exposure profiles and columns the genes differentially expressed. The goal is to organize profiles into clusters so that the instances in the same cluster are highly similar to each other and the instances from different clusters have low similarity to each other.

Due to the special characteristics of gene expression data, and the particular requirements from the biological domain, gene-based clustering presents several challenges. Firstly, cluster analysis is typically in data mining and knowledge discovery. The purpose of clustering gene expression data is to reveal the natural data structures and gain some initial insights regarding data distribution. Therefore, a good clustering algorithm should depend as little as possible on prior knowledge, which is usually not available before cluster analysis. For example, a clustering algorithm which can accurately estimate the "true" number of clusters in the data set would be more favored than one requiring the pre-determined number of clusters. Secondly, due to the complex procedures of microarray experiments, gene expression

Figure 3. Schematic illustration of the three popular ensemble methods

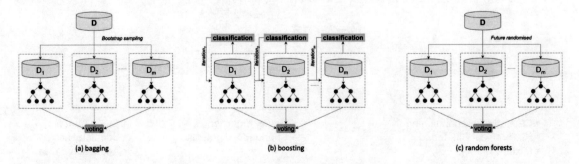

Figure 4. A sample mRNA expression profile

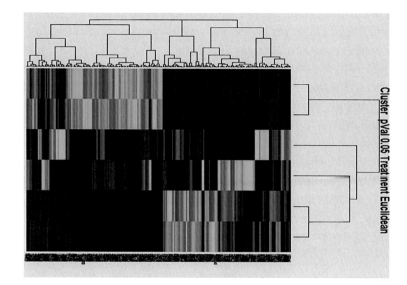

data often contain a huge amount of noise. Therefore, clustering algorithms for gene expression data should be capable of extracting useful information from a high level of background noise. Thirdly, gene expression data are often "highly connected" (Jiang, Pei, & Zhang, 2003b), and clusters may be highly intersected with each other or even embedded one in another (Jiang, Pei, & Zhang, 2003a). Therefore, algorithms for gene-based clustering should be able to effectively handle this situation. Finally, users of microarray data may not only be interested in the clusters of genes, but also be interested in the relationship between the clusters (e.g., which clusters are more close to each other, and which clusters are remote from each other) and the relationship between the genes within the same cluster (e.g., which gene can be considered as the representative of the cluster and which genes are at the boundary area of the cluster).

In this regard the available methods include the K-means algorithm (McQueen, 1967), the Self-organizing Map (SOP) method (Kohonen, 1984), Hierarchical clustering algorithms, Graph-theoretical approaches (Ben-Dor, 1999; Shamir & Sharan, 2000), pattern clustering methods (Seno & Karypis, 2001) and model-based clustering (Dasgupta & Raftery, 1998; Fraley & Raftery, 1998).

K-Means

The K-means algorithm (McQueen, 1967) is a typical partition-based clustering method. Given a pre-specified number K, the algorithm partitions the data set into K disjoint subsets which optimize the following objective function 1,

$$E = \sum_{i=1}^{K} \sum_{O \in c_i} \left| O - \mu_i \right|^2 \tag{1}$$

where O is a data object cluster C_i and μ_i is the centroid (mean of objects) of C_i. Hence according to the objective function 1, E is the minimized sum of the squared distances of objects from their cluster centres. The time complexity of the K-means method is $O(l*k*n)$, where l is the number of iterations and k is the number of clusters. While the K-means cluster converges after a small number of iterations, with regard to the gene-based clustering algorithm, several drawbacks are identified: firstly, the number of gene clusters in a gene expression data set is usually unknown in advance. To detect the optimal number of clusters, users usually run the algorithms repeatedly with different values of k and compare the clustering results. For a large gene expression data set which contains thousands of genes, this extensive parameter fine-tuning process may not be practical. Secondly, gene expression data typically contain a huge amount of noise; however, the K-means algorithm forces each gene into a cluster, which may cause the algorithm to be sensitive to noise (De Smet et al., 2002; Sherlock, 2000). Other clustering algorithms available to overcome the drawbacks of the K-means algorithms include those that typically use some global parameters to control the quality of resulting clusters (e.g., the maximal radius of a cluster and/or the minimal distance between clusters). However, the qualities of clusters in gene expression data sets may vary widely. Thus, it is often a difficult problem to choose the appropriate globally-constraining parameters. The implementation of the K-means algorithm is depicted in Figure 5.

SOM

The Self-Organizing Map (SOM) method (Kohonen, 1984) was developed on the basis of a single layered neural network. Accordingly, data objects are presented at the input, and the output neurons are organized with a simple neighborhood structure such as a two-dimensional p * q grid. Each neuron of the neural network is associated with a reference vector and each data point is "mapped" to the neuron with the "closest" reference vector. In the process of running the algorithm, each data object acts as a training sample which directs the movement of the reference vectors towards the denser areas of the input vector space, so that those reference vectors are trained to fit the distributions of the input data set. When the training is complete, clusters are identified by mapping all data points to the output neurons. The SOM method generates an intuitively-appealing map of a high-dimensional data set in 2D or 3D space and places similar clusters near each other. The neuron training process of SOM provides a relatively more

Figure 5. Implementation of the K-means algorithm to a data set

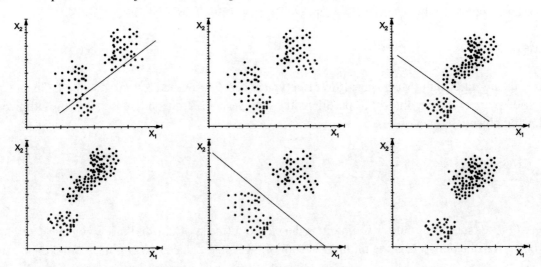

robust approach than K-means to the clustering of highly noisy data (Herrero, 2001; Tamayo, 1999). However, SOM requires users to input the number of clusters and the grid structure of the neuron map.

These two parameters are preserved through the training process; hence, improperly-specified parameters will prevent the recovering of the natural cluster structure. Furthermore, if the data set is abundant with irrelevant data points, such as genes or metabolites with invariant patterns, SOM will produce an output in which this type of data will populate the vast majority of clusters (Herrero, 2001). In this case, SOM is not effective because most of the interesting patterns may be merged into only one or two clusters and cannot be identified. Figure 6 illustrates how from a 4x4 array of neurons and a random weight initialization, the weights values aid to evaluate the final data profile grouping.

Hierarchical Clustering

Hierarchical clustering generates a hierarchical series of nested clusters which can be graphically represented by a tree, called dendrogram, as seen in Figure 7. The branches of a dendrogram not only record the formation of the clusters but also indicate the similarity between the clusters. By cutting the dendrogram at some level, we can obtain a specified number of clusters. By reordering the objects such that the branches of the corresponding dendrogram do not cross, the data set can be arranged with similar objects placed together. Hierarchical clustering algorithms can be further divided into agglomerative approaches and divisive approaches based on how the hierarchical dendrogram is formed. Agglomerative algorithms (bottom-up approach) initially regard each data object as an individual cluster, and at each step, merge the closest pair of clusters until all the groups are merged into one cluster. Divisive algorithms (top-down approach) starts with one cluster containing all the data objects, and at each step

Figure 6. Implementation of SOM to data profiles

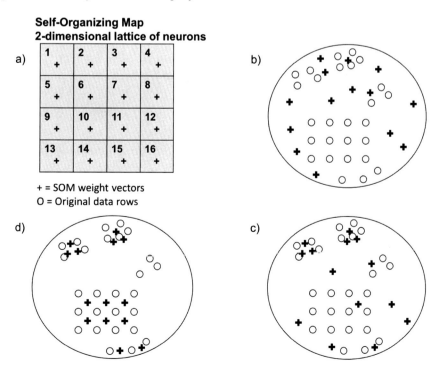

153

Figure 7. An example of hierarchical clustering

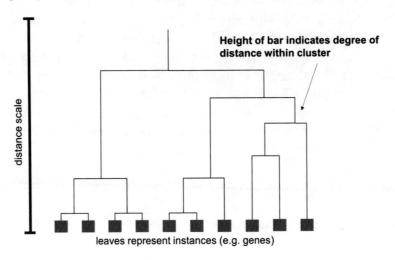

split a cluster until only singleton clusters of individual objects remain. For agglomerative approaches, different measures of cluster proximity, such as single link, complete link and minimum-variance (Dubes, 1988; Kaufman & Rousseeuw, 1990), derive various merging strategies. For divisive approaches, the essential problem is to decide how to split clusters at each step.

Graph-Theory Based Methods

Using graph-theoretical approaches, data are represented graphically using a proximity matrix P, where $P[I,j] = proximity [O_i, O_j]$ and a weighted graph $G(V,E)$ denoted as the proximity graph, where each data point corresponds to a vertex. Two general approaches are available, firstly each pair of objects is connected by an edge with weight assigned according to the proximity value between the objects (Shamir & Sharan, 2000; Xing, 2001) and secondly, proximity is mapped only to either or 0 or 1 on the basis of some threshold, and edges only exist between objects i and j, where $P[i,j]$ equals 1 (Ben-Dor, 1999; Hartuv & Shamir, 2000). It is noted that the Graph-theoretical clustering techniques are explicitly presented in terms of a graph, thus converting the problem of clustering a dataset into such graph theoretical problems as finding minimum cut or maximal cliques in the proximity graph G. Figure 8, depicts global and local clustering using graph-based methods. Graph vertices are grouped into cultures. From these representations the vertex similarity measures are estimated including distance, adjacency and the degree of connectivity. Other cluster fitness measures include density, conductance, modularity and centrality.

Pattern Discovery

Association rules can reveal biologically relevant associations between different genes or between environmental effects and gene expression. An association rule has the form LHS→RHS, where LHS and RHS are disjoint sets of items, the RHS set being likely to occur whenever the LHS set occurs. Items in gene expression data can include genes that are highly expressed or repressed, as well as relevant facts describing the cellular environment of the genes. It is hence a commonly used methodology for detecting

Figure 8. Global vs. local clustering in graph-based methods

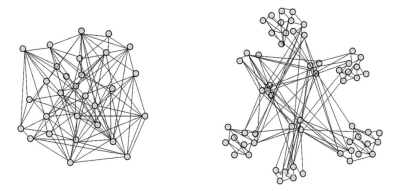

local patterns in unsupervised learning systems and represent feature-value conditions among the data. Analysis of large genomic data has two important goals:

- To determine how the expression of any particular gene might affect the expression of other genes; the genes involved in this case could belong to the same gene regulatory network. By this we mean a set of genes being expressed together in a non-random pattern to code for specific proteins regulating biological function.
- To determine what genes are expressed as a result of certain cellular conditions, e.g. what genes are expressed in diseased cells that are not expressed in healthy cells.

A number of different algorithms for pattern extraction are available including the Apriori, the FP-growth and the LPMiner used either independently or in combination.

Apriori

The most basic join-based algorithm is the *Apriori* method (Agrawal, 1994). The *Apriori* approach uses a level-wise approach in which all frequent item-sets of length k are generated before those of length $(k + 1)$. The main observation which is used for the *Apriori* algorithm is that every subset of a frequent pattern is also frequent. Therefore, candidates for frequent patterns of length $(k+1)$ can be generated from known frequent patterns of length k with the use of joins. A join is defined by pairs of frequent k-patterns that have at least $(k - 1)$ items in common. This method identifies the frequent items in the dataset: i.e. those items with minimum *Support*. Here Support (S) is defined as the proportion of records in the dataset which contain the item set. An advantage of this approach is the fact that it is bottom-up; as such it can be extended to larger item sets that appear often in the dataset. Figure 9 shows the implementation of the Apriori method in a database D.

FP-Growth

The most popular frequent itemset mining algorithm is FP-Growth (Han, Pei, & Yin, 2000). The main aim of this algorithm was to remove the bottlenecks of the Apriori algorithm in generating and testing candidate set. The problem of Apriori algorithm was dealt with, by introducing a novel, compact data

Figure 9. Implementation of the Apriori method from a database D

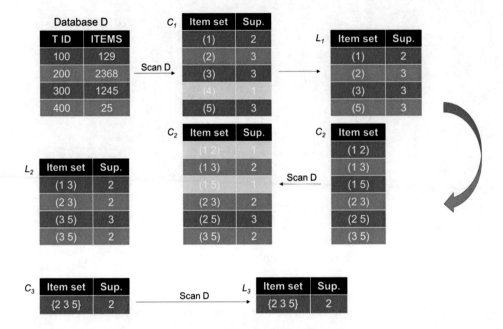

structure, called frequent pattern tree, or FP-tree then based on this structure an FP-tree-based pattern fragment growth method was developed. FP-growth uses a combination of the vertical and horizontal database layout to store the database in main memory. Instead of storing the cover for every item in the database, it stores the actual transactions from the database in a tree structure and every item has a linked list going through all transactions that contain that item. This new data structure is denoted by FP-tree (Frequent-Pattern tree) (Han et al., 2003). Essentially, all transactions are stored in a tree data structure. The advantages of this method are that it avoids the costly iterative scans and generations of large number of candidate pattern sets and produces a more compact pattern set.

LPMiner

The LPMiner approach (Seno & Karypis, 2001) is based on the FP-growth method, using false frequent patterns. The main idea behind is that the minimal frequency threshold decreases with the length of the pattern then a smaller number of false frequent patterns is generated. Therefore an additional constraint was introduced, the *length-decreasing support* constraint. Using this method, frequent items are found, the support of which decreases as a function of item length. This method combines the FP-tree data structure with pruning process and it is known to be faster than the FP-growth method. However, it has been found to be problematic when dealing with short item sets.

K-Nearest Neighbors

The simplest of all machine learning algorithms, is the K-nearest algorithm, based on instance based learning. Data classification is based on the methodology of k nearest neighbors where the output is object value equal to the average of the values of their k nearest neighbors. It is noted that weights are used to regulate the attribute's contribution, when k=1 the object is assigned to the class of the nearest neighbor. Selection of the Ks is crucial and in our case it is accomplished heuristically.

Decision Trees

Decision trees (Breiman et al., 1984; Quinlan, 1986) are among the most popular learning algorithms and they have been applied extensively in computational biology. The key ingredients of the success of these methods are their interpretability that makes their model transparent and understandable to human experts, their flexibility, that makes them applicable to a wide range of problems, and their ease of use, that makes them accessible even to non-specialists. Combined with ensemble methods, they furthermore often provide state-of-the-art results in terms of predictive accuracy. Common algorithms include the Classification And Regression Tree - CART (Breiman et al., 1984), the C4.5 (Quinlan, 1986) and the Random Forests (Breiman, 2001) methods. Importantly in the context of high-throughput data sets, tree-based methods are also highly scalable from a computational point of view. In its simplest form, a decision tree combines several binary tests in a tree structure. As an illustration, Figure 10 presents a bi-dimensional classification problem where the learning goal is to find a function which discriminates at best between red and green points.

Figure 11 plots a decision tree and the resulting decision boundary. Each interior node of this tree is labeled with a test, which compares the value of an input attribute to a threshold, and each terminal node is labeled with a class. To produce a classification for a new object whose attribute values are known, we simply propagate it into the tree from the top node according to the test answers. When a terminal node is reached, its corresponding class label is attributed to the object. By using such tests, the tree progressively partitions the input space into hyper-rectangular regions where the output is constant. The general idea behind tree induction algorithms is to find a simple tree that has good predictive performance on the learning sample. Since the enumeration of all possible trees is essentially intractable, most tree induction algorithms are based on heuristics. The most common heuristic is a greedy top-down recursive partitioning approach. This algorithm starts with a single node tree corresponding to the complete learning sample and finds a way to split this node by selecting a test among a set of candidate tests. The algorithm then precedes recursively to split the successors of this node. The whole process results in a partition of the learning sample into smaller and smaller subsets. The development of a branch is stopped when some stop-splitting criterion applies. Eventually, each terminal node of the tree is labeled with a prediction (class name or vector of class probabilities) which is computed based on the subset of objects

Figure 10. An illustrative two-dimensional supervised learning problem: From left to right: (a) tabular learning sample, (b) scatter-plot of the learning sample together with the optimal classification boundary for this problem, (c) the classification boundary for a too simple model and (d) of a too complex one

X1	X2	Y
0.19	0.35	Sick
0.44	0.94	Healthy
0.63	0.08	Sick
....		
0.20	0.63	Healthy

Figure 11. A decision tree and the corresponding decision boundary

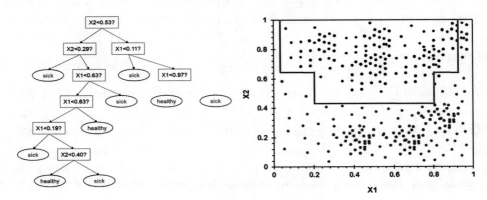

which reach this node. This tree growing step is then usually followed by a pruning stage which aims at removing unessential parts of the tree to avoid over-fitting. Possible application in exposome-based discovery include, the prediction of interactions between different types of bio-molecules, such as Protein-Protein Interactions (PPIs) and DNA protein interactions. Prediction of the PPIs requires adjustment of the tree learning algorithms, because each attribute is measured twice, once for each protein of a pair.

Artificial Neural Networks

Artificial neural networks (ANNs) are a family of statistical learning algorithms implemented in a computational model based on the structure and functions of biological neural networks. Information that flows through the network affects the structure of the ANN because a neural network changes - or learns, in a sense - based on that input and output. ANNs are considered nonlinear statistical data modelling tools, where complex relationships between inputs and outputs are modelled or patterns are found. ANNs have three layers that are interconnected.

The first layer consists of input neurons. Those neurons send data on to the second layer, which in turn sends the output neurons to the third layer. As ANNs are loosely based on the way a biological neuron is believed to organize and process information, they have many advantages in their ability to derive meaning from large complex datasets. Firstly, they do not rely on data to be normally distributed, an assumption of classical parametric analysis methods. They can process data containing complex (non-linear) relationships and interactions that are often too difficult or complex to interpret by conventional linear methods. Secondly, they are fault tolerant, i.e. they have the ability of handling noisy or fuzzy information, whilst also being able to endure data which is incomplete or contains missing values. Thirdly, they are capable of generalization (like other machine learning methods), so they can interpret information which is different to that of the training data, thus representing a 'real-world' solution to a given problem by their ability to predict future cases or trends based on what they have previously seen. Thus, trained ANNs can be used as standalone executable systems to predict the class of an unknown case of interest and therefore have the potential application in diagnosis. Finally, there are several techniques that can be used to extract knowledge from trained ANNs, and the importance of individual variables can be easily recovered using various methods such as the analysis of interconnecting network weights (Olden et al., 2004), sensitivity analysis and rule extraction (Silva et al., 2008).

Figure 12. Typical ANN architecture

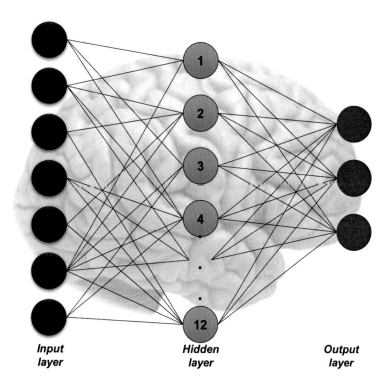

Input layer **Hidden layer** **Output layer**

ANNs also have their limitations: training of ANNs can potentially be time consuming depending on the complexity of the data being modelled, and as the number of hidden layers required to capture the features of the data increases, so does the time taken for training to complete. As such, only one or two hidden layers are commonly used. Over-fitting may be a problem in ANNs, which is a memorization of the training cases causing the network to perform poorly on future cases. The one major barrier which researchers usually associate with ANNs is that it is not always apparent how they reach a solution, and because of this they have been referred to as 'black boxes' (Duh et al., 1998; Smith et al., 2003; Tung et al., 2004; Wall et al., 2003). In addition, the quality of the model output is highly dependent upon the quality of the input data. If the input data is not representative of the 'real world' scenario, the model is compromised. To overcome these issues, several techniques for pre-processing the data have been proposed, and the reader is referred to (Barla et al., 2008; Phan et al., 2006; Wang, 2008; Wong et al., 2005; Wong et al., 2005b) for more examples.

Support Vector Machines

Support Vector Machines (SVM) are classification and regression prediction tools that use machine learning theory to maximize predictive accuracy while automatically avoiding data over-fitting. Neural networks (NN) and Radial Basis Functions (RBFs), both popular data mining techniques, can be viewed as a special case of SVMs. SVMs perform well on bioinformatics and bio-sequence analysis. Their introduction in the early 1990s led to an explosion of applications and deepening theoretical analysis that established SVM along with neural networks as one of the standard tools for machine learning and data mining. Figure 13 depicts the optimal hyperplane, which has the largest distance from the nearest training data of any class (functional margin). It is noted that the larger the margin the lower the SVM generalization error.

Bayesian Networks

Bayesian networks (Pearl 1988) represent the dependence structure between multiple interacting quantities (e.g., expression levels of different genes). Bayesian networks are a promising tool for analyzing gene expression patterns. First, they are particularly useful for describing processes composed of locally interacting components; that is, the value of each component directly depends on the values of a relatively small number of components. Second, statistical foundations for learning Bayesian networks from observations, and computational algorithms to do so are well understood and have been used successfully in many applications. Finally, Bayesian Networks provide models of causal influence.

Although Bayesian networks are mathematically defined strictly in terms of probabilities and conditional independence statements, a connection can be made between this characterization and the notion of direct causal influence (Pearl & Verma, 1991; Spirtes et al., 1993). Probabilistic graphical models are graphs in which nodes represent random variables, and the (lack of) arcs represent conditional independence assumptions. Hence they provide a compact representation of joint probability distributions. Undirected graphical models, also called Markov Random Fields (MRFs) or Markov Networks, have a simple definition of independence: two (sets of) nodes A and B are conditionally independent given a third set, C, if all paths between the nodes in A and B are separated by a node in C. By contrast, directed graphical models also called Bayesian Networks or Belief Networks (BNs), have a more complicated notion of independence, which considers the directionality of the arcs, as we explain below. Undirected graphical models are more popular with the physics and vision communities, and directed models are more popular with the AI and statistics communities. (It is possible to have a model with both directed and undirected arcs, which is called a chain graph.) Although directed models have a more complicated notion of independence than undirected models, they do have several advantages. The most important is that one can regard an arc from A to B as indicating that A ``causes'' B. This can be used as a guide to construct the graph structure. In addition, directed models can encode deterministic relationships, and are easier to learn (fit to data). For a directed model, we must also specify the Conditional Probability Distribution (CPD) at each node i.e.

Figure 13. Detection of the optimal hyperplane and the maximum margin in clustered data

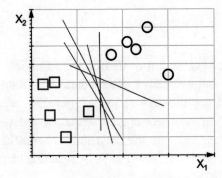 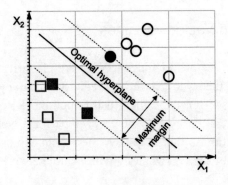

$$\Pr\left(V_i \Big| \pi\left(V_i\right)\right)$$

If the variables are discrete, this can be represented as a table (CPT), which lists the probability that the child node takes on each of its different values for each combination of values of its parents $\pi\left(V_i\right)$, as seen in equation 3.

$$\Pr\left(V_1,...,V_n\right) = \prod_{i=1}^{n} \Pr\left(V_i \Big| \pi\left(V_i\right)\right) \tag{3}$$

The advantages of the DAG models include their ability to handle efficiently incomplete datasets using novel sampling techniques (e.g. Gibbs sampling) and learn casual relationships for specific problem domains. Over-fitting can be avoided by embedding the prior knowledge to the model structure. Figure 14 depicts probabilistic inference, whereby it is possible to determine any probability of interest from an estimated Graphical model (direct acyclic graph, DAG) using a prior knowledge embedded to the model to avoid over-fitting.

Fuzzy Logic

A fuzzy subset of X as a function of A i.e. X-> [0, 1], is a characteristic function from X into the interval [0, 1], where the A(X) is called the membership function of the point x in the fuzzy set A, or the degree to which the point X belongs to the set A (Zadeh, 1965). The set of all fuzzy subsets (of X) is precisely the unit hypercube In = [0, 1] n, as any fuzzy subset μ determines a point P∈In given by

P=(μ(x1), ..., μ(xn)).

Figure 14. Implementation of the Bayesian networks

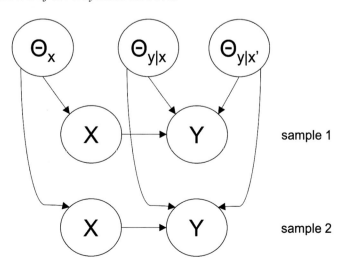

Reciprocally, any point A = (a1, ..., an) ∈ In, generates a fuzzy subset μ defined by μ(xi) = ai, with i = 1, ..., n. Non-fuzzy or crisp subsets of X are given by mappings μ: X → [0, 1], and are located at the 2n corners of the n-dimensional unit hypercube In.

Fuzzy logic has a number of successful applications in bioinformatics; some indicative ones are listed here: fuzzy logic has been used to increase the flexibility of protein motifs (Chang, 2002), to study differences between poly-nucleotides (Torres, 2003), to analyze experimental expression data (Tomida, 2002) using fuzzy adaptive resonance theory, to align sequences based on a fuzzy recast of a dynamic programming algorithm (Schlosshauer, 2002), for DNA sequencing using genetic fuzzy systems (Cordón, 2004), to cluster genes from microarray data (Belacel, 2004), to predict proteins sub-cellular locations from their dipeptide composition (Huang, 2004) using fuzzy k-nearest neighbors algorithm, to simulate complex traits influenced by genes with fuzzy-valued effects in pedigreed populations (Carleos, 2003), to attribute cluster membership values to genes (Dembele, 2003) applying a fuzzy partitioning method, fuzzy C-means, to map specific sequence patterns to putative functional classes since evolutionary comparison leads to efficient functional characterization of hypothetical proteins (Heger, 2003), others used a fuzzy alignment model, to analyze gene expression data (Woolf 2000), to unravel functional and ancestral relationships between proteins via fuzzy alignment methods (Blankenbecler, 2003), or using a generalized radial basis function neural network architecture that generates fuzzy classification rules(Lukac et al., 2005), to analyze the relationships between genes and decipher a genetic network (Agrawal, 1994), to process complementary deoxyribonucleic acid (cDNA) microarray images (Lukac et al., 2005) and to classify amino acid sequences into different super families (Bandyopadhyay, 2005).

SOLUTIONS AND RECOMMENDATIONS

Coupling Metabolomics with Transcriptomics towards Exposure Biology Analysis

Bioinformatics further advance the concept of the exposome, by integrating the omics responses of different omics levels, through mapping of regulatory networks and disease pathways. Functional integration of different omics results using bioinformatics tools aiming at development of adverse outcome pathways (AOPs) (Gutsell & Russell, 2013) for the endpoints addressed in EWAS. Different omics data that derived both from existing on-line databases and from *in vitro* laboratory experimentation are mapped onto regulatory pathways. They can be analysed using network visualization environments such as Agilent GeneSpring, Thompson-Reuters MetaCoreTM and Reactome/Functional Interaction network plug-in for Cytoscape, to create systems toxicology hypotheses from human data, related to the endpoints addressed in exposome-wide association studies, as well as to identify common nodes across several pathways of exposure to different compounds of relevance. This is especially important under the prism of cumulative exposure; metabolomics data, in combination with transcriptome data, show that the mechanism for the combined toxicity of several compounds exerting interactions beyond additivity occur at a network level (Roede et al., 2014).

Metabolic Pathway Analysis

Various statistical techniques can be combined in a proper way to identify potential biomarkers and demonstrate how useful the selected biomarkers are. A key issue for metabolomics studies is to avoid over-fitting the data. Because of the large number of metabolites and the relatively small sample size, a complex model can over-utilize (over-fit) the data specific information and show very good performance, but that good result is useless if it cannot be duplicated using a new set of test data. Proper model evaluation and validation is therefore a necessary step to understand the true performance of a model and the potential biomarkers. So, preprocessing methods, such as filtering, normalization and mean-centering, are crucial to pathway analysis. Mass Profiler Professional, an Agilent's software, provides the necessary tools for preprocessing steps, statistical analysis and pathway analysis.

Clustering Analysis

In Hierarchical Clustering Analysis (HCA), the multidimensional data obtained by untargeted metabolomics analysis is reduced to a correlation/distance matrix. Then, the samples are clustered together in a single dendogram and the distances between the samples reflect the similarities and differences between their metabolomic patterns.

Different distance measures (e.g. Euclidean, Pearson, Spearman) and clustering algorithms (e.g. average linkage, single linkage, complete linkage, ward, centroids) can be used in the development of HCA models. For this data set Euclidean will be used as distance metric and Wards as linkage rule. After that step, an entity list is created, which will be the sample data file for pathway analysis.

Pathway Analysis

The simple algorithms have present defaults to quickly create a pathway view for further investigation. On the other hand, the advanced algorithms provide the ability to specify several filter criteria for input data and relations.

Figure 15. HCA, similarity measure: Euclidean, number of clusters: 3, maximum number of iterations: 50

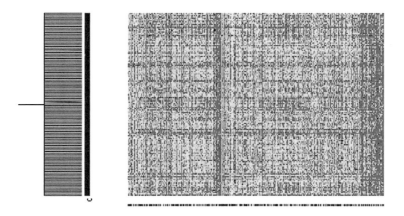

Simple Analysis

As input data will be used the identified biomarkers and metabolic pathways will be created with NLP Network discovery:

- **Workflow:** NLP Network Discover.
- Direct Interpretations.
- Matching statistics (Matched and redundant).
- **Analysis Filters:** Relation score ≥ 9.
- **Relation Types:** Member, transport, expression, regulation, binding, promoter binding, metabolism, protein modification.
- **Pathways From:** WikiPathways, KEGG, BioCyc.

Mass Profiler Professional first tries to find direct matches between the pathway entities (pathways from databases) and the entities in the selected list (input data). A direct match occurs only when entities from both pathways and entity lists have identifiers from the same annotation.

Advanced Analysis

Single Experiment Analysis (SEA) as the name implies, the SEA only identifies matching pathways for one experiment. In addition, the curated pathways options (for example WikiPathways, BioCyC pathways, KEGG, or BioPAX pathways) as well as NLP created pathways can also be individually selected as sources for pathway analysis.

Figure 16. Pathway from single experiment analysis: Butyrate-induced histone acetylation

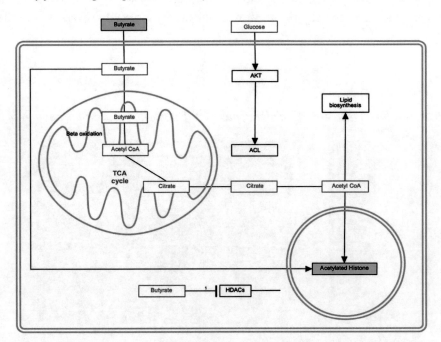

No p-values are computed for entities from metabolomics experiments during an SEA workflow to avoid a misrepresentation of the significance of matching pathways caused by the fact that Mass Profiler Professional uses the technology (All Entities list) as a reference for p-value computation. The technology of a metabolomics experiment is limited to only the measured metabolites with an observable abundance in the experiment. Pathways on the other hand are likely to contain many other metabolites that may not be present in the technology. This results in a pathway p-value computed with the technology as reference to be higher than a more realistic p-value computed with a comprehensive reference set of global entities.

Exposome-Wide Association Studies

A recently proposed analytic design to systematically associate exposures with disease is the "environment-wide association study" or "exposome-wide association study" (EWAS), analogous methodologically to the genome-wide association study (GWAS). In EWAS, multiple exposures are assessed simultaneously for their association with a phenotype or disease of interest. Multiple hypotheses are controlled using the false discovery rate (Benjamini and Hochberg 1995) and significant associations are validated in independent data (Patel et al. 2010, 2012, 2013b; Tzoulaki et al. 2012). The main advantage of this approach is that it systematically investigates an array of exposures and adjusts for multiple testing, thus avoiding selective reporting while enabling discovery. Just as the literature for genetic associations in disease has become more reproducible due to standardized and extensively validated analytical procedures (Ioannidis et al. 2011), we claim an analogous process to associate the exposome with disease and health outcomes will result in more robust environmental associations.

We introduce a novel approach towards defining causal associations between health status and environmental stressors through the integrated use of advanced statistical tools for environment-wide association studies (EWAS). Environmental factors that are correlated are not considered confounders; rather they are co-variates, which are in "linkage disequilibrium" with each other. EWAS findings could then be used to identify further factors that may be in "disequilibrium", for further detailed measurement and causal identification. Internal doses will be coupled to health impacts on the local population through advanced statistical methods to derive the dose–response functions which account for differences in exposure patterns, susceptibility differences and inter-individual variation in health response. The approach starts from the biomarker values measured in different biological matrices (urine and peripheral blood) to estimate through the application of the lifetime generic PBBK model the biological effective dose in the target tissue, which is consistent with the biomarker level measured. To estimate the health impact we will use a statistical approach based on survey-weighted logistic multivariate regression adjusted for different covariates (age, sex, socio-economic status etc.) linking internal doses with health effects or intermediate biological events that can be associated to health perturbations through pathway analysis considering the interdependence of the covariates (using as metric an analogy of the "linkage disequilibrium" metric used in genome-wide association studies). The general formulation of the approach is based on the mathematical linkage of health end points (expressed in terms of odds ratio, p) with different covariates (age sex, SES, lifestyle choices such as smoking, etc.) and the internal dose in the target tissue (X_{Factor}) such as the expression below:

$$\log it\left(\frac{p}{1-p}\right) = \alpha + \beta_0 \cdot \mathrm{cov}_1 + \beta_1 \cdot \mathrm{cov}_2 + \beta_2 \cdot X_{factor} \ldots + \beta_n \cdot \mathrm{cov}_n$$

where *cov* represents the different covariates used in the model and α and β are the regression coefficients which consider the interdependence between covariates.

Applications of EWAS in Case Studies

In this section, key examples of case studies stemming from HEALS and CROME, the largest exposome projects worldwide (together these multi-annual and multi-center exposome studies amount to a budget of 18-19 million EUR) are given. First, we shall illustrate the application of exposome-wide associations through the combined use of bioinformatics and big data analytics in the assessment of the association between:

1. Neurodevelopmental disorders and children's exposure to metals in Greece; and
2. Neurodevelopmental disorders and children's exposure to phthalates and metals in Greece.

The results of our analysis revealed the potentiation effect that phthalates exert on the neurotoxicity of heavy metals and identified the metabolic pathway that plays a key part in the adverse health outcome of combined exposure to phthalates and toxic metals at different ages.

Neurodevelopmental disorders and children's exposure to metals in Greece

For clustering the various exposure related data, the two different clustering techniques were used and the results are graphically illustrated in Figure 17.

The auto-correlations of the various parameters, are illustrated in both the heatmap (Figure 18a) and the correlation globe (Figure 18b).

The outcomes of the associations among the various exposure and sociodemographic factors for one selected indicative outcome of each test battery are illustrated in the following Figures.

EWAS analysis results relevant to the Child Behavioral CheckList (CBCL) test battery outcomes show that socio-cultural factors are strongly associated with child behavior. More specifically mother school title and age of the mothers at birth show both a robust statistical association (p-value<0.05 and in some cases p-value <0.01) with most of the CBCL indices considered. Looking at the respective

Figure 17. Hierarchical clustering using the (a) Hoeffding D and (b) the Pearson correlation methods respectively

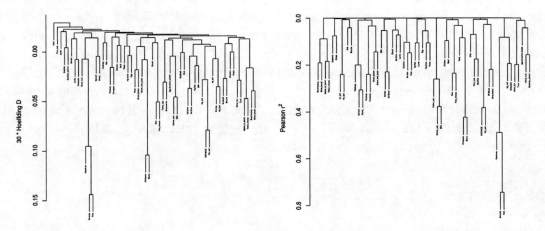

Figure 18. Heatmap of the exposure parameters and correlation globe of the environmental, dietary and exposure factors of an exposome study

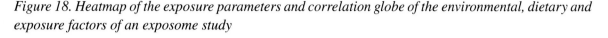
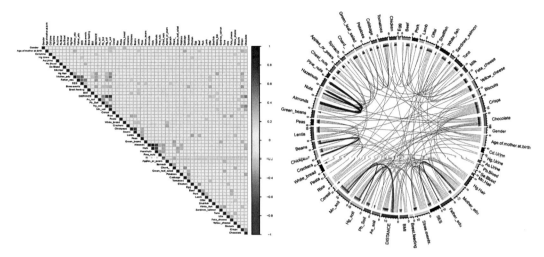

volcano plots both parameters show a negative association with the CBCL scores indicating that lower educational level of the mothers as well as a lower age of the mother at child birth may have negative impact on child behavior.

The stress index was derived by merging the total number of stressful events detected by the mother and their average intensity is also playing an important role on child behavior (p-value<0.05 and in some cases p-value<0.01) showing a negative effect on both internalizing and externalizing problems indices such as anxiety and depression, withdrawal and depression and somatic complaints, aggressive and rule-breaking behavior.

The concentration of lead in blood shows a strong statistical significance (p-value <0.05) with most of the CBCL indices analyzed. In this case the association shows a positive direction revealing a negative impact of higher blood concentration of lead on the on cognitive functions in children. This result is confirmed by a number of research studies which indicate exposure to lead as one of the most environmental determinants of neurodevelopmental disorders in children. On this subject the National Toxicology Program (NTP) has concluded that childhood lead exposure is associated with reduced cognitive function, including lower intelligence quotient (IQ) and reduced academic achievement (National Toxicology Program, 2012). The NTP has also concluded that childhood lead exposure is associated with attention-related behavioral problems (including inattention, hyperactivity, and diagnosed attention-deficit/hyperactivity disorder (ADHD)) and increased incidence of problem behaviors including delinquent, criminal, or antisocial behavior (National Toxicology Program, 2012).

Of opposite sign but still with robust statistical significance is the association of the concentration of selenium in blood which appears to act as beneficial element especially with regard to Internalizing Problems and ADHD as measured by CBCL battery indices. These results confirm the antioxidant properties of selenium which is a well-known regulator of brain function (Dominiak et al., 2016). These positive properties that selenium possesses are attributed to its ability to be incorporated into selenoproteins as an amino acid. Several selenoproteins are expressed in the brain, in which some of them, e.g. glutathione peroxidases (GPxs), thioredoxin reductases (TrxRs) or selenoprotein P (SelP), are strongly involved in antioxidant defense and in maintaining intercellular reducing conditions. Since increased oxidative stress has been implicated in neurological disorders higher levels of selenium in blood may be among the important factors protecting against those pathologies.

Breast feeding in the first months of children life is another parameter that shows a significant statistical association (p-value <0.05) especially with the internalizing problems as measured by CBCL battery indices. Also in this case the association shows a negative sign indicating that breastfeeding and especially its duration during the first year of life results in a beneficial effect on anxiety/depression, withdrawal/depression and somatic complaints as reported by the CBCL indices.

The concentration of mercury in hair reveals a strong association (p-value <0.05) with many CBCL indices considered, however its effect appears to have a controversial behavior as witnessed by its negative sign reported in the volcano plots indicating that higher concentration levels of Hg in hair may results in potential positive effect on the problem behavior in children.

CBCL indices as measured by teachers reveal slightly different patterns. Even though the socio- cultural factors such as mother school title still show robust associations with most of the Child Behavioral CheckList test battery outcomes, other variables appear to play an important role. Among them the distance of the residence address from the waste management site shows a strong association especially with the internalizing problems. The negative sign of the association corroborates the negative impact of living in areas close to the waste management site especially on anxiety/depression, withdrawal/ depression and somatic complaints.

Concentration of lead in blood is yet another significant variable (p-value <0.05) associated with Attention Deficit Hyperactivity Disorder while Breast feeding shows a strong association with Oppositional Defiant Disorder (ODD). Among the various food items considered, some of them show significant statistical association with CBCL indices. Consumption of pork appears to be inversely associated (p-value <0.05) with the CBCL indices related to externalizing problems such as aggressive and rule-breaking behavior as well as with association with Oppositional Defiant Disorder and with Conduct Problems. High consumption of chicken reveals a strong association with Attention Deficit Hyperactivity Disorder measured by the teachers. Consumption of cabbage and lentils appears to influence negatively Attention Deficit Hyperactivity Disorder, Oppositional Defiant Disorder and with Conduct Problems too. High consumption of coffee is associated with externalizing problems such as aggressive and rule-breaking behavior and with Attention Deficit Hyperactivity Disorder and Conduct Problems measured by the teachers. Higher consumption of pine nuts and nuts as well as of white and wheat bread indicates a beneficial effect on externalizing problems such as aggressive and rule-breaking behavior. Finally, higher consumption of eggs and of beans are also associated to beneficial effects on internalizing problems (i.e. anxiety/depression, withdrawal/depression and somatic complaints) indices.

EWAS analysis results relevant to the Cambridge Neuropsychological Test Automated Battery (CANTAB) test battery results show that concentration of Manganese in the hair is associated (p-value <0.05) with the Spatial Working Memory (SWM) with a positive sign revealing that higher Manganese levels in the hair increase error generation. Socio-cultural factors show again significant statistic association with the outcomes of the CANTAB test battery.

More in detail Mother School title appears to have a beneficial effect (p-value < 0.05) on the Stop Signal Task while Father School title on the spatial Working Memory Strategy index (p-value < 0.05). The stress index is also strongly associated (p-value <0.01) with the Spatial Working Memory (SWM) with a negative sign showing that higher stress levels decrease the error production.

Figure 19. Associations of (a) attention deficit / hyperactivity problems (from the CBCL test battery), (b) Stop Signal Task Mean correct RT on GO trials (from the CANTAB test battery), (c) Total score T / Teachers (from the Social Responsiveness Scale test battery) and (d) intelligence quotient (from the WISC-IV test battery) with the environmental, dietary and exposure factors

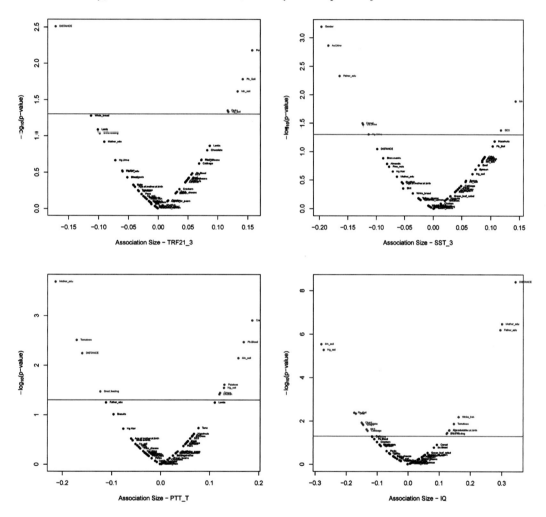

EWAS analysis results relevant to the Social Responsiveness Scale (SRS) test battery show that also in this case socio-cultural factors are strongly associated with the Social Responsiveness Scale outcomes considered. Mother school title (p-value <0.000) and to a lower extent Father school title (p-value < 0.05) show both a robust statistical association the T scores of both the parents and teachers. Moreover, the associations have a negative direction demonstrating that lower educational level of the parents may have negative impact on the Autism Spectrum Disorder (ASD) impairments of children.

Distance of the residence address from the waste management site shows a good association (p-value <0.001) with the T scores of the teachers. The negative sign of the association confirms the potential negative impact of living in the areas close to the waste management site on ASD impairments of children

Breastfeeding in the first months of children life also shows a good statistical association (p-value <0.05) with T scores as reported by teachers. The association shows a negative sign indicating the positive effect of breastfeeding, and especially its duration during the first year of life, on ASD impairments of children.

Among the biomonitoring data selenium in blood appears to be inversely associated (p-value < 0.05) with the T scores of the parents. The negative sign of the association supports the positive impact of selenium on the neurodevelopmental disorders. Mercury concentration in hair shows a significant statistical association (p-value < 0.05) with SRS battery indices and its effect appears to result in potential positive effect on ASD impairments.

Among the different food items higher consumption of pork (p < 0.01), coffee (p-value < 0.01), chicken (p < 0.05), crackers (p-value < 0.05) and lentils (p-value < 0.05) are associated with higher T scores of the SRS test battery indicating a potential negative effect on ASD impairments. On the contrary higher consumption of tomatoes (p-value < 0.001), fish (p-value < 0.01) and white cheese (p-value <0.05)) are related with lower T scores of the SRS test battery signifying a potential positive effect on ASD impairment of children.

EWAS analysis results relevant to the WISC-IV test results show that the variable distance of the residence address from the waste management site is a key factor associated with almost all the indices of the WISC IV test. More specifically this variable shows a robust statistical association (p-value <0.001) with the Intelligence Quotient (IQ), Verbal Comprehension index, Perceptual Reasoning index, Working Memory index. Analysis of the results show a positive association with the WISC IV scores indicating that living far from the waste management site has a positive impact on the children cognitive functions. Some interesting conclusions can be drawn from the analysis of food consumption patterns. Tomatoes consumption appears to be statistically (p-value <0.05) associated to QI, Verbal Comprehension index and Working Memory index while cereal consumption reveals a strong association (p-value < 0.01) with the Perceptual Reasoning index. Both these food items show a positive sign meaning that their consumption has potential positive effects on the cognitive functions of the children. Epidemiological evidence suggests that consumption of lycopene, natural antioxidant presents in tomatoes, is able to reduce the risk of chronic diseases such as cancer, cardiovascular diseases as well as psychiatric syndromes (Story et al., 2010). In another study (Li & Zhang, 2007) reported that low serum levels of lycopene have been associated with increased risk of psychiatric disorders. One review of 22 studies examining the association of breakfast cereal consumption and academic performance in children and adolescents concluded that breakfast consumption may improve cognitive function related to memory, test grades, and school attendance (Rampersaud et al., 2005).

Similarly to the CBCL test battery consumption of white fish appears to have positive effects on the IQ and Verbal Comprehension index (p-value < 0.001).

Neurodevelopmental Disorders and Children's Exposure to Phthalates and Metals in Poland

Investigation of the associations between the various neurodevelopment indices evaluated by the Bailey test revealed that different factors might have a negative, or a beneficial contribution.

Regarding cognitive development at one year of life (Figure 20a), it was found that child exposure to DEHP and BBzP result in lower cognitive scores, while the same occurs for the levels of glutathione peroxidase 3 in the mother plasma during pregnancy. On the other hand, the gestational age of the mother has beneficial effect, however causality (socio-developmental or physiology) should be further investigated. In the second year of age (Figure 20b), cognitive development is negatively affected by child exposure to DnBP and the presence of thiobarbituric acid reactive substances in the mother plasma during pregnancy. On the contrary, the presence of selenium during the third semester of pregnancy seem to be a significant beneficial parameter, followed by glutathione peroxidase 1 in the mother plasma during pregnancy. It is also very important to highlight that cognitive development strongly depends on child attendance of day care center; children hosted in day care centers present higher cognitive skills.

Child exposure to phthalates (BBzP) seems to affect negatively language development at one year of age (Figure 21a). Interestingly, presence of Zn (during all the trimesters of pregnancy), glutathione peroxidase 1 (during the second trimester) and Cu in maternal plasma acts beneficially in linguistic development. Language development at two years of age (Figure 21) is affected negatively by child exposure to DEP, DnBP and DinP, indicating once more the detrimental effects of children exposure to both low and high molecular phthalates. However, prenatal exposure to thiobarbituric acid reactive substances, glutathione peroxidase 3, glutathione peroxidase 1 and selenium during the last trimester of pregnancy, indicate the importance of this developmental period for the future language development of the child.

None of the environmental exposure factors seems to play a key role on motor development. At year one (Figure 22a), maternal alcohol consumption during pregnancy results in lower scores of motor development, while the presence of selenium (during the 1st and the 3rd trimester), contributes beneficially. In addition, child attendance in a day care center contributes beneficially as well. Regarding the motor development in the second year (Figure 22b), a very interesting finding is that increased maternal bodyweight during the 1st and the 3rd trimester result in lower motor development. On the other hand, the presence of thiobarbituric acid reactive substances and Hg in the mother plasma during the 3rd trimester result in higher motor development scores. Note that the presence of Hg does not act (in terms of physiology) positively in motor development; it is rather an indicator of high consumption of food items (e.g. fish), rich in Hg, but also in other nutrients (e.g. omega 3 fatty acids) that are beneficial for child development.

Figure 20. Association of the cognitive development at year one (a) and year two (b) of age with exposure and modifiers

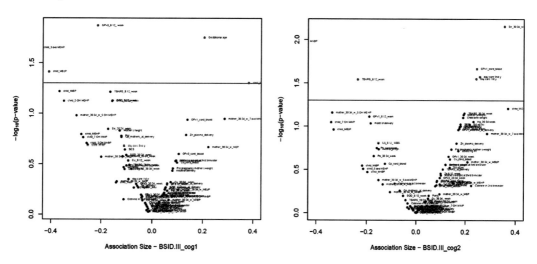

Figure 21. Association of the language development at year one (a) and year two (b) of age with exposure and modifiers

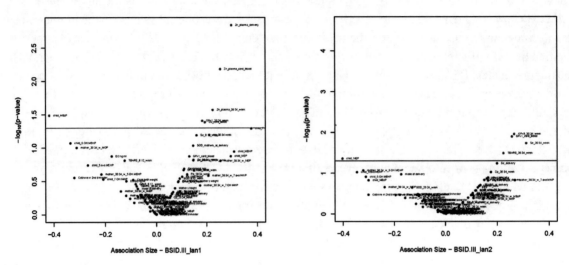

Figure 22. Association of the motor development at year one (a) and year two (b) of age with exposure and modifiers

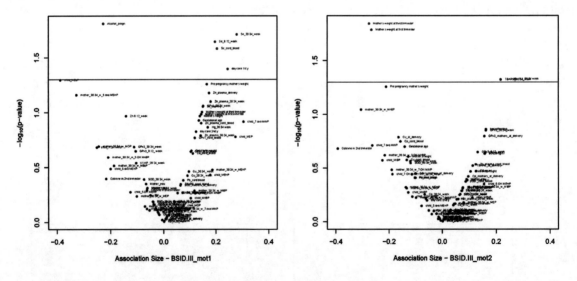

Application of the Computational Exposure Biology Framework to Real-Life Ambient Air Mixtures

Exposure to multiple stressors offers a comprehensive example of applying high throughput –omics data analysis to understand the effects of environmental burden on public health. Toxicity of chemical mixtures is only partially addressed by the current state of environmental health sciences. The so-called 'cocktail' effect becomes even more complex due to the large number of possible combinations of chemicals and other (physical or biological) stressors in the environment. This has hampered the development of rigorous methodologies for tackling the issue of environmental mixture safety. To date both our scientific understanding and policy for environmental mixtures are based largely on extrapolating from, and combining, data in the observable range of single chemical toxicity to lower environmental concentrations and composition - i.e. using higher dose data to extrapolate and predict lower dose toxicity. Thus, more precise approaches to characterize toxicity of mixtures are needed. A major obstacle to the development of effective mixture risk assessment methodologies is the possibly infinite ways of combining chemicals into actual environmental mixtures (Mason et al., 2007). It should be noted, however, that although in theory the number of combinations of chemicals or stressors is infinite, the number of biological processes is finite. Therefore, in considering an integrated approach for risk assessment, it makes more sense to work on the finite biological processes that may be affected by human exposure to these mixtures rather than the infinite combinations of chemicals and stressors (Liao et al., 2002). Integrated health impact assessment of environmental stressor mixtures would need to follow a 'full chain' approach to consider all relevant health stressors and their interaction. Application of the full chain approach entails considering all possible exposure pathways via the environment and lifestyle choices. It also encompasses considering the effects of co-exposure to relevant stressors and how risk modifying factors such as age, diet, gender, and time window of exposure affects the final physiological response. Successful application of this approach poses demanding data requirements both in terms of environmental monitoring and in terms of biological and clinical data interpretation. What is most important is the need for comprehensive data interpretation of the molecular, biochemical and physiological processes that couple exposure to health outcome.

This requires forging a new paradigm for interdisciplinary scientific work in environment and health. We shall call this the connectivity paradigm for chemical risk assessment, denoting an approach that builds on the exploration of the interconnections between the co-existence of multiple stressors and the different scales of biological organization explicitly described by omics that together produce the final adverse health effect (Workman et al., 2006). Connectivity marks a clear departure from the conventional paradigm, which seeks to shed light on the identification of singular cause-effect relationships between stressors and health outcomes. It entails creating a new way of combining health-relevant information coming from different disciplines, including (but not limited to) environmental science, epidemiology, toxicology, physiology, molecular biology, biochemistry, mathematics and computer science (Kitano, 2002a, 2002b). The integration of these different information classes into a unique framework to better inform and support public health impact assessment of chemical mixtures in the environment could serve as a good example for the integration of the omics in the risk assessment process and the evaluation of population health impact assessment.

In the context of applying systems biology approaches to chemical mixtures risk assessment, we move forward towards the definition of a combined-exposure biology using optimally physiology and systems biology based modelling and data mining and assimilation algorithms. The aim is to couple the systems biology approach to the gene-environment interactions with the corresponding "physiome" approach. The variable levels of biological organization involved in this holistic view of mixture toxicology and cumulative exposure and risk assessment suggest that different technologies need to be brought to bear to obtain a comprehensive view of how co-exposure to multiple chemicals affects the overall phenotypic response of individuals. Technological variability introduces the need for better data integration and assimilation and for the development of novel data analysis and hypothesis generation and testing procedures to best elucidate the biological mechanisms underlying mixture toxicity. On the basis of the data currently available, the best available techniques, and the need for data integration, a tiered approach has been developed and outlined herein to support the connectivity approach to the assessment of health risk associated to combined exposure to multiple chemical stressors (Sarigiannis, Gotti, Cimino Reale, & Marafante, 2009). This exposure biology approach to mechanism-based risk assessment of environmental chemical mixtures can be tackled with an integrated, multi-layer computational methodology, ideally comprising the following steps:

1. Characterization of exposure factors quantifying the parameters that affect human exposure to environmental chemicals, such as time-activity relationships, seasonal and climatic variation, and consumer choice. These exposure factors can be used to derive aggregate and cumulative exposure models, leading in probabilistic exposure assessments. Aggregation can be done across exposure pathways and routes and even across different exposure scenarios, if the relevant exposure metric or the imputable biological or physiological effect can be related to these scenarios. For instance, exposure to volatile organic compounds (VOCs) such as benzene or toluene and mixtures thereof may occur both from environmental media and in specific occupational settings. A cumulative exposure scenario for these substances would have to take stock of the actual variability of exposure across these different settings throughout typical days for the same period in an individual's lifespan.
2. Current toxicological state of the art combines estimations of biologically effective dose with early biological events to derive dose-effect models, which can be used in combination with the probabilistic exposure estimates to derive biomarkers of exposure and/or effect. Combined use of epidemiological, clinical and genetic analysis data may shed light on the effect of risk modifying factors such as lifestyle choices and DNA polymorphisms. Observation of real clinical data and/ or results of biomonitoring, if coupled with the exposure/effect biomarker discovery systems, can produce biomarkers of individual susceptibility and thus allow estimations of individual response to toxic insults. Toxicogenomics, comprising transcriptomics, proteomics and metabolomics, and adductomics (considering adducts of xenobiotics not only to DNA but also to proteins such as albumin) are key technologies to this kind of analytical and data interpretation process.
3. The analysis of the biomarker data (including results on biomarkers of exposure, effects and individual susceptibility) results in the integrated assessment of risk factors. Use of information on risk factors with molecular dosimetry data (i.e. estimation of the actual internal and biologically effective dose of xenobiotic substance found in the target organ and, indeed, perturbing cellular response) enables population risk studies to be done, by converting generic exposure profiles into population risk metrics having considered inter-individual variability of response and exposure uncertainty.

The connectivity approach was applied on data from Europe-wide campaigns on environmental and biological monitoring of a virtually ubiquitous mixture of volatile organic compounds, i.e. benzene, ethylbenzene, toluene and o-, m- and p-xylene, aldehydes such as formaldehyde and acetaldehyde and a complex mixture of polyaromatic hydrocarbons, which is typical of combustion products (Kotzias et al., 2009). The full array of –omics technologies outlined above were applied to samples of indoor air and dry blood spots and urine of exposed subjects from almost all European Union capitals. Exposure assessment was completed with detailed time activity diaries and questionnaires regarding smoking and dietary habits (especially with regard to alcohol consumption) (Sarigiannis, Karakitsios, Gotti, Liakos, & Katsoyiannis, 2011). Gene expression results were processed using clustering algorithms to derive heat maps demonstrating clearly the differences in the biological perturbations caused by parts of the indoor and ambient airborne chemical mixtures in the sampled sites.

Dry blood spot samples from a subset (n = 50) of the population which participated in the personal exposure study were analyzed with the –omics technologies and state-of-the-art bioinformatics software. Agilent MicroArray Express was used for analysis of the blood samples and comparison with controls and GeneSpring, the Agilent data analysis system, and in-house bioinformatics analysis software developed on R and Stata were used for –omics data analysis in EnvE Lab.

The sample analysis followed a hybrid, tiered approach starting from an agnostic search in whole genome mRNA extracted from the biological samples after appropriate sampling and storage at -80 ^{0}C. The population data were clustered by group of dominant source of exposure to airborne chemicals including ambient air in cities, typical airborne mixtures in dwellings, schools, kindergartens and other indoor professional environments (public buildings) and samples from people occupationally exposed to fly ash from coal-fired thermal power plants. $p < 0.005$ was used as test of statistical significance revealing the level of gene expression modulation against the controls – in this case only the genes that were up- or down-regulated by more than two-fold compared to the controls were selected. This agnostic search indicated the presence of exposure-specific signatures using gene expression data, especially when considering not just the number but also the loci of the genes that showed the most important differences in expression levels after exposure to the respective mixtures of xenobiotics. Both common parts and clearly distinct regions of the genes with significant modulation in expression were identified when comparing biological samples of subjects exposed to ambient air chemicals against the ones of subjects exposed non-professionally to indoor chemicals and professionally to fly ash (Figure 23). Comparative analysis showed that ambient air chemicals in urban settings across Europe affect a wide spectrum of genes (n=376), most of which are up-regulated (n' = 209); a significant number of genes in the same samples was down-regulated (n''=167). Fly ash had an almost as high an effect on the human genome. Here there were fewer genes that showed modulation in expression (n = 214). Unlike ambient urban air chemicals, fly ash from power plants resulted in limited up-regulation (n' = 66) and more important down-regulation of gene expression (n''=148). Indoor air chemicals had the smallest effect on gene expression modulation. In this case the total number of genes that modulated their expression levels was contained (n = 145). Up-regulated genes were dominant (n'=92) and down-regulated genes were relatively limited (n'' = 53). Several genes showed very distinct expression patterns when cross-comparing samples from subjects exposed to different types of airborne chemicals. These could be isolated to serve as exposure signatures at the molecular level. Clearly, such genomic biomarkers of exposure do not imply causal associations with adverse health outcomes. However, they may serve as seed information to the formation of biologically plausible mechanistic hypotheses on adverse outcome pathways (AOPs). These hypotheses help in limiting the investigation space for AOPs without compromising the agnostic nature of the initial analyses.

The results of the agnostic transcriptome search on biological samples regarding the identification of potential genomic signatures that can serve as reliable exposure biomarkers were corroborated by means of in vitro testing. For this reason, samples of the airborne chemicals taken in the various environments considered in this study were extracted and applied on cell lines covering both lung epithelial cells (A549) and skin keratinocytes (Ha-CaT). Cluster analysis of the gene expression results are depicted in the heat map shown in Figure 24. It is very clear that indoor chemicals show distinctly different patterns of gene expression modulation in both types of matrices, especially when compared to the mixture of indoor air chemicals and PAHs from the ambient air in urban settings. It should be noted that the latter corresponds

Figure 23. Comparison of gene expression modulation from biosamples of population exposed to different types of airborne chemical mixtures: (a) ambient air chemicals (top left); (b) characteristic airborne chemicals found in indoor settings (top right); (c) chemicals found in fly ash from thermal power plants using fossil fuel (bottom left). The table at the bottom right of the figure shows the total number of gene expressed differentially in subjects exposed to the different airborne chemical mixtures and the number of genes up- and down-modulated respectively

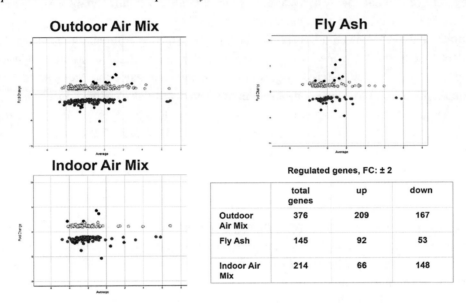

Regulated genes, FC: ± 2			
	total genes	up	down
Outdoor Air Mix	376	209	167
Fly Ash	145	92	53
Indoor Air Mix	214	66	148

Figure 24. Heat map representing comparative cluster analysis of gene expression after application of airborne chemical mixtures on dermal (Ha-CAT) and lung epithelial (A549) cells. IAM: indoor air mixture; PAHs: the mixture of 19 polyaromatic hydrocarbons commonly found in the ambient air in European metropolitan areas

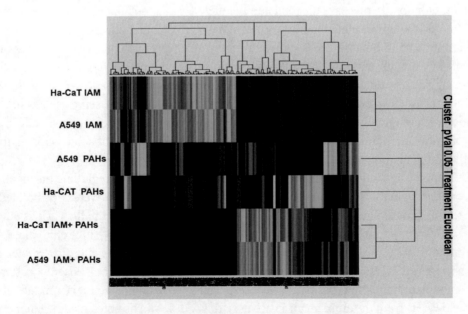

to realistic total exposure patterns of the human population in European metropolitan areas. Exposure to ambient air chemicals only shows intermediate results, indicating that co-exposure to ambient and indoor air chemical mixtures in cities may have more than additive effects on gene expression modulation.

After the agnostic tier, it is possible to identify not only single genes that have shown significant modulation in expression levels, but also determine the biological pathways that are regulated by gene networks that were significantly modulated with regard to their induction levels from exposure to xenobiotics. Pathway analysis using Agilent GeneSpring and the on-line PANTHER – Protein ANalysis THrough Evolutionary Relationships) Classification System (http://www.pantherdb.org) showed that two key pathways, *p53* (regulating cell cycle, senescence and apoptosis) and *oxidative stress induction* were differentially modulated from specific chemical families such as aldehydes, while specific genes or gene sequences could be characterized as molecular markers of exposure. In Figure 25 comparative analysis of the gene regulation induction after exposure to different chemical classes of xenobiotics, which comprise a large part of the indoor air mixture found in European dwellings is shown, focusing on the genetic network regulating oxidative stress response at the cellular level. More specifically, the samples of indoor air chemical mixtures taken from different European cities were decomposed and

Figure 25. Modulation of the oxidative stress pathway in blood samples of subjects exposed to different airborne chemical families reveals molecular signatures of co-exposure

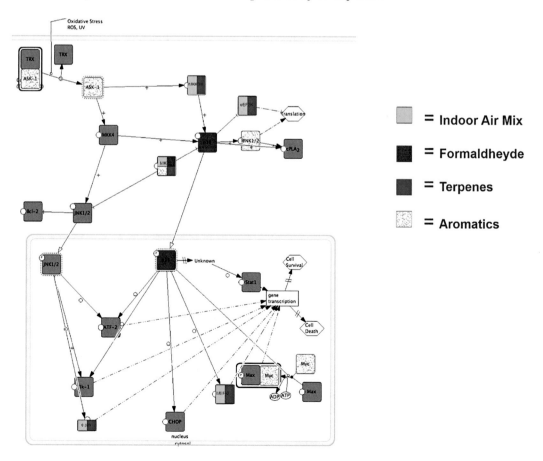

sequentially extracted to analyze separately the effect on gene expression of major chemical families, including: (a) carbonyl compounds such as aldehydes, (b) phenols and other aromatics, and (c) terpens.

Aromatics had the highest impact in terms of inducing oxidative stress responses. Terpens had the second highest impact in terms of activation of parts of the oxidative stress regulatory network. Aldehydes, and in particular formaldehyde, induced among others a specific gene, p38, which is central to the regulation of oxidative stress response in human cells. This gene (p38) could serve as a reliable biomarker of oxidative stress (intermediate effect) associated to exposure to formaldehyde, since no other treatment seemed to modulate its expression levels.

Similar results were found when exploring the modulation of the gene network that regulates the function of the p53 pathway, controlling thus cell cycle and death and thus the onset of carcinogenesis in case of faulty operation and down-regulation. In this case the indoor air chemical mixture as a whole has the highest impact. It seems to induce the expression of the overall regulatory network thus leading to significant up-regulation compared to the controls. Aromatics and terpens have similar size effects on gene network regulation. Terpens are more involved in processes regulating apoptosis, as well as inhibition of angiogenesis and metastasis. Aldehydes are involved in processes leading to inhibition of angiogenesis and metastasis too. Thus, different chemical families show different toxicity profiles, not only when associating them with phenotypes of disease such as cancer, but also, and possibly more importantly, when elucidating their role in biological pathways of toxicity that may (or may not) lead to adverse health outcomes.

From the chemical speciation of the air samples taken in the different European urban settings in this study, typical airborne chemical mixtures were identified for indoor and ambient air as a function of latitude. For example, regarding volatile organic chemicals, compounds that are essentially ubiquitous in Europe, air mixtures were richer in benzene in the south compared to the north of Europe, where toluene seemed to be more abundant. Following through to the biological processes that were perturbed by exposure to these airborne chemical mixtures we found that during acute (short-term) exposure signal transduction and mRNA transcription were modulated the most following an inverse dose-response function. When chronic (longer-term) exposure results were analyzed, protein metabolism, mRNA transcription regulation and cell proliferation and differentiation were the main mechanisms that were modulated following a normal dose-response behavior. The salient results of this tier of the connectivity analysis are given in Figure 26 for mixture A (the benzene-richer mixture, typical of the European south) and for mixture B (the one that was relatively richer in toluene and other chemically similar solvents, typical of central and northern Europe).

In addition, the mixtures that were richer with non-carcinogens were the ones that had the highest impact on the biological processes induced during short-term exposure; on the contrary, mixtures richer with carcinogens such as benzene induced a higher response in terms of biological process induction to the individuals who were exposed longer. This behavior was confirmed by untargeted metabolomics profiling, which showed a relative increase in benzene metabolites such as s- mercapturic acid as well as free, non-metabolized benzene. Phenotypic observations confirm that chronic exposure to carcinogenic VOCs such as benzene could increase the risk of leukemia. Considering the metabolic processes and interactions (e.g. competitive inhibition) that regulate the effective metabolism of the VOCs to which the European population was exposed we estimated the actual risk of cancer from the combined exposure to such airborne chemical mixtures released from fuel and consumer products. Focusing even further

Figure 26. Biological processes induced by the two characteristic types of indoor air mixtures in Europe

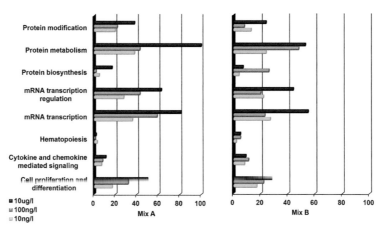

on the molecular underpinning of the induced modulation of the human capacity to metabolize VOCs under co-exposure conditions, targeted analysis of the CyP450 was performed using Taqman Fluidigm microarrays. Results showed a significant variation in the expression of genes involved in the coding of the enzymes involved in benzene and toluene metabolic chains. This variation results in reduction of the amount of available enzymes and thus enhances the effect of competitive inhibition for the limited amount of receptor sites at the metabolically active tissues. The results show suppression of CyP450 metabolic capacity after co-exposure to the four VOCs (Figure 27). These findings were translated into quantitative change in the metabolic rates captured in the biology-based dose-response (BBDR) model developed in-house to estimate cancer risk by applying dynamic flux balance analysis and coupling the gene regulatory network with the ADME model.

Figure 27. Comparison of CyP450 expression modulation for benzene-rich (black bar) and toluene-rich (white bar) quaternary BTEX mixtures after 4 (left figure) and 24 h (right figure) of exposure

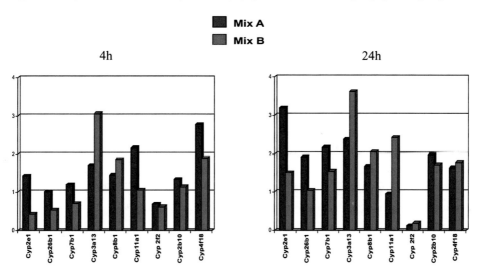

FUTURE RESEARCH DIRECTIONS

As discussed above a large variety of bioinformatics and big data analytics tools are available to explore the human exposome and how this affects human health through its interaction with the genome and the epigenome. Currently a small number of relatively large research projects on the exposome attempt to develop methodologies for meeting this goal. A couple of examples in case are given in earlier sections of this chapter. The progress in computational exposure biology notwithstanding, several directions for future research that would facilitate the transition to precision medicine and prevention are noted and given below:

- Development and implementation of deep learning algorithms coupled with advances in massive parallelization to approach efficiently the computational complexity of exposure biology.
- Enhancement of the application space of computational exposure biology to pose practical problems that will need to be solved. This will refine further and establish the EWAS approach as a valid, ground-breaking paradigm in environmental health science.
- Coupling of the bioinformatics and big data analytics methods described in this chapter with systems biology models to capture the dynamics of the interactions occurring on different levels of biological organization.
- Development of a dynamic flux balance analysis framework to link the observed modulations in gene expression (the transcriptome) with the resulting imbalances of metabolic fluxes.
- Enhancement of the application of causality-searching algorithms such as Bayesian belief networks to target the common nodes between different adverse outcome pathways.

CONCLUSION

The exposome represents the totality of exposure during lifespan, aiming at providing more accurate and comprehensive exposure estimates, towards a better understanding of the respective biological responses that will eventually end up into clinical phenotypes. Major challenges regarding the unravelling of the exposome comprise the following:

- The totality of exposures relates to combined exposure to multiple compounds, thus methods that will allow the realistic estimation (modelled or measured) of personal exposure or media contamination to multiple compounds play a key role in deciphering the human exposome.
- The accurate assessment of contamination of the media that people come into contact; these include outdoor and indoor air, drinking water, food items, soil and settled dust. In addition, consumer product affect human exposure either directly (e.g. clothes and personal care product), or indirectly (e.g. cleaning products and indoor air).
- The accurate assessment of the time people encounter various media (e.g. time spent driving) and the exposure conditions (e.g. intensity of activity). Sensor technologies and the algorithms for interpreting the big data collected by these sensors, are expected to provide the missing pieces for complementing individual exposome.

- Although the exposome is oriented towards assessing individual exposure, accurate extrapolation to population groups is equally important for large population studies; the extrapolation process should not be based only on probabilistic techniques, but also on the dynamic interactions among the members of the study population capturing individual behaviors, affecting both space-time trajectories and consumer choice. Thus, sociodemographic parameters should be explicitly addressed. In addition, the effect of this behavior on the environmental quality itself is something that must be accounted for.

- Another key component of the exposome is the internal exposome. People that are exposed to similar levels of environmental exposure, might be internally exposed to completely different levels to toxicants because of genetic factors, differentiated dietary patterns and health status (e.g. pre-existing disease hampering or modulating the metabolism of xenobiotics). In addition, internal dosimetry, allows the proper integration of uptake from different routes and within variant exposure regimes.

- In addition to the above, the use of biomonitoring data for understanding human exposure bears major advantages compared to bottom up approaches. However, this requires a proper computational framework and a valid biokinetics modelling platform that can cover a large part of the currently existing chemical space. The exposure reconstruction algorithm presented herein, provides unique opportunities for human biomonitoring data assimilation and it is expected to be extensively used in the European Human Biomonitoring Initiative (HBM4EU, 2017-2021). The development of such computationally and biostatistically advanced tools may overhaul the current practice in the use of human biomonitoring (HBM) data for chemical risk assessment. To date, HBM data are used readily as direct proxies of human exposure. This, however, is a gross approximation that does not support the more stringent requirements of internal exposome analysis. In that context, we need to properly translate HBM data into actual external exposure profiles for the study population, expressed in terms of patterns of dose and time profile of delivery.

- Considering the need for better internal dosimetry metrics and biomonitoring data assimilation of a vast number of compounds, computational methods that allow to expand the applicability domain of biokinetic models are of major importance as well.

REFERENCES

Aebersold, R., & Mann, M. (2003). Mass spectrometry-based proteomics. *Nature, 422*(6928), 198–207. doi:10.1038/nature01511 PMID:12634793

Agrawal, R., & Srikant, R. (1994). Fast Algorithms for Mining Association Rules in Large Databases. *Paper presented at the VLDB Conference.*

Allison, D. B., Cui, X., Page, G. P., & Sabripour, M. (2006). Microarray data analysis: From disarray to consolidation and consensus. *Nature Reviews. Genetics, 7*(1), 55–65. doi:10.1038/nrg1749 PMID:16369572

Altman, R. B., & Raychaudhuri, S. (2001). Whole-genome expression analysis: Challenges beyond clustering. *Current Opinion in Structural Biology, 11*(3), 340–347. doi:10.1016/S0959-440X(00)00212-8 PMID:11406385

Bandyopadhyay, S. (2005). An efficient technique for superfamily classification of amino acid sequences: Feature extraction, fuzzy clustering and prototype selection. *Fuzzy Sets and Systems, 152*(1), 5–16. doi:10.1016/j.fss.2004.10.011

Barla, A., Jurman, G., Riccadonna, S., Merler, S., Chierici, M., & Furlanello, C. (2008). Machine learning methods for predictive proteomics. *Briefings in Bioinformatics, 9*(2), 119–128. doi:10.1093/bib/bbn008 PMID:18310105

Belacel, N., Čuperlović-Culf, M., Laflamme, M., & Ouellette, R. (2004). Fuzzy J-Means and VNS methods for clustering genes from microarray data. *Bioinformatics (Oxford, England), 20*(11), 1690–1701. doi:10.1093/bioinformatics/bth142 PMID:14988127

Ben-Dor, A., Shamir, R., & Yakhini, Z. (1999). Clustering gene expression patterns. *Journal of Computational Biology, 63*(3/4), 281–297. doi:10.1089/106652799318274 PMID:10582567

Blankenbecler, R., Ohlsson, M., Peterson, C., & Ringner, M. (2003). Matching protein structures with fuzzy alignments. *Paper presented at the Proceedings of the National Academy of Sciences of the United States of America.*

Breiman, L. (1996). Bagging predictors. *Machine Learning, 24*(2), 123–140. doi:10.1007/BF00058655

Breiman, L. (1998). Arcing classifiers (with discussion). *Annals of Statistics, 26*(3), 801–849. doi:10.1214/aos/1024691079

Breiman, L. (2001). Random forests. *Machine Learning, 45*(1), 5–32. doi:10.1023/A:1010933404324

Breiman, L., Friedman, J., Olsen, R., & Stone, C. (1984). *Classification and Regression Trees.* California.

Carleos, C., Rodriguez, F., Lamelas, H., & Baro, J. A. (2003). Simulating complex traits influenced by genes with fuzzy-valued effects in pedigreed populations. *Bioinformatics (Oxford, England), 19*(1), 144–148. doi:10.1093/bioinformatics/19.1.144 PMID:12499304

Chang, B., & Halgamuge, S. K. (2002). Protein motif extraction with neuro-fuzzy optimization. *Bioinformatics (Oxford, England), 18*(8), 1084–1090. doi:10.1093/bioinformatics/18.8.1084 PMID:12176831

Cordón, O., Gomide, F., Herrera, F., Hoffmann, F., & Magdalena, L. (2004). Ten years of genetic fuzzy systems: Current framework and new trends. *Fuzzy Sets and Systems, 141*(1), 5–31. doi:10.1016/S0165-0114(03)00111-8

Dasgupta, A., & Raftery, A. E. (1998). Detecting features in spatial point processes with clutter via model-based clustering. *Journal of the American Statistical Association, 93*(441), 294–302. doi:10.1080/01621459.1998.10474110

De Smet, F., Mathys, J., Marchal, K., Thijs, G., De Moor, B., & Moreau, Y. (2002). Adaptive quality-based clustering of gene expression profiles. *Bioinformatics (Oxford, England), 18*(5), 735–746. doi:10.1093/bioinformatics/18.5.735 PMID:12050070

Dembele, D., & Kastner, P. (2003). Fuzzy C-means method for clustering microarray data. *Bioinformatics (Oxford, England), 19*(8), 973–980. doi:10.1093/bioinformatics/btg119 PMID:12761060

Dominiak, A., Wilkaniec, A., Wroczynski, P., & Adamczyk, A. (2016). Selenium in the Therapy of Neurological Diseases. Where is it Going? *Current Neuropharmacology, 14*(3), 282–299. doi:10.2174 /1570159X14666151223100011 PMID:26549649

Dong, G., Zhang, X., Wong, L., & Li, J. (1999). CAEP: Classification by aggregating emerging patterns. *Paper presented at the Proceedings of the Second International Conference on Discovery Science.*

Dubes, R. (1988). *Algorithms for Clustering Data.*

Duh, M. S., Walker, A. M., & Ayanian, J. Z. (1998). Epidemiologic interpretation of artificial neural networks. *American Journal of Epidemiology, 147*(12), 1112–1122. doi:10.1093/oxfordjournals.aje. a009409 PMID:9645789

Fayyad, U. M., Piatetsky-Shapiro, G., & Smyth, P. (1996). Knowledge Discovery and Data Mining: Towards a Unifying Framework. *Paper presented at the Proceedings of the Second International Conference on Knowledge Discovery and Data Mining.*

Fraley, C., & Raftery, A. E. (1998). How many clusters? Which clustering method? Answers via model-based cluster analysis. *The Computer Journal, 41*(8), 586–588. doi:10.1093/comjnl/41.8.578

Freund, Y., & Schapire, R. (1996). Experiments with a new boosting algorithm. *Paper presented at the Thirteenth National Conference on Machine Learning.*

Gasch, A., & Eisen, M. (2002). Exploring the conditional corregulation of yeast gene expression through fuzzy k-means clustering. *Genome Biology, 3*(11), 1–22. doi:10.1186/gb-2002-3-11-research0059 PMID:12429058

Gutsell, S., & Russell, P. (2013). The role of chemistry in developing understanding of adverse outcome pathways and their application in risk assessment. *Toxicological Reviews, 2*(5), 299–307.

Han, J., Pei, H., & Yin, Y. (2000). Mining Frequent Patterns without Candidate Generation. *Paper presented at the Conf. on the Management of Data,* Dallas.

Han, J., Pei, J., Yin, Y., & Mao, R. (2003). Mining frequent patterns without candidate generation: A frequent-pattern tree approach. *Paper presented at the Data Mining and Knowledge Discovery.*

Hartuv, E., & Shamir, R. (2000). A clustering algorithm based on graph connectivity. *Information Processing Letters, 76*(4–6), 175–181. doi:10.1016/S0020-0190(00)00142-3

Heger, A., & Holm, L. (2003). Sensitive pattern discovery with fuzzy alignments of distantly related proteins. *Bioinformatics (Oxford, England), 19*(Suppl. 1), i130–i137. doi:10.1093/bioinformatics/btg1017 PMID:12855449

Herrero, J., Valencia, A., & Dopazo, J. (2001). A hierarchical unsupervised growing neural network for clustering gene expression patterns. *Bioinformatics (Oxford, England), 17*(2), 126–136. doi:10.1093/ bioinformatics/17.2.126 PMID:11238068

Hirschhorn, J. N., & Daly, M. J. (2005). Genome-wide association studies for common diseases and complex traits. *Nature Reviews. Genetics, 6*(2), 95–108. doi:10.1038/nrg1521 PMID:15716906

Huang, Y., & Li, Y. (2004). Prediction of protein subcellular locations using fuzzy k-NN method. *Bioinformatics (Oxford, England), 20*(1), 21–28. doi:10.1093/bioinformatics/btg366 PMID:14693804

Jiang, D., Pei, J., & Zhang, A. D. (2003a, March 10-12). A Density-based Hierarchical Clustering Method for Timeseries Gene Expression Data. *Paper presented at the 3rd IEEE International Symposium on Bioinformatics and Bioengineering*, Bethesda, Maryland.

Jiang, D., Pei, J., & Zhang, A. D. (2003b). Interactive exploration of coherent patterns in time-series gene expression data. *Paper presented at the ACM SIGKDD International Conference on Knowledge Discovery and Data Mining*. doi:10.1145/956750.956820

Jones, D. T. (2001). Protein structure prediction in genomics. *Briefings in Bioinformatics, 2*(2), 111–125. doi:10.1093/bib/2.2.111 PMID:11465730

Kaufman, L., & Rousseeuw, P.J. (1990). *Finding Groups in Data: an Introduction to Cluster Analysis.*

Kitano, H. (2002a). Computational systems biology. *Nature, 420*(6912), 206–210. doi:10.1038/nature01254 PMID:12432404

Kitano, H. (2002b). Systems biology: A brief overview. *Science, 295*(5560), 1662–1664. doi:10.1126/science.1069492 PMID:11872829

Kohonen, T. (1984). *Self-Organization and Associative Memory.* Berlin: Spring-Verlag.

Kotzias, D., Geiss, O., Tirendi, S., Josefa, B. M., Reina, V., Gotti, A., . . . Sarigiannis, D. (2009). Exposure to multiple air contaminants in public buildings, schools and kindergartens-the European indoor air monitoring and exposure assessment (airmex) study. *Fresenius Environmental Bulletin, 18*(5A), 670-681.

Kuncheva, L. (2004). *Combining Pattern Classifiers: Methods and Algorithms.* Wiley. doi:10.1002/0471660264

Larranaga, P., Calvo, B., Santana, R., Bielza, C., & Galdiano, J. (2003). Machine learning in bioinformatics. *Briefings in Bioinformatics, 7*(1), 86–112. doi:10.1093/bib/bbk007 PMID:16761367

Li, Y., & Zhang, J. (2007). Serum concentrations of antioxidant vitamins and carotenoids are low in individuals with a history of attempted suicide. *Nutritional Neuroscience, 10*(1-2), 51–58. doi:10.1080/10284150701250747 PMID:17539483

Liao, K. H., Dobrev, I. D., Dennison Jr, J. E., Andersen, M. E., Reisfeld, B., Reardon, K. F., ... Yang, R. S. H. (2002). Application of biologically based computer modeling to simple or complex mixtures. *Environmental Health Perspectives, 110*(Suppl. 6), 957-963.

Lukac, R., Plataniotis, K., Smolka, B., & Venetsanopoulos, A. (2005). cDNA microarray image processing using fuzzy vector filtering framework. *Fuzzy Sets and Systems, 152*(1), 17–35. doi:10.1016/j.fss.2004.10.012

Martinez, R., & Collard, M. (2007). Extracted knowledge: Interpretation in mining biological data, a survey. *International Journal of Computer Science and Applications, 1*, 1–21.

Mason, A. M., Borgert, C. J., Bus, J. S., Moiz Mumtaz, M., Simmons, J. E., & Sipes, I. G. (2007). Improving the scientific foundation for mixtures joint toxicity and risk assessment: Contributions from the SOT mixtures project-Introduction. *Toxicology and Applied Pharmacology, 223*(2), 99-103.

McQueen, J. B. (1967). Some methods for classification and analysis of multivariate observations. *Paper presented at the Fifth Berkeley Symposium on Mathematical Statistics and Probability*, Berkeley.

National Toxicology Program. (2012). *NTP Monograph on Health Effects of Low-Level Lead.* Research Triangle Park, NC: National Institute of Environmental Health Sciences.

Olden, J. D., Joy, M. K., & Death, R. G. (2004). An accurate comparison of methods for quantifying variable importance in artificial neural networks using simulated data. *Ecological Modelling, 178*(3-4), 389–397. doi:10.1016/j.ecolmodel.2004.03.013

Pearl, J., & Verma, T. S. (1991). A theory of inferred causation. *Paper presented at the Principles of Knowledge Representation and Reasoning Second International Conference.*

Phan, J. H., Quo, C. F., & Wang, M. D. (2006). *Functional genomics and proteomics in the clinical neurosciences: data mining and bioinformatics. Progress in Brain Research*, 158, 83–108. doi:10.1016/S0079-6123(06)58004-5

Quinlan, J. (1986). C4.5: Programs for machine learning. San Mateo.

Rampersaud, G. C., Pereira, M. A., Girard, B. L., Adams, J., & Metzl, J. D. (2005). Breakfast habits, nutritional status, body weight, and academic performance in children and adolescents. *J Am Diet Assoc, 105*(5), 743-760; quiz 761-742. doi:10.1016/j.jada.2005.02.007

Roede, J. R., Uppal, K., Park, Y., Tran, V., & Jones, D. P. (2014). Transcriptome–metabolome wide association study (TMWAS) of maneb and paraquat neurotoxicity reveals network level interactions in toxicologic mechanism. *Toxicological Reviews*, 1, 435–444. doi:10.1016/j.toxrep.2014.07.006 PMID:27722094

Sarigiannis, D., Gotti, A., Cimino Reale, G., & Marafante, E. (2009). Reflections on new directions for risk assessment of environmental chemical mixtures. *International Journal of Risk Assessment and Management, 13*(3-4), 216–241. doi:10.1504/IJRAM.2009.030697

Sarigiannis, D. A., Karakitsios, S. P., Gotti, A., Liakos, I. L., & Katsoyiannis, A. (2011). Exposure to major volatile organic compounds and carbonyls in European indoor environments and associated health risk. *Environment International, 37*(4), 743–765. doi:10.1016/j.envint.2011.01.005 PMID:21354626

Schapire, R., Freund, Y., Bartlett, P., Lee, WS.,. (1998). Boosting the margin: A new explanation for the effectiveness of voting methods. *the Annals of Statistics, 26*(5), 1651–1686.

Schlosshauer, M., & Ohlsson, M. (2002). A novel approach to local reliability of sequence alignments. *Bioinformatics (Oxford, England), 18*(6), 847–854. doi:10.1093/bioinformatics/18.6.847 PMID:12075020

Seno, M., & Karypis, G. (2001). LPMiner: An Algorithm for Finding Frequent Itemsets Using Length-Decreasing Support Constraint. *Paper presented at the 1st IEEE Conference on Data Mining.* doi:10.1109/ICDM.2001.989558

Shamir, R., & Sharan, R. (2000). Click: A clustering algorithm for gene expression analysis. *Paper presented at the 8th International Conference on Intelligent Systems for Molecular Biology (ISMB '00).*

Shatkay, H., Edwards, S., Wilbur, W.J., & Boguski, M. (2000). Genes, themes, microarrays: using information retrieval for large-scale gene analysis. *Paper presented at the Int. Conf. Intell. Syst. Mol. Biol.*

Sherlock, G. (2000). Analysis of large-scale gene expression data. *Current Opinion in Immunology, 12*(2), 201–205. doi:10.1016/S0952-7915(99)00074-6 PMID:10712947

Silva, A., Cortez, P., Santos, M. F., Gomes, L., & Neves, J. (2008). Rating organ failure via adverse events using data mining in the intensive care unit. *Artificial Intelligence in Medicine, 43*(3), 179–193. doi:10.1016/j.artmed.2008.03.010 PMID:18486459

Smith, A. E., Nugent, C. D., & McClean, S. I. (2003). Evaluation of inherent performance of intelligent medical decision support systems: Utilising neural networks as an example. *Artificial Intelligence in Medicine, 27*(1), 1–27. doi:10.1016/S0933-3657(02)00088-X PMID:12473389

Spirtes, P., Glymour, C., & Scheines, R. (1993). *Causation, prediction, and search.*

Story, E. N., Kopec, R. E., Schwartz, S. J., & Harris, G. K. (2010). An update on the health effects of tomato lycopene. *Ann. Rev. Food Sci. Technol., 1*(1), 189–210. doi:10.1146/annurev.food.102308.124120 PMID:22129335

Tamayo, P., Solni, D., Mesirov, J., Zhu, Q., Kitareewan, S., Dmitrovsky, E., . . . Golub, T. R. I. (1999). Interpreting patterns of gene expression with self-organizing maps: Methods and application to hematopoietic differentiation. *Paper presented at the Natl. Acad. Sci.* doi:10.1073/pnas.96.6.2907

Tomida, S., Hanai, T., Honda, H., & Kobayashi, T. (2002). Analysis of expression profile using fuzzy adaptive resonance theory. *Bioinformatics (Oxford, England), 18*(8), 1073–1083. doi:10.1093/bioinformatics/18.8.1073 PMID:12176830

Torres, A., & Nieto, J. J. (2003). The fuzzy polynucleotide space: Basic properties. *Bioinformatics (Oxford, England), 19*(5), 587–592. doi:10.1093/bioinformatics/btg032 PMID:12651716

Tung, W. L., Quek, C., & Cheng, P. (2004). GenSo-EWS: A novel neural-fuzzy based early warning system for predicting bank failures. *Neural Networks, 17*(4), 567–587. doi:10.1016/j.neunet.2003.11.006 PMID:15109685

Valencia, A., & Pazos, F. (2002). Computational methods for the prediction of protein interactions. *Current Opinion in Structural Biology, 12*(3), 368–373. doi:10.1016/S0959-440X(02)00333-0 PMID:12127457

Wall, R., Cunningham, P., Walsh, P., & Byrne, S. (2003). Explaining the output of ensembles in medical decision support on a case by case basis. *Artificial Intelligence in Medicine, 28*(2), 191–206. doi:10.1016/S0933-3657(03)00056-3 PMID:12893119

Wang, J. (2008). Computational biology of genome expression and regulation - A review of microarray bioinformatics. *Journal of Environmental Pathology, Toxicology and Oncology, 27*(3), 157–179. doi:10.1615/JEnvironPatholToxicolOncol.v27.i3.10 PMID:18652564

Webb, G., & Zheng, Z. (2004). Multistrategy ensemble learning: Reducing error by combining ensemble learning techniques. *Paper presented at the IEEE Transactions on Knowledge and Data Engineering.* doi:10.1109/TKDE.2004.29

Wong, J. W. H., Cagney, G., & Cartwright, H. M. (2005). SpecAlign - Processing and alignment of mass spectra datasets. *Bioinformatics (Oxford, England), 21*(9), 2088–2090. doi:10.1093/bioinformatics/bti300 PMID:15691857

Wong, J. W. H., Durante, C., & Cartwright, H. M. (2005). Application of fast Fourier transform cross-correlation for the alignment of large chromatographic and spectral datasets. *Analytical Chemistry, 77*(17), 5655–5661. doi:10.1021/ac050619p PMID:16131078

Woolf, P., & Wang, Y. (2000). A fuzzy logic approach to analyzing gene expression data. *Physiological Genomics, 3*(1), 9–15. PMID:11015595

Workman, C. T., Mak, H. C., McCuine, S., Tagne, J. B., Agarwal, M., Ozier, O., … Ideker, T. (2006). A systems approach to mapping DNA damage response pathways. *Science, 312*(5776), 1054-1059.

Xing, E. P., & Karp, R. M. (2001). Cliff: Clustering of high-dimensional microarray data via iterative feature filtering using normalized cuts. *Bioinformatics (Oxford, England), 17*(Suppl. 1), 306–315. doi:10.1093/bioinformatics/17.suppl_1.S306 PMID:11473022

Zadeh, L. A. (1965). Fuzzy Sets. *Information and Control, 8*(3), 338–353. doi:10.1016/S0019-9958(65)90241-X

Zeng, J., Zhu, S., & Yan, H. (2009). Towards accurate human promoter recognition: A review of currently used sequence features and classification methods. *Briefings in Bioinformatics, 10*(5), 498–508. doi:10.1093/bib/bbp027 PMID:19531545

KEY TERMS AND DEFINITIONS

Bioinformatics: An interdisciplinary field that includes methods and computational tools for the interpretation of biological data.

Data Mining: Analysis of data from different perspectives and summarizing it into useful information towards relationships that have not previously been reported.

Exposome-Wide Association Studies: Association of multiple environmental, sociodemographic and genetic factors for explaining the environmental causes of human disease.

Machine Learning: Field of computer science that provides to the computers the ability to learn without straight forward programming for deterministic calculations.

Metabolomics: Large-scale study of small molecules, commonly known as metabolites, within cells, biofluids, tissues or organisms that specific cellular processes leave behind.

Pathway Analysis: Identification of the underlying biological processes of differentially expressed genes and proteins, translated into different metabolic profiles.

Pattern Recognition: Machine learning domain related to the recognition of patterns and regularities in data.

Chapter 8
Transcriptomics to Metabolomics:
A Network Perspective for Big Data

Ankush Bansal
Jaypee University of Information Technology, India

Pulkit Anupam Srivastava
Jaypee University of Information Technology, India

ABSTRACT

A lot of omics data is generated in a recent decade which flooded the internet with transcriptomic, genomics, proteomics and metabolomics data. A number of software, tools, and web-servers have developed to analyze the big data omics. This review integrates the various methods that have been employed over the years to interpret the gene regulatory and metabolic networks. It illustrates random networks, scale-free networks, small world network, bipartite networks and other topological analysis which fits in biological networks. Transcriptome to metabolome network is of interest because of key enzymes identification and regulatory hub genes prediction. It also provides an insight into the understanding of omics technologies, generation of data and impact of in-silico analysis on the scientific community.

INTRODUCTION

The appearance of majority of disease processes cannot be explained by modification in one gene, but involves the involvement of synchronized genes associated with same function using various network analyses. Since the advent of molecular biology, extensive progress has been made in the quest to grasp the mechanisms that lie beneath human disease. Consequently, to be unbeaten in drug development, scientific community must shift its focus from individual genes that carry disease-associated mutations towards a numerous gene association perspective of disease mechanisms.

No doubt that genomic sequencing resulted in high advancement in prognosis and personalized medicine but still leaves the elementary questions pertaining to genotype-phenotype relationships unresolved (Vidal, Cusick, and Barabási, 2011). The contributory changes that connect genotype-phenotype remain

DOI: 10.4018/978-1-5225-2607-0.ch008

usually unidentified, especially for complex attributes like gene loci and cancer related mutations. Though, when mutations are identified, it's still unclear how a perturbation function works and correlates with splicing, post translational modifications and other autocrine and paracrine cellular communications. Till date there is no justified answer discovered for functional association which merge the knowledge and construct a bridge between genotype to phenotype. To connect the dots of the unorganized information at genomic, proteomic level and find out their association with function variation we need to opt interdisciplinary approaches. Even after genome sequencing, there was need to align data with respect to condition variation. Also, analysis of multiple genes can be done at same point using differential gene expression analysis, which ultimately can give limelight to function prediction, co-expressed gene identification and functional validation (Zhu et al. 2012). Next generation sequencing based RNA-seq transcriptomic analysis answered almost all the questions as it was the need of decade.

During the past decade, tremendous development has been made in terms of speed, read length, and throughput, along with a sharp reduction in per-base cost. Together, these advances democratized NGS and paved the path for the development of a outsized number of novel NGS applications in basic science as well as in translational research areas such as clinical diagnostics, agrigenomics, and forensic science. The evolution of NGS and significant improvements in sequencing technologies and library preparation protocols benefited the way as expected to resolve from enormous bio-fields. But, transcriptome data has its own disadvantages like abnormality in transcripts alignment, annotation and abundance values in terms of TPM and FPKM, which turns the scientific community to think about alternative to resolve such big data.

As quantity of data increases, the variable associated with function also seems impossible to calculate through manual curation. A quantitative description of a complex system is intrinsically restricted by our capability to estimate the system's interior state from experimentally accessible outputs. Although the simultaneous measurement of all internal variables, such as all metabolite concentrations in a cell, offers a complete description of a system's state, in practice however experimental access is limited to only a subset of variables, or sensors. A system is called observable if its interior state could be reconstructed from its output. Here, we adopted a graphical approach derived from the dynamical laws that govern a system to determine the subset of variables that are obligatory to reconstruct the full interior state of a complex system. Before, scientist has applied this approach to biochemical reaction systems, and found that the identified sensors are not only essential but also enough for observability. The developed approach can also identify the optimal sensors for target or partial observability, helping us reconstruct selected state variables from appropriately chosen outputs, a pre-requirement for optimal biomarker design. Observability plays key role in complex systems; these results offer avenues to systematically discover the dynamics of a extensive range of natural, technological and socioeconomic systems.

Merely, combining big data complexity with network theory can assist in study of genotype-phenotype characteristics and identification of hub nodes may predict the impact of gene silencing method inclusion with disappearance with disease phenotype. Various studies which reflect the impact of random networks reflected that biological networks do not reciprocate the property of randomness. Biological network follow power law and hence regulation of biological and chemical pathways have patterns. Although, various software and tools are available in market, but optimization of these tools to resolve complexity of biological problems remains problematic till date.

Basic structural and spectral parametric analysis of complex networks gives an insight towards the study of network model behavior using metabolic networks, transcription regulatory networks, protein-protein interaction networks and gene regulatory networks. Bipartite network also shows controlling behavior through regulatory nodes in context to over-expression and under-expression using transcriptional activator or repressor. This chapter presents a review of transcriptomic analysis using various network derived from graph theory world to decipher the key association on the basis of parametric optimization. Connecting genotype-phenotype using transcriptomic to metabolomics analysis can represent the future condition of specific variation and modeling of same using simulation algorithm which may result in accurate prediction of variation factor with respect to function and metabolic pathway route change.

METHODS

Transcriptomics: Big Data Generation

The transcriptome is the complete set of RNA transcripts in a given cell for a specific developmental or physiological state (Ozsolak and Milos, 2011). To understand the underlying mechanism of disease development and to interpret the functional elements of the genome, it becomes necessary to comprehend the transcriptome. So far microarray technologies has served the purpose for high-throughput large-scale RNA-level studies however, hybridization-based limits the ability to catalog and quantify RNA molecules expressed under varied conditions. Meanwhile, advancement in parallel DNA sequencing technologies has enabled transcriptome sequencing (RNA-seq) by sequencing of cDNA. The reason behind the replacement of microarray technologies by RNA-seq is its better resolution and higher reproducibility besides it can be used to extend our knowledge of alternative splicing events (Wang et al., 2008), novel genes and transcripts (Denoeud et al., 2008), and fusion transcripts (Maher et al., 2009). Complete workflow of transcriptome analysis shown in Figure 1.

Raw Data Refinement

Similarly to sequence whole genome or exome, RNAseq data is formatted in FASTQ (sequence and base quality). During the library preparation, sequencing, and imaging steps (Robasky, Lewis, and Church, 2014), numerous erroneous sequence variants can be introduced which must be recognized and filtered out in the data analysis step. Therefore, to perform the initial step of routine RNA-seq, quality of raw data must be assessed, i.e. assessment of the overall and per-base quality for each read (i.e., read 1 and 2 in case of paired-end sequencing) in each sample must be performed by using tools such as FastQC ("Babraham Bioinformatics - FastQC A Quality Control Tool for High Throughput Sequence Data" 2016) and HTQC (Yang et al., 2013). Before aligning the RNA-seq data, read trimming can be performed depending on the approach used for construction of RNA-seq library. Two common approaches, namely, adapter and quality trimming can be applied to read trim the RNA-seq data. Generally, adapter trimming involves exclusion of the adapter sequence by masking unambiguous sequences used during library construction, while quality trimming removes the ends of reads where base quality scores have decreased to a level such that sequence errors and the resulting mismatches prevent reads from aligning. Typically, the adapter trimming step isn't necessary since most recent sequencers provide raw data

Figure 1. Workflow for transcriptome data analysis

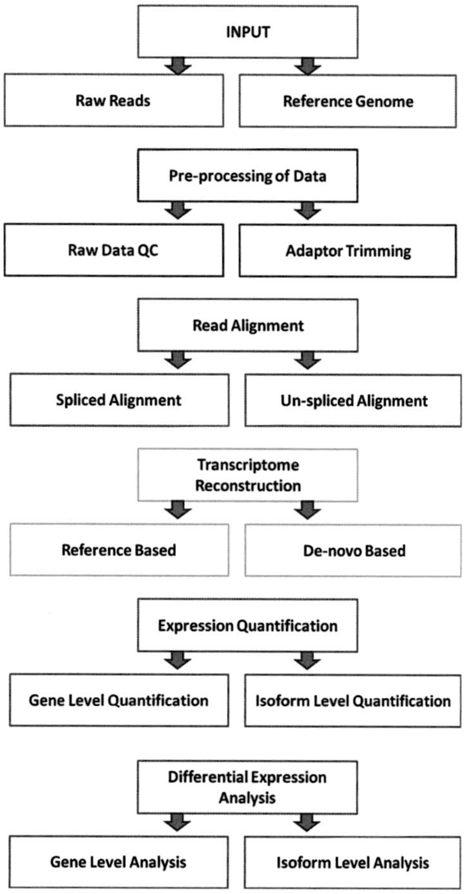

in which the adapters are already trimmed. In contrast, quality trimming may be an essential step and can be achieved through FASTX-Toolkit ("FASTX-Toolkit," 2016) and FLEXBAR (Dodt et al., 2012).

Alignment Performance

Read alignment step can be performed by using either genome or transcriptome as a reference. One can rely on unspliced aligners, such as Stampy, Mapping and Assembly with Quality (MAQ) (Li, Ruan, and Durbin, 2008), Burrow-Wheeler Aligner (BWA) (Li and Durbin, 2009), and Bowtie(Langmead et al., 2009), that do not allow large gaps for accurate read mapping while considering transcriptome as a reference. Despite of the advantages of unspliced aligners have, these alignments are limited to the identification of known exons and junctions as it cannot recognize splicing events involving novel exons. However, if reference used is genome, various spliced aligners that allows wide range of gaps, like TopHat (Trapnell, Pachter, and Salzberg, 2009), MapSplice (Wang et al., 2010), STAR (Dobin et al., 2013), and GSNAP (Wu and Nacu, 2010), can be employed because spliced aligners would split exons-exons junctions into two fragments and therefore may increase the probability of recognizing novel transcripts generated by alternative splicing.

RNA-Seq Transcriptomics Specific Quality Check

There are chances of introduction of several intrinsic biases including polymerase chain reaction bias, GC bias and nucleotide composition bias to RNA-seq data of clinical samples with low quality or quantity. Programs like RNA-SeQC (DeLuca et al., 2012), RSeQC (Wang, Wang, and Li, 2012), and Qualimap 2 (Okonechnikov, Conesa, and García-Alcalde, 2016) has been developed to evaluate the biases from RNA-seq data by examining following metrics: 5'-to-3' coverage of 5' and 3' ends, accuracy and biases in gene expression measurements, and percentage of exonic or rRNA reads (Adiconis et al., 2013).

Transcriptome Reconstruction Approaches

Transcriptome reconstruction includes two approaches to identify all transcripts that are expressed in a specimen. Among the two approaches, i.e. reference-guided approach and the reference-independent approach, the earlier is a two step process where raw reads are aligned to reference as described in previous section followed by assembly of overlapping reads. On the other hand, reference-independent approach uses a *de novo* assembly algorithm to directly construct consensus transcripts from short reads without aligning against the reference. Nevertheless, both approaches are used to reconstruct the transcriptome; reference-guided approach provides the best reconstruction when reference annotation information is well-known, such as in human and mouse, while reference-independent approach is useful when there is no known reference genome or transcriptome. Cufflinks (Trapnell et al., 2010), Scripture (Guttman et al., 2010), and StringTie (Pertea et al., 2015) can be used to reconstruct transcriptome using reference-guided approach besides Trinity (Grabherr et al., 2011), Oases (Schulz et al., 2012), and transABySS (Robertson et al., 2010) can be employed for reconstruction of transcriptome through reference-independent approach.

Quantification of Expression Values

Using RNA-seq data, several methods have been developed for expression quantification. These methods can further be classified on the basis of target levels: gene-level and isoform-level. Gene-level quantification is supported by enhanced read analysis of gene expression (ERANGE) (Mortazavi et al. 2008), Alternative expression analysis by sequencing (ALEXA-seq) (Griffith et al., 2010), and normalization by expected uniquely mappable area (NEUMA) (Lee et al., 2011). Isoform-level quantification methods are further sub-divided into three sub-groups based on the reference type and requirement of alignment results. Three sub-groups are as follows: (1) considers alignment results of reads by using transcriptome as a reference e.g., RSEM (B. Li and Dewey 2011); (2) considers alignment results of reads by using genome as a reference instead of transcriptome e.g., Cufflinks (Trapnell et al. 2010) and StringTie (Pertea et al., 2015); (3) uses alignment free method e.g., Sailfish (Patro, Mount, and Kingsford, 2014).

Differential Expression Analysis

A number of software packages and pipelines, such as edgeR (Robinson, McCarthy, and Smyth 2010), DESeq (Anders and Huber 2010), NOIseq (Tarazona et al., 2015), SAMseq (Li and Tibshirani, 2013), Cuffdiff (Trapnell et al., 2010), and EBSeq (Leng et al., 2013), have been developed for differential expression analysis using RNA-seq. Even though no single method may be optimal under all experimental conditions and exhibits large differences among themselves, as reported by one research group

(Seyednasrollah, Laiho, and Elo, 2015). Hence, it becomes difficult for users with no or weak statistical background to select a proper method. As a result of rapid accumulation of RNA-seq data, we look ahead for development of new bioinformatics tools for analyzing differential expression and also functions robustly under a wide range of conditions.

Transcriptome Complexity under Big Data and Complex Network Framework

Undoubtedly, above described transcriptomic methodology provides a strong support for efficient usage of transcriptome data. But the complexity lies in understanding and decoding the significance out of gene coding transcripts and their expression values based on their correlation. Hence, there is a need to incorporate other field theories where such big and complex data are being studied on regular basis. Currently, advancement in physics and chemistry has its root drawn from reductionist approaches where an atom or particle taken under consideration for further studies are scientifically isolated from rest of the world in a strictly controlled surroundings, on the other hand biology defies such models by encircling the whole array of spatial and temporal scales present in nature: varying from molecules being observed to the observer built from molecules. To address three major problems namely: (1) organization of ever increasing experimental results from biological system into appropriate relevant representations and models; (2) ability to replicate the dynamics of such models under varying conditions, so as to reveal significant biological patterns and structures; and (3) uncovering the ways for efficiently relating such models at the several spatial and time scales. Integrative attempts to resolve such problems are now part of the new area of systems biology. Transcriptome to metabolome network construction workflow shown in Figure 2.

One must consider the following three key concepts in order to understand complex biological systems (Aderem, 2005): (1) Emergence, since the study of individual elements such as genes, proteins and metabolites is not enough to elucidate the behavior of entire systems its indeed to discover links between elements of a system; (2) Robustness, biological systems retain their foremost functions even under perturbations imposed by the environment; and (3) Modularity, vertices sharing analogous functions are extremely associated. In complex networks research all these three features have been extensively studied, as for example, in the case of protein-protein interaction networks (Jeong et al., 2001) and Internet (null Albert, Jeong, and Barabasi, 2000). Consequently, complex networks theory can be basically applied for developing systems biology research for the reason that several tools for network characterization, modeling and simulation are already.

Ground Rules of Complex Systems

Representations of structure of complex networks can be done by using a *graph*, which is an ordered pair $G = (V, E)$ connected by a set $E \equiv \{e_1, e_2, ..., e_M\}$ of *edges*, or links, formed by a set $V \equiv \{1, 2, i, ..., N\}$ of *vertices*, or nodes (Bollobas, 2016; Diestel, 2016). Link between two vertices is represented by each edge, i.e., $e_p = (i, j)$ which indicates the association between the vertices i and j. In directed graph, the edges have direction and G is an ordered pair $G = (V, E^{\rightarrow})$, where V is the set of vertices and $E^{\rightarrow}$ is the set of ordered pairs of *arcs*, or arrows. In this case, each arc $e_p = (i, j)$ is a intended for edge extending from node i, called the *head*, to j, called the *tail*.

Figure 2. Transcriptomics to metabolomics network construction overview

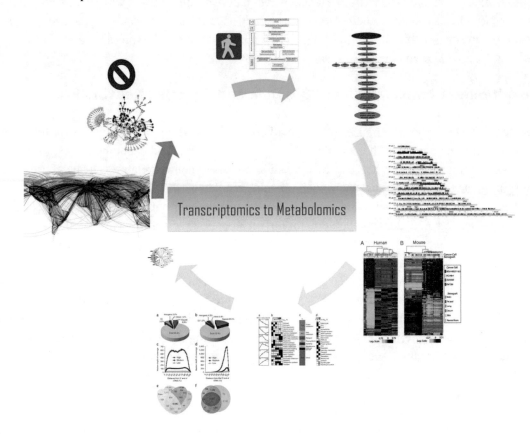

A directed and an undirected network are shown Figure 3 and the elements of their adjacency matrices can represented as a_{ij} equal to 0 whenever there is no edge connecting the vertices i and j, and equal to 1 otherwise. In case of undirected graph, the elements $a_{ij} = a_{ji}$ for any i and j, i.e., the adjacency matrix is symmetric.

Degree: A Basic Parameter for Quantification

In order to describe such complex networks, it is essential to take topological measurements into consideration, which can offer important insights about the structure of networks. Occurrence of cycles, distances between pairs of nodes and vertex connectivity are associated with basic network measurements, among other possibilities. Even though the vertex degree is a very basic measurement, it's particularly significant for network description. As in case of protein-protein interaction networks, highly connected proteins have a propensity to be necessary for the survival of the organism (Jeong et al., 2001). One of the global measurements of the connectivity of the network is average degree which corresponds to the average of the degrees of all vertices. *Hubs* are highly connected nodes, which are elementary for several imperative properties of networks, such as resilience adjacent to random failures (null Albert, Jeong, and Barabasi, 2000). Note that the notion of resilience in complex network theory cannot be straight away extended to biological networks, as, compared to other types of networks; organisms can be greatly susceptible to minute changes such as a missing gene or a defective protein.

Figure 3. Complex network implementation to metabolic network reconstruction

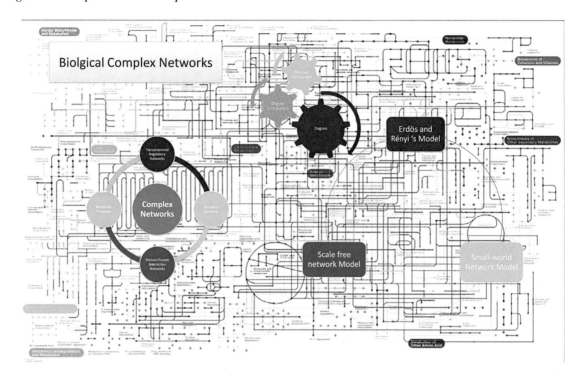

Degree Distribution

The *degree* distribution of a network, $P(k)$, can be obtained by including the number of nodes with a known connectivity and dividing by N, i.e., the probability that a chosen vertex has degree k. It can be used for network classification and to infer the overall connectivity. If the majority of vertices have a comparable degree, $P(k)$ will be a peak distribution. Since the majority of biological networks are scale-free, as a result of which their distribution of connections is irregular and approximates a power-law $P(k) \approx k^{-\gamma}$, where γ is a constant. In this case, enormous number of edges is concentrated in a small number of nodes, at the same time most vertices are little connected. Scale free networks possess higher probability of exhibiting hubs as shown in (Barabási and Albert, 1999).

Shortest Path Length

Another significant property of networks relates to the distances among pairs of vertices, which is calculated by the path length, i.e., the number of edges required to be crossed while going from one vertex to another in such a way that each one of the node is visited not more than once. The length of the shortest path that connects i and j gives the *shortest path length* $\left(\ell \right)$ between two vertices i and j. The average shortest path length is calculated by taking into consideration the distance matrix L, in which the entry ℓ_{ij} represents the length of the shortest paths between the nodes i and j. A universal feature of biological networks is their small-world property in which any two nodes in the system can be connected by relatively short paths along existing edges. For instance, the value of the average shortest path length in metabolic networks of *Saccharomyces cerevisiae* is $\ell \approx 3$ (Jeong et al., 2001) and in the protein-protein interaction network is $\ell \approx 7$. In case of metabolic networks, a biochemical pathway connecting two substrates corresponds to the paths. A proper explanation of small-worldness, which takes into account the increase of the shortest paths with the size of the network, can be found in (Newman, 2001).

Models for Complex Networks

Erdös and Rényi's Model

The elementary complex network model was projected by Paul Erdös and Alfred Rényi (Flory 1941). Stated model was commonly known as the random graph of Erdös and Rényi. Opening with a set of N disconnected nodes, edges were connected according to a fixed probability p (Erdös and Rényi, 1959). The distribution of generated connections of networks by mentioned model follows the Poisson distribution for large N. An built-in feature of this model is the extremely homogeneous number of connections at every node, which fallout in networks and can be characterized by respective average node degree. But. Randome model can't be represented for real life scenarios.

Small-World Network Model

Watts and Strogatz (1998) experimental process relected that unlike random networks the real-world networks shows many third-order cycles (Watts and Strogatz, 1998). Hence, they projected model called the small-world network model, which begins with a full regular network of N nodes in which each node is linked to its k nearest neighbors. Subsequently, each edge is randomly re-connected with probability p. This model fabricates between regularity and randomness. The time when p = 0, the structure of model is ordered with number third-order cycles i.e. high average clustering coefficient but larger average shortest path length. When p → 1, the network works similar to random graph. Though, stated model makes such networks whose degree distribution is homogeneous.

Scale Free Network Model

It has been observed that the internet network is not limited to Poisson distribution and do not behave as per random networks because a few nodes shows more association towards a large number of the network connections (Barabási and Albert, 1999) and the similar structure has been originate in the case of Internet (Faloutsos, Faloutsos, and Faloutsos, 1999) protein-protein interaction networks (Jeong et al., 2001), metabolic networks, and in networks of scientific collaboration and citation (Ravasz et al., 2002). The presence of hub genes is straightforwardly related to the scale-free distribution of node degrees, where a straight line is found in log-log plots of the node distribution.

To understand the irregular distribution of connectivity in real networks, a *scal*e-free network model has been proposed (Barabási and Albert, 1999), which is based on defined rules: (i) growth, and (ii) preferential attachment. The growth in which the network growing process begins with a set of m_0 nodes and grows at each succeeding step by the adding up of a new node with m links. Preferential attachment, represents the nodes receiving the new connection are chosen on the basisof a linear preferential attachment rule; which shows the probability of the new node i linking with an existing node j is proportional to the mentioned degree of j. In this scale-free model, the highly connected nodes have a greater probability of receiving new connections. In spite of the accomplishment in reproducing the scale-free degree distribution, the scale-free network model presents non-assortative networks through small average clustering coefficients. Therefore, this stated model is not appropriate for presenting some real networks (Costa et al. 2007).

Implications and Applicability of Complex Models on Biological Network Reconstruction

Biological Networks

The accessibility of entirely sequenced genomes and the expansion in molecular biology of high-throughput techniques like microarray technology (Schena et al., 1995; Ren et al., 2000) and two-hybrid systems (Fields and Song, 1989) have permitted genome-wide studies of biological processes that come about from complex communication between genetic entities, such as DNA RNA and proteins (Lockhart and Winzeler, 2000; Uetz and Hughes, 2000). These sub-cellular entities act together with one another as per their functional importance. For example, protein-protein connections, associated to cellular interactions by signal transduction, repress or activate the transcription of genes, altering the molecular symphony of the cell. These split modules are structural blocks of the biological systems, which works together to shape the phenotypic prototype of the cells and cell-organisms (Hartwell et al., 1999). Mapping of all the consistent modules helps us to understand model and their dynamical and topological properties (Barabási, 2007). The majority of networks use cellular systems to control the transcription, metabolism and protein-protein interaction (Barabási and Oltvai, 2004). Regardless of the great variety of networks in biology, networks contribute to several global properties. For example, many networks within the cell are presented by (i) Power Law: a scale-free degree (ii) Small World Network: a small average shortest path length between any two nodes (iii) a disassortative nature, (iv) a modular association and organization and a structural and dynamical robustness (Barabási and Oltvai, 2004; Albert, 2005). Figure 4 shows biological complex network and parameters for construction.

Constraint in biological networks examination is the noisy or incomplete data sample presented by missing edges and/or nodes and the existence of links and nodes that do not exist in a real world. These errors usually contribute to noise which might be contributed by manual technical errors. Even though sampling still remains a significant issue as current databases offer an incomparable opportunity to study control based regulatory network of the cell with the viewpoint of complex networks.

Transcriptional Regulatory Networks

The immense complication of species arises from consequence of well elaborated regulation of gene expression from differences genetic variations in context of the number of genes (Carroll, 2000; Levine and Tjian, 2003). The transcription network is a significant system that controls gene expression in a cell. Transcription regulation based map construction was performed on *Escherichia coli* (Milo et al., 2002; Huerta et al., 1998; Gama-Castro et al., 2008). The connections between Transcription Factors (TF) and Target Genes (TG) can be represented as a directed graph. The two types of nodes (TF and TG) are connected by directed arrows where regulatory interaction takes place in between regulator and targets (Teichmann and Babu, 2004; "An Introduction to Systems Biology: Design Principles of Biological Circuits," 2006). Transcriptional regulatory networks exhibit attractive properties that be capable

Figure 4. Overview of complex biological networks

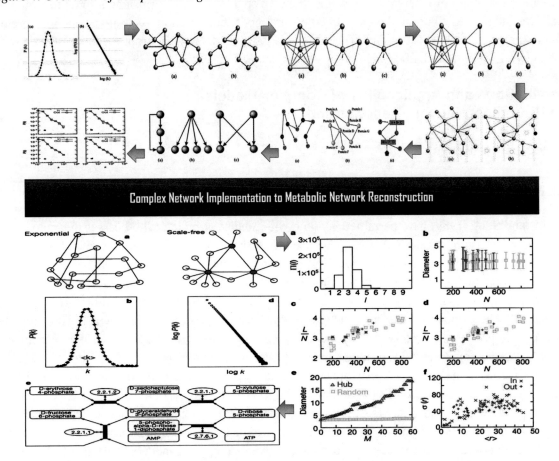

of interpreting in a biological systems in context to better comprehend the complex activities of gene regulatory networks. At a global network level, the out-degree distribution of TFs is measured scale-free distribution is experiential while the in-degree distribution of TGs shows exponential distribution (Guelzim et al., 2002). The scale-free network emphasize that most TFs regulate a few set of TGs but a few TFs interrelate with many TGs, though in the exponential network most of the TGs are regulated by the same TF (Barabási and Oltvai, 2004; Albert, 2005).

Protein-Protein Interaction Networks

In complex networks, every protein is shown as a node and the interactions between proteins are presented by edges in the network (Jeong et al., 2001). Few proteins have a large number of connections but most of the proteins have just one or two links as observed for yeast. Also. the similar type of topology was originated in the bacterium *Helicobacter pylori* (Rain et al., 2001). Discoveries lie this suggests that the scale-free nature of PPI networks is a common property of all organisms. Additionally, the scale-free structure, PPI also present the small-world network, modular organization (Barabási and Oltvai, 2004) and motifs (Milo et al. 2002). The utmost challenge in the post-genomic era is to predict the function of protein. Proteins that share connections in a PPI network be likely to have similar functions (Hishigaki et al., 2001). Experimental observations have indicated that 70- 80% of protein interaction nodes share at least one function (Schwikowski, Uetz, and Fields, 2000). By interpreting the neighborhood of known proteins, it is likely to infer a few functional roles of their direct neighbors. This approach called *majority rule assignment* and has been deeply improved by allowing higher neighborhood levels (Hishigaki et al., 2001) and by reducing the number of physical connections between different functional modules of proteins (Vázquez and Moreno, 2003).

Metabolic Networks

Genes, nutrition and environment mainly determines metabolism. It consists of chemical reactions catalyzed by enzymes to generate essential components such as sugars, lipids and amino acids, and also synthesizing the energy essential for construction of cellular components. In view of the fact that the chemical reactions are structured into metabolic pathways, in which one chemical is transformed into another by enzymes and co-factors, therefore such a structure can be logically modeled as a complex network. Thus, metabolic networks are directed and weighted graphs, where enzymes, metabolites and reactions represents vertices, and mass flow and catalytic reactions are represented by edges. Kyoto Encyclopedia of Genes and Genomes (KEGG) is one of the broadly considered catalogues of metabolic pathways. (Jeong et al., 2001) found that metabolic group is not random, but follows the scale-free degree distribution by characterizing the metabolic networks of 43 organisms from all three domains of life. Combined framework of OMICS tools for network construction shown in Figure 5. Metabolic networks are small-world $\left(\ell \approx 3 \right)$, as two metabolites can be connected by a small path – paths which correspond to the biochemical pathway connecting two substrates. For instance, (Wagner and Fell, 2001)

Figure 5. Tools for Omics analysis

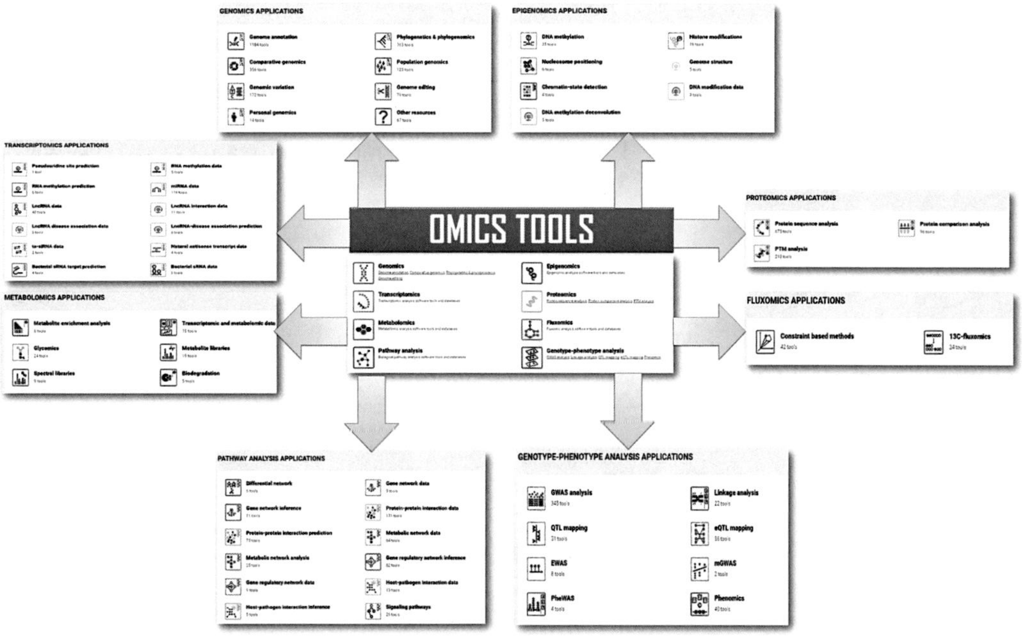

showed that the core of the *E. coli* metabolism map is glutamate and pyruvate, with a mean shortest path length equals to 2.46 and 2.59, respectively. (Jeong et al., 2001) found that the diameter of metabolic networks is the equal for all the 43 organisms analyzed, on the other hand diameter obtained for other types of networks increased logarithmically with the addition of new vertices. Undoubtedly, as the complexity of organisms grows, individual substrates tend to form additional connections with the intention of maintaining a relatively constant network diameter. Given that metabolic networks are scale-free, a high number of connections are concentrated in small number of hubs (Wagner and Fell, 2001) as a result of which it makes such a type of network tolerant to random failures, but susceptible to directed attacks. So, the sequential exclusion of nodes in decreasing order of degree increases the network diameter and rapidly separates the network into disconnected components.

CONCLUSION

Key changes have occurred in biological research during the last few decades, making progress all the way from genome sequencing to functional genomics, animal development and even medicine and ecology. Such an evolution has been mainly characterized by not only increasing complexity but also the need to integrate the dynamics of processes over wider time and space scales. One of the prime challenges in biological research concerns the incorporation of the different systems in an ordered and effective manner, therefore increasing the chances of discovering how significant biological properties come into sight. Although introduced into the biological sciences recently, complex networks research provides an influential tool for not only organizing the complexity of biological data but also incorporating the different subsystems involved and has been effectively applied for the representation, characterization and modeling of several biological systems. One of the most exciting prospects would be the comprehensive integration of the several biological subsystems so that more realistic models and simulations could be obtained. For example, it would be likely to consider the evolution of gene families under varied environmental changes and phylogenetic constraints, with possible implications for the advancement of new therapies. One of the most fascinating problem which may be beneficial from complex networks research is the study of the gene regulatory networks of stem cells while trying to recognize interactions conserved throughout diverse species which can pinpoint the basic framework of cell fate determination. All in one, complex networks are unbiased to provide one of the most significant keys to systems biology.

ACKNOWLEDGMENT

Authors thank Ashwani Kumar, Jaypee University of Information Technology for technical guidance and useful suggestion during critical review of manuscript.

REFERENCES

Aderem, A. (2005). Systems Biology: Its Practice and Challenges. *Cell*, *121*(4), 511–513. doi:10.1016/j.cell.2005.04.020 PMID:15907465

Adiconis, X., Borges-Rivera, D., Satija, R., DeLuca, D. S., Busby, M. A., Berlin, A. M., & Levin, J. Z. et al. (2013). Comparative Analysis of RNA Sequencing Methods for Degraded or Low-Input Samples. *Nature Methods*, *10*(7), 623–629. doi:10.1038/nmeth.2483 PMID:23685885

Albert, R. (2005). Scale-Free Networks in Cell Biology. *Journal of Cell Science*, *118*(Pt 21), 4947–4957. doi:10.1242/jcs.02714 PMID:16254242

Albert, R., Jeong, H., & Barabási, A.L. (2000). Error and Attack Tolerance of Complex Networks. *Nature*, *406*(6794), 378–382. doi:10.1038/35019019

Alon, U. (2006). An Introduction to Systems Biology: Design Principles of Biological Circuits. CRC Press. Retrieved from https://www.crcpress.com/An-Introduction-to-Systems-Biology Design-Principles-of-Biological-Circuits/Alon/p/book/9781584886426

Anders, S., & Huber, W. (2010). Differential Expression Analysis for Sequence Count Data. *Genome Biology*, *11*(10), R106. doi:10.1186/gb-2010-11-10-r106 PMID:20979621

Andrews, S. (2016). FastQC A Quality Control Tool for High Throughput Sequence Data. *Babraham Bioinformatics*. Retrieved from http://www.bioinformatics.babraham.ac.uk/projects/fastqc/

Barabási, A.-L. (2007). Network medicine from obesity to the diseasome. *The New England Journal of Medicine*, *357*(4), 404–407. doi:10.1056/NEJMe078114 PMID:17652657

Barabási, A.-L., & Albert, R. (1999). Emergence of Scaling in Random Networks. *Science*, *286*(5439), 509–512. doi:10.1126/science.286.5439.509 PMID:10521342

Barabási, A.-L., & Oltvai, Z. N. (2004). Network Biology: Understanding the Cells Functional Organization. *Nature Reviews. Genetics*, *5*(2), 101–113. doi:10.1038/nrg1272 PMID:14735121

Bollobas, B. (2016). *Modern Graph Theory*. Springer. Retrieved from http://www.springer.com/gp/book/9780387984889

Carroll, S. B. (2000). Endless Forms: The Evolution of Gene Regulation and Morphological Diversity. *Cell*, *101*(6), 577–580. doi:10.1016/S0092-8674(00)80868-5 PMID:10892643

Costa, L.D.F., Rodrigues, F.A., Travieso, G., & Villas Boas, P.R. (2007). Characterization of Complex Networks: A Survey of Measurements. *Advances in Physics*, *56*(1), 167–242. doi:10.1080/00018730601170527

DeLuca, D. S., Levin, J. Z., Sivachenko, A., Fennell, T., Nazaire, M.-D., Williams, C., & Getz, G. et al. (2012). RNA-SeQC: RNA-Seq Metrics for Quality Control and Process Optimization. *Bioinformatics (Oxford, England)*, *28*(11), 1530–1532. doi:10.1093/bioinformatics/bts196 PMID:22539670

Denoeud, F., Aury, J.-M., Da Silva, C., Noel, B., Rogier, O., Delledonne, M., & Artiguenave, F. et al. (2008). Annotating Genomes with Massive-Scale RNA Sequencing. *Genome Biology*, *9*(12), R175. doi:10.1186/gb-2008-9-12-r175 PMID:19087247

Diestel, R. (2016). *Graph Theory*. Springer. Retrieved from http://www.springer.com/gp/book/9783642142789

Dobin, A., Davis, C. A., Schlesinger, F., Drenkow, J., Zaleski, C., Jha, S., & Gingeras, T. R. et al. (2013). STAR: Ultrafast Universal RNA-Seq Aligner. *Bioinformatics (Oxford, England)*, *29*(1), 15–21. doi:10.1093/bioinformatics/bts635 PMID:23104886

Dodt, M., Roehr, J. T., Ahmed, R., & Dieterich, C. (2012). FLEXBAR-Flexible Barcode and Adapter Processing for Next-Generation Sequencing Platforms. *Biology*, *1*(3), 895–905. doi:10.3390/biology1030895 PMID:24832523

Erdös, P., & Rényi, A. (1959). On Random Graphs, I. *Publicationes Mathematicae (Debrecen)*, *6*, 290–297.

Faloutsos, M., Faloutsos, P., & Faloutsos, C. (1999). On Power-Law Relationships of the Internet Topology. *Proceedings of the Conference on Applications, Technologies, Architectures, and Protocols for Computer Communication SIGCOMM '99* (pp. 251–262). New York, NY, USA: ACM. doi:10.1145/316188.316229

FASTX-Toolkit. (2016). Retrieved from http://hannonlab.cshl.edu/fastx_toolkit/

Fields, S., & Song, O. (1989). A Novel Genetic System to Detect Protein-Protein Interactions. *Nature*, *340*(6230), 245–246. doi:10.1038/340245a0 PMID:2547163

Flory, P. J. (1941). Molecular Size Distribution in Three Dimensional Polymers. I. Gelation1. *Journal of the American Chemical Society*, *63*(11), 3083–3090. doi:10.1021/ja01856a061

Gama-Castro, S., Jiménez-Jacinto, V., Peralta-Gil, M., Santos-Zavaleta, A., Peñaloza-Spinola, M. I., & Contreras-Moreira, B. et al.. (2008). RegulonDB (Version 6.0): Gene Regulation Model of Escherichia Coli K-12 beyond Transcription, Active (Experimental) Annotated Promoters and Textpresso Navigation. *Nucleic Acids Research*, *36*(Database issue), D120–D124. doi:10.1093/nar/gkm994 PMID:18158297

Ren, B., Robert, F., Wyrick, J. J., Aparicio, O., Jennings, E. G., Simon, I., ... & Volkert, T. L. (2000). Genome-Wide Location and Function of DNA Binding Proteins. *Science*, *290*(5500), 2306–2309. doi:10.1126/science.290.5500.2306 PMID:11125145

Grabherr, M. G., Haas, B. J., Yassour, M., Levin, J. Z., Thompson, D. A., Amit, I., & Regev, A. et al. (2011). Full-Length Transcriptome Assembly from RNA-Seq Data without a Reference Genome. *Nature Biotechnology*, *29*(7), 644–652. doi:10.1038/nbt.1883 PMID:21572440

Griffith, M., Griffith, O. L., Mwenifumbo, J., Goya, R., Morrissy, A. S., Morin, R. D., & Marra, M. A. et al. (2010). Alternative Expression Analysis by RNA Sequencing. *Nature Methods*, *7*(10), 843–847. doi:10.1038/nmeth.1503 PMID:20835245

Guelzim, N., Bottani, S., Bourgine, P., & Képès, F. (2002). Topological and Causal Structure of the Yeast Transcriptional Regulatory Network. *Nature Genetics*, *31*(1), 60–63. doi:10.1038/ng873 PMID:11967534

Guttman, M., Garber, M., Levin, J. Z., Donaghey, J., Robinson, J., Adiconis, X., & Regev, A. et al. (2010). Ab Initio Reconstruction of Cell Type-Specific Transcriptomes in Mouse Reveals the Conserved Multi-Exonic Structure of lincRNAs. *Nature Biotechnology*, *28*(5), 503–510. doi:10.1038/nbt.1633 PMID:20436462

Hartwell, L. H., Hopfield, J. J., Leibler, S., & Murray, A. W. (1999). From Molecular to Modular Cell Biology. *Nature*, *402*(6761 Suppl.), C47–C52. doi:10.1038/35011540 PMID:10591225

Hishigaki, H., Nakai, K., Ono, T., Tanigami, A., & Takagi, T. (2001). Assessment of Prediction Accuracy of Protein Function from Protein Protein Interaction Data. *Yeast (Chichester, England), 18*(6), 523–531. doi:10.1002/yea.706 PMID:11284008

Huerta, A. M., Salgado, H., Thieffry, D., & Collado-Vides, J. (1998). RegulonDB: A Database on Transcriptional Regulation in Escherichia Coli. *Nucleic Acids Research, 26*(1), 55–59. doi:10.1093/nar/26.1.55 PMID:9399800

Jeong, H., Mason, S. P., Barabási, A.-L., & Oltvai, Z. N. (2001). Lethality and Centrality in Protein Networks. *Nature, 411*(6833), 41–42. doi:10.1038/35075138 PMID:11333967

Langmead, B., Trapnell, C., Pop, M., & Salzberg, S.L. (2009). Ultrafast and Memory Efficient Alignment of Short DNA Sequences to the Human Genome. *Genome Biology, 10*(3), R25. doi:.10.1186/gb-2009-10-3-r25

Lee, S., Seo, C. H., Lim, B., Yang, J. O., Oh, J., Kim, M., & Lee, S. et al. (2011). Accurate Quantification of Transcriptome from RNA-Seq Data by Effective Length Normalization. *Nucleic Acids Research, 39*(2), e9. doi:10.1093/nar/gkq1015 PMID:21059678

Leng, N., Dawson, J. A., Thomson, J. A., Ruotti, V., Rissman, A. I., Smits, B. M. G., & Kendziorski, C. et al. (2013). EBSeq: An Empirical Bayes Hierarchical Model for Inference in RNA-Seq Experiments. *Bioinformatics (Oxford, England), 29*(8), 1035–1043. doi:10.1093/bioinformatics/btt087 PMID:23428641

Levine, M., & Tjian, R. (2003). Transcription Regulation and Animal Diversity. *Nature, 424*(6945), 147–151. doi:10.1038/nature01763 PMID:12853946

Li, B., & Dewey, C. N. (2011). RSEM: Accurate Transcript Quantification from RNA-Seq Data with or without a Reference Genome. *BMC Bioinformatics, 12*(August), 323. doi:10.1186/1471-2105-12-323 PMID:21816040

Li, H., & Durbin, R. (2009). Fast and Accurate Short Read Alignment with Burrows-Wheeler Transform. *Bioinformatics (Oxford, England), 25*(14), 1754–1760. doi:10.1093/bioinformatics/btp324 PMID:19451168

Li, H., Ruan, J., & Durbin, R. (2008). Mapping Short DNA Sequencing Reads and Calling Variants Using Mapping Quality Scores. *Genome Research, 18*(11), 1851–1858. doi:10.1101/gr.078212.108 PMID:18714091

Li, J., & Tibshirani, R. (2013). Finding Consistent Patterns: A Nonparametric Approach for Identifying Differential Expression in RNA-Seq Data. *Statistical Methods in Medical Research, 22*(5), 519–536. doi:10.1177/0962280211428386 PMID:22127579

Lockhart, D. J., & Winzeler, E. A. (2000). Genomics, Gene Expression and DNA Arrays. *Nature, 405*(6788), 827–836. doi:10.1038/35015701 PMID:10866209

Maher, C. A., Kumar-Sinha, C., Cao, X., Kalyana-Sundaram, S., Han, B., Jing, X., ... & Chinnaiyan, A. M. (2009). Transcriptome Sequencing to Detect Gene Fusions in Cancer. *Nature, 458*(7234), 97–101. doi:10.1038/nature07638

Milo, R., Shen-Orr, S., Itzkovitz, S., Kashtan, N., Chklovskii, D., & Alon, U. (2002). Network Motifs: Simple Building Blocks of Complex Networks. *Science*, *298*(5594), 824–827. doi:10.1126/science.298.5594.824 PMID:12399590

Mortazavi, A., Williams, B. A., McCue, K., Schaeffer, L., & Wold, B. (2008). Mapping and Quantifying Mammalian Transcriptomes by RNA-Seq. *Nature Methods*, *5*(7), 621–628. doi:10.1038/nmeth.1226 PMID:18516045

Newman, M. E. J. (2001). The Structure of Scientific Collaboration Networks. *Proceedings of the National Academy of Sciences of the United States of America*, *98*(2), 404–409. doi:10.1073/pnas.98.2.404 PMID:11149952

Okonechnikov, K., Conesa, A., & García-Alcalde, F. (2016). Qualimap 2: Advanced Multi-Sample Quality Control for High-Throughput Sequencing Data. *Bioinformatics (Oxford, England)*, *32*(2), 292–294. doi:10.1093/bioinformatics/btv566 PMID:26428292

Ozsolak, F., & Milos, P. M. (2011). RNA Sequencing: Advances, Challenges and Opportunities. *Nature Reviews. Genetics*, *12*(2), 87–98. doi:10.1038/nrg2934 PMID:21191423

Patro, R., Mount, S. M., & Kingsford, C. (2014). Sailfish Enables Alignment-Free Isoform Quantification from RNA-Seq Reads Using Lightweight Algorithms. *Nature Biotechnology*, *32*(5), 462–464. doi:10.1038/nbt.2862 PMID:24752080

Pertea, M., Pertea, G. M., Antonescu, C. M., Chang, T.-C., Mendell, J. T., & Salzberg, S. L. (2015). StringTie Enables Improved Reconstruction of a Transcriptome from RNA-Seq Reads. *Nature Biotechnology*, *33*(3), 290–295. doi:10.1038/nbt.3122 PMID:25690850

Rain, J. C., Selig, L., De Reuse, H., Battaglia, V., Reverdy, C., Simon, S., & Legrain, P. et al. (2001). The Protein-Protein Interaction Map of Helicobacter Pylori. *Nature*, *409*(6817), 211–215. doi:10.1038/35051615 PMID:11196647

Ravasz, E., Somera, A. L., Mongru, D. A., Oltvai, Z. N., & Barabási, A. L. (2002). Hierarchical Organization of Modularity in Metabolic Networks. *Science*, *297*(5586), 1551–1555. doi:10.1126/science.1073374 PMID:12202830

Robasky, K., Lewis, N. E., & Church, G. M. (2014). The Role of Replicates for Error Mitigation in next-Generation Sequencing. *Nature Reviews. Genetics*, *15*(1), 56–62. doi:10.1038/nrg3655 PMID:24322726

Robertson, G., Schein, J., Chiu, R., Corbett, R., Field, M., Jackman, S. D., & Birol, I. et al. (2010). De Novo Assembly and Analysis of RNA-Seq Data. *Nature Methods*, *7*(11), 909–912. doi:10.1038/nmeth.1517 PMID:20935650

Robinson, M. D., McCarthy, D. J., & Smyth, G. K. (2010). edgeR: A Bioconductor Package for Differential Expression Analysis of Digital Gene Expression Data. *Bioinformatics (Oxford, England)*, *26*(1), 139–140. doi:10.1093/bioinformatics/btp616 PMID:19910308

Schena, M., Shalon, D., Davis, R. W., & Brown, P. O. (1995). Quantitative Monitoring of Gene Expression Patterns with a Complementary DNA Microarray. *Science*, *270*(5235), 467–470. doi:10.1126/science.270.5235.467 PMID:7569999

Schulz, M. H., Zerbino, D. R., Vingron, M., & Birney, E. (2012). Oases: Robust de Novo RNA-Seq Assembly across the Dynamic Range of Expression Levels. *Bioinformatics (Oxford, England), 28*(8), 1086–1092. doi:10.1093/bioinformatics/bts094 PMID:22368243

Schwikowski, B., Uetz, P., & Fields, S. (2000). A Network of Protein-Protein Interactions in Yeast. *Nature Biotechnology, 18*(12), 1257–1261. doi:10.1038/82360 PMID:11101803

Seyednasrollah, F., Laiho, A., & Elo, L. L. (2015). Comparison of Software Packages for Detecting Differential Expression in RNA-Seq Studies. *Briefings in Bioinformatics, 16*(1), 59–70. doi:10.1093/bib/bbt086 PMID:24300110

Tarazona, S., Furió-Tarí, P., Turrà, D., Di Pietro, A., Nueda, M. J., Ferrer, A., & Conesa, A. (2015). Data Quality Aware Analysis of Differential Expression in RNA-Seq with NOISeq R/Bioc Package. *Nucleic Acids Research, 43*(21), e140. doi:10.1093/nar/gkv711 PMID:26184878

Teichmann, S. A., & Madan Babu, M. (2004). Gene Regulatory Network Growth by Duplication. *Nature Genetics, 36*(5), 492–496. doi:10.1038/ng1340 PMID:15107850

Trapnell, C., Pachter, L., & Salzberg, S. L. (2009). TopHat: Discovering Splice Junctions with RNA-Seq. *Bioinformatics (Oxford, England), 25*(9), 1105–1111. doi:10.1093/bioinformatics/btp120 PMID:19289445

Trapnell, C., Williams, B. A., Pertea, G., Mortazavi, A., Kwan, G., van Baren, M. J., & Pachter, L. et al. (2010). Transcript Assembly and Quantification by RNA-Seq Reveals Unannotated Transcripts and Isoform Switching during Cell Differentiation. *Nature Biotechnology, 28*(5), 511–515. doi:10.1038/nbt.1621 PMID:20436464

Uetz, P., & Hughes, R. E. (2000). Systematic and Large-Scale Two-Hybrid Screens. *Current Opinion in Microbiology, 3*(3), 303–308. doi:10.1016/S1369-5274(00)00094-1 PMID:10851163

Vázquez, A., & Moreno, Y. (2003). Resilience to Damage of Graphs with Degree Correlations. *Physical Review E: Statistical, Nonlinear, and Soft Matter Physics, 67*(1 Pt 2), 15101. doi:10.1103/PhysRevE.67.015101 PMID:12636544

Vidal, M., Cusick, M. E., & Barabási, A.-L. (2011). Interactome Networks and Human Disease. *Cell, 144*(6), 986–998. doi:10.1016/j.cell.2011.02.016 PMID:21414488

Wagner, A., & Fell, D. A. (2001). The Small World inside Large Metabolic Networks. *Proceedings. Biological Sciences, 268*(1478), 1803–1810. doi:10.1098/rspb.2001.1711 PMID:11522199

Wang, E. T., Sandberg, R., Luo, S., Khrebtukova, I., Zhang, L., Mayr, C., & Burge, C. B. et al. (2008). Alternative Isoform Regulation in Human Tissue Transcriptomes. *Nature, 456*(7221), 470–476. doi:10.1038/nature07509 PMID:18978772

Wang, K., Singh, D., Zeng, Z., Coleman, S. J., Huang, Y., Savich, G. L., & Liu, J. et al. (2010). MapSplice: Accurate Mapping of RNA-Seq Reads for Splice Junction Discovery. *Nucleic Acids Research, 38*(18), e178. doi:10.1093/nar/gkq622 PMID:20802226

Wang, L., Wang, S., & Li, W. (2012). RSeQC: Quality Control of RNA-Seq Experiments. *Bioinformatics (Oxford, England), 28*(16), 2184–2185. doi:10.1093/bioinformatics/bts356 PMID:22743226

Watts, D. J., & Strogatz, S. H. (1998). Collective Dynamics of small-World Networks. *Nature*, *393*(6684), 440–442. doi:10.1038/30918 PMID:9623998

Wu, T. D., & Nacu, S. (2010). Fast and SNP-Tolerant Detection of Complex Variants and Splicing in Short Reads. *Bioinformatics (Oxford, England)*, *26*(7), 873–881. doi:10.1093/bioinformatics/btq057 PMID:20147302

Yang, X., Di Liu, F. L., Wu, J., Zou, J., Xiao, X., Zhao, F., & Zhu, B. (2013). HTQC: A Fast Quality Control Toolkit for Illumina Sequencing Data. *BMC Bioinformatics*, *14*(January), 33. doi:10.1186/1471-2105-14-33 PMID:23363224

Zhu, M., Deng, X., Joshi, T., Xu, D., Stacey, G., & Cheng, J. (2012). Reconstructing Differentially Co-Expressed Gene Modules and Regulatory Networks of Soybean Cells. *BMC Genomics*, *13*(1), 437. doi:10.1186/1471-2164-13-437 PMID:22938179

Chapter 9
Protein Docking and Drug Design

Aditi Gangopadhyay
Jhargram Raj College, India

Hirak Jyoti Chakraborty
Central Inland Fisheries Research Institute, India

Abhijit Datta
Department of Botany, Jhargram Raj College, India

ABSTRACT

Protein docking is integral to structure-based drug design and molecular biology. The recent surge of big data in biology, the demand for personalised medicines, evolving pathogens and increasing lifestyle-associated risks, asks for smart, robust, low-cost and high-throughput drug design. Computer-aided drug design techniques allow rapid screening of ultra-large chemical libraries within minutes. This is immensely necessary to the drug discovery pipeline, which is presently burdened with high attrition rates, failures, huge capital and time investment. With increasing drug resistance and difficult druggable targets, there is a growing need for novel drug scaffolds which is partly satisfied by fragment based drug design and de novo methods. The chapter discusses various aspects of protein docking and emphasises on its application in drug design.

INTRODUCTION

Docking the Big Data Surge to Drug Design

With decreasing costs in human genome sequencing, advances in exome sequencing, high-throughput peptide sequencing and a growing network of scientific collaborations, the golden age of Molecular Biology is presently sensing a massive big data surge. The cost of sequencing a single human genome dropped steeply after 2007 with the advent of next generation sequencers (Wetterstrand, 2016). Genome-wide studies are now possible, which feed information to the human diseasome (Hirschhorn & Daly,

DOI: 10.4018/978-1-5225-2607-0.ch009

2005; McCarthy et al., 2008). Colossal advances in genome informatics, personal genomes, make way for the field of personalised medicines, which hold the future of medicine and drug discovery (Agyeman & Ofori-Asenso, 2015; Ginsburg & McCarthy, 2001; Stein, 2010). However, the discovery of a single drug is presently a matter of years and billions of US dollars (Avorn, 2015). With personalised medicines out on the field, the future demands high-throughput drug design to stay at par with the big data explosion in biology and medicinal chemistry (Lusher, McGuire, van Schaik, Nicholson, & de Vlieg, 2014). As if this wasn't enough, the human race is constantly at battle with evolving viral strains, bacterial multidrug resistance, undruggable targets, epidemics and accelerated lifestyle-associated risks. Future drug design will demand smart and robust technologies capable of handling the five V's of biological big data: volume, velocity, variety, veracity and value. The discovery of computational power has been a blessing to Science. Computer-aided drug design (CADD) is presently able to screen chemical libraries in the order of millions, in minutes. An important technique in CADD is molecular docking, used in structure-based drug design. CADD is evolving rapidly and sharply, and probably by the time this book is published, there will be newer tools and techniques in the field. Molecular docking serves one of the most important objectives in drug design and molecular biology: to model and comprehend molecular interactions.

This chapter attempts to discuss the various aspects of protein docking: the kinds, purpose, algorithms, scoring functions, tools and some practical facets such as the docking tools, file formats, visualisation and computational time. The chapter places emphasis on the application of high-throughput protein docking for handling big data in CADD, and illustrates with case studies.

Background

The docking technique was first applied to biology in 1975 by Levinthal et al. to determine the interactions of sickle haemoglobin. The earliest mention of "molecular docking" in ScienceDirect is in a work by Luskey et al. in 1981. Today, "molecular docking" returns over 5,000 articles for the year 2016 alone in ScienceDirect, of which over 3,000 are linked to drug design. Docking is applied in CADD to model protein interactions to small molecules, fragments and peptides and to examine the structure of protein-protein and protein-nucleic complexes. The most commonly encountered docking computations in CADD are protein-small molecule and protein-fragment, usually on a high-throughput scale.

Molecular docking involves two steps: pose generation and scoring. One molecule can bind to the other molecule in n number of ways or poses. In pose generation, the *n* poses of one molecule with respect to the other are generated by the docking algorithm. The poses are scored by a scoring function. The optimum solution is selected on the basis of the score and other parameters (Lengauer, 2008). One of the main difficulties in any docking computation is identifying false positives and selecting the natural binding mode, which is a test of the power of the scoring function. Generally, the use of consensus scoring using different scoring functions and cross-platform docking with different algorithms is suggested to eliminate false positives and identify the correct binding mode.

Protein Docking: Getting Them Sorted

The individuality and dimensionality of biological problems makes every docking computation unique and each case requires an exclusive solution. This section will attempt to integrate protein docking computations into separate categories based on the nature of docked molecules, incorporation of structural flexibility and the purpose of the docking exercise.

1. **The Molecular Players - Splitting the Game:** Protein docking is applied to study protein interactions to diverse molecular classes: small molecules, fragments, peptides and to macromolecules such as nucleic acids and other proteins. This partitions the protein docking exercise into protein-small molecule, protein-fragment, protein-peptide, protein-protein and protein-nucleic acid docking computations.

    a. **Small Molecules - The Big Issue:** Protein-small molecule docking is mostly performed in structure-based virtual screening when the structure of the target site is known (Jorgensen, 2004; Shoichet, McGovern, Wei, & Irwin, 2002). It is also widely used to model protein-ligand complexes (Mobley & Dill, 2009). Virtual screening is a um of computational approaches employed to screen large chemical libraries against a target site in drug design. In docking-based virtual screening, chemical libraries are docked to the binding site and scored. Compounds that score well are further tested for *in vitro* or *in vivo* activities. The technique has been successful in the development of a number of drugs, such as HIV protease and DNA gyrase inhibitors (Jorgensen, 2004; Kuntz, 1992). Docking-based screening sometimes have higher hit rates than assay-based HTS (high-throughput screening) (Doman et al., 2002; Jorgensen, 2004). However, virtual screening and HTS have their own strengths and weaknesses, and success depends on the logical application to the problem at hand.

    b. **Fragment Docking - Building from Bits:** The chemical space is vast, diverse and most of its potential is untapped. Unexplored molecular frameworks might be potential scaffolds for new drugs. One of the subsets of the chemical space is the fragment space, fragments being structural subsets of larger compounds. Fragments ideally follow the rule of three: molecular weight < 300 Da, cLogP $\leq$ 3, number of hydrogen bond donors is $\leq$ 3, number of hydrogen bond acceptors is $\leq$ 3 (Congreve, Carr, Murray, & Jhoti, 2003). In fragment docking, the fragments are docked to the binding site and the top scorers are selected. Whole compounds are built by "growing" the fragments in steps, or by joining several fragments that are docked to the binding site. One of the greatest advantages of this technique is the combinations and permutations of fragments, which allows a greater exploration of the chemical space.

    c. **Macromolecular Docking - Still a Macro Challenge:** Macromolecular docking approaches model protein interactions to bio-macromolecules. Protein-protein interfaces (PPIs) are becoming increasingly popular targets for small molecule and peptide inhibitors (Bakail & Ochsenbein, 2016; Wells & McClendon, 2007). PPI inhibition is a therapeutic approach for disease-causing protein-protein associations in neuro-degeneration, prion diseases, genetic disorders like Huntington's and host-pathogen interactions (Aguzzi & O'Connor, 2010). The main focal points of interaction at PPIs are the "hotspots" which are the primary targets (Arkin, Tang, & Wells, 2014; Cukuroglu, Engin, Gursoy, & Keskin, 2014; Guo, Wisniewski, & Ji, 2014). Structural investigations required in the study of protein interactomes employ high-throughput protein-protein docking techniques (Mosca, Pons, Fernández-Recio, & Aloy, 2009). The CAPRI (Critical Assessment of PRedicted Interactions) is a community-wide blind experiment initiated in 2001 to evaluate protein-protein docking tools, hosted by the PDBe group of EMBL-EBI (Janin, 2002). The CAPRI results demonstrate that current protein docking tools are quite successful in modelling homodimeric complexes with large interfaces. However, the success rate in predicting heterodimeric complexes is lower (Lensink et al., 2016). For tetramers and proteins with problematic oligomeric state assignments, present docking tools show poor results (Lensink et al., 2016). The use of a combination of docking algorithms improves the reliability and correctness of protein-protein docking predictions (Vajda & Kozakov, 2009).

2. **Flexibility - To Be or Not to Be:** Docking computations are either rigid body or flexible computations. The structures are treated rigidly in rigid body docking (RBD), while flexible docking incorporates the flexibility of the molecules in the computation. RBD is a computationally faster method than flexible docking. Flexible dockings include the torsional degrees of freedom, which allow the molecules to explore a more extensive search space, also making the search computationally more expensive than RBD.

In protein-small molecule docking, it is a common practice to keep the protein receptor rigid, while treating the small molecules flexibly. However, molecular interactions in the cell require some degree of compromise on part of the protein as well, established by the "induced fit" and "conformational selection" models of protein-ligand binding. To deal with this, receptor flexibility in protein-small molecule docking is handled by keeping the receptor structure partially flexible: the binding site residues are flexible and the rest of the protein is rigid.

Since proteins and nucleic acids are large macromolecules, including the torsional degrees of freedom is massive computational affair. In these cases, an approximate structure of the complex is initially modeled by rigid docking, followed by flexible docking to improve model accuracy. Protein-macromolecule docking tools currently deal with side-chain and backbone flexibility. The flexibility of side-chains is tackled in the final stages of refinement and minimisation. Considering protein flexibility is particularly essential when the proteins are constructed by comparative or loop modelling techniques.

3. **Divided by Purpose:** The purpose of the docking computation is the most important thing to consider prior to designing a docking workflow. Docking studies are designed for various purposes such as structure-based virtual screening, drug repositioning, *de novo* drug design, studying protein-protein interactions, interfaces, complexes and investigating protein-nucleic acid interactions.

    a. High-Throughput Docking (HTD) - Big Data, Small Time: HTS (High-throughput screening) is an assay-based method where millions of compounds are rapidly screened for hit identification. However, HTS sometimes perform poorly and is uneconomical, requiring cheaper alternatives (Abagyan & Totrov, 2001). Docking-based virtual screening harnesses the power of molecular docking to identify structure-based antagonists. In high-throughput docking (HTD), molecular docking is applied on a large scale to screen large compound libraries as fast as possible. HTD is being increasingly used to identify leads, which are biologically therapeutic and has the potential of being developed into drugs (Abagyan & Totrov, 2001; Alvarez, 2004; Gane & Dean, 2000). The use of cluster computing to speed up HTD by parallelisation of docking runs has been used in the DOVIS (DOcking based VIrtual Screening) protocol that runs AutoDock on a Linux cluster (Jiang et al., 2008; Zhang et al., 2008). The Anchor-based Library TAiloring (ALTA) approach also performs high-throughput docking of large chemical libraries (Kolb, Kipouros, Huang, & Caflisch, 2008). In ALTA, the compound library is decomposed into fragments and the fragments are screened according to the binding site features. Screened fragments are docked into the binding site and ranked. Top ranking fragments are used to retrieve a subset of compounds from the library. The subset is next docked to the binding site using flexible docking approaches. The ALTA approach is used for creating focused libraries and prioritising fragments (Kolb et al., 2008).

b. **Ultra-High Throughput Docking (UHTD) - Ultra-Large Libraries, Ultra-Small Time:** Ultra-high throughput docking (UHTD) is a large-scale version of high-throughput docking. Here, ultra-large libraries in the order of millions are screened within a very short time with docking techniques. Several docking tools allow UHTD which are employed in structure-based virtual screening. Combined with powerful computational resources such as cluster computing, they allow ultra-large libraries in millions to be screened in a matter of hours. Ultra-high throughput structure-based virtual screening can be performed by combining docking with other computational approaches. A new approach for ultra-high throughput screening was demonstrated in the work of Johnson and Karanicolas (Johnson & Karanicolas, 2016). In the work, the protein pocket conformations were represented by exemplars: virtual pocket-complementary pseudo-ligands. The exemplars were used to screen libraries for similar compounds. Compounds initially identified with exemplar-matching were docked with existing docking tools. The exemplar method is ultra-fast and is an example of how molecular docking can be combined with other virtual screening approaches for ultra-high throughput screening of large compound libraries (Johnson & Karanicolas, 2016).

c. **Fragment Docking - As a Tool:** In the previous section, fragments were regarded as a molecular category and "fragment docking" was simply as case of docking fragments to proteins. In this section, "fragment docking" refers to the docking tool, which is variously applied in drug design. Fragment docking techniques in FBDD are commonly used for *de novo* drug design, drug repositioning, focusing libraries (as in ALTA) and virtual screening (Huameng Li et al., 2011, 2014; Huameng Li & Li, 2010a). Virtual screening and fragment based drug discovery is suggested to be more successful than high-throughput screening in the identification of inhibitors of PPIs (Sheng et al., 2015). In *de novo* drug design, drugs are made from scratch for generating new chemical entities (NCEs) (Schneider & Fechner, 2005). To name a few, FBDD was used in the discovery of the melanoma drug Vemurafenib and treatments for myeloma, stromal tumors and Alzheimer's disease (Baker, 2012; Erlanson, Fesik, Hubbard, Jahnke, & Jhoti, 2016). Several candidates identified by FBDD are in the trial phase of the drug discovery pipeline (Baker, 2012).

d. **Multiple Ligand Simultaneous Docking (MLSD) - The "Orchestrated Dancing of Ligands":** Molecular docking is generally used to model a bimolecular complex. However, within the cell, there are ions, cofactors, water molecules, substrates all floating in the cytoplasm along with the two docked molecules. The MLSD technique simulates this cellular environment by employing the Lamarckian genetic algorithm combined with Particle Swarm Optimisation for reaching the global minimum (Huameng Li et al., 2011, 2014; Huameng Li & Li, 2010a; Raghavendra, Aditya Rao, Kumar, & Ramesh, 2015). The core principle of the MLSD approach is effectively expressed in the words of Li and Li (2010) as the "Orchestrated dancing of ligands in binding sites of proteins" (Huameng Li & Li, 2010a). The MLSD approach combined with fragment docking is applied to drug repositioning (Huameng Li et al., 2011, 2014; Huameng Li & Li, 2010b).

e. **Drug Repositioning - Cutting the Cost of Drug Discovery:** In drug repositioning, a drug originally meant for one disease is "repositioned" to target another disease. This reduces the cost of drug discovery as repositioned drugs are already tested for human safety and biological activity and can enter the pipeline from phases II or III of clinical trial (Ashburn & Thor, 2004; Chong & Sullivan, 2007; Nosengo, 2016). Drug repositioning is estimated to cut the cost of drug design from 2-3 billion to 300 million US dollars and reduce the time from 15 years to 6 and a half (Nosengo, 2016). Estimates suggest that 75% of existing drugs can be repositioned. Another advantage of drug repositioning is that it can also make use of drugs which have failed in previous trials. These drugs are already tested for human safety and bioactivity and have a dormant potential that could be effective against other diseases. Molecular docking is employed to perform drug repositioning in various ways: docking-based screening of drug libraries, MLSD and fragment docking.

Protein Docking Algorithms: Choosing the Right Road to Success

Docking algorithms are broadly rigid body docking or flexible docking algorithms. The choice of the docking algorithm depends on the particular biological problem. Both ligands and macromolecules can be treated rigidly or flexibly as the case demands. This section will discuss algorithms for performing rigid and flexible protein dockings to rigid or flexible small molecules, fragments, proteins and nucleic acids.

1. **Small Molecule Docking - Big Share in CADD:** Protein-small molecule dockings can be rigid protein-rigid ligand, rigid protein-flexible ligand, partially flexible protein-flexible ligand or both flexible protein-flexible ligand computations. This section will discuss algorithms on how they deal with the flexibility of individual categories of molecules in small-molecule protein docking.

    a. **The Case of Rigid Ligands - Going with Geometry:** RBD algorithms are based on geometric complementarity between the ligand and the receptor binding site and include geometric hashing, clique detection, pose clustering and shape comparison methods. They are computationally faster and are used in combination with flexible docking methods.

Based on the Bron-Kerbosch algorithm (Bron & Kerbosch, 1973), clique detection matches a ligand feature to a protein feature, where the feature is a volume, distance, geometry or a hydrogen bond. The geometric hashing technique was applied in molecular docking by Fisher and coworkers (Fischer, Lin, Wolfson, & Nussinov, 1995; Lamdan & Wolfson, 1988). The three-dimensional geometric features of the ligand and the binding site are fed into a hash table and matched, the match with the highest votes is selected. The LUDI docking program uses pose clustering, where the interaction surface of the protein is represented with discrete points. These points are used to triangulate the binding site. Triangles of ligand atoms are matched to complementary triangles of the triangulated binding site. The results of triangle-matching are clustered by RMSD. The cluster with the largest population of triangle matches is used to determine ligand orientation in the binding site (Dhanik & Kavraki, 2012). Pose clustering is applied in fragment docking and *de novo* docking. The shape comparison method is a computationally faster geometry matching approach. It uses the overlapping volume and area between the protein and ligand to arrive at the optimum ligand conformation.

b. **The Case of Flexible Ligands - Freedom at Last:** RBD techniques are computationally cheaper than flexible docking techniques. While this helps to generate a quick estimate of the ligand pose, flexible docking allows a more extensive conformational search for selecting the optimum ligand pose.

  i. **Docking Conformational Ensembles - The Many Faces of a Lone Ligand:** In ensemble docking, an ensemble of ligand conformations is generated each conformation is rigidly docked to the receptor binding site. The computational time is directly proportional to the population of the ensemble.

  ii. **Docking by Fragmentation - Breaking to Bits, then Making from Bits:** The principle of docking by fragmentation involves fragmenting a ligand and docking the fragments for constructing the original ligand from the fragments. There are two ways of doing this: with place and join and incremental construction algorithms [Figure 1]. Place and join as the name indicates, first places (docks) the ligand fragments into the binding site followed by joining to construct the original ligand molecule. Fragment placing may be performed with RBD. One of the difficulties of this method is rebuilding the correct ligand structure while simultaneously safeguarding the fragment interactions to the binding site. This algorithm is generally used for molecules with fragments of average size and a moderate number of fragments. The more popular incremental construction algorithm uses the construction-by-increment strategy. The algorithm proceeds by first identifying the base (anchor) fragment to which the other fragments are attached. The base fragment is first docked into the binding site, which acts as an anchor for the construction of the rest of the ligand. The entire molecule is constructed by docking the remaining fragments one after the other in increments.

  iii. **The Genetic Algorithm - Inspired by Evolution:** The Genetic Algorithm draws inspiration from natural evolution [Figure 2]. In the Natural Algorithm, organisms (individuals) evolve through genetic modifications across generations. Natural selection follows the law of survival of the fittest, where the fittest organisms survive. In the Genetic Algorithm, the individuals are the different ligand conformations. The genes of a ligand encode the degrees of freedom: of translation, orientation and torsion, and

Figure 1. Flexible docking strategies by fragmentation

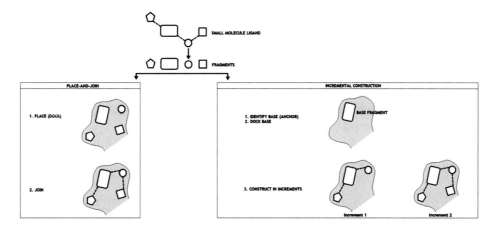

Figure 2. Comparing the genetic algorithm with natural evolution

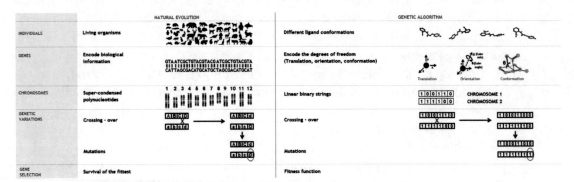

are represented by a chromosome. Translations are straight line ligand motions in the 3-dimensional space (x, y, z). Orientational degrees of freedom are measured by bond rotations and represented by quaternions (qx, qy, qz, qw) where qx, qy, qz represents the Euler axis and qw the Euler angle. The chromosome is a binary sequence encoding the ligand configuration is the order: x, y, z, qx, qy, qz, qw, Σt, where Σt is the total number of ligand torsions. Similar to the Natural Algorithm, genetic diversity occurs by cross-over and mutation between chromosomes. The population evolves over the generations and reaches an optimum ligand conformation. At each generation, the fittest offspring are selected by a fitness function.

In the multiple ligand simultaneous docking (MLSD) using the Lamarckian genetic algorithm (LGA), the chromosome is represented as: $(x, y, z, qx, qy, qz, qw, \Sigma t)_N$, where N is the total number of ligands being docked. The LGA uses an inverse phenotype-to-genotype mapping, similar to Lamarck's genetic theory that acquired phenotypes are incorporated in the genetic makeup. The LGA is better capable at handling flexible ligands (Morris et al., 1998).

c. **Simulation Methods - Mimicking the Cell:** The process of finding the minimum potential energy of a molecular system is called Molecular Mechanics (MM). MM generates an idealised geometry of motionless molecules. However, in practical scenarios, molecules undergo thermal motions and their geometries change. Biomolecules undergo abrupt conformational changes. The protein-ligand interaction is a good example where changes are observed not only in the conformations of protein-ligand complexes, but also in solvent rearrangements. In MM, information is derived from a single conformation of the molecular system whereas simulation uses millions of conformations of the same molecular system. There are various simulation techniques like Molecular Dynamics (MD), Monte Carlo (MC), simulated annealing which allows these fluctuations in conformation and energy, and calculates the thermodynamic properties. There are two approaches in molecular simulation: stochastic and deterministic. The MC is a stochastic approach while MD is a deterministic method. Simulations virtually mimic the behaviour of a real-life system over time.

i. **Molecular Dynamics (MD) Simulations - Observing Motion:** MD simulations are used to study the motional dynamics of the components of a system. MD can be applied to study the stability and dynamics of a protein-ligand complex over a period of time. To study the behaviour of docked complexes, the system is placed in a simulated biological environment. A perturbation is applied to this system and the atomic shifts are observed at specific time intervals (say δt). Atomic shifts are determined from Newton's laws of motion by calculating the velocities and acceleration at each time interval (δt). Each interval generates a new conformation of the complex, whose potential energy is measured by force field equations. The process is iterated for a certain period of time (t). The dynamics of the complex is studied from the trajectory, which gives a measure of the movement of the atoms over time t. Since MD simulations involve a lot of calculations at each step, it is computationally expensive and time consuming. The computational time is directly proportional to the system size (the number of atoms), the number of intervals and the total simulation time (t). Apart from its application in protein docking, MD plays an important role in drug design and is being increasingly used in recent times (Fox et al., 2016).

ii. **Simulated Annealing - Cooling Down:** Simulated annealing simulates the process of annealing, which is applied to harden materials like glass and metal by cooling slowly from a higher to lower temperature. Simulated annealing is applied in optimisation problems to search for the global optimum. The simulation starts with an initial configuration of the protein-ligand complex with an energy E_1, the initial temperature of the system being T. After a perturbation, the configuration makes a random move to a local configuration with energy E_2. The second configuration will be accepted on the basis of the Metropolis criterion, where the energy $E_2 < E_1$. If $E_2 \leq E_1$, then the second configuration is accepted with probability P, where $P = e^{-\left[\frac{|(E2-E1)|}{kB.T}\right]}$ and k_B is the Boltzman constant. As the simulation proceeds, T is gradually reduced. The process is iterated for a given number of cycles so that the system can move towards a global optimum (Lengauer, 2008).

iii. **Monte Carlo (MC) Simulations - Making Random Moves:** The Monte Carlo (MC) is a stochastic method which uses randomness to study the behaviour of a system. In the MC method, a system approaches a low-energy state with random local moves. Defining the degrees of freedom and energy scoring are two important factors in MC simulations. MC is sometimes combined with other energy minimisation techniques to achieve low energy states.

d. **The Case of Flexible Proteins:** Flexibility of protein structures are dealt with side chain flexibility, partial flexibility of binding sites, docking with conformational ensembles or with optimisation and simulation (Friesner et al., 2004; Meiler & Baker, 2006; Morris et al., 2009; Ravindranath, Forli, Goodsell, Olson, & Sanner, 2015).

In the ensemble method, the ligand is docked to an ensemble of feasible receptor conformations generated by NMR, crystallography or simulations techniques. Multiple conformations allow exploration of the receptor flexible space. Computational time is proportional to the ensemble size and can be reduced by working with only feasible receptor conformations.

2. **Protein-Fragment Docking - Drugs from Pieces:** Fragment docking is generally applied to screen large fragment libraries against a target, so the algorithms need to handle a large fragment population. Algorithms used for protein-fragment docking commonly include rigid body docking, place

and join, incremental construction, genetic algorithm, Lamarckian genetic algorithm, hierarchical search, global optimisation, Monte Carlo and Molecular Dynamics simulation (Wang et al., 2015). The place-and-join uses the principle of fragment linking while incremental construction is based on fragment growing in steps. Since the incremental construction algorithms grows the molecule step by step, there is a lesser chance of torsional strains in the ligand than the place-and-join method (Lengauer, 2008). Also, fragment joining generates leads which are difficult to synthesise, in contrast to fragment growing methods (Wang et al., 2015).

3. **Protein-Protein Docking - Still a Challenge:**

   a. **Rigid Body Docking (RBD) - Correlating Geometries:** Rigid body docking of protein-macromolecular complexes uses the shape complementarity of the binding surfaces, similar to the lock-and-key principle. RBD of protein-protein complexes are all geometry correlation techniques, where the surface of the protein is denoted by some representative form (grid, graph, sphere, points, polygons or topology). Geometry matching is performed by correlating the representative form. In RBD, generally one protein (the larger) is kept fixed, while the other is mobile in space and tries to find its optimum configuration with respect to the first.

      i. **Correlating Grids - FFT Makes It Faster:** Docking by correlation is based on geometry matching between the protein surfaces. The FFT-based correlation algorithm is widely used for modelling protein-protein complexes. Here, the proteins are represented on a grid and the geometries of the grid are correlated. The smaller protein is translated and rotated in space around the fixed larger protein. Each orientation of the proteins is evaluated from the score (geometry fitness value). The computational time is reduced by calculating the grid transformations with the fast Fourier transform (FFT). Attempts to accelerate the FFT-based approach for high-throughput dockings include the use of hardware accelerators such as GPUs and optimised FFTs (B. G. Pierce, Hourai, & Weng, 2011; Pons et al., 2012; D. W. Ritchie & Venkatraman, 2010).

      ii. **With Graphs:** In this method, the protein surfaces are represented on graphs and graph-correlation is performed to model the optimum structure of the protein-protein complex. The surface of the protein can be represented in some manner on the graph, such as by spheres (as in DOCK) or by points (Lengauer, 2008). These are superposed and the algorithm tries to find the optimum superposition from the score.

      iii. **Other Ways to Correlate Geometry - With Slices and Surfaces:** In the polygon representation of protein surfaces, the protein is first sliced and the slice boundaries are denoted by polygons. Polygon-matching and scoring drives the docking. The critical surface point method correlates surface topologies such as concavities, protrusions and flat surfaces. Each topology (flat, concavity or protrusion) is represented by a critical point, which is located centrally on the surface. The critical points are correlated, sometimes with geometric hashing (Lengauer, 2008).

      iv. **Hybrid Geometry Matching Methods - Mix and Match:** Several combined techniques such as genetic algorithms, soft docking and simulated annealing have been applied to geometry matching of protein surfaces. Methods for RBD of protein-protein complexes have been attempted with machine learning methods such as the basin hopping algorithm. The basin hopping approach is a combination of the Monte Carlo method with the Metropolis procedure for approaching the minima (Balbuena & Seminario, 2007).

Basin hopping methods have been combined with geometry matching for modelling protein-protein complexes (Hashmi & Shehu, 2012, 2015).

b. **Docking Proteins Flexibly - Because Proteins Really Are (Flexible):** Macromolecular complexes modeled by RBD strategies provide an approximate structure of the complex, and sometimes requires optimisation by flexible docking approaches. Protein flexibility is particularly important when the proteins have been constructed by homology or loop modelling methods. Generally, the top scoring complexes generated by RBD are optimised by flexible methods. Protein flexibility is realised on two levels: side-chain and backbone.

i. **Side-Chain Flexibility - Reaching for the Global Minimum:** Side-chain flexibility is dealt with in the final stages of optimisation and minimisation by side-chain positioning, which aims to arrive at the global optimum side-chain conformation at the protein-protein interface (PPI). This problem is a GMEC (Global Minimum-Energy Conformation) problem, which tries to identify the combination of side-chain rotamers corresponding to the global minimum energy.

Side-chain positioning methods begin by identifying the interface residues. For each residue, all possible rotameric states are derived from a rotamer library. A binary vector is used to denote the total of all possible rotamer conformations of the interface residues. The rotamers are combined in various ways and a potential energy function is applied to identify the lowest energy conformation. Since a large number of residues interact at PPIs, this would mean an even larger number of rotamers, making the search for the GMEC an extensive computational task. To reduce the breadth of computation, several approaches such as the Dead End Elimination (DEE), branch and bound methods are used.

Dead End Elimination (DEE): Eliminating Incompatibility: The DEE method exploits the fact that of all the rotamers, only some are compatible with the GMEC. In DEE, the incompatible rotamers are removed, thus reducing the rotamer population and computational expense. DEE works like this: say a side-chain (sc) has rotamers sc_1 and sc_2; if the lowest energy of sc_1 is larger than the highest energy of sc_2, then sc_1 is not a compatible rotamer with the GMEC (Desmet, Maeyer, Hazes, & Lasters, 1992).

Branch and Bound Algorithm: Picking the Best Leaf: In this method, all the rotamer combinations at the interface are represented by a rotamer tree with branches and finally terminating in leaves. Each node layer in the tree is a side chain. So the root layer would be side-chain 1 (sc_1), the next node layer is side-chain 2 (sc_2), the next sub-node layer is side-chain 3 (sc_3) and so on. The last side-chain N layer (sc_N) is in the leaves of the tree. Each side-chain can have a number of rotamers, so at each node-layer the nodes split-up on the basis of the number of rotamers.Each path from root to leaf is one rotamer combination at the PPI. After tree construction, the leaf with the lowest energy is searched for determining the GMEC.

Other Methods: Simulation with MC, simulated annealing, mean field optimisation, combination of DEE with dynamic programming, integer linear programming, geometry-prioritisation, machine learning and local homology modelling are applied to the side-chain optimisation problem (Fahmy & Wagner, 2011; Nagata, Randall, & Baldi, 2012; Ryu et al., 2016).

ii. **Backbone Flexibility - Flexing the Backbone Is Taxing:** The backbone flexibility is still a major challenge in protein-protein docking. Backbone flexibility is handled by four classes of algorithms that perform: soft docking, ensemble docking, hinge-bending and heuristic search (Andrusier, Mashiach, Nussinov, & Wolfson, 2008). Soft docking performs fast RBD while allowing some degree of penetration. This may introduce steric clashes, requiring post-docking optimisation. In ensemble docking, an ensemble of only the feasible protein conformations is docked. Hinge-bending algorithms divide the backbone into flexible hinges and rigid regions. The rotational degrees of freedom around the hinges are incorporated in the docking. The heuristic search algorithms search the entire flexible space of a protein to select the energetically preferred conformations.

4. **Guided Docking - Enlightened by Experiments:** Guided docking approaches use experimental data to guide the docking computation. This gives a "direction" to the docking computation, driving the virtual experiment towards the real-life search space. This reduces the cost of computational time spent in searching a larger conformational space and also the chance of irrelevant results.

    a. **Data-Driven Docking - Data Shows the Way:** Experimental data obtained from mutagenesis studies, mass spectrometry (MS), NMR and MS/NMR are used to define the protein-protein interface and guide the docking run. The incorporation of experimental data during docking generates more biologically relevant complexes and aids the scoring function while selecting true-positives (Van Dijk, Boelens, & Bonvin, 2005).

    b. **Template-Based Docking - When Comparison Isn't Bad:** In template-based docking, the docking computation is guided by a structural alignment with structure neighbours in the PDB (protein data bank). Template-based approaches are applied to model protein-protein and protein-RNA complexes (Muratcioglu, Guven-Maiorov, Keskin, & Gursoy, 2015; Szilagyi & Zhang, 2014).

5. **Protein-DNA Docking:** Geometry correlation-based rigid body techniques used for protein-protein docking are applied to model protein-DNA complexes. Flexibility of protein-DNA complexes is handled by Monte Carlo and simulated annealing methods (Lengauer, 2008; Tuszynska, Magnus, Jonak, Dawson, & Bujnicki, 2015). Hybrid methods combining geometric hashing, minimisation and MC are used to model protein-DNA complexes.

6. **Protein-RNA Docking - Young and Important:** Protein-RNA docking tools are still in the nascent stage. The difficulty of experimental techniques such as X-ray or NMR in determining the structures of protein-RNA complexes makes protein-RNA docking studies important to molecular biology (Puton, Kozlowski, Tuszynska, Rother, & Bujnicki, 2012). FFT-based correlation combined with guided docking approaches have been successful in modelling protein-RNA complexes (Madan et al., 2016; Zheng et al., 2016).

Scoring Functions: Mapping Reality From the Virtual

One of the aspects of working in a virtual space is anything can be possible. Docking solutions can afford to generate *n* numbers of structurally diverse combinations of biological complexes. This is possible since the virtual space allows a molecule to have *n* conformations with respect to the other molecule. However, only one (or perhaps more than one) binding mode is biologically feasible. The challenge here is to identify the biologically feasible binding mode from a large number of conformations. This is the test of the scoring function: to be able to identify the natural binding mode from multiple conformations. Ideally, a scoring function must be accurate, reliable and computationally fast (Lengauer, 2008).

1. **Protein-Small Molecule Complexes:** Scoring functions for protein-small molecule complexes are designed to compare and rank ligand binding modes. These are four types of scoring functions: force-field based, empirical, knowledge-based and machine learning.

Force-field functions calculate the total energy of the complex by adding the binding energy of the interaction with the internal strain. The binding energy is calculated from van der Waals and electrostatic terms. Bond stretching, angle bending, planar deviations, electrostatic and van der Waals interaction terms contribute to the total energy. Empirical scoring functions use the geometry and interactions of the protein-ligand interface to calculate the total energy. Hydrogen bonding, hydrophobic, ionic interaction terms, lipophilic contact surface area, metal binding, number of rotatable bonds and penalty terms (such as in GlideScore) are some of the contributions used by empirical functions.

$$GlideScore = 0.065v + 0.130C + L + Hb + M + BP + RotB + Site$$

where

vdW = van der Waals term,
C = Coulomb energy term,
L= Lipophilic term,
Hb = hydrogen bonding term,
M = Metal binding term,
BP = penalty for burying polar groups,
RotB = penalty term for freezing rotatable bonds,
Site = polar interaction term at the active site (Friesner et al., 2004; Halgren et al., 2004).

Knowledge-based functions derive protein-ligand pair potentials from existing protein-ligand complexes in databases. The protein-ligand interactions of the docked complex are determined and the total energy of the complex is computed from the pre-calculated pair potential. The machine learning scoring function is developed with a training data set and the function is validated with test data. Machine learning techniques such as SVMs (Support Vector Machines), random forest and neural networks are employed for the purpose (Ballester & Mitchell, 2010; Durrant, Friedman, Rogers, & McCammon, 2013; Kinnings et al., 2011; Li, Wang, & Meroueh, 2011). Machine learning scoring functions are sometimes more successful than classical scoring functions (Ain, Aleksandrova, Roessler, & Ballester, 2015; Ashtawy & Mahapatra, 2015). To improve the accuracy and reliability of a docking solution consensus scoring is used, employing different scoring functions to score the complex.

2. **Protein-Protein Complexes:** Empirical, force-field based, knowledge-based and machine learning scoring functions are applied to score protein-protein complexes. Empirical scoring functions use terms such as van der Waals, electrostatic free energy difference, hydrophobic interactions, hydrogen bonds, solvation energy difference, internal energy difference for calculating the free energy of binding. In knowledge-based scoring, the potentials of mean force (PMFs) for pairs of interacting amino acid residues or atoms are pre-calculated from existing protein-protein. This is later employed to calculate the free energy of binding of the docked complex. Machine learning scoring functions developed by SVMs have also been used (Bradford & Westhead, 2005).

3. **Protein-Nucleic Acids:** Knowledge-based scoring functions using statistical potentials derived from protein-DNA and protein-RNA complexes are used for scoring protein-nucleic acid complexes. Electrostatic terms, geometric fit and atomic desolvation terms are also incorporated.

DOCKING PREREQUISITES

1. **Docking Programs:** Docking programs generally employ a hybrid combination of algorithms for reaching the optimum docked solution (Table 1).
2. **Common Input File Formats:** The input molecules sometimes need to be prepared in accordance to the file format that a docking tool accepts. Table 2 provides a list of the file formats accepted by some of the commonly used tools.

Table 1. List of docking tools and web servers for different kinds of protein docking

Docking Program, Year of Publication (Standalone*/ Web Server ‡)	Algorithm	Scoring Function (s)	Application in Protein Docking
Protein-Ligand Docking Tools, Servers			
DOCK, 1982* (Ewing, Makino, Skillman, & Kuntz, 2001; Kuntz, Blaney, Oatley, Langridge, & Ferrin, 1982)	Incremental construction with random search	Several types of scoring: grid-based, contact, Zou GB/SA, Hawkins GB/SA, PB/SA, continuous, AMBER, descriptor, multi-grid FPS, SASA scores	Structure-based ligand screening, examine binding modes of protein-macromolecule complexes
ICM, 1994* (Neves, Totrov, & Abagyan, 2012)	Monte Carlo for global optimisation	ICM scoring function (Internal energy of ligand, van der Waals, free energy difference, hydrogen bond, desolvation, hydrophobic, solvation electrostatic, size correction terms)	Virtual screening
AutoDock, 1996*(Jiang et al., 2008; Morris et al., 2009; Morris, Goodsell, Huey, & Olson, 1996; Zhang et al., 2008)	Simulated Annealing/ Monte Carlo/ Genetic algorithm/ Lamarckian genetic algorithm	Grid-based semi-empirical free energy force field	Virtual screening (Forli et al., 2016), HTS with DOVIS
GOLD (Genetic Optimisation for Ligand Docking), 1997* (Jones, Willett, Glen, Leach, & Taylor, 1997)	Genetic algorithm	GoldScore, ChemScore, ASP, CHEMPLP, consensus and user-defined	Virtual screening, lead optimisation
FlexX, 1999* (Kramer, Rarey, & Lengauer, 1999)	Hybrid (pose clustering, incremental construction with hashing)	Empirical	High-throughput docking
Glide (Grid-based Ligand Docking with Energetics), 2004*(Friesner et al., 2004, 2006; Halgren et al., 2004)	Hybrid hierarchial search	Empirical	High-throughput docking, fragment docking, protein-peptide docking
ROSETTALIGAND, 2006* ‡(Meiler & Baker, 2006)	Ensemble docking with MC minimisation	Force field, includes van der Waals, explicit orientation hydrogen bond, electrostatics, implicit solvation terms	Protein-small molecule docking, with full side-chain flexibility
TarFisDock, 2006‡ (H. Li et al., 2006)	Based on DOCK version 4.0	DOCK interaction energy terms	Inverse docking against Potential Drug Target Database (PDTD)
ParDOCK, 2007 ‡(Gupta, Gandhimathi, Sharma, & Jayaram, 2007)	All-atom energy-based Monte Carlo	All-atom electrostatic, van der Waals, hydrophobic terms	Protein-ligand docking server

continued on next page

Table 1. Continued

Docking Program, Year of Publication (Standalone*/ Web Server ‡)	Algorithm	Scoring Function (s)	Application in Protein Docking
AutoDock Vina*, 2010(O Trott & Olson, 2010)	Iterated Local Search global optimiser using Broyden-Fletcher-Goldfarb-Shanno local optimiser	Weighted empirical scoring function	Virtual screening
idock, 2012 * ‡ (Hongjian Li, Leung, & Wong, 2012)	Derived from AutoDock Vina	Derived from AutoDock Vina	Docking-based virtual screening with flexible ligands
Galaxy7TM, 2016‡(Lee & Seok, 2016)	Combines ensemble receptor docking with GalaxyDock (global optimisation with conformational space annealling), refinement with GalaxyRefine (side-chain repacking and complex relaxation)	GalaxyDock energy (modified AutoDock 3.0 energy function)	Flexible GPCR-ligand docking
Protein-Protein Docking Tools, Servers			
Hex Protein Docking, 1999 * ‡ (Macindoe, Mavridis, Venkatraman, Devignes, & Ritchie, 2010; David W. Ritchie & Kemp, 1999)	FFT-based shape, electrostatics correlation	Shape-based	Protein-macromolecular docking
ZDOCK, 2003 ‡ (B. G. Pierce et al., 2014)	Global search with FFT	Statistical potential (IFACE/ACE), shape complementarity, electrostatics	Protein-protein docking
HADDOCK (High Ambiguity Driven protein-protein DOCKing), 2003* ‡ (Cyril Dominguez, Rolf Boelens, & Bonvin*, 2003)	Data-driven docking (biochemical/biophysical interaction data)	Static, van der Waals, and data-driven AIR (Ambiguous Interaction Restraints) terms	Protein-macromolecule docking
ClusPro, 2004 ‡(Comeau, Gatchell, Vajda, & Camacho, 2004)	Correlation with FFT	Empirical	Protein-protein docking
M-ZDOCK, 2005 ‡ (B. Pierce, Tong, & Weng, 2005)	Grid correlation with FFT	ACE statistical potential, shape complementarity, electrostatics	Radially symmetric multimers
GRAMM-X, 2005 ‡ (Tovchigrechko & Vakser, 2006)	Correlation with FFT, refinement	Knowledge-based	Protein-protein docking
PatchDock, 2005 ‡ (Schneidman-Duhovny, Inbar, Nussinov, & Wolfson, 2005)	Geometry correlation	Geometric fit and atomic desolvation terms	Protein-protein, protein-DNA
PIPER, 2006* (Kozakov, Brenke, Comeau, Vajda, & Vajda, 2006)	Multiple grid correlations with FFT	Knowledge based pairwise potentials	Protein-protein docking
FireDock, 2008 * ‡ (Andrusier, Nussinov, & Wolfson, 2007)	Side chain flexibility, MC rigid body minimisation	Multiple energy terms	Docking, refinement of docked protein-protein complexes

continued on next page

Table 1. Continued

Docking Program, Year of Publication (Standalone*/ Web Server ‡)	Algorithm	Scoring Function (s)	Application in Protein Docking
RosettaDock, 2008 * ‡ (Lyskov & Gray, 2008)	RBD, Monte Carlo (Simultaneous optimisation of rigid body and side chain conformations)	Low resolution phase: Residue contacts, knowledge-based contributions, residue-residue pair potentials. High resolution phase: van der Waals, hydrogen bonding, electrostatic energy, implicit Gaussian solvation, rotamer probability	Protein-protein docking
3D-Garden, 2008‡ (Lesk & Sternberg, 2008)	Conformational refinement of ensembles using the marching cubes algorithm	All-atom modified Lennard-Jones potential	Protein-protein docking
FiberDock, 2010* ‡ (Mashiach, Nussinov, & Wolfson, 2010)	Soft rigid docking, side-chain optimisation with ILP (integer linear programming), NMA (normal mode analysis)-based backbone refinement, rigid body Monte Carlo minimisation	Desolvation (atomic contact energy(ACE)), van der Waals, partial electrostatic, hydrogen and disulfide bond, pi-stacking, aliphatic Interaction terms	Protein-protein docking with side-chain and backbone flexibility
pyDockWEB, 2013‡ (Jiménez-García, Pons, & Fernández-Recio, 2013)	FFT-based rigid body docking	Electrostatics, desolvation terms (uses improved pyDock score)	Protein-protein rigid docking
DockTrina, 2013* (Popov, Ritchie, & Grudinin, 2014)	Pairwise rigid body docking with the Hex docking program	Pairwise contact, geometry-clash terms	For docking triangular protein trimers
SwarmDock, 2013‡ (Torchala, Moal, Chaleil, Fernandez-Recio, & Bates, 2013)	Hybrid particle swarm optimisation and local search, minimisation, clustering	Knowledge-based	Flexible protein-protein docking
VORFFIP-driven dock (V-D2OCK), 2015‡ (Segura et al., 2015)	Data-driven docking using PatchDock, clustering with GROMACS	PatchDock native score, ES3DC knowledge-based statistical potential, ZRANK (electrostatics, van der Waals, desolvation)	Data-driven protein-protein docking
pyDockSAXS, 2015‡ (Jiménez-García, Pons, Svergun, Bernadó, & Fernández-Recio, 2015)	Data-driven docking with FTDock (uses SAXS – small angle X-ray scattering data)	pyDock energy score (desolvation, electrostatics terms)	Data-driven protein-protein docking
CABS-Dock, 2015‡ (Kurcinski, Jamroz, Blaszczyk, Kolinski, & Kmiecik, 2015)	Simulation with replica Exchange Monte Carlo dynamics	Selection based on K-medoids clustering of bound states	Flexible protein-peptide docking from protein structure and peptide sequence
FRODOCK 2.0, 2016‡(Ramírez-Aportela, López-Blanco, & Chacón, 2016)	Improved version of FRODOCK (Fast Rotational Docking with FFT-based correlation and spherical harmonics based rotational search)	Knowledge-based potential	Fast protein-protein docking
PEPSI-Dock (Polynomial Expansion of Protein Structures and Interactions-Dock), 2016‡(Neveu, Ritchie, Popov, & Grudinin, 2016)	Data-driven FFT-based (Hex)	Knowledge-based	Protein-protein docking

continued on next page

Table 1. Continued

Docking Program, Year of Publication (Standalone*/ Web Server ‡)	Algorithm	Scoring Function (s)	Application in Protein Docking
InterEvDock, 2016‡ (Yu et al., 2016)	Based on FRODOCK	Knowledge-based InterEvScore (uses evolutionary information) and SOAP_PP (atom-based statistical potential)	Protein-protein docking using evolutionary information
Memdock, 2016‡ (Hurwitz, Schneidman-Duhovny, & Wolfson, 2016)	Modified from PatchDock, refinement with FiberDock	Scoring function designed for membrane proteins	Flexible membrane protein docking
Protein-Nucleic Acid Docking Tools, Servers			
ParaDock, 2011‡ (Banitt & Wolfson, 2011)	PatchDock with geometric complementarity	PatchDock score, electrostatic score and amino acid propensity-based score	Rigid protein flexible DNA
NPDock, 2015‡ (Tuszynska et al., 2015)	GRAMM algorithm	Knowledge based statistical potentials for protein-RNA (QUASI-RNP, DARD-RNP) and protein-DNA (QUASI-DNP) complexes (Tuszynska et al., 2011)	Protein-nucleic acid docking
Server for Protein Docking and Drug Design Tools			
ROSIE server, 2013‡ (Lyskov et al., 2013)	Different algorithms	Different scoring function	Server for antigen-antibody, protein-ligand, protein-protein, symmetric protein docking tools.

Table 2. Input file formats for some commonly used docking tools

Input Type	Input File Type	Description	Used by Docking Tool(s)
Small molecule ligand	.smi	Simplified Molecular Input Line Entry Specification (SMILES) chemical format	FlexX
	.mol	Chemical file format with atom, bond, connectivity, co-ordinate information	GOLD (MDL SD), Surflex, ICM
	.mol2	Chemical file format with bond, atom, substructure, coordinates	DOCK, GOLD, DOCK, Glide, FlexX, Surflex, ICM
	.sdf	Structure Data File (SDF) chemical file format, can contain multiple compounds	Glide, FlexX
	.mae, .maegz	Maestro format with input structures for docking	Glide
	.pdb	Protein Data Bank format	Glide, ICM (conversion to ICM object for docking preparation)
	.pdbqt	PDB file with partial charge (q) and atom typing (t)	AutoDock, AutoDock Vina
DNA ligand	.pdb	Protein Data Bank format	NPDock (also accepts CHARMM format)
RNA ligand	.pdb	Protein Data Bank format	NPDock (also accepts AMBER format)
	.mol2	Chemical file format	NPDock

continued on next page

Table 2. Continued

Input Type	Input File Type	Description	Used by Docking Tool(s)
Receptor (protein)	.mol2	Chemical file format	DOCK, GOLD, FlexX, Surflex
	.pdb	Protein Data Bank format	GOLD, Glide, FlexX, Surflex, ICM (conversion to ICM object for docking preparation), NPDock, ATTRACT
	.pdbq	PDB with partial charges (q)	AutoDock
	.pdbqt	PDBQ with atom typing (t)	AutoDock, AutoDock Vina
	.pdbqs	PDBQ with solvation parameters (s)	AutoDock
	.mae, .maegz	Maestro format with input structures for docking	Glide
	.rdf	Receptor Description File	
Other miscellaneous inputs	.gpf	Grid parameter file (grid size, centre, spacing, atom types)	AutoDock
	.in	Input command for grid job	Glide
	.inp	Input file for Impact (for molecular mechanics calculations)	Glide
	.zip	Zip file with receptor grid	Glide
	.dpf	Docking parameter file	AutoDock
	.txt	Configuration file (plain text file with instructions)	AutoDock Vina
	.conf	Configuration file (plain text file with details of docking calculation, ligand, receptor, docking parameters, scoring function, torsions)	GOLD
	.fxx	Project file	FlexX
	.edf	Ensemble description file	FlexX
	.map	3D3-dimensional map files	ICM, AutoDock

3. **Receptor Preparation:** Protein Prepping is Important: This is one of the most critical steps in molecular docking. The manner in which the receptor is prepared can affect the docking results. Differences in preparation steps can generate very different docking results. Receptor preparation commonly involves correction of missing atoms or bonds, removal of hetero atoms and water, hydrogen atom preparation, charge assignment and minimisaton. Flexible receptor residues are designated at this stage. The steps vary across different docking tools. The receptors need to be prepared according to what is optimum for the biological problem and the docking algorithm used. For instance, the removal of water depends on the character of the water molecules. Ordered waters are associated with the protein and serve as important bridges for protein-ligand interactions (Huang & Shoichet, 2008). Ordered water molecules are usually retained, while the free waters are removed (Lu, Wang, Yang, & Wang, n. d.). The same principle holds for hetero atoms and cofactors. In short, receptor preparation depends on the purpose of the docking run, the structural biology of the protein and the biological question.

4. **Preparing Ligands:** A ligand is a smaller molecule that binds to the larger receptor. Although the term "ligand" is commonly applied to small molecules only, small molecules, fragments, small

peptides, nucleic acids and smaller proteins are also ligands in protein docking. Small molecule ligand structures are retrieved from databases and repositories. Ligand preparation aims to generate 3-dimensional structures of ligands having proper charges and geometries. Desalting, protonation, geometry optimisation, energy minimisation, charge assignment, atom-typing are some of the common steps of small molecule ligand preparation. On a high-throughput scale it is sometimes necessary to filter compounds based on properties like drug-likeliness, fragment-likeliness or lead-likeliness. Similarity searches, use of molecular fingerprints, pharmacophores or fragments can create focused libraries which reduce and refine the number of compounds that need to be docked, saving unnecessary computational expense.

5. **Grid Settings:** For small molecule-protein docking, grids are sometimes employed to save time. The grid is represented by equally spaced *grid points* and the protein-ligand interaction energies are pre-calculated at each point. The grid is set around the receptor binding site. The molecular grid defines the conformational space where the ligand will search for its optimum pose. It is recommended to keep the grid slightly large, so that the ligand does not face space constraints while searching for its most comfortable conformation in the receptor. However, the use of larger grids increases computational time. The *grid space* is simply the space between the points in the grid and represents the density of points.

6. **Docking Runs, Resource and Time - Hands-On:** Computational times depend on several factors, such as the size and complexity of the molecular system, the algorithm, incorporation of flexibility, number of docking runs, scoring method and resource [Table 3]. For grid-based calculations, the computational time is directly proportional to the grid size, ligand size and number of torsions, and inversely proportional to grid spacing. In ensemble docking approaches, the time varies proportionately to the ensemble population.

7. **Output File Formats - What to Expect:** Different docking programs generate results in various ways. While some programs directly provide a structure of the docked complex, others generate separate files for the receptor and multiple docked conformations for the ligand. The common output formats of the commonly used docking programs are represented in Table 4.

8. **Result Analyses, Interaction Study, Visualisation:** The scoring function is aimed to identify the natural binding mode. However, the complexity and uniqueness of biological problems can prevent scoring functions from doing so. The selection of the optimum docking solution must be done carefully so as to avoid selecting false-positives or rejecting true positives. Consensus scoring and cross-platform docking with different algorithms are used to identify the optimum solution (Gangopadhyay & Datta, 2015). Prior to selection, the binding mode needs to be visually inspected and the chemical interactions must be sensible and appropriate. A number of tools for molecular visualisation and generating ligand interaction diagrams have been developed for this purpose. Experimental data such as binding residues or bioactivity data may guide the selection. In the context of drug design, analysing docked complexes serve various purposes such as:

a. Hit and lead identification,

b. Lead optimization,

c. *De novo* drug design,

d. Design of peptide inhibitors,

e. Structural analyses of protein-protein interfaces for druggability,

f. Structural investigations of protein-macromolecule complexes.

Table 3. The computational time depends on a number of factors as presented by the examples

Docking Tool/Program	Molecular System	Computational Resource and Time
Glide HTVS (High Throughput Virtual Screening)	Compound + active site of 1ETT (Bovine thrombin)	1.5 second/compound on 2.2 GHz Opteron processor
Glide SP (Standard Precision)	As above	15 seconds/compound on 2.2 GHz Opteron processor
Glide XP (Extra Precision)	As above	6 minutes/compound on 2.2 GHz Opteron processor
AutoDock	Protein-ligand (tested on 190 complexes). Ligand rotatable bonds from 0-32.	521.85 minutes on average on 2 quad-core 2.66GHz Xeon processors (Oleg Trott & Olson, 2010)
AutoDock 4 with DOVIS protocol	2.3 million ligands from ZINC with 259-amino acid protein target (binding site size 28 x 40 x 24 Å³), default AutoDock parameters	670 ligands/CPU/day on a 256 CPUs on a Linux cluster (Jiang et al., 2008)
AutoDock Vina	Protein-ligand (tested on 190 complexes). Ligand rotatable bonds from 0-32.	1.16 minutes/ligand on average on 2 quad-core 2.66GHz Xeon processors, 8 CPUs (Oleg Trott & Olson, 2010)
GOLD	10Å radius of active site of acetylserotonin-O-methyltransferase enzyme	1.66 seconds/compound (average) on a Linux workstation (openSUSE11.4), Intel Pentium D processor (3.0 GHz), 1 GB RAM (Azam & Abbasi, 2013)
FlexX	As above	5 seconds/compound (average) on Intel® Atom™ processor (1.67 GHz), 1GB of RAM, Windows 7 (Azam & Abbasi, 2013)
FlexX virtual HTS mode	Protein-small molecule docking	~ 1,000,000 compounds in ~ 8 hours on a 30-node cluster

Table 4: Output formats and their information content for the most commonly used docking tools

Output Type	Output File Type	Description	Used by Docking Tool(s)
Docked poses/ ligands/ results	.dlg	Docking log file with ligand poses	AutoDock
	.pdbqt	Multiple ligand poses	AutoDock Vina
	.mae, .maegz	Pose viewer (pv) file with receptor structure, followed by rank-wise ligand poses	Glide
	.mol2	Docked ligand	GOLD, FlexX
	.ob	ICM object file with best ranking poses of each ligand	ICM
	.cnf	Conformational stack file with multiple docked conformations, ranked by energy	ICM
Receptor information	.mol2	Binding site geometry	GOLD
Other miscellaneous file formats	.log	Standard log file	Glide, GOLD
	.rept	Plain text file with a table of ranked poses, scores, score components	Glide
	.out	Output file	Glide, FlexX
	.xpdes	Glide XP descriptor file	Glide (XP mode)
	Spreadsheet	Each row for one ligand conformation, with ranks, scores and other information	FlexX
	.rnk	Ranked fitness score for individual ligand	GOLD
	.lst	Ranked fitness score for multiple ligands (batch submission)	GOLD
	.err	Error messages	GOLD
	.ou	Output file. Various information, such as score	ICM

Docking tools generally include a graphical interface for analysing the docked solutions. However, several programs allow in-depth molecular visualisation and analyses of non-covalent interactions [Table 5].

CASE STUDIES OF PROTEIN DOCKING IN DRUG DESIGN

1. **Combining High-Throughput Docking (HTD) and Molecular Dynamics (MD) - 2 From 2 Million:** In a recent example, HTD was combined with MD to identify inhibitors of the CREB

Table 5. Commonly used programs for molecular visualisation and protein interactions

Program/Tool/Server	Applications	Available as
Molecular Visualisation		
RasMol (Sayle & Bissell, 1992)	Molecular visualisation	Standalone
RasTop	Molecular visualisation	Standalone
VMD (Visual Molecular Dynamics) (Humphrey, Dalke, & Schulten, 1996)	• Molecular visualisation, analysis • For large biomolecules (proteins, nucleic acids, lipid layers) • Interaction analysis	Standalone, by the Theoretical and Computational Biophysics Group, NIH
Swiss PDB Viewer (DeepView)(Guex & Peitsch, 1997)	• Several modelling applications • Visualisation, interaction study, surface analyses	Standalone, from the Swiss Institute of Bioinformatics
PMV (Python Molecular Viewer) (Sanner, 1999)	• Molecular visualisation • Molecular measurements, surface calculations	Standalone
Chimera (Pettersen et al., 2004)	• Molecular visualisation • In-depth analyses of molecular structures, simulations • Several molecular modelling applications	Standalone, by the UCSF
PyMol	Molecular visualisation, analysis	Standalone, open-source, maintained and distributed by Schrödinger
Maestro	• Molecular visualisation • Protein-ligand interaction diagrams	Standalone, free version for academics, by Schrödinger
iMol	Molecular visualisation for Mac OS X	Standalone
QuteMol (Tarini, Cignoni, & Montani, 2006)	Molecular visualisation	Standalone
BioBlender (Andrei et al., 2012)	• Molecular visualisation • Molecular dynamics simulations • Protein surface property visualisation	Standalone, open-source, by SciVis (Scientific Visualisation) group
Yasara View (Krieger & Vriend, 2014)	Molecular visualisation, modelling, analysis	Standalone
Chimera-X	Next-generation molecular visualisation program	Currently in development, by the UCSF
Interaction Studies		
Ligplot+ (Laskowski & Swindells, 2011)	• Protein-ligand interaction diagrams • Protein-protein interaction diagrams with DIMPLOT	Standalone
LeView (Caboche, 2013)	Ligand-biomacromolecule diagrammatic interactions	Standalone
Maestro	Protein-ligand interaction diagrams	Standalone
PLIP (Protein-Ligand Interaction Prolifier)(Salentin, Schreiber, Haupt, Adasme, & Schroeder, 2015)	Diagrammatic representation of non-covalent protein-ligand interactions	Server-based
PDBePISA (Krissinel & Henrick, 2007)	Studying protein-protein interfaces, surfaces, assemblies	Server-based, from Protein Data Bank, Europe

Binding Protein (CREBBP) from a library of 2 million (Xu et al., 2016) [Figure 3]. The binding site contains a conserved Asn, an important target residue. The Asn has two possible conformations, represented in PDB structures 3P1C and 3SVH. The binding site of both 3P1C and 3SVH were targeted using the ALTA (Anchor based Library Tailoring) approach.

A first, 2 million compounds from the ZINC leads now library were fragmented and screened to obtain ~97,000 fragments. Fragments were docked rigidly using the SEED program and minimised with CHARMM. The docked fragments were screened on the basis of SEED energy efficiency and hydrogen bond penalties. ~4000 top scoring fragment hits were selected against each PDB target. The 4000 fragment hits were used to retrieve ~81,000 and ~76,000 compounds against 3SVH and 3P1C respectively, from the initial ZINC leads now library. 81,000 and 76,000 compounds were docked flexibly against 3SVH and 3P1C respectively using AutoDock Vina. The compounds were rescored with SEED and the top scoring 1000 compounds were selected in each case. From these, 20 compounds were selected on the basis of interactions with the conserved Asn. MD simulations were performed with the 20 complexes, of which 17 formed stable complexes. 2 compounds were finally selected on the basis of a competitive binding assay.

2. **Fragment Docking in Drug Design - Resisting Antibiotic Resistance:** Gram-negatives produce beta-lactamase enzymes responsible for antibiotic resistance. A strategy for combating antibiotic resistance is through the inhibition of beta-lactamase. Studies show that fragment docking and virtual screening have more promise in the discovery of beta-lactamase (class C) inhibitors than assay-based HTS (Nichols, Renslo, & Chen, 2014). In a fragment docking approach for identifying novel beta-lactamase inhibitors, 137,639 fragments from the ZINC fragment library were docked against the structure of the beta-lactamase class C enzyme (PDB ID: 1KE4) using the DOCK algorithm. 500 top-scoring fragments were prioritised on the basis of receptor interactions, of which 48 were experimented *in vitro*. 23 of these showed promising enzyme inhibition, indicating a 48% hit-rate. The binding modes of 8 fragments strongly correlated with X-ray crystallography (Teotico et al., 2009).

3. **Multiple Ligand Simultaneous Docking (MLSD) and Drug Repositioning:** The MLSD approach combined with drug repositioning identified Celecoxib an inhibitor of STAT3 (Signal Transducer

Figure 3. Combining high-throughput docking, library focusing and molecular dynamics strategies in structure-based drug design: a case study

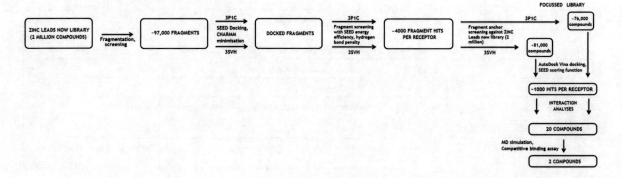

and Activator of Transcription) (Huameng Li et al., 2011). The STAT3 oncogene is constitutively activated in certain types of cancer. Structures of previously known STAT3 inhibitors were decomposed into fragments. Fragment-based similarity searches against the FDA-approved drug scaffold database helped prepare a privileged drug scaffold library for STAT3. The privileged library was docked to the STAT3 SH2 domain (PDB ID: 1BG1) using the MLSD approach with AutoDock. Scaffolds with a binding energy lesser than -8.2 Kcal/mol were retained for hit identification. Potential fragments were linked to generate virtual compounds that were optimised for drug-likeliness. The virtually linked compounds were re-docked, scored and ranked to identify hits. A similarity search (Tanimoto cut-off 0.5) was performed with the hits to identify drug analogues from DrugBank. The final hits were selected on the basis of their performance in re-docking studies. The drug Celecoxib and two compounds (T2 and T3) showed *in vitro* STAT3 inhibition (Huameng Li et al., 2011).

ISSUES, SOLUTIONS AND RECOMMENDATIONS

Some important facets of docking that need careful consideration are docking preparation, choosing the right number of docking runs, selecting the appropriate algorithm and scoring function. All of these demand a careful concern for the biological problem. Since scoring functions can deviate from identifying the correct natural binding mode, users need to be careful not to select false positives or reject true positives, by using an appropriate scoring function, consensus scoring and cross-checking with visualisation and interaction data. Docking protocols must be designed so that they are able to match the dimensionality of the system, by considering aspects such as system size, complexity or flexibility. The docking algorithm used must correspond to the nature of the biological question for generating relevant docking solutions.

FUTURE RESEARCH DIRECTIONS

The major challenges in protein docking are selecting the native binding pose, handling structural flexibility of proteins and macromolecules such as nucleic acids. Although guided docking provides successful results in protein-RNA docking, experimental data for performing guided docking are not always available.

Algorithms for protein-RNA docking are still at a nascent stage and need further development. There is a need for developing algorithms for docking protein-RNA, protein-DNA complexes. The future demands improved algorithms to handle the flexibility of proteins, DNA and RNA. Proteome-wide studies on protein interactions require high-throughput protein-macromolecular docking techniques. With respect to protein-macromolecular docking, the algorithms of the future need to consider structural flexibility accurately and return solutions at a high-throughput rate.

CONCLUSION

Recent progresses in protein docking provide solutions for drug discovery, drug repositioning, identifying novel drug scaffolds, designing virtual compounds and inhibitory peptides against disease-causing proteins. Docking studies are integral to structural investigations of protein-macromolecule interfaces and interactions for assessing druggability. The present big data surge demands smart, robust and high-throughput docking technologies not only for drug design, but also for providing accurate insights into protein structure, function, interactome networks and evolution. Although there are still some difficulties, protein docking approaches have come a long way and continue to evolve. Someday the intelligent application of computational technologies will perhaps be able to provide real-life results. When new personalised genomes get sequenced, or dangerous viral strains evolve, CADD will promptly present exclusive tailor-made drugs for specific purposes. At the rate CADD is evolving, the golden age of computational biology and bioinformatics is perhaps not far-off.

REFERENCES

Abagyan, R., & Totrov, M. (2001). High-throughput docking for lead generation. *Current Opinion in Chemical Biology*, *5*(4), 375–382. doi:10.1016/S1367-5931(00)00217-9 PMID:11470599

Aguzzi, A., & OConnor, T. (2010). Protein aggregation diseases: Pathogenicity and therapeutic perspectives. *Nature Reviews. Drug Discovery*, *9*(3), 237–248. doi:10.1038/nrd3050 PMID:20190788

Agyeman, A., & Ofori-Asenso, R. (2015). Perspective: Does personalized medicine hold the future for medicine? *Journal of Pharmacy and Bioallied Sciences*, *7*(3), 239. doi:10.4103/0975-7406.160040 PMID:26229361

Ain, Q. U., Aleksandrova, A., Roessler, F. D., & Ballester, P. J. (2015). Machine-learning scoring functions to improve structure-based binding affinity prediction and virtual screening. *Computational Molecular Science*, *5*(6), 405–424. doi:10.1002/wcms.1225 PMID:27110292

Alvarez, J. C. (2004). High-throughput docking as a source of novel drug leads. *Current Opinion in Chemical Biology*, *8*(4), 365–370. doi:10.1016/j.cbpa.2004.05.001 PMID:15288245

Andrei, R. R., Callieri, M., Zini, M. M., Loni, T., Maraziti, G., Pan, M., ... Scopigno, R. (2012). Intuitive representation of surface properties of biomolecules using BioBlender. *BMC Bioinformatics*, *13*(Suppl. 4), S16. Doi:<ALIGNMENT.qj></ALIGNMENT>10.1186/1471-2105-13-S4-S16

Andrusier, N., Mashiach, E., Nussinov, R., & Wolfson, H. J. (2008). Principles of flexible protein-protein docking. *Proteins*, *73*(2), 271–289. doi:10.1002/prot.22170 PMID:18655061

Andrusier, N., Nussinov, R., & Wolfson, H. J. (2007). FireDock: Fast interaction refinement in molecular docking. *Proteins*, *69*(1), 139–159. doi:10.1002/prot.21495 PMID:17598144

Arkin, M. R., Tang, Y., & Wells, J. A. (2014). Small-molecule inhibitors of protein-protein interactions: Progressing toward the reality. *Chemistry & Biology*, *21*(9), 1102–1114. doi:10.1016/j.chembiol.2014.09.001 PMID:25237857

Ashburn, T. T., & Thor, K. B. (2004). Drug repositioning: Identifying and developing new uses for existing drugs. *Nature Reviews. Drug Discovery*, *3*(8), 673–683. doi:10.1038/nrd1468 PMID:15286734

Ashtawy, H. M., & Mahapatra, N. R. (2015). A Comparative Assessment of Predictive Accuracies of Conventional and Machine Learning Scoring Functions for Protein-Ligand Binding Affinity Prediction. *IEEE/ACM Transactions on Computational Biology and Bioinformatics*, *12*(2), 335–347. doi:10.1109/TCBB.2014.2351824 PMID:26357221

Avorn, J. (2015). The $2.6 Billion Pill — Methodologic and Policy Considerations. *The New England Journal of Medicine*, *372*(20), 1877–1879. doi:10.1056/NEJMp1500848 PMID:25970049

Azam, S. S., & Abbasi, S. W. (2013). Molecular docking studies for the identification of novel melatoninergic inhibitors for acetylserotonin-O-methyltransferase using different docking routines. *Theoretical Biology & Medical Modelling*, *10*(1), 63. doi:10.1186/1742-4682-10-63 PMID:24156411

Bakail, M., & Ochsenbein, F. (2016). Targeting protein–protein interactions, a wide open field for drug design. *Comptes Rendus. Chimie*, *19*(1), 19–27. doi:10.1016/j.crci.2015.12.004

Baker, M. (2012). Fragment-based lead discovery grows up. *Nature Reviews. Drug Discovery*, *12*(1), 5–7. doi:10.1038/nrd3926 PMID:23274457

Balbuena, P. B., & Seminario, J. M. (2007). *Nanomaterials: design and simulation.* Elsevier.

Ballester, P. J., & Mitchell, J. B. O. (2010). A machine learning approach to predicting protein-ligand binding affinity with applications to molecular docking. *Bioinformatics (Oxford, England)*, *26*(9), 1169–1175. doi:10.1093/bioinformatics/btq112 PMID:20236947

Banitt, I., & Wolfson, H. J. (2011). ParaDock: A flexible non-specific DNArigid protein docking algorithm. *Nucleic Acids Research*, *39*(20), e135. doi:10.1093/nar/gkr620 PMID:21835777

Bradford, J. R., & Westhead, D. R. (2005). Improved prediction of protein-protein binding sites using a support vector machines approach. *Bioinformatics (Oxford, England)*, *21*(8), 1487–1494. doi:10.1093/bioinformatics/bti242 PMID:15613384

Bron, C., & Kerbosch, J. (1973). Algorithm 457: Finding all cliques of an undirected graph. *Communications of the ACM*, *16*(9), 575–577. doi:10.1145/362342.362367

Caboche, S. (2013). LeView: Automatic and interactive generation of 2D diagrams for biomacromolecule/ligand interactions. *Journal of Cheminformatics*, *5*(1), 40. doi:10.1186/1758-2946-5-40 PMID:23988161

Chong, C. R., & Sullivan, D. J. (2007). New uses for old drugs. *Nature*, *448*(7154), 645–646. doi:10.1038/448645a PMID:17687303

Comeau, S. R., Gatchell, D. W., Vajda, S., & Camacho, C. J. (2004). ClusPro: a fully automated algorithm for protein-protein docking. *Nucleic Acids Research, 32*(Web Server issue), W96-9. Doi:<ALIGNMENT.qj></ALIGNMENT>10.1093/nar/gkh354

Congreve, M., Carr, R., Murray, C., & Jhoti, H. (2003). A rule of three for fragment-based lead discovery? *Drug Discovery Today*, *8*(19), 876–877. Retrieved from http://www.ncbi.nlm.nih.gov/pubmed/14554012 doi:10.1016/S1359-6446(03)02831-9 PMID:14554012

Cukuroglu, E., Engin, H. B., Gursoy, A., & Keskin, O. (2014). Hot spots in protein–protein interfaces: Towards drug discovery. *Progress in Biophysics and Molecular Biology, 116*(2–3), 165–173. doi:10.1016/j.pbiomolbio.2014.06.003 PMID:24997383

Desmet, J., De Maeyer, M., Hazes, B., & Lasters, I. (1992). The dead-end elimination theorem and its use in protein side-chain positioning. *Nature, 356*(6369), 539–542. doi:10.1038/356539a0 PMID:21488406

Dhanik, A., & Kavraki, L. E. (2012). Protein-Ligand Interactions: Computational Docking. In eLS. Chichester, UK: John Wiley & Sons, Ltd. Doi:<ALIGNMENT.qj></ALIGNMENT>10.1002/9780470015902.a0004105.pub2

Doman, T. N., McGovern, S. L., Witherbee, B. J., Kasten, T. P., Kurumbail, R., Stallings, W. C., & Shoichet, B. K. et al. (2002). Molecular Docking and High-Throughput Screening for Novel Inhibitors of Protein Tyrosine Phosphatase-1B. *Journal of Medicinal Chemistry, 45*(11), 2213–2221. doi:10.1021/jm010548w PMID:12014959

Dominguez, C., Boelens, R., & Bonvin, A. M. (2003). HADDOCK: A Protein—Protein Docking Approach Based on Biochemical or Biophysical Information. Doi:<ALIGNMENT.qj></ALIGNMENT>10.1021/JA026939X

Durrant, J. D., Friedman, A. J., Rogers, K. E., & McCammon, J. A. (2013). Comparing neural-network scoring functions and the state of the art: Applications to common library screening. *Journal of Chemical Information and Modeling, 53*(7), 1726–1735. doi:10.1021/ci400042y PMID:23734946

Erlanson, D. A., Fesik, S. W., Hubbard, R. E., Jahnke, W., & Jhoti, H. (2016). Twenty years on: The impact of fragments on drug discovery. *Nature Reviews. Drug Discovery, 15*(9), 605–619. doi:10.1038/nrd.2016.109 PMID:27417849

Ewing, T. J. A., Makino, S., Skillman, A. G., & Kuntz, I. D. (2001). DOCK 4.0: Search strategies for automated molecular docking of flexible molecule databases. *Journal of Computer-Aided Molecular Design, 15*(5), 411–428. doi:10.1023/A:1011115820450 PMID:11394736

Fahmy, A., & Wagner, G. (2011). Optimization of van der Waals energy for protein side-chain placement and design. *Biophysical Journal, 101*(7), 1690–1698. doi:10.1016/j.bpj.2011.07.052 PMID:21961595

Fischer, D., Lin, S. L., Wolfson, H. L., & Nussinov, R. (1995). A Geometry-based Suite of Molecular Docking Processes. *Journal of Molecular Biology, 248*(2), 459–477. doi:10.1016/S0022-2836(95)80063-8 PMID:7739053

Forli, S., Huey, R., Pique, M. E., Sanner, M. F., Goodsell, D. S., & Olson, A. J. (2016). Computational protein–ligand docking and virtual drug screening with the AutoDock suite. *Nature Protocols, 11*(5), 905–919. doi:10.1038/nprot.2016.051 PMID:27077332

Fox, S. J., Li, J., Sing Tan, Y., Nguyen, M. N., Pal, A., & Ouaray, Z. … Kannan, S. (2016). The Multifaceted Roles of Molecular Dynamics Simulations in Drug Discovery. *Current Pharmaceutical Design, 22*(23), 3585–600. Retrieved from http://www.ncbi.nlm.nih.gov/pubmed/27108593

Friesner, R. A., Banks, J. L., Murphy, R. B., Halgren, T. A., Klicic, J. J., Mainz, D. T., & Shenkin, P. S. et al. (2004). Glide: A New Approach for Rapid, Accurate Docking and Scoring. 1. Method and Assessment of Docking Accuracy. *Journal of Medicinal Chemistry*, *47*(7), 1739–1749. doi:10.1021/jm0306430 PMID:15027865

Friesner, R. A., Murphy, R. B., Repasky, M. P., Frye, L. L., Greenwood, J. R., Halgren, T. A., & Mainz, D. T. et al. (2006). Extra precision glide: Docking and scoring incorporating a model of hydrophobic enclosure for protein-ligand complexes. *Journal of Medicinal Chemistry*, *49*(21), 6177–6196. doi:10.1021/jm051256o PMID:17034125

Gane, P. J., & Dean, P. M. (2000). Recent advances in structure-based rational drug design. *Current Opinion in Structural Biology*, *10*(4), 401–404. Retrieved from http://www.ncbi.nlm.nih.gov/pubmed/10981625 doi:10.1016/S0959-440X(00)00105-6 PMID:10981625

Gangopadhyay, A., & Datta, A. (2015). Identification of inhibitors against the potential ligandable sites in the active cholera toxin. *Computational Biology and Chemistry*, *55*, 37–48. doi:10.1016/j.compbiolchem.2015.02.011 PMID:25698576

Ginsburg, G. S., & McCarthy, J. J. (2001). Personalized medicine: Revolutionizing drug discovery and patient care. *Trends in Biotechnology*, *19*(12), 491–496. Retrieved from http://www.ncbi.nlm.nih.gov/pubmed/11711191 doi:10.1016/S0167-7799(01)01814-5 PMID:11711191

Guex, N., & Peitsch, M. (1997). SWISS-MODEL and the Swiss-Pdb Viewer: an environment for comparative protein modeling. *Electrophoresis*. Retrieved from http://onlinelibrary.wiley.com/doi/10.1002/elps.1150181505/full

Guo, W., Wisniewski, J. A., & Ji, H. (2014). Hot spot-based design of small-molecule inhibitors for protein–protein interactions. *Bioorganic & Medicinal Chemistry Letters*, *24*(11), 2546–2554. doi:10.1016/j.bmcl.2014.03.095 PMID:24751445

Gupta, A., Gandhimathi, A., Sharma, P., & Jayaram, B. (2007). ParDOCK: An all atom energy based Monte Carlo docking protocol for protein-ligand complexes. *Protein and Peptide Letters*, *14*(7), 632–646. Retrieved from http://www.ncbi.nlm.nih.gov/pubmed/17897088 doi:10.2174/092986607781483831 PMID:17897088

Halgren, T. A., Murphy, R. B., Friesner, R. A., Beard, H. S., Frye, L. L., Pollard, W. T., & Banks, J. L. (2004). Glide: A New Approach for Rapid, Accurate Docking and Scoring. 2. Enrichment Factors in Database Screening. *Journal of Medicinal Chemistry*, *47*(7), 1750–1759. doi:10.1021/jm030644s PMID:15027866

Hashmi, I., & Shehu, A. (2012). A basin hopping algorithm for protein-protein docking. *Proceedings of the 2012 IEEE International Conference on Bioinformatics and Biomedicine* (pp. 1–4). IEEE. http://doi.org/ doi:10.1109/BIBM.2012.6392725

Hashmi, I., & Shehu, A. (2015). idDock+: Integrating Machine Learning in Probabilistic Search for Protein–Protein Docking. *Journal of Computational Biology*, *22*(9), 806–822. doi:10.1089/cmb.2015.0108 PMID:26222714

Hirschhorn, J. N., & Daly, M. J. (2005). Genome-wide association studies for common diseases and complex traits. *Nature Reviews. Genetics*, *6*(2), 95–108. doi:10.1038/nrg1521 PMID:15716906

Huang, N., & Shoichet, B. K. (2008). Exploiting ordered waters in molecular docking. *Journal of Medicinal Chemistry*, *51*(16), 4862–4865. doi:10.1021/jm8006239 PMID:18680357

Humphrey, W., Dalke, A., & Schulten, K. (1996). VMD: Visual molecular dynamics. *Journal of Molecular Graphics*, *14*(1), 33–38. doi:10.1016/0263-7855(96)00018-5 PMID:8744570

Hurwitz, N., Schneidman-Duhovny, D., & Wolfson, H. J. (2016). Memdock: An α-helical membrane protein docking algorithm. *Bioinformatics (Oxford, England)*, *32*(16), 2444–2450. doi:10.1093/bioinformatics/btw184 PMID:27153621

Janin, J. (2002). Welcome to CAPRI: A Critical Assessment of PRedicted Interactions. *Proteins*, *47*(3), 257–257. doi:10.1002/prot.10111

Jiang, X., Kumar, K., Hu, X., Wallqvist, A., Reifman, J., Ghosh, S., & McCammon, J. et al. (2008). DOVIS 2.0: An efficient and easy to use parallel virtual screening tool based on AutoDock 4.0. *Chemistry Central Journal*, *2*(1), 18. doi:10.1186/1752-153X-2-18 PMID:18778471

Jiménez-García, B., Pons, C., & Fernández-Recio, J. (2013). pyDockWEB: A web server for rigid-body protein-protein docking using electrostatics and desolvation scoring. *Bioinformatics (Oxford, England)*, *29*(13), 1698–1699. doi:10.1093/bioinformatics/btt262 PMID:23661696

Jiménez-García, B., Pons, C., Svergun, D. I., Bernadó, P., & Fernández-Recio, J. (2015). pyDockSAXS: Protein-protein complex structure by SAXS and computational docking. *Nucleic Acids Research*, *43*(W1), W356-61. doi:10.1093/nar/gkv368 PMID:25897115

Johnson, D. K., & Karanicolas, J. (2016). Ultra-High-Throughput Structure-Based Virtual Screening for Small-Molecule Inhibitors of Protein–Protein Interactions. *Journal of Chemical Information and Modeling*, *56*(2), 399–411. doi:10.1021/acs.jcim.5b00572 PMID:26726827

Jones, G., Willett, P., Glen, R. C., Leach, A. R., & Taylor, R. (1997). Development and validation of a genetic algorithm for flexible docking. *Journal of Molecular Biology*, *267*(3), 727–748. doi:10.1006/jmbi.1996.0897 PMID:9126849

Jorgensen, W. L. (2004). The Many Roles of Computation in Drug Discovery. *Science*, *303*(5665), 1813–1818. doi:10.1126/science.1096361 PMID:15031495

Kinnings, S. L., Liu, N., Tonge, P. J., Jackson, R. M., Xie, L., & Bourne, P. E. (2011). A machine learning-based method to improve docking scoring functions and its application to drug repurposing. *Journal of Chemical Information and Modeling*, *51*(2), 408–419. doi:10.1021/ci100369f PMID:21291174

Kolb, P., Kipouros, C. B., Huang, D., & Caflisch, A. (2008). Structure-based tailoring of compound libraries for high-throughput screening: Discovery of novel EphB4 kinase inhibitors. *Proteins: Structure, Function, and Bioinformatics*, *73*(1), 11–18. doi:10.1002/prot.22028 PMID:18384152

Kozakov, D., Brenke, R., Comeau, S. R., Vajda, S., & Vajda, S. (2006). PIPER: An FFT-based protein docking program with pairwise potentials. *Proteins: Structure, Function, and Bioinformatics*, *65*(2), 392–406. doi:10.1002/prot.21117 PMID:16933295

Kramer, B., Rarey, M., & Lengauer, T. (1999). Evaluation of the FLEXX incremental construction algorithm for protein-ligand docking. *Proteins*, *37*(2), 228–241. doi:10.1002/(SICI)1097-0134(19991101)37:2<228::AID-PROT8>3.0.CO;2-8 PMID:10584068

Krieger, E., & Vriend, G. (2014). YASARA View - molecular graphics for all devices - from smartphones to workstations. *Bioinformatics (Oxford, England)*, *30*(20), 2981–2982. doi:10.1093/bioinformatics/btu426 PMID:24996895

Krissinel, E., & Henrick, K. (2007). Inference of Macromolecular Assemblies from Crystalline State. *Journal of Molecular Biology*, *372*(3), 774–797. doi:10.1016/j.jmb.2007.05.022 PMID:17681537

Kuntz, I. D. (1992). Structure-Based Strategies for Drug Design and Discovery. *Science*, *257*(5073), 1078–1082. doi:10.1126/science.257.5073.1078 PMID:1509259

Kuntz, I. D., Blaney, J. M., Oatley, S. J., Langridge, R., & Ferrin, T. E. (1982). A geometric approach to macromolecule-ligand interactions. *Journal of Molecular Biology*, *161*(2), 269–288. doi:10.1016/0022-2836(82)90153-X PMID:7154081

Kurcinski, M., Jamroz, M., Blaszczyk, M., Kolinski, A., & Kmiecik, S. (2015). CABS-dock web server for the flexible docking of peptides to proteins without prior knowledge of the binding site. *Nucleic Acids Research*, *43*(W1), W419-24. doi:10.1093/nar/gkv456 PMID:25943545

Lamdan, Y., & Wolfson, H. (1988). Geometric hashing: A general and efficient model-based recognition scheme. Retrieved from http://www.cs.utexas.edu/~grauman/courses/spring2007/395T/395T/papers/Lamdan88.pdf

Laskowski, R. A., & Swindells, M. B. (2011). LigPlot+: Multiple ligand-protein interaction diagrams for drug discovery. *Journal of Chemical Information and Modeling*, *51*(10), 2778–2786. doi:10.1021/ci200227u PMID:21919503

Lee, G. R., & Seok, C. (2016). Galaxy7TM: Flexible GPCR-ligand docking by structure refinement. *Nucleic Acids Research*, *44*(W1), W502-6. doi:10.1093/nar/gkw360 PMID:27131365

Lengauer, T. (2008). *Bioinformatics - From Genomes to Therapies* (Vol. 1). Bioinformatics - From Genomes to Therapies; doi:10.1002/9783527619368

Lensink, M. F., Velankar, S., Kryshtafovych, A., Huang, S.-Y., Schneidman-Duhovny, D., Sali, A., & Wodak, S. J. et al. (2016). Prediction of homoprotein and heteroprotein complexes by protein docking and template-based modeling: A CASP-CAPRI experiment. *Proteins. Structure, Function, and Bioinformatics*, *84*, 323–348. doi:10.1002/prot.25007 PMID:27122118

Lesk, V. I., & Sternberg, M. J. E. (2008). 3D-Garden: A system for modelling protein-protein complexes based on conformational refinement of ensembles generated with the marching cubes algorithm. *Bioinformatics (Oxford, England)*, *24*(9), 1137–1144. doi:10.1093/bioinformatics/btn093 PMID:18326508

Li, H., Gao, Z., Kang, L., Zhang, H., Yang, K., Yu, K., … Jiang, H. (2006). TarFisDock: a web server for identifying drug targets with docking approach. *Nucleic Acids Research, 34*(Web Server), W219–W224. http://doi.org/<ALIGNMENT.qj></ALIGNMENT>10.1093/nar/gkl114

Li, H., Leung, K.-S., & Wong, M.-H. (2012). idock: A multithreaded virtual screening tool for flexible ligand docking. *Proceedings of the 2012 IEEE Symposium on Computational Intelligence in Bioinformatics and Computational Biology (CIBCB)* (pp. 77–84). IEEE. http://doi.org/ doi:10.1109/CIBCB.2012.6217214

Li, H., & Li, C. (2010a). Multiple Ligand Simultaneous Docking: Orchestrated Dancing of Ligands in Binding Sites of Protein. *Journal of Computational Chemistry, 31*(10), 2014–2022. doi:10.10021/jcc.21486 PMID:20166125

Li, H., & Li, C. (2010b). Multiple ligand simultaneous docking: Orchestrated dancing of ligands in binding sites of protein. *Journal of Computational Chemistry, 31*(10), 2014–2022. doi:10.1002/jcc.21486 PMID:20166125

Li, H., Liu, A., Zhao, Z., Xu, Y., Lin, J., Jou, D., & Li, C. (2011). Fragment-based drug design and drug repositioning using multiple ligand simultaneous docking (MLSD): Identifying celecoxib and template compounds as novel inhibitors of signal transducer and activator of transcription 3 (STAT3). *Journal of Medicinal Chemistry, 54*(15), 5592–5596. doi:10.1021/jm101330h PMID:21678971

Li, H., Xiao, H., Lin, L., Jou, D., Kumari, V., Lin, J., & Li, C. (2014). Drug Design Targeting Protein–Protein Interactions (PPIs) Using Multiple Ligand Simultaneous Docking (MLSD) and Drug Repositioning: Discovery of Raloxifene and Bazedoxifene as Novel Inhibitors of IL-6/GP130 Interface. *Journal of Medicinal Chemistry, 57*(3), 632–641. doi:10.1021/jm401144z PMID:24456369

Li, L., Wang, B., & Meroueh, S. O. (2011). Support vector regression scoring of receptor-ligand complexes for rank-ordering and virtual screening of chemical libraries. *Journal of Chemical Information and Modeling, 51*(9), 2132–2138. doi:10.1021/ci200078f PMID:21728360

Lu, Y., Wang, R., Yang, C.-Y., & Wang, S. (n. d.). Analysis of ligand-bound water molecules in high-resolution crystal structures of protein-ligand complexes. *Journal of Chemical Information and Modeling, 47*(2), 668–75. Doi:<ALIGNMENT.qj></ALIGNMENT>10.1021/ci6003527

Lusher, S. J., McGuire, R., van Schaik, R. C., Nicholson, C. D., & de Vlieg, J. (2014). Data-driven medicinal chemistry in the era of big data. *Drug Discovery Today, 19*(7), 859–868. doi:10.1016/j.drudis.2013.12.004 PMID:24361338

Lyskov, S., Chou, F.-C., Conchúir, S. Ó., Der, B. S., Drew, K., Kuroda, D., & Meiler, J. et al. (2013). Serverification of Molecular Modeling Applications: The Rosetta Online Server That Includes Everyone (ROSIE). *PLoS ONE, 8*(5), e63906. doi:10.1371/journal.pone.0063906 PMID:23717507

Lyskov, S., & Gray, J. J. (2008). The RosettaDock server for local protein-protein docking. *Nucleic Acids Research, 36*(Web Server issue), W233-8. Doi:<ALIGNMENT.qj></ALIGNMENT>10.1093/nar/gkn216

Macindoe, G., Mavridis, L., Venkatraman, V., Devignes, M.-D., & Ritchie, D. W. (2010). HexServer: an FFT-based protein docking server powered by graphics processors. *Nucleic Acids Research, 38*(Web Server issue), W445-9. Doi:<ALIGNMENT.qj></ALIGNMENT>10.1093/nar/gkq311

Madan, B., Kasprzak, J. M., Tuszynska, I., Magnus, M., Szczepaniak, K., Dawson, W. K., & Bujnicki, J. M. (2016). Modeling of Protein–RNA Complex Structures Using Computational Docking Methods (pp. 353–372). Doi:<ALIGNMENT.qj></ALIGNMENT>10.1007/978-1-4939-3569-7_21

Mashiach, E., Nussinov, R., & Wolfson, H. J. (2010). FiberDock: Flexible induced-fit backbone refinement in molecular docking. *Proteins*, *78*(6), 1503–1519. doi:10.1002/prot.22668 PMID:20077569

McCarthy, M. I., Abecasis, G. R., Cardon, L. R., Goldstein, D. B., Little, J., Ioannidis, J. P. A., & Hirschhorn, J. N. (2008). Genome-wide association studies for complex traits: Consensus, uncertainty and challenges. *Nature Reviews. Genetics*, *9*(5), 356–369. doi:10.1038/nrg2344 PMID:18398418

Meiler, J., & Baker, D. (2006). ROSETTALIGAND: Protein-small molecule docking with full side-chain flexibility. *Proteins: Structure, Function, and Bioinformatics*, *65*(3), 538–548. doi:10.1002/prot.21086 PMID:16972285

Mobley, D. L., & Dill, K. A. (2009). Binding of small-molecule ligands to proteins: "what you" is not always "what you get." *Structure*, *17*(4), 489–98. Doi:<ALIGNMENT.qj></ALIGNMENT>10.1016/j.str.2009.02.010

Morris, G. M., Goodsell, D. S., Halliday, R. S., Huey, R., Hart, W. E., Belew, R. K., & Olson, A. J. (1998). Automated docking using a Lamarckian genetic algorithm and an empirical binding free energy function. *Journal of Computational Chemistry*, *19*(14), 1639–1662. doi:10.1002/(SICI)1096-987X(19981115)19:14<1639::AID-JCC10>3.0.CO;2-B

Morris, G. M., Goodsell, D. S., Huey, R., & Olson, A. J. (1996). Distributed automated docking of flexible ligands to proteins: Parallel applications of AutoDock 2.4. *Journal of Computer-Aided Molecular Design*, *10*(4), 293–304. doi:10.1007/BF00124499 PMID:8877701

Morris, G. M., Huey, R., Lindstrom, W., Sanner, M. F., Belew, R. K., Goodsell, D. S., & Olson, A. J. (2009). AutoDock4 and AutoDockTools4: Automated docking with selective receptor flexibility. *Journal of Computational Chemistry*, *30*(16), 2785–2791. doi:10.1002/jcc.21256 PMID:19399780

Mosca, R., Pons, C., Fernández-Recio, J., & Aloy, P. (2009). Pushing Structural Information into the Yeast Interactome by High-Throughput Protein Docking Experiments. *PLoS Computational Biology*, *5*(8), e1000490. doi:10.1371/journal.pcbi.1000490 PMID:19714207

Muratcioglu, S., Guven-Maiorov, E., Keskin, Ö., & Gursoy, A. (2015). Advances in template-based protein docking by utilizing interfaces towards completing structural interactome. *Current Opinion in Structural Biology*, *35*, 87–92. doi:10.1016/j.sbi.2015.10.001 PMID:26539658

Nagata, K., Randall, A., & Baldi, P. (2012). SIDEpro: A novel machine learning approach for the fast and accurate prediction of side-chain conformations. *Proteins*, *80*(1), 142–153. doi:10.1002/prot.23170 PMID:22072531

Neves, M. A. C., Totrov, M., & Abagyan, R. (2012). Docking and scoring with ICM: The benchmarking results and strategies for improvement. *Journal of Computer-Aided Molecular Design*, *26*(6), 675–686. doi:10.1007/s10822-012-9547-0 PMID:22569591

Neveu, E., Ritchie, D. W., Popov, P., & Grudinin, S. (2016). PEPSI-Dock: A detailed data-driven protein-protein interaction potential accelerated by polar Fourier correlation. *Bioinformatics (Oxford, England)*, *32*(17), i693–i701. doi:10.1093/bioinformatics/btw443 PMID:27587691

Nichols, D. A., Renslo, A. R., & Chen, Y. (2014). Fragment-based inhibitor discovery against β-lactamase. *Future Medicinal Chemistry*, *6*(4), 413–427. doi:10.4155/fmc.14.10 PMID:24635522

Nosengo, N. (2016). Can you teach old drugs new tricks? *Nature*, *534*(7607), 314–316. doi:10.1038/534314a PMID:27306171

Pettersen, E. F., Goddard, T. D., Huang, C. C., Couch, G. S., Greenblatt, D. M., Meng, E. C., & Ferrin, T. E. (2004). UCSF Chimera - A visualization system for exploratory research and analysis. *Journal of Computational Chemistry*, *25*(13), 1605–1612. doi:10.1002/jcc.20084 PMID:15264254

Pierce, B., Tong, W., & Weng, Z. (2005). M-ZDOCK: A grid-based approach for Cn symmetric multimer docking. *Bioinformatics*, *21*(8), 1472–1478. doi:10.1093/bioinformatics/bti229 PMID:15613396

Pierce, B. G., Hourai, Y., & Weng, Z. (2011). Accelerating Protein Docking in ZDOCK Using an Advanced 3D Convolution Library. *PLoS ONE*, *6*(9), e24657. doi:10.1371/journal.pone.0024657 PMID:21949741

Pierce, B. G., Wiehe, K., Hwang, H., Kim, B.-H., Vreven, T., & Weng, Z. (2014). ZDOCK server: Interactive docking prediction of protein-protein complexes and symmetric multimers. *Bioinformatics*, *30*(12), 1771–1773. doi:10.1093/bioinformatics/btu097 PMID:24532726

Pons, C., Jiménez-González, D., González-Álvarez, C., Servat, H., Cabrera-Benítez, D., Aguilar, X., & Fernández-Recio, J. (2012). Cell-Dock: High-performance protein-protein docking. *Bioinformatics*, *28*(18), 2394–2396. doi:10.1093/bioinformatics/bts454 PMID:22815362

Popov, P., Ritchie, D. W., & Grudinin, S. (2014). DockTrina: Docking triangular protein trimers. *Proteins: Structure, Function, and Bioinformatics*, *82*(1), 34–44. doi:10.1002/prot.24344 PMID:23775700

Puton, T., Kozlowski, L., Tuszynska, I., Rother, K., & Bujnicki, J. M. (2012). Computational methods for prediction of protein–RNA interactions. *Journal of Structural Biology*, *179*(3), 261–268. doi:10.1016/j.jsb.2011.10.001 PMID:22019768

Raghavendra, S., Aditya Rao, S. J., Kumar, V., & Ramesh, C. K. (2015). Multiple ligand simultaneous docking (MLSD): A novel approach to study the effect of inhibitors on substrate binding to PPO. *Computational Biology and Chemistry*, *59 Pt A*, 81–6. Doi:<ALIGNMENT.qj></ALIGNMENT>10.1016/j.compbiolchem.2015.09.008

Ramírez-Aportela, E., López-Blanco, J. R., & Chacón, P. (2016). FRODOCK 2.0: Fast protein-protein docking server. *Bioinformatics*, *32*(15), 2386–2388. doi:10.1093/bioinformatics/btw141 PMID:27153583

Ravindranath, P. A., Forli, S., Goodsell, D. S., Olson, A. J., & Sanner, M. F. (2015). AutoDockFR: Advances in Protein-Ligand Docking with Explicitly Specified Binding Site Flexibility. *PLoS Computational Biology*, *11*(12), e1004586. doi:10.1371/journal.pcbi.1004586 PMID:26629955

Ritchie, D. W., & Kemp, G. J. L. (1999). Fast computation, rotation, and comparison of low resolution spherical harmonic molecular surfaces. *Journal of Computational Chemistry*, *20*(4), 383–395. doi:10.1002/(SICI)1096-987X(199903)20:4<383::AID-JCC1>3.0.CO;2-M

Ritchie, D. W., & Venkatraman, V. (2010). Ultra-fast FFT protein docking on graphics processors. *Bioinformatics*, *26*(19), 2398–2405. doi:10.1093/bioinformatics/btq444 PMID:20685958

Ryu, J., Lee, M., Cha, J., Laskowski, R. A., Ryu, S. E., & Kim, D.-S. (2016). BetaSCPWeb: Side-chain prediction for protein structures using Voronoi diagrams and geometry prioritization. *Nucleic Acids Research, 44*(W1), W416-23. doi:10.1093/nar/gkw368 PMID:27151195

Salentin, S., Schreiber, S., Haupt, V. J., Adasme, M. F., & Schroeder, M. (2015). PLIP: Fully automated protein-ligand interaction profiler. *Nucleic Acids Research, 43*(W1), W443-7. doi:10.1093/nar/gkv315 PMID:25873628

Sanner, M. (1999). Python: a programming language for software integration and development. *J Mol Graph Model*. Retrieved from http://citeseerx.ist.psu.edu/viewdoc/download?doi=10.1.1.35.6459&rep =rep1&type=pdf

Sayle, R., & Bissell, A. (1992). RasMol: A program for fast, realistic rendering of molecular structures with shadows. *Proceedings of the 10th Eurographics UK*. Retrieved from http://mail.ccl.net/cca/ software/X-WINDOW/rasmol2.5/paper.ps

Schneider, G., & Fechner, U. (2005). Computer-based de novo design of drug-like molecules. *Nature Reviews. Drug Discovery, 4*(8), 649–663. doi:10.1038/nrd1799 PMID:16056391

Schneidman-Duhovny, D., Inbar, Y., Nussinov, R., & Wolfson, H. J. (2005). PatchDock and SymmDock: servers for rigid and symmetric docking. *Nucleic Acids Research, 33*(Web Server issue), W363-7. http:// doi.org/<ALIGNMENT.qj></ALIGNMENT>10.1093/nar/gki481

Segura, J., Marín-López, M. A., Jones, P. F., Oliva, B., Fernandez-Fuentes, N., Ewing, R., & Chikova, A. et al. (2015). VORFFIP-Driven Dock: V-D2OCK, a Fast and Accurate Protein Docking Strategy. *PLoS ONE, 10*(3), e0118107. doi:10.1371/journal.pone.0118107 PMID:25763838

Sheng, C., Dong, G., Miao, Z., Zhang, W., Wang, W., Arkin, M. R., & Sperandio, O. et al. (2015). State-of-the-art strategies for targeting protein–protein interactions by small-molecule inhibitors. *Chemical Society Reviews, 44*(22), 8238–8259. doi:10.1039/C5CS00252D PMID:26248294

Shoichet, B. K., McGovern, S. L., Wei, B., & Irwin, J. J. (2002). Lead discovery using molecular docking. *Current Opinion in Chemical Biology, 6*(4), 439–446. doi:10.1016/S1367-5931(02)00339-3 PMID:12133718

Stein, L. D. (2010). The case for cloud computing in genome informatics. *Genome Biology, 11*(5), 207. doi:10.1186/gb-2010-11-5-207 PMID:20441614

Szilagyi, A., & Zhang, Y. (2014). Template-based structure modeling of protein–protein interactions. *Current Opinion in Structural Biology, 24*, 10–23. doi:10.1016/j.sbi.2013.11.005 PMID:24721449

Tarini, M., Cignoni, P., & Montani, C. (2006). Ambient Occlusion and Edge Cueing for Enhancing Real Time Molecular Visualization. *IEEE Transactions on Visualization and Computer Graphics, 12*(5), 1237–1244. doi:10.1109/TVCG.2006.115 PMID:17080857

Teotico, D. G., Babaoglu, K., Rocklin, G. J., Ferreira, R. S., Giannetti, A. M., & Shoichet, B. K. (2009). Docking for fragment inhibitors of AmpC beta-lactamase. *Proceedings of the National Academy of Sciences of the United States of America, 106*(18), 7455–7460. doi:10.1073/pnas.0813029106 PMID:19416920

Torchala, M., Moal, I. H., Chaleil, R. A. G., Fernandez-Recio, J., & Bates, P. A. (2013). SwarmDock: A server for flexible protein-protein docking. *Bioinformatics (Oxford, England)*, *29*(6), 807–809. doi:10.1093/bioinformatics/btt038 PMID:23343604

Tovchigrechko, A., & Vakser, I. A. (2006). GRAMM-X public web server for protein-protein docking. *Nucleic Acids Research, 34*(Web Server issue), W310-4. Doi:<ALIGNMENT.qj></ALIGNMENT>10.1093/nar/gkl206

Trott, O., & Olson, A. J. (2010). AutoDock Vina. *Journal of Computational Chemistry*, *31*, 445–461. doi:10.1002/jcc.21334 PMID:19499576

Trott, O., & Olson, A. J. (2010). AutoDock Vina: Improving the Speed and Accuracy of Docking with a New Scoring Function, EfficientOptimization, and Multithreading. *Journal of Computational Chemistry*, *31*(2), 455–461. doi:10.1002/jcc PMID:19499576

Tuszynska, I., Bujnicki, J. M., Chen, Y., Varani, G., Lukong, K., Chang, K., & Bujnicki, J. et al. (2011). DARS-RNP and QUASI-RNP: New statistical potentials for protein-RNA docking. *BMC Bioinformatics*, *12*(1), 348. doi:10.1186/1471-2105-12-348 PMID:21851628

Tuszynska, I., Magnus, M., Jonak, K., Dawson, W., & Bujnicki, J. M. (2015). NPDock: A web server for protein-nucleic acid docking. *Nucleic Acids Research*, *43*(W1), W425-30. doi:10.1093/nar/gkv493 PMID:25977296

Vajda, S., & Kozakov, D. (2009). Convergence and combination of methods in protein-protein docking. *Current Opinion in Structural Biology*, *19*(2), 164–170. doi:10.1016/j.sbi.2009.02.008 PMID:19327983

Van Dijk, A. D. J., Boelens, R., & Bonvin, A. M. J. J. (2005). Data-driven docking for the study of biomolecular complexes. *The FEBS Journal*, *272*(2), 293–312. doi:10.1111/j.1742-4658.2004.04473.x PMID:15654870

Wang, T., Wu, M.-B., Chen, Z.-J., Chen, H., Lin, J.-P., & Yang, L.-R. (2015). Fragment-based drug discovery and molecular docking in drug design. *Current Pharmaceutical Biotechnology*, *16*(1), 11–25. Retrieved from http://www.ncbi.nlm.nih.gov/pubmed/25420726 doi:10.2174/138920101566614112220 4532 PMID:25420726

Wells, J. A., & McClendon, C. L. (2007). Reaching for high-hanging fruit in drug discovery at protein-protein interfaces. *Nature*, *450*(7172), 1001–1009. doi:10.1038/nature06526 PMID:18075579

Wetterstrand, K. A. (2016). DNA Sequencing Costs: Data from the NHGRI Genome Sequencing Program (GSP). Retrieved from www.genome.gov/sequencingcostsdata

Xu, M., Unzue, A., Dong, J., Spiliotopoulos, D., Nevado, C., & Caflisch, A. (2016). Discovery of CREBBP Bromodomain Inhibitors by High-Throughput Docking and Hit Optimization Guided by Molecular Dynamics. *Journal of Medicinal Chemistry*, *59*(4), 1340–1349. doi:10.1021/acs.jmedchem.5b00171 PMID:26125948

Yu, J., Vavrusa, M., Andreani, J., Rey, J., Tufféry, P., & Guerois, R. (2016). InterEvDock: A docking server to predict the structure of protein–protein interactions using evolutionary information. *Nucleic Acids Research*, *44*(W1), W542–W549. doi:10.1093/nar/gkw340 PMID:27131368

Zhang, S., Kumar, K., Jiang, X., Wallqvist, A., Reifman, J., Ghosh, S., & Holbeck, S. et al. (2008). DOVIS: An implementation for high-throughput virtual screening using AutoDock. *BMC Bioinformatics*, *9*(1), 126. doi:10.1186/1471-2105-9-126 PMID:18304355

Zheng, J., Kundrotas, P. J., Vakser, I. A., Liu, S., Kozomara, A., Griffiths-Jones, S., & Lapointe, J. et al. (2016). Template-Based Modeling of Protein-RNA Interactions. *PLoS Computational Biology*, *12*(9), e1005120. doi:10.1371/journal.pcbi.1005120 PMID:27662342

KEY TERMS AND DEFINITIONS

Docking: A computational approach used to model the structure of molecular complexes formed upon binding.

Docking Algorithm: The manner in which a docking computation is worked out.

Fragment: Smaller fractions of larger molecules. Usually these are the rigid portions from a larger molecule.

Library: A large collection of a certain category of compounds: small molecules, leads, fragments, drug-like compounds, and so on.

Ligand: The smaller molecule which binds to a bigger molecule (receptor). In protein docking, this generally includes small molecules, fragments, peptides, small proteins, nucleic acids.

Pose: the binding mode of one molecule with respect to the other.

Scoring Function: An equation used to evaluate ligand poses in order to select the optimum solution.

Structure-Based Drug Design: A drug design approach using the structure of the target site. This is possible when the structure of the target site is known.

Virtual Screening: A combination of computational approaches, aimed at high-throughput screening of compound libraries.

Section 3
Big Data Analytics for Medical and Health informatics

This section covers topics related to health analytics and informatics, medical and health informatics by using "-omics" data, system biology, disease control, predictive model of disease state, translational medicine, drug design, combinatorial drug discovery, proteomics in personalized medicine, image processing including medical imaging, healthcare and healthcare delivery, healthcare policy research, healthcare outcomes research, monitoring and evaluation, hospital information system, Electronic Medical Record and Electronic Health Record, population health management, decision support systems, telemedicine, Human-Machine Interfaces, ICT, Ageing and Disability, Mobile technologies for Healthcare applications (m-Health), Evaluation and use of Healthcare IT, Health Knowledge Management, Healthcare Management and Information Systems, Software Systems in Medicine, Data Mining and Visualization, Virtual Healthcare Teams, e-Health for Public Health integrating genetics with e-health.

Chapter 10
Effective and Efficient Business Intelligence Dashboard Design:
Gestalt Theory in Dutch Long-Term and Chronic Healthcare

Marco Spruit
Utrecht University, The Netherlands

Max Lammertink
Utrecht University, The Netherlands

ABSTRACT

This research focuses on the design process of an effective and efficient dashboard which displays management information for an Electronic Health Record (EHR) in Dutch long-term and chronic healthcare. It presents the actual design and realization of a management dashboard for the YBoard 2.0 system, which is a popular solution on the Dutch market. The design decisions in this investigation were based on human perception and computer interaction theory, in particular Gestalt theory. The empirical interviews with medical professionals supplemented valuable additional insights into what the users wanted to see most of all in a dashboard in their daily practices. This study successfully shows how effective and efficient dashboard design can benefit from theoretical insights related to human perception and computer interaction such as Gestalt theory, in combination with integrated end user requirements from daily practices.

INTRODUCTION

An electronic health record (EHR) can be viewed as an evolving concept defined as a systematic collection of electronic health information about individual patients or populations. It is a digital record with the information of patients of a particular group. By itself an EHR is just that, a record. It cannot do anything and a system is required to provide the functions that make the EHR useful. This combination is known as an electronic health record system (Moghaddasi, 2011). However, in daily practice,

DOI: 10.4018/978-1-5225-2607-0.ch010

the term EHR is often used to refer to both the electronic health record as well as the system. Most of the EHRs are able to (1) capture health information in a coded format, (2) track clinical conditions and quality reporting, (3) support clinical decision-making and healthcare coordination, and (4) eventually improves performance of the healthcare institute. Spruit, Vroon and Batenburg (2014) notably perform an exploratory analYBoard on HER information in long-term care institutions within The Netherlands.

In 2008 about 98% of the healthcare professionals in the Netherlands already made use of some sort of EHR (Jha et al, 2008). For now, these systems are mostly standalone systems, or linked with just a couple of other systems. For example, an EHR of a local general practitioner can be linked with the EHR of the local pharmacy, but it is most likely not linked with the EHR of a pharmacy in a different city or state. Furthermore, according to a survey by Goldberg et al. (2012) in Virginia, USA, 'Physicians and staff also repeatedly described their EHR systems as complex, having too many functions to navigate, numerous steps needed to complete a transaction, and difficult to customize.'

However, a recent survey shows that the Netherlands is a key player in adopting EHRs in ambulatory healthcare and hospital settings. The Dutch Ministry of Health aimed to establish a national infrastructure for data exchange between electronic patient records (EPRs). This way, healthcare providers which are connected will always have up-to-date information about a patient. The core of this infrastructure is the "national switch point" (LSP), an index with pointers to all registered EPRs of a patient (Tange, 2008). This project has now been taken over by the National IT Institute for Healthcare in the Netherlands. EHRs are a very hot topic in the Netherlands because of those relatively recent changes in the development of the national EHR.

Koopman et al (2011) show the benefits that dashboards can provide within an EHR in diabctcs healthcare. Their survey shows that the mouse clicks needed to find particular information about patients is reduced by 95% and the time needed to find the information wanted reduced by about 25%. Although this survey was held for an EHR used in diabetes healthcare, it may be assumed that this is not only the case for the diabetes EHR but also for non-diabetes EHRs like the EHR used in long-term and chronic healthcare. Meulendijk et al. (2013) similarly report on the high demand from general practitioners for integrated and visual systems to optimize polypharmacy in the Dutch primary care sector. On a broader level than healthcare, more research has been performed regarding the use of dashboards. A 2009 survey showed that over 80% of dashboard users think that a dashboard has a positive impact on business results (Eckerson, 2011). Finally, Wijaya et al. (2008) note that Web 2.0 technologies provide further opportunities to further enhance business values in online health systems.

BACKGROUND: DASHBOARD DESIGN

So, what exactly is a dashboard and how is it used? A dashboard is more than just a screen with some nice performance graphics in it. It is actually three applications in one, woven in a seamless fashion: (1) a monitoring application, (2) an analYBoard application, and (3) a management application. According to Eckerson (2011), the benefits of a dashboard appear to be endless; they can be used to communicate a company-wide strategy, refine and control that strategy and increase coordination and motivation throughout the company. With this taken into account, lots of companies decided to create or buy a dashboard systems tool.

Historically speaking, the first business intelligence dashboards where developed in the 1980s. Back then they were called Executive Information Systems (EIS). Those systems remained in offices of executives and there were only a few of them. The objectives of those EISs were to merely display key financial measures through a simple interface. Unfortunately, in most cases, the data used were not sufficiently complete to provide accurate information to the executives. Because of that, there were only a few dashboards available and no new dashboards where developed, until the required information became increasingly more available in the right quantities and qualities.

In the 1990s, technologies such as data warehousing, online analytical processing and business intelligence all tried to work together to group and analyse the sprawl of information and information systems within companies. It became more and more important to collect, correct, integrate and access the data as accurate and useful as possible. This created new approaches to management. Most notably, one new approach involved the identification and use of key performance indicators: the balanced scorecard (BSC; Kaplan & Norton, 1992).

One might argue that the big acknowledgement of dashboards came with the Enron scandal in 2001. This scandal put new pressure on corporations to closely monitor what was going on in their companies, thereby assuring shareholders they were in control of their companies. This increased accountability pressured Chief Information Officers to find new ways to help managers at all levels to monitor performance more easily and efficiently. The solution to this was to create or buy easy to understand dashboard systems. Most, if not all, of the Business Intelligence (BI) vendors nowadays offers some kind of dashboard solution. Some of them newly designed, some of them just adjustments or extensions to other systems.

Common Mistakes

Overall, the fundamental challenge of dashboard design is the need to squeeze a great deal of information into a small space, resulting in a display that is easily and immediately understandable (Few, 2006). This can be done in several ways; one of them is to check for common mistakes in dashboard design. The thirteen most common mistakes in dashboard design that Few (2006) identifies are related to either data handling or screen development issues.

Data handling mistakes include supplying inadequate context for the data. Data needs a supporting cast to be successfully transferred. For example, a total quarterly sale presented without any reference to the previous quarter does not supply much information. This mistake is commonly made in financial and qualitative dashboards. Also, displaying excessive detail or precision. Dashboards are normally used to gain a quick overview. Too much detail will only slow viewers down without providing them with any additional benefits. To provide the details needed in the dashboard, filters can be built in to the dashboard. In that way, details can be set on or off. Or, choosing a deficient measure. For data to be meaningful, it must be clear what is being measured and this must be expressed in the correct units. The measure is deficient when it is not the clearest and most efficient way to communicate that data. Although it can be accurate, it might not be the best choice for the message. Some information has to be communicated in exact numbers, and some in percentages to provide for a clear view of the information. Furthermore, choosing inappropriate display media. There are a lot of different ways to display data. It is very important to use the right display of data when showing information. This will be discussed in depth in the upcoming section 'Display of data'. Not to mention the issue of introducing meaningless variety. Some designers tend to think that using the same type of display medium multiple times will bore viewers. Therefore, they introduce different kinds of display medium, which will eventually just confuse the viewer. The means of display must be selected according to which display works best, even if that results in a dashboard filled with multiple instances of the same type of graph. The consistency in the display of data allows users to use the same perceptual strategy for interpreting the data, which saves time and energy. And what about encoding quantitative data inaccurately? Problems of this kind exist, for example, when the quantitative scale along the vertical axes for a bar graph does not start at 0. This gives a distorted view, so the start of the vertical axe should always be 0. The final data handling related problem in dashboard design is highlighting important data ineffectively or not at all. In a dashboard, attention should be drawn to information that is most relevant. This information has to be made visually attractive, in a way that it jumps out of the other, less useful, information.

Screen development issues include exceeding the boundaries of a single screen. Most information is picked up when the information is within eye span. Critical information can be lost when the user loses sight of some data by scrolling or switching screens. This is because people are able to hold just a little bit of information in their short-term memory. Therefore, people might not remember information that they no longer see. Also, misusing or overusing colour. When correctly used, colours can help viewers to understand the data in the dashboard. When incorrectly used however, colours can attract attention to the wrong parts of the dashboard. The use of colour will be discussed at a more detailed level in section 2.4. This is highly related to using poorly designed display media. A common mistake with poorly designed display media is using very bright colours, which creates overkill. Another mistake can be using too similar colours, making it difficult to distinguish between data sets. Apart from applying wrong colour schemes, there is also the problem of arranging the data poorly. Dashboards often need to present a large amount of information in a limited space. This data has to be organized well, or it will result in an unclear mess. The goal is not to simply make the dashboard look good, but to arrange the data in a manner that fits the way the dashboard is used. The most important data should be prominent on first sight. Data that requires immediate attention has to stand out. Data that should be compared has to be arranged and visually designed to encourage those comparisons. And another issue may be cluttering the display with useless decoration. Dashboards sometimes tend to be abundant with useless decoration. Attempts are made to make them look like a car dashboard or an electronic control panel. If this is not the main objective of the dashboard, it is just visual garbage that the viewer has to process before getting to the data. The final screen development related problem in dashboard design that Few (2006) discusses is designing an unattractive visual display. Some dashboards are just ugly. This can be a distraction when using the dashboard, so it should be avoided. When making the design of a dashboard, it must be kept simple, yet attractive.

In addition to the above mentioned thirteen common mistakes in dashboard design, there are three common early failures indicators. Those early failure symptoms were described by Eckerson (2011) and are leading factors within the design of dashboards. A developer designing a dashboard should always bear the following early failure symptoms in mind.

1. **Too Flat:** Dashboards can be considered too flat, when they do not provide enough data or analytical capabilities to let users explore the problems highlighted in the graphical indicators.
2. **Too Manual:** Some organizations tend to rely too heavily on manual methods to update dashboards with sizable amounts of information. In this way, people spend several days a week on collecting the data, instead of analysing it. Dashboards should provide methods for the automatic collection and delivery of information.
3. **Too Isolated:** Some dashboards do not show an enterprise a view of the whole system or organization. These dashboards only show management information on a small part of the organization, leading to confusion or tunnel vision with the managers.

Data Visualization

According to Eckerson (2011), a dashboard should consist of three layers: monitoring, analysing and drilling down. This approach is called the MAD-framework. With this technique, each layer provides additional details, views and perspectives. This layered approach gives the users access to additional information and conforms to the natural sequence in which users want to handle that information.

The first layer is used for monitoring, and to provide a graphical view of performance metrics, usually in the form of graphics. This layer is essentially a visual report.

The middle layer has to be optimized for analysing the data perceived in the monitoring layer, and consists of dimensional data and lets the users the possibility to drill down to the information in the bottom layer.

The bottom layer is used to drill down to detail. In this last layer it is possible to drill down to single persons or actions.

Typically, with the MAD framework, the number of metrics and users increases when moving down in the layers. The first layer is primarily used by executives, the second layer by analysts and the third layer by day-to-day workers. In smaller companies and dashboard systems, the MAD framework also works but with a greater overlay between the different layers. In the case of smaller companies, the third layer will be used as well by workers as by executives and the difference between the layers is less clear-cut.

A key point is: for strategic dashboards the quality of the data is key, not the quantity. Simon et al. (2006) show that dashboards in healthcare organizations are mostly used for clinical quality, efficiency, and safety in the organization.

Visual Perception

Vision is a very powerful human sense. Seeing and thinking are intimately connected. Vision dominates our sensory landscape, which is important to keep in mind when designing dashboards. The human visual system automatically looks for patterns. This quality can be translated into rules for displaying information. Following perception-based rules, we can present our data in such a way that the important and informative patterns stand out, which makes the overall dashboard much more comprehensible and useful.

Our eyes cannot register everything that is visible in the world around us, but only what is in their span of perception. The brain looks for tell-tale signs, and filters out the useful information. Only a portion of what our eyes sense becomes an object of focus. It is then transferred to the memory, which comes in three types (Few, 2006):

1. Iconic memory,
2. Short term memory,
3. Long term memory.

In the iconic memory, the information is briefly kept until it can be processed to the short-term memory. In this research, the short-term memory is the most important memory type, as the short-term memory stores the information for processing. The short-term memory can only store three to nine *chunks* of visual information at a time. When the short-term memory is full, some of those chunks have to move to the long-term memory or they have to be removed from the memory altogether. This is the reason that information which belongs together should never be fragmented into multiple screens and scrolling should not be required to see this information. Once the information is no longer seen, it can easily be removed from the short-term memory. In that case, the information is no longer available for the brain to process. You have to switch back to the previous view to see that information again. This makes it very difficult to make good comparisons between information.

What a 'chunk' of information constitutes depends on the nature of the objects we are seeing, their design and our familiarity with the objects. Well-designed graphical patterns for instance, can be stored as one chunk. Individual numbers are also stored as one chunk. This is one of the great advantages of using graphics over text. There are some visual rules on which dashboards can be designed to use a natural flow in the dashboard, and chunk information optimal together for the most efficient understanding and perception of the data. Those rules are discussed below.

Gestalt Psychology

It is important for a dashboard to work in a natural way. The design and display of information in a dashboard have a great share in this natural flow of information. Using a natural and clear flow in a dashboard facilitates an easier incorporation of knowledge than a dashboard that does not obey this natural way of working. Important work here has been done within the field of *Gestalt psychology*. The German word *Gestalt* simply means pattern in English. *Gestalt psychology* is a theory of mind and brain, started back in 1912, but it is still very useful today. The fundamental principle underlying *Gestalt*-perception is the Law of Prägnanz, which, in short, states that individuals tend to order things in their mind in a manner which is regular, orderly, symmetric, and simple. We discuss this with regard to the Law of Prägnanz and seven more laws in *Gestalt psychology* to help structure and organize the information in the mind below (Todorović, 2008; Gestalt psychology, 2016).

- **Law of Proximity:** According to the Law of Proximity, when a person sees multiple objects, the objects close to each other seem to form a group. According to this, several objects can be visually associated to form a group. Figure 1 (top-left) shows an example of the proximity law. In this image there are 72 circles, but instead of seeing those individual circles, the human mind perceives them as four separate groups of circles. Three separate groups of 12 circles on the right hand, and one big group of 36 on the left hand.
- **Law of Common Fate:** According to the Law of Common Fate, objects that move together belong together. When from each group of circles in Figure 1 one circle starts to move, it will be perceived that it is a group, even though it is not a group according to the one of the other laws.
- **Law of Similarity:** According to the Law of Similarity, multiple similar objects in a group of objects will be perceived as belonging together. This occurs whether or not this similarity really exists. The perceived similarity can occur on different levels, such as colour, form of shape, shading or other qualities. In the image at the top-right of Figure 1, there are 36 circles. For most people, the rows are grouped together consisting of coloured and not coloured circles, instead of seeing the circles apart.
- **Law of Closure**: According to the Law of Closure, individuals perceive objects as being whole even if they are not complete. This can occur with all kinds of objects such as shapes, letters, pictures, and the like. When parts of a whole picture are missing, our perception fills in the visual gap. In Figure 1, bottom-left, there is an example of the law of closure. People perceive to see a circle and a rectangle, wheras in fact there are none.

Figure 1. Gestalt principle examples
Reprinted from Gestalt psychology, 2016.

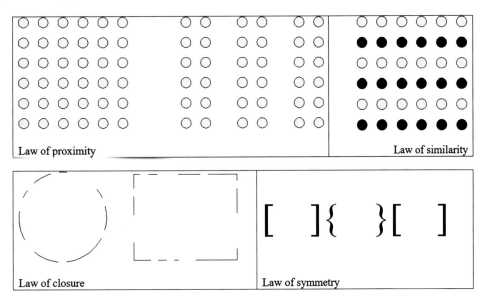

- **Law of Past Experience:** According to the Law of Past Experience, under some circumstances visual stimuli are categorized according to past experience of the mind. For example, if the mind has never seen an image before, it is still able to figure out what is on that image by pointing out the different known images from the larger image.
- **Law of Symmetry:** According to the Law of Symmetry, the mind perceives objects as being symmetrical and forming around one point. For the mind it is calmer to divide objects in to a number of symmetrical parts. The mind only has to remember one of those parts, to figure out what the counterpart is. When two symmetrical parts are unconnected, the mind perceived them to be connected to form a complete shape. Figure 1, bottom-right, shows six individual brackets, which are perceived to be three pairs of symmetrical brackets.
- **Law of Continuity:** According to the Law of Continuity, lines are perceived as if they are following the smoothest path. This occurs when we see a trend and we decide to follow it at a particular up or downwards scope. We tend continue following that line when we perceive them to be heading in an implied direction. When two lines intersect, the continuation of each line is still apparent.

When designing a dashboard, the above laws should be kept in mind. When the dashboard is designed with respect to those laws, it is more likely that the user will perceive the natural flow when using the dashboard, which likely results in a higher usability of the dashboard design.

Configurable Time Spans

Data in a dashboard can be viewed in different time frames. Typical examples are: current year to date, current week to date, current quarter to date, yesterday, and this month. Those time frames can be selected by quick choices. In dashboards, it should also be possible to select custom data. This makes the dashboard as flexible in time selection as possible. In that way, the user of the dashboard can adjust the time frame to the range needed at that moment.

Data Display

The layout of a dashboard is one of the major things contributing to its success. The basic structures for showing data are graphics, tables, and words. Often two or three of these devices should be combined (Tufte, 2007). Graphics, tables and words are different mechanisms with the same single purpose; the clear presentation of information. The best medium for displaying particular or specific data, however, will always be dependent on the nature of that data.

Graphics

An important thing to keep in mind is that graphics should only be used for richer, more complex, and more difficult statistical material. For less difficult statistical material, a table or textual overview is often better. According to Tufte and Roger (2007) graphical displays should at least always:

- Show the data,
- Induce the viewer to think about the content over form and methodology,
- Avoid distorting what the data has to say,
- Present many numbers in a small space,
- Make large datasets coherent,
- Encourage the eye to compare different pieces of data,
- Reveal the data at several levels of detail, from a broad overview to a finer structure,
- Serve a reasonable clear purpose: description, exploration, tabulation or decoration,
- Be closely integrated with the statistical and verbal description of the dataset.

There are a few principles to enhance graphical integrity. The two most important principles for this research are (1) that the representation of the numbers, as shown on the surface of the graphics itself, should be directly proportional to the numerical quantities represented, and (2) clear, detailed, and thorough labelling should be used to defeat graphical distortion and ambiguity. Any important data should be supported by written explanations on the graph.

Data-ink is the ink on the graph that represents the data in that graph. There is also ink called non-data-ink, which is used for grid lines and other information lines. According to Tufte (2007), when a graph serves as a look-up table, the grid lines should be muted or completely suppressed so that its presence is only implicit. In this way, the non-data-ink does not compete with the data-ink. If the diagram does not serve as a look-up table, the grid can be removed completely to show the data as clearly as possible.

Another very important thing about graphs is that graphs must be instantly understandable: 'if you have to explain it, don't use it.' Because of the user group of this particular medical system, it is very important to use easily understandable and clear graphics. Too much colour in a graph, for instance, often generates graphical puzzles. This is because the eye does not readily give a visual ordering to colours, except for red to reflect higher levels than other colours.

There are also some guidelines to create user-friendly data graphs. One of those guidelines deserves special attention and is about choosing colours which can be understood by people with a colour-deficiency or who suffer from colour-blindness. Colour-blindness affects a substantial portion of the human population. In individuals of Northern European ancestry, as many as 8% of men and 0.5% of women experience the common form of red-green colour blindness (Albrecht, 2010). For this reason, the colours picked for the graph used in the model should be suitable for colour-blind readers. The palette of eight colours shown in Figure 2 has good overall variability in colours and can be differentiated by individuals with red-green colour blindness. The P and D indicate simulated colours as seen by individuals with protanopia (P) and deuteranopia (D), respectively.

Shapes and Proportions

It is recommended to make the shape of the graphic more wide than tall. Wider-than-tall shapes usually make it easier for the eye to follow from left to right (Tukey, 1977). This is also in line with our normal sight. Our eye has evolved to detect deviations from the horizon, which is also more wide than tall. Graphics design should use this natural advantage. Furthermore, it is easier to write and read words from left to right. When the x-axis is wider than the y-axis, there is more space to write down the labels on the axis. The last point is that normally the causal influence is plotted on the horizontal axis. With a wider x-axis, there is more space to show the causal variable in more detail.

On a related note, a fifth century rule about the proportion of the axes is called the Golden Section. This rule states that the length of the horizontal axis should be approximately 1.618 times longer than the vertical axis. Most of the time, however, it should be taken into consideration how much the nature of the data suggests the shape of the diagram. This suggestion must be followed in designing the graphic (Livio, 2002).

Figure 2. Colors optimized for color-blind individuals

Color	Color name	RGB (1–255)	CMYK (%)	P	D
■	Black	0, 0, 0	0, 0, 0, 100	■	■
■	Orange	230, 159, 0	0, 50, 100, 0	■	■
■	Sky blue	86, 180, 233	80, 0, 0, 0	■	■
■	Bluish green	0, 158, 115	97, 0, 75, 0	■	■
■	Yellow	240, 228, 66	10, 5, 90, 0	■	■
■	Blue	0, 114, 178	100, 50, 0, 0	■	■
■	Vermillion	213, 94, 0	0, 80, 100, 0	■	■
■	Reddish purple	204, 121, 167	10, 70, 0, 0	■	■

Tables and Numbers

Tables are clearly the best way to show exact numerical values. In small datasets, this notation is preferable to graphics. According to Tufte (2007) and other designers, tables are nearly always better than the pie chart. Tables are known for their organized, sequential details, are easily readable and therefore tables also work well when the data requires many localized comparisons. The table is a good and straightforward method of showing data in the dashboard described in this paper.

Sentences and Words

In all dashboards, no matter how visually oriented, there is some information in the form of writing. However, the conventional sentence is considered a poor way to show more than two numbers because it prevents comparisons of data. The linearly organized flow of words, folded over at arbitrary points, offers only one effective dimension for organizing the data. For the reasons stated above, in this model should be made more use of tables and graphics and less use of sentences to describe the data.

Display Type

An important thing to take into consideration while designing an electronic dashboard, is on which kind of display it will be presented. The dashboard described in this research will be designed to be shown on a computer screen, rather than a tablet computer or mobile (smart) phone. This distinction is important because the screen resolution differs between systems. The most widely used screen resolution for computer screens in 2012 was 1024*768, and in 2016 is 1366*768, and higher (W3Schools, 2012). This made us design the system of our case study to be at most 1000 pixels in width, in order to prevent scrolling bars from appearing on the horizontal side of the computer screen. More key design considerations regarding BI implementations are provided in Verkooij & Spruit (2013).

SINGLE CASE STUDY RESEARCH

We performed a single case study at the Dutch SME CareSoft. Their product YBoard implements a dashboard which displays management information for an Electronic Health Record (EHR) in long-term and chronic healthcare. At the time of this research, their version 1.x series of YBoard has become a popular solution within the chronic and long-term care domain. However, due to various reasons, together with CareSoft we set out to completely redesign the EHR management solution to realize a more effective and usable 2.x series of the product.

Data Collection

To uncover how a more effective and sustainable management dashboard for YBoard should be designed, we first interviewed five of the end-users of the current system for their input in the functions and design of the management screens. This was done because different studies show that it is highly recommended that (potential) end-users are involved in the early design and creation of the dashboard. It is advisable because of the experience they have in their own organizations and the systems they use. With the help of end-users in the design of a dashboard, suggestions of functionalities and design questions can be incorporated which the designer would not normally think about.

End-users are typically great at articulating issues and problems with current systems, and identifying which features should be developed first and which are of lower priority. By interviewing end-users and using their suggestions there is a potentially high acceptance of the final product, because the users feel respected in their needs. A downside to this strategy is that users are usually not great in offering solutions, but they are great at identifying problems and needs. For most cases, problems are easily identifiable but solutions are harder to find.

Interviewing Method

For this research, two rounds of interviews were held with five current users of the YBoard system. Those users are handpicked by CareSoft. These five current users are representative for the end users of the management screens which need to be developed for the YBoard system. The first round of exploratory interviews was held in week 49 of 2012 and was intended to discover some key features of the system. The second round of evaluation interviews was held in week 10 of 2013 and was intended to discuss the designed prototype with the end-users, and to find improvements in this first design. The results of the exploratory interviews are described in this chapter under three different sub-headings. These are: General remarks, Selections and information and Comparisons. This subdivision follows the course of the interviews.

Users of YBoard were interviewed from five companies, as shown in Table 1.

The first and second interview in the first round progressed relatively unstructured. This approach was chosen in order to be certain that the interviewee was not pushed in a certain direction, and so to see what the interviewee would come up with. After the first two interviews, it appeared that this was not an ideal method because the interviewees asked for data in the management screen that was not (yet) available in YBoard. This probably occurred because they were confused with other systems in the organization. The last three interviews in the first round where held according to a more structured approach, with a list of managerial questions the interviewee was asked to prioritize. It appeared that this was a better approach to get the desired workable results. All the interviews started with a short introduction to explain the reason for the interview. Some interviews were held with just one person, the responsible manager and in others other people were present, such as a controller or another YBoard user. In the next paragraph, there is no distinction in the interviews with a single interviewee, and those where more people were involved.

Table 1. Interviewed YBoard customer organizations

Name	Location	Kind of Care	Total Clients	# of Locations
1PergaCare	Echt	Chronic	1400	36
2OsiraCare	Amsterdam	Long-term	3100	23
3ZuidoostCare	Drachten	Long-term	1500	14
4FlorenceCare	Rijswijk	Long-term	2200	45
5NoorderCare	Leeuwarden	Long-term	1400	15

Results of Exploratory Interviews

In all five interviews it was pointed out that a dashboard is a welcome and much needed addition to the current functionalities of the system. According to the interviewed professionals, a dashboard will save time in performing management and patient healthcare tasks.

Quotes on General Requirements

1. **PergaCare:** "We look for a better way to control and monitor specialized healthcare personnel, a management system will give me the information needed for this."
2. **OsiraCare:** "Even though we are still implementing YBoard and I am not yet working with it, a dashboard for overall management information is for me a key point to use YBoard. I am not that much interested in client information, but more in the whole picture. How is my team doing?"
3. **ZuidoostCare:** "Accumulated information would be great, but when I have a more overall overview it would already help a lot. It is important that it is possible to classify user between different user groups."
4. **FlorenceCare:** "There is a need for more information about the registered Diagnostic Treatment Combination (DBC) information. This information is already available at the client level in YBoard, but not yet available as management information. The information has to be real-time and up to date. An export of all the information in YBoard would be great for starters. In that way, our controllers can do their own calculations on the numbers."
5. **NoorderCare:** "We are very interested in such screens, especially for DBC information at the client level. Currently time is tracked by the healthcare providers in Excel and sent to the backoffice, which enters it in Excel. This is a very time consuming way of processing the information. If this could be done is YBoard and YBoard would give meaningful reports, it would save a lot of time."

Quotes on Selections and Information

1. **PergaCare:** "Selection criteria can be age, or nature of disease. It is important to classify the different groups clearly. "
2. **OsiraCare:** "Interesting information would be specific information about some key figures of the different locations. For example, the number of CPR-certificates filled in. Currently there is no automation available for acquiring this information."
3. **ZuidoostCare:** "It is important that there is a possibility to differentiate between different locations, because there are many differences between different (sub) locations. It is also important to classify users in different user groups."
4. **FlorenceCare:** "Interesting selection criteria would be ICPC codes and number of reports per employee. In that way, we can see if our employees do report their work and we can subdivide the different groups of clients."
5. **NoorderCare:** "Most interestingly are the reports about DBC information. An example is information about the mean treatment duration. Selections can be on diagnosis, or on age of gender. It would be good to add a number of different selections methods."

Quotes on Comparisons

1. **PergaCare:** "The treatment groups vary in our chronic healthcare centres, so it is difficult to make comparisons between those groups. It would be interesting to make comparisons in between groups between different locations or wards."
2. **OsiraCare:** "It should be possible to make comparisons between different target groups on different locations. To compare, for example, the personnel from a certain discipline on the one location in comparison to the personnel from that same discipline on another location."
3. **ZuidoostCare:** "With the selection made to differentiate the clients in different groups, it is important that it is possible to compare those groups with each other. In that way, we can find discrepancies between different groups or locations."
4. **FlorenceCare:** "For the DBC information, comparisons are not very important in the beginning. It is important however, it is more important that the system can export data for our own use."
5. **NoorderCare:** "Comparisons between different locations would be very useful, but there must be a possibility to select which clients or employees to compare."

CONCLUSIONS BASED ON EXPLORATORY INTERVIEWS

The first round of interviews confirmed that there was indeed a need for a management dashboard in YBoard. The interviews also gave some valuable insight into which kind of information is considered important for managers and controllers.

Some of the interviewed managers and controllers asked for a database export of the information of a selected user group, or all users. This suggests that those users or their subordinates have a thorough knowledge of Excel or another statistical program, and so they can perform their own queries on this export. With such an export, people can get all the possible information they want from the system.

Another insight is that there is a strong need for implementing the management screens, at least for DBC information. Because of an amendment of the law in the Netherlands, since January 1, 2013, healthcare providers only get paid for the medical rehabilitation healthcare they really provide and can prove. Therefore, all the medical professionals have to keep track of their hours in regard to rehabilitation healthcare to make it possible for the finance department to send the final bill to the health insurance of the specific clients. Even though it is already possible to track time in YBoard for DBC clients, it is also important to have a managerial overview of that information.

The interviews also showed that the choice of comparing different (sub) locations with each other received wide consensus. It should also be noted that the interviewees asked for a great range of selection criteria on the different (sub) locations, so that they can subdivide the big client or employee group of the different (sub) locations into smaller groups. With those smaller groups it is more useful and helpful to make comparisons.

The interviews also helped to prioritize the managerial questions, prepared by the CareSoft staff. With this prioritization, the implementation of the dashboard can be performed step-by-step. In this way, any (design) errors can be detected in an early stage before too much potential work is lost.

The last insight the interviews provided was that, for the managers, DBC is a very important group of clients. A DBC client is not just *a* client, but a 'special' client. When the DBC option is enabled in YBoard, these clients are given a different status and more / different options than other clients. For DBC clients, it is mandatory for employees to register time. It may be concluded from this information there are actually three groups of persons in YBoard; employees, clients and DBC-clients.

All in all, from the interviews conducted in this research, key data appeared to be having a good and clear selection process of the target group. With that selected target group, it must be possible to create a view of what kind of healthcare is provided to different selections of groups, and to compare this selection between locations and branches within the same organization.

THE BI DASHBOARD FOR YBOARD 2.0

YBoard is a major EHR system in long-term and chronic healthcare. According to CareSoft, other available systems are mostly just modules added to current accounting systems of healthcare institutes and these modules are not optimized for use as EHRs. The decision to use extension modules is often based on the idea of having just one supplier for all, or most, of the systems used.

YBoard is especially designed for use as an EHR in long-term and chronic healthcare, and therefore provides some specific functions which are not covered in the extension modules of other systems. YBoard is developed and tested by dozens of doctors, psychologists and paramedics in nursing homes and institutions for the mentally disabled. Because of this development in association with people who are actually using it, YBoard is specifically attuned to the needs of those users. YBoard is an EHR in the cloud, so all of the users automatically make use of the newest version available (*e.g.* Abdat, Spruit, & Bos, 2011). This is an advantage because there is no possibility of using an older, possibly more insecure and unstable, version of the system.

In the current version 1.0 of YBoard, decision making, healthcare coordination and improvement of performance are not yet used to its full potential. The information of the patients is available, but only on patient level. For managers, it is important to have an option to create an overview of the company as a whole. Therefore, the new version of YBoard needs a dashboard to display the medical information in a more efficient way.

User Group

The user group of YBoard consists of doctors and managers in the long-term and chronic healthcare branch of Medicare. Most of the medical professionals are used to working with computers and information systems (Lupiáñez-Villanueva et al., 2010). For the YBoard users, information systems knowledge is even more explicit because they already have experience in working with YBoard. Some of the users already have experience with other, in-house developed management screens. Therefore, it can be assumed that knowledge of computers and information systems is sufficient within this user group.

Notable constraints of this user group are that they mostly have a busy schedule, and do not have much time to learn a completely new system. Therefore, the management screens should be easily accessible, and clear within an instant of usage.

Dashboard Design

In dashboard design, the guiding principle should always be simplicity: the data must be displayed as simply and clearly as possible, and unnecessary and distracting decoration must be avoided. Because of this, dashboards have to be well organized, concise, customized to the user and they must communicate the data as clearly and directly as possible. The best way of condensing lots of information is via summarization. The most commonly used summarizations on a dashboard are summing and averaging.

Another important point in the design is to address the information in the vocabulary of the audience. The users of this particular dashboard are medical professionals, therefore, the terms used in the dashboard should match the language used in their profession and in the rest of this EHR.

For this dashboard, a step-by-step approach is used. In the first part, a selection is made of the data which is sought. In the second part, the data is shown. In practice, presumably the steps will be used interchangeably when the dashboard is online. This does not affect the working of the dashboard.

The starting point of this research project was to do research in order to develop a dashboard for the EHR of CareSoft. In the sections above, the background information about EHRs and creating and designing of dashboards was given. This chapter will describe the final design of the dashboard, and the live version as added to the actual online product YBoard 2.0.

In this dashboard there are three main variables, which have to be presented. The first variable is the selected population; this can either be Clients, Employees or DBC-clients. The second variable is the location. From which location(s) does the dashboard need to show the data? This can be up to two different locations, which are visually displayed by the line in the diagram. According to the interviewed end-users, comparing two locations was enough to start with. With two locations, it is most effective to make a clear comparison. Technically, when feedback shows that there is a need to, it is possible to add more locations to compare at a later moment. The third variable can differ, is easily expandable and is displayed on the X-axis. For example time; to what timescale does the data refer? The time is set to one month as standard, but can be adjusted to day, year, or any manually selected period. It can also be the (average) record time in the specific location; what is the average record time in the home for the elderly? This variable can be extended with other variables when suited.

The First Sketch

The first sketch of the design was made with Microsoft Visio, and is displayed in Figure 3. This sketch was based on the YBoard layout, and was made before any interviews were held. It was primarily based on literature and exploratory discussions with CareSoft. With the presentation of this first design, it quickly appeared that it was not clear for users within the first moment of sight. Because of this, it was decided to start again completely with creating a new design.

The Second Sketch

The next sketch was made after doing more literature research and the interviews held with the medical professionals and end-users of the system. This second sketch in Figure 4 was made in Excel and is the basis for the final design of the dashboard, which is described in this section. It was decided to split the dashboard selection up into three different steps. Those steps, and where you are in the selecting process, are visually displayed with the status bar in the top of the screen. Even though it is just a quick three-step

Figure 3. YBoard design version 1, sketched in MS Visio

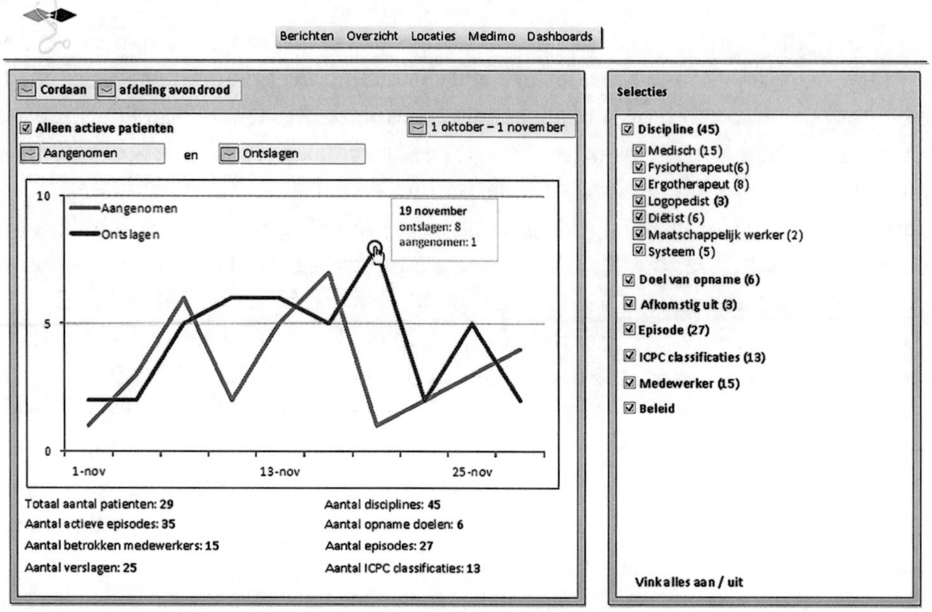

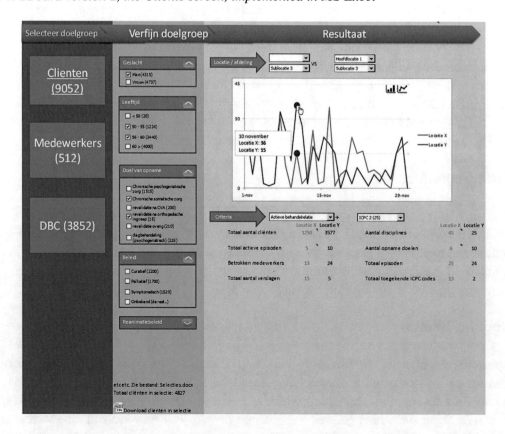

Figure 4. YBoard version 2, the Clients screen, implemented in MS Excel

selection process, it is still important to give users as much feedback as possible about progress. The layout of the dashboard is explained below following those steps.

The Third and Final Design

The final design of the management dashboard is a refinement of the second design as presented in Figure 4. The three steps in this dashboard are (1) select user group, (2) select population (of that user group) and (3) show the results of the selection. In this way, it is a very clear step-by-step approach to get to the final results. Figure 9 displays the steps in the selection process graphically. In the final design, the choice was made to always display the data with reference to one of more different branches or locations. This approach was tested with a couple of small use cases and specifically asked about in the interviews. The interviewees all reacted positively on the possibility of comparing different locations with each other.

The First Step

The first step in the dashboard is selecting the group whose data is shown in the next steps. The first step is shown in Figure 6.

This step allows the user to select the user group. This domain selection is about for which group you want to display information. There are three different groups in the domain selection; Clienten 'patients,' Medewerkers 'employees' and DBC 'Treatment codes'. This differentiation is made because these are the three main groups about which information is recorded in YBoard. In this case, DBC is a special group of clients and therefore a separate selection.

DBC-clients are a relative new kind of client, and there are a lot of questions about those clients from the YBoard-users. It could be technically possible to place DBCclients within the client selection, but in consultation with the medical professionals and the CareSoft team, the choice was made to approach DBC-clients as a separate group.

For any other system those groups can be extended or narrowed to fewer or more user groups, depending on the groups in the system. In other systems, it may make sense to use the selection 'men' or 'women' or 'in house clients' and 'external clients'. The main reason for this first selection is to narrow the group down to a specific target group, from where you can drill down as specific as wanted or needed.

Figure 5. Conceptual lay-out of YBoard

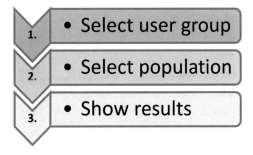

259

Figure 6. Step 1

The Second Step

In the second step shown in Figure 7, the user has to specify the population which he chose in the first step. The population can be selected by specific characters of the group selected. Specific characters applying to all groups are Geslacht 'sex' and Leeftijd 'age.' To give the user as much freedom as possible, the user can fill in an age range. Some selections are group-specific like Reanimatiebeleid 'CPR-policy' for clients or 'field of profession' for employees. All selection criteria, except for age, are checkboxes which means that it is possible to select more than one to make a selection as broad as possible. The advantage of working with a special step for making selections is that, in this way, the system is easily expandable. When more (patient or employee) information is added to YBoard, the selection step can easily be expanded with this information.

The different selection options are folded by default, and can be unfolded when needed. The selections in this step are filters, they apply when checked. Because in the YBoard system all selections are unchecked by default, it was decided to continue along this line in the dashboard so as to not confuse users. When none of the filters are active, the whole group selected in the first step is shown on the dashboard.

At the bottom of the selection, it is possible to download all the clients made in the selection above in a .csv file. This option was added in response to the specific wish of the interviewed end users.

Figure 7. Step 2

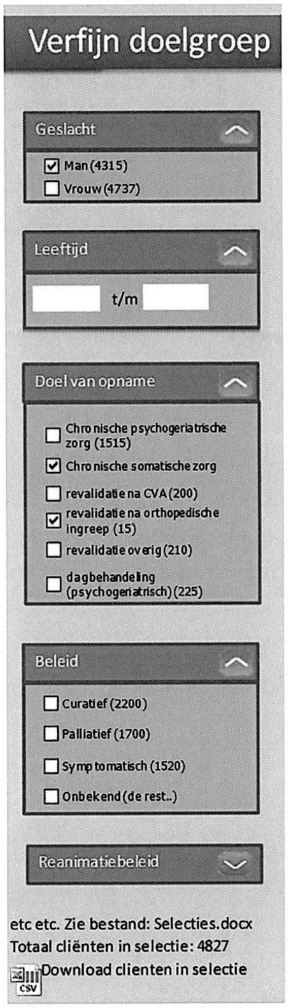

The Third Step

This last step is the result screen as shown in Figure 8. In this last step, it is possible to select two locations for comparison. The numbers underneath the location give the information of four key information points. This makes it easy to compare key data of the selected locations. It is also possible to select 'all' locations, for a company-wide overview. In a later stage, the two locations are easily expandable if needed. The colours used in this screen are colour-blind friendly colours.

When hovering with the mouse over a point in the graph, information about that specific point occurs. In the top right corner, it is possible to switch between a line and a bar graph. Underneath that switch, there is the possibility of quickly selecting different time frames. Time frames can be today, the past week, the past year or the last year. The time frame can also be selected with a slider on the X-axis. On top of the Y-axis, there is a switch between percentage and absolute numbers. This is needed when the user wants to compare two different locations with different numbers of clients.

For some kinds of data, it is better to have a different X-axis than a specific time frame. An example is the length of stay in a specific location. In that case, it is better to have the different times of stay on the X-axis and the number of clients staying that specific time. The type of graphic can be changed with the dropdown box in the lower right corner. The choice of using a dropdown box for this is because of the ease of expandability. In this first version of the dashboard, at client level, it is only possible to see the movement of the selection in a specific time frame and to see the average length of stay of the selection. At the DBC level, however, the possibility of viewing three different kinds of X-axis has already been implemented. It can be imagined that different kinds of graphics at client and employee level will be added in time.

Applied Laws from Gestalt Theory

Two of the greatest challenges in dashboard design are to make important data stand out, and to arrange disparate data in an effective way, giving it significance. The dashboard above is designed with regard to the *Prägnanz* principle, which means that following the steps in the dashboard has been made as regular, orderly, symmetric, and simple as possible. Therefore, most of the laws from *Gestalt* Theory are applied to the dashboard. This part describes which laws are applied and in what manner.

- **Law of Proximity:** The Law of Proximity is used in the design of the second step. This step is always built up from the header and the subs of a selection grouped together, i.e. sex and the two

Figure 8. Step 3

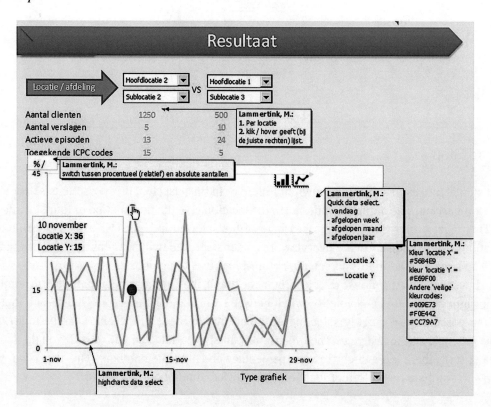

different sexes. Because of the colour and borders for the grouping used, it is clear that 'men' and 'women' are choices on the 'sex' header. The Law of Proximity is also used in the statistics underneath the different location in the third step. The name of the statistic and the corresponding number is placed next to each other with the location above, which suggests correctly that that name, number and location belong together.

- **Law of Similarity:** The first use of the Law of Similarity is that whatever first selection of user group is made, step two and three are the same. These steps may have different options, but the layout of step two and three is the same for all the groups selected in step one. Another application of the Law of Similarity is that in the second step all the different headers have the same layout. Therefore, the user concludes that underneath the other header(s) in that step there is some kind of submenu with a number of choices. A last application of the Law of Similarity is that the different locations are always the same colour, whatever selection criteria are chosen.

- **Law of Closure:** The Law of Closure is used in the choice of the line chart. The line chart suggests that the space underneath that chart belongs to the chart.

- **Law of Symmetry:** The Law of Symmetry is first of all applied in the width of the three columns. The first and second columns are both the same width, the last screen is three times that width. The selection boxes in the first and second step are also related to the same width, and therefore visually related to each other. This consistent use of sizes gives a feeling of symmetry to the system.

- **Law of Common Fate:** The three steps approach in the design indicates the position of the user in the selecting process. The active step is highlighted by a different colour than the previous and next step(s). In this way, the step in the selecting process is clear to the user in the blink of an eye. An arrow-shaped path was chosen to indicate the path to follow. The Law of Common Fate is also used in the choice of colours. The colour range selected for the three columns, dark to light, suggests following the path in that direction, from dark to light.

- **Law of Continuity:** This law is applied in the visual display of the data. The data is displayed in a line chart. The line charts can cross each other. For the user it is still clear what line they are following because of the colour and implied path of the line.

- **Law of Past Experience:** The Law of Past Experience is applied in order to show the users they are still in the YBoard system, this with respect to the colours used in other parts of the system. The Law of Past Experiences is also used in the graphic visualization of the system. Because widely known and accepted graphic visualizations such as line and bar charts are used, people recognize the visual presentation and are able to read it in the way they should without any additional schooling needed.

Avoided Common Mistakes

In the theoretical background to this research in Section 2, common mistakes in dashboard design were reviewed. This dashboard has been designed with those common mistakes in mind, to avoid making known errors again. Those common mistakes are briefly described again in this chapter, and thereby the solution found to it in this design.

- **Exceeding the Boundaries of a Single Screen:** In this design, all data are shown in one screen. This is done with the use of selections that can fold in and out, in order not to exceed the boundaries of the screen. The most commonly used resolution worldwide was also kept in mind.

- **Supplying Inadequate Context for the Data and Displaying Excessive Detail or Precision:** In the design it is possible to compare different locations. As stated, this mistake is more common in financial dashboards and does not really apply here. The design uses filtering methods to counter the excessive detail mistake. The main group can be as detailed or as broad as needed for the desired results.

- **Choosing a Deficient Measure, Choosing Inappropriate or Poorly Designed Display Media:** A mixture of visual and textual display was used to show the data. To easily compare key data between different locations possible, these data are displayed right underneath that location and next to each other. This allows the user to easily compare locations. This is, according to the theory and interviews, the most effective way of displaying the data.

- **Introducing Meaningless Variety or Encoding Quantitative Data Inaccurately:** There is no meaningless variety in the dashboard, because only tables, bar and line charts are used with the axes starting at the zero point. In this way, it is clear how the data displayed must be interpreted.

- **Arranging the Data Poorly**: The data are very well ordered. This refers to the step-by-step approach described earlier. Because of this step-by-step approach, it is clear where all data belong and what it adds to the overall view.

- **Highlighting Important Data Ineffectively or not at all:** In this dashboard, no highlighting data are used. This is because the dashboard does not give real-time day-to-day information to monitor.

- **Cluttering the Display with Useless Decoration or Design an Unattractive Display:** There is no useless decoration in the design. every bit of information is deliberately available and belongs in the dashboard.

- **Misusing or Overusing Colour:** The colours used in this dashboard are all colour-blind friendly colours. Attention has also been paid to the background colours, which help users in following the path in the selection process.

Initial YBoard Product Release

After a month of development, a first version of the management tool was made available for use by the developers behind YBoard. This first version is based on the mock-ups above and was designed in line with the encompassing YBoard system. Because YBoard is a SaaS EHR, it is constantly updated to the latest version. In this first version, only the DBC tool is available because of the great need for this tool in the long-term healthcare institutes. Since then, other functions of the management tool, like employee and client, have been added as well to the online version of the tool. Figure 9 shows a screenshot of the DBC screen of the management tool in YBoard as of April 9, 2013.

Results of Evaluation Interviews

The second round of interviews was held in week 10 of 2013 and was intended to discuss the designed prototype with the end-users, and to find improvements in this first design. The working prototype was barely finished that week, so the interview leaned largely on the sketches of the design. All of the interviews started with a short introduction about what was done in the last weeks. It was made clear that developing such a sytem in only a couple of weeks was something very unusual, and therefore special. Unfortunately, it was not possible for all of the interviewees from the first round to come to the second

Figure 9. Initial product release of the management dashboard in YBoard 2.0

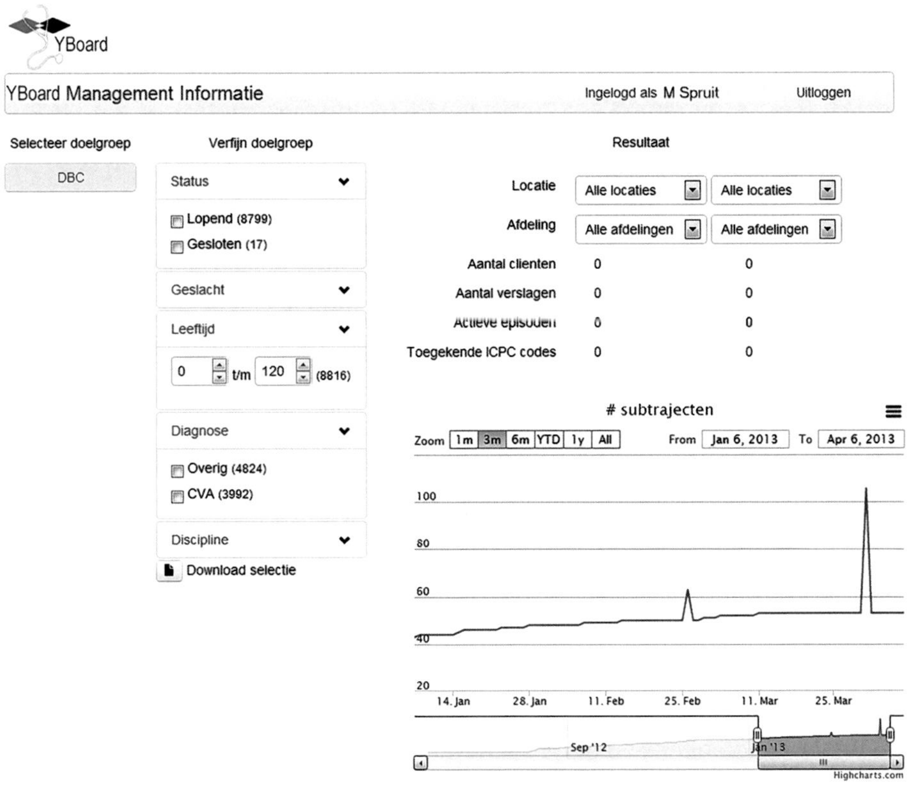

round of interviews. The three interviewees for the second round were employees from 4FlorenceCare, 5NoorderCare and 2OsiraCare.

The results of the interviews are described in this chapter under five different sub-headings. Those sub-headings are: General impression, Client selection, Employee selection, DBC selection and other remarks. This subdivision follows the pattern of the second round of interviews.

General Impression

- **4FlorenceCare:** "We already watched the prototype online and there a lot of ambiguities about the functionality of the management screens. We want more financial information in the system. We soon need to declare the first DBC costs out of YBoard. In our view, the layout is clear and simple, but there is still some work to do on the different selections. It is great however that we can download our selection in CSV format."
- **5NoorderCare:** "Unfortunately we did not have time to go through the system beforehand, so this will be the first impression. On this first impression it looks good, with a clear distinction between clients, employees and currently most importantly: DBC's."
- **2OsiraCare:** "We did not watch the management screens online, because we are still implementing YBoard. Not everybody has yet access to the YBoard system. What we see of the sketches is that it is very specific, maybe even too specific."

Client Selection

- **4FlorenceCare:** "In addition to the medical policy and reanimation headings, it is also important to add a heading for compulsory hospitalization. For some of the clients in the nursing homes the admission is compulsory, for example for elderly with dementia. It is important that the status of this is entered in the dossier. Further, the client selection is very extensive and most certainly helpful for doctors. It is a great tool to check the completeness of the dossier. "

- **5NoorderCare:** "The big absentee in this list of selections is the heading for compulsory hospitalization. This will get more and more important, because there is a change in the law on this point underway. The selection with the different therapists is in our case too extensive. In addition to a music therapist, we have certain other therapists. They do not have to be named all separately. This can be on a joint heading 'therapists.'"

- **2OsiraCare:** "This list with selections is extensive, maybe even too extensive. It is a good thing that the headings which are not used can be folded. This makes it stay clear. On certain wards it is mandatory to have a compulsory hospitalization declaration. A compulsory hospitalization heading is most certainly a good extension to the current list of selections. With this client selection, the record keeping per ward can be checked. This is a needed function."

Employee Selection

- **4FlorenceCare:** "The male/female selection is a unnecessary addition to the employee selection. Interesting information on the employee selection is in our view for example: How many physiotherapists have a treatment relation with a certain client. It would also be interesting to see a list of all the medical professionals to do comparisons on workload, and treatment relationships with clients."

- **5NoorderCare:** "It would be interesting to see if all the employees adhere to their own agreements. When there is the agreement to use certain forms in a particular group of employees, does everybody use those forms? It would also be useful to see the number of reports and clients per employee. This is useful for the managers, but also for the employees themselves."

- **2OsiraCare:** "Interesting information would be how much time employees spend on direct and indirect work. It would also be a good addition to see if there are enough reports written by the employees. It is not necessary to lead this back to certain employees; it would be enough to see this information by discipline per ward.

DBC Selection

- **4FlorenceCare:** "The DBC group is an important and a new group of clients. Depending on the amount of healthcare given to DBC clients, we get paid from the insurer. It is important that every employee keeps track and reports his or hers work regarding to DBC clients. What we miss in this screen is more financial information. A DBC route can be declared by the insurer when it is closed for 42 days. For us, it is important to see which routes are closed and are ready for declaration. In the screens now developed, we can see for how long clients are treated, but we cannot see how much that treatment will yield. We want to see of our costs and earnings are in line with each other. "

- **5NoorderCare:** "We compared the selection possibilities in the YBoard management screens with our own wishes, and that turned out to be in high accordance. We do not particularly want financial information in YBoard, because we have other systems to take care of that. An interesting point can be an overview in absence days. The absence days are visible per client, but an overall view per location can be interesting. This does not have priority. All in all, the selection criteria are complete enough for now."
- **2OsiraCare:** "The first use of this management tool is that we are able to see whether employees even register any hours. This is important for the declaration in a later stadium. In the diagnose heading, there is now a choice between only two options. There is a formal classification in four options, it would be better to use that formal classification."

Other Remarks

- **4FlorenceCare:** "It is very helpful that there is an export to Excel function. In that way we can do our own company-specific calculations on the data. The system now developed is a very extensive tool for doctors and other practitioners, but in our view not so much for other managers. We want to make our financial reports in YBoard, and use the management tool for these reports. Therefore, in our view it would be useful to make a fourth group in the first step, called financial."
- **5NoorderCare:** "Is would be a great addition when it is possible to make an Excel sheet from the information in the management tool. We are happy with what is developed now, although we see that there is still some work needed to be done. It is important to realize that the information now presented in a line chart, are in fact separate dots. A bar graph would be more appropriate on this point."
- **2OsiraCare:** "The answers you get on the interviews may be coloured because of the people you contacted for the interviews. It is possible that I focus on different points than other (future) users of the system. However, the first sketches are very promising and it is good to see that this first part of the system is ready for use. It is especially good to check the completeness of the client dossiers."

Evaluation Summary

The second round of interviews confirmed that a good start with designing the dashboard had been made, but there was still work to be done.

- **General Impression:** The overall general impression of the management screens appeared to be good. The team at *4FlorenceCare* however, indicated that they expected more financial information. If and how this financial information belongs in the YBoard management system is a point of discussion, because most of the YBoard clients do have other systems which provide them with financial management information from different sources. This is beyond the scope of this research.
- **Client Selection:** The client selection is one of the biggest and the most complete of the selections in the management screens. The interviewees endorsed the possibility of checking the records with this selection. They unanimously stressed the point that they missed the heading for compulsory hospitalization. This is a selection criterion which most certainly has to be added in the near future.

- **Employee Selection:** The employee selection was the one where the least selection criteria were possible. The most welcome addition here was to see which (groups of) practitioners had how many clinical relationships with clients. In that way, it is possible for the managers to see if there is any difference between different locations and practitioner groups. For most of the managers, it was not really needed to see this on an individual personnel level.

- **DBC Selection:** The DBC selection was the most discussed selection of all the interviews. This is because the DBC legislation is new since January 1ste 2013, and most of the companies have still to find their way of working with it. A welcome addition to the system would be an overview of which routes are ready to be invoiced. Those are the records which have been closed for at least 42 days. Another addition would be to show what the financial gains or losses are of the entire DBC sections. To accomplish this, a number of links between different systems are needed. It is not clear if this will be part of the YBoard system, being in essence an electronic healthcare record system.

- **Other Remarks:** As it has been shown, a welcome part of the system is the possibility of making an Excel export of the selection. Most of the managers, and controllers, in particular, want to do the calculations for their own company for a specific date, which is not possible without a database export. Also, ad-hoc hypothesis testing guided by knowledge discovery methods such as CRISP-DM or 3PM (e.g. Vleugel et al., 2010) needs to be accomodated. Furthermore, for the interviewees it was difficult to determine which parts belonged to the management screens and which to other YBoard system parts. The interviewer had to point out multiple times in each interview that the particular question was outside the scope of that interview.

Overall the interviewees where happy with the first results, but they stressed that it was important that more development needs to be done on the tool to support extra features.

CONCLUSION

This research focused on an effective and efficient dashboard design for chronic and long-term healthcare. The result of this work was the actual design and realization of the management dashboard for the YBoard 2.0 system. The design decisions in this investigation were based on human perception and computer interaction theory—in particular Gestalt theory—whereas the empirical interviews with medical professionals supplied valuable additional insights into what the users wanted to see in a dashboard in their daily practices. This study shows how effective and efficient dashboard design can benefit from theoretical insights related to human perception and computer interaction such as Gestalt theory, in combination with integrated end user requirements from daily practices.

FUTURE RESEARCH DIRECTIONS

A problem with this way of working is that all end users have different views on the dashboard, depending on his or her position within the organization. For a controller, financial information is essential. For a practitioner, completeness of the medical record is crucial. Future research could, therefore, focus on better alignment of Business Intelligence end-users, tasks and technologies (Tijssen et al., 2011). This, in turn, might then facilitate the transition towards a more data-driven health practice (Menger et al., 2016).

Obviously, it is really valuable to investigate a complete software development cycle within the scope of the research, to be able to interact with the end users from soliciting requirements to evaluating a working version of the proposed system. The evaluated version, however, remains under constant development and it is important for the developers to remain aware of the designs presented here. Otherwise, it is not unlikely that, should developers lose track of the reasoning behind certain design decisions over time, this might ultimately result in an increasingly less user-friendly system in the future. Future research could, therefore, focus on maturing the organization's software product management function to incrementally assess and improve the YBoard development process, taking into account requirements management, release planning, and product planning (Bekkers & Spruit, 2010). Ideally, this improvement process should be executed based on the organization's unique set of characteristics to avoid negative consequences such as unnecessary implementation of capabilities, and the wrong order of priority when implementing capabilities or over-implementing of capabilities (Baars et al., 2016).

To conclude, in the YBoard dashboard we attempted to take all the wishes of the potential end users of the system into account. It is designed to be flexible and extendable, i.e. with more specific selections and more kinds of X-axes. Extending the design will be an on-going process, as is the whole development of YBoard. Because of the design choice to position YBoard and the electronic health record 'in the cloud' as a SaaS solution, accomplishing this on-going extension process will be easy. One pitfall of this constant extension of the system may be to listen too much to users' wishes. In some cases, users want extensions to the dashboard which do not belong in this dashboard. An example of this is integration of extensive financial information. In most cases, users have other systems which should provide them with this financial information. After all, it is a dashboard for managers in the healthcare. Therefore, we argue that effective and efficient dashboard design should always build upon theoretical insights from relevant research fields related to human perception and computer interaction, as well as sollicit and integrate end user requirements from daily practices.

REFERENCES

W3Schools (2012). Browser Display Statistics. *W3Schools*. Retrieved from http://www.w3schools.com/browsers/browsers_display.asp

Abdat, N., Spruit, M., & Bos, M. (2011). Software as a Service and the Pricing Strategy for Vendors. In T. Strader (Ed.), Digital Product Management, Technology and Practice: Interdisciplinary Perspectives (pp. 154–192). Hershey, PA: IGI Global. doi:10.4018/978-1-61692-877-3.ch010

Albrecht, M. (2010). Color blindness. *Nature Methods*, *7*(10), 775–775. doi:10.1038/nmeth1010-775a PMID:20885436

Baars, T., Mijnhardt, F., Vlaanderen, K., & Spruit, M. (2016). An Analytics Approach to Adaptive Maturity Models using Organizational Characteristics. *Decision Analytics, 3*(5).

Bekkers, W., & Spruit, M. (2010, September 27). The Situational Assessment Method Put to the Test: Improvements Based on Case Studies. *Proceedings of the 4th International Workshop on Software Product Management*, Sydney, Australia (pp. 7–16). doi:10.1109/IWSPM.2010.5623871

Centre for Medicare & Medicaid services. (2011). The Medicare EHR Incentive Program. Retrieved from https://www.cms.gov/Regulations-and-Guidance/Legislation/EHRIncentivePrograms/index.html?redirect=/EHRIncentivePrograms/30_Mean-ingful_Use.asp

Eckerson, W. (2011). Performance Dashboards. Hoboken, New Jersey: John Wiley & Sons Inc.

Eckerson, W., & LaRow, M. (2009). Next Generation Performance Dashboards. *TDWI Research*. Retrieved from http://download.101com.com/pub/tdwi/Files/performance_dashboards092408final2.pdf

Elena, C. (2011). Business intelligence. *Journal of knowledge management, economics and information technology*, 2, 32-44.

Few, S. (2006). *Information Dashboard Design. The Effective Visual Communication of Data. California*. O'Reilly.

Goldberg, D. G., Kuzel, A. J., Feng, L. B., DeShazo, J. P., & Love, L. E. (2012). EHRs in Primary Care Practices: Benefits, Challenges, and Successful Strategies. *The American Journal of Managed Care*, *18*(2), 48–54. PMID:22435884

Gunter, T. D., & Terry, N. P. (2005). The Emergence of National Electronic Health Record Architectures in the United States and Australia: Models, Costs, and Questions. *Journal of Medical Internet Research*. Retrieved from http://www.ncbi.nlm.nih.gov/pmc/articles/PMC1550638/

Jha, A. K., Doolan, D., Grandt, D., Scott, T., & Bates, D. W. (2008). The use of health information technology in seven nations. *International Journal of Medical Informatics*, *77*(12), 848–854. doi:10.1016/j.ijmedinf.2008.06.007 PMID:18657471

Kaplan, R., & Norton, D. (1992). The Balanced Scorecard: Measures that Drive Performance. *Harvard Business Review*, *70*(1), 71–79. PMID:10119714

Koopman, R. J., Kochendorfer, K. M., Moore, J. L., Mehr, D. R., Wakefield, D. S., Yadamsuren, B., & Belden, J. L. et al. (2011). A Diabetes Dashboard and Physician Efficiency and Accuracy in Accessing Data Needed for High-Quality Diabetes Care. *Annals of Family Medicine*, *9*(5), 398–205. doi:10.1370/afm.1286 PMID:21911758

Kroch, E., Vaughn T., Koepke, M., Roman, S., Foster, D., Sinha, S. Levey, S. (2006). Hospital Boards and Quality Dashboards. *J. Patient Saf.*, *2*(1), 10-19.

Livio, M. (2002). *The Golden Ratio: The Story of Phi, The World's Most Astonishing Number*. New York: Broadway Books.

Lupiáñez-Villanueva, F., Hardey, M., Torrent, J., & Ficapal, P. (2010). The integration of Information and Communication Technology into medical practice. *International Journal of Medical Informatics*, *79*(7), 478–491. doi:10.1016/j.ijmedinf.2010.04.004 PMID:20472494

McGinn, C. A., Grenier, S., Duplantie, J., Shaw, N., Sicotte, C., Mathieu, L., Leduc, Y., & Légaré, F., & Gagnon, Mp. (2011). Comparison of user groups' perspectives of barriers and facilitators to implementing electronic health records: A systematic review. *BMC Medicine*, *9*(1), 46. PMID:21524315

Menger, V., Spruit, M., Hagoort, K., & Scheepers, F. (2016). Transitioning to a data driven mental health practice: Collaborative expert sessions for knowledge and hypothesis finding. *Computational and Mathematical Methods in Medicine*.

Meulendijk, M., Spruit, M., Drenth-van-Maanen, A., Numans, M., Brinkkemper, S., & Jansen, P. (2013). General practitioners attitudes towards decision-supported prescribing: An analysis of the Dutch primary care sector. *Health Informatics Journal, 19*(4), 247–263. doi:10.1177/1460458212472333 PMID:24255051

Moghaddasi, H., Hosseini, A., Asadi, F., & Ganjali, R. (2011). Infrastructures of the System for Developing Electronic Health record. *Journal of Paramedical Sciences, 2*, 48–55.

Negash, S. (2004). Business intelligence. *Communications of the Association for Information Systems, 13*, 177–195.

Simon, S. R., McCarthy, M. L., Kaushal, R., Jenther, C. A., Volk, L. A., Poon, E. G., & Bates, D. W. et al. (2006). Electronic health records: Which practices have them, and how are clinicians using them? *Journal of Evaluation in Clinical Practice, 14*(1), 43–47. doi:10.1111/j.1365-2753.2007.00787.x PMID:18211642

Spruit, M., Vroon, R., & Batenburg, R. (2014). Towards healthcare business intelligence in long-term care: an explorative case study in the Netherlands. *Computers in Human Behavior, 30*, 698–707.

Tange, H. (2008). Electronic patient records in the Netherlands. *Health Policy Monitor*. Retrieved from http://hpm.org/en/Surveys/BEOZ_Maastricht_-_Netherlands/12/Electronic_patient_records_in_the_Netherlands.html

Tijssen, R., Spruit, M., van de Ridder, M., & van Raaij, B. (2011). BI-FIT: Aligning Business Intelligence end-users, tasks and technologies. In M. Cruz-Cunha & J. Varajão (Eds.), *Enterprise Information Systems Design, Implementation and Management: Organizational Applications* (pp. 162–177). doi:10.4018/978-1-61692-020-3.ch011

Todorović, D. (2008). Gestalt principles. *Scholarpedia, 3*(12), 5345. doi:10.4249/scholarpedia.5345

Tufte, E., & Roger, J. (2007). *The Visual Display of Quantitative Information*. Cheshire, Connecticut: Graphics Press LLC.

Verkooij, K., & Spruit, M. (2013). Mobile Business Intelligence: Key considerations for implementation projects. *Journal of Computer Information Systems, 54*(1), 23–33. doi:10.1080/08874417.2013.11645668

Vleugel, A., Spruit, M., & van Daal, A. (2010). Historical data analysis through data mining from an outsourcing perspective: The three-phases method. *International Journal of Business Intelligence Research, 1*(3), 42–65. doi:10.4018/jbir.2010070104

Wijaya, S., Spruit, M., & Scheper, W. (2008). Webstrategy Formulation: benefiting from web 2.0 concepts to deliver business values. In M. Lytras, E. Damiani, & P. Ordóñez de Pablos (Eds.), *Web 2.0: The Business Model* (pp. 103–132). Springer. doi:10.1007/978-3-540-87781-3_41

Wikipedia. (2016). Gestalt psychology. Retrieved from https://en.wikipedia.org/wiki/Gestalt_psychology

Wong, B. (2011). Points of view: Color blindness. *Nature Methods, 8*(6), 441. doi:10.1038/nmeth.1618 PMID:21774112

Chapter 11
Role of Online Data from Search Engine and Social Media in Healthcare Informatics

M. Saqib Nawaz
Peking University, China

Raza Ul Mustafa
COMSATS Institute of IT, Sahiwal, Pakistan

M. Ikram Ullah Lali
University of Sargodha, Pakistan

ABSTRACT

Search engines and social media are two different online data sources where search engines can provide health related queries logs and Internet users' discuss their diseases, symptoms, causes, preventions and even suggest treatment by sharing their views, experiences and opinions on social media. This chapter hypothesizes that online data from Google and Twitter can provide vital first-hand healthcare information. An approach is provided for collecting twitter data by exploring contextual information gleaned from Google search queries logs. Furthermore, it is investigated that whether it is possible to use tweets to track, monitor and predict diseases, especially Influenza epidemics. Obtained results show that healthcare institutes and professional's uses social media to provide up-to date health related information and interact with public. Moreover, proposed approach is beneficial for extracting useful information regarding disease symptoms, side effects, medications and to track geographical location of epidemics affected area.

INTRODUCTION

Internet is now affecting and facilitating nearly every aspect of modern life, from healthcare and education to government and business. In past few years, healthcare organizations and professionals are using social media in order to promote, support and spread health related information and data for improving

DOI: 10.4018/978-1-5225-2607-0.ch011

both personal and community health practices (Househ, 2013; Chretien & Kind, 2013). Moreover, the younger generation also uses Internet especially social media for research and making health related decisions. In a survey (Health Fact Sheet, 2015), Internet users of approximately 72% checked online for information on health in past year. Online health seekers of about 77% used search engine. 11% said that they looked for health information at specialized health information site such as WebMD. 3% started their health related research at sites like Wikipedia and an additional 2% said that they used social networking sites such as Facebook and Twitter.

For health related applications and monitoring, the idea of using online data came from the estimation of Influenza incidence using logs of health related search engine queries (Eysenbach, 2006). Studies in (Ginsberg et al., 2009; Hulth et al., 2009; Palet et al., 2009; Achrekar et al, 2011, Aramaki et al., 2011; Polgreen et al., 2008) show that epidemics trend can be detected with information available on Web and there is a strong correlation in the frequency of online search queries and tweets with epidemics events (Xu et al., 2011). Hence, the behavior or pattern of when and how Internet users search may provide early indications or clues related to future concerns and expectations. For example, analysis conducted by Ettredge et al., (2005) on jobs and jobs opportunities related keywords searched by users over Internet has generated an accurate and useful statistics on the unemployment rate. These studies also suggested that people suffering from any kind of disease or health issues uses World Wide Web (WWW) to search for disease information. Logs of search queries (or terms) entered in search engines can provide valuable information on health related issues, especially the detection and monitoring of emerging epidemic diseases, as it is possible to track changes in the volumes of specific search queries.

However search query data is noisy, coarse and it does not provide any contextual information. People search for information related to health on search engine for various reasons, such as concern about oneself, friends or families. Some searches are done because of general interest that is usually initiated by a live event, news report or new scientific discovery (Signorini et al., 2011). Furthermore, errors discovered in Google Flu Trends serves as reminder that this big online data paradigm required further critical investigation and the development of more empirical methodologies for exploring the predictive utility of Internet data (Lazer et al., 2014a; Lazer et al., 2014b). One other limitation is that researchers and scientists do not have full access to search engines logs. Recently, social media data have been used effectively for disease surveillance as they contain contextual health information with diverse descriptions of health states. A study on "Twitter stream" (Twitter Study, 2009) revealed that despite high level of noise, a major proportion of Twitter message contain informative, links to the useful information and news content or spam and self-promotion.

In Natural Language Processing (NLP), opinion mining (also called sentiment analysis) is used for detection and extraction of subjective information from text documents (Liu & Zhang, 2012). Using sentiment analysis, one can find the overall contextual polarity about any topic in a document provided by its author. The challenging task in opinion mining is sentiment classification which is done by guessing opinion about anything such as book, movie, product, issues regarding politics and religion etc. These opinions can be in the form of sentence, document or feature, and the task is to label them as positive, negative or neutral. From developers and researchers point of view, various social media sites and search engine offers APIs (application programming interfaces) that can be used to collect data which later can be used for analysis. Moreover, we can combine these APIs to build our own applications. Therefore, opinion mining shares a strong fundament with the support of huge online data (Fang & Zhang, 2015).

For situation involving limited access to search logs, this chapter consider the use of search queries data to select tweets associated with health related information especially for Influenza epidemics. Main objective of this chapter is to show the correlation between Google search queries and Twitter data. Furthermore, an approach is proposed to describe that how Internet search query logs and Twitter data helps in detecting changes in real world disease activity. Influenza and flu related data that is searched on Google is collected first and then the same queries are used to get data from Twitter. Data (extracted tweets) filtering and source finding tasks are posed as classification tasks. For training and evaluation purposes, Support Vector Machine (SVM) classifier is used. The proposed approach can be beneficial for extracting useful information regarding side effects, medications and to track geographical location of epidemics affected area.

BACKGROUND

Infectious diseases spread directly or indirectly from person to person and these diseases are caused by viruses, bacteria, fungi or parasites. The list of the most common infectious diseases can be found in (WHO Infectious Disease Fact Sheet, 2015; MASS Fact Sheet of Infectious Disease, 2015). Here we gave a fact sheet on infectious disease Influenza. Influenza is a contagious viral infection that affects 5-10% adults and 20–30% children globally each year. This disease causes 3-5 Million cases of illness and approximately 0.25-0.5 Million deaths (Influenza Fact Sheet, 2015). Centre for Disease Control (CDC) in U.S and European Influenza Surveillance Scheme (EISS) in Europe are used to collect Influenza data from clinical diagnosis. However, CDC and EISS systems are almost entirely manual and it takes time leg of two weeks for acquisition of clinical data. CDC and EISS do not provide advance warning for disease outbreak as it identify and categorize disease as or after it occur. Moreover, their data regarding infectious disease activity are no longer current after it is released to general public and healthcare professionals. Public healthcare authorities need to predict the breakout of infectious diseases at the earliest time in order to ensure effective prevention mechanism.

Surveillance or monitoring of infectious diseases provides disease information to healthcare professionals, general public as well as patients. Information from surveillance reports enables effective monitoring of occurrence and distribution of disease, detection of outbreaks, monitoring of interventions, and prediction of emerging hazards. The surveillance reports contain analyses and interpretation of surveillance data, mainly from diseases that occurs commonly, influenza and sexually transmitted infections. However, the effectiveness of traditional monitoring systems for infectious diseases is limited by the nature of infectious diseases occurrence (Malik et al., 2011). On Internet, the availability of health information has also changed the searching pattern of public about health information (Leung, 2008). Such pattern changes offer a new approach for the detection and monitoring of infectious diseases. Digital monitoring of infectious diseases can improve the timeliness and sensitivity of detection of health events (Morse, 2012). Digital monitoring tries to provide knowledge on health issues by analyzing health information that is stored digitally and patterns and distribution governing access to these data.

With increasing dependencies on WWW and expansion of the Internet, various social media tools are now available for healthcare. The term 'social media' generally refers to online tools that offer both individuals and communities to share their opinions, useful information, ideas, images and other content (Ventola, 2014). Social media are helping people to create their own content, share it, participate in activities and live events, follow breaking news and keep up with friends and family. In recent years, social media has and is continuously changing the discourse of public in community and setting new agendas trends in topics that range from healthcare education and politics to technology, government and business (Asur & Huberman, 2010). Today, Facebook boasts more than 1.4 Billion users, Twitter has 280 Million registered users and more than 600 million tweets are sent each day. Furthermore, each day, 60 Million pictures are uploaded on Instagram and approximately 4 Billion videos are watched on YouTube (Wellons, 2015).

Search engines as well as social networks are widely used now to extract the right information at the time of need. Search engine is basically a program that Internet users' use for finding specific contents and information on the Web (Henzinger, 2004). Nowadays, different search engines exist each of them have distinct features and abilities. Google, MSN, Yahoo, Baidu and Bing are the famous search engines (Mustafa et al., 2015). Particularly, Google is considered by Internet users as the essential link between them and the information they want to seek online and approximately 4 Billion searches are performed every day (Google Search Statistics, 2016). On the other hand, Twitter is a social networking site that allows user to write messages (tweets) up to 140 characters. Twitter effectively takes part in any mega event happening around the world and is used before, during and after live events (Bollen et al., 2011).

Sentiment analysis has gained much attention in last couple of years. In sentiment analysis, one active area of research is to solve the problem of categorization of sentiment polarity (Pang & Lee, 2008; Choi & Cardie, 2009). For a piece of document or text, the problem of sentiment polarity categorization is to classify the document or text into one class: positive, negative or neutral. Three levels of sentiment polarity classification exist that are based on the scope of document or text: the entity (aspect) level, sentence level and document level (Liu & Zhang, 2012). The document level categorization deals with whether a whole document expresses negative or positive sentiment. On the other hand, sentence level categorization is concerned with finding the sentiment polarity of each sentence and entity level classification targets on investigating the like or dislike of people from their opinions. However, Google search engine queries and tweets have certain flaws that affect the sentiment analysis process. One of the flaw is that people can use Google to search anything or post content on Twitter, so the quality of their search and opinions cannot be guaranteed (Jindal & Liu, 2008; Mukherjee et al., 2012). Another main flaw is that ground truth for Google and Twitter data is not always available. A ground truth acts like a tag for certain opinions and it indicates whether the opinion belongs to positive class, negative class or neutral class.

In literature, one of the earliest studies carried out to assess the use of social media in healthcare focused the use of the Bulletin Board System for the education of nurses (Russin & Davis, 1990). Early work for creating new flu reporting system includes the use of different kinds of Influenza signals such as Telephone Calls (Espino et al., 2003) or drug cells (Magruder, 2003) for surveillance. Common approaches that are used to monitor the outbreaks by using the Internet include mining those newspaper articles where flu illnesses is mentioned (Collier et al., 2008; Grishman et al., 2002). Furthermore, the use of click-through data from search engines (Eysenbach, 2006), counting search queries that are submitted to a medical site (Hulth et al., 2009), visitors to health websites (Johnson et al., 2004) or clicks on a search keyword advertisement (Polgreen et al., 2008) are other common approaches used for web-based Influenza surveillance. Google's flu trends (Cook et al., 2011; Ginsberg et al., 2008) is a click based flu reporting system that offers Influenza activity estimates for more than 25 countries. However, it is no longer publishing estimates of Flu fever on the basis of search patterns. Carneiro & Mylonakis (2009) showed that Google Flu Trends can be used for detecting Influenza regional outbreaks 10 days before conventional CDC. Pervaiz et al., (2012) developed a system called FluBreaks for early epidemic detection.

Data obtained from Twitter has been effectively utilized in the prediction and explanation of various real-world phenomena, such as elections (Tumasjan et al., 2010), in stock market prediction (Bollen et al, 2011), opinion polls (O'connor et al., 2010) and sports (Godin et al., 2014). Twitter has already been proved to be quite useful for flu detection (Achrekar et al., 2011; Culotta, 2010; Li & Cardie, 2013). Ritterman et al., (2009), demonstrated that tweets can improve the forecasting models accuracy by offering early warnings of external events such as the outbreak of H1N1. Furthermore, De Quincey & Kostova (2009) have collected and characterize more than 13.5K tweets of H1N1 virus to demonstrate the Twitter potential for detection of an outbreak. Similarly, Chew & Eysenbach (2010) analyzed the content and sentiment of 2009 H1N1 outbreak tweets and showed the effectiveness of social media use for conducting infodemiology studies.

Despite using different data sources, different methodological approaches are employed for predictions. For example, Signorini et al., (2011) estimates Influenza activity by investigating public sentiment and applying SVM algorithms on Influenza A H1N1 pandemic tweets. Lamb et al., (2013) investigated multiple features in a supervised learning framework in order to find tweets that indicate flu in surrounding areas. Achrekar et al., (2011) build a system to monitor flu-related tweets by extracting relevant location and user demographic information. Other approaches for flu detection on Twitter involve supervised classification (Aramaki et al., 2011), unsupervised models (Paul & Dredze, 2011), and tracking geographic illness trend (Sadilek et al., 2012). Li & Cardie (2013) investigated the real-time flu detection problem on Twitter data by proposing unsupervised approached called as Flu Markov Network (Flu-MN) to identify the flu breakout at the earliest stage. Their proposed approach assumed the Twitter users as "sensors" and collective tweets that contain flu keywords as early indicators and robust predictors of Influenza. Lee et al., (2013) developed a surveillance system flu by using spatial, temporal and text mining on tweets to automatically track flu activities.

Existing approaches pay more attention to check how well Twitter data can fit real world CDC data, but less explored the disease breakout detection when government or health organizations should send out alarm for disease breakout. Existing research on disease detection tend to focus on a single social network i.e. Twitter. Current and future research in using online data in healthcare needs to focus more on approaches that can accurately identify the particular phases that are associated with diseases from highly informative Internet data. Focus in this chapter is to investigate the relevancy of search engine (Google) users' health related data with Twitter messages for early prediction and detection of disease outbreak.

RESEARCH DESIGN AND METHODOLOGY

Figure 1 is flowchart that depicts the proposed methodology. It consists of three stages: Data Collection and Pre-Processing, Data Modeling and Data Visualization. The stages are briefly explained next:

Data Collection

Influenza and flu related queries searched by users on Google over 12 months are gathered from 9 August 2014 to 9 August 2015 with Google AdWords tool (Google Adwords Keyword Tool, 2015) that provide keyword ideas and also give an estimate of monthly search volumes for keywords. Example of such Google queries and their estimated volume of search are listed in Table 1. These queries had high search volume in 12 months. Other search queries related to Influenza such as *'fluvir'* and *'vaccine side effects'* had search volume less than 3000.

Figure 1. Block diagram of methodology

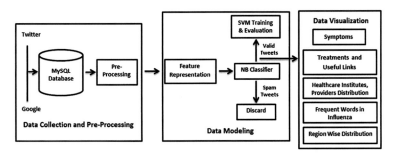

Table 1. Influenza related queries searched on Google from August 2014-August 2015

Search Query	Avg. Monthly Searches (Exact Match Only)	Search Query	Avg. Monthly Searches (Exact Match Only)
Influenza	301000	Influenza A symptoms	12100
Influenza A	60500	Influenza treatment	3600
Influenza B	27100	Influenza B symptoms	4400
Influenza symptoms	22200	Haemophilus Influenza	60500
Influenza virus	22200	Avian Influenza	12100
Influenza vaccine	14800	Swine flu	201000

The same queries are used to collect tweets from Twitter using Twitter search and stream API (Twitter Search API, 2015). This API can be used to collect relevant tweets that match a specific query. MySQL database and Twitter Search API application are used in the development of data collection server. Some of tweets attributes are used for sorting in database and some attributes are used for tracking geo-location such as time zones. Tweet timestamp is a string tagged to each tweets and shows the tweet generation time (e.g., Nov 13 05:21:45 +0000 2015). '+0000' represents that the time is in Greenwich Mean Time (GMT). The authors consider Twitter messages as a valuable source for tracking infectious diseases due to following reasons:

- High posting frequency of tweets by people enables up-to the minute analysis of an outbreak.
- As opposed to Google search query logs, tweets are longer, easily available and more descriptive.
- Tweets also contain time zone associated with them.
- Twitter also keeps information of retweets, tag inside tweets and who follows whom that offer discourse information.
- Twitter hashtags provide easy access for data gathering related to any topic or event

Hashtagify.me is a famous search engine for finding best Twitter hashtags for any topic of interest. Top hashtags are collected (listed in Table 2) for keyword '*influenza*' from hashtagify.me. These hashtags were also used for tweets collection from top Influenza trends on Twitter. Second and fourth columns in Table 2 show the correlation of the hashtag with Influenza. It is important to note that there is a clear similarity between trends collected from Twitter and queries that are searched on Google. People discuss

Table 2. Top ten trends discussions hash tags on Twitter

Hash Tag	Correlation From #Influenza in %	Hash Tag	Correlation From #Influenza in %
H1N1	2.1%	Vacunes	2.5%
Vaccine	2.5%	Virus	1.5%
Flue	17.1%	Infografia	2.4%
H7N9	5.1%	Bioterrorismo	2.1%
Ebola	1.6%	Aceitderateros	2%

their problems on social media and search for the complete detail related to the problem on search engine Google. In this case, people having any flu symptoms such as headache or fever, they use Google and type words "flu symptoms" to check whether they are suffering from Influenza or not.

Data Representation and Pre-Processing

In data representation, raw tweets are transformed into a format on which machine learning algorithms can be applied. This involves feature representation and weighting. Tokenization process is used for feature representation and TF-IDF (Salton & Buckley 1988) is used for weighting each feature. In tokenization, tweet is break into tokens (features). For example, tweet *"Headache may lead to Influenza"* is broke into *'Headache' 'may' 'lead'*, etc. TF-IDF scheme is used to assign weights to each feature and it consists of two parts: TF (term frequency) and IDF (inverse document frequency) and is computed with following equations:

$$\text{TF(t)} = \frac{\# \ of \ times \ term \ t \ appears \ in \ a \ tweet}{Total \ \# \ of \ terms \ in \ document} \tag{1}$$

$$\text{IDF(t)} = \log_e \frac{Total \ \# \ of \ tweets}{\# \ of \ tweets \ with \ term \ t \ in \ it} \tag{2}$$

The main objective of pre-processing is data cleaning, filtering and normalization. Data representation and pre-processing tasks have key importance in classification of textual data since proper representation and pre-processing not only improve the effectiveness of classifier but also make classifier time efficient. From tweets some attributes that plays no role in our classification such as *Friends Count, User ID, Screen Name, Display URL (Uniform Resource Locator), Statuses Count* are also removed in pre-processing.

Feature Selection

Methods for feature selection are generally used for dataset dimensionality reduction by removing those irrelevant features that plays no part in classification (Ikonomakis et al., 2005). Feature selection methods are important because it deals with curse of dimensionality or high dimensionality of feature space. The curse of dimensionality is popularly known to be one of the main reasons of over-fitting since classifiers have to learn very complex decision boundaries and therefore cannot generalize well. A widely recognized approach to deal with the issue is to reduce dimensionality. This not only improves the classification accuracy but also speeds up classifiers' training process. Feature subset selection methods use evaluation function for scoring features (Ikonomakis et al., 2005; Esuli & Sebastiani, 2006). The features are then ranked based on their scores (considered to be best features) for selecting the top ranked subset of features. The measure that we used for feature scoring is the Information Gain (IG) (Zia et al., 2015; Forman & Coehn, 2004).

IG is used to find the worth of a particular feature on the basis of its classification efficiency. IG is related to count the number of bits of information that will be used for prediction by checking the presence or absence of a term in a text or document, where the set of possible categories are $(c_1, c_2, c_3, ..., c_n)$. IG uses each distinctively term t that is calculated as follows:

$$IG(t) = \sum_{i=1}^{m} P(c_i).\log P(c_i) + P(t) \sum_{i=1}^{m} P(c_i \mid t).\log P(c_i) + P(t) \sum_{i=1}^{m} P(c_i \mid t).\log P(c_i \mid t) \qquad (3)$$

For already given features, $P(c_i)$ is the prior probability of category and $P(t)$ denotes the prior probability of a term. It can be projected from the tweets in the training set where term t is present.

Those features are selected that play critical role in the prediction such as *Retweet Count, Favorite Count* of that page and *Follower Count*. In these suggested features, *Retweet Count* has maximum IG, than *Followers Count* and at the end *Favorite Count*. So *Retweet Count* is the root node of IG in decision tree for accuracy. *Favorite Count* and *Follower Count* are identical to each other. Pages having maximum *Followers* are most likely to have maximum *Favorite Count*.

In the extracted dataset of 55K tweets, highest number of *Followers Count* is 991, *Favourites count* is 9991 and *Retweet count* is 99. The authors used *High (H), Medium* (M) and *Low (L)* frequencies to indicate the number of occurrences of these three features and used three different classes of data. For *High Followers Count,* the range 700-991 is considered, for *Medium* 300-699 and for *Low,* the considered range is 1-299. Similarly for *Favourites count,* ranges are 7000-9991, 3000-6999 and 1-2999 for *High, Medium and Low* respectively. For *Retweet count,* ranges which are selected are 70-99 (*High*), 20-69 (*Medium*) and 1-19 (*Low*). If a link has high frequency for these three features then that information shared in respective tweet is considered valid. Tweets that have valid information are mostly likely to be liked and shared by users on Twitter. In order to perform this task, Naive Bayes (NB) classifier is used due to its popularity in data filtering tasks especially when a reasonable size dataset is available (Kotsiantis, 2007). In Table 3, two classes for tweets are made: valid tweets and spam tweets on the basis of NB algorithm. For example, if *Followers Count* is *High, Favourites Count* is *High* and *Retweet Count* is *High,* then tweet is considered genuine as these features represent that tweet is posted from a valid page.

In Bayesian classifier, categorization of text (tweet in this work) is considered as calculating the posterior probabilities $P(c_i|d_j)$. Here, Bayesian classifier calculates that the probability that j^{th} tweet (represented as a weight vector $d_j = \left\langle q_{1j}, q_{2j}, ... q_{|T|j} \right\rangle$) belongs to the class c_i. Bayes theorem is used to calculate posterior probabilities as follows:

$$P\left(c_i \mid d_j\right) = \frac{P\left(d_j \mid c_i\right)P\left(c_i\right)}{P\left(d_j\right)} \tag{4}$$

$P(c_i)$ represents the probability of selecting an arbitrary tweet that belongs to c_i, probability $P(d_j)$ represents that a randomly selected tweet has weight vector d_j. Probability $P\left(d_j \mid c_i\right)$ represents that the tweet d_j belongs to class c_i. However, estimation of term $\left(d_j \mid c_i\right)$ involves large dimensional vector which makes the guessing of $\left(d_j \mid c_i\right)$ hard. To make estimation manageable, it is assumed that the co-ordinates of tweet vector are conditionally independent of one another. With this assumption, $\left(d_j \mid c_i\right)$ is estimated as follows:

$$P\left(d_j \mid c_i\right) = \prod_{k=1}^{|T|} P\left(W_{kj} \mid c_i\right) \tag{5}$$

On the basis of Table 3 and their respective ranges, a script is created which classify tweets into category which contains useful links for Influenza, but these tweets must contain words such as "*influenza*" and "*vaccine*". After this, it is checked that either these tweets contain some link for users where they can get necessary information such as vaccine, influenza early signs and precautions. Such tweets are annotated as positive examples (flu indicators, word *vaccine* is there and link is present) and negative ones (not indicative of the flu, link not present). The link finding task is also posed as classification task and SVM is employed to build the classifier. The reason for using SVM is its effectiveness under limited data as it rely on few instances (i.e. support vectors) to learn the decision boundary (Joachims, 1998; Zia et al., 2016). The classifier provides guarantee to learn hyper-plan with maximum margin from supporting vectors of classes.

Table 3. Supposed data set for valid information to classify tweets into two groups: valid and spam

Followers Count (Page)	Favourites Count (Page)	Retweet Count	Content Class
H	H	H	Valid
H	M	H	Valid
M	M	L	Spam
H	M	L	Valid
L	L	M	Spam
L	L	L	Spam
L	M	M	Valid
M	L	H	Valid
H	L	L	Spam

RESULTS AND DISCUSSION

The experimentation of this work was performed in WEKA (Hall et al., 2009) tool. There are several reasons due to which WEKA is selected to perform the experimentation. Firstly, it has state of the art built-in functionalities for tokenization, stop words removal, attribution selection, feature weighting, classification and classifier evaluation. Secondly, it is a popular tool used for text and NLP tasks such as language identification, named entity recognition, sentence boundary detection (Nadeau, 2005), word sense disambiguation and key phrase detection (Yeow, 2014).

Extracted tweets are separated on the basis of dataset mentioned in Table 3. Table 4 contains sample of tweets which are distributed into positive and negative category along with respective *Retweet count* and *Favourite count* values.

After labelling, a classifier with Support Vector Machine (SVM) is built to train the model. SVM method was primarily introduced by Joachims (Joachims, 1998) in text categorization problem. Risk minimization (RM) (Burges, 1998) principle is the basic idea of SVM. RM principle focuses on discovering a hypothesis having ability to assure lowest true error. Unless the true target is known to learner, it is very difficult to make direct estimation of true error. However, true error can be bounded with training error and hypothesis complexity. The main focus of SVM is the maximum reduction of true error of resultant hypothesis by controlling VC dimension efficiently where VC dimension (Vapnik Chervonenkis dimension) (Mitchell, 1997) is used to measure capacity of hypothesis space.

Standard 10 cross fold validation test is used for characterizing the performance of SVM. Cross validation is a technique to validate models (Chui et al., 2015) and it also investigate and evaluates the independent data set generalization over statistical results that are provided by the model. In 10 cross fold validation, dataset is randomly partitioned into 10 sub datasets. Out of 10, 1 sub dataset is selected as validation set for testing the model and the remaining 9 are used for model training. This process

Table 4. Useful links extracted from tweets using Bayesian Classifier

Tweet (Positive)	Retweet Count	Favourite Count
Advisory Panel of FDA Recommends Licensure of NVS Influenza Candidate Vaccine for Protection http://t.co/gu1SP0HQym	80	3000
Advisory Panel of FDA Recommends Licensure of NVS Influenza Candidate Vaccine for Protection Against Seasonal Influenza http://t.co/EXwdQLcJjL	70	10000
CDC Admits Flu Vaccine Does Not Work Influenza Outbreak on Fully Vaccinated Navy Ship http://t.co/xKsEmqkhoC	70	12000
Tweet (Negative)	**Retweet Count**	**Favorite Count**
RT @goodsam: Those 65 & older could see a 2nd stronger option for the flu vaccine this fall http://t.co/BLFyOgYrRR	1	201
Plan on getting your flu vaccine this year https://t.co/yra8VDjK0W	0	0
Failure of #H7N9 #Influenza #vaccine may be due to the immune camouflage, a study reveals http://t.co/ve4FXdA1WW	0	0

is repeated 10 times in total where each sub datasets is used exactly once as the validation set. Single estimation of the result is obtained by taking the average of 10 results.

Precision, recall and f-measure (evaluation measures) are used for evaluating SVM performance. As accuracy may not be an effective measure here for example, in binary classification problem, good accuracy can be obtained always by predicting negative class in data in presence of few positive cases. On the other hand, precision, recall and f-measure have the ability to evaluate a category wise prediction of the classifier. These measures with respect to positive class can be defined as given in equations 6, 7 and 8. SVM results are listed in Table 5.

$$Recall = \frac{\# \ of \ CPP}{\# \ of \ PE} \tag{6}$$

$$Precision = \frac{\# \ of \ CPP}{\# \ of \ PP} \tag{7}$$

$$F - measure = \frac{2 \times precision \times recall}{precision + recall} \tag{8}$$

In equation 6 and 7, *CPP* represents Correct Positive Predictions, *PE* and *PP* represents Positive Examples and Positive Predictions respectively.

Disaster phenomena detection and predicting the final stage nowadays becomes very important from the view point of risk analysis. Accurate estimates are provided by statistical methods in cases the data are given completely. The remaining tweets are used for further information gathering purpose. Each Google searched query and positive tweet is marked to check whether they contains one or more phrases or words describing medical symptoms given in a list by Yom-Tov & Gabrilovich (2013). Influenza symptoms that most people shared on Twitter are graphically represented in Figure 2. Most of the people described symptoms such as *Headaches, Fatigue, Fever, Vomiting, Diarrhea, Cough, Tiredness, Sore throat, Runny and Stuffy nose, Muscle* and *Body aches*. The authors collected tweets with specific keywords in it such as tweets where word symptoms exist. Furthermore, a sample of tweets that contain useful information related to Influenza that are posted by authorized healthcare institutes is listed in Appendix 1. Only those tweets are considered whose retweet count is more than 10, contains a link and specific keywords such as 'influenza' and 'flu' exist in the tweet.

Table 5. SVM results for classification of tweets into positive and negative class

Precision	Recall	F-Measure
0.90	0.95	0.94

Figure 2. Distribution of tweets for Influenza symptoms

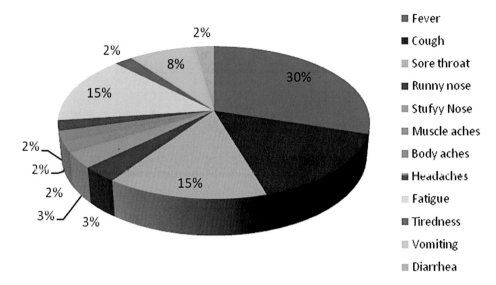

Tweet with words *worst*, *bad* and *side effects* were further classified. The word *side effects* have great importance in sense of medications. A regular expression is built to extract such information from tweets and tweets with maximum *Retweet count* are given importance. Some of extracted links and tweets liked by majority of users are listed in Table 6.

Healthcare institutes, providers and general public also post and share important medications and treatments for Influenza and Flu on Twitter. The authors also investigated that whether dataset of valid tweets has such information or not. For this, a regular expression is built to extract information related to medications and precautions for Influenza and Flu. Obtained results are shown in Table 7. Nearly 45% of valid tweets contain such information and in these tweets, 33% tweets suggested to use Influenza vaccination in order to tackle the disease before it breaks out.

Table 6. Tweets with word side effects and links extracted from micro posts

Links Extracted With Useful Information	Tweet Text
http://t.co/cn0g0T41Hb	Flublok® Influenza Vaccine is free of egg http://t.co/cn0g0T41Hb
http://t.co/nh03Uq0UhU	protein = fewer side effects http://t.co/nh03Uq0UhU
http://t.co/5slC4Uyhfz	Repost:: Facts about Influenza Vaccine (Flu Shot) Types and Side Effects http://t.co/5slC4Uyhfz
https://hepatitiscnewdrugs.blogspot.com/2013/09/hcv-influenza-and-you-flu-shots.html	HCV, Influenza Side Effects and You: Flu Shots Explained https://hepatitiscnewdrugs.blogspot.com/....
http://www.cdc.gov/flu/weekly/usmap.html	Side effects of Flu are widespread in some states, vaccine 59% effective: Weekly #Influenza Summary Update http://www.cdc.gov/flu/weekly/usmap.htm …
https://www.nia.nih.gov/alzheimers/publication/alzheimers-disease-medications-fact-sheet	Fact sheet for Alzheimer's Disease Medications > side effects + dosage > nia.nih.gov/alzheimers/pub...
http://articles.mercola.com/sites/articles/archive/2015/11/21/statin-nation-2.aspx	Statin Side Effects: Real Causes of Heart Disease? http://articles.mercola.com/sites/art... some great information in article.

Table 7. Percentage of medication/precaution suggested in tweets

Medication/Precaution	Occurrence in Tweets
Influenza Vaccination	33%
Medication (Tamiflu, Relenza, Fluvax, Rapivab)	29%
Rest, eating healthy food and drinking fluids	22%
Decongestants, Antihistamines	16%

The percentage of tweets posted and shared by healthcare institutes, healthcare providers and general public is also investigated. Obtained results are shown in Figure 3. More than 60% of tweets were posted from healthcare institutes, healthcare providers and healthcare communities, whereas 26% tweets were posted from public.

Moreover, the tweets are distributed ccording to most frequent word used in micro posts. For this, it is checked that the tweet must contain the word *Influenza*. Distribution of tweets for 5 mostly used words is shown in Figure 4. Regions where most people are suffered from flu have been visualized in Figure 5 using time zone property of tweets posted on Twitter. In total, there are 56 distinct time zones in which there is description of Influenza.

In Figure 5, EST represents Eastern Standard Time, PST represents Pacific Standard Time, CST represents Central Standard Time, AST stands for Atlantic Standard Time and MST stands for Mountain Standard Time. U.S and Canada regions are found to be most affected areas.

Figure 3. Tweets distribution for healthcare institutes, communities, providers and general public

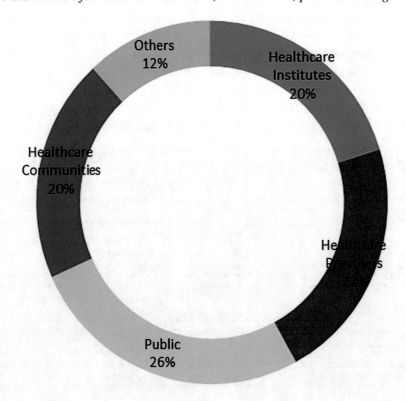

Figure 4. Most frequent words distribution

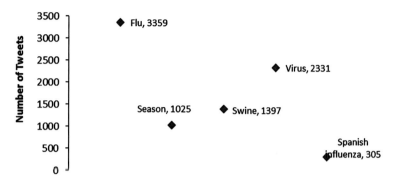

Figure 5. Tweets distribution according to time zone

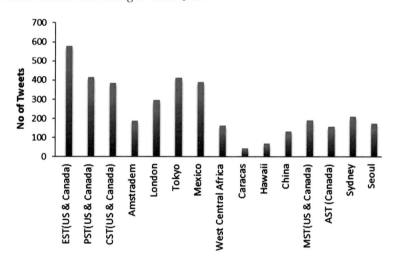

FUTURE RESEARCH DIRECTIONS

In this study, it is found that Influenza and flu related Google search queries correlates with twitter data. The results suggest that Google search query logs and tweets can be used effectively for providing low cost and informative Influenza surveillance. However, various challenges are faced when search engine and social media is used effectively by healthcare providers and general public. As discussed in Introduction Section, search query data is noisy and researchers do not have full access to query logs. The correlation of Google search queries and tweets can be improved with the search time series that precedes the surveillance data for one or two months. This phenomenon was consistent with some studies (Polgreen et al., 2008; Zhou et al., 2011; Cho et al., 2013), which suggested that the Influenza surveillance system based on these queries might detect the change of influenza activity before traditional virological surveillance networks. The prediction of disease outbreak can be enhanced further by including more social network information, such as friends and follower's network and making the filtration and classification process of collected data to be based on the culture based keywords and hashtags.

It is important to note here that search queries generally evolve with time as users' behavior and pattern of searching changes constantly. Searching terms and keywords entered by users may be influenced by a number of factors (Woo et al., 2016). Developing a robust and flexible disease monitoring model is probably the most difficult and important task to complete. One suggestion towards constructing such model is to select query logs using social media data, such as popular trends in Twitter. Social media data offers contextual information and important clues to understand those predictors that changes over time and their weight.

For general public and patients, main threat when looking for health information via social media is the spreading of false information either intentionally or unintentionally. On Twitter, some users or groups share spam on forums, instead of posting topic-related opinions. Majority of such spam opinions are irrelevant and meaningless at all and causes skew in the results. Moreover, ground truth is needed for tweets categorization into positive, negative and neutral classes. For classification of tweets related to product/brand, the ground truth of tweet Corpus (Stanford Sentiment 140) is used. For classification of people opinion related to health information, same kind of corpus is required. Another issue in this regard is the effect of online sharing or posting of personal health information, such as sexual, psychological and genetic information, as individual can be traced with such information if he/she does not take the proper precautions (Thompson et al., 2011).

For healthcare providers, interacting with community through social media has potential benefits; however, more research is needed for determining the impacts of the use of social media on healthcare outcomes, the quality of healthcare services and revenue or costs. Any conclusions based on the limited and anecdotal evidence available are premature (Househ, 2013). More robust evidence is needed to justify the case for healthcare organizations making social media an integral part of their healthcare service delivery models.

CONCLUSION

The purpose of this chapter was to investigate the impact of search engine and social media on healthcare professionals, general public and patients. An approach is proposed in order to demonstrate the positive role of search engine query and social network data in finding disease related information worldwide. Google queries and Twitter data are merged to investigate what people think about symptoms, causes, preventions and treatment for diseases especially in case of Influenza attacks. This data have also been used for early prediction of epidemics in a particular geographical region from where these searches and tweets are made. Moreover, the number of searched tweets and retweets from a particular region are related to probability of epidemics over there. A model has been trained experimentally in WEKA to extract valid information for surveillance against Influenza that is thought to be shared by people who experienced such disease. Important medicines have also been extracted that are used against such disease along with their side effects. Obtained results show that symptoms for early signs of critical diseases such as Influenza are also distributed according to people opinions on social media.

REFERENCES

Achrekar, H., Gandhe, A., Lazarus, R., Yu, S. H., & Liu, B. (2011). Predicting flu trends using Twitter data. *Proceedings of IEEE Conference on Computer Communications Workshops* (pp. 702-707).

Alwagait, E., & Shahzad, B. (2014). Maximization of Tweet's viewership with respect to time. *Proceedings of the 2014 World Symposium on Computer Applications & Research* (pp. 1-5). doi:10.1109/WSCAR.2014.6916776

Alwagait, E., & Shahzad, B. (2015). When are Tweets Better Valued? An Empirical Study. *Journal of Universal Computer Science, 20*(10), 1511–1521.

Aramaki, E., Maskawa, S., & Morita, M. (2011). Twitter catches the flu: Detecting Influenza epidemics using Twitter. *Proceedings of the Conference on Empirical Methods in Natural Language Processing* (pp. 1568-1576).

Asur, S., & Huberman, B. A. (2010). Predicting the future with social media. *Proceedings of 2010 International Conference on Web Intelligence and Intelligent Agent Technology* (pp. 492-499).

Bollen, J., Mao, H., & Zeng, X. J. (2011). Twitter mood predicts the stock market. *Journal of Computational Science, 2*(1), 1–8. doi:10.1016/j.jocs.2010.12.007

Burges, C. J. C. (1998). A tutorial on support vector machines for pattern recognition. *Data Mining and Knowledge Discovery, 2*(2), 121–167. doi:10.1023/A:1009715923555

Carneiro, H. A., & Mylonakis, E. (2009). Google Trends. A web-based tool for real-time surveillance of disease outbreaks. *Clinical Infectious Diseases, 49*(10), 15557–15564. doi:10.1086/630200 PMID:19845471

Chertien, C., & Kind, T. (2013). Social Media and clinical care: Ethical, professional and social implications. *Circulation, 127*(13), 1413–1421. doi:10.1161/CIRCULATIONAHA.112.128017 PMID:23547180

Chew, C., & Eysenbach, G. (2010). Pandemics in the age of Twitter: Content analysis of tweets during the 2009 H1N1 outbreak. *PLoS ONE, 5*(11), e14118. doi:10.1371/journal.pone.0014118 PMID:21124761

Cho, S., Sohn, C. H., Jo, M. W., Shin, S. Y., Lee, J. H., Ryoo, S. M., & Seo, D.-W. et al. (2013). Correlation between national influenza surveillance data and Google trends in South Korea. *PLoS ONE, 8*(12), e81422. doi:10.1371/journal.pone.0081422 PMID:24339927

Choi, Y., & Cardie, C. (2009). Adapting a polarity lexicon using integer linear programming for domain-specific sentiment classification. *Proceedings of the 2009 Conference on Empirical Methods in Natural Language Processing* (pp. 590–598). doi:10.3115/1699571.1699590

Chui, K.T., Tsang, K.F., Wu, C.K., Hung, F.H., Chi, H.R., Chung, H.S.H., & Ko, K.T. et al. (2015). Cardiovascular disease identification using electrocardiogram health identifier based on multiple criteria decision making. *Expert Systems with Applications, 42*(13), 5684–5695. doi:10.1016/j.eswa.2015.01.059

Collier, N. (2012). Uncovering text mining: A survey of current work on web-based epidemic intelligence. *Global Public Health: An International Journal for Research, Policy and Practice, 7*(7), 731–749. doi:10.1080/17441692.2012.699975 PMID:22783909

Collier, N., Doan, S., Kawazeo, A., Goodwin, R., Conway, M., Tateno, Y., & Taniguchi, K. et al. (2008). BioCaster: Detecting public health rumors with a web-based text mining system. *Bioinformatics (Oxford, England)*, *24*(24), 2940–2941. doi:10.1093/bioinformatics/btn534 PMID:18922806

Cook, S., Conrad, C., Fowlkes, A.L., & Mohebbi, M.H. (2011). Assessing Google flu trends performance in the United States during the 2009 Influenza virus A (H1N1) pandemic. *PLoS ONE*, *6*(8), e23610. doi:10.1371/journal.pone.0023610 PMID:21886802

Culotta, A. (2010). Towards detecting Influenza epidemics by analyzing Twitter messages. *Proceedings of the First Workshop on Social Media Analytics* (pp. 1515-1521). doi:10.1145/1964858.1964874

De Quincey, E. M., & Kostkova, P. (2009). Early warning and outbreak detection using social networking websites: The potential of Twitter, electronic healthcare. *Proceedings of 2nd International e-Health Conference*.

Espino, J. U., Hogan, W. R., & Wagner, M. M. (2003). Telephone triage: A timely data source for surveillance of Influenza-like diseases. *Proceedings of the AMIA Annual Symposium*.

Esuli, A., & Sebastiani, F. (2006). Sentiwordnet: A publicly available lexical resource for opinion mining. *Proceedings of the 5th Conference on Language Resources and Evaluation* (pp. 417-422).

Ettredge, M., Gerdes, J., & Karuga, G. (2005). Using web-based search data to predict macroeconomic statistics. *Communications of the ACM*, *48*(11), 87–92. doi:10.1145/1096000.1096010

Eysenbach, G. (2006). Infodemiology: Tracking flu-related searches on the web for syndromic surveillance. *Proceedings of the AMIA Annual Symposium* (pp. 244-248).

Fang, X., & Zhang, J. (2015). Sentiment analysis using product review data. *Journal of Big Data*, *2*(5), 1–14.

Forman, G., & Coehn, I. (2004). Learning from little: Comparison of classifiers given little training. Proceedings of Knowledge Discovery in Databases (pp. 161-172).

Ginsberg, J., Mohebbi, M. H., Patel, R. S., Brammer, L., Smolinski, M. S., & Brilliant, L. (2008). Detecting Influenza epidemics using search engine query data. *Nature*, *457*(7232), 1012–1014. doi:10.1038/nature07634 PMID:19020500

Godin, F., Zuallaert, J., Vandersmissen, B., Neve, W. D., & De Walle, R. V. (2014). Beating the bookmakers: Leveraging statistics and Twitter microposts for predicting soccer results. *Proceedings of KDD Workshop on Large-Scale Sports Analytics*.

Google Adwords Keyword Tool. (2015, November 11). Retrieved from https://www.google.com/adwords/

Google Search Statistics. (2016, January 10). Retrieved from http://www.internetlivestats.com/google-search-statsitics/

Grishman, R., Huttunen, S., & Yangarber, R. (2002). Information extraction for enhanced access to disease outbreak reports. *Journal of Biomedical Informatics*, *35*(4), 236–246. doi:10.1016/S1532-0464(03)00013-3 PMID:12755518

Hall, M., Frank, E., Holmes, G., Pfahringer, B., Reutemann, P., & Witten, L. H. (2009). The WEKA data mining software: An update. *ACM SIGKKD Exploration Newsletter*, *11*(1), 10–18. doi:10.1145/1656274.1656278

Health Fact Sheet. (2015, November 9). *Pew Research Centre*. Retrieved from http://www.pewinternet.org/fact-sheets/health-fact-sheet/

Henzinger, M. (2004). The past, present and future of web search engines. *Proceedings of 31st International Colloquium of Automata* (p. 3). Languages and Programming. doi:10.1007/978-3-540-27836-8_2

Househ, M. (2013). The use of social media in healthcare: Organizational, clinical and patient perspectives. *Studies in Health Technology and Informatics*, *18*(38), 244–248. PMID:23388291

Hulth, A., Rydevik, G., & Linde, A. (2009). Web queries as a source for syndromic surveillance. *PLoS ONE*, *4*(3), e4378. doi:10.1371/journal.pone.0004378 PMID:19197389

Ikonomakis, M., Kotsiantis, S., & Tampakas, V. (2005). Text classification using machine learning techniques. *WSEAS Transaction on Computers*, *8*(4), 966–974.

Influenza. (2015, October 21). Popularity, Trend, Related Hashtags-Hashtagify.me. Retrieved from http://hashtagify.me/

Influenza Fact Sheet. (2015, November 7). Retrieved from World Health Organization website: Retrieved from http://www.who.int/mediacentre/factsheets /fs211/en/

Jindal, N., & Liu, B. (2008). Opinion spam and analysis. *Proceedings of the 2008 International Conference on Web Search and Data Mining* (pp. 219–2300.

Joachims, T. (1998). Text categorization with support vector machine: Learning with many relevant features. *Proceedings of the 10th European Conference on Machine Learning* (pp. 137137-137142). doi:10.1007/BFb0026683

Johnson, H. A., Wagner, M. M., Hogan, W. R., Chapman, W., Olszewski, R. T., Dowling, J., & Barnas, G. (2004). Analysis of web access logs for surveillance of Influenza. *Studies in Health Technology and Informatics*, *107*(2), 1202–2066. PMID:15361003

Kotsiantis, S. B. (2007). Supervised machine learning: A review of classification techniques. *Informatica*, *21*, 249–268.

Lali, M. I. U., Mustafa, R. U., Saleem, K., Nawaz, M. S., Zia, T., & Shahzad, B. (2017). Finding Healthcare Issues with Search Engine Queries and Social Network Data. *International Journal on Semantic Web and Information Systems*, *13*(1), 48–62. doi:10.4018/IJSWIS.2017010104

Lamb, A., Paul, M. J., & Dredze, M. (2013). Separating fact from fear: Tracking flu infections on Twitter. *Proceedings of NAACL-HLT* (pp. 789-795).

Lazer, D., Kennedy, R., King, G., & Vespignani, A. (2014a). Big data. The parable of Google Flu: Traps in big data analysis. *Science*, *343*(6176), 1203–1205. doi:10.1126/science.1248506 PMID:24626916

Lazer, D., Kennedy, R., King, G., & Vespignani, A. (2014b). Twitter: Big data opportunities response. *Science*, *345*(6193), 148–149. doi:10.1126/science.345.6193.148-b PMID:25013053

Lee, K., Agarwal, A., & Choudhary, A. (2013). Real-time disease survelliance using Twitter Data. *Proceedings of the 2nd Workshop on Data Mining for Medicine and Healthcare.*

Leung, L. (2008). Internet embeddedness: Links with online health information seeking, expectancy value/quality of health information websites, and internet usage patterns. *Cyberpsychology & Behavior,* *11*(5), 565–569. doi:10.1089/cpb.2007.0189 PMID:18771393

Li, J., & Cardie, C. (2013). Early stage Influenza detection from Twitter. arXiv:1309.7340

Liu, B., & Zhang, L. (2012). A survey of opinion mining and sentiment analysis. In Mining Text Data (pp. 415-463).

Magruder, S. (2003). Evaluation of over-the-counter pharmaceutical sales as a possible early warning indicator of human disease. *Johns Hopkins University APL Technical Digest,* *24*(4), 349–353.

Malik, M. T., Gumelm, A., Thompson, L. H., Strome, T., & Mahmud, S. M. (2011). Google flu trends and emergency department triage data predicted the 2009 pandemic H1N1 waves in Manitoba. *Canadian Journal of Public Health,* *102*(4), 294–297. PMID:21913587

MASS Fact Sheet of Infectious Disease. (2015 December 9). Retrieved from http://www.mass.gov/eohhs/gov/departments/dph/programs/id/epidemiology/factsheets.html

Mitchell, T. (1997). *Machine Learning.* New York, USA: McGraw-Hill Publishers.

Morse, S. S. (2012). Public health surveillance and infectious disease detection. *Biosecurity and Bioterrorism,* *10*(1), 6–16. doi:10.1089/bsp.2011.0088 PMID:22455675

Mukherjee, A., Liu, B., & Glance, N. (2012). Spotting fake reviewer groups in consumer reviews. *Proceedings of the 21st International Conference on World Wide Web* (pp. 191–200). doi:10.1145/2187836.2187863

Mustafa, R. U., Nawaz, M. S., & Lali, M. I. (2015). Search engine optimization techniques to get high score in SERP's using recommended guidelines. *Science International,* *26*(6), 5079–5086.

Nadeau, B. D. (2005). *Baseline information extraction: Multilingual information extraction from text with Machine Learning and Natural Language techniques (Technical Report).* University of Ottawa.

O'Connor, B., Balasubramanyan, R., Routledge, B. R., & Smith, N. A. (2010). From tweets to polls: Linking text sentiment to public opinion time series. *Proceedings of Fourth International AAAI Conference on Weblogs and Social Media* (pp. 122-129).

Palet, C., Turbelin, C., Bar-Hen, A., Flahault, A., & Vallernon, A. (2009). More disease tracked by using Google Trends. *Emerging Infectious Diseases,* *15*(8), 1327–1328. doi:10.3201/eid1508.090299 PMID:19751610

Pang, B., & Lee, L. (2008). Opinion mining and sentiment analysis. *Foundation of Trends in Information Retrieval,* *2*(1-2), 1–135. doi:10.1561/1500000011

Paul, M. J., & Dredze, M. (2011). You are what you tweet: Analysing Twitter for public health. *Proceedings of Fifth International AAAI Conference on Weblogs and Social Media* (pp. 265-272).

Pervaiz, F., Pervaiz, M., Rehman, N. A., & Saif, U. (2012). FluBreaks: Early Epidemic detection system from Google Flu Trends. *Journal of Medical Internet Research, 14*(5), e125. doi:10.2196/jmir.2102 PMID:23037553

Polgreen, P. M., Chen, Y., Pennock, D. M., Nelson, F. D., & Weinstein, R. A. (2008). Using Internet searches for Influenza surveillance. *Clinical Infectious Diseases, 47*(11), 1433–1448. doi:10.1086/593098 PMID:18954267

Ritterman, J., Osborne, M., & Klein, E. (2009). Using prediction markets and Twitter to predict a swine flu pandemic. *Proceedings of 1st International Workshop on Mining Social Media* (p. 9).

Russin, M. M., & Davis, J. H. (1990). Continuing education electronic bulletin board system: Provider readiness and interest. *Journal of Continuing Education in Nursing, 21*(1), 7–23. PMID:2106537

Sadilek, A., Kautz, H. A., & Silenzio, V. (2012). Modelling spread of disease from social interactions. *Proceedings of 6th International AAAI conference on Web and Social Media.*

Sakaki, T., Okazaki, M., & Matsuo, Y. (2010). Earthquake shakes Twitter users: real-time event detection by social sensors. *Proceedings of the 19th International Conference on World Wide Web* (pp. 851-860). doi:10.1145/1772690.1772777

Salton, G., & Buckley, C. (1988). Term-weighting approaches in automatic text retrieval. *Information Processing & Management, 24*(5), 513–523. doi:10.1016/0306-4573(88)90021-0

Signorini, A., Segre, A. M., & Polgreen, P. M. (2011). The use of Twitter to track levels of disease activity and public concern in the U.S. during the Influenza A H1N1 pandemic. *PLoS ONE, 6*(5), e19467. doi:10.1371/journal.pone.0019467 PMID:21573238

Stanford Sentiment 140. (2014). Retrieved from http://www.sentiment140.com/

Tehseen, Z., Shehbaz, M. S., Nawaz, M. S., Shahzad, B., Abdullatif, A., Mustafa, R. U., & Lali, M. I. (2016). Identification of Hatred Speeches on Twitter. *Proceedings of 52nd The IRES International Conference* (pp. 27-32).

Thompson, L. A., Black, E., Duff, W. P., Black, N. P., Salibi, H., & Dawson, K. (2011). Protected Health Information on Social Networking Sites: Ethical and Legal Considerations. *Journal of Medical Internet Research, 13*(1), e8. doi:10.2196/jmir.1590 PMID:21247862

Tumasjan, A., Sprenger, T. O., Sandner, P. G., & Welpe, I. M. (2010). Predicting elections with Twitter: what 140 characters reveal about political sentiment. *Proceedings of Fourth International AAAI Conference on Weblogs and Social Media* (pp. 178-185).

Twitter Search, A. P. I. (2015, November 12). Retrieved from https://dev.Twitter.com/rest/public/search

Twitter Study. (2009, August 12). Retrieved from http://pearanalytics.com/wp-content/uploads/2009/08/Twitter-Study-August-2009.pdf

Ventola, C. L. (2014). Social media ad health care professionals: Benefits, risks and best practices. *Pharmacy & Therapeutics, 39*(7), 491–500. PMID:25083128

Wellons. W. C. (2015, January). 11 Predictions on the Future of Social Media. Retrieved from www. cnbc.com/id/102029041

WHO Infectious Disease Fact Sheet. (2015, December 8). Retrieved from http://www.who.int/topics/ infectious_diseases/factsheets/en/

Woo, H., Cho, Y., Shim, E., Lee, J. K., Lee, C. G., & Kim, S. H. (2016). Estimating Influenza Outbreaks Using Both Search Engine Query Data and Social Media Data in South Korea. *Journal of Medical Internet Research*, *18*(7), e177. doi:10.2196/jmir.4955 PMID:27377323

Xu, D., & Liu, Y., hang, M., Ma, S., Cui, A., & Ru, L. (2011). Predicting Epidemic tendency through search behaviour analysis. *Proceedings of 22th International Joint Conference on Artificial Intelligence* (pp. 2361-2366).

Yeow, W. L., Mahmud, R., & Raj, R. G. (2014). An application of case-based reasoning with machine learning for forensic autopsy. *Expert Systems with Applications*, *41*(7), 3497–3505. doi:10.1016/j. eswa.2013.10.054

Yom-Tov, E., & Gabrilovich, E. (2013). Postmarket drug surveillance without trial costs: Discovery of adverse drug reactions through large-scale analysis of web search queries. *Journal of Medical Internet Research*, *15*(6), e124. doi:10.2196/jmir.2614 PMID:23778053

Zhou, X., Ye, J., & Feng, Y. (2011). Tuberculosis surveillance by analyzing Google trends. *IEEE Transactions on Bio-Medical Engineering*, *58*(3), 2247–2254. doi:10.1109/TBME.2011.2132132 PMID:21435969

Zia, T., Akhter, M. P., & Abbas, Q. (2015). Comparative study of feature selection approaches for Urdu text Categorization. *Malaysian Journal of Computer Science*, *28*(2), 93–109.

KEY TERMS AND DEFINITIONS

Epidemic: Widespread occurrence and spreading of an infectious disease at a particular time such as flu epidemic.

Google: A popular search engine company that also offers Internet-related products and services.

Healthcare Institution: An authorized public or private entity that provides health care related services.

Healthcare Providers: An authorized individual that can provide health related services in a systematic way to people, families or communities.

Influenza: A contagious viral infection of respiratory passages that causes fever, severe headache, aching, and catarrh, etc.

Search Engine: A set of programs that searches the World Wide Web for finding specific information and contents entered by users through keywords.

Sentiment Analysis/Opinion Mining: A process in natural language processing to identify and categorize opinions that are present in a piece of text or document.

Social Media: Online platforms that are used by Internet users for communication and to create online communities for information, ideas and personal opinion sharing.

Twitter: Popular social media site that offers users to post and read short 140-character messages also known as 'tweets'.

APPENDIX 1

herbury.com/flu-cold-fighters/... #Flu and #Cold Help

The benefit of early antiviral #influenza and #flu treatment 4 pregnant women hospitalized with laboratory-confirmed. ow.ly/YSuBP.

ACIP: #Influenza #vaccine 59% effective to date goo.gl/Q2YKdk

#H1N1 ? What you need to know; national #influenza plan is activated: http://bit.ly/1QcdlwL

So you've got the #flu. Now what? http://1.usa.gov/1nmYvfJ#FluSeason

This year's #flu #vaccine is ~ 60% effective, according to US CDC idse.net/Immunology--Vaccination/Article/02-16/CDC-Flu-Vaccine-Nearly-60-Effective/35441 ... #influenza

There are 3 ways to make #flu #vaccinations: egg-based, cell-based, & recombinant. Learn about each method: http://1.usa.gov/1vMoOvX

This Season #Influenza Vaccine Nearly 60% Effective. 1.usa.gov/1oGrGKw

#Flu prevention tip: avoid touching your mouth/nose/eyes in order to avoid spreading germs: http://j.mp/1Set96b

Separating fact from fiction about the #flu vaccine – 2015 - http://bit.ly/1XgoFAn#TeamVax #VaccinesWork #influenza

APPENDIX 2

Google Query Data Correlation with other Social Networking Sites such as Facebook.

Collection of Latest Online Health Related Data and Training WEKA Models.

State of the Art Literature Review on the use of Online Data in Healthcare.

Building a Corpus for Classification of People Opinion Related to Health Information.

Data Collection of Health Information from Crowd Sources and Analyze it in WEKA.

Chapter 12

An Optimized Semi–Supervised Learning Approach for High Dimensional Datasets

Nesma Settouti
Tlemcen University, Algeria

Mohammed El Amine Bechar
Tlemcen University, Algeria

Mostafa El Habib Daho
Tlemcen University, Algeria

Mohammed Amine Chikh
Tlemcen University, Algeria

ABSTRACT

The semi-supervised learning is one of the most interesting fields for research developments in the machine learning domain beyond the scope of supervised learning from data. Medical diagnostic process works mostly in supervised mode, but in reality, we are in the presence of a large amount of unlabeled samples and a small set of labeled examples characterized by thousands of features. This problem is known under the term "the curse of dimensionality". In this study, we propose, as solution, a new approach in semi-supervised learning that we would call Optim Co-forest. The Optim Co-forest algorithm combines the re-sampling data approach (Bagging Breiman, 1996) with two selection strategies. The first one involves selecting random subset of parameters to construct the ensemble of classifiers following the principle of Co-forest (Li & Zhou, 2007). The second strategy is an extension of the importance measure of Random Forest (RF; Breiman, 2001). Experiments on high dimensional datasets confirm the power of the adopted selection strategies in the scalability of our method.

INTRODUCTION

One of the strongest problems afflicting current machine learning techniques is dataset dimensionality. Nowadays, with the advance of technologies, in many applications of real world problems, we deal with data from a few dozen to many thousands of dimensions. The analysis of higher dimensional datasets is difficult, not only because they are large in terms of the number of observations, but also because of the large number of variables (features) that can be generated with the modern automatic acquisition methods. In fact, most applications allow to obtain many features and samples at low cost. However,

DOI: 10.4018/978-1-5225-2607-0.ch012

the relevant features are often more difficult to be obtain than the others. This is particularly true in the prediction problems.

In these application fields, the learning task is confronted with another important detail where, new samples are easily generated; nevertheless, labeling data can be costly and time consuming. For example, with the fast development of the Internet, it is easy to get billions of Web pages from Web servers. However, the classification of web pages into classes is a long and difficult task. Also in the field of speech recognition, registration gives a huge amount of audio data whose cost is negligible. However, labeling them requires someone to listen and understand later. Similar situations apply to remote sensing, face recognition, medical imaging, image search by content (Zhou and Goldman, 2004) and intrusion detection in computer networks (Roli, 2005).

The availability of unlabeled data and the difficulty of obtaining labels, make the semi-supervised learning methods gained great importance. The question that arises is whether the knowledge of points with labels is sufficient to construct a decision function that can correctly predict the labels of unlabeled points. Different approaches propose to deduct unlabeled points of additional information and include them in the learning problem.

Different kinds of approaches have been developed to achieve the semi-supervised learning task. There are mainly three paradigms (Chapelle, O. et al., 2006; Cornuéjols and Miclet, 2010) that address the problem of combination of labeled and unlabeled to improve the performances. Therefore, we include in brief these categories:

- **Semi-Supervised Learning (SSL):** Refers to methods that attempt to exploit unlabeled data for supervised learning where unlabeled examples are different from test examples; or exploiting labeled data for unsupervised learning.
- **The Transductive Learning:** Assemble methods that attempt also to exploit the unlabeled examples, but assuming unlabeled examples are exactly the test examples.
- **The Active Learning:** Refers to methods that select unlabeled examples that are the most important, and an oracle can be proposed for the labeling of these instances; the objective is to minimize the labeling data (Freund, Y. et al., 1997). Sometimes it is called selective sampling or sample selection.

In this paper, we focus on improving the performance of supervised classification using unlabeled data (SSL). In this context the two main contributions of this work are the treatment of the following questions: "How to judge the relevance of a model using unlabeled data? " And "How to improve the performance of the model ?".

Many semi-supervised learning (SSL) algorithms have been proposed, among which the *"Co-forest"* algorithms are widely used. We present in this work an optimized *Co-forest* algorithm. It uses a relevant random subspace method to form an initial ensemble of classifiers, where each classifier is trained with different relevant subspace of the original feature space. Unlike the prior work of (Li and Zhou, 2007) on *Co-forest*, our method uses a feature importance measure in semi-supervised learning by the ensemble of classifiers. Each classifier's prediction on new unlabeled data with relevant features are combined and then used to enlarge the training set of others. The classifiers ensemble are refined through the enlarged training set. Experiments on high and small data sets show the ability and effectiveness of *Optim Co-forest* to select and measure importance to improve the performance of the ensemble of classifiers learned with a small amount of labeled samples by exploiting unlabeled samples. A comparative result also corroborates, to study our approach as a feature selection method in semi-supervised learning. Results indicate an overall significant improvement of our method compared to the existing semi-supervised feature selection approaches.

This work introduces the *Optim Co-forest* algorithm, which leads us to organize this paper as follows: at first, a state of art of semi-supervised learning techniques is summarized in section 1. A review of some ensemble methods in the semi-supervised field is performed in section 2. We expose in detail the evolution of this latter as well as its advantages and limitations. We then describe in section 3, the *Co-forest* algorithms and its improved version *ADE-Co-forest*. In section 4, we present the general process of our proposed approach and its different strategies. We validate our algorithm and the choices we have made in an experimental phase in section 5. We show in section 6, the ability of our method to improve the classification performance by comparing them with the representative literature methods on high dimensional datasets. Finally, we conclude in section 7 by summarizing the contributions made and the tracks defining possible opportunities for future work, also the difficulties faced in the realization of this work.

BACKGROUND OF ENSEMBLE METHODS IN SEMI-SUPERVISED LEARNING

The semi-supervised learning emphasizes the assumption that unlabeled data will improve learning process. However, this is not always true (Zhu, 2005; Chapelle, O. et al., 2006), distinguish three hypotheses that data points must satisfy to take advantage of unlabeled examples.

The hypothesis of similarity: the standard similarity measure used by learning algorithms is the Euclidean distance. Semi-supervised learning algorithms rely on the intuition that two data points are similar to each other if they are connected by a high-density region.

- **The Hypothesis of Class:** The points are on the same cluster, they are likely to be of the same class,
- **The Hypothesis of Subspace:** The (high-dimensional) data lie generally on a low dimensional variety.

The first hypothesis is a condition that data must fill in to enable generalization from a small number of labels. Indeed, data for which two examples are very close, located in dense regions of the learning space, wouldn't be more likely to have common labels become data whose nature prevent a semi-supervised learning. The other two hypotheses specify the conditions that the data may fulfill and under which it is possible to generalize from a few labeled examples: the data are grouped either into homogeneous classes, or in dense, homogeneous subspaces. The difference between these two hypotheses concerns mainly the space in which the distance is measured between two examples.

Among the methods that take advantage of these assumptions (Zhu, 2005), we have distinguished several families (Figure. 1). Most methods assume an underlying structure that correlates the unlabeled data with label class and thus making them instructive. This class of methods has a direct link with the ensemble methods since it uses several classifiers to handle unlabeled examples. The first to emerge in this category is the *co-Training* algorithm proposed by Blum and Mitchell, 1998 for semi-supervised classification web pages.

Figure 1. The different multiple approaches for semi-supervised learning SSL

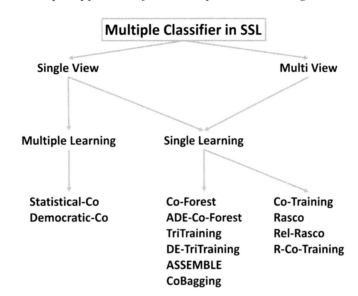

The *co-Training*, assumes that features are naturally partitioned into two sets $x = (x_1, x_2)$. For example, in the Web pages we consider all hyperlinks and all content under the following hypothesis:

- Each component is sufficient for classification,
- All components are conditionally independent of the class,

Blum and Mitchell, 1998 shows the guarantees of the Probably Approximately Correct (PAC) type (Valiant, 1984) on learning process in the presence of labeled and unlabeled data (Algorithm1).

The authors also showed that the independence of the two subsets of attributes is a necessary condition for improving the prediction provided by the *co-Training* algorithm. However, in practice, it is not always possible to obtain two independent subsets of attributes relative to the label, which makes it difficult to generalize *co-Training*.

To overcome this difficulty, (Zhou and Goldman, 2004) proposed to adapt this strategy to a set of heterogeneous classifiers *statistical Co-learning*. Their method follows the procedure introduced by (Blum and Mitchell, 1998), even if they are constrained to check the quality of newly labeled examples before adding them permanently to relearning.

With three classifiers instead of two, (Zhou and Li, 2005) proposed *tri-Training* learning algorithm, which do not requires a sufficient and redundant subsets of attributes, as well as no supervised learning algorithms that could divide the special space for example in a set of equivalence classes. It realizes the prediction by majority vote rather than a handset classifier or a stacking.

Otherwise, an improved *co-Training* have emerged lately as the *RASCO* algorithm (Random Subspace Method for Co-training, (Wang, J. et al., 2008). *RASCO* gets different distributions of characteristics using the method of random subspace RSM (Ho, 1998). This change brought an important reduction of learning error in comparison with traditional algorithms *co Training* and *tri-Training*. In its principle, *RASCO* uses the random distributions to train different classifiers. Samples of unlabeled data are labeled and added to the learning based on the combination of classifiers trained on different distributions of

Algorithm 1. co-Training pseudo-code for document classification

```
1: Input: an initial collection of labeled documents
2: Repeat until it is no longer document without label.
- Building the classifier C1 using the x₁ portion of each document
- Building the classifier C2 using the x₂ portion of each document
for each class k,
Add to the collection of labeled documents the unlabeled documents classified
as Class k by the classifier C1 with the highest probability.
end
for each class k,
Add to the collection of labeled documents the unlabeled documents classified
as Class k by the classifier C2 with the highest probability.
end
end
3: Output: Two classifiers, C1 and C2, which predict the label of new docu-
ments.
4: These predictions may then be combined.
```

features. However, in the presence of many irrelevant features, *RASCO* can select subspaces, which are unsuitable characteristics for a good classification. In (Yaslan and Cataltepe, 2010), they propound to apply relevant features random subspace for learning *co-Training*. The algorithm, called *Rel-RASCO* produces relevant random subspaces using relevance calculation from dozens of features. The relevance of a feature is obtained by calculating the mutual information between the feature and its class label.

On the other hand, a new algorithm that extends the paradigm of *co-Training* using *Random Forest* (Breiman, 2001) was introduced by (Li and Zhou, 2007) for the detection of micro calcifications to breast cancer diagnosis. This algorithm named *Co-forest* uses $N > 3$ instead of 3 classifiers in *Tri training*. $N - 1$ classifiers are used to determine examples of trust, called concomitant Set $H_i = H_{N-1}$. The confidence of unlabeled example, can be simply estimated by the degree of agreement on labeling, i.e. the number of classifiers that agree with the label assigned by H_i.

The approaches proposed by (Blum and Mitchell, 1998), (Zhou and Goldman, 2004), (Zhou and Li, 2005) attest the advantage of using multiple classifiers. Which means, learning these classifiers involves predicting the unlabeled examples before using them. Therefore, the algorithm of Li and Zhou, offers the best compromise in the semi-supervised approach.

Recently, (Deng and Guo, 2011) provide an improvement of *Co-forest* with a very interesting results by integrating an adaptive filtering method "Adaptive DATA Editing", the algorithm is called *ADE-Co-forest*. *ADE-Co-forest* uses the *RemoveOnly* editing approach (Jiang and Zhou, 2004) to identify and eliminate the "suspect" noisy mislabeled examples in the subset of newly certified learning ones.

The principle of *RemoveOnly* is as follows: for each example x newly labeled in L_i, k nearest neighbors of x of learning $L \cup L_i$ are selected under the nearest neighbor rule. It then checks if at least k' neighbors from the k nearest neighbors of x hold the same class label as x, otherwise the concerned example x is identified as mislabeled and removed from L_i.

The first observation we can deduct from these data editing (filter approach) methods is that they have advantages in terms of their computational efficiency and robustness against the over fitting. However, these methods do not take into account the interactions between the elements, and tend to select examples with rather than redundant information. In addition, the data editing approaches do not absolutely reflect the choices made for the classification method. Instead, this later deplete the entire re-learning instead of enriching it with new elements to strengthen learning.

Through the background ensemble methods in the semi-supervised learning, we also proposed an improvement of *Co-forest* algorithm, but unlike *ADE-Co-forest* (Deng and Guo, 2011), which is based on calculating distance to the removal of noisy elements, we include an selecting approach (embedded approach) of relevant features in the process of re-learning classifiers, which will keep all the newly labeled elements but with a relevancy ranking of features to reconstruct decision trees in the random forest.

METHODS

The *Optim Co-forest* algorithm is an improvement of the *Co-forest* method (Li and Zhou, 2007) for semi-supervised classification. We propose to optimize the approach by integrating a relevant feature subset in the process of re-learning in addition to make some corrections to the observed boundaries in *Co-forest* and *ADE-Co-forest*; but before discussing the steps of our approach, we firstly present the *Co-forest* algorithm and its improved version *ADE-Co-forest*.

Co-Forest Algorithm

(Li and Zhou, 2007) proposed the *Co-forest* algorithm, it extends the *co-Training* paradigm (Blum and Mitchell, 1998) by the well know ensemble method *Random Forest* (Breiman, 2001).

We denote by L and U the set of labeled and unlabeled data respectively. In *co-Training* two classifiers are trained from L, then each of them selects the most confident examples in U for relearning, from their own ranking function or by separating hyper-plane. Thus, an important part of *co-Training* is in the way to estimate the confidence of the prediction. In other words, for improving the prediction we must know *how to estimate or obtain the confidence of an unlabeled example*.

In *Co-forest*, a set of N classifiers designated as H^* is used in *co-Training* instead of two classifiers. In this way, we can effectively estimate the confidence of each classifier. If we want to considering the example labeled the more confident by a classifier h_i $(i = 1,2,...,n)$ of the set H^*, we use all the other classifiers exception h_i, called concomitant ensemble of h_i and denoted by H_i.

Therefore, the confidence of the labeling step may be calculated as the degree of agreement on the labeling, i.e. the number of classifiers agree with the label assigned by H_i. The general idea of *Co-forest* is to first form a set of classifiers labeled L data and refine each classifier with unlabeled ones by its concomitant ensemble.

More specifically, in each iteration of learning around *Co-forest*, the concomitant ensemble h_i will test each example in U. For an unlabeled example xu, if the number of classifiers that agree on a particular label exceeds a predefined threshold θ, this new label is assigned to the example and then it will be copied in the new set L'. In the next iteration, L' is used for refining h_i. Hereafter, we note that the unlabeled examples U are not deleted, so they can be selected by other $H_j (j = i)$ in the following iterations.

A problem that can affect the overall performance of *Co-forest* is that all unlabeled data whose confidence is above θ will be added to L_i, making L_i large enough in the future. Nevertheless, in the case where a classifier cannot represent the underlying distribution; a huge amount of labeled data becomes detrimental to performance, instead of improving the prediction accuracy.

This phenomenon has been discovered in several semi-supervised learning algorithms. Inspired by (Nigam and Ghani, 2000), *Co-forest* also incorporates the principle of assigning a weight to each unlabeled example. A sample is weighted according to the predictive confidence concomitant ensemble. This approach reduces the influence of θ, even if θ is small, the examples having a low predictive confidence may be limited.

$$\frac{\hat{e}_{i,t}}{\hat{e}_{i,t-1}} < \frac{w_{i,t-1}}{w_{i,t}} < 1 \tag{1}$$

According to (Li and Zhou, 2007) in two iterations $((t-1)$ with $t > 1)$, a condition (eq. 1) for updating the training set should be satisfied to iteratively improve the generalization ability. Presuming that the classifier h_i is reconstructed (relearning phase) on the dataset $L_i \cup L'_{i,t}$ in t i-th iteration. And $\hat{e}_{i,t}$ is the error rate of H^* on $L'_{i,t}$, also that $\hat{e}_{i,t} w_{i,t}$ is the weighted average of the mislabeled examples by H^*.

Assumptions that $\hat{e}_{i,t} < \hat{e}_{i,t-1}$ and $w_{i,t-1} < w_{i,t}$, $w_{i,t} < \frac{\hat{e}_{i,t-1} w_{i,t-1}}{\hat{e}_{i,t}}$ should be satisfied at the same time.

However, even if this requirement is met, $\hat{e}_{i,t} W_{i,t} < \hat{e}_{i,t-1} W_{i,t-1}$ might still be violated since $w_{i,t}$ might be much larger than $w_{i,t-1}$. To verify the equation (1) in this case, the new labeled data $L_{i,t}$ must be subsampled so that $w_{i,t}$ is less than $\frac{\hat{e}_{i,t-1} w_{i,t-1}}{\hat{e}_{i,t}}$.

According to (Krogh and Vedelsby, 1995), an ensemble exhibits its generalization power when the average error rate of component classifiers is low and the diversity between component classifiers is high.

To maintain the diversity in the semi-supervised learning process, (Li and Zhou, 2007) introduce two strategies:

1. Firstly, the *Random Forest* ensemble method (Breiman, 2001) is used to construct the ensemble in *Co-forest*. Since *Random Forest* injects certain randomness in the tree learning process, any two trees in the Random Forest could still be diverse even if their training data are similar.
2. Secondly, the diversity is further maintained when the concomitant ensembles select the unlabeled data to label. Specifically, not all the examples in U will be examined by concomitant ensemble.

Instead, a subset of unlabeled examples with the total weight less than $\frac{\hat{e}_{i,t-1} w_{i,t-1}}{\hat{e}_{i,t}}$ is randomly selected from U. Then confident examples are further selected from the subset. Note that the subset not only offers diversity to some extent, but also acts as a pool to reduce the chance of being trapped in a local minimum, just as a similar strategy employed in *co-Training* (Blum and Mitchell, 1998).

In summary, the principle of the algorithm *Co-forest* (Figure 2) consists of N random trees that are first formed on a labeled bootstrap[1] training set L to create in first a random forest. Then, at each itera-

Figure 2. Diagram representing the overall operating principle of co-forest

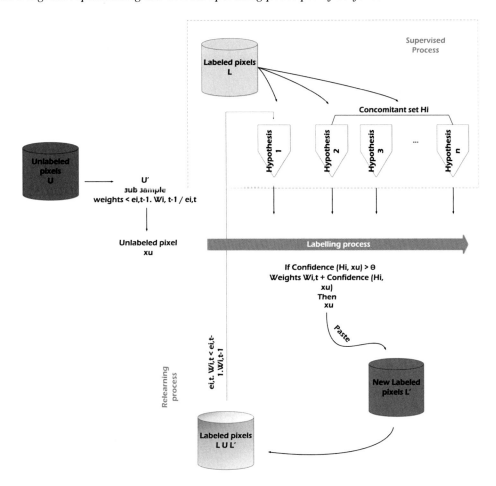

tion, each random tree will be refined with the newly labeled by its concomitant ensemble, where the confidence of the labeled example exceeds a certain threshold θ. Therefore, when we use only unlabeled data, this procedure will reduce the chances of a biased tree in the *Random Forest*. For a more detailed description of the algorithm *Co-forest* algorithm, we refer the reader to articles (Li and Zhou, 2007) and (Deng and Guo, 2011).

ADE Co-Forest Algorithm

The authors (Deng and Guo, 2011) highlighted a problem that may affect *Co-forest* as well as other algorithms such as *co-Training*, worth knowing, that the unlabeled examples may be mislabeled and introduced into the learning process. This is due to the limited number of examples initially labeled that usually generates low classifiers, which lacks precision and diversity. In their article, (Deng and Guo, 2011) proposed a new algorithm that combines *Co-forest* with an adaptive data editing technique called *ADE-Co-forest*.

ADE-Co-forest uses specific technical data editing to identify and possibly eliminate mislabeled examples through iterations of *co-labeling*, but also uses an adaptive strategy to decide according to different cases when trigger the editing operation. Adaptive strategy combines five theorems (pre-conditions), all ensure an iterative reduction of classification error and an increase in the scale of new learning sets under PAC learning theory (Valiant, 1984).

In *ADE Co-forest* the *Remove Only* data editing technical (Algorithm 2) (Jiang and Zhou, 2004) is used to identify mislabeled data. Its principle shall that the label of each unlabeled instance is not only determined by multiple classifiers, but also by the nearest neighbor rule. If the label is compatible with those selected from a minimum of k' nearest neighbor data, the unlabeled instance data with the greatest confidence are added to the training set. Otherwise, they are rejected and removed from the set of re-learning.

OPTIM CO-FOREST ALGORITHM

In the context of high dimensional datasets, applications, the features can be correlated, redundant or perhaps noisy and therefore not relevant. In this case, *Co-forest* may select these features and thereby learn about the erroneous data resulting poor classification performance. This disadvantage can be avoided by the selection of the most relevant features.

The measure importance method in the paradigm of *Random Forest* (RF) (Breiman, 2001) had a great influence on our proposed approach. In this study, we show that these ideas are also applicable to feature selection in semi-supervised. Therefore, we propose a method for evaluating features of importance in semi-supervised based on the principle of *Co-forest* called *Optim Co-forest*.

The algorithm classifies the features through a framework consisting of ensemble methods, in which the relevance of an element is evaluated by its predictive accuracy drawing on labeled and unlabeled data.

In *Co-forest*, measuring feature importance can be estimated only from Out-Of-Bag (OOB) samples[2], since the sample used to bootstrap the learning of each random tree is changed after the first iteration. Out-Of-Bag (OOB) dataset are all labeled. However, given the very small amount of labeled data, diversity in OOB data is not sufficient. OOB estimates are biased because they depend on too few data.

Therefore, we also mention two necessary conditions for the success of ensemble methods, where it is necessary that each individual classifier should be a relatively good predictor; and that individual predictors should be different from each other. Simpler, it is necessary that the individual predictors are good classifiers; and where a predictor is mistaken, the other must take over without making mistakes.

Algorithm 2. Remove Only Data editing technical

```
1: Input: Let S = X
2: For each x_i ∈ X
Find the k nearest neighbor of xi in (X − x_i)
If no class label is shared with at least k' neighbors
Then remove x_i from S
end
```

Thereby, to maintain the diversity among members in *Co-forest*, two strategies have been implemented in our proposed approach. *Optim Co-forest* combines a re-sampling data methods (Bagging) (Breiman, 1996) and two selection strategies. The first involves the intelligent selection of a subset of random parameters based on the *Rel-RASCO* approach (Yaslan and Cataltepe, 2010) to generate the set of classifiers according to the principle of *Co-forest*. This will conserve the diversity of classifiers and their ability to produce the best discrimination for each class. Once each member of the ensemble is obtained, the second strategy is applied that consist of an extension of the measure importance of RF (Breiman, 2001). It uses a labeled and unlabeled data set to measure the relevance of features. A ranking of features is finally realized with respect to their relevance in semi-supervised classifiers. The combination of these two strategies in the construction of all semi-supervised classifiers leads to explore a larger solution space and beyond retrieve a predictor that reflects all this exploration.

In this article, we propose to establish relevant random subspaces for *Co-forest*. The proposed algorithm, *Optim Co-forest* (Algorithm 3) produces relevant random subspaces using the features relevance score obtained by calculating the mutual information between the features and class labels. To also maintain diversity (randomness), each feature of a subspace is selected as a proportional function to the relevance scores of features probability.

In our proposal *Optim Co-forest* (Algorithm 3 line 2), the first step is to build the classical random forest method proposed by (Breiman, 2001), it sets up an improved bagging (Breiman, 1996) with an induction algorithm *Random Forest* (Forest-RI: Random forest - random Input). It uses the randomization principle "Random Feature Selection" proposed by (Amit and Geman, 1997) to generate a set of trees doubly disrupted using a randomization operating both on the training sample and at internal partitions.

Each tree is thus generated at first from a sub-sample (a bootstrap sample (Efron, 1979)) of the complete training set, similar to the techniques of bagging (Breiman, 1996). Then, the tree is constructed using the CART methodology (Breiman, L. et al., 1984) with the difference that at each node, the selection of the best split, based on the Gini index, is performed not on the complete set of attributes M but on a randomly selected subset of it. The size K of this subset is established prior to the execution of the procedure ($1 \leq K \leq M$) (Sirikulviriya and Sinthupinyo, 2011).

To set the parameter K of the *Random Forest* algorithm, several works in the literature (Breiman, 2001), (Zhou, Z. et al., 2002), have shown that a number of attributes equals to $\sqrt{M}$ is a good compromise to produce an efficient forest.

Strategy One: Relevant Random Subspaces Approach.

In *Optim Co-forest* (Algorithm 3 line 2), we introduce the measure of relevant subspaces on the K randomly selected subset of attributes (Figure. 3). We relied on the principle of generating subsets of the algorithm *Rel-RESCO* (Yaslan and Cataltepe, 2010) because it has the ability to randomly select through a calculation of relevance. This approach helps to bring more diversity to the classifiers while producing as many subspaces as necessary.

For this, we assume that we have a C class problem of classification. Entries $x \in R^2$ is of dimension K. Labels l are represented using an encoding $\in 1,...,C$. It comprises a Bag of labeled data Bag_L which consists of N samples with replacement from L. Our goal is to select O feature subspaces (with $O = Ntree$) $S_1,...,S_O$ (Algorithm 3 line 2), (Figure. 3), so that we can train classifiers on each of these subspaces and combine their outputs to produce an improved ensemble learning for the new examples.

Algorithm 3. Optimized Co-forest Algorithm

Input: The labeled set L, the unlabeled set U, the confidence threshold θ, O: number of relevant random subspaces, the number of random trees $NTree$.

1: Process:

2: Construct a random forest H consisting $NTree$ random trees on O relevent random subspaces.

3: $I \leftarrow$ Measure of feature importance using H

4: for $i = 1 \to NTree$ do

5: $\qquad \hat{e}_{i,0} \leftarrow 0.5$

6: $\qquad w_{i,0} \leftarrow 0$

7: end for

8: $t \leftarrow 0$

9: Repeat Until none of the trees in Forest changes

10: $t \leftarrow t + 1$

11: for $i = 1 \to NTree$ do

12: $\qquad \hat{e}_{i,t} \leftarrow EstimateError\ (H_i, OOB_L)$

13: $\qquad L^1_{i,t} \leftarrow \varnothing$

14: $\qquad$ if $(\hat{e}_{i,t} < \hat{e}_{i,t-1})$ then

15: $\qquad\qquad U^1_{i,t} \leftarrow Subsample\left(U, \dfrac{\hat{e}_{i,t-1} w_{i,t-1}}{\hat{e}_{i,t}}\right)$

16: $\qquad\qquad U^2_{i,t} \leftarrow Subsample\left(U, \dfrac{\hat{e}_{i,t-1} w_{i,t-1}}{\hat{e}_{i,t}}\right)$

17: $\qquad\qquad$ for $x_u \in U^1_{i,t}$ do

18: $\qquad\qquad\qquad$ if $Confidence\ (H_i, x_u) > \theta$ then

19: $\qquad\qquad\qquad L^1_{i,t} \leftarrow L^1_{i,t} \cup (x_u, H_i(x_u))$

20: $\qquad\qquad\qquad w_{i,t} \leftarrow w_{i,t} + Confidence\ (H_i, x_u)$

21: $\qquad\qquad\qquad$ end if

22: $\qquad\qquad$ end for

23: $\qquad$ end if

24: end for

25: for $i = 1 \to NTree$ do

26: $\qquad$ if $(\hat{e}_{i,t} w_{i,t} < \hat{e}_{i,t-1} w_{i,t-1})$ then

27: $\qquad h_i \leftarrow LearnRandomTree\ (L \cup (L^1_{i,t}, I))$

28: $\qquad$ end if

29: end for

30: for $i = 1 \to NTree$ do

31: $\qquad$ for each *feature* f do

32: $\qquad I_{i,t}(f) \leftarrow Measure\ of\ Importance\ (f,\ (OOB_{i,t} \cup U_{i,t}^2))$

33: $\qquad$ end for

34: end for

continued on next page

Algorithm 3. Continued

```
35: for each feature f do
```

$$I(f) \leftarrow \frac{\sum I_{i,t}(f)}{NTree}$$

```
36:
37: end for
38: end of Repeat
```

$$H * (x) \leftarrow \arg\max_{y \in label} \sum_{i:h_i(x)} 1$$

```
39: Output:
```

Figure 3. The relevant subspaces method process

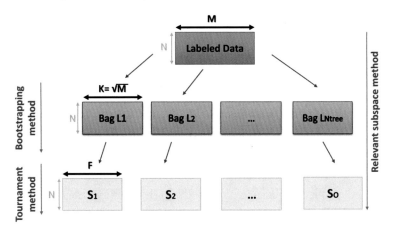

During the production of each feature subspace, the *Relevant Random Subspace* algorithm selects each feature, according to its relevance score achieved from the mutual information between the feature and the labels class (Algorithm 4).

If we note $V_j, j = \{1,2,...,K\}$ the feature vector at N dimensions for the j th feature. Relevance $Rel(V_j)$ of feature V_j, i.e. mutual information $MI(V_j, l)$ between V_j and l target classes can be evaluated as follows:

$$Rel(V_j) = MI(V_j, l) = \sum_{n,c} p(V_{n,c}, l_{n,c}) \log \rightarrow \frac{p(V_{n,c}, l_{n,c})}{p(V_{n,c})p(l_{n,c})} \qquad (2)$$

where $V_{i,j}$ is the $j - th$ feature and $l_{n,c}$ is the label c for the n th training sample.

To be able to calculate the probabilities in equation (2), we have to go through a phase of discretization. Therefore, we will resume the principle used by *Rel-RASCO* (Yaslan and Cataltepe, 2010). Where 10 subsets of equal size are placed between the minimum and maximum values observed for a feature V_j in the labeled training set. We approximate the probability by the average number of samples in each subset.

We create in the first place O subspace $S_1,...,S_O$ each of them containing $m > 0$ features. Secondly, we apply the *tournament* selection method by (Goldberg and Deb, 1991) between pairs of relevant scores of each feature (with size *tournament* fixed to 2) to implement the feature subspaces.

Algorithm 4. Relevant Random Subspace Algorithm

```
1: Inputs: discretized L, Ntree: number of Trees, F: number of features to se-
lect in each bag, labels l.
2: For O = 1 until Ntree Do
    Rel = score relevance (Bag_LO, l) % mutual information between the K fea-
tures and class labels l
For m = 1 until F Do
S_O ←tournament (Rel,m)
end
3: end
```

Selection by *tournament* is performed as follows: Two features are randomly selected from the K set of available features. Of these, two features, one of which has a higher relevance score is added to the selected subset of features. The selected feature is derived from the available features set and the procedure is repeated until all of the selected sets reach the F required number of features (Figure. 4).

The *Optim Co-forest* process continues to build its committee by learning classifiers on O relevant feature subspaces sets, by reference to the principle of *Co-forest*.

We bring some modifications on the computation error $\hat{e}_{i,t}$ of *Co-forest*, where is accurately assessed only in the first iteration based on the estimation Out-Of-Bag error (OOB). The following iterations tend to be underestimated and erroneous because it depends on the training set.

Should be noted that the Out-Of-Bag error (OOB) was already calculated by the Bagging algorithm (Breiman, 1996); hence, the presence of "Bag". The calculation procedure of this error is as follows: From a training set A of N examples, bootstraps samples are generated by drawing N samples with replacement from A (Efron, 1979). On average, for each bootstrap sample 63.2% are unique examples of A, the rest being duplicates (Breiman, 2001). So for each sub base, about 1/3 samples of A are not selected and are called OOB data. They will be used in internal evaluation of the forest (estimated classification generalization error of forest) or as a measure to calculate the feature of importance as a feature selection method.

In *Optim Co-forest* the error is calculated at all levels on the elements *Out Of Bag* (Algorithm 3 line 12), to ensure that the error achieved is unbiased and thus more accurate.

Figure 4. The tournament principle

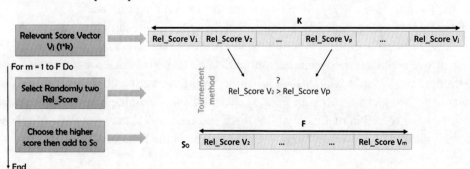

Strategy Two: Measure of Feature Importance by the OOB Estimation.

The second selection strategy that we developed in *Optim Co-forest* is a measure of feature importance from *Out-Of-Bag* sets, which are the samples not used for the construction of the corresponding model; this will lead to an unbiased estimate (Algorithm 3 line 30-36).

First, we construct the set *Out Of Bag* for each classifier, we select then the well predicted examples from labeled OOB_l with the newly labeled examples in a subset will be called U^2 (Algorithm 3 line 16).

Second, we took the confidence of each selected example, measured by the *Confidence* function (Algorithm 5). Note that the confidence of labeled examples if the class label given by h_i is the real label, is set to 1. For unlabeled examples, their confidences will be calculated on the degree of agreement with the label among the members of concomitant H^*.

Finally, the values for each feature V_i are swapped randomly, and h_i is used to predict the class of this new model *Out Of Bag Perm*. The procedure is repeated for each feature $V \in V_1 ... V_i$ (Figure. 5).

At the end of the procedure, the sum of confident examples where the label predicted in *Out Of Bag Perm* differs from the first initial label in *Out Of Bag* is calculated. This last value is averaged over *NTree* (the size of the committee) (Algorithm 3 line 36). The value thus obtained is taken as the importance of the feature V. The key idea of our approach is the use of the confidence of the label in the assessment of importance feature measure. Thus, unlabeled examples play an important role in the importance feature assessment.

Figure 5. Measure importance features procedure

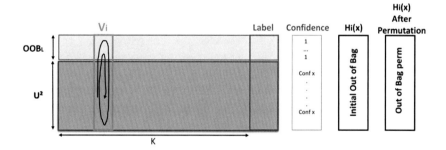

Algorithm 5. Confidence function

```
1: Input: Unlabeled training example x, H_x: committee where x is out of bag,
number of classes C.
2: Apply H_x to generate the class probability distribution for x as P(x) =
{pc(x): c =1...,C}
3: conf (x)= max1≤c≤CP(x)
4: label(x)= argmax1≤c≤CP(x)
5: Output: conf (x) and label(x)
```

The Advantages of Our Approach

The interest of our approach summarizes the various advantages offered compared the state of art algorithms as: *Co-forest*, *ADE-Co-forest* and *Random Forest*.

- First, *Optim Co-forest* outperforms RF when the set of available labeled learning is low. *Random Forest* is based on the learning data available to encourage diversity. Therefore, if the size of the training set is small as is the case with semi-supervised, accordingly diversity among members of the set will be limited. Thus, the overall error will be small. *Optim Co-forest* gradually added newly labeled examples certified by the confident measure to the learning set by building in areas relevant features. However, *Optim Co-forest* can improve the diversity and the average error of all members built by RF (Breiman, 2001), *Co-forest* (Li and Zhou, 2007), *ADE-Co-forest* (Deng and Guo, 2011) and also improves the measurement of feature importance.
- Second, *Optim Co-forest* uses a method of creating diverse set, the feature importance measure based on a set of classifier (calculation of trust) is more accurate than using one classifier.
- Finally, we also note that the feature importance measure is done differently in our approach than *Random Forest*, *Co-forest* (Li and Zhou, 2007) and *ADE-Co-forest* (Deng and Guo, 2011).

In *Co-forest*, measuring feature importance cannot be estimated from *OOB* samples, since the bootstrap sample used to form each random tree is rejected after the first iteration. However, given that the amount of labeled data is very small, the diversity of data *Out Of Bag* is insufficient. Estimates *Out Of Bag* are biased because they depend on a limited number of data.

EXPERIMENTS

The same benchmark data consisting of 10 databases of UCI repository (Newman, D. et al., 1998) where, (Li and Zhou, 2007) and (Deng and Guo, 2011) have made their experiments to evaluate the performance of their algorithms *Co-forest* and *ADE-Co-forest* is used in this paper. The details of these datasets are shown in Table 1.

For each dataset, a 10 cross validation is carried out for evaluation. The training data are randomly divided into two sets: L labeled and unlabeled U determined by a rate (μ), which is calculated by the size of U on the size of $L \cup U$. To simulate different amounts of unlabeled data, four different *unlabeled rates* $\mu = 20\%, 40\%, 60\%$ and 80%, are studied. Also, we note that the distributions of class in L and U are maintained similar to the original set.

In the following experiments, the value of N is 6 trees. Confidence level θ is set at 0.75, i.e, a newly labeled example is considered trusted if more than three quarters of the trees are agreements on its assigned label. To estimate the accuracy on each dataset, we have predetermined a set of labeled examples. For each set, the algorithm is evaluated on its ability to correctly predict the labels of unlabeled examples. The labeled samples were randomly selected, with the only constraint being the presence of at least one example of each class for each set.

To compare the performances of *Optim Co-forest* to *Co-forest*, *Random Forest* and *ADE-Co-forest*, improvements are averaged over all datasets in all unlabeled examples, and improved overall performance is achieved. For each dataset with a specific *unlabeled rate* μ, a cross-validation is repeated ten times,

Table 1. Description of experimental bases

Bases	#instances	#features	#class
Bupa	345	7	2
Colic	368	22	2
Diabetes	768	8	2
Hepatitis	155	19	2
Hypothyroid	3163	25	2
Ionosphere	351	34	2
kr-vs-kp	3196	36	2
Sonar	208	60	2
Vote	435	16	2
Wpbc	194	33	2

and the results are averaged and recorded. Tables 2, 3, 4 and 5 summarize the mean accuracy rate of the ensemble classifiers learned on the different μ.

Tables 2, 3, 4 and 5 show that, compared to the average accuracy rate of *Random Forest* on different rates of μ, the three versions of *Co-forest* in semisupervised learning is able to operate the unlabeled data in order to improve the initial hypothesis learned by *RF* only on labeled data.

For each unlabeled rate μ, *Optim Co-forest* shows the greatest improvement, while *Random Forest* has highlighted the smallest performances of the four algorithms. *Optim-Co-forest* have significantly improved performance compared to *Random Forest, Co-forest* and *ADE-Co-forest*. This can be seen at a different unlabeled rate μ, especially when the rate is high, i.e, the labeled data are very limited.

The obtained results are very interesting and its differences depend on the database. For example, the performance of *Optim Co-forest* on *Sonar, kr − vs − kp* and *Ionosphere* are quite remarkable. Furthermore, *Optim Co-forest* gives equivalent or almost mediocre results on *Diabetes* and *Bupa* datasets. This can

Table 2. The average error of the compared algorithms with an unlabeled rate $\mu= 80\%$

Dataset	Optim Co-Forest		Random Forest (RF)		Co-Forest		ADE-Co-Forest	
	Mean±Std	T(s)	Mean±Std	T(s)	Mean±Std	T(s)	Mean±Std	T(s)
Bupa	0.675 ± 0.0408	2.035	0.464 ± 0.0596	0.103	0.670 ± 0.0530	1.944	0.663 ± 0.0428	1.954
Colic	0.843 ± 0.0073	5.814	0.570 ± 0.0200	0.108	0.841 ± 0.0167	4.643	0.840 ± 0.0218	5.546
Diabetes	0.742 ± 0.0215	4.633	0.372 ± 0.0084	0.134	0.740 ± 0.0268	3.393	0.742 ± 0.0257	4.334
Hepatitis	0.835 ± 0.0208	0.921	0.653 ± 0.0409	0.081	0.832 ± 0.0434	0.663	0.841 ± 0.0667	0.886
Hypothyroid	0.990 ± 0.0044	36.153	0.500 ± 0.0054	0.307	0.989 ± 0.0043	16.284	0.990 ± 0.0048	34.398
Ionosphere	0.931 ± 0.0149	1.973	0.481 ± 0.0287	0.094	0.929 ± 0.0221	1.461	0.928 ± 0.0300	1.671
kr-vs-kp	0.987 ± 0.0529	0.785	0.477 ± 0.1805	0.046	0.983 ± 0.0686	0.453	0.986 ± 0.0610	0.681
Sonar	0.799 ± 0.0283	1.548	0.526 ± 0.0611	0.097	0.797 ± 0.0189	1.106	0.796 ± 0.0664	1.218
Vote	0.958 ± 0.0073	0.980	0.567 ± 0.0274	0.085	0.954 ± 0.0277	0.913	0.956 ± 0.0289	0.882
Wpbc	0.793 ± 0.0073	1.237	0.263 ± 0.0173	0.088	0.788 ± 0.0328	1.247	0.796 ± 0.0311	1.074
Average rank	**1.3**		**4**		**2.6**		**2.1**	

Table 3. The average error of the compared algorithms with an unlabeled rate µ= 60%

Dataset	Optim Co-Forest		Random Forest (RF)		Co-Forest		ADE-Co-Forest	
	Mean±Std	T(s)	Mean±Std	T(s)	Mean±Std	T(s)	Mean±Std	T(s)
Bupa	0.674 ± 0.0169	2.154	0.642 ± 0.0420	0.082	0.660 ± 0.0290	0.935	0.662 ± 0.0586	2.096
Colic	0.842 ± 0.0559	2.915	0.821 ± 0.0117	0.091	0.838 ± 0.0170	3.045	0.84 ± 0.0241	2.894
Diabetes	0.75 ± 0.0290	3.365	0.730 ± 0.0353	0.104	0.743 ± 0.0250	2.584	0.749 ± 0.0239	3.207
Hepatitis	0.828 ± 0.0159	0.622	0.811 ± 0.0631	0.069	0.828 ± 0.0750	0.462	0.831 ± 0.0253	0.536
Hypothyroid	0.988 ± 0.0000	26.453	0.987 ± 0.0031	0.286	0.988 ± 0.0059	12.767	0.988 ± 0.0040	25.835
Ionosphere	0.921 ± 0.0061	1.246	0.909 ± 0.0300	0.076	0.921 ± 0.0496	1.161	0.92 ± 0.0668	1.193
kr-vs-kp	0.983 ± 0.0039	2.012	0.976 ± 0.0359	0.095	0.980 ± 0.0282	0.952	0.981 ± 0.0177	1.827
Sonar	0.785 ± 0.0256	0.598	0.738 ± 0.0915	0.072	0.777 ± 0.0625	0.726	0.782 ± 0.0769	0.550
Vote	0.955 ± 0.0485	0.494	0.945 ± 0.0283	0.074	0.951 ± 0.0396	0.472	0.957 ± 0.0544	0.446
Wpbc	0.753 ± 0.0011	0.601	0.689 ± 0.0380	0.071	0.746 ± 0.0407	0.621	0.754 ± 0.0420	0.597
Average rank	**1.5**		**4**		**2.7**		**1.8**	

Table 4. The average error of the compared algorithms with an unlabeled rate µ=40%

Dataset	Optim Co-Forest		Random Forest (RF)		Co-Forest		ADE-Co-Forest	
	Mean±Std	T(s)	Mean±Std	T(s)	Mean±Std	T(s)	Mean±Std	T(s)
Bupa	0.65 ± 0.0061	2.183	0.626 ± 0.0420	0.082	0.645 ± 0.0290	0.935	0.651 ± 0.0586	2.096
Colic	0.839 ± 0.0061	2.921	0.812 ± 0.0117	0.091	0.829 ± 0.0170	3.045	0.832 ± 0.0241	2.894
Diabetes	0.739 ± 0.0043	3.256	0.733 ± 0.0353	0.104	0.741 ± 0.0250	2.584	0.74 ± 0.0239	3.207
Hepatitis	0.833 ± 0.0163	0.554	0.805 ± 0.0631	0.069	0.818 ± 0.0750	0.462	0.825 ± 0.0253	0.536
Hypothyroid	0.988 ± 0.0010	26.946	0.986 ± 0.0031	0.286	0.987 ± 0.0059	12.767	0.987 ± 0.0040	25.835
Ionosphere	0.931 ± 0.0467	1.354	0.898 ± 0.0300	0.076	0.921 ± 0.0496	1.161	0.923 ± 0.0668	1.193
kr-vs-kp	0.982 ± 0.0107	2.014	0.968 ± 0.0092	0.097	0.976 ± 0.0231	0.105	0.978 ± 0.0294	1.986
Sonar	0.778 ± 0.0199	0.659	0.721 ± 0.0915	0.072	0.757 ± 0.0625	0.726	0.764 ± 0.0769	0.550
Vote	0.957 ± 0.0045	0.499	0.945 ± 0.0283	0.074	0.953 ± 0.0396	0.472	0.955 ± 0.0544	0.446
Wpbc	0.75 ± 0.0334	0.603	0.718 ± 0.0380	0.071	0.724 ± 0.0407	0.621	0.735 ± 0.0420	0.597
Average rank	**1.3**		**4**		**2.75**		**1.95**	

be explained by the small number of attributes in their data set. In fact, each tree in the random forest is constructed using the best attribute among several attributes randomly selected for internal distribution at each node. More the number of attributes is small in subsets, more there is a high chance that some attributes are selected. Therefore, there is more chance that the internal distribution of the tree is the same. Thus, a random forest with an ensemble of trees generated with a minimal number of attributes could be less diverse compared to those formed on other attributes.

In Table 2, we can see that the *Diabetes* dataset have only 8 attributes and *Bupa* has 6 features while the *Hepatitis* and *Wpbc* have a more important number of features. This may explain the performances on *Diabetes* and *Bupa* which tend to be lower than *Ionosphere* and *Sonar* Tables 2, 3, 4 and 5.

Table 5. The average error of the compared algorithms with an unlabeled rate μ=20%

Dataset	Optim Co-Forest		Random Forest (RF)		Co-Forest		ADE-Co-Forest	
	Mean±Std	T(s)	Mean±Std	T(s)	Mean±Std	T(s)	Mean±Std	T(s)
Bupa	0.623 ± 0.0142	1.136	0.604 ± 0.0098	0.077	0.615 ± 0.0613	0.985	0.62 ± 0.0323	1.127
Colic	0.831 ± 0.0028	2.298	0.793 ± 0.0640	0.078	0.822 ± 0.0794	2.058	0.821 ± 0.0820	2.233
Diabetes	0.75 ± 0.0147	2.301	0.721 ± 0.0129	0.086	0.737 ± 0.0272	1.983	0.745 ± 0.0219	2.297
Hepatitis	0.825 ± 0.0114	0.256	0.792 ± 0.0286	0.077	0.813 ± 0.0363	0.392	0.82 ± 0.0481	0.229
Hypothyroid	0.986 ± 0.0119	18.023	0.983 ± 0.0129	0.251	0.984 ± 0.0137	8.845	0.985 ± 0.0035	17.626
Ionosphere	0.912 ± 0.0323	0.773	0.869 ± 0.0549	0.071	0.908 ± 0.0195	0.730	0.911 ± 0.0430	0.715
kr-vs-kp	0.971 ± 0.0123	1.126	0.95 ± 0.0133	0.065	0.966 ± 0.0347	0.923	0.9691 ± 0.0283	1.025
Sonar	0.754 ± 0.0097	0.432	0.678 ± 0.0831	0.062	0.705 ± 0.0664	0.522	0.747 ± 0.0831	0.402
Vote	0.953 ± 0.0118	0.487	0.94 ± 0.0477	0.070	0.944 ± 0.0559	0.614	0.949 ± 0.0424	0.457
Wpbc	0.751 ± 5.8514E-17	0.389	0.697 ± 0.0462	0.063	0.75 ± 0.0395	0.466	0.757 ± 0.0666	0.340
Average rank	**1.1**		**4**		**2.9**		**2**	

When performance is important, as it often is, we also need to choose an algorithm that runs quickly and uses the available computing resources efficiently. We shall, in fact, take the efficiency of the compared algorithms by measuring the mean of the amount of time they take. Tables 2, Table 3, Table 4 and Table 5 indicate the run time T(s) with the same execution hardware (i7-4720HQ CPU @ 2.60GHz) of the four algorithms for each unlabeled rates. We notice that, *Optim Co-forest* records slightly more running time than the three others approaches, the two strategies applied to optimize *Co-forest* explains the slight difference in the application of small databases.

In order to better assess the results obtained for each algorithm, we adopt in this study the post-hoc Friedman test methodology proposed by (Demsar, 2006) for the comparison of several algorithms over multiple datasets.

Friedman Post-Hoc Comparison

The Friedman test is a non-parametric test (free distribution) used to compare observations repeated on the same subjects. This is also called a nonparametric randomized block analysis of variance. The statistical test for the Friedman's test is a chi-square with $a - 1$ degrees of freedom, where a is the number of repeated measures. When the $p-value$ for this test is small (usually lower than 0.05), we have evidence to reject the null hypothesis.

Firstly, we used the non-parametric Friedman test to evaluate the rejection of the hypothesis that all the classifiers perform equally well for a given level. It ranks the algorithms for each dataset separately, the best performing algorithm getting the lower rank, for example, in our case with 4 classifiers it equals to 1, the second best rank 2, etc.

Then, the Friedman test compares the average ranks of the algorithms and calculates the Friedman statistic. In our case, with four algorithms and 10 datasets, Friedman statistic (distributed according to chi-square with 3 degrees of freedom): is 27.72 for $\mu = 20\%$, 24.33 for $\mu = 40\%$, 22.68 for $\mu = 60\%$ and

23.16 for μ= 80%. P-value computed by Friedman Test: 0.000004, 0.000021, 0.000047 and 0.000037 respectively, so the null hypothesis is rejected at a high level of significance for all μ.

If a statistically significant difference in the performance is detected, which means that some of the hypotheses in the experimentation have different distribution from one another, therefore, our next step will be to try and find out which pairs of our algorithms are significantly different then each other. We proceed with a post-hoc test.

Demsar shown in his study (Demsar, 2006), that the power of the post-hoc test is much greater when all classifiers are compared only to a control classifier and not among themselves. We thus should not make pairwise comparisons when we in fact, only test whether a newly proposed method is better than the existing ones.

When all classifiers are compared with a control classifier, we can instead use one of the general procedures for controlling the family-wise error in multiple hypothesis testing, such as the Bonferroni correction. Although this method is generally conservative, more flexible and easy test to use (Demsar, 2006).

A *p*-value provides information about whether a statistical hypothesis test is significant or not, and it also indicates something about how significant the result is: the smaller the *p*-value, the stronger the evidence against the null hypothesis. Most importantly, it does this without committing to a particular level of significance.

According to (Garcıa, D. et al., 2010), when a *p*-value is considered in a multiple comparison, it reflects the probability of error of a certain comparison, but it does not take into account the remaining comparisons belonging to the family. (Garcıa, S. et al., 2010) recommend the use of adjusted p-values (APVs) due to the fact that they provide more information in a statistical analysis.

In this paper, the statistical tests are conducted once, assuming that the results come from an aggregation based on the means of several repetitions. In our case, we measured the performance of each classifier by means of its accuracy in test data by using 5 repetitions of 10-fold cross validation, so each result belonging to the sample analyzed by the statistical tests actually represents the mean of 50 runs of the algorithm in question. The Adjusted *p*-values obtained by applying post-hoc methods over the results of Friedman procedure are summarized in Table 6).

The Bonferroni-Dunn's procedure rejects the hypotheses that have an unadjusted p-value ≤ 0.016667. At $\mu = 20$ and 40% unlabeled rate for small dimensional datasets, the test found *Random forest* and *Co-forest* significantly different from *Optim Co-forest*, the test found *ADE-Co-forest* and *Optim Co-forest* too similar. Therefore, at the 60 and 80% unlabeled rate, *Optim Co-forest*, *ADE-Co-forest* and *Random forest* are too similar, the test rejects only the *Random forest*.

Application on High Dimensional Datasets

As mentioned earlier in the presentation of *Optim Co-forest* algorithm, our proposed approach is more focused and geared on high dimensional datasets, where features can be correlated, redundant or perhaps noisy and thus irrelevant. In this case, *Optim Co-forest* can smoothly select the most relevant features, providing a more interesting performance. Hence, we confirm this hypothesis by the following tests.

We have selected a set of 10 high dimensional databases from ASU repository (Zafarani and Liu, 1998) and UCI (Newman, D. et al., 1998); their characteristics are summarized in Table 7. To study the effectiveness of *Optim Co-forest* on high dimensional datasets in semi-supervised learning, the performance of *RF*, *Co-forest* and *ADE-Co-forest* are also analyzed.

Table 6. Post-hoc comparison Table for $\alpha = 0.05$ (Friedman)

μ	i	Algorithm	$z = (R_0 - R_i)/SE$	Unadjusted p
20%	3	RF	5.022947	0.000001
	2	Co-forest	3.117691	0.001823
	1	ADE-Co-forest	1.558846	0.119033
40%	3	RF	4.676537	0.000003
	2	Co-forest	2.511474	0.012023
	1	ADE-Co-forest	1.125833	0.260236
60%	3	RF	4.330127	0.000015
	2	Co forest	2.078461	0.037667
	1	ADE-Co-forest	0.519615	0.603332
80%	3	RF	4.676537	0.000003
	2	Co-forest	2.251666	0.024343
	1	ADE-Co-forest	1.385641	0.165857

Table 7. Description of experimental high dimensional datasets

Bases	#instances	#features	#class
Arcene	200	10000	2
BaseHock	1993	4862	2
CNAE-9	1080	856	9
Leukemia	73	7129	2
Madelon	2598	500	2
Musk	476	166	2
Ovarian	54	1536	2
PCMAC	1943	3289	2
Relathe	1427	4322	2
Toxicology	171	5748	4

The results were performed with the following parameters: the number of tree N equals to 100 trees, the confidence level θ fixed to 0.75. The 10 cross-validation method is applied, the tests follow the same simulation strategy as above with different amounts of *unlabeled rates μ* variant from 20% to 80%, with a distribution of class L and U similar to the original dataset.

It can be seen from Tables 8, 9, 10 and 11 that, *Optim Co-forest* is able to improve the performance of hypothesis learned from different rates of unlabeled data. The average accuracy of the four unlabeled rates μ of the various tables was improved respectively.

We also note that *ADE-Co-forest* has performed significantly lower than *Co-forest* when scaling on different μ. In another scenario, *Optim Co-forest* making significant performance even in the most extreme conditions with a rate of unlabeled $\mu = 80\%$ (Table 8); which brings us back, citing the *CNAE*

Table 8. The average accuracy of the compared algorithms on large dimensional datasets with unlabeled rate μ = 80%

Dataset	Optim Co-Forest		Random Forest (RF)		Co-Forest		ADE-Co-Forest	
	Mean±Std	T(s)	Mean±Std	T(s)	Mean±Std	T(s)	Mean±Std	T(s)
Arcene	0.5118 ± 0.0777	3.1632	0.4647 ± 0.0503	0.1371	0.5176 ± 0.0369	1.3980	0.4706 ± 0.0716	2.8093
BaseHock	0.8547 ± 0.0359	996.2300	0.5700 ± 0.0116	1.3317	0.6243 ± 0.0124	98.2694	0.6201 ± 0.0642	956.8076
CNAE-9	0.6889 ± 0.0282	26.2365	0.3722 ± 0.0449	0.5091	0.4922 ± 0.0528	14.4724	0.4778 ± 0.0654	24.0344
Leukemia	0.7231 ± 0.0114	0.5313	0.6538 ± 0.0583	0.0942	0.6538 ± 0.0798	0.2811	0.6769 ± 0.0570	0.4775
Madelon	0.5621 ± 0.0158	85.2317	0.5002 ± 0.0126	0.5012	0.5007 ± 0.0309	14.3252	0.5005 ± 0.0148	81.2428
Musk	0.5100 ± 0.0100	1.9855	0.4812 ± 0.0565	0.1601	0.5112 ± 0.0518	1.5900	0.4975 ± 0.0617	1.6966
Ovarian	0.6000 ± 0.0031	0.3564	0.4778 ± 0.0609	0.0961	0.5000 ± 0.0497	0.0998	0.4778 ± 0.0248	0.2320
PCMAC	0.8040 ± 0.0568	1235.6480	0.5260 ± 0.0346	2.1784	0.5473 ± 0.0476	62.2557	0.5488 ± 0.0598	1098.6757
Relathe	0.6587 ± 0.0389	276.5900	0.5673 ± 0.0190	1.5407	0.6059 ± 0.0438	69.3345	0.5908 ± 0.0512	252.3587
Toxicology	0.3053 ± 0.0130	1.4632	0.2632 ± 0.0517	0.1706	0.2667 ± 0.0505	0.3165	0.2667 ± 0.0147	1.2165
Average rank	1.2		3.9		2.1		2.8	

− 9 for example, only 15 individuals labeled with 7129 features and yet an average improvement of 19% on performances.

The feature importance measure adopted in *Optim Co-forest* had made significant improvements, distinguishing as an excellent candidate in the semi-supervised classification of high dimensional dataset. Furthermore, in term of computing time T(s) (Tables 8, 9, 10 and 11), we can see clearly that, in high dimensional dataset application, *Optim Co-forest* is greedier, this especially on the bases with a large number of attributes, which which is connected to the computational complexity of the two adopted selections strategies.

The Friedman post-hoc comparison of the four algorithms with the Adjusted P-values over the results of Friedman procedure is summery in Table 12. For high dimensional datasets, the Bonferroni-Dunn's procedure rejects those hypotheses that have an unadjusted p-value ≤ 0.016667, at each unlabeled rate μ. Thereby, the test found at $\mu = 20,40$ and 80% unlabeled rate *Random forest* and *ADE-Co-forest* significantly different from *Optim Co-forest*, and a similarity in measure performances between *Optim Co-forest* and *Co-forest*.

Therefore, at the 60% unlabeled rate, *Optim Co-forest*, *ADE-Co-forest* are too similar, the test rejects the *Random forest* and *Co-forest* algorithms. This can be explained by the editing data approach applied by *ADE-Co-forest* allowing it to remove the noisy data and surpass *Co-forest* at some level of available labeled dataset.

Table 9. The average accuracy of the compared algorithms on high dimensional datasets with unlabeled rate μ = 60%

Dataset	Optim Co-Forest		Random Forest (RF)		Co-Forest		ADE-Co-Forest	
	Mean±Std	T(s)	Mean±Std	T(s)	Mean±Std	T(s)	Mean±Std	T(s)
Arcene	0.5165 ± 0.0256	10.7892	0.4412 ± 0.0411	0.3282	0.4824 ± 0.0483	1.8689	0.4912 ± 0.0305	9.2982
BaseHock	0.8718 ± 0.0111	1965.3546	0.5471 ± 0.0153	4.7914	0.6321 ± 0.0063	149.3320	0.6351 ± 0.0195	1871.3423
CNAE-9	0.7189 ± 0.0618	61.2355	0.3567 ± 0.0191	0.7362	0.4633 ± 0.0341	24.6943	0.4878 ± 0.0388	59.4440
Leukemia	0.7385 ± 0.0150	1.5688	0.6538 ± 0.0834	0.1373	0.6611 ⊥ 0.0632	0.5043	0.6741 ± 0.0608	1.0460
Madelon	0.5095 ± 0.0147	160.0256	0.5000 ± 0.0279	1.1366	0.5042 ± 0.0208	21.4946	0.5090 ± 0.0163	158.7042
Musk	0.4587 ± 0.0163	2.8955	0.4375 ± 0.0476	0.1277	0.4450 ± 0.0307	2.3389	0.4463 ± 0.0162	2.4255
Ovarian	0.7289 ± 0.0932	0.8623	0.4556 ± 0.1204	0.1407	0.5089 ± 0.0633	0.4353	0.5137 ± 0.1009	0.5000
PCMAC	0.7954 ± 0.0280	1112.0135	0.5214 ± 0.0348	4.2671	0.5501 ± 0.0176	54.0222	0.5498 ± 0.0219	1002.7259
Relathe	0.6516 ± 0.0253	402.8965	0.5572 ± 0.0125	2.8730	0.5954 ± 0.0280	47.6561	0.5820 ± 0.0306	390.1300
Toxicology	0.3158 ± 0.0480	3.4786	0.2667 ± 0.0419	0.2570	0.2772 ± 0.0563	1.6305	0.2667 ± 0.0419	3.2478
Average rank	**1**		**3.95**		**2.7**		**2.35**	

To further support these rank comparisons, we compared, on each dataset the hegemony of *Optim Co-forest* with each pair of methods. We use the paired t-test (with $p = 0.05$) on the accuracy values in Tables 8, 9, 10 and 11 for respectively μ 20, 40, 60 and 80%. The results of these pairwise comparisons are depicted in Table 13 in terms of "Win — Tie — Loss" statuses [24] of our approach with each pair of methods; the three values in each cell indicate how many times the *Optim Co-forest* is significantly better/not significantly different/significantly worse than the other method over the 10 high dimensional datasets.

It can be clearly seen from Pairwise t-test comparisons Table 13, that *Optim Co-forest* significantly outperforms *Co-forest* and *ADE-Co-forest* for high dimensional data set.

Overall, these experimentations, however, a question remains, would it not be a better idea to use a standard feature selection as a preprocessing step in semi-supervised learning for better performance. Therefore, we have established an evaluation of our approach as a semi-supervised feature selection approach on an extended version of our study.

Next, we experiment *Optim Co-forest* as a feature selection method in semi-supervised learning. The evaluations are made on several high dimensional databases from ASU and UCI to prove the effectiveness of *Optim Co-forest* as a feature selection method, and confirm its ability to select and measure importance to improve the performance of the hypothesis learned with a small amount of labeled samples by exploiting unlabeled samples.

Table 10. The average accuracy of the compared algorithms on high dimensional datasets with unlabeled rate μ = 40%

Dataset	Optim Co-Forest		Random Forest (RF)		Co-Forest		ADE-Co-Forest	
	Mean±Std	T(s)	Mean±Std	T(s)	Mean±Std	T(s)	Mean±Std	T(s)
Arcene	0.6453 ± 0.0297	12.1003	0.5076 ± 0.0460	0.4207	0.5877 ± 0.0403	2.2795	0.6043 ± 0.0197	11.4293
BaseHock	0.8092 ± 0.0133	7025.6955	0.5862 ± 0.0195	8.0011	0.7051 ± 0.0068	110.3242	0.6698 ± 0.0152	6866.1659
CNAE-9	0.6303 ± 0.0294	87.2365	0.3878 ± 0.0370	1.4157	0.5239 ± 0.0159	24.4810	0.4264 ± 0.0146	85.6367
Leukemia	0.7231 ± 0.0498	1.9632	0.6538 ± 0.0885	0.1528	0.6654 ± 0.0918	0.5478	0.6538 ± 0.0501	1.6467
Madelon	0.5635 ± 0.0218	183.2152	0.5016 ± 0.0174	1.4692	0.5089 ± 0.0280	24.0347	0.5066 ± 0.0189	171.2990
Musk	0.6469 ± 0.0346	3.9965	0.4781 ± 0.0591	0.1535	0.6231 ± 0.0214	1.8201	0.5725 ± 0.0347	3.5546
Ovarian	0.7111 ± 0.0778	0.5123	0.4944 ± 0.0843	0.1362	0.5944 ± 0.0556	0.3709	0.5722 ± 0.0633	0.4694
PCMAC	0.6435 ± 0.0204	6324.5980	0.5367 ± 0.0150	6.9202	0.5857 ± 0.0158	90.4668	0.5678 ± 0.0182	6182.8384
Relathe	0.7623 ± 0.0334	1121.3587	0.5723 ± 0.0179	5.5956	0.6551 ± 0.0135	47.3533	0.6166 ± 0.0387	1074.2383
Toxicology	0.4228 ± 0.0509	5.4237	0.3649 ± 0.0771	0.3383	0.4000 ± 0.0603	1.8807	0.3877 ± 0.0400	5.0429
Average rank	1		3.95		2.1		2.95	

CONCLUSION

This work presented an optimized semi-supervised ensemble method *Optim Co-forest* that improves the performances of *Co-forest* algorithm in high dimensional dataset applications, whilst considering sources of information from labeled as well as unlabeled data. In this semi-supervised learning task, we developed our research according to two distinct approaches. The first one is based on the idea of eliminating irrelevant features by the selection of relevant random subspaces for *Co-forest*. In order to also maintain randomness, each feature for a subspace is selected based on probabilities proportional to relevance scores of features. The second approach is the feature importance measure to establish the relevance of features by the out of Bag estimation. The combination of these two strategies in the construction of all semi-supervised classifiers led to the exploration of a larger solution space and beyond have a more competitive and adequate predictor for high dimensional spaces.

Experiments on small and high dimensional datasets from the UCI verify the effectiveness of *Optim Co-forest*. They clearly show that the principle of *Optim Co-forest* is more interesting and powerful and, thereby, stands out in the case of high dimensional dataset. Like all methods, *Optim Co-forest* has advantages, drawbacks and specific technical characteristics that have to be taken into account when applying it to the problems. Depending on the own problem characteristics our method will be more interesting rather than others. For example, it will depend on the type of available data, the quantity of

Table 11. The average accuracy of the compared algorithms on high dimensional datasets with unlabeled rate μ = 20%

Dataset	Optim Co-Forest		Random Forest (RF)		Co-Forest		ADE-Co-Forest	
	Mean±Std	T(s)	Mean±Std	T(s)	Mean±Std	T(s)	Mean±Std	T(s)
Arcene	0.5809 ± 0.0497	26.8956	0.4706 ± 0.0524	0.5852	0.5574 ± 0.0682	2.8265	0.5603 ± 0.0472	25.4365
BaseHock	0.8020 ± 0.0167	1533.2555	0.5775 ± 0.0162	6.3920	0.6985 ± 0.0086	39.5137	0.661 ± 0.0115	1496.3231
CNAE-9	0.5006 ± 0.0213	122.3255	0.3281 ± 0.0145	1.7349	0.4550 ± 0.0352	353.5539	0.3872 ± 0.0201	120.8174
Leukemia	0.7615 ± 0.099	1.7524	0.6538 + 0.0699	0.1562	0.6692 ± 0.0926	0.4856	0.6577 ± 0.0632	1.7313
Madelon	0.5470 ± 0.0302	210.2354	0.5008 ± 0.0139	2.2302	0.5106 ± 0.0371	337.9970	0.5088 ± 0.0458	202.7113
Musk	0.5969 ± 0.0515	4.7859	0.4763 ± 0.0421	0.1903	0.5825 ± 0.0428	2.8359	0.53 ± 0.0456	4.5300
Ovarian	0.7056 ± 0.1049	0.6234	0.4722 ± 0.0304	0.1232	0.5611 ± 0.1009	0.4204	0.5389 ± 0.1204	0.5704
PCMAC	0.7287 ± 0.0295	1678.9560	0.5341 ± 0.0258	8.5303	0.5804 ± 0.0159	49.0181	0.5624 ± 0.0150	1654.5269
Relathe	0.7216 ± 0.0171	963.2540	0.5581 ± 0.0240	7.4081	0.6365 ± 0.0182	51.7928	0.599 ± 0.0149	943.0689
Toxicology	0.4351 ± 0.0574	5.2364	0.3789 ± 0.0771	0.3383	0.3947 ± 0.0603	1.8807	0.3807 ± 0.0400	5.0429
Average rank	**1**		**4**		**2.1**		**2.9**	

Table 12. Post-hoc comparison Table for α = 0.05 (Friedman)

μ	i	Algorithm	$z = (R_0 - R_i)/SE$	Unadjusted p
20%	3	RF	5.196152	0
	2	ADE-Co-forest	3.290897	0.000999
	1	Co-forest	1.905256	0.056747
40%	3	RF	5.10955	0
	2	ADE-Co-forest	3.377499	0.000731
	1	Co-forest	1.905256	0.056747
60%	3	RF	5.10955	0
	2	Co-forest	2.944486	0.003235
	1	ADE-Co-forest	2.338269	0.019373
80%	3	RF	4.676537	0.000003
	2	ADE-Co-forest	2.771281	0.005584
	1	Co-forest	1.558846	0.119033

Table 13. Pairwise t-test comparisons of Optim Co-forest method with the 3 others approaches in terms of accuracy

Algorithm	Random Forest			Co-Forest			ADE-Co-Forest		
Paired t-Test (with $t = 0.05$)	Win	Tie	Loss	Win	Tie	Loss	Win	Tie	Loss
$\mu\% = 20$	10	0	0	7	3	0	9	1	0
$\mu\% = 40$	10	0	0	7	3	0	9	1	0
$\mu\% = 60$	10	0	0	7	2	1	7	3	0
$\mu\% = 80$	10	0	0	8	2	0	9	1	0

data (labeled and unlabeled), the proportions between each type of data, the nature of these data, the way how it is measured, the type of study, the objectives, and the available resources like time, hardware, etc.

When unlabeled data are labeled iteratively, the ensemble accuracy of *Optim Co-forest* is better than *Co-forest* or *ADE Co-forest*. Unlike *ADE Co-forest,* which applies the principle of data editing to discard noisy examples, *Optim Co-forest* is more focus on selecting the important and relevant features for a better ensemble learning and therefor, a better discrimination of noisy examples especially in the context of high dimensional dataset. *Optim Co-forest* performs significantly better than *co-Forest* or *ADE Co-forest* when there are many irrelevant features or when high number of features are used for each classifier. The same pronouncement can be done as semi supervised feature selection approach.

However, there are some points that deserve some discussion and further development in future works. We must say that the main limitation of our method is the long time processing, which makes it useless in big problems. One of the proposed solutions to deal with this problem is the parallel programming. Indeed, our algorithm allows us to use a master /slave architecture. Further work is currently underway, with new experiments on biological databases with thousands of features and can assess the stability in feature selection methods (Kuncheva, 2007) when small changes are made to the data.

The other point in the same method that deserves some attention is the feature importance measure based on the Random forest Out-Of-Bag measure; the score importance step needs to be improved. The way in which it is implemented only perform a univariate filter, analyzing individually the importance of each feature. It must be interesting to develop or to use some multivariate measure because the features that are irrelevant alone may be very important when considered together with other features and such change can improve the method performances.

ACKNOWLEDGMENT

This research was partially supported by LIMOS, CNRS, UMR 6158, 63173, Aubiere, France. Their contributions are sincerely appreciated and gratefully acknowledged. However, we would like to express our deep appreciation and indebtedness to Dr. Haytham Elghazel, Université de Lyon, CNRS. Université Lyon 1, LIRIS UMR 5205, F-69622, France, the initiator of this study, to sharing his expertise and knowledge in this field.

REFERENCES

Amit, Y., & Geman, D. (1997). Shape quantization and recognition with randomized trees. *Neural Computation*, *9*(7), 1545–1588. doi:10.1162/neco.1997.9.7.1545

Blum, A., & Mitchell, T. (1998). Combining labeled and unlabeled data with co-training. *Proceedings of the eleventh annual conference on Computational learning theory*, 92–100. doi:10.1145/279943.279962

Breiman, L. (1996). Bagging predictors. *Machine Learning*, *24*(2), 123–140. doi:10.1007/BF00058655

Breiman, L. (2001). Random forests. *Machine Learning*, *45*(1), 5–32. doi:10.1023/A:1010933404324

Breiman, L., Friedman, J. H., Olshen, R. A., & Stone, C. J. (1984). *Classification And Regression Trees*. New York: Chapman and Hall.

Chapelle, O., Scholkopf, B., & Zien, A. (2006). *Semi-Supervised Learning*. Cambridge, MA: MIT Press. doi:10.7551/mitpress/9780262033589.001.0001

Cornuejols, A., & Miclet, L. (2010). *Apprentissage artificiel: Concepts et algorithmes*. Eyrolles.

Demsar, J. (2006). Statistical comparisons of classifiers over multiple datasets. *Journal of Machine Learning Research*, *7*, 1–30.

Deng, C., & Guo, M. (2011). A new co-training-style random forest for computer aided diagnosis. *Journal of Intelligent Information Systems*, *36*(3), 253–281. doi:10.1007/s10844-009-0105-8

Efron, B. (1979). Bootstrap methods: Another look at the jackknife. *Annals of Statistics*, *7*(1), 1–26. doi:10.1214/aos/1176344552

Freund, Y., Seung, H. S., Shamir, E., & Tishby, N. (1997). Selective sampling using the query by committee algorithm. *Machine Learning*, *28*(2-3), 133–168. doi:10.1023/A:1007330508534

Garcia, S., Fernandez, A., Luengo, J., & Herrera, F. (2010). Advanced non-parametric tests for multiple comparisons in the design of experiments in computational intelligence and data mining: Experimental analysis of power. *Inf. Sci.*, *180*(10), 2044–2064. doi:10.1016/j.ins.2009.12.010

Goldberg, D. E., & Deb, K. (1991). A comparative analysis of selection schemes used in genetic algorithms. In *Foundations of Genetic Algorithms* (pp. 69–93). Morgan Kaufmann. doi:10.1016/B978-0-08-050684-5.50008-2

Hindawi, M., Elghazel, H., & Benabdeslem, K. (2013). Efficient semi-supervised feature selection by an ensemble approach. *International Workshop on Complex Machine Learning Problems with Ensemble Methods COPEM@ECML/PKDD'13*, 41–55.

Ho, T. K. (1998). The random subspace method for constructing decision forests. *IEEE Transactions on Pattern Analysis and Machine Intelligence*, *20*(8), 832–844. doi:10.1109/34.709601

Jiang, Y., & Hua, Z. (2004). Editing training data for KNN classifiers with neural network ensemble. *Lecture Notes in Computer Science*, *3173*, 356–361.

Krogh, A., & Vedelsby, J. (1995). Neural network ensembles cross validation, and active learning. *Advances in Neural Information Processing Systems, 7*, 231–238.

Kuncheva, L. I. (2007). A stability index for feature selection. *Proceedings of the 25th IASTED International Multi-Conference: Artificial Intelligence and Applications*, 390–395.

Leskes, B., & Torenvliet, L. (2008). The value of agreement a new boosting algorithm. *Journal of Computer and System Sciences, 74*(4), 557–586. doi:10.1016/j.jcss.2007.06.005

Li, M., & Zhou, Z.-H. (2007). Improve computer-aided diagnosis with machine learning techniques using undiagnosed samples. *Trans. Sys. Man Cyber. Part A, 37*(6), 1088–1098. doi:10.1109/TSMCA.2007.904745

Newman, D., Hettich, S., Blake, C., & Merz, C. (1998). *Uci repository of machine learning databases.* Academic Press.

Nigam, K., & Ghani, R. (2000). Analyzing the effectiveness and applicability of co-training. *Proceedings of the Ninth International Conference on Information and Knowledge Management,* 86–93. doi:10.1145/354756.354805

Roli, F. (2005). Semi-supervised multiple classifier systems: Background and research directions. Lecture Notes in Computer Science, 3541, 1–11.

Sheskin, D. J. (2007). Handbook of Parametric and Nonparametric Statistical Procedures (4th ed.). Chapman & Hall/CRC.

Sirikulviriya, N., & Sinthupinyo, S. (2011). Integration of rules from a random forest. *International Conference on Information and Electronics Engineering IPCSIT,* 6.

Valiant, L. G. (1984). A theory of the learnable. *Communications of the ACM, 27*(11), 1134–1142. doi:10.1145/1968.1972

Wang, J., Luo, S., & Zeng, X. (2008). A random subspace method for co-training. In *IJCNN* (pp. 195–200). IEEE.

Yaslan, Y., & Cataltepe, Z. (2010). Co-training with relevant random sub-spaces. *Neurocomput., 73*(10-12), 1652–1661. doi:10.1016/j.neucom.2010.01.018

Zafarani, R., & Liu, H. (1998). *Asu repository of social computing databases.* Academic Press.

Zhou, Y., & Goldman, S. (2004). Democratic co-learning. *Proceedings of the 16th IEEE International Conference on Tools with Artificial Intelligence, ICTAI '04,* 594–202. doi:10.1109/ICTAI.2004.48

Zhou, Z.-H., & Li, M. (2005). Tri-training: Exploiting unlabeled data using three classifiers. *IEEE Transactions on Knowledge and Data Engineering, 17*(11), 1529–1541. doi:10.1109/TKDE.2005.186

Zhou, Z.-H., Wu, J., & Tang, W. (2002). Ensembling neural networks: Many could be better than all. *Artificial Intelligence, 137*(1-2), 239–263. doi:10.1016/S0004-3702(02)00190-X

Zhu, X. (2005). *Semi-Supervised learning literature survey. Technical report, Computer Sciences.* University of Wisconsin-Madison.

ENDNOTES

[1]   A bootstrap sample L is, for example, obtained by randomly drawing n observations with replacement from the training sample L_n each observation with a probability 1/n to be drawn.

[2]   Each bootstrap sample leaves out about 37% of the examples. These left-out examples are the Out-Of-Bag (OOB) samples

Chapter 13
Predicting Patterns in Hospital Admission Data

Jesús Manuel Puentes Gutiérrez
Universidad de Alcalá, Spain

Miguel-Angel Sicilia
University of Alcalá, Spain

Salvador Sánchez-Alonso
Universidad de Alcalá, Spain

Elena García Barriocanal
Universidad de Alcalá, Spain

ABSTRACT

Predicting patterns to extract knowledge can be a tough task but it is worth. When you want to accomplish that task you have to take your time analysing all the data you have and you have to adapt it to the algorithms and technologies you are going to use after analysing. So you need to know the type of data that you own. When you have finished making the analysis, you also need to know what you want to find out and, therefore, which methodologies you are going to use to accomplish your objectives. At the end of this chapter you can see a real case making all that process. In particular, a Classification problem is shown as an example when using machine learning methodologies to find out if a hospital patient should be admitted or not in Cardiology department.

INTRODUCTION

In this chapter we roughly discuss how to derive conclusions from hospital admission data. We describe a process to identify patterns in the data as well as the description of several concepts needed to carry out that objective. We use different Big Data analytics techniques to achieve our goal. Big Data analytics allowed us to uncover hidden patterns and unknown correlations to start working with available datasets. Then, we are able to improve the operational efficiency and obtain business benefits, in order to follow a system of work. Similar conclusions were reached according to (Powers, Meyer, Roebuck, & Vaziri, 2005), where they use advanced econometric cost modelling techniques to predict healthcare costs using pharmacy data.

Initially, it is advisable to make a study of correlation indexes from the attributes we are going to use. These indexes will give us a better idea about the most appropriate attributes and will allow us to obtain conclusions with the selected dataset.

DOI: 10.4018/978-1-5225-2607-0.ch013

Once we have decided what are the answers we want to know and the type of study we want to accomplish, we need to begin studying the type of data and the type of structure that we have in our dataset. This means that an important part of the available time to develop the study was devoted to prepare our data for the algorithms we would use. For that reason, section 2 details the type of data we can find and how it usually appears.

After preparing the dataset environment, we needed to use the appropriate Machine Learning techniques depending on the type of data we had and on which conclusions we wanted to obtain. In the present day, other studies are using machine learning techniques to predict behaviours in health systems and they select their appropriate techniques to reach them. As an example of this, some researchers would like to know if patients are going to re-enter during the next twelve months as it is done in (Vaithianathan, Jiang, & Ashton, 2012), where they used multivariate logistic regression. Or, perhaps, they would like to predict hospital admissions depending on patient-specific medical history using several types of classification algorithms, according to Wuyang et al. (2015). Since several years ago, those techniques have gradually been introduced in different studies thanks to their effectiveness when making predictions, as we can observe in (Wuyang et al., 2015) too.

At the end of this chapter, we will describe the process followed in a real research with the dataset provided by a Spanish hospital. As we will see, while developing this research, the same procedure described in this chapter was followed to obtain the conclusions. In the following sections we describe everything that is required to carry out such research. Each technique permits to decide which algorithm is appropriated in each case. Specifically, in that research a "yes or no" question type was answered but it is extendable to other types of similar questions. All this also depends on what kind of information we were treating with. In that case, it was generic data from the hospital information system. On that point, we needed to analyse the dataset to know what conclusions we can derive and what kind of answers we expect to obtain. In the mentioned research we had a supervised machine learning problem, because of the type of question we have to answer (which is of the "yes or no" type in this case). We studied a Classification problem because the results we wanted to obtain used labelled data. In that case we already had answers to the questions raised. In other words, we have a dataset where we know what happened previously and then we want to predict what is it going to happen in the next unknown cases. This can be observed in (Valverde, Tejada, & Cuadros, 2015), where the authors use some methodologies comparing several supervised Classification algorithms to predict and analyse feelings. As we have a dataset where we know what happened previously, we can split the dataset in two groups of data, one to train the learning algorithm and another one to use it lately in a testing process, avoiding the overfitting effect. In this way, after the training and testing process, we can compare predicted results with real ones. That means that we can validate the selected algorithm and determine the success rate that it is obtained with its use. Finally, we can observe the best algorithms that can be used with that particular dataset. The rest of this chapter is organized as follows. Section 2 defines the types of data we can find in a dataset and how to classify them. It is important to know where to use it and how. In section 3 we describe machine learning techniques. We have to know when we should use supervised or unsupervised learning methods to achieve the objectives that we had planned. Then, we talk about the different algorithms that can be used to predict our objectives according to the types of data that we have and to the type of technique. Section 4 describes the process followed in a recent research to find out potential assignments in a hospital department, being assisted by the different sections in this chapter. Finally, in sections 5 and 6, we find the conclusions and the references, respectively.

1. DIFFERENT TYPES OF DATA

The study of our available datasets is an important part of the specific problem analysis. That particular part of the analysis, which takes a long part of study time, is influenced by the own data analyst experience. That experience supposes being able to see additional opportunities for new studies with the available datasets, in addition to save working time. It also would influence the detection of incorrect information when dealing with dataset, as could be typing errors or missing data. According to the type of mistakes, these mistakes could be corrected or you'll have to exclude those records.

You are going to need a previous treatment of your dataset to prepare it for the different algorithms or tools you are going to use to extract knowledge, depending on the type of data you have to work with. It sometimes happens that you have labelled data e.g. using the values "Yes" or "No" as data type, or may be "True" or "False" or perhaps colours such as Red, Green or Blue. But then you realize that the algorithm you have to use only accepts numeric data. In such cases you can customize the dataset and use 0 instead of No (or False), and 1 instead of Yes (or True). In the case of colours, you can assign a numeric code to every colour, where each number corresponds to a different colour. Another typical case you could often find are dates. They can vary depending on the format you apply or depending on your country format. In those cases, you can transform them to numeric codes where the date format could be YYYYMMDD (YYYY for Year, MM for Month with 2 digits and DD for Day with 2 digits). Using this type of formatting, the bigger the numeric code is, the later is the time it represents. So, if you use comparison operators you will be able to compare dates directly and you will be able to know which one will be the previous and the later date. In such a way, you won't need to use more complex functions.

Typically, generic machine learning algorithms need structured data to work with, but data can be found in different formats in sites like market trends, customer preferences, web server logs, survey responses, etc. For those reasons, we find structured data that we have to know and differentiate between them. That will help us to deal with them.

Most of the data generated today is unstructured data, but still exists an important part of structured data generated in all companies that is generated and adapted to current technologies. Specifically, that type of data is filtered information that every organization store in their business intelligence and financial structures, in their Customer Relationship Management systems, etc. However, unstructured and semi structured data come in multiple types of formats, which can have a basic structure or not. These other types of data are stored in non-transactional systems. They come from machines, sensors and interactions between customers in multiple ways. Besides, that data is growing very fast and it is becoming increasingly important. Although there is currently a predisposition for many people to think the future is unstructured data due to large data volumes created in applications today. The fact is that every data is equally important and necessary, despite generating a considerable amount of data or not. The significant progress is actually being able to deal with all those types of data using current analytical applications regardless of the type, with cheaper and more effective machines. This allows us to give bigger consideration to make analytical studies previously unthinkable and only accessible to big companies.

Also you have to bear in mind that sometimes data can be converted from unstructured to structured data in case of necessity. Previously, it is likely to make a treatment so you can adapt algorithms instead of creating new ones.

1.1. Structured Data

It can be defined as any type of data inside a field in a record or in a file. That field is in turn organised with a defined length and a fixed format, such as dates and numbers. Typically, structured data is stored in tables inside relational databases or inside spreadsheets. Structured data usually is associated with a given data model, which is a business data model. In that business model data will be stored, processed and accessed. That model also includes a definition of what fields will be stored and in which way, namely the type of data (numeric, currency, alphabetic, date, etc.) and any kind of restriction on the entry data (number of characters or restricted ones to a specific format).

The main advantage of structured data is the facility for managing it (i.e. introducing, storing, listing and analysing the data). In the recent past, structuring data was the only way of managing data efficiently due to high cost and limitations with efficient storage, memory and processing. All the information that couldn't be fitted to existing data structure should find an alternative storage. Usually, structured data is managed with a structured query language (SQL). This language was stablished to manage and consult data in relational database management systems.

Although structured data was a big breakthrough and it remains as important today as it was, all kind of information is equally important, including the one that doesn't fit to the fixed format in structured data. These types of information are defined as unstructured and semi structured data and they are used in many applications. Nowadays, that type of information is constantly growing in size.

1.2. Unstructured Data

Unstructured data is all kind of information that neither cannot be easily classified nor adapted to a fixed format. In this classification are included pictures, videos, photos, streaming instrument data, web pages, PDF files, emails, blog entries, etc. Despite its lack of any defined structure, it is usually packaged as an object, such as files or documents framed in a structure of their own but containing unstructured data in their definition code.

In customer-facing businesses the information contained in unstructured data is usually used to analyse how to improve customer relationship management (CRM) and relationship marketing. The term "Big Data" is mostly associated with unstructured data. Big Data concerns to very large datasets which are difficult to analyse with traditional tools, although Big Data can deal and analyse both types of data.

The general idea when you use unstructured data is to extract useful information by processing the natural language and by semantic analysis. So you can find patterns, understand behaviours and graphically display results. All this can be achieved if we previously prepare data and establish objectives that will allow us to reach previously sought conclusions. Otherwise we can lose perspective of the results that you want to obtain and even extract unhelpful information.

1.3. Semi Structured Data

Semi structured data are those data that cannot be organized in a specialized repository, as can be a database, but nevertheless they have certain information associated as metadata. That metadata makes semi structured data easier to process than unstructured data. Although semi structured data does not allow an analysis or a sophisticated access, it allows an access to the contents of the addressable elements through labelling metadata. In some forms of semi structured data there is no separate schema, although in others this schema does exists but only places loose constraints on the data.

Examples of semi structured data are web pages, files/documents based or written in mark-up languages as XML, JSON or emails. In those examples you can see they contain distinguishable semantic elements that can appear or not, have different elements and the order is not important.

An advantage of this type of data is that the data model can be simplified, because they allow to deal with them through hierarchical structures as tree-shaped ones. This enables the building of relations between different elements. The same idea with semi structured data is used in (Buneman, 1997), but allowing cycles in the data to generate graphs as trees. This type of data, while it is easy to implement, it is difficult to display or to optimize. The disadvantages include they can have data with unavoidable errors that should be corrected and they can increase exponentially in size.

2. MACHINE LEARNING TECHNIQUES

Machine Learning is a method to analyse data that uses algorithms to learn iteratively from data, with the aim to find hidden patterns of behaviour. Those algorithms are able to independently adapt themselves and to learn from previous iterations, obtaining reliable and efficient results.

Machine Learning evolved from pattern recognition studies and from computational learning theory in artificial intelligence. Besides, it is closely associated with computational statistics and it is focused on making predictions by means of computers. Sometimes it combines with data mining focusing on exploratory data analysis. When it is combined with data analytics, it allows to make models and algorithms which give predictions by themselves and it is known as predictive analytics.

When we combine Big Data and Machine Learning, we can predict, for example, what patients admitted to a hospital are referred to that hospital department. This can be done when we use patient hospital datasets to search any behavioural patterns while we try to find out what patients have to be referred to Cardiology department. Besides, the algorithm you decide to use will be learning from the available data until generating a new modified algorithm that predicts the behaviour we are looking for. Thus, thanks to those predictions, you can make better decisions, both on a human scale and in terms of business.

Depending on the type of data we own to make our study and depending on the results we want to obtain, we will need to use a different category of technique and, therefore, a number of different suitable algorithms for each occasion.

2.1. Supervised Learning

When we want to make a learning process on a dataset where you know the output variable, then we have to use supervised learning algorithms. In this approach, the data we own are learning samples and you have records as pairs of samples where one part of the pair is usually an object in a vector shape, with several variables and the other part is an output value. For example, the object in a vector shape, as the first part in the pair, could be the results in a medical lab test and the second part in the pair (or the output value) could be the result of having a disease.

Supervised learning algorithms analyse training data and generate a function that allows to create new ones. That function is called *classifier* when the output is discrete data and it is called *regression* when the output is continuous data. In such a way, that function will allow you to predict an approximate result, regardless of the input data.

When working with supervised learning, you generally have to take into account several aspects in reference to the training data you are going to use. In that training data, there must be a balance between variability and data bias. In case of excessive variability, the learning algorithm can produce different results in different datasets and if it exists an excessive bias, the algorithm will adapt itself to every dataset differently producing, therefore, a high variability. In that way, there should be a balance between both parameters. The sum of them is the aspect that will define the prediction error in a supervised algorithm as also stated in (Gareth, 2003). Also, the amount of available training data related to the complexity of the function used in the supervised learning algorithm, needs to be taken into consideration. If that function is a simple one, then a high bias and low variability learning algorithm will be able to learn with a little amount of data. Otherwise, if you use a complex function, you will need a large amount of training data, with low bias and high variability. So you will have to fit the function you will use with the amount of available data. Another factor to bear in mind is the input vector dimensionality. If that input vector has many dimensions, the learning problem evolves into a highly complex problem. This situation can confuse the learning algorithm, making it to acquire a high variability. Therefore, whenever you have an input vector with many dimensions, you will have to adjust your function to have low variability and high bias. In practice, it is better to avoid unnecessary features in the input vector. Finally, another important factor to consider is the presence of noisy data in the output values. If output values are often wrong, either by human mistakes or by sensors mistakes, then the learning algorithm is not going to find a suitable function to the training dataset. For that reason, in this case it is better to use a function with low variability and high bias.

The following sections will detail the main algorithms used in supervised learning, depending on their use of either Classifier or Regression functions.

2.1.1. Classification

When the task of prediction consists of classifying the observed data in a finite set of labels, e. g. to give a name to observed data, then we find ourselves facing a Classification task. That task consists in building a concise model from the distribution of class labels as predictive features. Then, the resulting classifier is used to assign class labels to testing entities where the values of predictive features are known, but the value of the class label is unknown. The best way to test classifiers is often based in the accuracy of predictions, namely the percentage of correct predictions divided by the total number of predictions.

Most algorithms that are used in Classifications tasks, can also be used in Regression tasks. The difference between them depend on the training speed, the prediction speed, the accuracy of prediction or the type of learning, among others. The main Classification algorithms are also valid in Regression algorithms excluding Logistic Regression and Naïve Bayes, which are exclusive to Classification tasks. These algorithms are:

- **KNN (K – Nearest Neighbours):** KNN is a simple and efficient classifier that allows to obtain good results. This method uses an algorithm that calculates the Euclidean distance between different examples and orders the output depending on nearest distances between different samples. Then one object or sample is assigned to the detected class and predicts what class it belongs to.

- **Logistic Regression:** This method is one of the most popular classification methods. It calculates the probability of a register to belong to one of the output classes. A logistic function is used whose input is a linear combination of their input variables. Besides, this model considers the prediction variables to be independent between them.

- **Decision Tree Classifier:** an effective and efficient system base on an algorithm which generates a tree with simple decision rules inferred from the entry data features. Decision rules will be more complex according to the depth of the generated tree. The depth levels in the generated trees vary depending on the dataset you use to execute the algorithm.

- **Random Forest**: In this method multiple decision trees are used with low depth level. After generating decision trees, the best class is selected from the ones chosen by every decision tree as the best option. Several estimators are used independently and later prediction is made with the average of those estimators.

- **Support Vector Machines (SVM):** This group of methods belongs to the discriminant models family. They try to find a set of samples to build a plane maximizing the limit between two specified classes. The way of regulating this limit is made by a parameter which indicates the number of samples that are used around the separator line between classes. A low value in this parameter means that there are many samples around that line. An additional parameter is used to set the influence effect of a single training record. Although this group of methods are used in classification, they can be used in regression too. The reason for using different types of function (each function is usually called kernel) is that classes are not always linearly separable and thus can have a better fitting depending on the use of other types of separation kernels. Some of the most common algorithms used in this group of methods are:

  ○ **Polynomial Kernel:** A polynomial function is used to make predictions. Several degrees can be used in the algorithms polynomials, but it supposes a high computational cost.

  ○ **RBF Kernel:** This RBF (Radial Basis Function) method is one of the most commonly used methodologies. It uses a radial kernel around samples through an exponential mathematical function. The adjustment which is usually applied is made using a gamma (γ) value of 0.7, which corresponds to a constant value in the formula used in this algorithm ($exp(-\gamma|x - x'|^2)$). A regularisation parameter of 1.0 is also a common value used to control the number of samples used for calculations around the separation limit line between classes.

  ○ **Non Linear Kernel:** A non linear function based in a RBF kernel with degree 3 and a gamma self-adjusting parameter is used. The method applies a strategy called "one-against-one", which basically classifies an unknown pattern comparing one class against another class in a group of different classes. So, the best class receives a vote. The class with the higher number of votes is chosen between all the pairs of classes compared.

  ○ **Linear Kernel:** This method is based on the use of a linear mathematical function. The operating strategy consists in a multiclass technique called "one-vs-the-rest". This technique builds a classifier per class, where it is trained to differentiate the samples of a class from the samples of the remaining classes. Finally, the best classifier is chosen.

- ◦ **Naïve Bayes:** A classifier assumes that all features are independent of each other. In that way, only a few samples can be used to train the algorithm and estimate output parameters. Besides, considering features as independent, we only need to calculate the variance of each class. When this method is implemented, it is accepted that all values in every class follow a Gaussian distribution because almost all natural phenomena follow approximately this type of Normal distribution.
- **Neural Networks:** Using neural networks in your classification process allows an adaptive learning, self organization and being immune to noise. Also it is clear that it is an efficient method, thanks to parallel processes with a great number of nodes and a high level of connectivity between them. The whole idea is to build acyclic graphs in those networks to obtain the expected results. Usually, a sigmoidal function is used to generate neural networks. In particular, that function is often a hyperbolic tangent. In the context of neural networks, a common algorithm is "backpropagation", where the input pattern in the trained network is transmitted through the different layers of neurons (nodes), until an output is obtained. That output unit is calculated using the observed error. After that, in the training or learning process, the weights of the network are altered to match the desired output with the output obtained in the network. Other models of neural networks, use a "softmax" function as final layer in the network with the aim to normalize output data. In this last network, nodes are distributed in three layers: input, hidden and output layer.

2.1.2. Regression

When the objective is to predict a continuous output variable, then we are dealing with a Regression task. Here, it is relevant to characterize the variation produced in the dependent variable (or the variable to predict between independent variables) around the Regression function. That function can be described by a probability distribution. In such case, the results are not defined classes which belong to independent variables, but statistically projected real values.

The algorithms used in Regression tasks are the same ones that in Classification tasks, excepting Logistic Regression and Naïve Bayes, in addition to Linear Regression which is unique in this case. A description of this algorithm follows:

- **Linear Regression:** This algorithm uses a model that assumes a linear relationship between the input variables and a single output variable. More specifically, that variable can be calculated from a linear combination of the input variables. When a single input variable is used, the method is called simple linear regression. On the other hand, it is called multiple linear regression when several input variables are used. The linear equation used in this algorithm assigns one scale factor to each input value, called coefficient (shown as the B letter). One additional coefficient is also added, giving the line an additional degree of freedom which is also called the intercept or the bias coefficient. In that way, the equation obtained for this algorithm would be $y = B0 + B1 * x$, where y represents the output variable and x the input variable. In higher dimensions, when we have more than one input (x), more coefficients (B) appear in that equation and then we do not obtain a line to define that relationship but a plane or an also called hyperplane. The complexity in this Linear Regression algorithm refers to the number of coefficients used in the model. When a coefficient becomes zero, it removes the influence of the input variable on the model and, therefore, the complexity is also reduced.

2.2. Unsupervised Learning

When the input data vector has no explicit outputs, then we face a problem or a study about unsupervised learning. In this case, you have samples that are sent in the input of the learner algorithm and where they are not labelled. The purpose of this type of learning is modelling the data structure and its distribution, which is defined. This model tries to explain the behaviour of data features. In that way, this type of learning does not seek to predict a concrete result given that there are no associated output variables. Instead, it tries to discover patterns where data is grouped and so it discovers behaviours in the samples or specific subgroups between samples. That methodology that seeks behaviours makes unsupervised learning technics be more subjective that supervised learning technics. In such a way, there is not an only way to make a data analysis, as in the case of predicting with an entry data.

An advantage you can find in this type of learning is that frequently it is easier finding samples without labels in a computer or from laboratory instruments than finding them labelled, where human intervention is required. It is also complicated to calculate feelings or tastes automatically about a particular product. In that way, it is perhaps more correct to group results by types of behaviour.

In essence, the only thing that unsupervised learning methods have to work with are the observed input samples. Those ones often are supposed to be independent samples in an underlying and unknown probability distribution, which are based on implicit or explicit information, over the most important part of that information. So, you can extract regular behaviours in the information or, sometimes, it is more relevant the irregularities you can find.

2.2.1. Clustering

Clustering processes consist of finding subgroups (called *clusters*) in a dataset as also affirmed in (Ullman, Poggio, Harari, Zysman, & Seibert, 2014). The procedure requires to partition the data in different groups so the samples that belong to each group of data are sufficiently dissimilar from each other or sufficiently similar inside the same group. Although clustering is hard to estimate, in practice it has useful applications such as the cataloguing of similar objects, people faces recognition, detecting similar objects in images (as lumps), and the like.

When you need to make clusters analysis you need a function that measures the similarity between two different samples, as the properties of each sample. Also you need a function that measures the dissimilarity between samples, as could be the distance between them. Then you need a criterion that assesses if a cluster is more or less appropriate. In such a way, we need an algorithm to calculate the clustering process so that it optimizes the criterion function. In order to evaluate the clusters obtained, you have to measure the cohesion degree between samples inside the same cluster. That is accomplished by measuring the similarity between samples in respect of a reference sample or centroid, or measuring the sum of squared errors. It is also evaluated by measuring the spacing between clusters, in such a way that they are sufficiently distant from each other, measuring spacing between centroids.

Another factor to consider is which one is the appropriate number of different groups you have to obtain. Many clustering algorithms require the specification of the number of clusters to produce in the input data set, prior to the execution of the algorithm. Barring knowledge of the proper value beforehand, the appropriate value must be determined. This can be done by fixing a specific number of clusters and the best amount is later calculated depending on the criterion function which has been previously defined. The Elbow criterion is one of the more commonly used ones. It is a common rule to determine what number of clusters should be chosen, for example for k-means and agglomerative hierarchical clustering. This criterion says that you should choose a number of clusters so that adding another cluster does not add sufficient information. More precisely, if you graph the percentage of variance explained by the clusters against the number of clusters, the first clusters will add much information, but at some point the marginal gain will drop, giving an angle in the graph.

The different clustering algorithms can be classified depending on which clustering techniques are used. Within each category you can find some of the most used ones.

- **Hierarchical:** This category seeks interrelated clusters of data between other ones previously defined. It creates a hierarchical decomposition of the dataset using some criterion. The key step in a hierarchical clustering is to select a distance measure. The most common distances used in these algorithms are the Manhattan distance, equal to the sum of absolute distances for each variable, and the Euclidean distance, computed by finding the square of the distance between each variable. An advantage of this category is that you do not need to specify the number of clusters in advance. As disadvantages, it must be said that does not scale well due to its complexity ($O(n^2)$) and that the interpretation of results is subjective. This type of algorithms can be further divided into two types, depending on the working procedure:
  - ○ **Divisive (Top Down):** This group begins with a unique cluster that includes to all the data we have, then it splits the data into smaller clusters depending on the distance between them. This procedure is applied recursively until each sample is in its own single cluster. Sometimes, when taking the first split, this group of algorithms can find the best possible split in two parts. As it has access to all the samples, it can have a better overview of the global structure of the data. Top-down clustering is conceptually more complex than bottom-up clustering since we need a second flat clustering algorithm as a subroutine. It has the advantage of being more efficient if we do not generate a complete hierarchy all the way down to individual sample leaves.
  - ○ **Agglomerative (Bottom Up):** This group of algorithms considers each sample as a unique cluster. It works making bigger groups depending on similarities between samples. It finds the best pair of clusters to merge it into a new cluster. Then, this process is repeated until all clusters become unified together. In these algorithms, when clustering with minimum distance, a minimum spanning tree is generated and the algorithms encourage growth of elongated clusters. Instead, when clustering with maximum distance, they encourage compact clusters and do not work well if elongated clusters are present. One of their disadvantages is that they are very sensitive to noise.
- **Bayesian:** The algorithms try to generate a distribution between all partitions of data. The framework of Bayesian inference can be used to provide a rational, coherent and automatic way of answering many questions. This means that, given a complete specification of the prior assumptions, there is an automatic procedure (based on Bayes rule) which provides a unique answer. Of course, if the prior assumptions are very poor, the answers obtained could be useless. For that reason, you have to think carefully about the prior assumptions before using these types of Bayesian algorithms. In these algorithms, you draw conclusions by analysing the posterior distribution over these quantities given the observed data. They provide a way of defining flexible models of real world phenomena. The key ingredient of Bayesian methods is not the prior, but the idea of averaging over different possibilities.

- **Partitional:** This group of techniques calculate the different clusters needed at once and then it adjusts them. These algorithms build several partitions and then evaluate them by some criterion. In this group, each instance is placed in exactly one of K non-overlapping clusters. Besides, since the output is only one set of clusters, the user has to specify the desired number of clusters (K). They can be used as Divisive algorithms inside the Hierarchical category. The typical algorithm in this group is the K-means that we detail below:
  - ◦ **K-Means:** This algorithm attempts to make different groups of samples by calculating the distance between a sample and the current group average of each feature. We start with one sample which has two features (A and B) with their respective averages. The K-means algorithm then evaluates another sample. If you asked for two groups, then sample 1 and sample 2 would be their own groups after two steps. The algorithm then takes another sample (sample 3), and measures the distance on a graph between their feature A (x - value) and the current average x – value for Group A vs. Group B. Whichever it is closest to, it is added to that group, and then a new mean for that group is calculated. It then does this with every other sample, adding them to whichever group their measurements are closest to. This algorithm is simple and efficient, with a complexity of $O(tkn)$, where k is the number of clusters and t is the number of iterations. As disadvantages, we can name that it is necessary to specify the k value (number of clusters) and that it is sensitive to outliers.

2.2.2. Density Estimation, Dimensionality Reduction

This section discusses the second classic example in unsupervised learning process. It deals with dimensionality reduction and density estimation. This second one looks for predicting a continuous density field from a group of points which have been collected as discrete points from that density field. In particular, statistical models are built (as could be Bayesian nets), where the underlying causes which produce the input data are explained. The techniques used to extract the data features try to search statistical regularities or irregularities directly from input data.

As with previous methodologies, it does not exist a unique model which can be named as the most appropriate for all types of datasets. The suitable process to develop machine learning models is to choose the most appropriate one for the dataset you are analysing, which has several desirable properties. For instance, in large dimension datasets it may be suitable choosing models where making a dimensionality reduction is necessary. It may also be suitable choosing another model which allows to view the different groups with different densities through more or less soft distributions that have been adapted to the analysed data. In that way, the chosen model is going to be more or less appropriated depending on how the data is adapted to the density estimation.

The algorithms you can find in this unsupervised learning section can be classified depending on their structure:

- **Density Estimation:** These algorithms attempt to measure a continuous field of density samples based on a group of discrete samples which are drawn as different points in that field of density. These algorithms are devised to discover arbitrary-shaped clusters. In this approach, a cluster is regarded as a region in which the density of data objects exceeds a threshold. Depending on the techniques used, we could use density estimation histograms, density estimation kernels, where they use positive mathematical functions as kernels, Extreme Deconvolution, which mistakes and projections are taken into account, and, finally, density estimation where the near neighbours are taken into account.

- **Dimensionality Reduction:** When you have a high number of features inside your dataset, it can be useful to reduce this number before analysing data with other supervised techniques. In this group of algorithms, you can use different reduction techniques as Principal Component Analysis (PCA), which finds a lineal combination of variables that have the maximum variance and they are not correlated, Random Projections, used in smaller sizes and higher speed of process, and, finally, Feature Agglomeration, which groups features that behave in a similar way.

3. REAL CASE: HOSPITAL ADMISSION DATA TO PREDICT POTENTIAL PATIENT DISEASES OR POTENTIAL ASSIGNMENTS IN HOSPITAL STRUCTURE

A recent survey (Wuyang et al., 2015) observed that it is possible to predict, with a reasonably high percentage of success, if patients in a hospital will be admitted or not to Cardiology department, starting out with some basic data from each patient. The dataset was provided by a Spanish hospital at the request of its Cardiology department. Then, since we have the hospital dataset and we also have a 5 years tracking historical dataset, we know the patients that were transferred to the Cardiology department previously. For that reason, we are facing a supervised learning problem so we are going to try to predict if future patients should be transferred or not to the Cardiology department or not, as we discovered with analysis. Besides, once we select and run our prediction algorithms, we will also be able to know the percentage rate of success provided by those algorithms and thanks to the data we already know.

In order to work with all algorithms used in this research, a data pre-processing is made, so that it can be obtained fitted information and without typographical or missing data mistakes. Once we selected the data to work with, we splitted it in two parts, a 67% for training and a 33% for testing purposes. The training data allows to prepare the algorithms to predict future samples, and the testing data permits us to check the effectiveness of results by predicting them. In order to avoid over/underfitting effects, we use this method of data selection. Besides, we avoid losing the ability to learn, thanks to the use of that data selection method every time an algorithm is used.

As a result of this survey, it will be possible to search other patterns of behaviour and to predict which specific department should be transferred the new patients admitted in that hospital. Therefore, we will be able to know which type of diseases are likely to have those patients as a result of knowing which particular hospital department should be transferred to.

As we know that the type of data we want to obtain is a "Yes" or "No" answer (or a "0" or "1" answer type, depending on the algorithm used), we are also facing a Classification problem, where the output data is a discrete or labelled data. Even though the available type of data for that research was structured data, data pre-processing was needed in order to adapt the data to the algorithms that were used. We had to adapt a data format that, in principle, it was detected as a real type. We needed to convert it to a labelled format that in fact it was a numerical code to identify a particular medical diagnosis. Also, several adjustments in data formats were made in order to avoid other particular country formats. Other necessary adjustments were made to delete errors as the lack of information in some fields from some records. Some time of analysis was saved and the work made was facilitated, thanks to data dump from hospital databases and thanks to structured format data in tables with fixed and well defined formats. As we are dealing with a supervised learning problem where we want to predict what is going to happen with future output data from new input data, the dataset was split as it was explained previously. In such a way, the objectiveness of algorithms used is maximized because the test data is unknown and all this data is new for the algorithm.

Once the was identified and listed, we proceed to use the appropriate group of algorithms. In this case, as we know, we are dealing with a Classification supervised learning problem. So, the specifically methods used in that research were KNN with k nearest neighbours, Logistic Regression, Decision Tree Classifier, Random Forest, Neural Networks and, the ones used form the Support Vector Machines group, were Polynomial Kernel, RBF Kernel, No Lineal Kernel, Lineal Kernel and Naïve Bayes. All these methods are used in Classification problems and some of them are common to both Classification and Regression. When this research was made, some algorithms did not produce the desired results, because not all of them are suitable for all conditions. It also depends on the type of the dataset (size, type of data, etc.) that you have.

According to the type of data that we had, the SVM techniques group with polynomial kernels was not appropriate to deal with that Classification problem. Several polynomials with different grades were used, which did not deliver satisfactory results. So, a polynomial function is not appropriate to separate data into groups and to be able to classify them properly. Instead, when exponential or lineal functions were used, the results were most suitable for distributing the classes in the dataset. While this algorithm is simpler, it is more appropriate than the previous ones. The fact of measuring the distances between samples depending on the features of each different sample was suitable to get good results. The name of this algorithm is KNN with K Nearest Neighbours, where it is predicted the results of future samples depending on their features, choosing the nearest ones to the most frequent used models.

Overall, the results were positive, among which outstand those ones that use decision trees in their algorithms, as are Random Forest and Decision Tree Classifier. These ones use decision trees to choose the final result. These trees generate decision rules that allow to classify samples and, at the same time, they allow to descend through the branches of those trees, choosing the most appropriate way for each particular sample. These algorithms yielded high prediction successful rates when predicting if a patient should be referred to the Cardiology department. In such a way, the healthcare system could form the basis in a decision-making system that allows to save costs referring patients to that hospital department, with generic initial assessment procedures and without using other types of more expensive medical procedures. Also it allows us to make earlier medical diagnosis saving time that can be essential when detecting diseases, being able to save a higher number of human lives.

CONCLUSION

The combination of Big data analytics and machine learning techniques provides a powerful tool to discover behaviour patterns and to predict what it is going to happen with a good enough successful rate to make decisions. Even if some of these techniques are not new, today they are becoming more and more important due to the great increase of data produced in part by remote mobile applications and by Internet applications. All that quantity of data allows to extract information and knowledge which can help making decisions, identifying behaviour patterns, objects, classifying types of subjects, etc.

We must also anticipate that a data mining process is needed to adapt data to algorithms and to discover possible relations between features. For that reason, we need to know the type of data that we are working with, so we are able to know the kind of tool, type of database, etc., needed in each case. It is also important to know what methodology to choose in each situation to reach our goal.

As an example of the kind of things you can achieve with those methodologies, we have shown a real case about the admission data in hospitals. This real case has many valuable uses in medicine and in many areas. It is also becoming really important in autonomous systems which require artificial intelligence to make decisions, where predicting what is going to happen becomes an important part of the system, as well as the learning capabilities provided by the machine learning algorithms.

Many other examples can be mentioned to show the machine learning techniques relevance, such as analysis of X-ray and colour images to classify the type of object we are analysing. It allows to predict with a reasonable margin of certainty if we are treating with a regular organ tissue or with another type. Other example is evaluating and predicting diseases by making blood tests and analysing specific parameters that we know they are the main causes of a particular disease. Then we study those cases where the disease appeared previously and we can offer a success ratio in future cases. As we can observe, there are many applications to be investigated, and in many other areas.

SOLUTIONS AND FUTURE RECOMMENDATIONS

According to the available dataset from the Spanish hospital, it has been observed that the most common admission cause doubles the second one. This cause was coronary atherosclerosis, so it is interesting to study all the data in future researches to look for patterns that can predict this disease, in order to prevent it and to save costs as well.

Any line of research that helps to prevent any heart disease is a good idea to reduce the high mortality rates that these types of diseases produce everyday. It can also be interesting to research the influence of patient age in heart diseases, studying the most common cases, but also the isolated ones.

Another interesting option would be to research about detecting different types of objects in an image, such as types of tissues. It can be helpful to know that there is a high percentage of success identifying a particular tissue where it is difficult to detect it by the human eye.

REFERENCES

Buneman, P. (1997). *Semistructured Data. Department of Computer and Information Science*. University of Pennsylvania.

Dai, W., Brisimi, T. S., Adams, W. G., Mela, T., Saligrama, V., & Ch, I. (2015). Prediction of Hospitalization Due to Heart Diseases by Supervised Learning Methods. *International Journal of Medical Informatics*, *84*(3), 189–197. doi:10.1016/j.ijmedinf.2014.10.002 PMID:25497295

James Gareth, M. (2003). *Variance and Bias for General Loss Functions. Marshall School of Business*. University of California.

Powers, C. A., Meyer, C. M., Roebuck, M. C., & Vaziri, B. (2005). Predictive Modeling of Total Healthcare Costs Using Pharmacy Claims: A Comparison of Alternative Econometric Cost Modeling Techniques. *Medical Care*, *43*(11), 1065–1072. doi:10.1097/01.mlr.0000182408.54390.00 PMID:16224298

Ullman, S., Poggio, T., Harari, D., Zysman, D., & Seibert, D. (2014). *Unsupervised Learning: Clustering. In Center for Brains, Minds & Machines. Document 9.54 used in Class 13*. Massachusetts Institute of Technology.

Vaithianathan, R., Jiang, N., & Ashton, T. (2012). *A Model for Predicting Readmission Risk in New Zealand. Faculty of Business and Law*. AUT University.

Valverde, J., Tejada, J., & Cuadros, E. (2015). *Comparing Supervised Learning Methods for Classifying Spanish Tweets*(Vol. 1397). Universidad Católica San Pablo.

Chapter 14
Selection of Pathway Markers for Cancer Using Collaborative Binary Multi-Swarm Optimization

Prativa Agarwalla
Heritage Institute of Technology, India

Sumitra Mukhopadhyay
Institute of Radiophysics and Electronics, India

ABSTRACT

Pathway information for cancer detection helps to find co-regulated gene groups whose collective expression is strongly associated with cancer development. In this paper, a collaborative multi-swarm binary particle swarm optimization (MS-BPSO) based gene selection technique is proposed that outperforms to identify the pathway marker genes. We have compared our proposed method with various statistical and pathway based gene selection techniques for different popular cancer datasets as well as a detailed comparative study is illustrated using different meta-heuristic algorithms like binary coded particle swarm optimization (BPSO), binary coded differential evolution (BDE), binary coded artificial bee colony (BABC) and genetic algorithm (GA). Experimental results show that the proposed MS-BPSO based method performs significantly better and the improved multi swarm concept generates a good subset of pathway markers which provides more effective insight to the gene-disease association with high accuracy and reliability.

INTRODUCTION

Genes control the different functioning of a cell, like growth, division, death etc. When the normal profile of a gene is changed or damaged, it causes the abnormal behavior of the cell and we, in generic sense, call it as cancer. Cancer is nothing but out-of-control cell growth due to change in the expression profile of genes. Advancement of microarray technology has made the genomic study more fast and

DOI: 10.4018/978-1-5225-2607-0.ch014

efficient by analysing the expression of thousands of genes in a single chip (Zhang et.al, 2008). But, the huge dimension of the gene expression data leads to statistical and analytical challenges to identify differentially expressed genes in different classes for the study of their effect on diseases. So the selection of the most relevant genes is very essential for the proper medical diagnosis as well as for drug target prediction and in this context, different aspects of big data processing and analysis come into play. Big data analysis is one of the very popular and recent day technologies, used for examining large dataset. It helps to reveal hidden pattern and correlations information of the data which can be used in the field of computational biology to analyze huge biological data for extracting the relevant information and to enrich the knowledge related to the biological system. While exploring small number of significant genes participating in a tumour progression, it has been observed that those genes are functioning similar and work as a group to form a certain cancer. The set of genes having identical biological functioning is known as a pathway. To understand the biological functioning of those groups of genes, involved in tumour progression and the phonotypical changes at the pathway level is a very interesting research topic now a day. But, the dataset contains high amount of noise and overlapping samples which decreases classification accuracy and the identification of dominant genes related to the disease suffers. Proper and efficient identification of those differentially expressed genes at the pathway level is very crucial for the treatment of the prior disease related to the pathway.

Different approaches have been developed by the researchers for finding the pathway marker genes related to different diseases (Khunlertgit, 2013; Ma, 2009; Mandal, 2015; Mukhopadhyay, 2014). The statistical approaches like mean, median are widely applied for this purpose (Guo et.al, 2005). Principal component analysis is used in the literature (Ma et.al, 2009). However, the uses of different statistical tests lack functionality (Mandal et.al, 2015). In another literature, Log-Likelihood Ratio (LLR) is implemented for accurate and reliable classification of cancer through the identification of pathway markers (Su et.al, 2009). Another method named as Condition Responsive Genes (CORGs) is proposed for delivering optimal discriminative power for the disease phenotype (Lee et.al, 2008). A family of bio-inspired algorithms, like particle swarm optimization algorithm (PSO), genetic algorithm (GA), artificial bee colony optimization (ABC), differential evolution (DE), ant colony optimization (ACO) etc. have also been applied by formulating the problem as a global optimization problem (Das et.al, 2008) where the position of a particle is termed as the solution which is associated with some fitness function. Binary version of PSO (Mandal et.al, 2015) has been adopted to find the pathway activity where the mean t-score of the pathways are computed as the metric of evaluation, that is the fitness function has to be maximized (Bandhopadhyay et.al, 2014). Again, Multi-objective particle swarm optimization (MOPSO) has also been designed to select significant pathway features for cancer identification (Mukhopadhyay et.al, 2014). Generally, the performance of meta-heuristic algorithms deteriorates as the dimension of the real world problem increases. So, involving a single group of swarm and using an average fitness value as a solution of the problem may fail to produce more accurate results for the problem of gene selection from the huge microarray data. In case of generalized optimization problems, multi-swarm concept (Niu et.al, 2007) working in a collaborative way produces better result than the conventional single swarm based methods (Eberhart et.al, 1995). In multi-swarm concept, total population is divided into several groups and each group searches for a new promising solution. The interactions between the groups influence the balance between exploration and exploitation and maintain a suitable diversity in the population, reducing the risk of pre-convergence. Therefore, a novel pathway gene selection technique using multi-swarm binary particle swarm optimization technique (MS-BPSO) is proposed where the groups of swarms are working in a collaborative way to find out the most relevant genes that are involved in the development of a particular type of cancer. In the similar way, the multi group concept is embedded with other meta-heuristic evolutionary and swarm algorithms such as genetic algorithm (GA) (Tan et.al, 2006), artificial bee colony optimization (ABC) (Amaratunga et.al, 2008), differential evolution (DE) (Das et.al, 2011) to have a comparative study of the performance of all those algorithms for the cancer pathway marker selection. Binary version of the algorithms is adopted as to select the relevant genes from the dataset by removing the irrelevant genes for computation.

In this work, the authors introduce a collaborative approach for the gene selection methodology and rather searching for the solution of huge dimensional problem at a time, the dimension of the problem is partitioned based on the pathway activity. Multiple swarm or groups are involved and each group actively searches for the respective pathway. The technique helps to gain better searching capability as each group is working on small dimension independently. It also provides better fitness value to the swarm unlike the other fitness functions where the average result has been used which causes suffering in the computation for pathway activity. At the last stage, the result of each group is combined and based on the final combined result, the fitness value is calculated. This whole scheme helps the particles to have a faster searching capability and the result is more accurate. The proposed methodology is associated with binary PSO and so is termed as MS-BPSO that efficiently finds the pathway marker genes which are significantly associated with the disease at the pathway level.

The experimental dataset consist of microarray data of prostate (Singh et.al, 2002), child_all (Cheoket.al, 2003), lymphoma- leukemia (Raetz et.al, 2006), gastric cancer (Hippo et.al, 2002). Initially, the performance of the proposed gene selection technique is compared with other existing pathway based methods for four real life cancer dataset. The proposed MS-BPSO establishes good result in all respect over other comparative methods, indicating its ability to produce more robust gene selection activity. Effectiveness of multi-swarm concept in BPSO technique is also demonstrated along with other different evolutionary and bio-inspired algorithms such as GA (Tan et.al, 2006), binary coded differential evolution (BDE) (Das et.al, 2011), binary coded artificial bee colony (BABC) (Amaratunga et.al, 2008) optimization algorithm etc. For the purpose, the results have been categorized into two ways. In the first phase, single swam based searching for all those above mentioned algorithms are considered and in the second phase multi-swarm concept is introduced for all those methodologies and then the experimental process is performed. The idea validates the performance of multi-swarm based work over the single swarm based methodology. The comparative result indicates that overall the proposed gene selection method works well to detect the relevant pathway genes for all the different types of dataset. As authors are interested to obtain the biologically relevant pathway genes, the biological significance of the selected genes are validated and demonstrated at the end of the chapter. Result shows that those genes are very highly functioning pathway genes for the corresponding type of cancer and the information helps to understand that the outcome does not come by chance.

The remaining section of the chapter is organized as follows: First an overview of microarray dataset is presented. Next, a brief review of the related work is presented followed by the description of usage of proposed technique (MS-BPSO) for pathway marker selection. After that, the result of the proposed technique is demonstrated. Next, the biological relevance of the result is also given. Finally the work has been concluded.

BACKGROUND

Microarray technology (Zhang, 2008; Kanehisa, 2000) is a recently developed advanced technology which is used to analyse the changes in gene at molecular level. For visualization of the changes occurs in gene level this technology is widely used by the researches so that any change in gene expression level can be identified for the progression of a disease to find out some informative content and subsequently, conclusion can be made by investigating the expression level. Researchers have developed different methodologies for this purpose and significant conclusions are made for biological interpretation of those gene expression levels. A brief description of microarray dataset and related research works performed in this field are given below.

Microarray Database

DNA microarray is nothing but the arrangement of hundreds or thousands of gene sequences on a single microscope slide. Microarray dataset is prepared by comparing the genes of cancerous cell with the genes of normal cell to find out the abnormality in their expression level. First samples are collected both from cancerous and normal cells and after dyeing with different fluorescent, they are put to hybridize with their synthetic complementary DNAs attached on the microarray slide. Now, using a scanner, the fluorescent intensity for each area on the microarray slide is scanned. If a particular gene is very active, it will generate a very bright fluorescent area. The information related to the intensity of the spot provides the information of thousand of genes and helps in parallel analysis of gene expression level simultaneously. The processing steps are demonstrated in Figure 1. Over the years, there has been a lot of generation of microarray data related to the gene expression through the examination of microarray slides. Different public websites are there to make those data available for public research. One of the

Figure 1. Preparation steps of microarray database

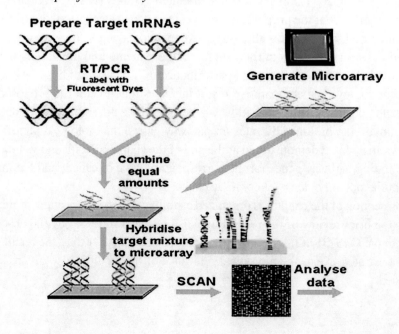

most reliable sources is the National Centre for Biotechnology Information (NCBI) and it has developed the Gene Expression Omnibus or GEO to make this data easy to access for public use. It is a data repository facility which includes data on gene expression from varied sources.

For the experimental study, the microarray dataset for different types of cancer of human being are collected. Each dataset consists of two classes of samples. A brief description of the dataset is given below.

- **Prostate Cancer:** The prostate cancer is related to the abnormal cell growth in the prostate. The dataset (Singh et.al, 2002) is prepared using gene expression measurements for prostate tumors and for the adjacent normal tissue of prostate. Total 102 samples are collected. Among which 50 samples are of prostate tumors and 52 are of non-canerous prostate tissues. The expression matrix consists of 12533 numbers of genes. Gene expressions are measured.
- **GSE412 (Child-ALL):** The gene expression dataset is for the childhood acute lymphoblastic leukemia cells based on changes in gene expression before and after treatment, regardless of the type of treatment used. The dataset childhood ALL includes 110 childhood acute lymphoblastic leukemia samples having 8280 genes (Cheok et.al, 2003). Among them, 50 examples are of type before therapy and 60 examples are of type after therapy.
- **Gastric Cancer (GSE2685):** In Gastric cancer, tumor cells form in the stomach lining. This dataset (Hippo et.al, 2002) is constructed by combining the diffuse and intestinal advanced gastric tumor samples into one class (22 samples) and noncancerous samples into another class (8 samples). The dataset contains 4522 genes.
- **Lymphoma & Leukemia (GSE1577):** The malignant cells in T-cell acute lymphoblastic leukemia (T-ALL) and T-cell lymphoblastic lymphoma (T-LL) are morphologically indistinguishable, and they share the expression of common cell surface antigens and cytogenetic characteristics. However, despite these similarities, differences in the clinical behavior of T-ALL and T-LL are observed. This dataset (Raetz et.al, 2006) is made of expression levels of 15434 genes across 19 examples. It has 9 examples of T-LL type and 10 examples of T-ALL type.

Review Work

Handling of big data and extracting the useful information from it is a hot topic of recent day research. Microarray data is one of them which grab enough attention to the researchers. The problem can be treated as the feature selection problem that can be addressed as an optimization problem or it can be constructed as a clustering problem where the centers of the clusters are the selected features of the problem. Those features are applied for the classification or pattern reorganizations of the disease as well as helping it for gene discovery and drug prediction for the treatment. Few of the examples of the related work are given below. For the selection of features, different statistical methods are used to filter the irrelevant genes such as t-test (Golub et.al, 1999), i-test (Bassat et.al, 1982), F-test (Bandyopadhyay et.al, 2014), information gain ratio (Bassat ct.al, 1982), significancc analysis of microarrays (SAM), Bayes t-test (eBayes), t-tests relative to a threshold (TREAT) (Yang et.al, 2014), entropy based filter (Pal et.al, 2016), mutual information (Chow et.al, 2005), Markov blanket filter (Koller et.al, 1996), correlation based filter (CFS) (Hall et.al, 1999), maximum predictive-minimum redundancy, maximum relevancy-minimum redundancy (MRMR) (Arevalillo et.al, 2013), etc. Those filter based approaches provide fast and scalable output but ignores the feature dependencies as there is no interaction with classifiers. Different classifier dependent statistical learning are proposed in this regards such as Fisher linear classifier

(Iizuka, 2003), Support vector machine (SVM) (Statnikov et.al, 2005), KNN etc. Again, researchers have come up with different wrapper based approaches which may be of two types. In the first type, some deterministic algorithms are used and in the second type, some random stochastic algorithms are applied for the problem. Few examples of deterministic type wrapper based work are sequential forward selection (SFS), sequential backward elimination (SBE) (Kittler, 1978) etc. Also, there are different types of randomized algorithms are used for the feature selection problem such as randomized hill climbing (Shalak et.al, 1994), estimation of distributed algorithm (Inza et.al, 2004), simulated annealing (SA), memetic algorithm (Zibakhsh et.al, 2013) having a fuzzy concept, ant bee colony (Amaratunga et.al, 2008), genetic algorithm (Tan, 2006), particle swarm optimization (Mandal et.al, 2015), binary ant colony optimization (Wan, 2016) etc. Generally, those works involve different statistical filter based techniques as a part of their computation. Again, few works are developed considering various classifiers as their computation tools such as GA using SVM (Kleftogiannis et.al, 2015), GA with KNN (Lee et.al, 2011), PSO with decision tree (Chen et.al, 2014) and so on. The main advantages of those stochastic methods are that they are less prone to local optima and having model feature dependencies as well as interact with classifiers. But the computational complexity and higher risk of over-fitting motivates researchers for the further improvement of work in this field. Recently, some hybrid approaches are proved to be very effective where both the filters and the classifiers are implemented along with the randomized algorithms. For an example, hybrid multi-filter embedded technique is proposed (Huerta, 2016) where GA along with the tabu-search algorithm is implemented using SVM on the dataset. In another approach CFS-tauchi-genetic algorithm with SVM classifier (Chauang et.al, 2011) is proposed. The described methods use the filter output or the classifier output as the solution of the objective function that has to be gained. Another totally different approach is present in the literatures where the problem is formulated as a clustering problem. Among them, fuzzy C-means (Dembele et.al, 2003), Self-organising map (SOM) (Toronen et.al, 1999) are very popular and efficient methodologies. Recursive cluster elimination based on support vector machine (pang et.al, 2007) is used for the classification purposes. Again, LDA technique (Ye et.al, 2004) is applied for the relevant gene selection purpose. Rough-fuzzy clustering for grouping functionally similar genes from microarray data (Maji et.al, 2013), simulated annealing based on fuzzy fitness function (Saha et.al, 2013) are also applied. However, the results are still not satisfying to solve large amounts of high dimensional gene expression data and the resulting top ranked genes or features are often redundant.

Different pathway activity inference methodologies have been proposed in this context for the identification of gene markers. Some approaches use gene expression parametrically by representing pathway activity with a function evaluating the expression values of member genes (Guo et.al, 2005). These methods have demonstrated classification accuracies that are comparable to conventional gene based classifiers, while providing a good interpretation of how the expression profile of genes is associated with a disease. For example, prior pathway knowledge is compiled into database inferring pathway activity on a sample, then statistical approaches like mean or median expression value of the member genes are computed to infer the pathway activity (Guo et.al, 2005). Ma et.al, (2009) used principal component analysis of the member genes to estimate the activity of a given pathway. Lee et al. (2008) proposed a method to predict the pathway activity using some CORGs in the pathway. Again, probabilistic inference of pathway activities is estimated by the log-likelihood ratio between different classes by Su et.al in 2009. A brief review of the different methodologies used for study of the genomic expression profile is given in the Table 1. In this work, authors have implemented a new multi-swarm binary swarm technique for the selection of differentially expressed genes from two classes of cancer. the result are compared using

Table 1. Brief review of different methodologies used for feature gene identification

Category	Authors	Year	Used Methodology
Filtering based	M. Ben-Bassat et.al	1982	i-test
	M. Ben-Bassat et.al	1982	Information gain ratio
	D. Koller et.al	1996	Markov blanket filter
	Golub et. al	1999	t-test
	M. Hall et.al	1999	Correlation based filter (CFS)
	Chow et.al	2005	Mutual information
	J.M Arevalillo et.al	2013	Maximum predictive-minimum redundancy
	J.M Arevalillo et.al	2013	Maximum relevancy-minimum redundancy (MRMR)
	S. Bandyopadhyay et.al	2014	F-test
	D. Yang et.al	2014	Significance analysis of microarrays (SAM)
	D. Yang et.al	2014	Bayes t-test (eBayes), t-tests relative to a threshold (TREAT)
	S.pal et.al	2016	Fuzzy rough based entropy based filter
Classifier Based	N. Iizuka et. al	2003	Fisher linear classifier
	A. Statnikov et.al	2005	Support vector machine (SVM)
Wrapper + filter	J. Kittler et.al	1978	Sequential forward selection (SFS)
	J. Kittler et.al	1978	Sequential backward elimination (SBE)
	D. Skalak et.al	1994	Randomized hill climbing
	I. Inza et.al	2004	Estimation of distributed algorithm
	F. Tan et.al	2006	Genetic algorithm
	D. Amaratunga et.al	2008	Artificial bee colony
	A. Zibakhsh et.al	2013	Memetic algorithm having a fuzzy concept
	M. Mandal et.al	2015	Binary PSO
	Y. Wan et.al	2016	Binary ant colony optimization
Wrapper + classifiers	C. P. Lee	2011	GA using KNN
	K.H. chen et.al	2014	PSO with decision tree
	D. Kleftogiannis et.al	2015	Adaptive GA with SVM
Hybrid approach	Chuang et. al	2011	CFS-taguchi-genetic algorithm with SVM
	B. Huerta et.al	2016	Multifilter+GA along with the tabu-search algorithm+SVM
Clustering Based	P. Toronen et.al	1999	Self-Organizing Map
	D. Dembele et.al	2003	Fuzzy C-means
	S. Pang et.al	2007	Recursive cluster using support vector machine
	J. Ye et. al	2004	LDA technique
	P. Maji et.al	2013	Rough-Fuzzy Clustering
	S. Saha et.al	2013	Simulated annealing based on fuzzy fitness function
	V. Elyasigomari et. al	2015	Cuckoo optimization algorithm + Genetic algorithm
Pathway marker based	Z. Guo et. al	2005	Mean
	Z. Guo et. al	2005	Median
	S. Ma et.al	2009	Principle component analysis (PCA)
	J. Su et. al	2009	Log-Likelihood ratio (LLR)
	E. Lee et. al	2008	Condition responsive genes (CORG)
	M. Mandal et.al	2015	Binary PSO
	C. Zheng et.al	2016	Multi-objective genetic algorithm

both the single swarm and multi swarm based different approaches to establish the effectiveness of the proposed concept to identify most significant genes for cancer progression.

PROPOSED GENE SELECTION METHOD

Raw microarray data (Singh, 2002; Cheok, 2003; Hippo, 2002) obtained from different types of cancer related tests is used for experimental purposes. Now, the work of examining the huge dimension of the dataset having the expression level of thousands of genes is quite cumbersome and time consuming. First, the data is pre-processed and the pathway activity is inferred. Then, using different computational procedure like single swarm or multi- swarm techniques, as primarily used in this paper, the normalized data is computed and significant pathway genes are extracted. A better solution can be achieved using the multi-swarm activity. So, the multi-swarm PSO based concept is implemented along with binary version of GA (Tan et.al, 2006), DE (Das et.al, 2011), ABC (Amaratunga et.al, 2008) algorithms and a comparative study is performed both for the single swarm and multi-swarm based stochastic computational methods. The schematic diagram of the proposed methodology is shown in Figure 2 and the process selection of pathway markers from gene expression profile is described below.

Processing Microarray Data

Microarray data contains many irrelevant and noisy data. Again, there remain many such genes whose expression level is not changing from one class to another class. As a consequence, they are not carrying any information regarding the cancer development and progression and they may be eliminated. So, the data has been pre-processed before computation by eliminating the genes having missing value in the dataset. To analyse the large amount of data, a statistical analysis is conducted so that the genes which are mostly differentially expressed in two classes can be identified. This technique in turns will remove the uninformative and redundant genes from the dataset. As, authors are interested in differentially expressed genes in two classes, two sample t-test (Bandyopadhyay et.al, 2014) is employed and based on the t-score, the genes are arranged in descending order and then top 1000 genes are selected for computation.

For the two different classes, t-test over the sample for a particular gene is very effective to select the differentially expressed genes which need attention for medical diagnosis. It uses means and standard deviations of two samples to make a statistical comparison. The formula for t-test is given below:

$$t = \frac{\mu_1 - \mu_2}{\sqrt{\frac{sd_1}{n_1^2}} + \sqrt{\frac{sd_2}{n_2^2}}} \tag{1}$$

μ_1, μ_2 are the mean of gene expression of a particular gene over the samples of 1st class and 2nd class respectively. sd_1, sd_2 are the standard deviation of gene expression of a particular gene over the samples of 1st and 2nd class respectively. n_1, n_2 are the total number of samples present in the first and the second class correspondingly.

Figure 2. Computational methods using multi-swarm based approach

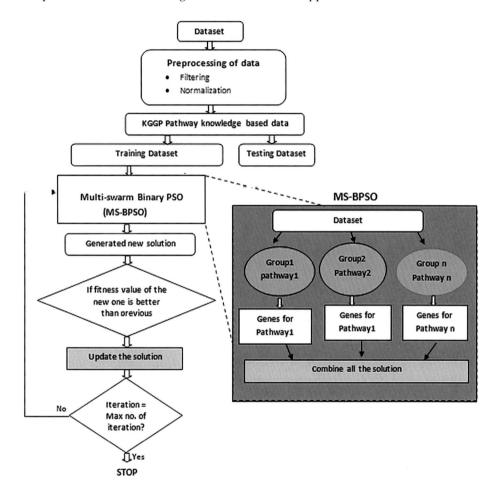

Gathering Pathway Information

In the next stage, those selected 1000 genes affymetrix IDs are searched in the http://david.abcc.ncif-crf.gov/tools.jsp website and the corresponding KEGG pathway information is collected (Kanehisa et.al, 2000), (Mandal et.al, 2015). For biological interpretation of the functioning of genes and their molecular-level information, KEGG pathway is a very strong tool which is used extensively for the gene discovery and for the diagnosis of the related diseases. For those 1000 genes corresponding pathway level information is gathered and then the pathways are arranged according to the ascending order of their P-values. P-value is calculated using Wilcoxon Rank Sum Test (Bandyopadhyay et.al, 2014). It is a nonparametric hypothetical test used to determine the statistical difference between two class having independent samples. Now top 50% pathways having p value at a significance level of 5% are chosen for calculation. The expressions of the genes which are present in the top 50% pathway activity are collected from the DNA microarray dataset.

Normalization Process

As the values of the gene expression are ranging from very high numerical values to very low value, authors have normalized the resultant dataset using min-max normalization (Bandyopadhyay et.al, 2014). If the expression of a gene over the samples is represented by the variable x, then the min-max normalization formula for a data point x_i is described by Eq.(2). Thus a data matrix D_{mxn} is formed for k number of pathways where n represents the number of genes and m is the number of sample. This generated data matrix is used for the next level of computation.

$$x_i(normalized) = \frac{x_i - \min(x)}{\max(x) - \min(x)} \tag{2}$$

Collaborative Multi-Swarm Binary Particle Swarm Optimization (MS-BPSO)

The normalized data matrix is now processed using MS-BPSO. Before going to the details of the processing phase for gene selection, a brief idea of PSO and its development to multi-swarm based binary PSO is described below.

Concept of Particle Swarm Optimization (PSO)

To solve the optimization problem, Particle Swarm Optimization (PSO) has been developed by Eberhart and Kennedy in 1995 being inspired by the social behavior of a bird flock. In the PSO algorithm, a swarm consists of many agents or particles whose location in the multi-dimensional problem space represents the possible solutions for the f(x). The particles fly with a velocity and the direction of the flying is influenced by its own past experience as well as other particles make an impact. The velocity and direction of each particle moving along each dimension of the problem space will be altered with each generation of movement. The velocity and position update rule for i^{th} particle at t^{th} generation are given below.

$$v^i\left(t\right) = w * v^i\left(t-1\right) + c_1 * rand * \left(p_{best}^i - x^i\right) + c_2 * rand * \left(g_{best}^i - x^i\right) \tag{3}$$

$$x^i\left(t\right) = x^i(t-1) + v^i\left(t\right) \tag{4}$$

where c_1, the cognitive learning factor, represents the attraction of a particle toward its own success p_{best} and c_2, social learning factor, represents the attraction of a particle toward the swarm's best position g_{best}, and w is the inertia weight.

Concept of Collaborative Multi-Swarm Binary Particle Swarm Optimization (MS-BPSO)

Basic PSO itself is a very efficient and simpler technique for optimization but it suffers from little deficiency. The main problem with it is the local trapping due to scarcity of diversity leads to pre-mature convergence. So, the solution which is found after searching may not be the optimized solution rather it could be a solution of local optima. The selection of gene from the microarray data is itself a large dimensional problem. To address the large dimension of the pathway gene expression data, PSO has to be modified and some sort of diversity has to be introduced for the betterment of the result. One of the possible solutions is to introduce multi-swarm concept (Niu et.al, 2007) which is very effective to introduce diversity in searching as it works with many numbers of groups. If one group is stuck to local optima then other groups are there to get it out of the situation by sharing its search either co-operatively or collaboratively. So, as a whole the performance of the algorithm is accelerated and the problem of fast pre-mature convergence will be overcome and a better optimized result of the problem can be obtained. In multi-swarm based techniques, the whole swarm is divided into groups and each group is searching for the solution separately. Now they can share the knowledge of searching at every iteration or after an interval based on different methodologies. Being motivated by this concept, a collaborative approach is integrated for searching of the pathway markers from the cancer dataset. The scheme is discussed below.

In this work, the authors have partitioned the total dimension according to the pathway activity and the total swarm is divided into groups where each group is searching for the solution for each partition. For an example, suppose 200 pathway genes are present in total 10 number of pathway activities, then the whole swarm are divided into 10 groups. Each group searches independently for each separate pathway activity and at the end of the searching, the ultimate result is the aggregation of the result collected from each group. The proposed approach is similar to the collaborative approach where total work load is distributed among the workers and the results are collected from each groups and combined to get the final output. The velocity and the position update rule for the member of a group is same as Eq. (3) and Eq. (4). The best result among the particle of a group is termed as g_{best}. Thus at every iteration, g_{best} from each group is collected and then they are combined to get a result as a whole which represents the pathway markers. If the fitness value of the combined result $g_{best-combined}$ is better than the result of the previous iteration then the archive is updated. A binary version of the optimization algorithm is used to handle the prescribed problem as to select few genes which are to be present in the computation. Keeping this in mind, if the solution is in binary 1 and 0 format then the genes corresponding to 1 indicates that they are used for computation and if 0 then they are not included in processing. The initial position and the velocity of the swarm are taken randomly within a range of 0 and 1. After getting the best solution at the end of each iteration, the position vector g_{best} of each group is used for the selection of genes of the particular pathway based on Algorithm 1. If the value of the jth dimension of the solution is greater than 0.5 then it is taken as 1 otherwise 0. The overall MS-BPSO technique is described in the following Algorithm 2.

Selection of Pathway Markers Using MS-BPSO

Now, for the problem of identifying the pathway marker genes, selection of those genes which are differentially expressed in different classes is necessary. So, the fitness function used for the computation is chosen such that the separation between two classes is maximized when those proper pathway genes

Algorithm 1. Implementation of binary concept

```
for j=1:dimension of (g_best)
   if g_best (j) > 0.5
        g_best (j)=1;
   else g_best (j)=0;
   end;
end;
```

Algorithm 2. MS-BPSO

```
1.          Initialization
   a) Divide the total N swarm into k number of groups (k= number of
      pathways)                    /*in a group N/k particles are present*/
   b) Randomly initialize the position and the velocity of all the
      particle
 2. Termination check
if the termination criterion holds go to step 6
else go to step 3
 3. Set t=1(t=iteration counter)        /*start of iteration*/
      for group= 1,2…k do              /*updation of a group*/
       for i= 1,2…N/k  do              /*updation of a particle*/
a)       Calculate the fitness of i^th particle.
b)       Update the position and the velocity according to (3) & (4)
c)       If f(x_i^k) is better than previous, update local best p_i^k
          end for                       /*end of udation of a group*/
   Update g_best^k of the k^th group=arg{min f(x_i^k) }
    end for                            /*end of udation of a group*/
   g_best_combined = Horizontal concatenation of g_best^k of all groups
   Calculate the fitness f(g_best_combined)
   if f(g_best_combined) is better than previous, update the archive
  4. Set t=t+1.                        /*increment of iteration*/
  5. go to step 2
  6. Solution is the g_best_combined.
```

are selected by the proposed technique. The mean expression of those selected genes over the samples for both the classes is calculated. Then the difference of the two mean expressions is computed. A fitness function for PSO based computation is used which is described in Eq. (5) where μ_1 and sd_1 represent the mean and the standard deviation value of the 1st class respectively. Similarly, μ_2 and sd_2 represent the mean and the standard deviation value of the 2nd class. Higher fitness function indicates the better selectivity of genes. Now for each iteration, new subset of genes for each pathway is selected. The best result of each group is then combined to get a complete resultant gene subset which is considered as the pathway marker genes.

$$fitness = \frac{\mu_1 - \mu_2}{sd_1 + sd_2} \qquad (5)$$

The use of the proposed approach for marker genes selection activity is given in Figure 3 where for one swarm group, the corresponding computational scheme is shown. The mean expression of those selected genes over the samples for both the classes is calculated. Then the difference of the two mean expressions is computed. Now, the authors have to select the particular portion of the differential expression which in turn selects those genes which are differentially expressed in two classes. Higher fitness function indicates the better selectivity of genes. For each iteration, new subset of genes for each pathway is selected. The best result g_{best} of each group is then combined to get a complete resultant gene subset which is considered as the pathway marker genes.

Other Comparative Methods for the Selection of Pathway Markers

To make an impartial comparison, few other evolutionary and swarm intelligence algorithms such as genetic algorithm (GA) (Tan et.al, 2006), differential evolution (DE) (Das et.al, 2011) and Artificial Bee Colony (ABC) (Amaratunga et.al, 2008) based marker gene selection methods are also carried out in the paper. All of the algorithms adopt the binary form here. As discussed, simple single swarm PSO-based approach may result in premature convergence and local trapping, some strategies like multi-swarm based methodology has been adopted to prevent premature convergence of PSO. This multi-swarm concept as implemented for MS-BPSO, is now integrated for all other evolutionary and swarm algorithms to get a fair comparison of performance. Authors have designed and implemented Multi-group Genetic Algorithm (MG-GA), Multi-group Binary Differential Evolution (MG-BDE), Multi-swarm Binary artificial Bee Colony (MS-BABC) method for the selection of genes from microarray dataset. In the next subsection, the methodologies are discussed in brief.

Multi-Group Genetic Algorithm (MG-GA)

GA is based on the natural principle of "survival of the fittest". It constitutes of a number of steps like initial population generation, fitness evaluation, parent selection, crossover, and mutation (Tan et al., 2006). The algorithm first starts with few solution termed as chromosome. Now, the chromosomes having promising fitness values are selected to form a set called mating pool for a number of genetic operations to create new solutions. The fittest chromosome survives and it is assigned as the optimal solution of the objective function. Now to implement the multi group concept for the selection of genes authors start with different set of chromosome and each set finds for the solution for each separate pathway. For MG-GA, the process of pathway marker selection is kept same as Figure 2, only the dash box will be replaced by the MG-GA.

Multi-Group Binary Differential Evolution (MG-BDE)

DE is a population-based stochastic optimization method which adopts mutation and crossover operators to search for new promising areas in the search space (Das et.al, 2011). Simple binomial crossover operator is used here and the algorithm is initialized with a number of groups where each group is searching

Figure 3. Computational method pathway data matrix using MS-BPSO

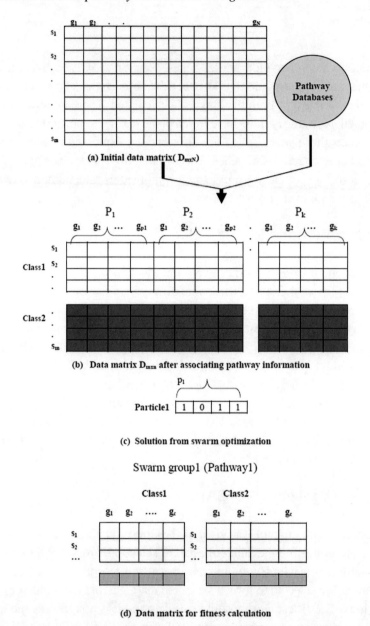

for the pathways separately. The ultimate solution is the aggregation of the solution collected from the each group. The binary format is implemented as done early using Algorithm-1 and the process of gene selection is same as described in Figure 2 except that the dash box MS-BPSO is replaced by MG-BDE.

Multi-Swarm Binary Artificial Bee Colony (MS-BABC)

Artificial Bee Colony (ABC) algorithm is based on the foraging behaviour of honey bees for numerical optimization problems (Amaratunga et.al, 2008). Three groups of bees: employee bees, onlooker bees and scout bees are involved in searching process. The employee bee produces a modification on the position (solution) and depending on the nectar amount (fitness value), the new source is memorized. Onlooker bee chooses a food source having higher probability of getting nectar. The best possible source is the optimized solution of the functions. Multiple swarms are involved in the search process and binary format is adopted as described in Algorithm1. MS-BAC is applied on cancer dataset similar to the process as described in Figure 2 just replacing the block of MS-BPSO by MS-BABC.

The parameter settings of all other stochastic algorithms are given in the Table 2. Here, the basic parameters are provided and the group or swarm number changes according to the number of pathway activity involved in the experimental dataset.

EXPERIMENTAL RESULTS

The proposed methodology is applied on different cancer dataset and the corresponding relevant significant pathway genes are identified which are used for the classification purposes. As mentioned above, the problem is formulated as optimization problem and selected differentially expressed genes are considered as the pathway marker genes which are evaluated using 10-fold cross validation and the decision tree is used as the classifier. The corresponding sensitivity, specificity, accuracy, and, F-score are considered as performance metric and they are evaluated. The definition of all the metrics are given in due course of discussion. In the first experimental set up, different pathway based marker gene selection approaches, reported in the literatures, are used for validating the efficiency of the proposed work. In the next set of experiment, the authors have used different stochastic bio-inspired algorithms for the comparative study. Here, two different approaches are involved which are described as follows. At first, binary version of DE, ABC, GA and PSO are implemented having single swarm concept. After that, different features of multiple swarm concepts are integrated for the searching of optimal solution for all those bio-inspired algorithms such as MG-GA, MG-BDE, MS-BABC and a comparative analysis is performed. In every experiment, we have used k-fold cross validation, where in this case we have considered k=10. Initially, all the samples are considered together and they are randomly partitioned into k subsets. One partition is taken as testing set whereas remaining (k-1) subsets are used for training

Table 2. Parameters used in different swarm and evolutionary algorithms

Algorithms	Parameters	Explanation	Value
MS-BPSO	N	Number of particle(s) in one swarm	10
	c_1, c_2	Acceleration constants	1.49
	w	Inertia	0.7
	r_1, r_2	Random numbers	[0,1]
MG-GA	N	Number of genetic(s) in one group	10
	Ps	Selection ratio	0.8
	Pc	Crossover ratio	0.9
	Pm	Mutation ratio	0.01
MG-BDE	N	Number of individual(s) in one group	10
	fm	Mutation factor	0.6
	CR	Crossover rate	0.9
MS-BABC	N	Number of bee(s) in one swarm	10
	L	Limit for scout phase	100

purpose and the number of false positives (f_p), true negatives (t_n), false negatives (f_n) and true positives (t_p) are figured out for the testing samples. Thereafter using these four numbers, sensitivity (Eq. (6)), specificity (Eq. (7)), accuracy (Eq. (8)), and F-score (Eq. (9)), are determined. Sensitivity is termed as the percentage of genes which are correctly identified in the specified class. Specificity is termed as the percentages of the genes which are not belonging to the specified class are correctly identified. The accuracy indicates the error in classification. Higher the accuracy means more accurate classification. Precision is termed as the deviation of result from the true value and is defined in the Eq. (10). Those metrics are very effective to evaluate the performance a technique for classifying a testing sample. Next, the top 20% pathway marker genes are searched in a disease-gene association database http://www.disgenet.org/ and disease information related to these top ranked differentially expressed genes are given to validate the biological significance of our work.

$$Sensitivity = \frac{t_p}{t_p + f_n} \tag{6}$$

$$Specificity = \frac{t_n}{t_n + f_p} \tag{7}$$

$$Accuracy = \frac{t_n + t_p}{t_n + t_p + f_p + f_n} \tag{8}$$

$$Fscore = \frac{2 * precision * sensitivity}{precision + sensitivity} \tag{9}$$

$$precision = \frac{t_p}{t_p + f_p} \tag{10}$$

Result and Discussion

Experiment 1: Result of Comparison With Other Pathway Based Methodologies

The proposed MS-PSO based gene selection technique is applied on prostate, child_all, gastric and lymphoma & leukemia dataset and the results are compared with other some existing statistical techniques and BPSO based techniques. Mean, median are two popular statistical techniques used by Guo et. al in 2005. Here, after inferring the pathway activity, all the member gene expression values for a pathway are summarized through mean and median respectively whereas the proposed MS-BPSO uses only those genes which are correspond to binary bit 1. Again, Su et.al, (2009) implemented a method named as LLR for all the constituent genes of a pathway using log-likelihood ratio. Recently, Mandal et.al (2015) proposed a BPSO for the identification of pathway genes from data matrix using t-score. The authors have run the experiment for mean, median and BPSO techniques along with the MS-BPSO. Fitness value achieved by other different technique is compared for the dataset and result of comparison is given in the form of bar chart in Figure 4. A higher fitness value of objective function indicates better optimization ability. The bar chart shows that the fitness value obtained by the proposed MS-BPSO based technique is best among all the techniques for LL dataset and Gastric cancer dataset. For prostate dataset, it has achieved the second best result. Mean and median provides nearly same result whereas the performance of BPSO based technique is poor. For the Child_ALL data the performance of the proposed technique is little bit compromising. The proposed method establishes good result in all respect over other comparative methods, indicating its ability to produce more robust gene selection activity. Now, the selected genes are considered as the pathway marker genes which are evaluated using 10-fold cross validation and the decision tree is used as the classifier. The corresponding sensitivity, specificity, accuracy, and, F-score are considered as performance metrics and they are reported in Table 3. These metrics measure the proportion of genes that are correctly identified for all the dataset. The result is also compared with the result obtained by the mean, median, LLR (Su et.al, 2009) and BPSO techniques. For the mean and the median techniques, all the genes are considered for the pathway activity calculation where as in the proposed method and in BPSO based techniques selected few numbers of genes are considered as pathway markers. So, rather considering all the genes as the features of the classification, top 75% genes are considered based on their ranking for mean and median technique. The result of Table 3 indicates that the proposed gene selection method works well to detect the relevant pathway genes for all the different types of dataset.

The good value of the sensitivity obtained by the proposed method validates the good performance of the proposed work for identification of those genes which are correctly belonging to the given class. The value of the specificity is highest compared to other techniques for all the reveals and it signifies that

Figure 4. Result of comparison of fitness value for different methods for the four cancer dataset

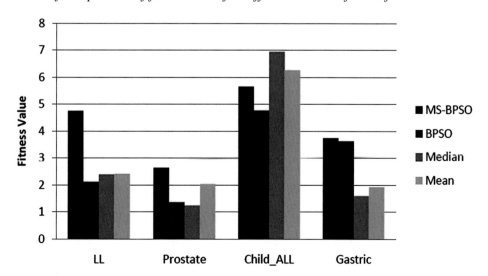

Table 3. Result of comparison with other pathway based methodologies for different cancer dataset

Dataset	Algorithms	Sensitivity	Specificity	Accuracy	F-Score
Gastric	Proposed	**1.00**	**1.00**	**1.00**	**1.00**
	BPSO	0.82	0.8	0.8	0.85
	Mean	0.85	0.9	0.86	0.88
	Median	0.81	0.8	0.79	0.84
	LLR	1.00	0.50	0.86	0.92
LL	Proposed	0.9	**1.00**	**0.95**	0.93
	BPSO	0.80	**1.00**	0.88	0.87
	Mean	**1.00**	0.9	0.95	**0.94**
	median	0.86	0.77	0.73	0.70
	LLR	0.80	1.00	0.89	0.88
Child_ALL	Proposed	0.80	**0.81**	**0.81**	**0.83**
	BPSO	0.73	0.53	0.63	0.67
	Mean	**0.81**	0.69	0.75	0.78
	Median	0.75	0.66	0.71	0.72
	LLR	0.76	0.72	0.73	0.72
Prostate	Proposed	0.77	**0.85**	0.79	0.79
	BPSO	0.72	0.81	0.77	0.73
	Mean	0.71	0.73	0.72	0.72
	Median	0.74	0.79	0.75	0.74
	LLR	**0.90**	**0.85**	**0.88**	**0.88**

the genes which are not belonging to the given class are correctly identified. Again, higher the accuracy value compared to all the other techniques indicates the amount of uncertainty or error is less. The results are also compared through the bar charts in Figure 5 to get a better insight in the result of classification.

Experiment 2: Comparative Result of Different Single and Multi-Swarm Based Approaches

In order to have an intuitional comparison the experimental evaluation is performed in two ways. First, GA, binary coded PSO (BPSO) and binary coded DE (BDE), binary coded artificial bee colony (BABC) are all used with its standard mode having a single group. Second, the multi-swarm concept based swarm and evolutionary computational algorithms are used. Here authors use MG-GA, MG-BDE, MS-ABC and MS-BPSO for experimental purposes. As discussed above, multi-swarm concept provides more diversity and more reliable solution, so its advantage over single group based concept is demonstrated through experiments. Among these algorithms, MB-BPSO has a better performance on an average and the result of classification is higher than the other techniques. Result of comparison is shown in Table 4. For the single group concept, the proposed MS-BPSO works simply as a BPSO technique. So, for that category, comparative analysis is performed among BPSO, BDE, BABC and GA. For prostate cancer dataset, BABC, BPSO, GA all are working good but better result is achieved when multi group concept

Figure 5. Comparative result of classification using different methods for the four cancer dataset

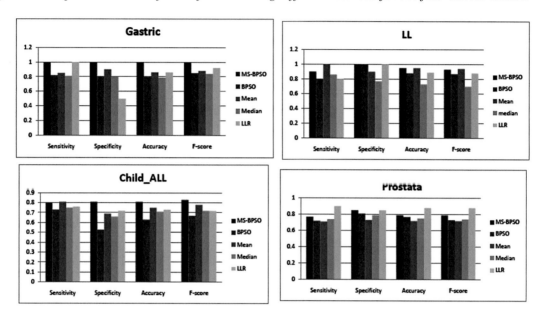

Table 4. Result of comparison with different swarm and evolutionary algorithms

Dataset		Single Swarm				Multi Swarm				
	Algorithms	Sensitivity	Specificity	Accuracy	F-Score	Algorithms	Sensitivity	Specificity	Accuracy	F-Score
Prostate	BPSO	**0.81**	0.76	0.78	**0.81**	MS-BPSO	0.77	**0.85**	0.79	0.79
	BABC	0.80	**0.80**	**0.80**	0.80	MS-BABC	0.81	0.76	0.78	0.80
	BDE	0.41	0.77	0.64	0.43	MG-BDE	0.68	0.82	0.77	0.67
	GA	0.74	**0.80**	0.77	0.76	MG-GA	**0.86**	0.84	**0.85**	**0.85**
LL	BPSO	0.9	**1.00**	**0.93**	**0.93**	MS-BPSO	0.90	**1.00**	0.95	0.93
	BABC	0.90	0.90	0.88	0.89	MS-BABC	0.80	0.90	0.81	0.80
	BDE	0.80	0.80	0.80	0.78	MG-BDE	**1.00**	0.70	0.86	0.89
	GA	**1.00**	0.90	0.88	0.89	MG-GA	0.90	0.90	0.90	0.89
Child_ ALL	BPSO	0.73	0.53	0.63	0.67	MS-BPSO	**0.80**	**0.81**	**0.81**	**0.83**
	BABC	0.73	**0.60**	**0.67**	**0.71**	MS-BABC	0.70	0.74	0.71	0.72
	BDE	0.66	**0.60**	0.63	0.66	MG-BDE	0.65	0.70	0.67	0.68
	GA	**0.76**	0.52	0.65	0.70	MG-GA	0.70	0.70	0.70	0.71
Gastric	BPSO	0.82	**0.80**	0.80	0.85	MS-BPSO	**1.00**	**1.00**	**1.00**	**1.00**
	BABC	0.86	**0.80**	0.82	0.87	MS-BABC	**1.00**	**1.00**	**1.00**	**1.00**
	BDE	0.87	0.70	0.80	0.86	MG-BDE	**1.00**	**1.00**	**1.00**	**1.00**
	GA	**1.00**	0.60	**0.90**	**0.94**	MG-GA	**1.00**	**1.00**	**1.00**	**1.00**

is implemented. The similar pattern is noticed for all other dataset also, where it can be said that multi group or swarm concept is providing better result of classification compared to single swarm or group based performance. For LL and child_all dataset, MS-BPSO is performing outstandingly compared to all other meta-heuristic algorithms. For gastric cancer dataset, the entire multi group algorithms are providing the best result. Overall, it can be said that MS-BPSO is able to achieve more reliable and accurate result of classification for more number of microarray dataset compared to other algorithms.

Biological Relevance

To demonstrate the biological relevance of the selected pathway markers by the proposed method, Wilcoxon signed rank test (Bandyopadhyay et.al, 2014) is performed on the gene expression data of the two classes and the corresponding P-value is collected. The pathway marker genes are arranged according to the ascending order of the P-value and top 20% genes are selected for biological significance validation. The authors have searched for the top 20% pathway marker genes in a disease-gene association database http://www.disgenet.org/. Also the information about the number of Pubmed citations of the disease-gene association is also collected from the database. In the Table 5, few disease information related to these top ranked differentially expressed genes are given. These genes, which are given in the table, are very highly functioning pathway genes for the corresponding type of cancer and the information helps to understand that the outcome does not come by chance.

CONCLUSION

In sum, a pathway gene selection method optimized with MS-BPSO algorithm is proposed in this chapter. Here collaborative multi-swarm PSO based technique has been introduced and the concept is implemented for GA, ABC and DE algorithm also. The proposed methodology is potentially useful in the context of medical diagnostics as it identifies marker genes of pathway activities which are signifi-

Table 5. Biological significance for gene-disease association

Dataset	Associated Diseases	Gene Symbol
Prostate	Prostatic Neoplasms	KLK3(62), INS(2), IGF1(14), AOX(1)
	Protate Carcinoma,	KLK3(677), INS(30), IGF2(16)
	Malignant neoplasm of Prostate	KLK3(681), INS(31), IGF1(58), PIK3R3(1)
LL	Carcinoma	NDUFA1(1), ABL1(7), SKP2(13), UQCRFSL1(3)
	Heart disease	UQCRFSL1(1), YWHAQ(1)
	Lymphomas	AKAP17A(1), ABL1(183), RHOA(4), SKP2(5)
Child_ALL	Leukemia	ABL1(1407), BCR(364), CCNB1 (3), CAMK2G(2)
	Lymphomas	PLK1(5), FGF2(4), AURKA(2)
	Lymphoblastic Leukemia	ABL1(183),BCR(64), AURKA(2)
Gastric	Malignant Neoplasm of Stomach	ADH7(1), HSP90AA1 (5), SPP1(20)
	Stomach Carcinoma	HSP90AA1 (6), SPP1(21), MCM2(3)

cantly associated with the disease. The generated resultant gene subset reveals insights into biological processes that may be valuable for functional genomics in cancer progression. The results and graphs reflect that the proposed method shows promising result in compare to other existing pathway marker selection techniques. Results are compared with some other classification techniques optimized by MG-GA, MS-BABC and MS-BDE. In general, it is observed that multi-group evolutionary algorithm and multi-swarm intelligence algorithm can be well used to solve the problem as well providing better classification accuracy compared to single group evolutionary algorithm and single swarm intelligence algorithm. Among this muti-swarm category of algorithms, MS-BPSO has a better performance on an average and it is more appropriate to be employed to reduce the data dimension to extract the useful information related to the pathway markers. The proposed method is able to keep a good balance on the efficiency and classification accuracy, which makes it more suitable for some other features election applications.

FUTURE RESEARCH DIRECTIONS

In the near future, the method can be applied for finding more robust pathway gene marker selection technique for different classes of cancer. Again, it is observed that those genes which are selected as pathway level genes through some statistical objective function are sometime not efficient for the job of classification and identification of cancer. This is because of the fact that pathway activity concludes about the consequences prior to disease and their collective effect on the growth of a disease, so it may cause to include many of the genes which are active at pathway level but may not be good enough for disease classification. As a remedy, the pitfall can be handled using some multi-objective function where both the situation can be taken care of. Some multi-objective evolutionary and swarm algorithms can be used as a possible approach to obtain a pareto-optimal solution set to balance between different statistical filtering and classification functioning.

Again, the reduction of noise from data and implementation of some good transforming techniques to differentiate between two overlapping sample can be helpful to improve the performance of the classification. MicroRNAs (miRNAs), small non-coding RNAs, play a significant role in gene regulation. Gene expression studies indicate that abnormal miRNA homeostasis is linked to many diseases. Predicting miRNA genes is also a challenging problem for the estimation of pathway for cancer.

REFERENCES

Amaratunga, D., Cabrera, J., & Kovtun, V. (2008). Microarray learning with ABC. *Biostatistics (Oxford, England)*, *9*(1), 128–136. doi:10.1093/biostatistics/kxm017 PMID:17573363

Arevalillo, J. M., & Navarro, H. (2013). Exploring correlations in gene expression microarray data for maximum predictive - minimum redundancy biomarker selection and classification. *Computers in Biology and Medicine*, *43*(10), 1437–1443. doi:10.1016/j.compbiomed.2013.07.005 PMID:24034735

Bandyopadhyay, S., Mallik, S., & Mukhopadhyay, A. (2014). A survey and comparative study of statistical tests for identifying differential expression from microarray data. *IEEE/ACM Transactions on Computational Biology and Bioinformatics*, *11*(1), 95–115. doi:10.1109/TCBB.2013.147 PMID:26355511

Ben-Bassat, M. (1982). Pattern recognition and reduction of dimensionality. Handbook of Statistics, 2, 773-910.

Chen, K. H., Wang, K. J., Tsai, M. L., Wang, K. M., Adrian, A. M., Cheng, W. C., & Chang, K. S. (2014). Gene selection for cancer identification: A decision tree model empowered by particle swarm optimization algorithm. *BMC Bioinformatics, 15*(1), 1–12. doi:10.1186/1471-2105-15-49 PMID:24555567

Cheok, M. H., Yang, W., Pui, C. H., Downing, J. R., Cheng, C., Naeve, C. W., & Evans, W. E. (2003). Treatment-specific changes in gene expression discriminate in vivo drug response in human leukemia cells. *Nature Genetics, 34*(1), 85–90. doi:10.1038/ng1151 PMID:12704389

Chow, T. W., & Huang, D. (2005). Estimating optimal feature subsets using efficient estimation of high-dimensional mutual information. *IEEE Transactions on Neural Networks, 16*(1), 213–224. doi:10.1109/TNN.2004.841414 PMID:15732401

Chuang, L. Y., Yang, C. H., Wu, K. C., & Yang, C. H. (2011). A hybrid feature selection method for DNA microarray data. *Computers in Biology and Medicine, 41*(4), 228–237. doi:10.1016/j.compbiomed.2011.02.004 PMID:21376310

Das, S., Abraham, A., & Konar, A. (2008). Swarm intelligence algorithms in bioinformatics. In *Computational Intelligence in Bioinformatics* (pp. 113–147). Springer Berlin Heidelberg. doi:10.1007/978-3-540-76803-6_4

Das, S., & Suganthan, P. N. (2011). Differential evolution: A survey of the state-of-the-art. *IEEE Transactions on Evolutionary Computation, 15*(1), 4–31. doi:10.1109/TEVC.2010.2059031

Dembele, D., & Kastner, P. (2003). Fuzzy C-means method for clustering microarray data. *Bioinformatics, 19*(8), 973-980.

Eberhart, R. C., & Kennedy, J. (1995, October). A new optimizer using particle swarm theory. *Proceedings of the Sixth International Symposium on Micro Machine and Human Science, 1*, 39-43. doi:10.1109/MHS.1995.494215

Elyasigomari, V., Mirjafari, M. S., Screen, H. R. C., & Shaheed, M. H. (2015). Cancer classification using a novel gene selection approach by means of shuffling based on data clustering with optimization. *Applied Soft Computing, 35*, 43–51. doi:10.1016/j.asoc.2015.06.015

Golub, T. R., Slonim, D. K., Tamayo, P., Huard, C., Gaasenbeek, M., Mesirov, J. P., & Bloomfield, C. D. (1999). Molecular classification of cancer: Class discovery and class prediction by gene expression monitoring. *Science, 286*(5439), 531–537. doi:10.1126/science.286.5439.531 PMID:10521349

Guo, Z., Zhang, T., Li, X., Wang, Q., Xu, J., Yu, H., & Wang, Q. (2005). Towards precise classification of cancers based on robust gene functional expression profiles. *BMC Bioinformatics, 6*(1), 1–8. doi:10.1186/1471-2105-6-58 PMID:15774002

Hall, M. A. (1999). *Correlation-based feature selection for machine learning* (Doctoral dissertation). The University of Waikato.

Hippo, Y., Taniguchi, H., Tsutsumi, S., Machida, N., Chong, J. M., Fukayama, M., & Aburatani, H. (2002). Global gene expression analysis of gastric cancer by oligonucleotide microarrays. *Cancer Research*, *62*(1), 233–240. PMID:11782383

Huerta, E., Hernández-Montiel, A., Morales-Caporal, R., & Arjona-López, M. (2016). Hybrid framework using multiple-filters and an embedded approach for an efficient selection and classification of microarray data. *IEEE/ACM Transactions on Computational Biology and Bioinformatics*, *13*(1), 12–26. doi:10.1109/TCBB.2015.2474384 PMID:26336138

Iizuka, N., Oka, M., Yamada-Okabe, H., Nishida, M., Maeda, Y., Mori, N., & Hamada, K. (2003). Oligonucleotide microarray for prediction of early intrahepatic recurrence of hepatocellular carcinoma after curative resection. *Lancet*, *361*(9361), 923–929. doi:10.1016/S0140-6736(03)12775-4 PMID:12648972

Inza, I., Larrañaga, P., Blanco, R., & Cerrolaza, A. J. (2004). Filter versus wrapper gene selection approaches in DNA microarray domains. *Artificial Intelligence in Medicine*, *31*(2), 91–103. doi:10.1016/j.artmed.2004.01.007 PMID:15219288

Kanehisa, M., & Goto, S. (2000). KEGG: Kyoto encyclopedia of genes and genomes. *Nucleic Acids Research*, *28*(1), 27–30. doi:10.1093/nar/28.1.27 PMID:10592173

Khanesar, M. A., Teshnehlab, M., & Shoorehdeli, M. A. (2007, June). A novel binary particle swarm optimization. In *Control & Automation, 2007. MED'07. Mediterranean Conference on* (pp. 1-6). IEEE.

Khunlertgit, N., & Yoon, B. J. (2013). Identification of robust pathway markers for cancer through rank-based pathway activity inference. *Advances in Bioinformatics*. PMID:23533400

Kittler, J. (1978). Feature set search algorithms. *Pattern Recognition and Signal Processing*, 41-60.

Kleftogiannis, D., Theofilatos, K., Likothanassis, S., & Mavroudi, S. (2015). YamiPred: A novel evolutionary method for predicting pre-miRNAs and selecting relevant features. *IEEE/ACM Transactions on Computational Biology and Bioinformatics*, *12*(5), 1183–1192. doi:10.1109/TCBB.2014.2388227 PMID:26451829

Koller, D., & Sahami, M. (1996). *Toward optimal feature selection*. Academic Press.

Kong, M., & Tian, P. (2005, December). A binary ant colony optimization for the unconstrained function optimization problem. In *International Conference on Computational and Information Science* (pp. 682-687). Springer Berlin Heidelberg. doi:10.1007/11596448_101

Lee, C. P., Lin, W. S., Chen, Y. M., & Kuo, B. J. (2011). Gene selection and sample classification on microarray data based on adaptive genetic algorithm/k-nearest neighbor method. *Expert Systems with Applications*, *38*(5), 4661–4667. doi:10.1016/j.eswa.2010.07.053

Lee, E., Chuang, H. Y., Kim, J. W., Ideker, T., & Lee, D. (2008). Inferring pathway activity toward precise disease classification. *PLoS Computational Biology*, *4*(11), e1000217. doi:10.1371/journal.pcbi.1000217 PMID:18989396

Liu, X., Krishnan, A., & Mondry, A. (2005). An entropy-based gene selection method for cancer classification using microarray data. *BMC Bioinformatics*, *6*(1), 1. doi:10.1186/1471-2105-6-1 PMID:15790388

Ma, S., & Kosorok, M. R. (2009). Identification of differential gene pathways with principal component analysis. *Bioinformatics (Oxford, England)*, *25*(7), 882–889. doi:10.1093/bioinformatics/btp085 PMID:19223452

Maji, P., & Paul, S. (2013). Rough-fuzzy clustering for grouping functionally similar genes from microarray data. *IEEE/ACM Transactions on Computational Biology and Bioinformatics*, *10*(2), 286–299. doi:10.1109/TCBB.2012.103 PMID:22848138

Mandal, M., Mondal, J., & Mukhopadhyay, A. (2015). A PSO-based approach for pathway marker identification from gene expression data. *IEEE Transactions on Nanobioscience*, *14*(6), 591–597. doi:10.1109/TNB.2015.2425471 PMID:25935045

Mukhopadhyay, A., & Mandal, M. (2014). Identifying non-redundant gene markers from microarray data: A multiobjective variable length pso-based approach. *IEEE/ACM Transactions on Computational Biology and Bioinformatics*, *11*(6), 1170–1183. doi:10.1109/TCBB.2014.2323065 PMID:26357053

Niu, B., Zhu, Y., He, X., & Wu, H. (2007). MCPSO: A multi-swarm cooperative particle swarm optimizer. *Applied Mathematics and Computation*, *185*(2), 1050–1062. doi:10.1016/j.amc.2006.07.026

Pal, J. K., Ray, S. S., Cho, S. B., & Pal, S. K. (2016). Fuzzy-Rough Entropy Measure and Histogram Based Patient Selection for miRNA Ranking in Cancer. *IEEE/ACM Transactions on Computational Biology and Bioinformatics*, 1. doi:10.1109/TCBB.2016.2623605 PMID:27831888

Pang, S., Havukkala, I., Hu, Y., & Kasabov, N. (2007). Classification consistency analysis for bootstrapping gene selection. *Neural Computing & Applications*, *16*(6), 527–539. doi:10.1007/s00521-007-0110-1

Raetz, E. A., Perkins, S. L., Bhojwani, D., Smock, K., Philip, M., Carroll, W. L., & Min, D. J. (2006). Gene expression profiling reveals intrinsic differences between T-cell acute lymphoblastic leukemia and T-cell lymphoblastic lymphoma. *Pediatric Blood & Cancer*, *47*(2), 130–140. doi:10.1002/pbc.20550 PMID:16358311

Saha, S., Ekbal, A., Gupta, K., & Bandyopadhyay, S. (2013). Gene expression data clustering using a multiobjective symmetry based clustering technique. *Computers in Biology and Medicine*, *43*(11), 1965–1977. doi:10.1016/j.compbiomed.2013.07.021 PMID:24209942

Singh, D., Febbo, P. G., Ross, K., Jackson, D. G., Manola, J., Ladd, C., & Lander, E. S. (2002). Gene expression correlates of clinical prostate cancer behavior. *Cancer Cell*, *1*(2), 203–209. doi:10.1016/S1535-6108(02)00030-2 PMID:12086878

Skalak, D. B. (1994, February). Prototype and feature selection by sampling and random mutation hill climbing algorithms. *Proceedings of the eleventh international conference on machine learning*, 293-301. doi:10.1016/B978-1-55860-335-6.50043-X

Statnikov, A., Aliferis, C. F., Tsamardinos, I., Hardin, D., & Levy, S. (2005). A comprehensive evaluation of multicategory classification methods for microarray gene expression cancer diagnosis. *Bioinformatics (Oxford, England)*, *21*(5), 631–643. doi:10.1093/bioinformatics/bti033 PMID:15374862

Su, J., Yoon, B. J., & Dougherty, E. R. (2009). Accurate and reliable cancer classification based on probabilistic inference of pathway activity. *PLoS ONE*, *4*(12), 155–161. doi:10.1371/journal.pone.0008161 PMID:19997592

Tan, F., Fu, X., Zhang, Y., & Bourgeois, A. G. (2006, July). Improving feature subset selection using a genetic algorithm for microarray gene expression data. In *2006 IEEE International Conference on Evolutionary Computation* (pp. 2529-2534). IEEE.

Toronen, P., Kolehmainen, M., Wong, G., & Castren, E. (1999). Analysis of gene expression data using self-organizing maps. *FEBS Letters*, *451*(2), 142–146. doi:10.1016/S0014-5793(99)00524-4 PMID:10371154

Wan, Y., Wang, M., Ye, Z., & Lai, X. (2016). A feature selection method based on modified binary coded ant colony optimization algorithm. *Applied Soft Computing*, *49*, 248–258. doi:10.1016/j.asoc.2016.08.011

Yang, D., Parrish, R. S., & Brock, G. N. (2014). Empirical evaluation of consistency and accuracy of methods to detect differentially expressed genes based on microarray data. *Computers in Biology and Medicine*, *46*, 1–10. doi:10.1016/j.compbiomed.2013.12.002 PMID:24529200

Ye, J., Li, T., Xiong, T., & Janardan, R. (2004). Using uncorrelated discriminant analysis for tissue classification with gene expression data. *IEEE/ACM Transactions on Computational Biology and Bioinformatics*, *1*(4), 181–190. doi:10.1109/TCBB.2004.45 PMID:17051700

Zhang, L., Kuljis, J., & Liu, X. (2008). Information visualization for DNA microarray data analysis: A critical review. *IEEE Transactions on Systems, Man and Cybernetics. Part C, Applications and Reviews*, *38*(1), 42–54. doi:10.1109/TSMCC.2007.906065

Zheng, C. H., Yang, W., Chong, Y. W., & Xia, J. F. (2016). Identification of mutated driver pathways in cancer using a multi-objective optimization model. *Computers in Biology and Medicine*, *72*, 22–29. doi:10.1016/j.compbiomed.2016.03.002 PMID:26995027

Zibakhsh, A., & Abadeh, M. S. (2013). Gene selection for cancer tumor detection using a novel memetic algorithm with a multi-view fitness function. *Engineering Applications of Artificial Intelligence*, *26*(4), 1274–1281. doi:10.1016/j.engappai.2012.12.009

KEY TERMS AND DEFINITIONS

Biological Pathway: A series of activities related to biological process whose collective effect leads to the growth of a disease.

Cancer: A collection of disease due to abnormal proliferation of cell.

Classification: A process to categorize the objects so that they can be differentiated from others.

DNA Microarray: The gene expression level of thousand genes collected from different samples in a single microscopic chip.

Evolutionary Algorithm: A set of meta-heuristic, population-based optimization techniques that uses nature inspired processes such as selection, reproduction, recombination, mutation, etc.

Feature Selection: A commonly used machine learning process for selecting redundant subset of feature or attributes which can be used for modeling a system.

p-Value: A statistical null hypothetical test that helps to determine the probability how the result differs from the observed values.

t-Test: A non parametric statistical test that can be used for the differentiation between two observations based on their mean and standard deviation.

APPENDIX

Handling large data like gene expression microarray data or pre-miRNA sequences have become an area of intense research. Different works in this field can be targeted by the researchers. Few of the topics are stated as follows.

- Multi-swarm bio-inspired algorithm for the cancer detection and classification from microarray data.
- Clustering of gene expression data for the feature selection of cancer classification.
- Multi-objective Optimization for the pathway marker selection from gene expression data.
- FPGA based embedded system implementation for the classification of cancer from microarray data.
- Prediction of miRNA from pre-miRNA sequences for cancer detection using Mono-, multi, many-objective bio-inspired algorithm.

Chapter 15

Applying Bayesian Networks in the Early Diagnosis of Bulimia and Anorexia Nervosa in Adolescents:
Applying Bayesian Networks in Early Diagnosis in Adolescents

Placido Rogerio Pinheiro
University of Fortaleza, Brazil

Marley Costa Marques
University of Fortaleza, Brazil

Mirian Caliope Dantas Pinheiro
University of Fortaleza, Brazil

Raquel Souza Bino Araújo
University of Fortaleza, Brazil

Victor Câmera Damasceno
University of Fortaleza, Brazil

Layane Mayara Gomes Castelo Branco
University of Fortaleza, Brazil

ABSTRACT

The diseases and health problems are concerns of managers of the Unified Health System has costs in more sophisticated care sector are high. The World Health Organization focused on prevention of chronic diseases to prevent millions of premature deaths in the coming years, bringing substantial gains in economic growth by improving the quality of life. Few countries appear to be aimed at prevention, if not note the available knowledge and control of chronic diseases and may represent an unnecessary risk to future generations. Early diagnosis of these diseases is the first step to successful treatment in any age group. The objective is to build a model, from the establishment of a Bayesian network, for the early diagnosis of nursing to identify eating disorders bulimia and anorexia nervosa in adolescents, from the characteristics of the DSM-IV and Nursing Diagnoses The need for greater investment in technology in public health actions aims to increase the knowledge of health professionals, especially nurses, contributing to prevention, decision making and early treatment of problems.

DOI: 10.4018/978-1-5225-2607-0.ch015

INTRODUCTION

The diseases and health problems are concerns of managers of the Unified Health System, in Brazil, has costs in more sophisticated care sector are high. Currently, the World Health Organization focused on prevention of chronic diseases to prevent millions of premature deaths in the coming years, bringing substantial gains in economic growth by improving the quality of life. Few countries appear to be aimed at prevention, if not note the available knowledge and control of chronic diseases and may represent an unnecessary risk to future generations. Early diagnosis of these diseases is the first step to successful treatment in any age group.

Considering, in the last decades, per the Brazilian Institute of Geography and Statistics, Census 2010, there has been an increase in the adolescent population representing 20% of the population, a total of 34,157,633 children (Brazil, 2013). Due to this population growth, multiple and complex needs of programs and public policies, health care is required because vulnerabilities are present in this age group. Also, per the Statute of Children and Adolescents, adolescence comprises the age group of 12 to 18 years old, and the Ministry of Health are all individuals aged 10 to 19 years (Brazil, 2012).

Adolescence is a stage of human development which is characterized by various transformations. Moreover, it is at this age that diseases may determine severe damage on the psychological, emotional, physical and social development of increased morbidity and mortality. The occurrence of eating disorders, bulimia, and anorexia, the prognosis is guarded. Among the severe pathologies detected in modernity that has been affecting the biopsychosocial development of the adolescent, especially females, Eating Disorders have been in evidence in the clinical and psychological field, particularly Anorexia Nervosa and Bulimia Nervosa, due to the complexity of causal factors, symptomatology, and diagnostic difficulties. The adolescent population has the highest prevalence of detected cases. McCabe and Ricciardelli (2003) point out that such an occurrence may be because it is precisely at this stage of life that the young person feels particularly pressured by the demands and impositions of society and is, therefore, vulnerable and insecure about the acceptance of his body, which can lead you to a process of distortion of your body image.

The phase of adolescence is a period characterized by the occurrence of major transformations of a bio psychophysiological nature, with which the adolescent needs to be able to cope. In this phase, the young person begins to build his identity and to recognize himself as a social subject. This task becomes even more arduous when faced with models of behaviors and behaviors pre-established by society, which then influences their choices and the way they view their body image McCabe and Ricciardelli (2003).

The distorted perception of one's own body image, coupled with the fact that the adolescent is very vulnerable to external influences, often ends up directly affecting the process of constructing his identity and fostering the emergence of eating disorders, because, to fit the standards of beauty imposed by the media, young people can adopt a destructive eating behavior, in the attempt to conquer the ideal body, as the realization of radical diets that can bring damage to their health, as reported by Fiates and Salles (2001). On the other hand, when reporting that Anorexia Nervosa brings "at first, dehydration and malnutrition. Although patients deny hunger, they present constant complaints due to fatigue, weakness, dizziness and blurred vision.

Moreover, to approximate the lean aesthetic pattern adopted by models and celebrities and thus feel socially accepted, some women tend to develop Eating Disorders such as Anorexia Nervosa and Bulimia Nervosa. What does not seem to happen to men, considering that they do not care so much about having an extremely thin body, just as young anorexics want, but they seek to construct, often in an obsessive way, an exaggeratedly muscular body, as it is the case of young people affected by Body Dysmorphic Disorder. In the case of Eating Disorders which are phenomena characterized by excessive preoccupation with weight, body, and food, of multidimensional nature, these are the result of the interaction of personal, family and socio-cultural factors.

Furthermore, Saikali et al. (2004) define the Eating Disorders as pathologies characterized by disturbances in body perception, severe changes in dietary pattern and obsession in weight control. They present a high degree of morbidity and can result in loss or excessive weight gain. Eating disorders are psychiatric diseases characterized by numerous and serious changes in eating behavior, which cause serious damages to the physical, mental and psychological health of the patient, increasing the incidence of morbidity and mortality, especially in the adolescent population.

Also, Morgan et al. (2002) corroborate and complement that among the multiple causal factors that characterize Eating Disorders, it is possible to identify those factors that influence its onset, characteristic symptoms and those that define the period of its action. Also, the authors highlighted the groups of factors responsible for the predisposition, precipitation, and maintenance of the Eating Disorders. Thus, they describe the predisposing factors as those that can increase the possibilities of the emergence of an Eating Disorders; The precipitants as the ones responsible for accelerating or anticipating this pathology, initiating the manifestation of its specific symptomatology; And, finally, the maintenance factors, which will determine the duration of each Eating Disorders (Morgan et al, 2002).

For a better understanding of the mode of action of each of these three groups in the process of development of Eating Disorders such as Anorexia Nervosa and Bulimia Nervosa, for example, since they have been the most frequently detected, especially in adolescents, (Morgan et al., 2002).

These disorders require attention to adolescent health for present prevalence from 0.5 to 3.7% for anorexia nervosa and 1.1 to 4.2% for bulimia nervosa, and both affect both the female and the male with an average prevalence in man-woman 1:10, even 1:20, respectively (Costa & Souza, 2002).

On the other hand, the socio-cultural aspects have influenced the emergence of eating disorders because of the demands of contemporary society that determines a perfect body pattern, thin and poorly defined forms. With this, the teenagers' risk of developing psychological and emotional problems, coming to practice excessive exercise and restrictive diets to get a slim body at any cost and be accepted by the group. The diagnosis and treatment of both disorders require a multidisciplinary team using a clinical, nutritional and psychosocial approach, to develop an integrated and efficient work. This way the adolescent phenomenon, bringing itself essential condition of vulnerability and need of physical, mental, moral protection, and, therefore, an entire attention, especially in the case of involvement of these disorders. The diagnosis and treatment of both disorders require a multidisciplinary team using a clinical, nutritional and psychosocial approach, to develop an integrated and efficient work. This way the adolescent phenomenon, bringing itself essential condition of vulnerability and need of physical, mental, moral protection, and, therefore, full attention, especially in the case of involvement of these disorders (Crespin & Reato, 2007). Therefore, resurfaced the following questions:

- What are the characteristics of bulimia and anorexia nervosa?
- What are the benefits of computational tool structured in Bayesian as networks for early diagnosis of bulimia and anorexia in adolescence?

The objective is to build a model, from the establishment of a Bayesian network, for the early diagnosis of nursing to identify eating disorders bulimia and anorexia nervosa in adolescents, from the characteristics of the Diagnostic and Statistical Manual of Mental Disorders (DSM) and North American Nursing Diagnosis Association (NANDA), respectively. The need for greater investment in technology in public health actions can increase the knowledge of health professionals, especially nurses, in identifying early diagnosis contributing to prevention, decision making and early treatment of disorders or health problems actual or potential. It is emphasized that this model could be applied to evaluate other nursing diagnoses of the NANDA taxonomy and DSM-IV, both for Brazilian adolescents how many other countries (Araújo & Neto, 2013; NANDA, 2015).

EATING DISORDERS IN ADOLESCENCE: ANOREXIA NERVOSA AND BULIMIA NERVOSA

The study of a theoretical correlation, whose purpose was to identify the similarities between NANDA and DSM, through an analysis of the convergences of the parameters involved.

NANDA is a standardized and flexible taxonomy that seeks to classify nursing diagnoses. Its structure includes a definition of diagnosis, defining characteristics and related factors. The DSM consists basically of a list of diagnoses categorized as a glossary that brings the clinical description of each diagnostic category.

Initially, a national and international bibliographic survey was carried out on books, articles, and manuals, from 2011 to 2016, to determine if there were studies that established correlations between these NANDA and DSM diagnoses. For this purpose, the texts were selected according to three fundamental stages: material exploration, data analysis, and interpretation. It was searched in the NANDA taxonomy and in the classification of the DSM specific aspects and the similarities of both diagnoses referring to eating disorders. It was organized and identify possible corrections between them.

The findings were analyzed and interpreted in the light of existing theoretical references on the subject, compiled and correlated to approximate the two diagnoses with the objective of elaborating two tables of the correlations for the two main disorders. Taking into consideration the hierarchy of the parameters to classify in order and the degree of importance.

The whole history of medicine and health is marked by the clinical reasoning in which one judges, groups diseases that share the same signs and symptoms and are the bases for formulating diagnoses for diseases and diseases to predict and seek means of follow-up and Healing of the sick.

However, unlike medical diagnosis, NANDA diagnoses are made by the clinical judgment of individual, family, or community responses to actual or potential health problems. And in the case of eating disorders, it aims at a clinical and behavioral assessment of individuals to be diagnosed for altered nutrition, whether for then the individual's bodily needs. Although studies of the NANDA diagnosis are frequently reviewed and validated, they are not related to bulimia and anorexia nervosa disorders. On the other hand, the DSM proposes to serve as a tool to help a precise clinical diagnosis assisting researchers of different areas, biological, psychodynamic, cognitive, behavioral, interpersonal, family / systemic. Being used fully for the training of students and professionals in the appropriate areas. Seeking a language for communication of essential characteristics for disorders presented by their patients. Moreover, what is its magnitude?

Clinical Features of Bulimia and Anorexia

Individual predispositions involve personality traits of the affected subject, presenting low self-esteem, obsessive and perfectionist traits, with marked impulsiveness and affective instability. Sometimes it has a clinical history of psychiatric disorders, such as depression and anxiety, and may also be associated with chemical dependence. Sometimes it comes from hormonal changes that lead to obesity due to changes in noradrenergic neurotransmitters and serotonin. Also, episodes of binge eating that interfere with the metabolism of glucose and insulin. It may also arise from family events of disintegration, violence, rigidity, intrusiveness, disorganization and lack of care, as well as stressful events such as illness, pregnancy, sexual and physical abuse. Regarding cultural aspects, he observes the social patterns of thinness, inappropriate diets, exaggerations in physical exercises in academies, in search of the perfect body.

On the other hand, Anorexia Nervosa is an eating disorder that has the characteristics of weight loss intentionally forced by a minimally caloric diet, coupled with a persistent desire to build an ideal body, extremely thin, as idealized by the media, which elects anorexic models as standard of beauty; A distorted vision of the body image, refusal to maintain a weight within the norms of normality for height and age; and the presence of alterations in the menstrual cycle or amenorrhea (DOYLE; BRYANT-WAUGH, (2000)); (SAITO (2001)).

Furthermore, per Diagnostic and Statistical Manual of Mental Disorders - DSM-IV there are three diagnostic characteristics of Anorexia Nervosa:

1. Persistent restriction of caloric intake;
2. Intense fear of gaining weight or gaining weight or persistent behavior that interferes with weight gain;
3. Perturbation in the perception of one's own weight or form.

Other factors add to Anorexia Nervosa, which can present in a restrictive way about forced diet, or purgative for episodes of food compunction associated with food compensation methods, such as induction to vomit and the use of laxatives and diuretics. Among the symptoms reported by patients affected by this eating disorder are lethargy, cold feet, and hands, amenorrhea, difficulty concentrating, cold intolerance, fatigue, hair loss, constipation, abdominal pain, anorexia and others.

Anorexia nervosa and bulimia nervosa are diseases belonging to the group of emotional eating disorders that usually affect the young adult population, but more strikingly to those who experience adolescence, especially the female sex. From the 1970s onwards, they became the two main types of Eating Disorder identified in adolescents. Both disorders, because they present an identification of common characteristic symptoms, allow a greater understanding of the development process of these eating disorders, when already installed, since in both there is a same prevalent idea related to an excess of preoccupation with the weight, an unjustified fear and unhealthy to gain weight and a distorted view of one's own body image, even though it is not always possible to perform their diagnosis effectively, in many cases because of patients refusing to seek professional help or because they deny the disease or even Believe that they have it under control and can and treat it alone.

As for the age group of adolescents who develop Eating Disorders, there are discrepancies, since the beginning of Anorexia Nervosa, for example, occurs around the age of 13, culminating from 17 to 18 years of age, whereas Bulimia Nervosa only presents later, around the last years of the teenage phase, usually around the age of 20, often as a sequel to persistent Anorexia, which does not imply that an inverse movement cannot occur, that is, the appearance of Anorexia as a sequel to Bulimia.

For Stenzel (2006), it is possible to identify other significant discrepancies between Bulimia Nervosa and Anorexia Nervosa, referring to the distortion of body image, because in Anorexia the individual presents a distortion in the perception of the own body, on the weight and the form, that takes it to a state of negation of real low weight, by looking in the mirror and judging himself fat. On the other hand, in Bulimia, this same distortion leads him to believe in a fanciful way that he is immensely far from achieving weight and ideal form.

In the aspect of Bulimia Nervosa, the analyses in Table 1 point to the existence of a correlation between the two diagnoses. For NANDA, considering the period from 1975 onwards, unbalanced nutrition presents greater than bodily needs and for Obesity in its defining characteristics of Body mass index greater than 30% for ages and sex, and related factors, for both diagnoses. For example, the defining characteristics of anthropometry beyond normality patterns, eating in response to internal and external stimuli, inadequate eating behavior and disordered eating perception, are equivalent to DSM-IV and V criteria for bulimia nervosa, regarding behavior and sensation lack of control over intake, excessive intake of compulsive eating episodes, among others. Similarly, the relationship is established in the definition of the NANDA diagnosis nutrient intake that exceeds metabolic needs and obesity, correlating with bulimia nervosa due to episodes of compulsive eating, improper eating behavior, the amount of food greater than Most individuals would consume during the same period under similar circumstances (NANDA, 2015). Let us see the correlations of both diagnoses in Table 1.

Also, per NANDA in the situation of an individual who does not present the sensation of hunger, but the internal stimuli other than hunger converges to the process of compulsion by the anxiety of the individual, and thus having a dysfunctional pattern. Implicitly is characteristic of bulimia nervosa, per the DSM criteria. Another fact is that the NANDA there is an association of anxiety with binge eating, which follows as a common antecedent to individuals who present concerns related to body weight and shape and food. However, such concerns are as extreme as the distortions perceived by anorexic individuals, including triggers such as interpersonal stressors, dietary restrictions, negative feelings related to body weight, body shape and food, and boredom.

There is also a factor that NANDA correlates to DSM that would address adherence to diets followed by binge eating and purging or other compensatory behaviors. For these individuals, vomiting and the most common inappropriate compensatory behavior and its immediate effects include relieving physical discomfort and reducing the fear of gaining weight. In some cases, vomiting causes the individual's compulsive eating to vomit after ingesting and satisfying his or her final desire, using methods such as the use of fingers and an instrument to induce and stimulate reflexes of vomiting. Other purging behaviors include the misuse of laxatives and diuretics.

The analysis of Table 2 on the NANDA for Unbalanced Nutrition: less than the bodily needs 1975 onwards, in its defining characteristics, such as anthropometric data below normality, lack of interest in eating, finds equivalences to the DSM criteria for anorexia nervosa with regard to eating aversion behaviors, exaggerated fear of eating and restriction of calorie intake, food intake less than the Recommended Daily Standard, as well as persistent behavior that interferes with the gain of weight, even when weighing significantly low for age, among others.

Therefore, the relationship between the two diagnoses is established in the related factor Psychological disorder and defining characteristics, such as insufficient intake of nutrients to meet metabolic needs,

Table 1. Correlations between the defining characteristics of NANDA and the DSM criteria for Bulimia Nervosa

NANDA: Unbalanced Nutrition More Than Body Needs 1975 onwards. Definition: Intake of nutrients that exceeds metabolic needs in NANDA (2009-2011). NANDA: Obesity. Definition: Conditions in which the individual accumulates abnormal or excessive fat for age and sex, which is overweight in NANDA (2015-2017)	DSM-IV and V Criteria Bulimia Nervosa
Related Factors	
Eating in response to external stimuli (e.g., time of day, social situation);	Excessive intake of compulsive episodes, induction of vomiting and laxatives to compensate for excess ingestion, within a given period (e.g. within each two-hour period), of a larger amount of food than most of the individuals would consume during the same period under similar circumstances.
Inadequate food behavior.	The sensation of lack of control over intake during the episode (e.g., feeling of being unable to stop eating or controlling what and how much you are ingesting).
Eat in response to internal stimuli other than hunger (e.g. anxiety);	• Shape and body weight unduly influence Self-assessment. • The disorder does not occur exclusively during episodes of anorexia nervosa.
Dysfunctional eating pattern (e.g. associates food with other activities).	Recurring inappropriate compensatory behaviors to prevent weight gain, such as self-induced vomiting, misuse of laxatives, diuretics or other medications, fasting, or excessive exercise.
• Disordered food perception. • Weight 20% above ideal for age and complexion. • Triceps skin fold greater than 22mm in women and greater than 15mm in men	Binge eating motivated by a negative perception of body image.

and its defining characteristics for aversion to eating and disturbance in the way the weight or body shape are experienced, and thus relating the characteristics of DSM to anorexia nervosa due to the exaggerated fear of fattening and restriction of caloric intake. Let us look at the correlations of both diagnoses in Table 2, which follow: (NANDA, 2011-2015) and its related factor of Psychological Disorder, and DSM criteria, own diagnoses

The defining diagnostic characteristics of NANDA are related to the rigid refusal of the individual to maintain a body weight at a minimum level of normality. The DSM associates this exaggerated fear of getting fat with the disturbance and perception of the shape and size of your body, which in turn ends up being distorted by the individual. It is estimated that they make these perceptions independent by establishing persistent behaviors that will prevent weight gain.

However, the distortion of body image perception has as a characteristic sign, lean individuals who believe that some parts of the body such as arm, leg, stomach, among others, would be fat. Usually, weight loss is achieved by obsessiveness, anxiety, depression and the regulation of appetite of almost all food consumption. Most of them go on an extremely poor diet. Also, they adopt the excessive practice of exercises and irrational rules for what they eat. Thus, in restricting intake, many of them use binge eating and purging, even if the compulsion is minimal.

Table 2. Correlations between the defining characteristics of NANDA and the DSM criteria for Anorexia nervosa

NANDA - Unbalanced nutrition: less than the bodily needs 1975 onwards. Definition: Insufficient intake of nutrients to meet metabolic needs. NANDA (2009-2011, 2015-2017)	DSM-IV and V Criteria Anorexia Nervosa
Defining Characteristics and Related Factors	
• Aversion to eating. • Food intake less than recommended daily standard (PDR).	Restriction of calorie intake, leading to a significantly low body weight in the context of age, gender, development trajectory and physical health.
Abdominal pain	Induction of vomiting and laxative abuse.
Lack of information	Disturbance in the way one's own weight or body shape is experienced, undue influence of weight or body shape on self-assessment or persistent absence of recognition of current low body weight severity.
• Lack of interest in food. • Psychological disorder.	Exaggerated fear of gaining weight, or persistent behavior that interferes with weight gain, even with a significantly low weight.
Weakness of muscles needed for swallowing or chewing	Weight below the minimum is defined as a weight below the minimum normal weight or, in the case of children and adolescents, less than the minimum expected.
Wrong ideas	Disturbance in the way one's own weight or body shape is experienced, undue influence of weight or body shape on self-assessment or persistent absence of recognition of current low body weight severity.
Incorrect Information	Purgative behavior such as induction of vomiting and abuse of laxatives.
Pale mucous membranes	Purgative behavior such as induction of vomiting and laxative abuse.
Excessive hair loss	Food restriction pattern.
Body weight 20% or more below ideal	Weight below the minimum is defined as a weight below the minimum normal weight or, in the case of children and adolescents, less than the minimum expected.
Report of inadequate food intake less than PDR (recommended area portion)	The pattern of food restriction with episodes of compulsive eating.
Imperative bowel sounds	Purgative behavior with induction of vomiting and laxative abuse.
Satiety immediately after ingestion	Exaggerated fear of gaining weight, or persistent behavior that interferes with weight gain, even with a significantly low weight.
Unsatisfactory muscle tone.	Weight below the minimum is defined as a weight below the minimum normal weight or, in the case of children and adolescents, less than the minimum expected.

DECISION METHODOLOGY

The applications of Bayesian Networks in health research began about 30 years ago. Since the 90's this methodology has been applied in this area with quite positive results. In this project, we will present a Bayesian model that uses the Netica-J API. The creation of the Bayesian network can ensure greater accuracy and assist health professionals in diagnoses of various diseases. The probability may help in the case of data that are not present in the databases or that do not have total integrity, since the lack of data or incoherence of them.

Bayesian Networks is a graphical model that represents in a simple way the causal relations of the variables of a system. In the Bayesian Network constructed for this work the direction of the arcs represents the relations between the nodes. For example, if vertex "A" is connected to vertex "B", it means that what happens with "A" will directly influence the result of "B". Knowledge is represented using a graph, where each edge represents a direct relation to the influence of one vertex to another.

The model is based on the calculation of the conditional probability of events. Considering two events called "A" and "B", the probability of "A" occurring given "B" has been calculated, and vice versa. Each event has an initial probability that can change if the another event happens. For example, it is likely to rain on any given day, but if we get additional information that the weather is cloudy, the probability of rain is changed. Similarly, if it rains the probability of being cloudy is also changed.

Two types of probability are considered. The first type is unconditional probability, a priori probability: P (A), P (B) are probabilities of an "A" event or a "B" event occurring independently of any other, respectively. The second is the conditional probability, a posteriori probability: P (A | B), which is the conditional probability of "A" given "B", i.e. is the probability of an event "A" given that an event "B " It happened. The Bayes' Theorem allows us to calculate the following probability:

$$P(A \mid B) = P(B \mid A) \cdot P(A) / P(B)$$

The Application Support Methodologies Decision that aims to improve the performance of expert systems from the creation of a Bayesian network for the early diagnosis of nursing to eating disorders such as bulimia and anorexia nervosa related to psychological factors in the age of adolescence. Bayesian Networks is a good strategy to deal with problems involving uncertainty in complex domains, very common in the medical field, where prior knowledge about the problem is not enough to draw conclusions. It allows representing and manipulating uncertainty based on well-founded probabilistic principles. Bayesian Network offers an approach to probabilistic reasoning, which includes graph theory for the establishment of relations between sentences and probability theory, for assigning levels of reliability (Fenton, N. and Neil, M., (2007), Lee, S. and Abbott, P. A., (2003)).

The Netica-J provides the complete Netica API (Application Programmer Interface) in Java. The Netica APIs are a set of powerful toolkits for working with Bayesian Networks. They allow you to build your own Bayesian Networks and Influence Diagrams, make the probabilistic inference, learn nets from data, modify nets, and save and restore nets. It allows direct connection to most database software. Netica is a powerful tool for building Bayesian Network, simple, intuitive, reliable and high performance. Bayesian Networks have shown high performance when used in the medical field. Prognosis of head injuries in (Sakellaropoulos, G. C. and Nikiforidis, G. C.(1999)), pneumonia in (Aronsky, D. and Haug, P. J., 2000) and diagnosis of breast cancer (Burnside, E., Rubin, D. and Shachter, R., 2000) are some examples of successful applications of Bayesian Network. Apply Bayesian Networks to represent the relationship between the parameters for the diagnosis and establish the probability of each one occurs. Justified the application of computational models in the study, as we have seen successfully applied in support of health professionals decision-making in the search for early diagnosis of diseases, namely the diagnosis of Psychological Disorders (Nunes et al., 2009) and (Nunes, L.C., Pinheiro, P.R, Pequeno, T.P., Pinheiro, M.C.D., 2011), Alzheimer's diagnosis (Castro, A. K. A., Pinheiro, P.R., Pinheiro, M.C.D., 2007, 2008, 2009), (Castro et al. 2011), (Tamanini, I., Pinheiro, P.R., Pinheiro, M.C.D., 2011) and diabetes diagnosis (Menezes, A.C., Pinheiro, P.R., Pinheiro, M.C.D., Pequeno, T. C., 2012a, 2012b, 2013).

In the construction of the model will be initially identified parameters for the diagnosis of bulimia and anorexia disorders, according to DSM-IV and the study of Toro et al. (2006). In the approach brings the DSM-IV criteria grouped in the data collection instruments, such is demographics partner information of Spanish and Mexican adolescents in the ages of 11 to 12 years old and 17-10 years (age, class social, family building (the teenager lives with whom). The questions regarding the history of mental illness in the family, eating habits of adolescents, restrictive diets, concerns of adolescents with body and weight, the skin of the abdomen crease, buttocks, arms, legs and way of dressing in this age group. The study of these authors is an exploratory and comparative between two population groups to identify the prevalence of eating disorders related to sociocultural risk factors.

The sample was constructed of 467 Spanish adolescents and 329 Mexicans. It was also used the diagnosis of NANDA, Nutrition Diagnosis Changed: more than body requirements involving the clinical DSM-IV. The characteristics listed in the study Toro et al. (2006) for the disorder bulimia nervosa, and similarly for the Amended diagnosis Nutrition: less than the body needs (Table 3) Therefore, the construction of an Expert System aims at supporting professionals in decision-making that aims at to seek the diagnosis of disorders to be studied.

The proposed model aggregates featured methodologies have validation processes. The methods presented are intended to make available to the decision maker, techniques, and tools that make it possible to structure the parameters for the diagnosis analysis and prioritize these parameters for the proper classification in order of degree of importance of each of the decision-making search process diagnosis.

RESULTS AND DISCUSSIONS

The results in Table 3 made it possible to perform a comparative analysis of the defining characteristics of unbalanced nutrition for less or more, respectively, for the bodily needs of Nursing Diagnoses applied North American Nursing Diagnosis Association (NANDA) and characteristics the Diagnostic and Statistical Manual of Mental Disorders (DSM) in special to use DSM-IV for anorexia and bulimia nervosa. As applied to database listed in the study Toro et al. (2006) for building the model Bayesian as networks.

In Figures 1 and 2 showing eating disorders anorexia having the purpose of early diagnosis of these disorders. In this context, we observe a comparative approach associated with each possible diagnosis of anorexia considering the aspect of the NANDA and DSM-IV. In the addition, in Figure 1 indicates that the Bayesian network on NANDA presents a diagnosis 40% chance of having anorexia compared to 60% of not having the disorder.

On the other hand, in the Figure 2 for the DSM-IV, the percentages ranged from 49.4% to have the disorder from 50.6% not to have anorexia.

Moreover, in Figure 3 and 4 presents, similarly, a Bayesian network NANDA unbalanced nutrition with a possible diagnosis of 28.6% having bulimia against 71.4% of non-disturbance. In both cases, a 10% discrepancy is observed a possible arrangement for the early diagnosis of NANDA compared DSM-IV.

Table 3. Comparatives data: Nursing diagnosis of the North American Nursing Diagnosis Association (NANDA) and characteristics the Diagnostic and Statistical Manual of Mental Disorders - DSM-IV for bulimia and anorexia

NANDA – Imbalanced Nutrition: Less than Body Requirements	Anorexia – DSM-IV (Eating Disorders)	NANDA – Imbalanced Nutrition: More than Body Requirements	Bulimia – DSM-IV (Eating Disorders)
Characteristics	Characteristics	Characteristics	Characteristics
It has weight 20% or more below the ideal.	Significant nutritional deficiency.	Weight 20% above ideal for height and build.	Overweight in childhood
Account of inadequate food intake, less than the recommended daily allowance.	• Patient feeds pressure from parents to gain weight. • The patient receives criticism and jokes from family members related to the body, weight or eating. • Amenorrhea.	The fold of the skin triceps 25mm larger in women, most 15mm in men.	The patient feels that some part of the body is too fat.
Inability perceived to ingest food.	• Afraid of gaining weight even the patient being too skinny. • The patient feels fat even telling others that it is thin. • The frequent concern with body or weight.	Eating in response to internal stimuli beyond hunger.	• Restrictive diets. • Vomiting to prevent weight gain. • Attacks of eating uncontrollably.
Erroneous concepts.	• The reason for dieting. • Physical activity to lose weight.	Food intake concentrated at the end of the day.	• Eating habits. • Breakfast. • Lunch. • Snack. • Dinner.
Abhorrence to the act of eating.	Excluding certain foods.	Eating in response to external stimuli (time of day, social situation).	• Worries about the body and weight. • The patient feels pressure from parents to lose weight. • The patient believes that if she loses weight, she would be more popular. • Marked psychological interference. • Family members living in the same household who are on a diet or dieted ever to lose weight.
Lack of interest in food.	Stress caused by body appearance.	-	-

CONCLUSION AND RESEARCH DIRECTIONS

The research points out that studying the NANDA diagnoses and their correlation with DSM, made possible the convergences and approximation to the diagnoses of bulimia nervosa and anorexia nervosa. As well as, the need to expand the knowledge of the health team, especially the nurse, contributing to discussions and reflections on early diagnosis and prevention of nutritional disorders. Studies on nursing

Figure 1. Bayesian network on NANDA presents a diagnosis anorexia

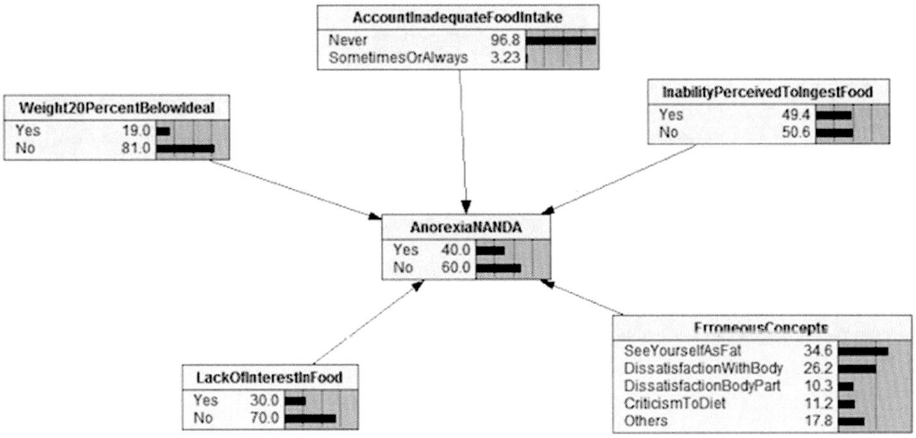

Figure 2. Bayesian network on DSM-IV presents a diagnosis anorexia

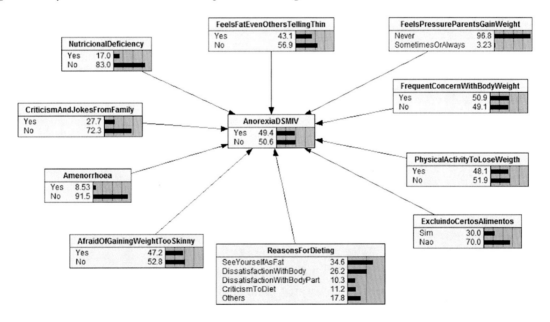

diagnosis, although periodically reviewed and validated, are not specifically endorsed for bulimia and anorexia, DSM eating disorders, because the NANDA diagnoses in their definition are not intended to diagnose diseases, but to conduct a clinical judgment of the responses of the patients. Individuals, families, and communities, to vital processes or actual or potential health problems The model applying Bayesian networks can direct the professional to detect early diagnosis of both eating disorders. In this regard, it may support other diagnostic possibilities considering criteria such as socio-demographic information, mental illness of a family history and cultural habits. Contributions diagnosis of nutritional disorders obtained through consolidated methodologies as Bayesian as networks and impact in several countries may also contribute to Nursing Diagnoses: Definitions and Classification and Diagnostic (NANDA).

Figure 3. Bayesian network on DSM-IV presents a diagnosis Bulimia

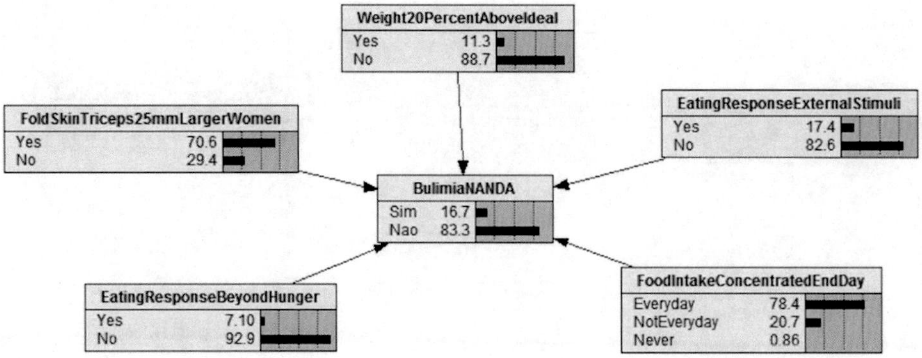

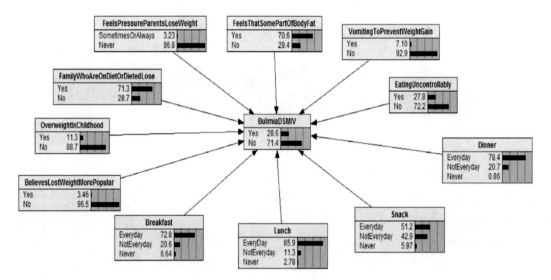

Figure 4. Bayesian network on NANDA presents a diagnosis Bulimia

It also emphasizes that the model could be applied to other databases in different countries because the nursing diagnosis is essential for all those working in nursing. As future work the model to help in the diagnosis of other pathologies. It is expected that other studies of this nature will be carried out since no bibliographical references were found in the studied literature to address the correlation between one or the other. Broadening the view of researchers in this area of so great importance for the quality of nursing care in its various areas of scientific knowledge.

ACKNOWLEDGMENT

The first and the second authors are thankful to the National Counsel of Technological and Scientific Development (CNPq) for the support received from this project, and the authors are grateful to the Edson Queiroz Foundation.

REFERENCES

Araújo, C. A., & Neto, F. L. (2013). A nova classificação para os transtornos mentais – DSM-V. *Jornal de Psicanálise.*, *46*(85), 99–116.

Aronsky, D., & Haug, P. J. (2000). Automatic identification of patients eligible for a pneumonia guideline. *Proceedings of the American Medical Informatics Association*, *1067*, 12–16. PMID:11079835

Brasil. Estatuto da Criança e do Adolescente (ECA). (2012). *Lei Federal nº 8069, de 13 de julho de 1990.* Brasília: Câmara dos Deputados, Edições Câmara.

Brasil. Instituto Brasileiro de Geografia e Estatística (IBGE). Censo demográfico 2010. (2013). Disponível em: http://7a12.ibge.gov.br/vamos-conhecer-o-brasil/nosso-povo/caracteristicas-da-populacao

Burnside, E., Rubin, D., & Shachter, R. (2000) A Bayesian Network for Mammography. *Proceedings of the American Medical Informatics Association*, 106-110.

Costa, M. C. O., & de Souza, R. P. (2002). *Adolescência: Aspectos clínicos e psicossociais.* Porto Alegre: Artmed Editora.

Crespin, J., & Reato, L. F. N. (2007). *Hebiatria: Medicina da Adolescência.* São Paulo: Rocco.

de Castro, A. K. A. (2008). Um Modelo Híbrido Aplicado ao Diagnóstico da Doença de Alzheimer. (Dissertação). Universidade de Fortaleza, Fortaleza.

De Castro, A. K. A., Pinheiro, P. R., & Pinheiro, M. C. D. (2007). Applying a Decision Making Model in the Early Diagnosis of Alzheimers Disease. *Lecture Notes in Computer Science*, *4481*, 149–156. doi:10.1007/978-3-540-72458-2_18

De Castro, A. K. A., Pinheiro, P. R., & Pinheiro, M. C. D. (2009). An Approach for the Neuropsychological Diagnosis of Alzheimers Disease: A Hybrid Model in Decision Making. *Lecture Notes in Computer Science*, *5589*, 216–223. doi:10.1007/978-3-642-02962-2_27

De Castro, A. K. A., Pinheiro, P. R., Pinheiro, M. C. D., & Tamanini, I. (2011). Towards the Applied Hybrid Model in Decision Making: A Neuropsychological Diagnosis of Alzheimers Disease Study Case. *International Journal of Computational Intelligence Systems*, *4*(1), 89–99. doi:10.1080/1875689 1.2011.9727766

Diagnostic and Statistical Manual of Mental Disorders (DSM). (2013). American Psychiatric Association Publishing.

Doyle, J., & Bryant-Waugh, R. (2000). Epidemiology. In Anorexia Nervosa and Related Eating Disorders in Childhood and Adolescence (2nd ed.). Psychology Press.

Fenton, N. E., Ncil, M., & Caballero, J. G. (2007). Using Ranked nodes to model qualitative judgments in Bayesian Networks. *IEEE Transactions on Knowledge and Data Engineering*, *19*(10), 1420–1432. doi:10.1109/TKDE.2007.1073

Fiates, G.M.R., & Salles, R.K. (2001). Fatores de Risco para o Desenvolvimento de distúrbios alimentares: Um Estudo em universitárias. *Revista de Nutrição*, *14*(3), 3-6.

Johson, M. (2009). Ligações entre NANDA, NOC E NIC: Diagnóstico, resultados e intervenções de enfermagem. *The Art of Medication*.

Lee, S., & Abbott, P. A. (2003). Bayesian networks for knowledge discovery in large datasets: Basics for nurse researchers. *Journal of Biomedical Informatics*, *36*(4-5), 389–399. doi:10.1016/j.jbi.2003.09.022 PMID:14643735

Mccabe, M. P., & Ricciardelli, L. A. (2003). Sociocultural influences on body image and body changes among adolescente boys and girls. *The Journal of Social Psychology*, *143*(1), 5–26. doi:10.1080/00224540309598428 PMID:12617344

Menezes, A. C., Pinheiro, P. R., Pinheiro, M. C. D., & Cavalcante, T. P. (2012a). A Hybrid Model to Support the Early Diagnosis of Diabetes. 5th World Summit on the Knowledge Society.

Menezes, A. C., Pinheiro, P. R., Pinheiro, M. C. D., & Cavalcante, T. P. (2012b). Towards the Applied Hybrid Model in Decision Making: Support the Early Diagnosis of Type 2 Diabetes. *3rd International Conference on Information Computing and Applications*, 648-655. doi:10.1007/978-3-642-34062-8_84

Menezes, A. C., Pinheiro, P. R., Pinheiro, M. C. D., & Cavalcante, T. P. (2013). A Hybrid Model to Support the Diagnosis of Disease: A Case Study for Diabetes. *IEEE Canadian Conference on Electrical and Computer Engineering*.

Morgan, C. M., Vecchiatti, I. R., & Negrão, A. B. (2002). Etiologia dos transtornos alimentares: Aspectos biológicos, psicológicos e sócio-culturais. *Revista Brasileira de Psiquiatria (Sao Paulo, Brazil)*, *24*(3), 18–23. doi:10.1590/S1516-44462002000700005

NANDA International Nursing Diagnosis. (2015). Definitions and Classifications 2015-2017 (10th ed.). Wiley-Blackwell.

Netica Application, Norsys Software Corp. (1998). Available in 08/2016, http://www.norsys.com

Nunes, L. C. (2010). *Um Modelo Híbrido para Apoio ao Diagnóstico de Transtornos Psicológicos*. Universidade de Fortaleza, Ceará: Dissertação, Mestrado em Informática Aplicada.

Nunes, L. C., Pinheiro, P. R., & Pequeno, T. C. (2009). An Expert System Applied to the Diagnosis of Psychological Disorders. *IEEE International Conference on Intelligent Computing and Intelligent Systems*, *3*, 363-367. doi:10.1109/ICICISYS.2009.5358164

Nunes, L. C., Pinheiro, P. R., Pequeno, T. C., & Pinheiro, M. C. D. (2011). Towards an Applied to the Diagnosis of Psychological Disorders. *Advances in Experimental Medicine and Biology*, *696*, 573–580. doi:10.1007/978-1-4419-7046-6_58 PMID:21431598

Saikali, C.J., et al. (2004). Imagem corporal nos transtornos alimentares. *Revista de Psiquiatria Clínica*, *31*(4), 154-156.

Saito, S., Kita, K., Morioka, C. Y., & Watanabe, A. (1999). Rapid recovery from anorexia nervosa after a life-threatening episode with severe thrombocytopenia: Report of three cases. *International Journal of Eating Disorders, Austin*, *25*(1), 113–118. doi:10.1002/(SICI)1098-108X(199901)25:1<113::AID-EAT15>3.0.CO;2-D PMID:9924661

Sakellaropoulos, G. C., & Nikiforidis, G. C. (1999). Development of a Bayesian Network for the prognosis of head injuries using graphical model selection techniques. *Methods of Information in Medicine, 38*(1), 37–42. PMID:10339962

Stenzel, L. M. (2006). A influência da imagem corporal no desenvolvimento e manutenção dos transtornos alimentares. In *Transtornos alimentares e obesidade* (pp. 73–81). Porto Alegre: Artmed.

Tamanini, I., Castro, A. K. A., Pinheiro, P. R., & Pinheiro, M. C. D. (2011). Verbal Decision Analysis Applied on the Optimization of Alzheimers Disease Diagnosis: A Study Case Based on Neuroimaging. *Advances in Experimental Medicine and Biology, 696*, 555–564. doi:10.1007/978-1-4419-7046-6_56 PMID:21431596

Toro, J., Gomez, G., Sentis, J., & Rodriguez, R. (2006). Eating disorders and body image in Spanish and Mexican female adolescents. *Social Psychiatry and Psychiatric Epidemiology, 41*(7), 556–565. doi:10.1007/s00127-006-0067-x PMID:16685478

Chapter 16

Image Processing Including Medical Liver Imaging:
Medical Image Processing from Big Data Perspective, Ultrasound Liver Images, Challenges

Suganya Ramamoorthy
Thiagarajar College of Engineering, India

Rajaram Sivasubramaniam
Thiagarajar College of Engineering, India

ABSTRACT

Medical diagnosis has been gaining importance in everyday life. The diseases and their symptoms are highly varying and there is always a need for a continuous update of knowledge needed for the doctors. The diseases fall into different categories and a small variation of symptoms may leave to different categories of diseases. This is further supplemented by the medical analysts for a continuous treatment process. The treatment generally starts with a diagnosis and further goes through a set of procedures including X-ray, CT-scans, ultrasound imaging for qualitative analysis and diagnosis by doctors. A small level of error in disease identification introduces overhead in diagnosis and difficult in treatment. In such cases, an automated system that could retrieve medical images based on user's interest. This chapter deals with various techniques, methodologies that correspond to the classification problem in data analysis process and its methodological impacts to big data.

INTRODUCTION

Fast development in the field of medical and healthcare sector is focused on the diagnosis, prevention and treatment of illness directly related to every citizen's quality of life. Medical imaging is a key tool in clinical practice, where generalized analysis methods such as image pre-processing, feature extraction, segmentation, registration and classification are applied. A huge number of varied radiological and patho-

DOI: 10.4018/978-1-5225-2607-0.ch016

logical illustrations in digital format are generated by hospitals and medical centers with sophisticated image acquisition devices. Anatomical imaging techniques such as Ultrasound, Computed Tomography and Magnetic Resonance Imaging are used daily over the world for non-invasive human examinations.

All the above imaging techniques are of intense significance in several domains such as computer-aided diagnosis, pathology follow-up, treatment planning and therapy modification. The information extracted from images may include functional descriptions, geometric models of anatomical structures, and diagnostic assessment. Different solutions such as Picture Archive and Communication Systems (PACS) and specialized systems for image databases address the problem of archiving those medical image collections. The obtained classification results can serve further for several clinical applications such as growth monitoring of diseases and therapy. The main contribution of this research is to address the accuracy of ultrasound liver image classification & retrieval by machine learning algorithms. Among all medical imaging modalities, ultrasound imaging still remains one of the most popular techniques due to its non-ionizing and low cost characteristics (Nicolas Dobigeon, Adrian Basarab, Denis Kouame, & Jean-Yves Tourneret 2012)

The image processing plays an important role in the medical field that comprises of image pre-processing, feature extraction, image segmentation, image classification & retrieval. Medical diagnosis is often a categorization (classification) of medical images according to the nature of a specific object namely pathology bearing region or entire region. The primary motivation behind this book is to develop an image retrieval framework focused on image classification according to the nature of the PBR. The PBR helps to classify the liver diseases based on gray texture. The diseases and their symptoms are drastically changing and there is always a need for a continuous update of knowledge for the doctors and the medical analyst. In such cases, an automated learning that could enhance retrieval of medical images based on the physician's and the radiologist's interest of making a final decision about the diseases is needed. This type of learning could be a semi supervised or unsupervised learning process. The learning mechanism has to be properly developed, since an improper design will result in large amount of misclassifications. This provides motivation on improving the learning capabilities of the model considering the fuzzy nature of the dataset.

This chapter deals with various types of liver images, challenges in medical imaging, pre-processing, registration, feature extraction and classification of liver images based on the diagnosis using different machine learning methodologies that correspond to the classification problem in data analysis process and its methodological impacts to big data (Lee, Yuan-Chang Chen & Kai-Sheng Hsieh 2003).

Medical Image Processing from Big Data Perspective

Medical imaging offers important information on anatomy and organ function besides detecting diseases states. Moreover, it is utilized for identifying tumors in liver, disease diagnosis, cancer detection and so forth. In these applications, image processing techniques such as registration, segmentation, and speckle reduction in addition to machine learning methods are employed. As the size and dimensionality of data increase drastically, understanding the dependencies among the data and designing efficient, accurate, and computationally effective methods demand new computer-aided techniques and platforms. The rapid growth in the number of healthcare sectors as well as the number of patients has resulted in the greater use of medical investigative and recommender support systems in clinical domain. Many areas in health care such as diagnosis, registration, and screening can be improved by utilizing computational intelligence. The integration of computer analysis with appropriate care has potential to help physicians improve diagnostic accuracy. The integration of medical images with other types of electronic health record (EHR) data and genomic data can also improve the accuracy and reduce the time taken for a diagnosis.

Modalities of Medical Imaging

Medical imaging includes a wide range of different image acquirement methodologies typically exploited for a variety of medical applications. For example, visualizing tumor structure can be performed using ultrasound, MRI, CT Scans. From a data dimension point of view, medical images might have PET, CT, 3D ultrasound, and functional MRI is considered as multidimensional medical data.

Medical Liver Imaging

The liver is the largest internal organ of the human body weighing 1.5kg and is located in the upper left of the abdomen that plays a vital role in various body metabolisms. The parenchymal echoes are mid-grey and consists of a uniform, sponge like pattern interrupted by the vessels. The structure of the liver hilum is accompanied by a number of ventrally and dorsally located lymph nodes that can be routinely demonstrated by ultrasound. Some important functions of liver include metabolizing drugs, clearing toxins from the blood and producing blood proteins and bile to aid digestion. Therefore, liver diseases have attracted much attention for a long time as the nature of diseases is highly varying and complex in terms of the characteristic and reasons. National Liver Foundation (NLF) is a voluntary, non-profit organization promoting awareness and prevention of liver diseases (Nimer Assy, Gattas Nasser, Agness Djibre, Zaza Beniashvili, Saad Elias & Jamal Zidan 2009). It is estimated that liver diseases are among the top ten killer diseases in India, causing lakhs of deaths every year. In medical image classification and retrieval system, subtle differences between images are considered highly relevant for diagnosis.

Types of Liver Diseases

Liver pathologies can be classified into two main categories according to the degree of dispersion of the disease. The first category is the focal liver disease in which the pathology is concentrated in small area, while the rest of the liver tissue remains normal. The second category is the diffuse liver disease in which the pathology is distributed all over the liver tissue. Visual interpretation of liver images by specialized physician contributes to the decision whether liver tissue is normal or abnormal. The decision depends on the ability of the sonographer to distinguish certain characteristics of the image and compare them with those from different pathologies.

The type of liver diseases analyzed in this work is presented below

1. **Liver Cyst:** Simple cysts are usually described as congenital lesions. Simple hepatic cysts are usually solitary that have a thin epithelial lining and contain watery fluid. Their size varies from less than 1 cm to more than 20cm in diameter. Cysts are found 4 times more frequently in females than males (Levine, E, Cook, LT, & Granthem, JJ 1985). Liver cysts are characterized by typically round, anechoic, smoothly delineated structures with refraction shadows at the edges of the liver.
2. **Fatty Liver:** Fatty liver, also known as fatty liver disease (FLD) is a reversible condition, where large vacuoles of triglyceride fat accumulate in liver cells. This is the commonest alcohol induced liver injury. Fatty liver is an excessive accumulation of fat inside the liver cells. Morphologically,

it is difficult to distinguish an alcoholic FLD from a non alcoholic FLD since both show micro-vesicular and macro vesicular fatty changes at different stages (Baker, MK, Wenker, JC, Cockerill, EM, & Ellis, JH 1985).

3. **Hepatic Hemangioma:** Hepatic Hemangioma is known to be the most common benign liver tumors with an incidence in autopsy & imaging studies of up to 7%. A typical hemangioma has uniformly well circumscribed hyperechoic mass less than 3 cm in diameter. These lesions are often small and can be multiple that is shown in Figure 1.3. The increased echogenicity has been related to the numerous interfaces between the walls of the abdomen liver. Hemangioma is four to six times more common in women than in men. A Female hormone promotes the formation and growth of hemangioma.

4. **Hepatoma:** Hepatoma or Hepatocellular carcinoma (HCC) is the most common type of liver cancer, comprising 80% of primary liver malignancies in the United States (Parkin, DM, Bray, F, Ferlay, J & Pisani, P 2005). The visual property of hepatoma is irregular- shaped with vague contours, complex structure of vessels and tissue heterogeneity as shown in Figure 1.4. The surface of the hepatoma tissues is coarser than normal tissues. In ultrasound imaging some gray levels in hepatoma tissues might be similar to parts of the hemangioma liver tissues and the contours of the hepatoma tissues vary from case to case. So it is not easy to discriminate the hepatoma tissues from the hemangioma tissues.

5. **Alcoholic Cirrhosis:** Alcoholic cirrhosis is the permanent destruction of normal liver tissue result-ing in non-functioning scar tissue. The severity of liver disease depends on the quantity of alcohol the patient consumes. The accuracy of ultrasound in the correct diagnosis of "liver cirrhosis" in patients with complications is high up to 30%. Sonographic signs of liver cirrhosis include inho-mogeneous echo texture and irregular-nodular liver surface delineation

Challenges in Medical Liver Imaging

Image Pre-Processing

Among all medical imaging modalities, ultrasound imaging still remains one of the most popular tech-niques due to its low power, easy-to-use nature and low cost characteristics. As ultrasound waves pass through a body, they are reflected back due to constructive and destructive interference of the ultrasound machine in different ways, based on the characteristics of the tissues encountered. One of the major problems of ultrasound images is the presence of noise, having the form of a granular pattern, called speckle. Automatic interpretation of ultrasound images however is extremely difficult because of its low signal to noise ratio (SNR). One of the main reasons for this low SNR is the presence of speckle noise. Speckle noises tend to obscure diagnostically important features and degrade the image quality and thus increase the difficulties in diagnosis. The automated recognition of meaningful image compo-nents, anatomical structures, and other pathology bearing region, is typically achieved using some kind of speckle reduction techniques.

The characteristics of the imaging system based on the spatial distribution of speckles can be divided speckles into three classes as given below:

1. The fully formed speckle pattern occurs when many random distributed scattering exists within the resolution cell of the imaging system. Example- Blood cells.

2. The second class of tissue scatters is random distribution with long-range order. Example of this type is lobules in liver parenchyma.
3. The last class occurs when invariant coherent structure is present within the random scatter region like organ surfaces and blood vessels.

Diagnostic usage for ultrasound has greatly expanded over the past couple of decades because its advantages over low cost and non-invasive nature. Ultrasound, however, suffers from an inherent imaging artifact called speckle. Speckle is created by a complex interference of ultrasound echoes made by reflectors. A speckle depends up on the ultrasound system's resolution limit. The ability of diagnosing ultrasound images to detect low contrast lesions is fundamentally limited by speckles. Speckle is a granular pattern formed due to constructive and destructive coherent interferences of backscattered signals due to unresolved tissue in-homogeneity. The speckle pattern depends on the structure of the imaged tissue and various imaging parameters, e.g., the frequency and geometry of the ultrasound transducer. Because of its dependence on the microstructure of the tissue parenchyma, speckle is often used in diagnosis such as focal and diffuse liver diseases. Since, speckle typically shows up as noise, it reduces image contrast and obscures image details. So, handling speckles in ultrasound images is a critical task in medical image processing. Laplacian pyramid non linear diffusion filter is used to remove speckles present in the medical images. The procedure for pre-processing the medical image is discussed below.

Step 1: Decomposition of a given input image into its Laplacian pyramid domain by using EXPAND and REDUCE operators.
   a. REDUCE: it performs 2D low pass filtering followed by a sub-sampling factor of two in both directions using the equation G_1 =REDUCE [G_{1-1}].
   b. EXPAND: it enlarges an image into twice its size in both directions by up sampling using equation L_1= G_1 – EXPAND [G_{1-1}].

Step 2: Calculation of pyramid coefficient values by modified diffusivity function for nonlinear diffusion in order to remove speckles from an image.

Apply Gaussian low pass-filter to each subband to estimate gradient ▼I by equation

$$\partial I / \partial t = div[c(\|▼(G(\sigma) * I)\|. ▼I]$$

   b. The selection of σ provides noise suppression and structure preservation. Compute modified diffusivity function in equation C2($\|▼I\|$) = exp [1-($\|▼I\|^2/(2\lambda +1))^2$]

Step 3: Reconstruction of the diffused laplacian pyramid by applying Gaussian low pass filter.

MAD estimator and its new decision role on the gradient threshold λ for the proposed LPND is computed by eqn λ = MAD($\|▼I\|$)/0.6745 and (I) λ = 1/0.6745. MAD ($\|▼I\|$.Sqrt 2log ((l+1)/2l))

After removing speckles present in ultrasound images, depending up on the user needs, the image is passed into either Image registration for growth monitoring of pathology changes in liver or Feature extraction for classification & retrieval.

Image Registration

Registration of medical images is done to investigate the disease process and understand normal development and aging. To analyze the image from different scanners, all the images need to be aligned into the same location, where the structure of tissues can be compared. Patient information is accumulated over years and has details in the form of ultrasound images. This needs to be stored and retrieved when required. Traditional mechanism for storage and retrieval suffers from redundancy that could be eliminated during image registration. In modern radiology, image registration is important for diagnosis, surgical planning and treatment control.

For classification & retrieval of ultrasound liver images, image registration helps to reduce the computational time and improve the accuracy of retrieval for diagnosis purposes. Mutual information is a popular similarity measure for medical image registration. Image registration reduces the redundancy of retrieval images and increases the response rate that motivates this work

Image Registration is the process of transforming different sets of medical image data into one co-ordinate system. The classification of medical image registration techniques is shown in Table 1. Data may have different scan images from different times or from different viewpoints. Registration is necessary in order to compare or integrate the data obtained from these different measurements. A common task within medical image analysis is the automatic registration of 2D/ 3D images of a patient taken

Table 1. Classification of medical image registration techniques

Based on Image Alignment Algorithm	
Intensity based image registration	It compares intensity patterns in images via correlation or mutual information metrics. It registers entire image or sub image.
Feature based image registration	This method finds correspondence between image features such as points, lines, and contours. It establishes a correspondence between a numbers of especially distinct points in images.
Based on Transformation Models	
Rigid-body transformation	Also called linear transformations, which includes rotation, scaling, and other affine transforms.
Non-rigid transformation	Also called elastic transformation, which includes radial basis functions, physical continuum models, and large deformation models.
Based on Domain Methods	
Spatial domain methods	Spatial methods operate in the image domain, by matching intensity patterns or features in images by using control points.
Frequency domain methods	Frequency-domain methods find the transformation parameters for registration of the images while working in the transform domain, such as translation, rotation, and scaling.
Based on Modalities	
Mono-modal	Single-modality methods tend to register images in the same modality acquired by the same scanner/ sensor type
Multi-modal	multi-modality registration methods tend to register images acquired by different scanner/sensor types
Based on Automation Methods	
Automatic image registration methods	Automatic methods provide tools to align the images itself without any user.
Interactive image registration methods	Interactive methods reduce user bias by performing certain key operations automatically while still relying on the user to guide the registration

at different times / different positions, i.e. Mono-modality case. This task is very useful to detect any pathological evolution and to compute quantitative measures of this evolution. The most important application is the matching of images taken from different modalities, i.e. different sensing devices called as multi-modal registration. This process allows the physician to combine information visually from any combination of imaging modalities and will prove to be extremely beneficial for the surgeon during any decision making processes. The classification of medical image registration techniques are shown below proposed by (Maintz, JBA, Meijering, EHW & Viergever, MA 1998).

This work concentrates on mono-modal image registration. During classification & retrieval, if the patient wants to know about his history from the database, his new ultrasound image will be generated using mutual information based image registration technique.

The main components of image registration technique are:

1. Similarity measures to determine the quality of match of the two images.
2. Transformations that relate the two images. The most representative transformation models include rigid, affine, projective and curved.
3. Optimization techniques to determine the optimal value of the transformation parameters as a function of the similarity measure.

Mutual information has the following properties:

1. **I (A, B) = I (B, A):** It is symmetric; otherwise it would not be mutual information. However, it is a logical property in theory; mutual information is not symmetric in practice. Implementation aspects of a registration method, such as interpolation and number of samples, can result in differences in outcomes when registering A to B or B to A.
2. **I (A, A) = H (A):** The information image A contains about itself is equal to the information (entropy) of image A.
3. **I(A, B) ≤ H(A):**
    a. **I (A, B) ≥ H (B):** The information that the images contain about each other can never be greater than the information in the images themselves.
    b. **I(A,B) ≥ 0:** The uncertainty about A cannot be increased by learning about B.
4. **I (A, B) = 0:** if and only if A and B are independent. When A and B are not related in any way, no knowledge is gained about one image when the other is given.

The following steps involved in MM-MI based image registration are:

1. **Image Pre-Processing for Speckle Reduction:** Pre-process both reference image (ultrasound-Liver) and target image (ultrasound-Liver) of the same patient by using S-Mean filter i.e. (SRAD and Median filter) in order to remove speckle noise present in the images.
2. **Similarity Measures:** Calculate MI value by entropy measure, that is necessary for intensity based image registration for both target and reference image.
3. **Geometric Transformation:** Perform rigid body transformation for target image that involves translation, rotation and affine which helps to align source image.

4. **Optimization Techniques:** Apply Optimization techniques on rigid body – DIRECT and Nelder-Mead method to optimize the registration at minimum value. The optimization algorithm is used to search for the best alignment data.

MI based Image registration should match the ultrasound liver images at the point- to- point level and small variation in the input image should result in small variations in the output image. But in practical applications, with the higher resolution and the more details obtained from the image, it is more difficult to realize the image registration. The fundamental technique for mono-modal image registration involves pre-processing, similarity measures by mutual information, rigid body transformation, and optimization methods by DIRECT and Nelder-Mead. The optimization method can quickly produce optimal solutions that reduce the computation time of the registration and error rate during classification. This overcomes the issue of redundancy that is inherent in liver images during retrieval. The retrieved results support the physicians to track the growth of liver diseases for taking quick decisions.

Feature Extraction

In medical image processing, selecting a minimal set of features based on texture pattern is a special form of dimensionality reduction. Transforming the input image into the set of features is called feature extraction. If the features extraction is chosen carefully, then it is expected to extract the relevant information from the pathology bearing region (PBR) of the input image in order to perform the desired task using this reduced representation instead of the full size image. Features often contain information relative to gray shade, texture, shape or context. In this work, to classify ultrasound liver diseases present in the form of texture in an image, features must be extracted.

Texture analysis algorithms are applied in two stages. First, the entire image is considered for the calculation of these metrics. Second the infected region will be selected by radiologist and that particular region (32 x 32 pixels PBR) is considered for the calculation of twelve Haralick's features by experience physician so as to avoid deviation in image statistics. A number of texture features may be extracted from the GLCM (Haralick, RM, Shanmugam, K & Dinstein, I, 1973).

The use of feature extraction in medical imaging has been proved to be important for Ultrasound modality. Ultrasonic echoes from human tissues are displayed as B-scan images that form texture patterns indicating the imaging system and tissue that is being scanned. The B-mode ultrasound that is generally the first choice of imaging technique for the liver has serious limitations in detection and characterization of liver lesions. The focal and diffuse lesions in ultrasound images are clinically differentiated based on the echo texture patterns. Image texture present in ultrasound images describes internal structure of human tissues or organs as well as pathological changes.

Experienced radiologists visualize the various texture features in liver ultrasound images to characterize the focal lesions and Normal (NOR) liver tissues. The features that are extracted from texture echo variation in ultrasound images are used to distinguish various liver diseases. So selection of minimal set of features plays a major role in classification & retrieval. Basically, feature selection is the process of removing features from the dataset that are irrelevant or redundant with respect to the task that is to be performed. It can be extremely useful in reducing the dimensionality of the data to be processed by a certain classifier thereby reducing execution time, and improving predictive accuracy. Diverse feature selection techniques have been proposed in the machine learning literature, such as Principal Component

Analysis (PCA), Correlation –based feature selection (CFS) methods, Support vector machine feature elimination etc.

Features Selection by CFS

Feature selection plays an important role in classification problems. It can be extremely useful in reducing the dimensionality of the data to be processed by a certain classifier, reducing execution time or even improving predictive accuracy. Diverse feature selection techniques have been proposed in the matching learning literature, such as principal component analysis (PCA), correlation-based feature selection methods, Support vector machine feature elimination etc. The Correlation Feature Selection (CFS) measure evaluates subsets of features on the basis of the following hypothesis: "Good feature subsets contain features highly correlated with the classification". The author suggested the use of CFS method to extract minimal set of features that are more suitable for ultrasound liver image detection and classifications. Haralick's defined twelve features based on gray level co-occurrence matrix- Contrast, Correlation, Auto correlation, homogeneity, dissimilarity, cluster shade, cluster prominence, energy, entropy, Angular Second Moment, mean and variance to analyze gray scale texture pattern in ultrasound images. All its mathematical formula and its importance over medical dataset are discussed above. CFS defined in equation is applied over GLCM. Correlation feature selection method is used to reduce the space complexity for medical image classification process.

Image Classification and Retrieval

Several image classification & retrieval systems such as supervised and unsupervised are being built in the field of medical imaging for the appropriate diagnosis and treatment of various diseases. The state-of-the-art Support Vector Machine (SVM) based on statistical learning theory is widely used in supervised learning and classification problem providing a good performance in classification. Compared to Artificial Neural network, the SVM has the advantage of being usable under different kernel functions and highly accurate classification based on parameter selection. Relevance Feedback (RF) is a supervised learning and query modification technique is used to capture the user's needs through iterative feedback and query refinement. In the absence of reliable framework for characterizing high level semantics of images and human subjectivity of perception, the user's feedback provides a way to learn case-specific query semantics.

A Self-Organizing Map (SOM) is a way to represent higher dimensional data in a 2-D/3-D manner, such that same categories of data are grouped together. The Kohonen (SOM) is an unsupervised learning that utilizes the concepts of competitive learning (Christodoulou, CI, Pattichis, CS, Kyriacou, E & Nicolaides, A et al 2010). Competitive learning is an adaptive process, in which the neurons gradually become sensitive to different input categories. SOM is different from Artificial Neural Network; in the way they use a neighborhood function to preserve the topological properties of the input space.

In Image Classification & Retrieval, the proposed work concentrates on improving the learning capabilities of the model considering the fuzzy nature of the dataset. Hence in order to predict the extent of damage, it is essential to eliminate this imprecision. Elimination of this imprecision can be done by employing the concept of fuzzy logic. The approach of fuzzy logic for this research can eliminate imprecision and can give accurate results for the submitted query image. Fuzzy classifier plays an important role in dealing uncertainty with medical applications. The accuracy helps the physician for proper and accurate diagnosis thereby enhancing the treatment of the patient.

Machine learning algorithm plays an important role in the medical imaging field, including computer-aided diagnosis, image segmentation, image registration, image-guided therapy and image classification. Recently, the application of machine learning techniques to medical image retrieval has received more attention. Due to the rapid development of computer technology, it is becoming more and more convenient to acquire, digitally store and transfer medical imagery. Nowadays, many hospitals need to manage several tera-bytes of medical image data each year. Therefore, categorization of medical images is becoming imperative for a variety of medical systems, especially in the application of digital radiology such as CAD and Case-based reasoning. This book deals with different machine learning algorithms namely – Support Vector Machine, Self Organizing Map, Relevance feedback and fuzzy for classification & retrieval of ultrasound liver images.

1. **Supervised Learning Algorithm:** The Support Vector Machine, stemming from statistical learning theory, involves state-of-the-art machine learning. The SVM based on statistical learning theory is widely used in supervised learning and classification problem, invariably providing a good performance in medical image classification problems. Compared to conventional neural network, the SVM has the advantage of being usable under different kernel functions and highly accurate classification based on parameter selection. The kernel function $k(x, y)$ is used as a mapping or a transformation function. The separation of data can be either linear or non-linear. The different types of kernel function are linear, nonlinear, polynomial, RBF, and quadratic. The SVM classifier is a part of computer aided diagnosis, which assists radiologists in accurately diagnose liver diseases.

2. **Unsupervised Learning Algorithm:** The Self Organizing Map (SOM) is an unsupervised learning algorithm where the input patterns are freely distributed over the output node matrix. SOM utilizes the concept of competitive learning for medical image classification. Competitive learning is an adaptive process in which the neurons gradually become sensitive to different input categories. The SOM is a type of artificial neural network to produce a low-dimensional discretized representation of the input space of the training samples called a map. SOM uses a neighborhood function to preserve the topological properties of the input space.

3. **Relevance Feedback (RF):** In the past years, relevance feedback techniques have evolved from early heuristic weighting adjustment techniques to various machine learning techniques for medical image classification and retrieval. Relevance Feedback (RF) is a query modification technique, originating in information retrieval that attempts to capture the user's precise needs through iterative feedback and query refinement.Most research in relevance feedback uses one or both of the following approaches: 1) query-point moving and 2) weight updating. The query-point moving approach tries to improve the estimation of the ideal query point by moving the current query point (i.e., estimate) by a certain amount based on user feedback. The weight updating approach is a refinement method based on modifying the weights or parameters used in the computation of similarity based on the user's feedback.

4. **Fuzzy Classifier:** Fuzzy classifier plays an important role in dealing with uncertainty decision making in medical applications. Classification of medical image objects is based on association of a given object with one of several classes (i.e., diagnoses). Fuzzy logic is a form of mathematical logic in which truth can take continuous values between 0 and 1. (Jesus Chamorro Martinez,

Pedro Manuel Martinez Jimenez & Jose Manuel Soto Hidalgo 2010) showed that the propositions of the fuzzy logic can be represented with degrees of truthfulness and falsehood. A Membership Function (MF) is a curve that defines how each point in the input space is mapped to a membership value (or degree of membership) between 0 and 1. The input space is sometimes referred to as the universe of discourse. He discussed that the membership function is similar to the indicator function in classical sets.

From the above discussion, Computer-based classification & retrieval of medical image data using machine learning algorithm can simplify the difficult interpretation of medical images and provide additional information to the physician. In order to be appropriate in clinical practice, it has to cope with the following two requirements:

1. During the training phase, untypical cases (due to imaging errors, abnormal physiological parameters of the patients, or untypical symptoms) have to be considered with a lower weighing factor so that the knowledge acquired during the training contains the typical characteristics of the classes.
2. The result of classification of unknown cases has to contain information on how reliable the computer-based diagnosis is.

Both requirements are not met by conventional classifiers. This work concentrates more on the accuracy of classification & retrieval of ultrasound liver images for automated decision making. The motivation behind this research is aimed at image classification according to the nature of pathology bearing region (PBR) that appears across a given image dataset containing liver images. The proposed work concentrates on classifying liver diseases like Cyst, Fatty Liver, Hepatoma, Hemangioma, and Cirrhosis from ultrasound Normal images.

Applications of Big Data in Medical Imaging

In this book, three application domains of big data analytics in medicine are discussed. These three areas do not broadly replicate the application of big data analytics in medicine; instead they are proposed to offer a broad view, popular areas of research where the concepts of big data analytics are currently being applied.

1. **Image Processing:** Medical images are a vital source of data regularly used for diagnosis, therapy conclusion and planning for surgery. Ultrasound, CT, MRI, X-ray, molecular imaging, fluoroscopy, positron emission tomography-computed tomography (PET-CT), and mammogram are some of the modalities of imaging techniques. Medical image data can range anywhere from a few megabytes for a single study (e.g., histology images) to hundreds of megabytes/terabytes per study (CT scan for Brain). Such data necessitates huge storage capacities if accumulated for long term. It also insists quick and precise algorithms if any recommender supports system were to be performed using the data. In addition, if alternate sources of data acquired for each patient are also utilized during the acquisition, diagnoses, screening test, and further treatment /surgery procedure, then the problem of providing unified storage and expanding efficient methods competent of encapsulating the wide range of data becomes a challenge.

2. **Signal Processing:** Related to medical images, medical signals also pretense huge volume and high velocity impediments especially during continuous, high-resolution acquirement and storage from a huge number of checks associated to each patient. However, besides the data size issues, physiological signals also create complexity of a spatiotemporal nature. Examining of physiological signals is often more significant when offered along with situational context consciousness which needs to be embedded into the development of continuous monitoring and prognostic systems to make sure its effectiveness and robustness. At present healthcare systems use numerous dissimilar and continuous supervising devices that utilize singular physiological waveform data or discretized vital information to provide attentive mechanisms in case of obvious occurrences.

3. **Genomics:** The cost to series the human genome is speedily decreasing with the development of high-throughput sequencing technology. With inferences for current public health policies and liberation of care, analyzing genome-scale / DNA data for expanding actionable recommendations in a timely manner is a significant challenge to the field of computational biology. Cost and time to distribute recommendations are crucial in a clinical setting. A decision making approach involves (i) analyzing genome-scale/DNA datasets to establish disease states, (ii) moving towards blood based diagnostic tools for continuous monitoring of a subject, (iii) exploring new approaches to drug target discovery, developing tools to deal with big data challenges of capturing, validating, storing, mining, integrating, and finally (iv) modeling data for each individual.

Big Data Challenges in Healthcare

1. Gathering knowledge from complex heterogeneous patient sources.
2. Understanding unstructured medical reports in the correct semantic context.
3. Managing large volumes of medical imaging data and extracting useful information from it.
4. Analyzing genomic data is a computationally intensive task
5. Capturing the patient's behavioural data through several wireless network sensors

FUTURE RESEARCH DIRECTIONS

The future scope of this book is as follows: Liver images in this work could be extended for considering other category of diseases. More level of issues arises in the preprocessing part that could also be addressed as part of the research. Multimodal Image Registration could also be analyzed and proposed in the work. Feature Extraction could be done with other techniques. Fuzzy classifier can be modified with Neuro Fuzzy classifier and their performance could be analyzed. A complete integration of all the steps in the thesis could be provided as a single system to the doctor community.

CONCLUSION

The existing challenges under Classification & Retrieval of ultrasound liver images include speckle noise, semantic gap, computational time, dimensionality reduction and accuracy of retrieval images from large dataset. All these issues are critical in nature and they have been addressed in each phase of the work. In this book, an attempt is made to address these issues and appropriate methods are proposed at each step and validated with the medical specialist in the relevant field. To conclude, most of the machine learning algorithms for today's medical imaging system have originally been both spawned and incubated to provide well designed and efficient solutions for classification of pathological lesions and cyst. The book proposes new methods for speckle reduction, image registration, feature extraction; classification & retrieval algorithms facilitate automated diagnosis, so as to improve the diagnostic accuracy of ultrasound liver diseases

REFERENCES

Assy, Nasser, Djibre, Beniashvili, Elias, & Zidan. (2009). Characteristics of common solid liver lesions and recommendations for diagnostic workup. *World Journal of Gastroenterology, 15*(26), 3217-3227.

Baker, M. K., Wenker, J. C., Cockerill, E. M., & Ellis, J. H. (1985). Focal fatty infiltration of the liver: diagnostic imaging. Radiographic, 5(6), 923-929.

Christodoulou, C. I., Pattichis, C. S., Kyriacou, E., & Nicolaides, A. (2010). Image retrieval and classification of carotid plaque ultrasound images. The Open Cardiovascular Imaging Journal, 2, 18-28.

Dobigeon, N., Basarab, A., Kouame, D., & Tourneret, J.-Y. (2012). Regularized bayesian compressed sensing in ultrasound imaging. *IEEE Signal Processing Conference*, 2600-2604.

Haralick, R. M., Shanmugam, K., & Dinstein, I. (1973). Textural features for image classification. IEEE Transactions on Systems, Man, and Cybernetics, 3(6), 610-621.

Lee, Y.-C. C., & Hsieh, K.-S. (2003). Ultrasonic Liver Tissues Classification by Fractal Feature Vector based on M-band Wavelet Transform. *IEEE Transactions on Medical Imaging, 22*(3), 382–392.

Levine, E., Cook, L.T., & Granthem, J.J. (1985). Liver Cysts in autosomal-dominant polycystic kidney disease. Clinical and computer topographic study. *American Journal of Roentgenlogy, 145*(2), 229-233.

Maintz, J. B. A., Meijering, E. H. W., & Viergever, M. A. (1998). General multimodal elastic registration based on mutual information. In *Medical imaging: Image processing* (pp. 144–154). SPIE Press.

Martinez, Martinez Jimenez, & Soto Hidalgo. (2010). Retrieving Texture Images Using Coarseness Fuzzy Partitions. *CCIS, 81*, 542-551.

Parkin, D. M., Bray, F., Ferlay, J., & Pisani, P. (2005). Global cancer statistics. CA: A Cancer Journal for Clinicians, 55(2), 74-108.

Compilation of References

Abagyan, R., & Totrov, M. (2001). High-throughput docking for lead generation. *Current Opinion in Chemical Biology*, *5*(4), 375–382. doi:10.1016/S1367-5931(00)00217-9 PMID:11470599

Abagyan, R., Totrov, M., & Kuznetsov, D. (1994). ICM - A new method for protein modeling and design: Applications to docking and structure prediction from the distorted native conformation. *Journal of Computational Chemistry*, *15*(5), 488–506. doi:10.1002/jcc.540150503

Abba, M., Mudduluru, G., & Allgayer, H. (2012). MicroRNAs in cancer: Small molecules, big chances. *Anti-cancer Agents in Medicinal Chemistry*, *12*(7), 733–743. doi:10.2174/187152012802650273 PMID:22292749

Abdat, N., Spruit, M., & Bos, M. (2011). Software as a Service and the Pricing Strategy for Vendors. In T. Strader (Ed.), Digital Product Management, Technology and Practice: Interdisciplinary Perspectives (pp. 154–192). Hershey, PA: IGI Global. doi:10.4018/978-1-61692-877-3.ch010

Abraham, M. H. (1993). Application of solvation equations to chemical and biochemical processes. *Pure and Applied Chemistry*, *65*(12), 2503–2512. doi:10.1351/pac199365122503

Achrekar, H., Gandhe, A., Lazarus, R., Yu, S. H., & Liu, B. (2011). Predicting flu trends using Twitter data. *Proceedings of IEEE Conference on Computer Communications Workshops* (pp. 702-707).

Aderem, A. (2005). Systems Biology: Its Practice and Challenges. *Cell*, *121*(4), 511–513. doi:10.1016/j.cell.2005.04.020 PMID:15907465

Adiconis, X., Borges-Rivera, D., Satija, R., DeLuca, D. S., Busby, M. A., Berlin, A. M., & Levin, J. Z. et al. (2013). Comparative Analysis of RNA Sequencing Methods for Degraded or Low-Input Samples. *Nature Methods*, *10*(7), 623–629. doi:10.1038/nmeth.2483 PMID:23685885

Aebersold, R., & Mann, M. (2003). Mass spectrometry-based proteomics. *Nature*, *422*(6928), 198–207. doi:10.1038/nature01511 PMID:12634793

Agrawal, R., & Srikant, R. (1994). Fast Algorithms for Mining Association Rules in Large Databases. *Paper presented at the VLDB Conference.*

Agrawal, V. (Accessed 2016). Securing Big Data On Cloud – Tools and Measures. Retrieved from http://www.exeideas.com/2015/09/securing-big-data-on-cloud.html

Aguzzi, A., & OConnor, T. (2010). Protein aggregation diseases: Pathogenicity and therapeutic perspectives. *Nature Reviews. Drug Discovery*, *9*(3), 237–248. doi:10.1038/nrd3050 PMID:20190788

Agyeman, A., & Ofori-Asenso, R. (2015). Perspective: Does personalized medicine hold the future for medicine? *Journal of Pharmacy and Bioallied Sciences*, *7*(3), 239. doi:10.4103/0975-7406.160040 PMID:26229361

Ain, Q. U., Aleksandrova, A., Roessler, F. D., & Ballester, P. J. (2015). Machine-learning scoring functions to improve structure-based binding affinity prediction and virtual screening. *Computational Molecular Science, 5*(6), 405–424. doi:10.1002/wcms.1225 PMID:27110292

Al-Ageel, N., Al-Wabil, A., Badr, G., & AlOmar, N. (2015). Human factors in the design and evaluation of bioinformatics tools. *Procedia Manufacturing, 3*, 2003–2010. doi:10.1016/j.promfg.2015.07.247

Albert, R., Jeong, H., & Barabási, A.L. (2000). Error and Attack Tolerance of Complex Networks. *Nature, 406*(6794), 378–382. doi:10.1038/35019019

Albert, R. (2005). Scale-Free Networks in Cell Biology. *Journal of Cell Science, 118*(Pt 21), 4947–4957. doi:10.1242/jcs.02714 PMID:16254242

Albrecht, M. (2010). Color blindness. *Nature Methods, 7*(10), 775–775. doi:10.1038/nmeth1010-775a PMID:20885436

Al-Lazikani, B., Jung, J., Xiang, Z., & Honig, B. (2001). Protein structure prediction. *Current Opinion in Chemical Biology.* doi:10.1016/S1367-5931(00)00164-2

Allison, D. B., Cui, X., Page, G. P., & Sabripour, M. (2006). Microarray data analysis: From disarray to consolidation and consensus. *Nature Reviews. Genetics, 7*(1), 55–65. doi:10.1038/nrg1749 PMID:16369572

Alon, U. (2006). An Introduction to Systems Biology: Design Principles of Biological Circuits. CRC Press. Retrieved from https://www.crcpress.com/An-Introduction-to-Systems-Biology-Design-Principles-of-Biological-Circuits/Alon/p/book/9781584886426

Alpaydin, E. (2010). *Introduction to machine learning.* Cambridge, MA: MIT Press.

Altman, R. B. (2012). Translational bioinformatics: Linking the molecular world to the clinical world. *Clinical Pharmacology and Therapeutics, 91*(6), 994–1000. doi:10.1038/clpt.2012.49 PMID:22549287

Altman, R. B., & Raychaudhuri, S. (2001). Whole-genome expression analysis: Challenges beyond clustering. *Current Opinion in Structural Biology, 11*(3), 340–347. doi:10.1016/S0959-440X(00)00212-8 PMID:11406385

Alvarez, J. C. (2004). High-throughput docking as a source of novel drug leads. *Current Opinion in Chemical Biology, 8*(4), 365–370. doi:10.1016/j.cbpa.2004.05.001 PMID:15288245

Alwagait, E., & Shahzad, B. (2014). Maximization of Tweet's viewership with respect to time. *Proceedings of the 2014 World Symposium on Computer Applications & Research* (pp. 1-5). doi:10.1109/WSCAR.2014.6916776

Alwagait, E., & Shahzad, B. (2015). When are Tweets Better Valued? An Empirical Study. *Journal of Universal Computer Science, 20*(10), 1511–1521.

Alyass, A., Turcotte, M., & Meyre, D. (2015). From Big Data analysis to personalized medicine for all: Challenges and opportunities. *BMC Medical Genomics, 8*(33). PMID:26112054

Amaratunga, D., Cabrera, J., & Kovtun, V. (2008). Microarray learning with ABC. *Biostatistics (Oxford, England), 9*(1), 128–136. doi:10.1093/biostatistics/kxm017 PMID:17573363

Amit, Y., & Geman, D. (1997). Shape quantization and recognition with randomized trees. *Neural Computation, 9*(7), 1545–1588. doi:10.1162/neco.1997.9.7.1545

Anderson, N. L., & Anderson, N. G. (1998). Proteome and proteomics: New technologies, new concepts, and new words. *Electrophoresis, 19*(11), 1853–1861. doi:10.1002/elps.1150191103 PMID:9740045

Anders, S., & Huber, W. (2010). Differential Expression Analysis for Sequence Count Data. *Genome Biology, 11*(10), R106. doi:10.1186/gb-2010-11-10-r106 PMID:20979621

Andra, S. S., Charisiadis, P., Karakitsios, S., Sarigiannis, D. A., & Makris, K. C. (2015). Passive exposures of children to volatile trihalomethanes during domestic cleaning activities of their parents. *Environmental Research, 136*(0), 187–195. doi:10.1016/j.envres.2014.10.018 PMID:25460636

Andrei, R. R., Callieri, M., Zini, M. M., Loni, T., Maraziti, G., Pan, M., … Scopigno, R. (2012). Intuitive representation of surface properties of biomolecules using BioBlender. *BMC Bioinformatics, 13*(Suppl. 4), S16. Doi:<ALIGNMENT. qj></ALIGNMENT>10.1186/1471-2105-13-S4-S16

Andrews, S. (2016). FastQC A Quality Control Tool for High Throughput Sequence Data. *Babraham Bioinformatics.* Retrieved from http://www.bioinformatics.babraham.ac.uk/projects/fastqc/

Andrusier, N., Mashiach, E., Nussinov, R., & Wolfson, H. J. (2008). Principles of flexible protein-protein docking. *Proteins, 73*(2), 271–289. doi:10.1002/prot.22170 PMID:18655061

Andrusier, N., Nussinov, R., & Wolfson, H. J. (2007). FireDock: Fast interaction refinement in molecular docking. *Proteins, 69*(1), 139–159. doi:10.1002/prot.21495 PMID:17598144

Angiuoli, S. V., Matalka, M., Gussman, A., Galens, K., Vangala, M., Riley, D. R., & Fricke, W. F. et al. (2011). CloVR: A virtual machine for automated and portable sequence analysis from the desktop using cloud computing. *BMC Bioinformatics, 12*(1), 356. doi:10.1186/1471-2105-12-356 PMID:21878105

Antelmann, H. (2001, September 1). A proteomic view on genome-based signal peptide predictions. *Genome Research, 11*(9), 1484–1502. doi:10.1101/gr.182801 PMID:11544192

Aramaki, E., Maskawa, S., & Morita, M. (2011). Twitter catches the flu: Detecting Influenza epidemics using Twitter. *Proceedings of the Conference on Empirical Methods in Natural Language Processing* (pp. 1568-1576).

Araújo, C. A., & Neto, F. L. (2013). A nova classificação para os transtornos mentais – DSM-V. *Jornal de Psicanálise., 46*(85), 99–116.

Arevalillo, J. M., & Navarro, H. (2013). Exploring correlations in gene expression microarray data for maximum predictive - minimum redundancy biomarker selection and classification. *Computers in Biology and Medicine, 43*(10), 1437–1443. doi:10.1016/j.compbiomed.2013.07.005 PMID:24034735

Arkin, M. R., Tang, Y., & Wells, J. A. (2014). Small-molecule inhibitors of protein-protein interactions: Progressing toward the reality. *Chemistry & Biology, 21*(9), 1102–1114. doi:10.1016/j.chembiol.2014.09.001 PMID:25237857

Aronsky, D., & Haug, P. J. (2000). Automatic identification of patients eligible for a pneumonia guideline. *Proceedings of the American Medical Informatics Association, 1067*, 12–16. PMID:11079835

Ashburn, T. T., & Thor, K. B. (2004). Drug repositioning: Identifying and developing new uses for existing drugs. *Nature Reviews. Drug Discovery, 3*(8), 673–683. doi:10.1038/nrd1468 PMID:15286734

Ashtawy, H. M., & Mahapatra, N. R. (2015). A Comparative Assessment of Predictive Accuracies of Conventional and Machine Learning Scoring Functions for Protein-Ligand Binding Affinity Prediction. *IEEE/ACM Transactions on Computational Biology and Bioinformatics, 12*(2), 335–347. doi:10.1109/TCBB.2014.2351824 PMID:26357221

Assy, Nasser, Djibre, Beniashvili, Elias, & Zidan. (2009). Characteristics of common solid liver lesions and recommendations for diagnostic workup. *World Journal of Gastroenterology, 15*(26), 3217-3227.

Asur, S., & Huberman, B. A. (2010). Predicting the future with social media. *Proceedings of 2010 International Conference on Web Intelligence and Intelligent Agent Technology* (pp. 492-499).

Avorn, J. (2015). The $2.6 Billion Pill — Methodologic and Policy Considerations. *The New England Journal of Medicine*, *372*(20), 1877–1879. doi:10.1056/NEJMp1500848 PMID:25970049

Azam, S. S., & Abbasi, S. W. (2013). Molecular docking studies for the identification of novel melatoninergic inhibitors for acetylserotonin-O-methyltransferase using different docking routines. *Theoretical Biology & Medical Modelling*, *10*(1), 63. doi:10.1186/1742-4682-10-63 PMID:24156411

Baars, T., Mijnhardt, F., Vlaanderen, K., & Spruit, M. (2016). An Analytics Approach to Adaptive Maturity Models using Organizational Characteristics. *Decision Analytics*, *3*(5).

Bacardit, J., Widera, P., Lazzarini, N., & Krasnogor, N. (2014). Hard data analytics problems make for better data analysis algorithms: Bioinformatics as an example. *Big Data*, *2*(3), 164–176. doi:10.1089/big.2014.0023 PMID:25276500

Badotti, F., Barbosa, A. S., Reis, A. L. M., do Valle, Í. F., Ambrósio, L., & Bitar, M. (2014). Comparative modeling of proteins: A method for engaging students interest in bioinformatics tools. *Biochemistry and Molecular Biology Education*, *42*(1), 68–78. doi:10.1002/bmb.20721 PMID:24167006

Bair, E. (2013). Identification of significant features in DNA microarray data. *Wiley Interdisciplinary Reviews: Computational Statistics*, *5*(4), 309–325. doi:10.1002/wics.1260 PMID:24244802

Bakail, M., & Ochsenbein, F. (2016). Targeting protein–protein interactions, a wide open field for drug design. *Comptes Rendus. Chimie*, *19*(1), 19–27. doi:10.1016/j.crci.2015.12.004

Baker, M. K., Wenker, J. C., Cockerill, E. M., & Ellis, J. H. (1985). Focal fatty infiltration of the liver: diagnostic imaging. Radiographic, *5*(6), 923-929.

Baker, M. (2012). Fragment-based lead discovery grows up. *Nature Reviews. Drug Discovery*, *12*(1), 5–7. doi:10.1038/nrd3926 PMID:23274457

Balbuena, P. B., & Seminario, J. M. (2007). *Nanomaterials: design and simulation*. Elsevier.

Ballester, P. J., & Mitchell, J. B. O. (2010). A machine learning approach to predicting protein-ligand binding affinity with applications to molecular docking. *Bioinformatics (Oxford, England)*, *26*(9), 1169–1175. doi:10.1093/bioinformatics/btq112 PMID:20236947

Bandyopadhyay, S. (2005). An efficient technique for superfamily classification of amino acid sequences: Feature extraction, fuzzy clustering and prototype selection. *Fuzzy Sets and Systems*, *152*(1), 5–16. doi:10.1016/j.fss.2004.10.011

Bandyopadhyay, S., Mallik, S., & Mukhopadhyay, A. (2014). A survey and comparative study of statistical tests for identifying differential expression from microarray data. *IEEE/ACM Transactions on Computational Biology and Bioinformatics*, *11*(1), 95–115. doi:10.1109/TCBB.2013.147 PMID:26355511

Banitt, I., & Wolfson, H. J. (2011). ParaDock: A flexible non-specific DNArigid protein docking algorithm. *Nucleic Acids Research*, *39*(20), e135. doi:10.1093/nar/gkr620 PMID:21835777

Bankes, S. C. (2002). Agent-based modeling: A revolution? *Paper presented at the National Academy of Sciences of the United States of America*.

Banwait, J. K., & Bastola, D. R. (2015). Contribution of bioinformatics prediction in microRNA-based cancer therapeutics. *Advanced Drug Delivery Reviews*, *81*, 94–103. doi:10.1016/j.addr.2014.10.030 PMID:25450261

Barabási, A.-L. (2007). Network medicine from obesity to the diseasome. *The New England Journal of Medicine, 357*(4), 404–407. doi:10.1056/NEJMe078114 PMID:17652657

Barabási, A.-L., & Albert, R. (1999). Emergence of Scaling in Random Networks. *Science, 286*(5439), 509–512. doi:10.1126/science.286.5439.509 PMID:10521342

Barabási, A.-L., & Oltvai, Z. N. (2004). Network Biology: Understanding the Cells Functional Organization. *Nature Reviews. Genetics, 5*(2), 101–113. doi:10.1038/nrg1272 PMID:14735121

Barla, A., Jurman, G., Riccadonna, S., Merler, S., Chierici, M., & Furlanello, C. (2008). Machine learning methods for predictive proteomics. *Briefings in Bioinformatics, 9*(2), 119–128. doi:10.1093/bib/bbn008 PMID:18310105

Bartoli, L., Fariselli, P., Krogh, A., & Casadio, R. (2009). CCHMM_PROF: A HMM-based coiled-coil predictor with evolutionary information. *Bioinformatics (Oxford, England), 25*(21), 2757–2763. doi:10.1093/bioinformatics/btp539 PMID:19744995

Beaudouin, R., Micallef, S., & Brochot, C. (2010). A stochastic whole-body physiologically based pharmacokinetic model to assess the impact of inter-individual variability on tissue dosimetry over the human lifespan. *Regulatory Toxicology and Pharmacology, 57*(1), 103–116. doi:10.1016/j.yrtph.2010.01.005 PMID:20122977

Becker, J., Maes, F., Wehenkel, L., Anfinsen, C., Matsumura, M., & Signor, G., … Frasconi, P. (2013). On the Relevance of Sophisticated Structural Annotations for Disulfide Connectivity Pattern Prediction. *PLoS ONE, 8*(2). doi:10.1371/journal.pone.0056621

Bekkers, W., & Spruit, M. (2010, September 27). The Situational Assessment Method Put to the Test: Improvements Based on Case Studies. *Proceedings of the 4th International Workshop on Software Product Management*, Sydney, Australia (pp. 7–16). doi:10.1109/IWSPM.2010.5623871

Belacel, N., Čuperlović-Culf, M., Laflamme, M., & Ouellette, R. (2004). Fuzzy J-Means and VNS methods for clustering genes from microarray data. *Bioinformatics (Oxford, England), 20*(11), 1690–1701. doi:10.1093/bioinformatics/bth142 PMID:14988127

Belcaid, M., & Toonen, R. J. (2015). Demystifying computer science for molecular ecologists. *Molecular Ecology, 24*(11), 2619–2640. doi:10.1111/mec.13175 PMID:25824671

Ben-Bassat, M. (1982). Pattern recognition and reduction of dimensionality. Handbook of Statistics, 2, 773-910.

Ben-Dor, A., Shamir, R., & Yakhini, Z. (1999). Clustering gene expression patterns. *Journal of Computational Biology, 63*(3/4), 281–297. doi:10.1089/106652799318274 PMID:10582567

Benkert, P., Tosatto, S. C. E., & Schomburg, D. (2008). QMEAN: A comprehensive scoring function for model quality assessment. *Proteins: Structure, Function, and Bioinformatics, 71*(1), 261–277. doi:10.1002/prot.21715

Berendsen, H. J. C., van der Spoel, D., & van Drunen, R. (1995). GROMACS: A message-passing parallel molecular dynamics implementation. *Computer Physics Communications, 91*(1), 43–56. doi:10.1016/0010-4655(95)00042-E

Beutler, E., Dern, R. J., & Alving, A. S. (1955). The hemolytic effect of premaquine. VI. An invitro test for sensitivity of erythrocytes to premaquine. *The Journal of Laboratory and Clinical Medicine, 45*, 40–50. PMID:13233626

BGI. (2016) Retrieved from http://www.bgi.com/

Bhattacharya, A., Tejero, R., & Montelione, G. T. (2006). Evaluating protein structures determined by structural genomics consortia. *Proteins: Structure, Function, and Bioinformatics, 66*(4), 778–795. doi:10.1002/prot.21165

Bhattacharya, D., Nowotny, J., Cao, R., & Cheng, J. (2016). 3Drefine: An interactive web server for efficient protein structure refinement. *Nucleic Acids Research, 44*(W1), W406–W409. doi:10.1093/nar/gkw336 PMID:27131371

Biasini, M., Bienert, S., & Waterhouse, A. (2014). SWISS-MODEL: modelling protein tertiary and quaternary structure using evolutionary information. *Nucleic Acids*. Retrieved from http://nar.oxfordjournals.org/content/early/2014/04/29/nar.gku340.short

Blanco, M. A., Leroy, G., Khan, Z., Aleckovic, M., Zee, B. M., Garcia, B. A., & Kang, Y. (2012). Global secretome analysis identifies novel mediators of bone metastasis. *Cell Research, 22*(9), 1339–1355. doi:10.1038/cr.2012.89 PMID:22688892

Blanke, C. A. (2015). The (Big) Data-security assemblage: Knowledge and critique. *Big Data & Society*.

Blankenbecler, R., Ohlsson, M., Peterson, C., & Ringner, M. (2003). Matching protein structures with fuzzy alignments. *Paper presented at the Proceedings of the National Academy of Sciences of the United States of America.*

Blaszczyk, M., Jamroz, M., Kmiecik, S., & Kolinski, A. (2013). CABS-fold: Server for the de novo and consensus-based prediction of protein structure. *Nucleic Acids Research, 41*(W1), W406–W411. doi:10.1093/nar/gkt462 PMID:23748950

Blum, A., & Mitchell, T. (1998). Combining labeled and unlabeled data with co-training. *Proceedings of the eleventh annual conference on Computational learning theory*, 92–100. doi:10.1145/279943.279962

Bois, F. Y., Jamei, M., & Clewell, H. J. (2010). PBPK modelling of inter-individual variability in the pharmacokinetics of environmental chemicals. *Toxicology, 278*(3), 256–267. doi:10.1016/j.tox.2010.06.007 PMID:20600548

Bollen, J., Mao, H., & Zeng, X. J. (2011). Twitter mood predicts the stock market. *Journal of Computational Science, 2*(1), 1–8. doi:10.1016/j.jocs.2010.12.007

Bollobas, B. (2016). *Modern Graph Theory*. Springer. Retrieved from http://www.springer.com/gp/book/9780387984889

Börner, J., Buchinger, S., & Schomburg, D. (2007). A high-throughput method for microbial metabolome analysis using gas chromatography/mass spectrometry. *Analytical Biochemistry, 367*(2), 143–151. doi:10.1016/j.ab.2007.04.036 PMID:17585867

Bowers, K., Chow, E., Xu, H., Dror, R., Eastwood, M., & Gregersen, B. … Shaw, D. (2006). Scalable Algorithms for Molecular Dynamics Simulations on Commodity Clusters. *Proceedings of ACM/IEEE SC 2006 Conference (SC'06)* (pp. 43–43). IEEE. doi:10.1109/SC.2006.54

Bradford, J. R., & Westhead, D. R. (2005). Improved prediction of protein-protein binding sites using a support vector machines approach. *Bioinformatics (Oxford, England), 21*(8), 1487–1494. doi:10.1093/bioinformatics/bti242 PMID:15613384

Brasil. Estatuto da Criança e do Adolescente (ECA). (2012). *Lei Federal nº 8069, de 13 de julho de 1990*. Brasília: Câmara dos Deputados, Edições Câmara.

Brasil. Instituto Brasileiro de Geografia e Estatística (IBGE). Censo demográfico 2010. (2013). Disponível em: http://7a12.ibge.gov.br/vamos-conhecer-o-brasil/nosso-povo/caracteristicas-da-populacao

Breiman, L. (1996). Bagging predictors. *Machine Learning, 24*(2), 123–140. doi:10.1007/BF00058655

Breiman, L. (1998). Arcing classifiers (with discussion). *Annals of Statistics, 26*(3), 801–849. doi:10.1214/aos/1024691079

Breiman, L. (2001). Random forests. *Machine Learning, 45*(1), 5–32. doi:10.1023/A:1010933404324

Breiman, L., Friedman, J. H., Olshen, R. A., & Stone, C. J. (1984). *Classification And Regression Trees*. New York: Chapman and Hall.

Breiman, L., Friedman, J., Olsen, R., & Stone, C. (1984). *Classification and Regression Trees*. California.

Brett Hannan, X. Z. (2014, August 11-14). iHANDs: Intelligent Health Advising and Decision-Support Agent. *Proceedings of the 2014 IEEE/WIC/ACM International Joint Conferences on Web Intelligence (WI) and Intelligent Agent Technologies (IAT)* (Vol. 3, pp. 294 – 301).

Broderick, J. A., & Zamore, P. D. (2011). MicroRNA therapeutics. *Gene Therapy*, *18*(12), 1104–1110. doi:10.1038/gt.2011.50 PMID:21525952

Bron, C., & Kerbosch, J. (1973). Algorithm 457: Finding all cliques of an undirected graph. *Communications of the ACM*, *16*(9), 575–577. doi:10.1145/362342.362367

Brooks, B. R., Brooks, C. L., Mackerell, A. D., Nilsson, L., Petrella, R. J., & Roux, B. … Karplus, M. (2009). CHARMM: The biomolecular simulation program. *Journal of Computational Chemistry, 30*(10), 1545–1614. doi:10.1002/jcc.21287

Brooks, B. R., Bruccoleri, R. E., Olafson, B. D., States, D. J., Swaminathan, S., & Karplus, M. (1983). CHARMM: A program for macromolecular energy, minimization, and dynamics calculations. *Journal of Computational Chemistry*, *4*(2), 187–217. doi:10.1002/jcc.540040211

Brown, D. G. (2006). In H. Geist (Ed.), *The Earth's changing land: An encyclopaedia of land-use and land-cover change Agent-based models* (pp. 7–13). Greenwood Publishing Group.

Brusic, V., Marina, O., Wu, C. J., & Reinherz, E. L. (2007). Proteome informatics for cancer research: From molecules to clinic. *Proteomics*, *7*(6), 976–991. doi:10.1002/pmic.200600965 PMID:17370257

Buchan, D. W. A., Ward, S. M., Lobley, A. E., Nugent, T. C. O., Bryson, K., & Jones, D. T. (2010). Protein annotation and modelling servers at University College London. *Nucleic Acids Research, 38*(Web Server issue), W563-8. doi:10.1093/nar/gkq427

Buettner, V. L., Hill, K. A., Halangoda, A., & Sommer, S. S. (1999). Tandem-based mutations occur in mouse liver and adipose tissue preferentially as G:C to T: A transversions and accumulate with age. *Environmental and Molecular Mutagenesis*, *33*(4), 320–324. doi:10.1002/(SICI)1098-2280(1999)33:4<320::AID-EM9>3.0.CO;2-S PMID:10398380

Buneman, P. (1997). *Semistructured Data. Department of Computer and Information Science*. University of Pennsylvania.

Burges, C. J. C. (1998). A tutorial on support vector machines for pattern recognition. *Data Mining and Knowledge Discovery*, *2*(2), 121–167. doi:10.1023/A:1009715923555

Burnside, E., Rubin, D., & Shachter, R. (2000) A Bayesian Network for Mammography. *Proceedings of the American Medical Informatics Association*, 106-110.

Caboche, S. (2013). LeView: Automatic and interactive generation of 2D diagrams for biomacromolecule/ligand interactions. *Journal of Cheminformatics*, *5*(1), 40. doi:10.1186/1758-2946-5-40 PMID:23988161

Caccia, D., Dugo, M., Callari, M., & Bongarzone, I. (2013). Bioinformatics tools for secretome analysis. *Biochimica et Biophysica Acta (BBA). Proteins and Proteomics*, *1834*(11), 2442–2453. doi:10.1016/j.bbapap.2013.01.039

Campos, L. M. (2010). Combining content-based and collaborative recommendations: A hybrid approach based on Bayesian networks. *International Journal of Approximate Reasoning*, *51*(7), 785–799. doi:10.1016/j.ijar.2010.04.001

Cannataro, M., Guzzi, P. H., & Sarica, A. (2013). Data mining and life sciences applications on the grid. *Data Mining and Knowledge Discovery*, *3*(3), 216–238.

Cannataro, M., & Veltri, P. (2007). MS-Analyzer: Preprocessing and data mining services for proteomics applications on the Grid. *Concurrency and Computation*, *19*(15), 2047–2066. doi:10.1002/cpe.1144

Carleos, C., Rodriguez, F., Lamelas, H., & Baro, J. A. (2003). Simulating complex traits influenced by genes with fuzzy-valued effects in pedigreed populations. *Bioinformatics (Oxford, England), 19*(1), 144–148. doi:10.1093/bioinformatics/19.1.144 PMID:12499304

Carneiro, H. A., & Mylonakis, E. (2009). Google Trends. A web-based tool for real-time surveillance of disease outbreaks. *Clinical Infectious Diseases, 49*(10), 15557–15564. doi:10.1086/630200 PMID:19845471

Carpenter, E. P., Beis, K., Cameron, A. D., & Iwata, S. (2008). Overcoming the challenges of membrane protein crystallography. *Current Opinion in Structural Biology.* doi:10.1016/j.sbi.2008.07.001

Carroll, A. P., Goodall, G. J., & Liu, B. (2014). Understanding principles of miRNA target recognition and function through integrated biological and bioinformatics approaches. *Wiley Interdisciplinary Reviews: RNA, 5*(3), 361–379. doi:10.1002/wrna.1217 PMID:24459110

Carroll, S. B. (2000). Endless Forms: The Evolution of Gene Regulation and Morphological Diversity. *Cell, 101*(6), 577–580. doi:10.1016/S0092-8674(00)80868-5 PMID:10892643

Centre for Medicare & Medicaid services. (2011). The Medicare EHR Incentive Program. Retrieved from https://www.cms.gov/Regulations-and-Guidance/Legislation/EHRIncentivePrograms/index.html?redirect=/EHRIncentivePrograms/30_Mean-ingful_Use.asp

Ceroni, A., Passerini, A., Vullo, A., & Frasconi, P. (2006). DISULFIND: a disulfide bonding state and cysteine connectivity prediction server. *Nucleic Acids Research, 34*(Web Server issue), W177-81. doi:10.1093/nar/gkl266

Chandrashekar, R. M. K. (2015). Integration of Big Data in Cloud computing environments for enhanced data processing capabilities. *International Journal of Engineering Research and General Science, 3*(3 Part 2), 2091–2730.

Chang, B., & Halgamuge, S. K. (2002). Protein motif extraction with neuro-fuzzy optimization. *Bioinformatics (Oxford, England), 18*(8), 1084–1090. doi:10.1093/bioinformatics/18.8.1084 PMID:12176831

Changqing Ji, Y. L. (2012). Big Data Processing in Cloud Computing Environments. *Proceedings of the 2012 International Symposium on Pervasive Systems, Algorithms and Networks.*

Chapelle, O., Scholkopf, B., & Zien, A. (2006). *Semi-Supervised Learning.* Cambridge, MA: MIT Press. doi:10.7551/mitpress/9780262033589.001.0001

Chaves, S. (2011). The Risks Issue in Cloud Computing. doi:10.2139/ssrn.1991156

Chen J, Qian F, Yan W, et al. (2013). Translational biomedical informatics in the cloud: present and future. *Biomed Res Int.*

Chen J, Qian F, Yan W. (2013). Translational biomedical informatics in the cloud: present and future. *Biomed Res Int.* 658925.

Chen, C.-C., Chang, Y.-J., Chung, W.-C., Lee, D.-T., & Ho, J.-M. (2013). CloudRS: an error correction algorithm of high-throughput sequencing data based on scalable framework. *Proceedings of the IEEE International Conference on Big Data,* Santa Clara, California (pp. 717–722). doi:10.1109/BigData.2013.6691642

Chen, V. B., Arendall, W. B., Headd, J. J., Keedy, D. A., Immormino, R. M., & Kapral, G. J. … Richardson, D. C. (2010). MolProbity: All-atom structure validation for macromolecular crystallography. *Acta Crystallographica Section D: Biological Crystallography, 66*(1), 12–21. doi:10.1107/S0907444909042073

Cheng, J., Randall, A. Z., Sweredoski, M. J., & Baldi, P. (2005). SCRATCH: a protein structure and structural feature prediction server. *Nucleic Acids Research, 33*(Web Server issue), W72-6. doi:10.1093/nar/gki396

Cheng, J., Saigo, H., & Baldi, P. (2005). Large-scale prediction of disulphide bridges using kernel methods, two-dimensional recursive neural networks, and weighted graph matching. *Proteins: Structure, Function, and Bioinformatics, 62*(3), 617–629. https://doi.org/10.1002/prot.20787

Chen, K. H., Wang, K. J., Tsai, M. L., Wang, K. M., Adrian, A. M., Cheng, W. C., & Chang, K. S. (2014). Gene selection for cancer identification: A decision tree model empowered by particle swarm optimization algorithm. *BMC Bioinformatics, 15*(1), 1–12. doi:10.1186/1471-2105-15-49 PMID:24555567

Chen, L., Weixing, S., Sheng, S., & Zhilong, A. (2013). Gene expression patterns combined with bioinformatics analysis identify genes associated with cholangiocarcinoma. *Computational Biology and Chemistry, 47*, 192–197. doi:10.1016/j.compbiolchem.2013.08.010 PMID:24140882

Chen, Q. F., & Chen, Y. P. P. (2006). Mining frequent patterns for AMP-activated protein regulation on skeletal muscle. *BMC Bioinformatics, 7*(394), 1–14. PMID:16939655

Chen, Q., & Deng, Q. (2009). Cloud computing and its key techniques. *Journal of Computer Applications, 29*(9), 2562–2567. doi:10.3724/SP.J.1087.2009.02562

Chen, Q., Luo, H., Zhang, C., & Chen, Y. P. P. (2015). Bioinformatics in protein kinases regulatory network and drug discovery. *Mathematical Biosciences, 262*, 147–156. doi:10.1016/j.mbs.2015.01.010 PMID:25656386

Cheok, M. H., Yang, W., Pui, C. H., Downing, J. R., Cheng, C., Naeve, C. W., & Evans, W. E. (2003). Treatment-specific changes in gene expression discriminate in vivo drug response in human leukemia cells. *Nature Genetics, 34*(1), 85–90. doi:10.1038/ng1151 PMID:12704389

Chertien, C., & Kind, T. (2013). Social Media and clinical care: Ethical, professional and social implications. *Circulation, 127*(13), 1413–1421. doi:10.1161/CIRCULATIONAHA.112.128017 PMID:23547180

Chew, C., & Eysenbach, G. (2010). Pandemics in the age of Twitter: Content analysis of tweets during the 2009 H1N1 outbreak. *PLoS ONE, 5*(11), e14118. doi:10.1371/journal.pone.0014118 PMID:21124761

Choi, Y., & Cardie, C. (2009). Adapting a polarity lexicon using integer linear programming for domain-specific sentiment classification. *Proceedings of the 2009 Conference on Empirical Methods in Natural Language Processing* (pp. 590–598). doi:10.3115/1699571.1699590

Chong, C. R., & Sullivan, D. J. (2007). New uses for old drugs. *Nature, 448*(7154), 645–646. doi:10.1038/448645a PMID:17687303

Cho, S., Sohn, C. H., Jo, M. W., Shin, S. Y., Lee, J. H., Ryoo, S. M., & Seo, D.-W. et al. (2013). Correlation between national influenza surveillance data and Google trends in South Korea. *PLoS ONE, 8*(12), e81422. doi:10.1371/journal.pone.0081422 PMID:24339927

Chou, P. Y., & Fasman, G. D. (1974). Prediction of protein conformation. *Biochemistry, 13*(2), 222–245. doi:10.1021/bi00699a002 PMID:4358940

Chow, T. W., & Huang, D. (2005). Estimating optimal feature subsets using efficient estimation of high-dimensional mutual information. *IEEE Transactions on Neural Networks, 16*(1), 213–224. doi:10.1109/TNN.2004.841414 PMID:15732401

Christodoulou, C. I., Pattichis, C. S., Kyriacou, E., & Nicolaides, A. (2010). Image retrieval and classification of carotid plaque ultrasound images. The Open Cardiovascular Imaging Journal, 2, 18-28.

Chuang, L. Y., Yang, C. H., Wu, K. C., & Yang, C. H. (2011). A hybrid feature selection method for DNA microarray data. *Computers in Biology and Medicine, 41*(4), 228–237. doi:10.1016/j.compbiomed.2011.02.004 PMID:21376310

Chui, K.T., Tsang, K.F., Wu, C.K., Hung, F.H., Chi, H.R., Chung, H.S.H., & Ko, K.T. et al. (2015). Cardiovascular disease identification using electrocardiogram health identifier based on multiple criteria decision making. *Expert Systems with Applications*, *42*(13), 5684–5695. doi:10.1016/j.eswa.2015.01.059

Clements, P., & Northrop, L. (2002). *Software product lines: Practices and patterns*. Boston, MA: Addison–Wesley.

Cohen, P. (2002). Protein kinases: The major drug targets of the twenty-first century? *Nature Reviews. Drug Discovery*, *1*(4), 309–315. doi:10.1038/nrd773 PMID:12120282

Coissac, E., Riaz, T., & Puillandre, N. (2012). Bioinformatic challenges for DNA metabarcoding of plants and animals. *Molecular Ecology*, *21*(8), 1834–1847. doi:10.1111/j.1365-294X.2012.05550.x PMID:22486822

Collier, N. (2012). Uncovering text mining: A survey of current work on web-based epidemic intelligence. *Global Public Health: An International Journal for Research, Policy and Practice*, *7*(7), 731–749. doi:10.1080/17441692.2012.6999 75 PMID:22783909

Collier, N., Doan, S., Kawazeo, A., Goodwin, R., Conway, M., Tateno, Y., & Taniguchi, K. et al. (2008). BioCaster: Detecting public health rumors with a web-based text mining system. *Bioinformatics (Oxford, England)*, *24*(24), 2940–2941. doi:10.1093/bioinformatics/btn534 PMID:18922806

Combet, C., Jambon, M., Deléage, G., & Geourjon, C. (2002). Geno3D: Automatic comparative molecular modelling of protein. *Bioinformatics (Oxford, England)*, *18*(1), 213–214. doi:10.1093/bioinformatics/18.1.213 PMID:11836238

Comeau, S. R., Gatchell, D. W., Vajda, S., & Camacho, C. J. (2004). ClusPro: a fully automated algorithm for protein-protein docking. *Nucleic Acids Research, 32*(Web Server issue), W96-9. Doi:<ALIGNMENT.qj></ALIGNMENT>10.1093/nar/gkh354

Congreve, M., Carr, R., Murray, C., & Jhoti, H. (2003). A rule of three for fragment-based lead discovery? *Drug Discovery Today*, *8*(19), 876–877. Retrieved from http://www.ncbi.nlm.nih.gov/pubmed/14554012 doi:10.1016/S1359-6446(03)02831-9 PMID:14554012

Cook, S., Conrad, C., Fowlkes, A.L., & Mohebbi, M.H. (2011). Assessing Google flu trends performance in the United States during the 2009 Influenza virus A (H1N1) pandemic. *PLoS ONE*, *6*(8), e23610. doi:10.1371/journal.pone.0023610 PMID:21886802

Cordón, O., Gomide, F., Herrera, F., Hoffmann, F., & Magdalena, L. (2004). Ten years of genetic fuzzy systems: Current framework and new trends. *Fuzzy Sets and Systems*, *141*(1), 5–31. doi:10.1016/S0165-0114(03)00111-8

Cornuejols, A., & Miclet, L. (2010). *Apprentissage artificiel: Concepts et algorithmes*. Eyrolles.

Costa, L.D.F., Rodrigues, F.A., Travieso, G., & Villas Boas, P.R. (2007). Characterization of Complex Networks: A Survey of Measurements. *Advances in Physics, 56*(1), 167–242. doi:10.1080/00018730601170527

Costa, G. C. B., Braga, R., David, J. M. N., & Campos, F. (2015). A scientific software product line for the bioinformatics domain. *Journal of Biomedical Informatics*, *56*, 239–264. doi:10.1016/j.jbi.2015.05.014 PMID:26079262

Costa, M. C. O., & de Souza, R. P. (2002). *Adolescência: Aspectos clínicos e psicossociais*. Porto Alegre: Artmed Editora.

Couclelis, H. (2001). Why I no longer work with agents: A challenge for ABMs of human-environment interactions. *Paper presented at the Proceeding of Special Workshop on Land-Use/Land-Cover Change.*

Courcelles, M., Lemieux, S., Voisin, L., Meloche, S., & Thibault, P. (2011). ProteoConnections: A bioinformatics platform to facilitate proteome and phosphoproteome analyses. *Proteomics*, *11*(13), 2654–2671. doi:10.1002/pmic.201000776 PMID:21630457

Crespin, J., & Reato, L. F. N. (2007). *Hebiatria: Medicina da Adolescência*. São Paulo: Rocco.

Cserzö, M., Eisenhaber, F., Eisenhaber, B., & Simon, I. (2002). On filtering false positive transmembrane protein predictions. *Protein Engineering*, *15*(9), 745–752. doi:10.1093/protein/15.9.745 PMID:12456873

Cukuroglu, E., Engin, H. B., Gursoy, A., & Keskin, O. (2014). Hot spots in protein–protein interfaces: Towards drug discovery. *Progress in Biophysics and Molecular Biology*, *116*(2–3), 165–173. doi:10.1016/j.pbiomolbio.2014.06.003 PMID:24997383

Culotta, A. (2010). Towards detecting Influenza epidemics by analyzing Twitter messages. *Proceedings of the First Workshop on Social Media Analytics* (pp. 1515-1521). doi:10.1145/1964858.1964874

Czarnecki, K., Kim, C. H. P., & Kalleberg, K. T. (2006). *Feature models are views on ontologies*. Paper presented at the 10th International on Software Product Line Conference (SPLC 2006), Washington, DC. doi:10.1109/SPLINE.2006.1691576

Dai, W., Brisimi, T. S., Adams, W. G., Mela, T., Saligrama, V., & Ch, I. (2015). Prediction of Hospitalization Due to Heart Diseases by Supervised Learning Methods. *International Journal of Medical Informatics*, *84*(3), 189–197. doi:10.1016/j.ijmedinf.2014.10.002 PMID:25497295

Dalpé, G., & Joly, Y. (2014). Opportunities and challenges provided by cloud repositories for bioinformatics-enabled drug discovery. *Drug Development Research*, *75*(6), 393–401. doi:10.1002/ddr.21211 PMID:25195583

Dan Foresee, F., & Hagan, M. T. (1997, June 9-12). Gauss-Newton approximation to Bayesian learning. *Paper presented at the International Conference on Neural Networks*.

Dasgupta, A., & Raftery, A. E. (1998). Detecting features in spatial point processes with clutter via model-based clustering. *Journal of the American Statistical Association*, *93*(441), 294–302. doi:10.1080/01621459.1998.10474110

Das, S., Abraham, A., & Konar, A. (2008). Swarm intelligence algorithms in bioinformatics. In *Computational Intelligence in Bioinformatics* (pp. 113–147). Springer Berlin Heidelberg. doi:10.1007/978-3-540-76803-6_4

Das, S., & Suganthan, P. N. (2011). Differential evolution: A survey of the state-of-the-art. *IEEE Transactions on Evolutionary Computation*, *15*(1), 4–31. doi:10.1109/TEVC.2010.2059031

Dastmalchi, S., Beheshti, S., Morris, M. B., & Bret Church, W. (2007). Prediction of rotational orientation of transmembrane helical segments of integral membrane proteins using new environment-based propensities for amino acids derived from structural analyses. *The FEBS Journal*, *274*(10), 2653–2660. doi:10.1111/j.1742-4658.2007.05800.x PMID:17451441

de Castro, A. K. A. (2008). Um Modelo Híbrido Aplicado ao Diagnóstico da Doença de Alzheimer. (Dissertação). Universidade de Fortaleza, Fortaleza.

De Castro, A. K. A., Pinheiro, P. R., & Pinheiro, M. C. D. (2007). Applying a Decision Making Model in the Early Diagnosis of Alzheimers Disease. *Lecture Notes in Computer Science*, *4481*, 149–156. doi:10.1007/978-3-540-72458-2_18

De Castro, A. K. A., Pinheiro, P. R., & Pinheiro, M. C. D. (2009). An Approach for the Neuropsychological Diagnosis of Alzheimers Disease: A Hybrid Model in Decision Making. *Lecture Notes in Computer Science*, *5589*, 216–223. doi:10.1007/978-3-642-02962-2_27

De Castro, A. K. A., Pinheiro, P. R., Pinheiro, M. C. D., & Tamanini, I. (2011). Towards the Applied Hybrid Model in Decision Making: A Neuropsychological Diagnosis of Alzheimers Disease Study Case. *International Journal of Computational Intelligence Systems*, *4*(1), 89–99. doi:10.1080/18756891.2011.9727766

de Koning, A.P., Gu, W., Castoe, T.A., Bazter, M.A., & Pollock, D. D. (2011). Repetitive Elements May Comprise Over Two-Thirds of the Human Genome. *PLOS Genetics, 7*(12). doi:10.1371/journal.pgen.1002384 de Nazelle, A., Seto, E., Donaire-Gonzalez, D., Mendez, M., Matamala, J., Nieuwenhuijsen, M. J., & Jerrett, M. (2013). Improving estimates of air pollution exposure through ubiquitous sensing technologies. *Environmental Pollution, 176*, 92–99. doi:10.1016/j.envpol.2012.12.032 PMID:23416743

De Quincey, E. M., & Kostkova, P. (2009). Early warning and outbreak detection using social networking websites: The potential of Twitter, electronic healthcare. *Proceedings of 2nd International e-Health Conference.*

De Smet, F., Mathys, J., Marchal, K., Thijs, G., De Moor, B., & Moreau, Y. (2002). Adaptive quality-based clustering of gene expression profiles. *Bioinformatics (Oxford, England), 18*(5), 735–746. doi:10.1093/bioinformatics/18.5.735 PMID:12050070

Dean, J. G. C. (2013). Large Scale Distributed Deep Networks. *Advances in Neural Information Processing Systems.*

Deb, B., & Srirama, S. N. (2013). Social networks for eHealth solutions on cloud. *Frontiers in Genetics, 4*, 171. doi:10.3389/fgene.2013.00171 PMID:24027578

Deligiannis, P., Loidl, H.-W., & Kouidi, E. (2012). Improving the diagnosis of mild hypertrophic cardiomyopathy with MapReduce. *Proceedings of Third International Workshop on MapReduce and its Applications Date*, Delft, Netherlands (pp. 41–48). ACM. doi:10.1145/2287016.2287025

Delorenzi, M., & Speed, T. (2002). An HMM model for coiled-coil domains and a comparison with PSSM-based predictions. *Bioinformatics (Oxford, England), 18*(4), 617–625. Retrieved from http://www.ncbi.nlm.nih.gov/pubmed/12016059 doi:10.1093/bioinformatics/18.4.617 PMID:12016059

DeLuca, D. S., Levin, J. Z., Sivachenko, A., Fennell, T., Nazaire, M.-D., Williams, C., & Getz, G. et al. (2012). RNA-SeQC: RNA-Seq Metrics for Quality Control and Process Optimization. *Bioinformatics (Oxford, England), 28*(11), 1530–1532. doi:10.1093/bioinformatics/bts196 PMID:22539670

Dembele, D., & Kastner, P. (2003). Fuzzy C-means method for clustering microarray data. *Bioinformatics, 19*(8), 973-980.

Dembele, D., & Kastner, P. (2003). Fuzzy C-means method for clustering microarray data. *Bioinformatics (Oxford, England), 19*(8), 973–980. doi:10.1093/bioinformatics/btg119 PMID:12761060

Demsar, J. (2006). Statistical comparisons of classifiers over multiple datasets. *Journal of Machine Learning Research, 7*, 1–30.

Deng, X., Eickholt, J., Cheng, J., Tompa, P., Receveur-Bréchot, V., & Bourhis, J. … McGuffin, L. (2009). PreDisorder: ab initio sequence-based prediction of protein disordered regions. *BMC Bioinformatics, 10*(1), 436. doi:10.1186/1471-2105-10-436

Deng, C., & Guo, M. (2011). A new co-training-style random forest for computer aided diagnosis. *Journal of Intelligent Information Systems, 36*(3), 253–281. doi:10.1007/s10844-009-0105-8

Dennis, J. E. J., & Schnabel, R. B. (1996). *Numerical Methods for Unconstrained Optimization and Nonlinear Equations*: Soc for Industrial &. *Applications of Mathematics.*

Denoeud, F., Aury, J.-M., Da Silva, C., Noel, B., Rogier, O., Delledonne, M., & Artiguenave, F. et al. (2008). Annotating Genomes with Massive-Scale RNA Sequencing. *Genome Biology, 9*(12), R175. doi:10.1186/gb-2008-9-12-r175 PMID:19087247

Desmet, J., De Maeyer, M., Hazes, B., & Lasters, I. (1992). The dead-end elimination theorem and its use in protein side-chain positioning. *Nature, 356*(6369), 539–542. doi:10.1038/356539a0 PMID:21488406

Dhanik, A., & Kavraki, L. E. (2012). Protein-Ligand Interactions: Computational Docking. In eLS. Chichester, UK: John Wiley & Sons, Ltd. Doi:<ALIGNMENT.qj></ALIGNMENT>10.1002/9780470015902.a0004105.pub2

Diagnostic and Statistical Manual of Mental Disorders (DSM). (2013). American Psychiatric Association Publishing.

Diestel, R. (2016). *Graph Theory*. Springer. Retrieved from http://www.springer.com/gp/book/9783642142789

Dieterich, C., & Stadler, P. F. (2013). Computational biology of RNA interactions. *Wiley Interdisciplinary Reviews: RNA*, *4*(1), 107–120. doi:10.1002/wrna.1147 PMID:23139167

Dill, K. A., Ozkan, S. B., Shell, M. S., & Weikl, T. R. (2008). The protein folding problem. *Annual Review of Biophysics*, *37*(1), 289–316. doi:10.1146/annurev.biophys.37.092707.153558 PMID:18573083

Disfani, F. M., Hsu, W.-L., Mizianty, M. J., Oldfield, C. J., Xue, B., & Dunker, A. K. … Kurgan, L. (2012). MoRFpred, a computational tool for sequence-based prediction and characterization of short disorder-to-order transitioning binding regions in proteins. *Bioinformatics (Oxford, England)*, *28*(12), i75-83. doi:10.1093/bioinformatics/bts209

Dobigeon, N., Basarab, A., Kouame, D., & Tourneret, J.-Y. (2012). Regularized bayesian compressed sensing in ultrasound imaging. *IEEE Signal Processing Conference*, 2600-2604.

Dobin, A., Davis, C. A., Schlesinger, F., Drenkow, J., Zaleski, C., Jha, S., & Gingeras, T. R. et al. (2013). STAR: Ultrafast Universal RNA-Seq Aligner. *Bioinformatics (Oxford, England)*, *29*(1), 15–21. doi:10.1093/bioinformatics/bts635 PMID:23104886

Dobson, L., Reményi, I., & Tusnády, G. E. (2015). CCTOP: A Consensus Constrained TOPology prediction web server. *Nucleic Acids Research*, *43*(W1), W408–W412. doi:10.1093/nar/gkv451 PMID:25943549

Dodt, M., Roehr, J. T., Ahmed, R., & Dieterich, C. (2012). FLEXBAR-Flexible Barcode and Adapter Processing for Next-Generation Sequencing Platforms. *Biology*, *1*(3), 895–905. doi:10.3390/biology1030895 PMID:24832523

Doman, T. N., McGovern, S. L., Witherbee, B. J., Kasten, T. P., Kurumbail, R., Stallings, W. C., & Shoichet, B. K. et al. (2002). Molecular Docking and High-Throughput Screening for Novel Inhibitors of Protein Tyrosine Phosphatase-1B. *Journal of Medicinal Chemistry*, *45*(11), 2213–2221. doi:10.1021/jm010548w PMID:12014959

Dominguez, C., Boelens, R., & Bonvin, A. M. (2003). HADDOCK: A Protein—Protein Docking Approach Based on Biochemical or Biophysical Information. Doi:<ALIGNMENT.qj></ALIGNMENT>10.1021/JA026939X

Dominiak, A., Wilkaniec, A., Wroczynski, P., & Adamczyk, A. (2016). Selenium in the Therapy of Neurological Diseases. Where is it Going? *Current Neuropharmacology*, *14*(3), 282–299. doi:10.2174/1570159X14666151223100011 PMID:26549649

Doncheva, N. T., Kacprowski, T., & Albrecht, M. (2012). Recent approaches to the prioritization of candidate disease genes. *Wiley Interdisciplinary Reviews: Systems Biology and Medicine*, *4*(5), 429–442. PMID:22689539

Dong, G., Zhang, X., Wong, L., & Li, J. (1999). CAEP: Classification by aggregating emerging patterns. *Paper presented at the Proceedings of the Second International Conference on Discovery Science*.

Doolittle, R. F. (1994). Convergent evolution: The need to be explicit. *Trends in Biochemical Sciences*, *19*(1), 15–18. Retrieved from http://www.ncbi.nlm.nih.gov/pubmed/8140615 doi:10.1016/0968-0004(94)90167-8 PMID:8140615

Dorn, M. E., Silva, M. B., Buriol, L. S., & Lamb, L. C. (2014). Three-dimensional protein structure prediction: Methods and computational strategies. *Computational Biology and Chemistry*. doi:10.1016/j.compbiolchem.2014.10.001

dos Reis, M. A., Aparicio, R., & Zhang, Y. (2011). Improving Protein Template Recognition by Using Small-Angle X-Ray Scattering Profiles. *Biophysical Journal*, *101*(11), 2770–2781. doi:10.1016/j.bpj.2011.10.046 PMID:22261066

Dosztanyi, Z., Csizmok, V., Tompa, P., & Simon, I. (2005). IUPred: Web server for the prediction of intrinsically unstructured regions of proteins based on estimated energy content. *Bioinformatics (Oxford, England), 21*(16), 3433–3434. doi:10.1093/bioinformatics/bti541 PMID:15955779

Douglas, C., Goulding, R., Farris, L., & Atkinson-grosjean, J. (2011). Socio-cultural characteristics of usability of bioinformatics databases and tools. *Interdisciplinary Science Reviews, 36*(1), 55–71. doi:10.1179/030801811X12941390545726

Doyle, J., & Bryant-Waugh, R. (2000). Epidemiology. In Anorexia Nervosa and Related Eating Disorders in Childhood and Adolescence (2nd ed.). Psychology Press.

Drozdetskiy, A., Cole, C., Procter, J., & Barton, G. J. (2015). JPred4: A protein secondary structure prediction server. *Nucleic Acids Research, 43*(W1), W389-94. doi:10.1093/nar/gkv332 PMID:25883141

Dubes, R. (1988). *Algorithms for Clustering Data.*

Duh, M. S., Walker, A. M., & Ayanian, J. Z. (1998). Epidemiologic interpretation of artificial neural networks. *American Journal of Epidemiology, 147*(12), 1112–1122. doi:10.1093/oxfordjournals.aje.a009409 PMID:9645789

Durbin, R.M., Abecasis, G.R., Altshuler, D.L., Auton, A., Brooks, L.D., …, McVean, G.A. (2010). A map of human genome variation from population-scale sequencing. *Nature, 467*(7319), 1061–1073. doi:10.1038/nature09534

Durrant, J. D., Friedman, A. J., Rogers, K. E., & McCammon, J. A. (2013). Comparing neural-network scoring functions and the state of the art: Applications to common library screening. *Journal of Chemical Information and Modeling, 53*(7), 1726–1735. doi:10.1021/ci400042y PMID:23734946

Eberhart, R. C., & Kennedy, J. (1995, October). A new optimizer using particle swarm theory. *Proceedings of the Sixth International Symposium on Micro Machine and Human Science, 1*, 39-43. doi:10.1109/MHS.1995.494215

Ebina, T., Toh, H., & Kuroda, Y. (2009). Loop-length-dependent SVM prediction of domain linkers for high-throughput structural proteomics. *Biopolymers, 92*(1), 1–8. doi:10.1002/bip.21105 PMID:18844295

Eckerson, W. (2011). Performance Dashboards. Hoboken, New Jersey: John Wiley & Sons Inc.

Eckerson, W., & LaRow, M. (2009). Next Generation Performance Dashboards. *TDWI Research.* Retrieved from http://download.101com.com/pub/tdwi/Files/performance_dashboards092408final2.pdf

Edelman, L. B., Eddy, J. A., & Price, N. D. (2010). In Silico models of cancer. Wiley Interdisciplinary Reviews: Systems Biology and Medicine, 2(4), 438–459. doi:10.1002/wsbm.75

Edginton, A. N., & Ritter, L. (2009). Predicting plasma concentrations of bisphenol A in children younger than 2 years of age after typical feeding schedules, using a physiologically based toxicokinetic model. *Environmental Health Perspectives, 117*(4), 645–652. doi:10.1289/ehp.0800073 PMID:19440506

Efron, B. (1979). Bootstrap methods: Another look at the jackknife. *Annals of Statistics, 7*(1), 1–26. doi:10.1214/aos/1176344552

Eisenberg, D., Lüthy, R., & Bowie, J. U. (1997). VERIFY3D: Assessment of protein models with three-dimensional profiles. *Methods in Enzymology, 277*, 396–404. Retrieved from doi:10.1016/S0076-6879(97)77022-8 PMID:9379925

Eissing, T., Kuepfer, L., Becker, C., Block, M., Coboeken, K., Gaub, T., . . . Lippert, J. (2011). A computational systems biology software platform for multiscale modeling and simulation: Integrating whole-body physiology, disease biology, and molecular reaction networks. *Frontiers in Physiology, FEB.*

Elena, C. (2011). Business intelligence. *Journal of knowledge management, economics and information technology, 2*, 32-44.

Elyasigomari, V., Mirjafari, M. S., Screen, H. R. C., & Shaheed, M. H. (2015). Cancer classification using a novel gene selection approach by means of shuffling based on data clustering with optimization. *Applied Soft Computing, 35*, 43–51. doi:10.1016/j.asoc.2015.06.015

Emily, M., Talvas, A., Delamarche, C., Jiménez, J., Guijarro, J., & Orlova, E. …Chiti, F. (2013). MetAmyl: A METa-Predictor for AMYLoid Proteins. *PLoS ONE, 8*(11). doi:10.1371/journal.pone.0079722

Erdös, P., & Rényi, A. (1959). On Random Graphs, I. *Publicationes Mathematicae (Debrecen), 6*, 290–297.

Erixon, P., & Oxelman, B. (2008). Whole-gene positive selection, elevated synonymous substitution rates, duplication, and indel evolution of the chloroplast clpP1 gene. PLoS ONE, 3(1). doi:10.1371/journal.pone.0001386

Erlanson, D. A., Fesik, S. W., Hubbard, R. E., Jahnke, W., & Jhoti, H. (2016). Twenty years on: The impact of fragments on drug discovery. *Nature Reviews. Drug Discovery, 15*(9), 605–619. doi:10.1038/nrd.2016.109 PMID:27417849

Espino, J. U., Hogan, W. R., & Wagner, M. M. (2003). Telephone triage: A timely data source for surveillance of Influenza-like diseases. *Proceedings of the AMIA Annual Symposium.*

Esuli, A., & Sebastiani, F. (2006). Sentiwordnet: A publicly available lexical resource for opinion mining. *Proceedings of the 5th Conference on Language Resources and Evaluation* (pp. 417-422).

Eswar, N., John, B., Mirkovic, N., Fiser, A., Ilyin, V. A., & Pieper, U. … Sali, A. (2003). Tools for comparative protein structure modeling and analysis. *Nucleic Acids Research, 31*(13), 3375–80. doi:10.1093/NAR/GKG543

Ettredge, M., Gerdes, J., & Karuga, G. (2005). Using web-based search data to predict macroeconomic statistics. *Communications of the ACM, 48*(11), 87–92. doi:10.1145/1096000.1096010

European Bioinformatics Institute (EBI). (2016) Retrieved from http://www.ebi.ac.uk/

European Bioinformatics Institute (EBI). (2016). Retrieved November 21, 2016, from http://www.ebi.ac.uk/

Ewing, T. J. A., Makino, S., Skillman, A. G., & Kuntz, I. D. (2001). DOCK 4.0: Search strategies for automated molecular docking of flexible molecule databases. *Journal of Computer-Aided Molecular Design, 15*(5), 411–428. doi:10.1023/A:1011115820450 PMID:11394736

Eysenbach, G. (2006). Infodemiology: Tracking flu-related searches on the web for syndromic surveillance. *Proceedings of the AMIA Annual Symposium* (pp. 244-248).

Fahmy, A., & Wagner, G. (2011). Optimization of van der Waals energy for protein side-chain placement and design. *Biophysical Journal, 101*(7), 1690–1698. doi:10.1016/j.bpj.2011.07.052 PMID:21961595

Faloutsos, M., Faloutsos, P., & Faloutsos, C. (1999). On Power-Law Relationships of the Internet Topology. *Proceedings of the Conference on Applications, Technologies, Architectures, and Protocols for Computer Communication SIGCOMM '99* (pp. 251–262). New York, NY, USA: ACM. doi:10.1145/316188.316229

Fan, X., & Kurgan, L. (2014). Accurate prediction of disorder in protein chains with a comprehensive and empirically designed consensus. *Journal of Biomolecular Structure and Dynamics*. Retrieved from http://www.tandfonline.com/doi/abs/10.1080/07391102.2013.775969

Fang, X., & Zhang, J. (2015). Sentiment analysis using product review data. *Journal of Big Data, 2*(5), 1–14.

Fariselli, P., Riccobelli, P., & Casadio, R. (1999). Role of evolutionary information in predicting the disulfide-bonding state of cysteine in proteins. *Proteins, 36*(3), 340–346. Retrieved from http://www.ncbi.nlm.nih.gov/pubmed/10409827 doi:10.1002/(SICI)1097-0134(19990815)36:3<340::AID-PROT8>3.0.CO;2-D PMID:10409827

FASTX-Toolkit. (2016). Retrieved from http://hannonlab.cshl.edu/fastx_toolkit/

Fayyad, U. M., Piatetsky-Shapiro, G., & Smyth, P. (1996). Knowledge Discovery and Data Mining: Towards a Unifying Framework. *Paper presented at the Proceedings of the Second International Conference on Knowledge Discovery and Data Mining.*

Feng, J. X., Onafeso, B., & Liu, E. (2016). *Computer and Information Technology; Ubiquitous Computing and Communications; Dependable, Autonomic and Secure Computing.* Pervasive Intelligence and Computing.

Fenstermacher, D. (2005). Introduction to bioinformatics. *Journal of the American Society for Information Science and Technology, 56*(5), 440–446. doi:10.1002/asi.20133

Fenton, N. E., Neil, M., & Caballero, J. G. (2007). Using Ranked nodes to model qualitative judgments in Bayesian Networks. *IEEE Transactions on Knowledge and Data Engineering, 19*(10), 1420–1432. doi:10.1109/TKDE.2007.1073

Ferrè, F., & Clote, P. (2005). DiANNA: a web server for disulfide connectivity prediction. *Nucleic Acids Research, 33*(Web Server issue), W230-2. doi.org/10.1093/nar/gki412

Few, S. (2006). *Information Dashboard Design. The Effective Visual Communication of Data. Californica.* O'Reilly.

Fiates, G.M.R., & Salles, R.K. (2001). Fatores de Risco para o Desenvolvimento de distúrbios alimentares: Um Estudo em universitárias. *Revista de Nutrição, 14*(3), 3-6.

Fiehn, O. (2002). Metabolomics–the link between genotypes and phenotypes. *Plant Molecular Biology, 48*(1/2), 155–171. doi:10.1023/A:1013713905833 PMID:11860207

Fields, S., & Song, O. (1989). A Novel Genetic System to Detect Protein-Protein Interactions. *Nature, 340*(6230), 245–246. doi:10.1038/340245a0 PMID:2547163

Fischer, D., Lin, S. L., Wolfson, H. L., & Nussinov, R. (1995). A Geometry-based Suite of Molecular Docking Processes. *Journal of Molecular Biology, 248*(2), 459–477. doi:10.1016/S0022-2836(95)80063-8 PMID:7739053

Fiser, A. (2010). Template-based protein structure modeling. *Methods in Molecular Biology (Clifton, N.J.), 673*, 73–94. doi:10.1007/978-1-60761-842-3_6 PMID:20835794

Fiser, A., & Sali, A. (2003). ModLoop: Automated modeling of loops in protein structures. *Bioinformatics (Oxford, England), 19*(18), 2500–2501. Retrieved from http://www.ncbi.nlm.nih.gov/pubmed/14668246 doi:10.1093/bioinformatics/btg362 PMID:14668246

Flory, P. J. (1941). Molecular Size Distribution in Three Dimensional Polymers. I. Gelation1. *Journal of the American Chemical Society, 63*(11), 3083–3090. doi:10.1021/ja01856a061

Fogel, G., & Corne, D. W. (2003). *Evolutionary computation in bioinformatics.* San Francisco, CA: Morgan Kaufmann Publishers.

Forli, S., Huey, R., Pique, M. E., Sanner, M. F., Goodsell, D. S., & Olson, A. J. (2016). Computational protein–ligand docking and virtual drug screening with the AutoDock suite. *Nature Protocols, 11*(5), 905–919. doi:10.1038/nprot.2016.051 PMID:27077332

Forman, G., & Coehn, I. (2004). Learning from little: Comparison of classifiers given little training. Proceedings of Knowledge Discovery in Databases (pp. 161-172).

Fox, S. J., Li, J., Sing Tan, Y., Nguyen, M. N., Pal, A., & Ouaray, Z. ... Kannan, S. (2016). The Multifaceted Roles of Molecular Dynamics Simulations in Drug Discovery. *Current Pharmaceutical Design, 22*(23), 3585–600. Retrieved from http://www.ncbi.nlm.nih.gov/pubmed/27108593

Fraley, C., & Raftery, A. E. (1998). How many clusters? Which clustering method? Answers via model-based cluster analysis. *The Computer Journal*, *41*(8), 586–588. doi:10.1093/comjnl/41.8.578

Freund, Y., & Schapire, R. (1996). Experiments with a new boosting algorithm. *Paper presented at the Thirteenth National Conference on Machine Learning*.

Freund, Y., Seung, H. S., Shamir, E., & Tishby, N. (1997). Selective sampling using the query by committee algorithm. *Machine Learning*, *28*(2-3), 133–168. doi:10.1023/A:1007330508534

Friesner, R. A., Banks, J. L., Murphy, R. B., Halgren, T. A., Klicic, J. J., Mainz, D. T., & Shenkin, P. S. et al. (2004). Glide: A New Approach for Rapid, Accurate Docking and Scoring. 1. Method and Assessment of Docking Accuracy. *Journal of Medicinal Chemistry*, *47*(7), 1739–1749. doi:10.1021/jm0306430 PMID:15027865

Friesner, R. A., Murphy, R. B., Repasky, M. P., Frye, L. L., Greenwood, J. R., Halgren, T. A., & Mainz, D. T. et al. (2006). Extra precision glide: Docking and scoring incorporating a model of hydrophobic enclosure for protein-ligand complexes. *Journal of Medicinal Chemistry*, *49*(21), 6177–6196. doi:10.1021/jm051256o PMID:17034125

Fu, L. M., & Fu, K. A. (2015). Analysis of Parkinson's disease pathophysiology using an integrated genomics-bioinformatics approach. *Pathophysiology*, *22*(1), 15–29. doi:10.1016/j.pathophys.2014.10.002 PMID:25466606

Gama-Castro, S., Jiménez-Jacinto, V., Peralta-Gil, M., Santos-Zavaleta, A., Peñaloza-Spinola, M. I., & Contreras-Moreira, B. et al.. (2008). RegulonDB (Version 6.0): Gene Regulation Model of Escherichia Coli K-12 beyond Transcription, Active (Experimental) Annotated Promoters and Textpresso Navigation. *Nucleic Acids Research*, *36*(Database issue), D120–D124. doi:10.1093/nar/gkm994 PMID:18158297

Gana, N. H. T., Victoriano, A. F. B., & Okamoto, T. (2012). Evaluation of online miRNA resources for biomedical applications. *Genes to Cells*, *17*(1), 11–27. doi:10.1111/j.1365-2443.2011.01564.x PMID:22077698

Gane, P. J., & Dean, P. M. (2000). Recent advances in structure-based rational drug design. *Current Opinion in Structural Biology*, *10*(4), 401–404. Retrieved from http://www.ncbi.nlm.nih.gov/pubmed/10981625 doi:10.1016/S0959-440X(00)00105-6 PMID:10981625

Gangopadhyay, A., & Datta, A. (2015). Identification of inhibitors against the potential ligandable sites in the active cholera toxin. *Computational Biology and Chemistry*, *55*, 37–48. doi:10.1016/j.compbiolchem.2015.02.011 PMID:25698576

Gao, C., Goind, R., & Tabak, H. H. (1992). Application of the group contribution method for predicting the toxicity of organic chemicals. *Environmental Toxicology and Chemistry*, *11*(5), 631–636. doi:10.1002/etc.5620110506

Garcia-Garcia, J., Bonet, J., Guney, E., Fornes, O., Planas, J., & Oliva, B. (2012). Networks of protein–protein interactions: From uncertainty to molecular details. *Molecular Informatics*, *31*(5), 342–362. doi:10.1002/minf.201200005 PMID:27477264

Garcia, S., Fernandez, A., Luengo, J., & Herrera, F. (2010). Advanced non-parametric tests for multiple comparisons in the design of experiments in computational intelligence and data mining: Experimental analysis of power. *Inf. Sci.*, *180*(10), 2044–2064. doi:10.1016/j.ins.2009.12.010

Garnier, J., Gibrat, J. F., & Robson, B. (1996). GOR method for predicting protein secondary structure from amino acid sequence. *Methods in Enzymology*, *266*, 540–553. Retrieved from http://www.ncbi.nlm.nih.gov/pubmed/8743705 doi:10.1016/S0076-6879(96)66034-0 PMID:8743705

Gasch, A., & Eisen, M. (2002). Exploring the conditional corregulation of yeast gene expression through fuzzy k-means clustering. *Genome Biology*, *3*(11), 1–22. doi:10.1186/gb-2002-3-11-research0059 PMID:12429058

Gatto, L., Breckels, L. M., Naake, T., & Gibb, S. (2015). Visualization of proteomics data using R and Bioconductor. *Proteomics*, *15*(8), 1375–1389. doi:10.1002/pmic.201400392 PMID:25690415

Gelbart, W. M., Lewontin, R. C., Griffiths, A. J. F., & Miller, J. H. (2002). *Modern genetic analysis: integrating genes and genomes*. New York: W.H. Freeman and CO.

Georgopoulos, P. G., Sasso, A. F., Isukapalli, S. S., Lioy, P. J., Vallero, D. A., Okino, M., & Reiter, L. (2009). Reconstructing population exposures to environmental chemicals from biomarkers: Challenges and opportunities. *Journal of Exposure Science & Environmental Epidemiology*, *19*(2), 149–171. doi:10.1038/jes.2008.9 PMID:18368010

Georgopoulos, P. G., Wang, S. W., Yang, Y. C., Xue, J., Zartarian, V. G., McCurdy, T., & Ozkaynak, H. (2008). Biologically based modeling of multimedia, multipathway, multiroute population exposures to arsenic. *Journal of Exposure Science & Environmental Epidemiology*, *18*(5), 462–476. doi:10.1038/sj.jes.7500637 PMID:18073786

Ghosh, S., Matsuoka, Y., Asai, Y., Hsin, K. Y., & Kitano, H. (2013). Toward an integrated software platform for systems pharmacology. *Biopharmaceutics & Drug Disposition*, *34*(9), 508–526. doi:10.1002/bdd.1875 PMID:24150748

Gieger, C., Geistlinger, L., Altmaier, E., Hrabé de Angelis, M., Kronenberg, F., Meitinger, T., & Wichmann, H.-E. et al. (2008). Genetics meets metabolomics: A genome-wide association study of metabolite profiles in human serum. *PLOS Genetics*, *4*(11), e1000282. doi:10.1371/journal.pgen.1000282 PMID:19043545

Ginsberg, J., Mohebbi, M. H., Patel, R. S., Brammer, L., Smolinski, M. S., & Brilliant, L. (2008). Detecting Influenza epidemics using search engine query data. *Nature*, *457*(7232), 1012–1014. doi:10.1038/nature07634 PMID:19020500

Ginsburg, G. S., & McCarthy, J. J. (2001). Personalized medicine: Revolutionizing drug discovery and patient care. *Trends in Biotechnology*, *19*(12), 491–496. Retrieved from http://www.ncbi.nlm.nih.gov/pubmed/11711191 doi:10.1016/S0167-7799(01)01814-5 PMID:11711191

Glasser, M. F., Coalson, T. S., Robinson, E. C., Hacker, C. D., Harwell, J., Yacoub, E., & Van Essen, D. C. et al. (2016). A multi-modal parcellation of human cerebral cortex. *Nature*, *536*(7615), 171–178. doi:10.1038/nature18933 PMID:27437579

Global Alliance for Genomics and Health (GA4GH). (2016). Retrieved November 21, 2016, from http://www.ebi.ac.uk/about/news/press-releases/ewan-birney-leads-global-alliance-genomics-and-health

Global Alliance for Genomics and Health. (GA4GH). (2016). Retrieved from http://genomicsandhealth.org

Godin, F., Zuallaert, J., Vandersmissen, B., Neve, W. D., & De Walle, R. V. (2014). Beating the bookmakers: Leveraging statistics and Twitter microposts for predicting soccer results. *Proceedings of KDD Workshop on Large-Scale Sports Analytics*.

Godzik, A. (2003). Fold recognition methods. *Methods of Biochemical Analysis*, *44*, 525–546. Retrieved from http://www.ncbi.nlm.nih.gov/pubmed/12647403 PMID:12647403

Goldberg, D. E., & Deb, K. (1991). A comparative analysis of selection schemes used in genetic algorithms. In *Foundations of Genetic Algorithms* (pp. 69–93). Morgan Kaufmann. doi:10.1016/B978-0-08-050684-5.50008-2

Goldberg, D. G., Kuzel, A. J., Feng, L. B., DeShazo, J. P., & Love, L. E. (2012). EHRs in Primary Care Practices: Benefits, Challenges, and Successful Strategies. *The American Journal of Managed Care*, *18*(2), 48–54. PMID:22435884

Golub, T. R., Slonim, D. K., Tamayo, P., Huard, C., Gaasenbeek, M., Mesirov, J. P., & Bloomfield, C. D. (1999). Molecular classification of cancer: Class discovery and class prediction by gene expression monitoring. *Science*, *286*(5439), 531–537. doi:10.1126/science.286.5439.531 PMID:10521349

Gonzalez, K. D., Hill, K. A., Li, K., Li, W., Scaringe, W. A., Wang, J.-C., & Sommer, S. S. et al. (2007, January). Somatic microindels: Analysis in mouse soma and comparison with the human germline. *Human Mutation, 28*(1), 69–80. doi:10.1002/humu.20416 PMID:16977595

Google Adwords Keyword Tool. (2015, November 11). Retrieved from https://www.google.com/adwords/

Google Search Statistics. (2016, January 10). Retrieved from http://www.internetlivestats.com/google-search-statsitics/

Gopalakrishnan, K., Sowmiya, G., Sheik, S. S., & Sekar, K. (2007). Ramachandran plot on the web (2.0). *Protein and Peptide Letters, 14*(7), 669–671. Retrieved from http://www.ncbi.nlm.nih.gov/pubmed/17897092 doi:10.2174/092986607781483912 PMID:17897092

Grabherr, M. G., Haas, B. J., Yassour, M., Levin, J. Z., Thompson, D. A., Amit, I., & Regev, A. et al. (2011). Full-Length Transcriptome Assembly from RNA-Seq Data without a Reference Genome. *Nature Biotechnology, 29*(7), 644–652. doi:10.1038/nbt.1883 PMID:21572440

Gracy, J., Le-Nguyen, D., Gelly, J.-C., Kaas, Q., Heitz, A., & Chiche, L. (2008). KNOTTIN: The knottin or inhibitor cystine knot scaffold in 2007. *Nucleic Acids Research, 36*(Database issue), D314–D319. doi:10.1093/nar/gkm939 PMID:18025039

Greene, A. C., Giffin, K. A., Greene, C. S. & Moore, J. H. (2015). Adapting bioinformatics curricula for Big Data. *Briefings in Bioinformatics-Bioinformatics Curricula,* 1-8.

Greene, A. C., Giffin, K. A., Greene, C. S. & Moore, J. H. (2015). Adapting bioinformatics curricula for Big Data. *Briefings in Bioinformatics-Bioinformatics Curricula.*

Gregory, T. R. (2004, January). Insertion-deletion biases and the evolution of genome size. *Gene, 324,* 15–34. doi:10.1016/j.gene.2003.09.030 PMID:14693368

Griffith, M., Griffith, O. L., Mwenifumbo, J., Goya, R., Morrissy, A. S., Morin, R. D., & Marra, M. A. et al. (2010). Alternative Expression Analysis by RNA Sequencing. *Nature Methods, 7*(10), 843–847. doi:10.1038/nmeth.1503 PMID:20835245

Grignard, A., Taillandier, P., Gaudou, B., Vo, D., Huynh, N., & Drogoul, A. (2013). GAMA 1.6: Advancing the Art of Complex Agent-Based Modeling and Simulation. In G. Boella, E. Elkind, B. Savarimuthu, F. Dignum, & M. Purvis (Eds.), *PRIMA 2013: Principles and Practice of Multi-Agent Systems, LNCS* (Vol. 8291, pp. 117–131). Berlin, Heidelberg: Springer. doi:10.1007/978-3-642-44927-7_9

Grishman, R., Huttunen, S., & Yangarber, R. (2002). Information extraction for enhanced access to disease outbreak reports. *Journal of Biomedical Informatics, 35*(4), 236–246. doi:10.1016/S1532-0464(03)00013-3 PMID:12755518

Gruber, T. R. (1995). Toward principles for the design of ontologies used for knowledge sharing. *International Journal of Human-Computer Studies, 43*(5/6), 907–928. doi:10.1006/ijhc.1995.1081

Guan, D., Yuan, W., Ma, T., & Lee, S. (2014). Detecting potential labeling errors for bioinformatics by multiple voting. *Knowledge-Based Systems, 66,* 28–35. doi:10.1016/j.knosys.2014.04.013

Guelzim, N., Bottani, S., Bourgine, P., & Képès, F. (2002). Topological and Causal Structure of the Yeast Transcriptional Regulatory Network. *Nature Genetics, 31*(1), 60–63. doi:10.1038/ng873 PMID:11967534

Guerler, A., Govindarajoo, B., & Zhang, Y. (2013). Mapping Monomeric Threading to Protein–Protein Structure Prediction. *Journal of Chemical Information and Modeling, 53*(3), 717–725. https://doi.org/10.1021/ci300579r doi:10.1021/ci300579r PMID:23413988

Guex, N., & Peitsch, M. (1997). SWISS-MODEL and the Swiss-Pdb Viewer: an environment for comparative protein modeling. *Electrophoresis*. Retrieved from http://onlinelibrary.wiley.com/doi/10.1002/elps.1150181505/full

Gullotto, D., Nolassi, M. S., Bernini, A., Spiga, O., & Niccolai, N. (2013). Probing the protein space for extending the detection of weak homology folds. *Journal of Theoretical Biology*, *320*, 152–158. doi:10.1016/j.jtbi.2012.12.005 PMID:23261396

Gunter, T. D., & Terry, N. P. (2005). The Emergence of National Electronic Health Record Architectures in the United States and Australia: Models, Costs, and Questions. *Journal of Medical Internet Research*. Retrieved from http://www.ncbi.nlm.nih.gov/pmc/articles/PMC1550638/

Guo, H., Ingolia, N. T., Weissman, J. S., & Bartel, D. P. (2010). Mammalian microRNAs predominantly act to decrease target mRNA levels. *Nature*, *466*(7308), 835–840. doi:10.1038/nature09267 PMID:20703300

Guo, W., Wisniewski, J. A., & Ji, H. (2014). Hot spot-based design of small-molecule inhibitors for protein–protein interactions. *Bioorganic & Medicinal Chemistry Letters*, *24*(11), 2546–2554. doi:10.1016/j.bmcl.2014.03.095 PMID:24751445

Guo, Z., Kozlov, S., Lavin, M. F., Person, M. D., & Paull, T. T. (2010). ATM activation by oxidative stress. *Science*, *330*(6003), 517–521. doi:10.1126/science.1192912 PMID:20966255

Guo, Z., Zhang, T., Li, X., Wang, Q., Xu, J., Yu, H., & Wang, Q. (2005). Towards precise classification of cancers based on robust gene functional expression profiles. *BMC Bioinformatics*, *6*(1), 1–8. doi:10.1186/1471-2105-6-58 PMID:15774002

Gupta, A., Gandhimathi, A., Sharma, P., & Jayaram, B. (2007). ParDOCK: An all atom energy based Monte Carlo docking protocol for protein-ligand complexes. *Protein and Peptide Letters*, *14*(7), 632–646. Retrieved from http://www.ncbi.nlm.nih.gov/pubmed/17897088 doi:10.2174/092986607781483831 PMID:17897088

Gutsell, S., & Russell, P. (2013). The role of chemistry in developing understanding of adverse outcome pathways and their application in risk assessment. *Toxicological Reviews*, *2*(5), 299–307.

Guttman, M., Garber, M., Levin, J. Z., Donaghey, J., Robinson, J., Adiconis, X., & Regev, A. et al. (2010). Ab Initio Reconstruction of Cell Type-Specific Transcriptomes in Mouse Reveals the Conserved Multi-Exonic Structure of lincRNAs. *Nature Biotechnology*, *28*(5), 503–510. doi:10.1038/nbt.1633 PMID:20436462

Hack, C., & Kendall, G. (2005). Bioinformatics: Current practice and future challenges for life science education. *Biochemistry and Molecular Biology Education*, *33*(2), 82–85. doi:10.1002/bmb.2005.494033022424 PMID:21638550

Haddad, S., Charest-Tardif, G., & Krishnan, K. (2000). Physiologically based modeling of the maximal effect of metabolic interactions on the kinetics of components of complex chemical mixtures. *Journal of Toxicology and Environmental Health. Part A.*, *61*(3), 209–223. doi:10.1080/00984100050131350 PMID:11036509

Hagan, M. T., & Menhaj, M. B. (1994). Training feedforward networks with the Marquardt algorithm. *IEEE Transactions on Neural Networks*, *5*(6), 989–993. doi:10.1109/72.329697 PMID:18267874

Haga, S. W., & Wu, H. F. (2014). Overview of software options for processing, analysis and interpretation of mass spectrometric proteomic data. *Journal of Mass Spectrometry*, *49*(10), 959–969. doi:10.1002/jms.3414 PMID:25303385

Hagos, D. (2016). Software-Defined Networking for Scalable Cloud-based Services to Improve System Performance of Hadoop-based Big Data Applications. *International Journal of Grid and High Performance Computing*, *8*(2), 1–22. doi:10.4018/IJGHPC.2016040101

Halangoda, A., Still, J. G., Hill, K. A., & Sommer, S. S. (2001). Spontaneous microdeletions and microinsertions in a transgenic mouse mutation detection system: Analysis of age, tissue, and sequence specificity. *Environmental and Molecular Mutagenesis*, *37*(4), 311–323. doi:10.1002/em.1038 PMID:11424181

Halgren, T. A., Murphy, R. B., Friesner, R. A., Beard, H. S., Frye, L. L., Pollard, W. T., & Banks, J. L. (2004). Glide: A New Approach for Rapid, Accurate Docking and Scoring. 2. Enrichment Factors in Database Screening. *Journal of Medicinal Chemistry*, *47*(7), 1750–1759. doi:10.1021/jm030644s PMID:15027866

Hall, M. A. (1999). *Correlation-based feature selection for machine learning* (Doctoral dissertation). The University of Waikato.

Hall, M., Frank, E., Holmes, G., Pfahringer, B., Reutemann, P., & Witten, L. H. (2009). The WEKA data mining software: An update. *ACM SIGKKD Exploration Newsletter*, *11*(1), 10–18. doi:10.1145/1656274.1656278

Han, J., Pei, H., & Yin, Y. (2000). Mining Frequent Patterns without Candidate Generation. *Paper presented at the Conf. on the Management of Data*, Dallas.

Han, J., Pei, J., Yin, Y., & Mao, R. (2003). Mining frequent patterns without candidate generation: A frequent-pattern tree approach. *Paper presented at the Data Mining and Knowledge Discovery*.

Hanks, S. K., & Hunter, T. (1995). Protein kinases 6. The eukaryotic protein kinase superfamily: Kinase (catalytic) domain structure and classification. *The FASEB Journal*, *9*(8), 576–596. PMID:7768349

Haralick, R. M., Shanmugam, K., & Dinstein, I. (1973). Textural features for image classification. IEEE Transactions on Systems, Man, and Cybernetics, 3(6), 610-621.

Hardin, C., Pogorelov, T. V., & Luthey-Schulten, Z. (2002). Ab initio protein structure prediction. [pii]. *Current Opinion in Structural Biology*, *12*(2), 176–181. doi:10.1016/S0959-440X(02)00306-8 PMID:11959494

Hartuv, E., & Shamir, R. (2000). A clustering algorithm based on graph connectivity. *Information Processing Letters*, *76*(4–6), 175–181. doi:10.1016/S0020-0190(00)00142-3

Hartwell, L. H., Hopfield, J. J., Leibler, S., & Murray, A. W. (1999). From Molecular to Modular Cell Biology. *Nature*, *402*(6761 Suppl.), C47–C52. doi:10.1038/35011540 PMID:10591225

Hashmi, I., & Shehu, A. (2012). A basin hopping algorithm for protein-protein docking. *Proceedings of the 2012 IEEE International Conference on Bioinformatics and Biomedicine* (pp. 1–4). IEEE. http://doi.org/ doi:10.1109/BIBM.2012.6392725

Hashmi, I., & Shehu, A. (2015). idDock+: Integrating Machine Learning in Probabilistic Search for Protein–Protein Docking. *Journal of Computational Biology*, *22*(9), 806–822. doi:10.1089/cmb.2015.0108 PMID:26222714

Hastings, P. J.; Lupski, J. R.; Roseberg, S. M.; Ira, G. (2009). Mechanisms of change in gene copy number. *Nature Reviews Genetics*. 10, 551–564. doi:10.1038/nrg2593

Health Fact Sheet. (2015, November 9). *Pew Research Centre*. Retrieved from http://www.pewinternet.org/fact-sheets/health-fact-sheet/

He, C., Fan, X., & Li, Y. (2013). Toward ubiquitous healthcare services with a novel efficient cloud platform. *IEEE Transactions on Bio-Medical Engineering*, *60*(1), 230–234. doi:10.1109/TBME.2012.2222404 PMID:23060318

Heger, A., & Holm, L. (2003). Sensitive pattern discovery with fuzzy alignments of distantly related proteins. *Bioinformatics (Oxford, England)*, *19*(Suppl. 1), i130–i137. doi:10.1093/bioinformatics/btg1017 PMID:12855449

Henzinger, M. (2004). The past, present and future of web search engines. *Proceedings of 31st International Colloquium of Automata* (p. 3). Languages and Programming. doi:10.1007/978-3-540-27836-8_2

Heo, L., Park, H., & Seok, C. (2013). GalaxyRefine: Protein structure refinement driven by side-chain repacking. *Nucleic Acids Research*, *41*(W1), W384–W388. doi:10.1093/nar/gkt458 PMID:23737448

Herrero, J., Valencia, A., & Dopazo, J. (2001). A hierarchical unsupervised growing neural network for clustering gene expression patterns. *Bioinformatics (Oxford, England)*, *17*(2), 126–136. doi:10.1093/bioinformatics/17.2.126 PMID:11238068

Hesper, B., ... (1970). Bioinformatica: een werkconcept (In Dutch.). Kameleon. 1(6), 28–29.

Hess, S. (2013). The emerging field of chemo- and Pharmacoproteomics. *Proteomics. Clinical Applications*, *7*(1-2), 171–180. doi:10.1002/prca.201200091 PMID:23184895

Hill, K. A., Wang, J., Farwell, K. D., & Sommer, S. S. (2003, January). Spontaneous tandem-base mutations (TBM) show dramatic tissue, age, pattern and spectrum specificity. *Mutation Research*, *534*(1–2), 173–186. doi:10.1016/S1383-5718(02)00277-2 PMID:12504766

Hindawi, M., Elghazel, H., & Benabdeslem, K. (2013). Efficient semi-supervised feature selection by an ensemble approach. *International Workshop on Complex Machine Learning Problems with Ensemble Methods COPEM@ECML/PKDD'13*, 41–55.

Hippo, Y., Taniguchi, H., Tsutsumi, S., Machida, N., Chong, J. M., Fukayama, M., & Aburatani, H. (2002). Global gene expression analysis of gastric cancer by oligonucleotide microarrays. *Cancer Research*, *62*(1), 233–240. PMID:11782383

Hirak, K., Hasin, A. A., Nazrul, H., Swarup, R. & Dhruba, K. B. (2014). Big Data Analytics in Bioinformatics: A Machine Learning Perspective. *Journal of Latex class files, 13*(9), 1-20.

Hirak, K., Hasin, A. A., Nazrul, H., Swarup, R. & Dhruba, K. B. (2014). Big Data Analytics in Bioinformatics: A Machine Learning Perspective. *Journal of Latex Class Files, 13*(9), 1-20.

Hirschhorn, J. N., & Daly, M. J. (2005). Genome-wide association studies for common diseases and complex traits. *Nature Reviews. Genetics*, *6*(2), 95–108. doi:10.1038/nrg1521 PMID:15716906

Hishigaki, H., Nakai, K., Ono, T., Tanigami, A., & Takagi, T. (2001). Assessment of Prediction Accuracy of Protein Function from Protein Protein Interaction Data. *Yeast (Chichester, England)*, *18*(6), 523–531. doi:10.1002/yea.706 PMID:11284008

Hofmann, K., & Stoffel, W. (1993). TMbase-A database of membrane spanning protein segments. Retrieved from http://en.journals.sid.ir/ViewPaper.aspx?ID=118765

Holland, J. H. (1975). *Adaptation in natural and artificial systems*. Ann Arbor, MI: University of Michigan Press.

Hooda, Y., & Kim, P. M. (2012). Computational structural analysis of protein interactions and networks. *Proteomics*, *12*(10), 1697–1705. doi:10.1002/pmic.201100597 PMID:22593000

Hooft, R., Vriend, G., Sander, C., & Abola, E. (1996). Errors in protein structures. *Nature*. Retrieved from http://www.cheric.org/research/tech/periodicals/view.php?seq=221219

Hospital, A., Andrio, P., Fenollosa, C., Cicin-Sain, D., Orozco, M., & Gelpí, J. L. (2012). MDWeb and MDMoby: An integrated web-based platform for molecular dynamics simulations. *Bioinformatics (Oxford, England)*, *28*(9), 1278–1279. doi:10.1093/bioinformatics/bts139 PMID:22437851

Ho, T. K. (1998). The random subspace method for constructing decision forests. *IEEE Transactions on Pattern Analysis and Machine Intelligence*, *20*(8), 832–844. doi:10.1109/34.709601

Househ, M. (2013). The use of social media in healthcare: Organizational, clinical and patient perspectives. *Studies in Health Technology and Informatics*, *18*(38), 244–248. PMID:23388291

Hu, H., Wen, Y., Chua, T. S., & Li, X. (2014). Toward Scalable Systems for Big Data Analytics: A Technology Tutorial.

Huang, H., Tata, S., & Prill, R. J. (2013). BlueSNP: R package for highly scalable genome-wide association studies using Hadoop clusters. *Bioinformatics (Oxford, England), 29*(1), 135–136. doi:10.1093/bioinformatics/bts647 PMID:23202745

Huang, N., & Shoichet, B. K. (2008). Exploiting ordered waters in molecular docking. *Journal of Medicinal Chemistry, 51*(16), 4862–4865. doi:10.1021/jm8006239 PMID:18680357

Huang, W., Li, L., Myers, J. R., & Marth, G. T. (2012). ART: A next-generation sequencing read simulator. *Bioinformatics (Oxford, England), 28*(4), 593–594. doi:10.1093/bioinformatics/btr708 PMID:22199392

Huang, Y., & Li, Y. (2004). Prediction of protein subcellular locations using fuzzy k-NN method. *Bioinformatics (Oxford, England), 20*(1), 21–28. doi:10.1093/bioinformatics/btg366 PMID:14693804

Huerta, A. M., Salgado, H., Thieffry, D., & Collado-Vides, J. (1998). RegulonDB: A Database on Transcriptional Regulation in Escherichia Coli. *Nucleic Acids Research, 26*(1), 55–59. doi:10.1093/nar/26.1.55 PMID:9399800

Huerta, E., Hernández-Montiel, A., Morales-Caporal, R., & Arjona-López, M. (2016). Hybrid framework using multiple-filters and an embedded approach for an efficient selection and classification of microarray data. *IEEE/ACM Transactions on Computational Biology and Bioinformatics, 13*(1), 12–26. doi:10.1109/TCBB.2015.2474384 PMID:26336138

Hulth, A., Rydevik, G., & Linde, A. (2009). Web queries as a source for syndromic surveillance. *PLoS ONE, 4*(3), e4378. doi:10.1371/journal.pone.0004378 PMID:19197389

Humphrey, W., Dalke, A., & Schulten, K. (1996). VMD: Visual molecular dynamics. *Journal of Molecular Graphics, 14*(1), 33–38. doi:10.1016/0263-7855(96)00018-5 PMID:8744570

Hunter, L. (1993). *Artificial intelligence and molecular biology*. Cambridge, MA: MIT Press.

Hurwitz, N., Schneidman-Duhovny, D., & Wolfson, H. J. (2016). Memdock: An α-helical membrane protein docking algorithm. *Bioinformatics (Oxford, England), 32*(16), 2444–2450. doi:10.1093/bioinformatics/btw184 PMID:27153621

Iizuka, N., Oka, M., Yamada-Okabe, H., Nishida, M., Maeda, Y., Mori, N., & Hamada, K. (2003). Oligonucleotide microarray for prediction of early intrahepatic recurrence of hepatocellular carcinoma after curative resection. *Lancet, 361*(9361), 923–929. doi:10.1016/S0140-6736(03)12775-4 PMID:12648972

Ikonomakis, M., Kotsiantis, S., & Tampakas, V. (2005). Text classification using machine learning techniques. *WSEAS Transaction on Computers, 8*(4), 966–974.

Influenza Fact Sheet. (2015, November 7). Retrieved from World Health Organization website: Retrieved from http://www.who.int/mediacentre/factsheets /fs211/en/

Influenza. (2015, October 21). Popularity, Trend, Related Hashtags-Hashtagify.me. Retrieved from http://hashtagify.me/

Inza, I., Larrañaga, P., Blanco, R., & Cerrolaza, A. J. (2004). Filter versus wrapper gene selection approaches in DNA microarray domains. *Artificial Intelligence in Medicine, 31*(2), 91–103. doi:10.1016/j.artmed.2004.01.007 PMID:15219288

Ioannidis, J. P., Loy, E. Y., Poulton, R., & Chia, K. S. (2009). Researching genetic versus nongenetic determinants of disease: A comparison and proposed unification. *Science Translational Medicine, 1*(7), 7ps8. doi:10.1126/scitranslmed.3000247 PMID:20368180

Iorio, M. V., & Croce, C. M. (2012). MicroRNA dysregulation in cancer: Diagnostics, monitoring and therapeutics. A comprehensive review. *EMBO Molecular Medicine, 4*(3), 143–159. doi:10.1002/emmm.201100209 PMID:22351564

Ishida, T., & Kinoshita, K. (2007). PrDOS: prediction of disordered protein regions from amino acid sequence. *Nucleic Acids Research, 35*(Web Server), W460–W464. doi:10.1093/nar/gkm363

Isukapalli, S., Roy, A., & Georgopoulos, P. (2000). Efficient sensitivity/uncertainty analysis using the combined stochastic response surface method and automated differentiation: Application to environmental and biological systems. *Risk Analysis, 20*(5), 591–602. doi:10.1111/0272-4332.205054 PMID:11110207

Jacobson, M. P., Pincus, D. L., Rapp, C. S., Day, T. J. F., Honig, B., Shaw, D. E., & Friesner, R. A. (2004). A hierarchical approach to all-atom protein loop prediction. *Proteins: Structure, Function, and Bioinformatics, 55*(2), 351–367. doi.org/10.1002/prot.10613

Jain, K. K. (2004). Role of Pharmacoproteomics in the development of Personalized medicine. *Pharmacogenomics, 5*(3), 331–336. doi:10.1517/phgs.5.3.331.29830 PMID:15102547

Jain, K. K. (2015). *Proteomics: technologies, markets and companies.* Basel: Jain PharmaBiotech.

James Gareth, M. (2003). *Variance and Bias for General Loss Functions. Marshall School of Business.* University of California.

Jamroz, M., Kolinski, A., & Kmiecik, S. (2013). CABS-flex: Server for fast simulation of protein structure fluctuations. *Nucleic Acids Research, 41*(Web Server issue), W427-31. https://doi.org/10.1093/nar/gkt332

Janin, J. (2002). Welcome to CAPRI: A Critical Assessment of PRedicted Interactions. *Proteins, 47*(3), 257–257. doi:10.1002/prot.10111

Jayaram, B., Bhushan, K., Shenoy, S. R., Narang, P., Bose, S., & Agrawal, P. ... Pandey, V. (2006). Bhageerath: an energy based web enabled computer software suite for limiting the search space of tertiary structures of small globular proteins. *Nucleic Acids Research, 34*(21), 6195–204. doi:10.1093/nar/gkl789

Jeong, H., Mason, S. P., Barabási, A.-L., & Oltvai, Z. N. (2001). Lethality and Centrality in Protein Networks. *Nature, 411*(6833), 41–42. doi:10.1038/35075138 PMID:11333967

Jewett, M. C., Hofmann, G., & Nielsen, J. (2006). Fungal metabolite analysis in genomics and phenomics. *Current Opinion in Biotechnology, 17*(2), 191–197. doi:10.1016/j.copbio.2006.02.001 PMID:16488600

Jha, A. K., Doolan, D., Grandt, D., Scott, T., & Bates, D. W. (2008). The use of health information technology in seven nations. *International Journal of Medical Informatics, 77*(12), 848–854. doi:10.1016/j.ijmedinf.2008.06.007 PMID:18657471

Jiang, D., Pei, J., & Zhang, A. D. (2003a, March 10-12). A Density-based Hierarchical Clustering Method for Timeseries Gene Expression Data. *Paper presented at the 3rd IEEE International Symposium on Bioinformatics and Bioengineering,* Bethesda, Maryland.

Jiang, D., Pei, J., & Zhang, A. D. (2003b). Interactive exploration of coherent patterns in time-series gene expression data. *Paper presented at the ACM SIGKDD International Conference on Knowledge Discovery and Data Mining.* doi:10.1145/956750.956820

Jiang, Y., & Hua, Z. (2004). Editing training data for KNN classifiers with neural network ensemble. *Lecture Notes in Computer Science, 3173,* 356–361.

Jiang, X., Kumar, K., Hu, X., Wallqvist, A., Reifman, J., Ghosh, S., & McCammon, J. et al. (2008). DOVIS 2.0: An efficient and easy to use parallel virtual screening tool based on AutoDock 4.0. *Chemistry Central Journal, 2*(1), 18. doi:10.1186/1752-153X-2-18 PMID:18778471

Jiménez-García, B., Pons, C., & Fernández-Recio, J. (2013). pyDockWEB: A web server for rigid-body protein-protein docking using electrostatics and desolvation scoring. *Bioinformatics (Oxford, England), 29*(13), 1698–1699. doi:10.1093/bioinformatics/btt262 PMID:23661696

Jiménez-García, B., Pons, C., Svergun, D. I., Bernadó, P., & Fernández-Recio, J. (2015). pyDockSAXS: Protein-protein complex structure by SAXS and computational docking. *Nucleic Acids Research*, *43*(W1), W356-61. doi:10.1093/nar/gkv368 PMID:25897115

Jindal, N., & Liu, B. (2008). Opinion spam and analysis. *Proceedings of the 2008 International Conference on Web Search and Data Mining* (pp. 219–2300.

Joachims, T. (1998). Text categorization with support vector machine: Learning with many relevant features. *Proceedings of the 10th European Conference on Machine Learning* (pp. 137137-137142). doi:10.1007/BFb0026683

Johnson, D. K., & Karanicolas, J. (2016). Ultra-High-Throughput Structure-Based Virtual Screening for Small-Molecule Inhibitors of Protein–Protein Interactions. *Journal of Chemical Information and Modeling*, *56*(2), 399–411. doi:10.1021/acs.jcim.5b00572 PMID:26726827

Johnson, H. A., Wagner, M. M., Hogan, W. R., Chapman, W., Olszewski, R. T., Dowling, J., & Barnas, G. (2004). Analysis of web access logs for surveillance of Influenza. *Studies in Health Technology and Informatics*, *107*(2), 1202–2066. PMID:15361003

Johson, M. (2009). Ligações entre NANDA, NOC E NIC: Diagnóstico, resultados e intervenções de enfermagem. *The Art of Medication*.

Jones, D. T. (1999). GenTHREADER: An efficient and reliable protein fold recognition method for genomic sequences. *Journal of Molecular Biology*, *287*(4), 797–815. doi:10.1006/jmbi.1999.2583 PMID:10191147

Jones, D. T. (2001). Protein structure prediction in genomics. *Briefings in Bioinformatics*, *2*(2), 111–125. doi:10.1093/bib/2.2.111 PMID:11465730

Jones, G., Willett, P., Glen, R. C., Leach, A. R., & Taylor, R. (1997). Development and validation of a genetic algorithm for flexible docking. *Journal of Molecular Biology*, *267*(3), 727–748. doi:10.1006/jmbi.1996.0897 PMID:9126849

Jongeneelen, F. J., & Berge, W. F. T. (2011). A generic, cross-chemical predictive PBTK model with multiple entry routes running as application in MS Excel; design of the model and comparison of predictions with experimental results. *The Annals of Occupational Hygiene*, *55*(8), 841–864. PMID:21998005

Joonsang B., Q. H. (2015, April/June). A Secure Cloud Computing Based Framework for Big Data Information Management of Smart Grid. *IEEE Transactions On Cloud Computing*, *3*(2).

Jorgensen, W. L. (2004). The Many Roles of Computation in Drug Discovery. *Science*, *303*(5665), 1813–1818. doi:10.1126/science.1096361 PMID:15031495

Jourdren, L., Bernard, M., Dillies, M.-A., & Le Crom, S. (2012). A cloud computing-based framework facilitating high throughput sequencing analyses. *Bioinformatics (Oxford, England)*, *28*(11), 1542–1543. doi:10.1093/bioinformatics/bts165 PMID:22492314

Judson, R. S., Kavlock, R. J., Setzer, R. W., Cohen Hubal, E. A., Martin, M. T., Knudsen, T. B., & Dix, D. J. et al. (2011). Estimating toxicity-related biological pathway altering doses for high-throughput chemical risk assessment. *Chemical Research in Toxicology*, *24*(4), 451–462. doi:10.1021/tx100428e PMID:21381849

Kahsay, R. Y., Gao, G., & Liao, L. (2005). An improved hidden Markov model for transmembrane protein detection and topology prediction and its applications to complete genomes. *Bioinformatics (Oxford, England)*, *21*(9), 1853–1858. doi:10.1093/bioinformatics/bti303 PMID:15691854

Källberg, M., Margaryan, G., Wang, S., Ma, J., & Xu, J. (2014). *RaptorX server: A Resource for Template-Based Protein Structure Modeling*. doi:10.1007/978-1-4939-0366-5_2

Källberg, M., Wang, H., Wang, S., Peng, J., Wang, Z., Lu, H., & Xu, J. (2012). Template-based protein structure modeling using the RaptorX web server. *Nature Protocols*, *7*(8), 1511–1522. doi:10.1038/nprot.2012.085 PMID:22814390

Kanehisa, M., & Goto, S. (2000). KEGG: Kyoto encyclopedia of genes and genomes. *Nucleic Acids Research*, *28*(1), 27–30. doi:10.1093/nar/28.1.27 PMID:10592173

Kaneko, T., Tahara, S., & Matsuo, M. (1996, May). Non-linear accumulation of 8-hydroxy-2-deoxyguanosine, a marker of oxidized DNA damage, during aging. *Mutation Research*, *316*(5–6), 277–285. doi:10.1016/S0921-8734(96)90010-7 PMID:8649461

Kaplan, R., & Norton, D. (1992). The Balanced Scorecard: Measures that Drive Performance. *Harvard Business Review*, *70*(1), 71–79. PMID:10119714

Karikari, T. K., & Aleksic, J. (2015). Neurogenomics: An opportunity to integrate neuroscience, genomics and bioinformatics research in Africa. *Applied & Translational Genomics*, *5*, 3–10. doi:10.1016/j.atg.2015.06.004 PMID:26937352

Kasemsap, K. (2016a). Mastering big data in the digital age. In M. Singh & D. G. (Eds.), Effective big data management and opportunities for implementation (pp. 104–129). Hershey, PA: IGI Global. doi:10.4018/978-1-5225-0182-4.ch008

Kasemsap, K. (2015a). The role of cloud computing adoption in global business. In V. Chang, R. Walters, & G. Wills (Eds.), *Delivery and adoption of cloud computing services in contemporary organizations* (pp. 26–55). Hershey, PA: IGI Global. doi:10.4018/978-1-4666-8210-8.ch002

Kasemsap, K. (2015b). Adopting cloud computing in global supply chain: A literature review. *International Journal of Social and Organizational Dynamics in IT*, *4*(2), 49–62. doi:10.4018/IJSODIT.2015070105

Kasemsap, K. (2015c). The role of data mining for business intelligence in knowledge management. In A. Azevedo & M. Santos (Eds.), *Integration of data mining in business intelligence systems* (pp. 12–33). Hershey, PA: IGI Global. doi:10.4018/978-1-4666-6477-7.ch002

Kasemsap, K. (2016b). Multifaceted applications of data mining, business intelligence, and knowledge management. *International Journal of Social and Organizational Dynamics in IT*, *5*(1), 57–69. doi:10.4018/IJSODIT.2016010104

Kasemsap, K. (2017a). Software as a service, Semantic Web, and big data: Theories and applications. In A. Turuk, B. Sahoo, & S. Addya (Eds.), *Resource management and efficiency in cloud computing environments* (pp. 264–285). Hershey, PA: IGI Global. doi:10.4018/978-1-5225-1721-4.ch011

Kasemsap, K. (2017b). Mastering intelligent decision support systems in enterprise information management. In G. Sreedhar (Ed.), *Web data mining and the development of knowledge-based decision support systems* (pp. 35–56). Hershey, PA: IGI Global. doi:10.4018/978-1-5225-1877-8.ch004

Kasemsap, K. (2017c). Mastering web mining and information retrieval in the digital age. In A. Kumar (Ed.), *Web usage mining techniques and applications across industries* (pp. 1–28). Hershey, PA: IGI Global. doi:10.4018/978-1-5225-0613-3.ch001

Kasemsap, K. (2017d). Text mining: Current trends and applications. In G. Sreedhar (Ed.), *Web data mining and the development of knowledge-based decision support systems* (pp. 338–358). Hershey, PA: IGI Global. doi:10.4018/978-1-5225-1877-8.ch017

Kaufman, L., & Rousseeuw, P.J. (1990). *Finding Groups in Data: an Introduction to Cluster Analysis*.

Kaur, M., & Singh, R. (2013). Implementing Encryption Algorithms to Enhance Data Security of Cloud in Cloud Computing. *International Journal of Computers and Applications*, *70*(18), 16–21. doi:10.5120/12167-8127

Kelley, L. A., Mezulis, S., Yates, C. M., Wass, M. N., & Sternberg, M. J. E. (2015). The Phyre2 web portal for protein modeling, prediction and analysis. *Nature Protocols*, *10*(6), 845–858. doi:10.1038/nprot.2015.053 PMID:25950237

Khanesar, M. A., Teshnehlab, M., & Shoorehdeli, M. A. (2007, June). A novel binary particle swarm optimization. In *Control & Automation, 2007. MED'07. Mediterranean Conference on* (pp. 1-6). IEEE.

Khor, B. Y., Tye, G. J., Lim, T. S., Choong, Y. S., Wu, S., & Zhang, Y. … Zhang, Y. (2015). General overview on structure prediction of twilight-zone proteins. *Theoretical Biology and Medical Modelling, 12*(1), 15. doi:10.1186/s12976-015-0014-1

Khoury, G. A., Tamamis, P., Pinnaduwage, N., Smadbeck, J., Kieslich, C. A., & Floudas, C. A. (2014). Princeton_TIGRESS: Protein geometry refinement using simulations and support vector machines. *Proteins: Structure, Function, and Bioinformatics, 82*(5), 794–814. doi:10.1002/prot.24459

Khunlertgit, N., & Yoon, B. J. (2013). Identification of robust pathway markers for cancer through rank-based pathway activity inference. *Advances in Bioinformatics*. PMID:23533400

Kim, J. K., Bamba, T., Harada, K., Fukusaki, E., & Kobayashi, A. (2007). Time-course metabolic profiling in *Arabidopsis thaliana* cell cultures after salt stress treatment. *Journal of Experimental Botany*, *58*(3), 415–424. doi:10.1093/jxb/erl216 PMID:17118972

Kinch, L. N., Li, W., Monastyrskyy, B., Kryshtafovych, A., & Grishin, N. V. (2016). Evaluation of free modeling targets in CASP11 and ROLL. *Proteins: Structure, Function, and Bioinformatics, 84*, 51–66. doi:10.1002/prot.24973

Kind, T., Tolstikov, V. V., Fiehn, O., & Weiss, R. H. (2007). A comprehensive urinary metabolomic approach for identifying kidney cancer. *Analytical Biochemistry*, *363*(2), 185–195. doi:10.1016/j.ab.2007.01.028 PMID:17316536

Kinnings, S. L., Liu, N., Tonge, P. J., Jackson, R. M., Xie, L., & Bourne, P. E. (2011). A machine learning-based method to improve docking scoring functions and its application to drug repurposing. *Journal of Chemical Information and Modeling*, *51*(2), 408–419. doi:10.1021/ci100369f PMID:21291174

Kitano, H. (2002a). Computational systems biology. *Nature*, *420*(6912), 206–210. doi:10.1038/nature01254 PMID:12432404

Kitano, H. (2002b). Systems biology: A brief overview. *Science*, *295*(5560), 1662–1664. doi:10.1126/science.1069492 PMID:11872829

Kitano, H. (2007). A robustness-based approach to systems-oriented drug design. *Nature Reviews. Drug Discovery*, *6*(3), 202–210. doi:10.1038/nrd2195 PMID:17318209

Kittler, J. (1978). Feature set search algorithms. *Pattern Recognition and Signal Processing*, 41-60.

Kleftogiannis, D., Theofilatos, K., Likothanassis, S., & Mavroudi, S. (2015). YamiPred: A novel evolutionary method for predicting pre-miRNAs and selecting relevant features. *IEEE/ACM Transactions on Computational Biology and Bioinformatics*, *12*(5), 1183–1192. doi:10.1109/TCBB.2014.2388227 PMID:26451829

Ko, J., Park, H., Seok, C., Zhang, Y., Marti-Renom, M., & Stuart, A. … Zhou, Y. (2012). GalaxyTBM: template-based modeling by building a reliable core and refining unreliable local regions. *BMC Bioinformatics*, *13*(1), 198. doi:10.1186/1471-2105-13-198

Kohonen, T. (1984). *Self-Organization and Associative Memory*. Berlin: Spring-Verlag.

Kolb, P., Kipouros, C. B., Huang, D., & Caflisch, A. (2008). Structure-based tailoring of compound libraries for high-throughput screening: Discovery of novel EphB4 kinase inhibitors. *Proteins: Structure, Function, and Bioinformatics*, *73*(1), 11–18. doi:10.1002/prot.22028 PMID:18384152

Koller, D., & Sahami, M. (1996). *Toward optimal feature selection*. Academic Press.

Kondrashov, A. S., & Rogozin, I. B. (2004, February). Context of deletions and insertions in human coding sequences. *Human Mutation*, *23*(2), 177–185. doi:10.1002/humu.10312 PMID:14722921

Kong, M., & Tian, P. (2005, December). A binary ant colony optimization for the unconstrained function optimization problem. In *International Conference on Computational and Information Science* (pp. 682-687). Springer Berlin Heidelberg. doi:10.1007/11596448_101

Koopman, R. J., Kochendorfer, K. M., Moore, J. L., Mehr, D. R., Wakefield, D. S., Yadamsuren, B., & Belden, J. L. et al. (2011). A Diabetes Dashboard and Physician Efficiency and Accuracy in Accessing Data Needed for High-Quality Diabetes Care. *Annals of Family Medicine*, *9*(5), 398–205. doi:10.1370/afm.1286 PMID:21911758

Kotsiantis, S. B. (2007). Supervised machine learning: A review of classification techniques. *Informatica*, *21*, 249–268.

Kotzias, D., Geiss, O., Tirendi, S., Josefa, B. M., Reina, V., Gotti, A., . . . Sarigiannis, D. (2009). Exposure to multiple air contaminants in public buildings, schools and kindergartens-the European indoor air monitoring and exposure assessment (airmex) study. *Fresenius Environmental Bulletin*, *18*(5A), 670-681.

Kozakov, D., Brenke, R., Comeau, S. R., Vajda, S., & Vajda, S. (2006). PIPER: An FFT-based protein docking program with pairwise potentials. *Proteins: Structure, Function, and Bioinformatics*, *65*(2), 392–406. doi:10.1002/prot.21117 PMID:16933295

Kozlowski, L. P., Bujnicki, J. M., Dunker, A., Oldfield, C., Meng, J., & Romero, P. ... Dunker, A. (2012). MetaDisorder: a meta-server for the prediction of intrinsic disorder in proteins. *BMC Bioinformatics, 13*(1), 111. doi:10.1186/1471-2105-13-111

Kramer, B., Rarey, M., & Lengauer, T. (1999). Evaluation of the FLEXX incremental construction algorithm for protein-ligand docking. *Proteins*, *37*(2), 228–241. doi:10.1002/(SICI)1097-0134(19991101)37:2<228::AID-PROT8>3.0.CO;2-8 PMID:10584068

Krampis, K., Booth, T., Chapman, B., Tiwari, B., Bicak, M., Field, D., & Nelson, K. E. (2012). Cloud BioLinux: Pre-configured and on-demand bioinformatics computing for the genomics community. *BMC Bioinformatics*, *13*(42), 3448–3449. PMID:22429538

Krauss, M., Schaller, S., Borchers, S., Findeisen, R., Lippert, J., & Kuepfer, L. (2012). Integrating Cellular Metabolism into a Multiscale Whole-Body Model. *PLoS Computational Biology*, *8*(10), e1002750. doi:10.1371/journal.pcbi.1002750 PMID:23133351

Krauth, F., Ihling, C. H., Ruttinger, H. H., & Sinz, A. (2009). Heterobifunctional isotope-labeled amine-reactive photo-cross-linker for structural investigation of proteins by matrix-assisted laser desorption/ionization tandem time-of-flight and electrospray ionization LTQ-Orbitrap mass spectrometry. *Rapid Communications in Mass Spectrometry*, *23*(17), 2811–2818. doi:10.1002/rcm.4188 PMID:19653199

Krieger, E., Joo, K., Lee, J., Lee, J., Raman, S., & Thompson, J. ... Karplus, K. (2009). Improving physical realism, stereochemistry, and side-chain accuracy in homology modeling: Four approaches that performed well in CASP8. *Proteins: Structure, Function, and Bioinformatics*, *77*(S9), 114–122. doi:10.1002/prot.22570

Krieger, E., & Vriend, G. (2014). YASARA View - molecular graphics for all devices - from smartphones to workstations. *Bioinformatics (Oxford, England)*, *30*(20), 2981–2982. doi:10.1093/bioinformatics/btu426 PMID:24996895

Krissinel, E., & Henrick, K. (2007). Inference of Macromolecular Assemblies from Crystalline State. *Journal of Molecular Biology*, *372*(3), 774–797. doi:10.1016/j.jmb.2007.05.022 PMID:17681537

Kroch, E., Vaughn T., Koepke, M., Roman, S., Foster, D., Sinha, S. Levey, S. (2006). Hospital Boards and Quality Dashboards. *J. Patient Saf.*, *2*(1), 10-19.

Krogh, A., Larsson, B., von Heijne, G., & Sonnhammer, E. L. (2001). Predicting transmembrane protein topology with a hidden markov model: application to complete genomes11Edited by F. Cohen. *Journal of Molecular Biology, 305*(3), 567–580. doi:10.1006/jmbi.2000.4315

Krogh, A., & Vedelsby, J. (1995). Neural network ensembles cross validation, and active learning. *Advances in Neural Information Processing Systems*, *7*, 231–238.

Kumar, C., & Mann, M. (2009). Bioinformatics analysis of mass spectrometry-based proteomics data sets. *FEBS Letters*, *583*(11), 1703–1712. doi:10.1016/j.febslet.2009.03.035 PMID:19306877

Kuncheva, L. I. (2007). A stability index for feature selection. *Proceedings of the 25th IASTED International Multi-Conference: Artificial Intelligence and Applications*, 390–395.

Kuncheva, L. (2004). *Combining Pattern Classifiers: Methods and Algorithms*. Wiley. doi:10.1002/0471660264

Kuntz, I. D. (1992). Structure-Based Strategies for Drug Design and Discovery. *Science*, *257*(5073), 1078–1082. doi:10.1126/science.257.5073.1078 PMID:1509259

Kuntz, I. D., Blaney, J. M., Oatley, S. J., Langridge, R., & Ferrin, T. E. (1982). A geometric approach to macromolecule-ligand interactions. *Journal of Molecular Biology*, *161*(2), 269–288. doi:10.1016/0022-2836(82)90153-X PMID:7154081

Kunz, M., Xiao, K., Liang, C., Viereck, J., Pachel, C., Frantz, S., & Dandekar, T. et al. (2015). Bioinformatics of cardio-vascular miRNA biology. *Journal of Molecular and Cellular Cardiology*, *89*, 3–10. doi:10.1016/j.yjmcc.2014.11.027 PMID:25486579

Kurcinski, M., Jamroz, M., Blaszczyk, M., Kolinski, A., & Kmiecik, S. (2015). CABS-dock web server for the flexible docking of peptides to proteins without prior knowledge of the binding site. *Nucleic Acids Research*, *43*(W1), W419-24. doi:10.1093/nar/gkv456 PMID:25943545

Lali, M. I. U., Mustafa, R. U., Saleem, K., Nawaz, M. S., Zia, T., & Shahzad, B. (2017). Finding Healthcare Issues with Search Engine Queries and Social Network Data. *International Journal on Semantic Web and Information Systems*, *13*(1), 48–62. doi:10.4018/IJSWIS.2017010104

Lamb, A., Paul, M. J., & Dredze, M. (2013). Separating fact from fear: Tracking flu infections on Twitter. *Proceedings of NAACL-HLT* (pp. 789-795).

Lambert, C., Léonard, N., De Bolle, X., & Depiereux, E. (2002). ESyPred3D: Prediction of proteins 3D structures. *Bioinformatics (Oxford, England)*, *18*(9), 1250–1256. doi:10.1093/bioinformatics/18.9.1250 PMID:12217917

Lamdan, Y., & Wolfson, H. (1988). Geometric hashing: A general and efficient model-based recognition scheme. Retrieved from http://www.cs.utexas.edu/~grauman/courses/spring2007/395T/395T/papers/Lamdan88.pdf

Langmead, B., Trapnell, C., Pop, M., & Salzberg, S.L. (2009). Ultrafast and Memory-Efficient Alignment of Short DNA Sequences to the Human Genome. *Genome Biology, 10*(3), R25. doi:.10.1186/gb-2009-10-3-r25

Larraaga, P., Calvo, B., Santana, R., Bielza, C., Galdiano, J., & Inza, I., & Robles, V. et al. (2006). Machine learning in bioinformatics. *Briefings in Bioinformatics*, *7*(1), 86–112. doi:10.1093/bib/bbk007 PMID:16761367

Laskowski, R. A., MacArthur, M. W., Moss, D. S., Thornton, J. M., & Cr, I. U. (1993). PROCHECK: A program to check the stereochemical quality of protein structures. *Journal of Applied Crystallography*, *26*(2), 283–291. doi:10.1107/S0021889892009944

Laskowski, R. A., & Swindells, M. B. (2011). LigPlot+: Multiple ligand-protein interaction diagrams for drug discovery. *Journal of Chemical Information and Modeling, 51*(10), 2778–2786. doi:10.1021/ci200227u PMID:21919503

Laukens, K., Naulaerts, S., & Berghe, W. V. (2015). Bioinformatics approaches for the functional interpretation of protein lists: From ontology term enrichment to network analysis. *Proteomics, 15*(5/6), 981–996. doi:10.1002/pmic.201400296 PMID:25430566

Lazer, D., Kennedy, R., King, G., & Vespignani, A. (2014a). Big data. The parable of Google Flu: Traps in big data analysis. *Science, 343*(6176), 1203–1205. doi:10.1126/science.1248506 PMID:24626916

Lazer, D., Kennedy, R., King, G., & Vespignani, A. (2014b). Twitter: Big data opportunities response. *Science, 345*(6193), 148–149. doi:10.1126/science.345.6193.148-b PMID:25013053

Lee, K., Agarwal, A., & Choudhary, A. (2013). Real-time disease survelliance using Twitter Data. *Proceedings of the 2nd Workshop on Data Mining for Medicine and Healthcare.*

Lee, C. P., Lin, W. S., Chen, Y. M., & Kuo, B. J. (2011). Gene selection and sample classification on microarray data based on adaptive genetic algorithm/k-nearest neighbor method. *Expert Systems with Applications, 38*(5), 4661–4667. doi:10.1016/j.eswa.2010.07.053

Lee, E., Chuang, H. Y., Kim, J. W., Ideker, T., & Lee, D. (2008). Inferring pathway activity toward precise disease classification. *PLoS Computational Biology, 4*(11), e1000217. doi:10.1371/journal.pcbi.1000217 PMID:18989396

Lee, G. R., & Seok, C. (2016). Galaxy7TM: Flexible GPCR-ligand docking by structure refinement. *Nucleic Acids Research, 44*(W1), W502-6. doi:10.1093/nar/gkw360 PMID:27131365

Lee, J., Wu, S., & Zhang, Y. (2009). Ab Initio Protein Structure Prediction. In *From Protein Structure to Function with Bioinformatics* (pp. 3–25). Dordrecht: Springer Netherlands. doi:10.1007/978-1-4020-9058-5_1

Lee, P. A., Tullman-Ercek, D., & Georgiou, G. (2006). The bacterial twin-arginine translocation pathway. *Annual Review of Microbiology, 60*(1), 373–395. doi:10.1146/annurev.micro.60.080805.142212 PMID:16756481

Lee, S., & Abbott, P. A. (2003). Bayesian networks for knowledge discovery in large datasets: Basics for nurse researchers. *Journal of Biomedical Informatics, 36*(4-5), 389–399. doi:10.1016/j.jbi.2003.09.022 PMID:14643735

Lee, S., Seo, C. H., Lim, B., Yang, J. O., Oh, J., Kim, M., & Lee, S. et al. (2011). Accurate Quantification of Transcriptome from RNA-Seq Data by Effective Length Normalization. *Nucleic Acids Research, 39*(2), e9. doi:10.1093/nar/gkq1015 PMID:21059678

Lee, Y.-C. C., & Hsieh, K.-S. (2003). Ultrasonic Liver Tissues Classification by Fractal Feature Vector based on M-band Wavelet Transform. *IEEE Transactions on Medical Imaging, 22*(3), 382–392.

Lengauer, T. (2008). *Bioinformatics - From Genomes to Therapies* (Vol. 1). Bioinformatics - From Genomes to Therapies; doi:10.1002/9783527619368

Leng, N., Dawson, J. A., Thomson, J. A., Ruotti, V., Rissman, A. I., Smits, B. M. G., & Kendziorski, C. et al. (2013). EBSeq: An Empirical Bayes Hierarchical Model for Inference in RNA-Seq Experiments. *Bioinformatics (Oxford, England), 29*(8), 1035–1043. doi:10.1093/bioinformatics/btt087 PMID:23428641

Lensink, M. F., Velankar, S., Kryshtafovych, A., Huang, S.-Y., Schneidman-Duhovny, D., Sali, A., & Wodak, S. J. et al. (2016). Prediction of homoprotein and heteroprotein complexes by protein docking and template-based modeling: A CASP-CAPRI experiment. *Proteins. Structure, Function, and Bioinformatics, 84*, 323–348. doi:10.1002/prot.25007 PMID:27122118

Leskes, B., & Torenvliet, L. (2008). The value of agreement a new boosting algorithm. *Journal of Computer and System Sciences*, *74*(4), 557–586. doi:10.1016/j.jcss.2007.06.005

Lesk, V. I., & Sternberg, M. J. E. (2008). 3D-Garden: A system for modelling protein-protein complexes based on conformational refinement of ensembles generated with the marching cubes algorithm. *Bioinformatics (Oxford, England)*, *24*(9), 1137–1144. doi:10.1093/bioinformatics/btn093 PMID:18326508

Leung, L. (2008). Internet embeddedness: Links with online health information seeking, expectancy value/quality of health information websites, and internet usage patterns. *Cyberpsychology & Behavior*, *11*(5), 565–569. doi:10.1089/cpb.2007.0189 PMID:18771393

Levine, E., Cook, L.T., & Granthem, J.J. (1985). Liver Cysts in autosomal-dominant polycystic kidney disease. Clinical and computer topographic study. *American Journal of Roentgenlogy, 115*(2), 229 233.

Levine, M., & Tjian, R. (2003). Transcription Regulation and Animal Diversity. *Nature, 424*(6945), 147–151. doi:10.1038/nature01763 PMID:12853946

Levy, S. (1993). *Artificial Life: A Report from the Frontier Where Computers Meet Biology*. Random House Inc.

Lewis, S., Csordas, A., Killcoyne, S., Hermjakob, H., Hoopmann, M. R., Moritz, R. L., & Boyle, J. et al. (2012). Hydra: A scalable proteomic search engine which utilizes the Hadoop distributed computing framework. *BMC Bioinformatics*, *13*(1), 324. doi:10.1186/1471-2105-13-324 PMID:23216909

Li, H., Gao, Z., Kang, L., Zhang, H., Yang, K., Yu, K., … Jiang, H. (2006). TarFisDock: a web server for identifying drug targets with docking approach. *Nucleic Acids Research, 34*(Web Server), W219–W224. http://doi.org/<ALIGNMENT.qj></ALIGNMENT>10.1093/nar/gkl114

Li, H., Leung, K.-S., & Wong, M.-H. (2012). idock: A multithreaded virtual screening tool for flexible ligand docking. *Proceedings of the 2012 IEEE Symposium on Computational Intelligence in Bioinformatics and Computational Biology (CIBCB)* (pp. 77–84). IEEE. http://doi.org/ doi:10.1109/CIBCB.2012.6217214

Li, J., & Cardie, C. (2013). Early stage Influenza detection from Twitter. arXiv:1309.7340

Li, Y., & Zhang, Y. (2009). REMO: A new protocol to refine full atomic protein models from C-alpha traces by optimizing hydrogen-bonding networks. *Proteins: Structure, Function, and Bioinformatics, 76*(3), 665–676. doi:10.1002/prot.22380

Liao, K. H., Dobrev, I. D., Dennison Jr, J. E., Andersen, M. E., Reisfeld, B., Reardon, K. F., … Yang, R. S. H. (2002). Application of biologically based computer modeling to simple or complex mixtures. *Environmental Health Perspectives, 110*(Suppl. 6), 957-963.

Li, B., & Dewey, C. N. (2011). RSEM: Accurate Transcript Quantification from RNA-Seq Data with or without a Reference Genome. *BMC Bioinformatics*, *12*(August), 323. doi:10.1186/1471-2105-12-323 PMID:21816040

Li, H., & Durbin, R. (2009). Fast and Accurate Short Read Alignment with Burrows-Wheeler Transform. *Bioinformatics (Oxford, England)*, *25*(14), 1754–1760. doi:10.1093/bioinformatics/btp324 PMID:19451168

Li, H., & Li, C. (2010a). Multiple Ligand Simultaneous Docking: Orchestrated Dancing of Ligands in Binding Sites of Protein. *Journal of Computational Chemistry*, *31*(10), 2014–2022. doi:10.10021/jcc.21486 PMID:20166125

Li, H., & Li, C. (2010b). Multiple ligand simultaneous docking: Orchestrated dancing of ligands in binding sites of protein. *Journal of Computational Chemistry*, *31*(10), 2014–2022. doi:10.1002/jcc.21486 PMID:20166125

Li, H., Liu, A., Zhao, Z., Xu, Y., Lin, J., Jou, D., & Li, C. (2011). Fragment-based drug design and drug repositioning using multiple ligand simultaneous docking (MLSD): Identifying celecoxib and template compounds as novel inhibitors of signal transducer and activator of transcription 3 (STAT3). *Journal of Medicinal Chemistry, 54*(15), 5592–5596. doi:10.1021/jm101330h PMID:21678971

Li, H., Ruan, J., & Durbin, R. (2008). Mapping Short DNA Sequencing Reads and Calling Variants Using Mapping Quality Scores. *Genome Research, 18*(11), 1851–1858. doi:10.1101/gr.078212.108 PMID:18714091

Li, H., Xiao, H., Lin, L., Jou, D., Kumari, V., Lin, J., & Li, C. (2014). Drug Design Targeting Protein–Protein Interactions (PPIs) Using Multiple Ligand Simultaneous Docking (MLSD) and Drug Repositioning: Discovery of Raloxifene and Bazedoxifene as Novel Inhibitors of IL-6/GP130 Interface. *Journal of Medicinal Chemistry, 57*(3), 632–641. doi:10.1021/jm401144z PMID:24456369

Li, J., & Tibshirani, R. (2013). Finding Consistent Patterns: A Nonparametric Approach for Identifying Differential Expression in RNA-Seq Data. *Statistical Methods in Medical Research, 22*(5), 519–536. doi:10.1177/0962280211428386 PMID:22127579

Li, L. (2015). The potential of translational bioinformatics approaches for pharmacology research. *British Journal of Clinical Pharmacology, 80*(4), 862–867. doi:10.1111/bcp.12622 PMID:25753093

Li, L., Wang, B., & Meroueh, S. O. (2011). Support vector regression scoring of receptor-ligand complexes for rank-ordering and virtual screening of chemical libraries. *Journal of Chemical Information and Modeling, 51*(9), 2132–2138. doi:10.1021/ci200078f PMID:21728360

Li, M., & Zhou, Z.-H. (2007). Improve computer-aided diagnosis with machine learning techniques using undiagnosed samples. *Trans. Sys. Man Cyber. Part A, 37*(6), 1088–1098. doi:10.1109/TSMCA.2007.904745

Lima, A. O. S., & Garcês, S. P. S. (2006). Intrageneric primer design: Bringing bioinformatics tools to the class. *Biochemistry and Molecular Biology Education, 34*(5), 332–337. doi:10.1002/bmb.2006.494034052641 PMID:21638710

Lindahl, E., Azuara, C., Koehl, P., & Delarue, M. (2006). NOMAD-Ref: visualization, deformation and refinement of macromolecular structures based on all-atom normal mode analysis. *Nucleic Acids Research, 34*(Web Server issue), W52-6. doi:10.1093/nar/gkl082

Linding, R., Jensen, L. J., Diella, F., Bork, P., Gibson, T. J., & Russell, R. B. (2003). Protein disorder prediction: implications for structural proteomics. *Structure, 11*(11), 1453–9. Retrieved from http://www.ncbi.nlm.nih.gov/pubmed/14604535

Linding, R., Russell, R. B., Neduva, V., & Gibson, T. J. (2003). GlobPlot: Exploring protein sequences for globularity and disorder. *Nucleic Acids Research, 31*(13), 3701–3708. doi:10.1093/nar/gkg519 PMID:12824398

Lin, W., Dou, W., Zhou, Z., & Liu, C. (2015). A cloud-based framework for home-diagnosis service over big medical data. *Journal of Systems and Software, 102*, 192–206. doi:10.1016/j.jss.2014.05.068

Liu, B., & Zhang, L. (2012). A survey of opinion mining and sentiment analysis. In Mining Text Data (pp. 415-463).

Liu, B., Madduri, R. K., Sotomayor, B., Chard, K., Lacinski, L., Dave, U. J., & Foster, I. T. et al. (2014). Cloud-based bioinformatics workflow platform for large-scale next-generation sequencing analyses. *Journal of Biomedical Informatics, 49*, 119–133. doi:10.1016/j.jbi.2014.01.005 PMID:24462600

Liu, X., Krishnan, A., & Mondry, A. (2005). An entropy-based gene selection method for cancer classification using microarray data. *BMC Bioinformatics, 6*(1), 1. doi:10.1186/1471-2105-6-1 PMID:15790388

Livio, M. (2002). *The Golden Ratio: The Story of Phi, The World's Most Astonishing Number.* New York: Broadway Books.

Li, Y., & Zhang, J. (2007). Serum concentrations of antioxidant vitamins and carotenoids are low in individuals with a history of attempted suicide. *Nutritional Neuroscience*, *10*(1-2), 51–58. doi:10.1080/10284150701250747 PMID:17539483

Lobley, A., Sadowski, M. I., & Jones, D. T. (2009). pGenTHREADER and pDomTHREADER: New methods for improved protein fold recognition and superfamily discrimination. *Bioinformatics (Oxford, England)*, *25*(14), 1761–1767. doi:10.1093/bioinformatics/btp302 PMID:19429599

Lockhart, D. J., & Winzeler, E. A. (2000). Genomics, Gene Expression and DNA Arrays. *Nature*, *405*(6788), 827–836. doi:10.1038/35015701 PMID:10866209

López-Blanco, J. R., Canosa-Valls, A. J., Li, Y., & Chacón, P. (2016). RCD+: Fast loop modeling server. *Nucleic Acids Research*, *44*(W1), W395-400. doi:10.1093/nar/gkw395 PMID:27151199

Lu, Y., Wang, R., Yang, C.-Y., & Wang, S. (n. d.). Analysis of ligand-bound water molecules in high-resolution crystal structures of protein-ligand complexes. *Journal of Chemical Information and Modeling, 47*(2), 668–75. Doi:<ALIGNMENT.qj></ALIGNMENT>10.1021/ci6003527

Lukac, R., Plataniotis, K., Smolka, B., & Venetsanopoulos, A. (2005). cDNA microarray image processing using fuzzy vector filtering framework. *Fuzzy Sets and Systems*, *152*(1), 17–35. doi:10.1016/j.fss.2004.10.012

Luo, J., Wu, M., Gopukumar, D., & Zhao, Y. (2016). Big Data Application in Biomedical Research and Health Care: A Literature Review. *Biomedical Informatics Insights*, *8*, 1–10. doi:10.4137/BII.S31559 PMID:26843812

Lupas, A., Van Dyke, M., & Stock, J. (1991). Predicting coiled coils from protein sequences. *Science*, *252*(5009), 1162–1164. doi:10.1126/science.252.5009.1162 PMID:2031185

Lupiáñez-Villanueva, F., Hardey, M., Torrent, J., & Ficapal, P. (2010). The integration of Information and Communication Technology into medical practice. *International Journal of Medical Informatics*, *79*(7), 478–491. doi:10.1016/j.ijmedinf.2010.04.004 PMID:20472494

Lusher, S. J., McGuire, R., van Schaik, R. C., Nicholson, C. D., & de Vlieg, J. (2014). Data-driven medicinal chemistry in the era of big data. *Drug Discovery Today*, *19*(7), 859–868. doi:10.1016/j.drudis.2013.12.004 PMID:24361338

Lyskov, S., & Gray, J. J. (2008). The RosettaDock server for local protein-protein docking. *Nucleic Acids Research, 36*(Web Server issue), W233-8. Doi:<ALIGNMENT.qj></ALIGNMENT>10.1093/nar/gkn216

Lyskov, S., Chou, F.-C., Conchúir, S. Ó., Der, B. S., Drew, K., & Kuroda, D. … Meiler, J. (2013). Serverification of Molecular Modeling Applications: The Rosetta Online Server That Includes Everyone (ROSIE). *PLoS ONE, 8*(5), e63906. doi:10.1371/journal.pone.0063906

Lyskov, S., Chou, F.-C., Conchúir, S. Ó., Der, B. S., Drew, K., Kuroda, D., & Meiler, J. et al. (2013). Serverification of Molecular Modeling Applications: The Rosetta Online Server That Includes Everyone (ROSIE). *PLoS ONE, 8*(5), e63906. doi:10.1371/journal.pone.0063906 PMID:23717507

Macdonald, M., Ambrose, C. M., Duyao, M. P., Myers, R. H., Lin, C., Srinidhi, L., & Groot, N. et al. (1993). A novel gene containing a trinucleotide repeat that is expanded and unstable on Huntington's disease chromosomes. *Cell, 72*(6), 971–983. doi:10.1016/0092-8674(93)90585-E PMID:8458085

Machuka, J. (2004). Agricultural genomics and sustainable development: Perspectives and prospects for Africa. *African Journal of Biotechnology*, *3*(2), 127–135.

Macindoe, G., Mavridis, L., Venkatraman, V., Devignes, M.-D., & Ritchie, D. W. (2010). HexServer: an FFT-based protein docking server powered by graphics processors. *Nucleic Acids Research, 38*(Web Server issue), W445-9. Doi:<ALIGNMENT.qj></ALIGNMENT>10.1093/nar/gkq311

Madan, B., Kasprzak, J. M., Tuszynska, I., Magnus, M., Szczepaniak, K., Dawson, W. K., & Bujnicki, J. M. (2016). Modeling of Protein–RNA Complex Structures Using Computational Docking Methods (pp. 353–372). Doi:<ALIGNMENT.qj></ALIGNMENT>10.1007/978-1-4939-3569-7_21

Madden, S. (2012, May). From Databases to Big Data. *IEEE Internet Computing, 16*(3), 4–6. Retrieved from http://ieeexplore.ieee.org/lpdocs/epic03/wrapper.htm?arnumber=6188576 doi:10.1109/MIC.2012.50

Magruder, S. (2003). Evaluation of over-the-counter pharmaceutical sales as a possible early warning indicator of human disease. *Johns Hopkins University APL Technical Digest, 24*(4), 349–353.

Maher, C. A., Kumar-Sinha, C., Cao, X., Kalyana-Sundaram, S., Han, B., Jing, X., ... & Chinnaiyan, A. M. (2009). Transcriptome Sequencing to Detect Gene Fusions in Cancer. *Nature, 458*(7234), 97–101. doi:10.1038/nature07638

Maintz, J. B. A., Meijering, E. H. W., & Viergever, M. A. (1998). General multimodal elastic registration based on mutual information. In *Medical imaging: Image processing* (pp. 144–154). SPIE Press.

Maji, P., & Paul, S. (2013). Rough-fuzzy clustering for grouping functionally similar genes from microarray data. *IEEE/ACM Transactions on Computational Biology and Bioinformatics, 10*(2), 286–299. doi:10.1109/TCBB.2012.103 PMID:22848138

Makridakis, M., & Vlahou, A. (2010). Secretome proteomics for discovery of cancer biomarkers. *Journal of Proteomics, 73*(12), 2291–2305. doi:10.1016/j.jprot.2010.07.001 PMID:20637910

Malhis, N., Jacobson, M., & Gsponer, J. (2016). MoRFchibi SYSTEM: Software tools for the identification of MoRFs in protein sequences. *Nucleic Acids Research, 44*(W1), W488-93. doi:10.1093/nar/gkw409 PMID:27174932

Malik, M. T., Gumelm, A., Thompson, L. H., Strome, T., & Mahmud, S. M. (2011). Google flu trends and emergency department triage data predicted the 2009 pandemic H1N1 waves in Manitoba. *Canadian Journal of Public Health, 102*(4), 294–297. PMID:21913587

Mallory, A. C., Dugas, D. V., Bartel, D. P., & Bartel, B. (2004). MicroRNA regulation of NAC-domain targets is required for proper formation and separation of adjacent embryonic, vegetative, and floral organs. *Current Biology, 14*(12), 1035–1046. doi:10.1016/j.cub.2004.06.022 PMID:15202996

Mamitsuka, H. (2012). Mining from protein–protein interactions. *Wiley Interdisciplinary Reviews: Data Mining and Knowledge Discovery, 2*(5), 400–410. doi:10.1002/widm.1065

Mandal, M., Mondal, J., & Mukhopadhyay, A. (2015). A PSO-based approach for pathway marker identification from gene expression data. *IEEE Transactions on Nanobioscience, 14*(6), 591–597. doi:10.1109/TNB.2015.2425471 PMID:25935045

Mandal, S. (2013). Enhanced Security Framework to Ensure Data Security in Cloud using Security Blanket Algorithm. *International Journal of Research in Engineering and Technology, 2*(10), 225–229. doi:10.15623/ijret.2013.0210033

Mank, R., Wilson, M. D., Rubio, J. M., & Post, R. J. (2004, March). A molecular marker for the identification of Simulium squamosum (Diptera: Simuliidae). *Ann. Trop. Med. Parasitol., 98*(2), 197–208. doi:10.1179/000349804225003118

Mao, W., & McEnhimer, S. (2010). *Survey: The application of GMOD in bioinformatics research.* Paper presented at the 4th International Conference on Bioinformatics and Biomedical Engineering (iCBBE 2010), Chengdu, China. doi:10.1109/ICBBE.2010.5516243

Mardia, K. V. (2013). Statistical approaches to three key challenges in protein structural bioinformatics. *Journal of the Royal Statistical Society. Series C, Applied Statistics, 62*(3), 487–514. doi:10.1111/rssc.12003

Margolis, R., Derr, L., Dunn, M., Huerta, M., Larkin, J., Sheehan, J., & Green, E. D. et al. (2014). The National Institutes of Healths Big Data to Knowledge (BD2 K) initiative: Capitalizing on biomedical Big Data. *Journal of the American Medical Informatics Association, 21*(6), 957–958. doi:10.1136/amiajnl-2014-002974 PMID:25008006

Markonis, D., Schaer, R., Eggel, I., ... (2012). Using MapReduce for large-scale medical image analysis. *Proceedings of the 2012 IEEE Second International Conference on Healthcare Informatics, Imaging and Systems Biology (HISB)*, La Jolla, California. IEEE. doi:10.1109/HISB.2012.8

Martinez, Martinez Jimenez, & Soto Hidalgo. (2010). Retrieving Texture Images Using Coarseness Fuzzy Partitions. *CCIS, 81*, 542-551.

Martinez, R., & Collard, M. (2007). Extracted knowledge: Interpretation in mining biological data, a survey. *International Journal of Computer Science and Applications, 1*, 1–21.

Ma, S., & Kosorok, M. R. (2009). Identification of differential gene pathways with principal component analysis. *Bioinformatics (Oxford, England), 25*(7), 882–889. doi:10.1093/bioinformatics/btp085 PMID:19223452

Mashiach, E., Nussinov, R., & Wolfson, H. J. (2010). FiberDock: Flexible induced-fit backbone refinement in molecular docking. *Proteins, 78*(6), 1503–1519. doi:10.1002/prot.22668 PMID:20077569

Mason, A. M., Borgert, C. J., Bus, J. S., Moiz Mumtaz, M., Simmons, J. E., & Sipes, I. G. (2007). Improving the scientific foundation for mixtures joint toxicity and risk assessment: Contributions from the SOT mixtures project-Introduction. *Toxicology and Applied Pharmacology, 223*(2), 99-103.

MASS Fact Sheet of Infectious Disease. (2015 December 9). Retrieved from http://www.mass.gov/eohhs/gov/departments/dph/programs/id/epidemiology/factsheets.html

Mccabe, M. P., & Ricciardelli, L. A. (2003). Sociocultural influences on body image and body changes among adolescente boys and girls. *The Journal of Social Psychology, 143*(1), 5–26. doi:10.1080/00224540309598428 PMID:12617344

Mccarroll, S. A., & Altshuler, D. M. (2007). Copy-number variation and association studies of human diseases. *Nature Genetics, 39*(7s), 37–42. doi:10.1038/ng2080 PMID:17597780

McCarthy, M. I., Abecasis, G. R., Cardon, L. R., Goldstein, D. B., Little, J., Ioannidis, J. P. A., & Hirschhorn, J. N. (2008). Genome-wide association studies for complex traits: Consensus, uncertainty and challenges. *Nature Reviews. Genetics, 9*(5), 356–369. doi:10.1038/nrg2344 PMID:18398418

McDonnell, A. V., Jiang, T., Keating, A. E., & Berger, B. (2006). Paircoil2: Improved prediction of coiled coils from sequence. *Bioinformatics (Oxford, England), 22*(3), 356–358. doi:10.1093/bioinformatics/bti797 PMID:16317077

McGinn, C. A., Grenier, S., Duplantie, J., Shaw, N., Sicotte, C., Mathieu, L., Leduc, Y., & Légaré, F., & Gagnon, Mp. (2011). Comparison of user groups' perspectives of barriers and facilitators to implementing electronic health records: A systematic review. *BMC Medicine, 9*(1), 46. PMID:21524315

McGuffin, L. J., Buenavista, M. T., & Roche, D. B. (2013). The ModFOLD4 server for the quality assessment of 3D protein models. *Nucleic Acids Research, 41*(Web Server issue), W368-72. doi:10.1093/nar/gkt294

McGuffin, L. J., Bryson, K., & Jones, D. T. (2000). The PSIPRED protein structure prediction server. *Bioinformatics (Oxford, England), 16*(4), 404–405. doi:10.1093/bioinformatics/16.4.404 PMID:10869041

McQueen, J. B. (1967). Some methods for classification and analysis of multivariate observations. *Paper presented at the Fifth Berkeley Symposium on Mathematical Statistics and Probability*, Berkeley.

Meiler, J., & Baker, D. (2006). ROSETTALIGAND: Protein-small molecule docking with full side-chain flexibility. *Proteins: Structure, Function, and Bioinformatics, 65*(3), 538–548. doi:10.1002/prot.21086 PMID:16972285

Menezes, A. C., Pinheiro, P. R., Pinheiro, M. C. D., & Cavalcante, T. P. (2012a). A Hybrid Model to Support the Early Diagnosis of Diabetes. 5th World Summit on the Knowledge Society.

Menezes, A. C., Pinheiro, P. R., Pinheiro, M. C. D., & Cavalcante, T. P. (2012b). Towards the Applied Hybrid Model in Decision Making: Support the Early Diagnosis of Type 2 Diabetes. *3rd International Conference on Information Computing and Applications*, 648-655. doi:10.1007/978-3-642-34062-8_84

Menezes, A. C., Pinheiro, P. R., Pinheiro, M. C. D., & Cavalcante, T. P. (2013). A Hybrid Model to Support the Diagnosis of Disease: A Case Study for Diabetes. *IEEE Canadian Conference on Electrical and Computer Engineering*.

Menger, V., Spruit, M., Hagoort, K., & Scheepers, F. (2016). Transitioning to a data driven mental health practice: Collaborative expert sessions for knowledge and hypothesis finding. *Computational and Mathematical Methods in Medicine*.

Meng, F., & Kurgan, L. (2016). DFLpred: High-throughput prediction of disordered flexible linker regions in protein sequences. *Bioinformatics (Oxford, England), 32*(12), i341–i350. doi:10.1093/bioinformatics/btw280 PMID:27307636

Merelli, I., Pérez-Sánchez, H., Gesing, S., & D'Agostino, D. (2014). Latest advances in distributed, parallel, and graphic processing unit accelerated approaches to computational biology. *Concurrency and Computation, 26*(10), 1699–1704. doi:10.1002/cpe.3111

Mészáros, B., Simon, I., Dosztányi, Z., Wright, P., Dyson, H., & Dyson, H. …Pliska, V. (2009). Prediction of Protein Binding Regions in Disordered Proteins. *PLoS Computational Biology, 5*(5), e1000376. doi:10.1371/journal.pcbi.1000376

Meulendijk, M., Spruit, M., Drenth-van-Maanen, A., Numans, M., Brinkkemper, S., & Jansen, P. (2013). General practitioners attitudes towards decision-supported prescribing: An analysis of the Dutch primary care sector. *Health Informatics Journal, 19*(4), 247–263. doi:10.1177/1460458212472333 PMID:24255051

Miller, B. T., Singh, R. P., Klauda, J. B., Hodoscek, M., Brooks, B. R., Woodcock, H. L., & III. (2008). CHARMMing: a new, flexible web portal for CHARMM. *Journal of Chemical Information and Modeling, 48*(9), 1920–9. doi:10.1021/ci800133b

Milo, R., Shen-Orr, S., Itzkovitz, S., Kashtan, N., Chklovskii, D., & Alon, U. (2002). Network Motifs: Simple Building Blocks of Complex Networks. *Science, 298*(5594), 824–827. doi:10.1126/science.298.5594.824 PMID:12399590

Mirel, B. (2007). *Usability and usefulness in bioinformatics: Evaluating a tool for querying and analyzing protein interactions based on scientists' actual research questions*. Paper presented at 2007 IEEE International Professional Communication Conference (IPCC 2007), Seattle, WA. doi:10.1109/IPCC.2007.4464064

Mirel, B. (2009). Supporting cognition in systems biology analysis: Findings on users' processes and design implications. *Journal of Biomedical Discovery and Collaboration, 4*(2), 1–17. PMID:19216777

Mitchell, T. (1997). *Machine Learning*. New York, USA: McGraw-Hill Publishers.

Mobley, D. L., & Dill, K. A. (2009). Binding of small-molecule ligands to proteins: "what you" is not always "what you get." *Structure, 17*(4), 489–98. Doi:<ALIGNMENT.qj></ALIGNMENT>10.1016/j.str.2009.02.010

Moghaddasi, H., Hosseini, A., Asadi, F., & Ganjali, R. (2011). Infrastructures of the System for Developing Electronic Health record. *Journal of Paramedical Sciences, 2*, 48–55.

Moles, C. G., Mendes, P., & Banga, J. R. (2003). Parameter estimation in biochemical pathways: A comparison of global optimization methods. *Genome Research, 13*(11), 2467–2474. doi:10.1101/gr.1262503 PMID:14559783

Møller, M. F. (1993). A scaled conjugate gradient algorithm for fast supervised learning. *Neural Networks, 6*(4), 525–533. doi:10.1016/S0893-6080(05)80056-5

Monastyrskyy, B., D'Andrea, D., Fidelis, K., Tramontano, A., & Kryshtafovych, A. (2016). New encouraging developments in contact prediction: Assessment of the CASP11 results. *Proteins: Structure, Function, and Bioinformatics, 84*(S1), 131–144. doi:10.1002/prot.24943

Moore, J. H. (2007). Bioinformatics. *Journal of Cellular Physiology, 213*(2), 365–369. doi:10.1002/jcp.21218 PMID:17654500

Morcos, F., Pagnani, A., Lunt, B., Bertolino, A., Marks, D. S., & Sander, C. …Weigt, M. (2011). Direct-coupling analysis of residue coevolution captures native contacts across many protein families. *Proceedings of the National Academy of Sciences of the United States of America, 108*(49), E1293-301. doi:10.1073/pnas.1111471108

Morgan, C. M., Vecchiatti, I. R., & Negrão, A. B. (2002). Etiologia dos transtornos alimentares: Aspectos biológicos, psicológicos e sócio-culturais. *Revista Brasileira de Psiquiatria (Sao Paulo, Brazil), 24*(3), 18–23. doi:10.1590/S1516-44462002000700005

Morris, G. M., Goodsell, D. S., Halliday, R. S., Huey, R., Hart, W. E., Belew, R. K., & Olson, A. J. (1998). Automated docking using a Lamarckian genetic algorithm and an empirical binding free energy function. *Journal of Computational Chemistry, 19*(14), 1639–1662. doi:10.1002/(SICI)1096-987X(19981115)19:14<1639::AID-JCC10>3.0.CO;2-B

Morris, G. M., Goodsell, D. S., Huey, R., & Olson, A. J. (1996). Distributed automated docking of flexible ligands to proteins: Parallel applications of AutoDock 2.4. *Journal of Computer-Aided Molecular Design, 10*(4), 293–304. doi:10.1007/BF00124499 PMID:8877701

Morris, G. M., Huey, R., Lindstrom, W., Sanner, M. F., Belew, R. K., Goodsell, D. S., & Olson, A. J. (2009). AutoDock4 and AutoDockTools4: Automated docking with selective receptor flexibility. *Journal of Computational Chemistry, 30*(16), 2785–2791. doi:10.1002/jcc.21256 PMID:19399780

Morse, S. S. (2012). Public health surveillance and infectious disease detection. *Biosecurity and Bioterrorism, 10*(1), 6–16. doi:10.1089/bsp.2011.0088 PMID:22455675

Mortazavi, A., Williams, B. A., McCue, K., Schaeffer, L., & Wold, B. (2008). Mapping and Quantifying Mammalian Transcriptomes by RNA-Seq. *Nature Methods, 5*(7), 621–628. doi:10.1038/nmeth.1226 PMID:18516045

Mosca, R., Pons, C., Fernández-Recio, J., & Aloy, P. (2009). Pushing Structural Information into the Yeast Interactome by High-Throughput Protein Docking Experiments. *PLoS Computational Biology, 5*(8), e1000490. doi:10.1371/journal.pcbi.1000490 PMID:19714207

Motiwalla, L. (2010). Value Added Privacy Services for Healthcare Data.

Moult, J., Fidelis, K., Kryshtafovych, A., Schwede, T., & Tramontano, A. (2016). Critical assessment of methods of protein structure prediction: Progress and new directions in round XI. *Proteins: Structure, Function, and Bioinformatics, 84*(S1), 4–14. doi:10.1002/prot.25064

Mount, D. W. (2004). *Bioinformatics: sequence and genome analysis*. Cold Spring Harbor Laboratory Press.

Muhtaroglu, F. C. P., Demir, S., Obali, M., & Girgin, C. (2013, October 6-9). Business model canvas perspective on big data applications. *Proceedings of the 2013 IEEE International Conference on Big Data*, Silicon Valley, CA (pp. 32 – 37).

Mukherjee, A., Liu, B., & Glance, N. (2012). Spotting fake reviewer groups in consumer reviews. *Proceedings of the 21st International Conference on World Wide Web* (pp. 191–200). doi:10.1145/2187836.2187863

Mukherjee, S., & Zhang, Y. (2011). Protein-Protein Complex Structure Predictions by Multimeric Threading and Template Recombination. *Structure (London, England)*, *19*(7), 955–966. doi:10.1016/j.str.2011.04.006 PMID:21742262

Mukhopadhyay, A., & Mandal, M. (2014). Identifying non-redundant gene markers from microarray data: A multiobjective variable length pso-based approach. *IEEE/ACM Transactions on Computational Biology and Bioinformatics*, *11*(6), 1170–1183. doi:10.1109/TCBB.2014.2323065 PMID:26357053

Muller, M. Q., Dreiocker, F., Ihling, C. H., Schafer, M., & Sinz, A. (2010). Fragmentation behavior of a thiourea-based reagent for protein structure analysis by collision-induced dissociative chemical cross-linking. *Journal of Mass Spectrometry*, *45*(8), 880–891. doi:10.1002/jms.1775 PMID:20607845

Muratcioglu, S., Guven-Maiorov, E., Keskin, Ö., & Gursoy, A. (2015). Advances in template-based protein docking by utilizing interfaces towards completing structural interactome. *Current Opinion in Structural Biology*, *35*, 87–92. doi:10.1016/j.sbi.2015.10.001 PMID:26539658

Mustafa, R. U., Nawaz, M. S., & Lali, M. I. (2015). Search engine optimization techniques to get high score in SERP's using recommended guidelines. *Science International*, *26*(6), 5079–5086.

Muzic, R. F. Jr, & Christian, B. T. (2006). Evaluation of objective functions for estimation of kinetic parameters. *Medical Physics*, *33*(2), 342–353. doi:10.1118/1.2135907 PMID:16532939

Nadeau, B. D. (2005). *Baseline information extraction: Multilingual information extraction from text with Machine Learning and Natural Language techniques (Technical Report)*. University of Ottawa.

Nagasaki, H., Mochizuki, T., Kodama, Y., Saruhashi, S., Morizaki, S., Sugawara, H., & Nakamura, Y. et al. (2013). DDBJ read annotation pipeline: A cloud computing-based pipeline for high-throughput analysis of next-generation sequencing data. *DNA Research*, *20*(4), 383–390. doi:10.1093/dnares/dst017 PMID:23657089

Nagata, K., Randall, A., & Baldi, P. (2012). SIDEpro: A novel machine learning approach for the fast and accurate prediction of side-chain conformations. *Proteins*, *80*(1), 142–153. doi:10.1002/prot.23170 PMID:22072531

Nakamura, H., Muro, T., Imamura, S., & Yuasa, I. (2009, March). Forensic species identification based on size variation of mitochondrial DNA hypervariable regions. *International Journal of Legal Medicine*, *123*(2), 177–184. doi:10.1007/s00414-008-0306-7 PMID:19052767

NANDA International Nursing Diagnosis. (2015). Definitions and Classifications 2015-2017 (10th ed.). Wiley-Blackwell.

National Toxicology Program. (2012). *NTP Monograph on Health Effects of Low-Level Lead*. Research Triangle Park, NC: National Institute of Environmental Health Sciences.

Negash, S. (2004). Business intelligence. *Communications of the Association for Information Systems*, *13*, 177–195.

Netica Application, Norsys Software Corp. (1998). Available in 08/2016, http://www.norsys.com

Nevado, B., & Perez-Enciso, M. (2015). Pipeliner: Software to evaluate the performance of bioinformatics pipelines for next-generation resequencing. *Molecular Ecology Resources*, *15*(1), 99–106. doi:10.1111/1755-0998.12286 PMID:24890372

Neves, M. A. C., Totrov, M., & Abagyan, R. (2012). Docking and scoring with ICM: The benchmarking results and strategies for improvement. *Journal of Computer-Aided Molecular Design*, *26*(6), 675–686. doi:10.1007/s10822-012-9547-0 PMID:22569591

Neveu, E., Ritchie, D. W., Popov, P., & Grudinin, S. (2016). PEPSI-Dock: A detailed data-driven protein-protein interaction potential accelerated by polar Fourier correlation. *Bioinformatics (Oxford, England)*, *32*(17), i693–i701. doi:10.1093/bioinformatics/btw443 PMID:27587691

Newman, D., Hettich, S., Blake, C., & Merz, C. (1998). *Uci repository of machine learning databases*. Academic Press.

Newman, M. E. J. (2001). The Structure of Scientific Collaboration Networks. *Proceedings of the National Academy of Sciences of the United States of America, 98*(2), 404–409. doi:10.1073/pnas.98.2.404 PMID:11149952

Ng, K., Ghoting, A., Steinhubl, S. R., Stewart, W. F., Malin, B., & Sun, J. (2014). PARAMO: A PARAllel predictive MOdeling platform for healthcare analytic research using electronic health records. *Journal of Biomedical Informatics, 48*, 160–170. doi:10.1016/j.jbi.2013.12.012 PMID:24370496

Nibbe, R. K., Chowdhury, S. A., Koyutürk, M., Ewing, R., & Chance, M. R. (2011). Protein–protein interaction networks and subnetworks in the biology of disease. Wiley Interdisciplinary Reviews: Systems Biology and Medicine, 3(3), 357–367. doi:10.1002/wsbm.121

Nichols, D. A., Renslo, A. R., & Chen, Y. (2014). Fragment-based inhibitor discovery against β-lactamase. *Future Medicinal Chemistry, 6*(4), 413–427. doi:10.4155/fmc.14.10 PMID:24635522

Nielsen, M., Lundegaard, C., & Lund, O. (2010). CPHmodels-3.0—remote homology modeling using structure-guided sequence profiles. *Nucleic Acids*. Retrieved from http://nar.oxfordjournals.org/content/early/2010/06/11/nar.gkq535.short

Niemenmaa, M., Kallio, A., Schumacher, A., Klemela, P., Korpelainen, E., & Heljanko, K. (2012). Hadoop-BAM: Directly manipulating next generation sequencing data in the cloud. *Bioinformatics (Oxford, England), 28*(6), 876–877. doi:10.1093/bioinformatics/bts054 PMID:22302568

Nieuwenhuijsen, M. J., Donaire-Gonzalez, D., Foraster, M., Martinez, D., & Cisneros, A. (2014). Using Personal Sensors to Assess the Exposome and Acute Health Effects. *International Journal of Environmental Research and Public Health, 11*(8), 7805–7819. doi:10.3390/ijerph110807805 PMID:25101766

Nigam, K., & Ghani, R. (2000). Analyzing the effectiveness and applicability of co-training. *Proceedings of the Ninth International Conference on Information and Knowledge Management,* 86–93. doi:10.1145/354756.354805

NIH. (2016). The Precision Medicine Initiative (PMI) Cohort Program. Retrieved from https://www.nih.gov/precision-medicine-initiative-cohort-program

Niu, B., Zhu, Y., He, X., & Wu, H. (2007). MCPSO: A multi-swarm cooperative particle swarm optimizer. *Applied Mathematics and Computation, 185*(2), 1050–1062. doi:10.1016/j.amc.2006.07.026

Noble, M. E., Endicott, J. A., & Johnson, L. N. (2004). Protein kinase inhibitors: Insights into drug design from structure. *Science, 303*(5665), 1800–1805. doi:10.1126/science.1095920 PMID:15031492

Nosengo, N. (2016). Can you teach old drugs new tricks? *Nature, 534*(7607), 314–316. doi:10.1038/534314a PMID:27306171

Nunes, L. C. (2010). *Um Modelo Híbrido para Apoio ao Diagnóstico de Transtornos Psicológicos*. Universidade de Fortaleza, Ceará: Dissertação, Mestrado em Informática Aplicada.

Nunes, L. C., Pinheiro, P. R., & Pequeno, T. C. (2009). An Expert System Applied to the Diagnosis of Psychological Disorders. *IEEE International Conference on Intelligent Computing and Intelligent Systems, 3*, 363-367. doi:10.1109/ICICISYS.2009.5358164

Nunes, L. C., Pinheiro, P. R., Pequeno, T. C., & Pinheiro, M. C. D. (2011). Towards an Applied to the Diagnosis of Psychological Disorders. *Advances in Experimental Medicine and Biology, 696*, 573–580. doi:10.1007/978-1-4419-7046-6_58 PMID:21431598

O'Connor, B., Balasubramanyan, R., Routledge, B. R., & Smith, N. A. (2010). From tweets to polls: Linking text sentiment to public opinion time series. *Proceedings of Fourth International AAAI Conference on Weblogs and Social Media* (pp. 122-129).

Ogurtsov, A.Y., Sunyaev, S., & Kondrashov, A.S. (2004, August). Indel-based evolutionary distance and mouse-human divergence. *Genome Res.*, *14*(8), 1610–1616. doi:10.1101/gr.2450504

Ojo, O. O., & Omabe, M. (2011). Incorporating bioinformatics into biological science education in Nigeria: Prospects and challenges. *Infection, Genetics and Evolution*, *11*(4), 784–787. doi:10.1016/j.meegid.2010.11.015 PMID:21145989

Okonechnikov, K., Conesa, A., & García-Alcalde, F. (2016). Qualimap 2: Advanced Multi-Sample Quality Control for High-Throughput Sequencing Data. *Bioinformatics (Oxford, England)*, *32*(2), 292–294. doi:10.1093/bioinformatics/btv566 PMID:26428292

Olden, J. D., Joy, M. K., & Death, R. G. (2004). An accurate comparison of methods for quantifying variable importance in artificial neural networks using simulated data. *Ecological Modelling*, *178*(3-4), 389–397. doi:10.1016/j.ecolmodel.2004.03.013

Omer, A., Singh, P., Yadav, N. K., & Singh, R. K. (2015). microRNAs: Role in leukemia and their computational perspective. Wiley Interdisciplinary Reviews: RNA, 6(1), 65–78. PubMed 10.1002/wrna.1256

Orobitg, M., Guirado, F., Cores, F., Llados, J., & Notredame, C. (2015). High performance computing improvements on bioinformatics consistency-based multiple sequence alignment tools. *Parallel Computing*, *42*, 18–34. doi:10.1016/j.parco.2014.09.010

Oveland, E., Muth, T., Rapp, E., Martens, L., Berven, F. S., & Barsnes, H. (2015). Viewing the proteome: How to visualize proteomics data? *Proteomics*, *15*(8), 1341–1355. doi:10.1002/pmic.201400412 PMID:25504833

Overington, J. P., Al-Lazikani, B., & Hopkins, A. L. (2006). How many drug targets are there? *Nature Reviews. Drug Discovery*, *5*(12), 993–996. doi:10.1038/nrd2199 PMID:17139284

Ozsolak, F., & Milos, P. M. (2011). RNA Sequencing: Advances, Challenges and Opportunities. *Nature Reviews. Genetics*, *12*(2), 87–98. doi:10.1038/nrg2934 PMID:21191423

P.R. (2012). Third Party Data Protection Applied To Cloud and Xacml Implementation in the Hadoop Environment With Sparql.

Palagi, P. M., Hernandez, P., Walther, D., & Appel, R. D. (2006). Proteome informatics I: Bioinformatics tools for processing experimental data. *Proteomics*, *6*(20), 5435–5444. doi:10.1002/pmic.200600273 PMID:16991191

Palet, C., Turbelin, C., Bar-Hen, A., Flahault, A., & Vallernon, A. (2009). More disease tracked by using Google Trends. *Emerging Infectious Diseases*, *15*(8), 1327–1328. doi:10.3201/eid1508.090299 PMID:19751610

Pal, J. K., Ray, S. S., Cho, S. B., & Pal, S. K. (2016). Fuzzy-Rough Entropy Measure and Histogram Based Patient Selection for miRNA Ranking in Cancer. *IEEE/ACM Transactions on Computational Biology and Bioinformatics*, 1. doi:10.1109/TCBB.2016.2623605 PMID:27831888

Panchaud, A., Singh, P., Shaffer, S. A., & Goodlett, D. R. (2010). xComb: A cross-linked peptide database approach to protein-protein interaction analysis. *Journal of Proteome Research*, *9*(5), 2508–2515. doi:10.1021/pr9011816 PMID:20302351

Pandith, M. (2014). Data Security and Privacy Concerns in Cloud Computing. *IOTCC*, *2*(2), 6. doi:10.11648/j.iotcc.20140202.11

Pang, B., & Lee, L. (2008). Opinion mining and sentiment analysis. *Foundation of Trends in Information Retrieval, 2*(1-2), 1–135. doi:10.1561/1500000011

Pang, S., Havukkala, I., Hu, Y., & Kasabov, N. (2007). Classification consistency analysis for bootstrapping gene selection. *Neural Computing & Applications, 16*(6), 527–539. doi:10.1007/s00521-007-0110-1

Park, H., Lee, G. R., Heo, L., Seok, C., Fiser, A., & Do, R. … Dill, K. (2014). Protein Loop Modeling Using a New Hybrid Energy Function and Its Application to Modeling in Inaccurate Structural Environments. *PLoS ONE, 9*(11), e113811. doi:10.1371/journal.pone.0113811

Parkin, D. M., Bray, F., Ferlay, J., & Pisani, P. (2005). Global cancer statistics. CA: A Cancer Journal for Clinicians, 55(2), 74-108.

Parveen, I., Moorby, J. M., Fraser, M. D., Allison, G. G., & Kopka, J. (2007). Application of gas chromatography-mass spectrometry metabolite profiling techniques to the analysis of heathland plant diets of sheep. *Journal of Agricultural and Food Chemistry, 55*(4), 1129–1138. doi:10.1021/jf062995w PMID:17249687

Patel, C., & Manrai, A. K. (2015). Development of exposome correlation globes to map out environment-wide associations. *Paper presented at the Pac Symp Biocomput.*

Patel, C. J., & Ioannidis, J. P. (2014). Placing epidemiological results in the context of multiplicity and typical correlations of exposures. *Journal of Epidemiology and Community Health, 68*(11), 1096–1100. doi:10.1136/jech-2014-204195 PMID:24923805

Patro, R., Mount, S. M., & Kingsford, C. (2014). Sailfish Enables Alignment-Free Isoform Quantification from RNA-Seq Reads Using Lightweight Algorithms. *Nature Biotechnology, 32*(5), 462–464. doi:10.1038/nbt.2862 PMID:24752080

Paul, M. J., & Dredze, M. (2011). You are what you tweet: Analysing Twitter for public health. *Proceedings of Fifth International AAAI Conference on Weblogs and Social Media* (pp. 265-272).

Payne, M. P., & Kenny, L. C. (2002). Comparison of models for the estimation of biological partition coefficients. *Journal of Toxicology and Environmental Health. Part A., 65*(13), 897–931. doi:10.1080/00984100290071171 PMID:12133236

Pearl, J., & Verma, T. S. (1991). A theory of inferred causation. *Paper presented at the Principles of Knowledge Representation and Reasoning Second International Conference.*

Pearlman, D. A., Case, D. A., Caldwell, J. W., Ross, W. S., Cheatham, T. E., & DeBolt, S. … Kollman, P. (1995). AMBER, a package of computer programs for applying molecular mechanics, normal mode analysis, molecular dynamics and free energy calculations to simulate the structural and energetic properties of molecules. *Computer Physics Communications, 91*(1), 1–41. doi:10.1016/0010-4655(95)00041-D

Peng, K., Radivojac, P., Vucetic, S., Dunker, A. K., & Obradovic, Z. (2006). Length-dependent prediction of protein intrinsic disorder. *BMC Bioinformatics, 7*(1), 208. doi:10.1186/1471-2105-7-208 PMID:16618368

Perco, P., Rapberger, R., Siehs, C., Lukas, A., Oberbauer, R., Mayer, G., & Mayer, B. (2006). Transforming omics data into context: Bioinformatics on genomics and proteomics raw data. *Electrophoresis, 27*(13), 2659–2675. doi:10.1002/elps.200600064 PMID:16739231

Pereira, F., Carneiro, J., Matthiesen, R., van Asch, B., Pinto, N., Gusmao, L., & Amorim, A. (2010, October 4). Identification of species by multiplex analysis of variable-length sequences. *Nucleic Acids Research, 38*(22), e203–e203. doi:10.1093/nar/gkq865 PMID:20923781

Perry, D. (2012). Most organizations unaware of employees with admin rights. Retrieved from http://www.tomsitpro.com/articles/administrator_rights-admin_rights-malware-IT_security_professionals,1-353.html

Pertea, M., Pertea, G. M., Antonescu, C. M., Chang, T.-C., Mendell, J. T., & Salzberg, S. L. (2015). StringTie Enables Improved Reconstruction of a Transcriptome from RNA-Seq Reads. *Nature Biotechnology, 33*(3), 290–295. doi:10.1038/nbt.3122 PMID:25690850

Pervaiz, F., Pervaiz, M., Rehman, N. A., & Saif, U. (2012). FluBreaks: Early Epidemic detection system from Google Flu Trends. *Journal of Medical Internet Research, 14*(5), e125. doi:10.2196/jmir.2102 PMID:23037553

Petersen, B., Lundegaard, C., & Petersen, T. N. GD, G. R., Smith, J., Milner-White, E. J., ... Ho, T. (2010). NetTurnP – Neural Network Prediction of Beta-turns by Use of Evolutionary Information and Predicted Protein Sequence Features. *PLoS ONE, 5*(11), e15079. doi:10.1371/journal.pone.0015079

Petersen, B., Petersen, T., Andersen, P., Nielsen, M., Lundegaard, C., & Lundegaard, C. ... Sander, C. (2009). A generic method for assignment of reliability scores applied to solvent accessibility predictions. *BMC Structural Biology, 9*(1), 51. doi:10.1186/1472-6807-9-51

Peterson, R., Grinyer, J., & Nevalainen, H. (2011). Secretome of the coprophilous fungus Doratomyces stemonitis C8, isolated from koala feces. *Applied and Environmental Microbiology, 77*(11), 3793–3801. doi:10.1128/AEM.00252-11 PMID:21498763

Pettersen, E. F., Goddard, T. D., Huang, C. C., Couch, G. S., Greenblatt, D. M., Meng, E. C., & Ferrin, T. E. (2004). UCSF Chimera - A visualization system for exploratory research and analysis. *Journal of Computational Chemistry, 25*(13), 1605–1612. doi:10.1002/jcc.20084 PMID:15264254

Peyret, T., & Krishnan, K. (2011). QSARs for PBPK modelling of environmental contaminants. *SAR and QSAR in Environmental Research, 22*(1-2), 129–169. doi:10.1080/1062936X.2010.548351 PMID:21391145

Pham, D. V., Halgamuge, M. N., Syed, A., & Mendis, P. (2010). Optimizing windows security features to block malware and hack tools on USB storage devices. Proceedings of Progress in electromagnetics research symposium (pp. 350-355).

Pham, D. V., Syed, A., Mohammad, A., & Halgamuge, M. N. (2010, June 14-16). Threat Analysis of Portable Hack Tools from USB Storage Devices and Protection Solutions. *Proceedings of the International Conference on Information and Emerging Technologies*, Karachi, Pakistan. doi:10.1109/ICIET.2010.5625728

Pham, D. V., Syed, A., & Halgamuge, M. N. (2011). Universal serial bus based software attacks and protection solutions. *Digital Investigation, 7*(3), 172–184. doi:10.1016/j.diin.2011.02.001

Phan, J. H., Quo, C. F., & Wang, M. D. (2006). *Functional genomics and proteomics in the clinical neurosciences: data mining and bioinformatics. Progress in Brain Research*, 158, 83–108. doi:10.1016/S0079-6123(06)58004-5

Phillips, J. C., Braun, R., Wang, W., Gumbart, J., Tajkhorshid, E., & Villa, E. ... Schulten, K. (2005). Scalable molecular dynamics with NAMD. *Journal of Computational Chemistry, 26*(16), 1781–1802. doi:10.1002/jcc.20289

Pierce, B. G., Hourai, Y., & Weng, Z. (2011). Accelerating Protein Docking in ZDOCK Using an Advanced 3D Convolution Library. *PLoS ONE, 6*(9), e24657. doi:10.1371/journal.pone.0024657 PMID:21949741

Pierce, B. G., Wiehe, K., Hwang, H., Kim, B.-H., Vreven, T., & Weng, Z. (2014). ZDOCK server: Interactive docking prediction of protein-protein complexes and symmetric multimers. *Bioinformatics, 30*(12), 1771–1773. doi:10.1093/bioinformatics/btu097 PMID:24532726

Pierce, B., Tong, W., & Weng, Z. (2005). M-ZDOCK: A grid-based approach for Cn symmetric multimer docking. *Bioinformatics, 21*(8), 1472–1478. doi:10.1093/bioinformatics/bti229 PMID:15613396

Pietra, F. (2002). Evolution of the secondary metabolite versus evolution of the species. *Pure and Applied Chemistry, 74*(11), 2207–2211. doi:10.1351/pac200274112207

Pinho, J., Sobral, J. L., & Rocha, M. (2013). Parallel evolutionary computation in bioinformatics applications. *Computer Methods and Programs in Biomedicine*, *110*(2), 183–191. doi:10.1016/j.cmpb.2012.10.001 PMID:23127284

Pitchai, R., Jayashri, S., & Raja, J. (2016). Searchable Encrypted Data File Sharing Method Using Public Cloud Service for Secure Storage in Cloud Computing. *Wireless Personal Communications*, *90*(2), 947–960. doi:10.1007/s11277-016-3273-1

Polgreen, P. M., Chen, Y., Pennock, D. M., Nelson, F. D., & Weinstein, R. A. (2008). Using Internet searches for Influenza surveillance. *Clinical Infectious Diseases*, *47*(11), 1433–1448. doi:10.1086/593098 PMID:18954267

Pollastri, G., & McLysaght, A. (2005). Porter: A new, accurate server for protein secondary structure prediction. *Bioinformatics (Oxford, England)*, *21*(8), 1719–1720. doi:10.1093/bioinformatics/bti203 PMID:15585524

Pons, C., Jiménez-González, D., González-Álvarez, C., Servat, H., Cabrera-Benítez, D., Aguilar, X., & Fernández-Recio, J. (2012). Cell-Dock: High-performance protein-protein docking. *Bioinformatics*, *28*(18), 2394–2396. doi:10.1093/bioinformatics/bts454 PMID:22815362

Pontius, J., Richelle, J., & Wodak, S. J. (1996). Deviations from Standard Atomic Volumes as a Quality Measure for Protein Crystal Structures. *Journal of Molecular Biology*, *264*(1), 121–136. doi:10.1006/jmbi.1996.0628 PMID:8950272

Popov, P., Ritchie, D. W., & Grudinin, S. (2014). DockTrina: Docking triangular protein trimers. *Proteins: Structure, Function, and Bioinformatics*, *82*(1), 34–44. doi:10.1002/prot.24344 PMID:23775700

Powers, C. A., Meyer, C. M., Roebuck, M. C., & Vaziri, B. (2005). Predictive Modeling of Total Healthcare Costs Using Pharmacy Claims: A Comparison of Alternative Econometric Cost Modeling Techniques. *Medical Care*, *43*(11), 1065–1072. doi:10.1097/01.mlr.0000182408.54390.00 PMID:16224298

Prakash, P., Ghosliya, D., & Gupta, V. (2014). Identification of conserved and novel microRNAs in *Catharanthus roseus* by deep sequencing and computational prediction of their potential targets. *Gene*, *554*(2), 181–195. doi:10.1016/j.gene.2014.10.046 PMID:25445288

Price, K., & Krishnan, K. (2011). An integrated QSAR-PBPK modelling approach for predicting the inhalation toxicokinetics of mixtures of volatile organic chemicals in the rat. *SAR and QSAR in Environmental Research*, *22*(1-2), 107–128. doi:10.1080/1062936X.2010.548350 PMID:21391144

Pugalenthi, G., Shameer, K., Srinivasan, N., & Sowdhamini, R. (2006). HARMONY: a server for the assessment of protein structures. *Nucleic Acids Research, 34*(Web Server), W231–W234. https://doi.org/10.1093/nar/gkl314

Puton, T., Kozlowski, L., Tuszynska, I., Rother, K., & Bujnicki, J. M. (2012). Computational methods for prediction of protein–RNA interactions. *Journal of Structural Biology*, *179*(3), 261–268. doi:10.1016/j.jsb.2011.10.001 PMID:22019768

Puzyn, T., Leszczynski, J., & Cronin, M. T. D. (2010). Recent Advances in QSAR Studies. New York: Springer Science+Business Media. doi:10.1007/978-1-4020-9783-6

Quinlan, J. (1986). C4.5: Programs for machine learning. San Mateo.

Raetz, E. A., Perkins, S. L., Bhojwani, D., Smock, K., Philip, M., Carroll, W. L., & Min, D. J. (2006). Gene expression profiling reveals intrinsic differences between T cell acute lymphoblastic leukemia and T-cell lymphoblastic lymphoma. *Pediatric Blood & Cancer*, *47*(2), 130–140. doi:10.1002/pbc.20550 PMID:16358311

Raghavendra, S., Aditya Rao, S. J., Kumar, V., & Ramesh, C. K. (2015). Multiple ligand simultaneous docking (MLSD): A novel approach to study the effect of inhibitors on substrate binding to PPO. *Computational Biology and Chemistry*, *59 Pt A*, 81–6. Doi:<ALIGNMENT.qj></ALIGNMENT>10.1016/j.compbiolchem.2015.09.008

Raimondo, F., Morosi, L., Chinello, C., Magni, F., & Pitto, M. (2011). Advances in membranous vesicle and exosome proteomics improving biological understanding and biomarker discovery. *Proteomics, 11*(4), 709–720. doi:10.1002/pmic.201000422 PMID:21241021

Rain, J. C., Selig, L., De Reuse, H., Battaglia, V., Reverdy, C., Simon, S., & Legrain, P. et al. (2001). The Protein-Protein Interaction Map of Helicobacter Pylori. *Nature, 409*(6817), 211–215. doi:10.1038/35051615 PMID:11196647

Ramamoorthy, S. (2013). Optimized Data Analysis in Cloud using BigData Analytics Techniques. Proceedings of 4th ICCCNT.

Raman, S., Vernon, R., Thompson, J., Tyka, M., Sadreyev, R., & Pei, J. ... Baker, D. (2009). Structure prediction for CASP8 with all-atom refinement using Rosetta. *Proteins, 77*(Suppl. 9), 89–99. doi:10.1002/prot.22540

Ramírez-Aportela, E., López-Blanco, J. R., & Chacón, P. (2016). FRODOCK 2.0: Fast protein-protein docking server. *Bioinformatics, 32*(15), 2386–2388. doi:10.1093/bioinformatics/btw141 PMID:27153583

Rampersaud, G. C., Pereira, M. A., Girard, B. L., Adams, J., & Metzl, J. D. (2005). Breakfast habits, nutritional status, body weight, and academic performance in children and adolescents. *J Am Diet Assoc, 105*(5), 743-760; quiz 761-742. doi:10.1016/j.jada.2005.02.007

Randic, M., Novic, M., & Plavsic, D. (2013). Milestones in graphical bioinformatics. *International Journal of Quantum Chemistry, 113*(22), 2413–2446.

Rathod, K. R. (2016). Cloud Computing - Key Pillar for Digital India. *International Journal of Information, 6*(1/2), 27–33.

Ravasz, E., Somera, A. L., Mongru, D. A., Oltvai, Z. N., & Barabási, A. L. (2002). Hierarchical Organization of Modularity in Metabolic Networks. *Science, 297*(5586), 1551–1555. doi:10.1126/science.1073374 PMID:12202830

Ravindranath, P. A., Forli, S., Goodsell, D. S., Olson, A. J., & Sanner, M. F. (2015). AutoDockFR: Advances in Protein-Ligand Docking with Explicitly Specified Binding Site Flexibility. *PLoS Computational Biology, 11*(12), e1004586. doi:10.1371/journal.pcbi.1004586 PMID:26629955

Reddy, P. J., Jain, R., & Paik, Y. K. et al.. (2011). Personalized medicine in the age of Pharmacoproteomics: A close up on India and need for social science engagement for responsible innovation in post proteomic biology. *Curr. Pharm. Pers. Med., 9*, 67–75. PMID:22279515

Reimand, J., Hui, S., Jain, S., Law, B., & Bader, G. D. (2012). Domain-mediated protein interaction prediction: From genome to network. *FEBS Letters, 586*(17), 2751–2763. doi:10.1016/j.febslet.2012.04.027 PMID:22561014

Remmel, H., Paech, B., Engwer, C., & Bastian, P. (2011). *Supporting the testing of scientific frameworks with software product line engineering: A proposed approach.* Paper presented at the 4th International Workshop on Software Engineering for Computational Science and Engineering (SE–CSE 2011), Waikiki, HI. doi:10.1145/1985782.1985785

Ren, B., Robert, F., Wyrick, J. J., Aparicio, O., Jennings, E. G., Simon, I., ... & Volkert, T. L. (2000). Genome-Wide Location and Function of DNA Binding Proteins. *Science, 290*(5500), 2306–2309. doi:10.1126/science.290.5500.2306 PMID:11125145

Ren, Y. a. (2012, October 30-November 1). A Service Integrity Assurance Framework For Cloud Computing Based On Mapreduce. *Proceedings of IEEE CCIS'12,* Hangzhou (pp. 240 –244).

Ribeiro, J. V., Bernardi, R. C., Rudack, T., Stone, J. E., Phillips, J. C., & Freddolino, P. L. ... Schulten, K. (2016). QwikMD — Integrative Molecular Dynamics Toolkit for Novices and Experts. *Scientific Reports, 6,* 26536. doi:10.1038/srep26536

Riedmiller, M., & Braun, H. (1993). A direct adaptive method for faster backpropagation learning: the RPROP algorithm. *Paper presented at the IEEE International Conference on Neural Networks.*

Ritchie, D. W., & Kemp, G. J. L. (1999). Fast computation, rotation, and comparison of low resolution spherical harmonic molecular surfaces. *Journal of Computational Chemistry, 20*(4), 383–395. doi:10.1002/(SICI)1096-987X(199903)20:4<383::AID-JCC1>3.0.CO;2-M

Ritchie, D. W., & Venkatraman, V. (2010). Ultra-fast FFT protein docking on graphics processors. *Bioinformatics, 26*(19), 2398–2405. doi:10.1093/bioinformatics/btq444 PMID:20685958

Ritterman, J., Osborne, M., & Klein, E. (2009). Using prediction markets and Twitter to predict a swine flu pandemic. *Proceedings of 1st International Workshop on Mining Social Media* (p. 9).

Robasky, K., Lewis, N. E., & Church, G. M. (2014). The Role of Replicates for Error Mitigation in next-Generation Sequencing. *Nature Reviews. Genetics, 15*(1), 56–62. doi:10.1038/nrg3655 PMID:24322726

Robertson, G., Schein, J., Chiu, R., Corbett, R., Field, M., Jackman, S. D., & Birol, I. et al. (2010). De Novo Assembly and Analysis of RNA-Seq Data. *Nature Methods, 7*(11), 909–912. doi:10.1038/nmeth.1517 PMID:20935650

Robinson, M. D., McCarthy, D. J., & Smyth, G. K. (2010). edgeR: A Bioconductor Package for Differential Expression Analysis of Digital Gene Expression Data. *Bioinformatics (Oxford, England), 26*(1), 139–140. doi:10.1093/bioinformatics/btp616 PMID:19910308

Robinson, T., Killcoyne, S., Bressler, R., & Boyle, J. (2011). SAMQA: Error classification and validation of high-throughput sequenced read data. *BMC Genomics, 12*(1), 419. doi:10.1186/1471-2164-12-419 PMID:21851633

Rodrigues, J. P. G. L. M., Levitt, M., & Chopra, G. (2012). KoBaMIN: A knowledge-based minimization web server for protein structure refinement. *Nucleic Acids Research, 40*(W1), W323–W328. doi:10.1093/nar/gks376 PMID:22564897

Roede, J. R., Uppal, K., Park, Y., Tran, V., & Jones, D. P. (2014). Transcriptome–metabolome wide association study (TMWAS) of maneb and paraquat neurotoxicity reveals network level interactions in toxicologic mechanism. *Toxicological Reviews, 1*, 435–444. doi:10.1016/j.toxrep.2014.07.006 PMID:27722094

Roessner, U., & Beckles, D. M. (2009). Metabolite measurements. In J. Schwender (Ed.), *Plant Metabolic Networks.* NY: Springer. doi:10.1007/978-0-387-78745-9_3

Roli, F. (2005). Semi-supervised multiple classifier systems: Background and research directions. Lecture Notes in Computer Science, 3541, 1–11.

Rose, B. A., Force, T., & Wang, Y. (2010). Mitogen-activated protein kinase signaling in the heart: Angels versus demons in a heart-breaking tale. *Physiological Reviews, 90*(4), 1507–1546. doi:10.1152/physrev.00054.2009 PMID:20959622

Rosenthal, A., Mork, P., Li, M. H., Stanford, J., Koester, D., & Reynolds, P. (2010). Cloud computing: A new business paradigm for biomedical information sharing. *Journal of Biomedical Informatics, 43*(2), 342–353. doi:10.1016/j.jbi.2009.08.014 PMID:19715773

Rost, B. (1999). Twilight zone of protein sequence alignments. *Protein Engineering, 12*(2), 85–94. doi:10.1093/protein/12.2.85 PMID:10195279

Rost, B., & Sander, C. (1993). Prediction of Protein Secondary Structure at Better than 70% Accuracy. *Journal of Molecular Biology, 232*(2), 584–599. doi:10.1006/jmbi.1993.1413 PMID:8345525

Roy, A., Weisel, C. P., Gallo, M., & Georgopoulos, P. (1996). Studies of multiroute exposure/dose reconstruction using physiologically based pharmacokinetic models. *Journal of Clean Technology. Environmental Toxicology and Occupational Medicine, 5*(4), 285–295.

Russin, M. M., & Davis, J. H. (1990). Continuing education electronic bulletin board system: Provider readiness and interest. *Journal of Continuing Education in Nursing, 21*(1), 7–23. PMID:2106537

Ryu, J., Lee, M., Cha, J., Laskowski, R. A., Ryu, S. E., & Kim, D.-S. (2016). BetaSCPWeb: Side-chain prediction for protein structures using Voronoi diagrams and geometry prioritization. *Nucleic Acids Research, 44*(W1), W416-23. doi:10.1093/nar/gkw368 PMID:27151195

Sadilek, A., Kautz, H. A., & Silenzio, V. (2012). Modelling spread of disease from social interactions. *Proceedings of 6th International AAAI conference on Web and Social Media.*

Saha, S., Ekbal, A., Gupta, K., & Bandyopadhyay, S. (2013). Gene expression data clustering using a multiobjective symmetry based clustering technique. *Computers in Biology and Medicine, 43*(11), 1965–1977. doi:10.1016/j.compbiomed.2013.07.021 PMID:24209942

Saikali, C.J., et al. (2004). Imagem corporal nos transtornos alimentares. *Revista de Psiquiatria Clínica, 31*(4), 154-156.

Saito, S., Kita, K., Morioka, C. Y., & Watanabe, A. (1999). Rapid recovery from anorexia nervosa after a life-threatening episode with severe thrombocytopenia: Report of three cases. *International Journal of Eating Disorders, Austin, 25*(1), 113–118. doi:10.1002/(SICI)1098-108X(199901)25:1<113::AID-EAT15>3.0.CO;2-D PMID:9924661

Sakaki, T., Okazaki, M., & Matsuo, Y. (2010). Earthquake shakes Twitter users: real-time event detection by social sensors. *Proceedings of the 19th International Conference on World Wide Web* (pp. 851-860). doi:10.1145/1772690.1772777

Sakellaropoulos, G. C., & Nikiforidis, G. C. (1999). Development of a Bayesian Network for the prognosis of head injuries using graphical model selection techniques. *Methods of Information in Medicine, 38*(1), 37–42. PMID:10339962

Salentin, S., Schreiber, S., Haupt, V. J., Adasme, M. F., & Schroeder, M. (2015). PLIP: Fully automated protein-ligand interaction profiler. *Nucleic Acids Research, 43*(W1), W443-7. doi:10.1093/nar/gkv315 PMID:25873628

Salton, G., & Buckley, C. (1988). Term-weighting approaches in automatic text retrieval. *Information Processing & Management, 24*(5), 513–523. doi:10.1016/0306-4573(88)90021-0

Salzberg, S. L., Phillippy, A. M., Zimin, A., Puiu, D., Magoc, T., Koren, S., & Yorke, J. A. et al. (2012). A critical evaluation of genome assemblies and assembly algorithms. *Genome Research, 22*(3), 557–567. doi:10.1101/gr.131383.111 PMID:22147368

Sanner, M. (1999). Python: a programming language for software integration and development. *J Mol Graph Model.* Retrieved from http://citeseerx.ist.psu.edu/viewdoc/download?doi=10.1.1.35.6459&rep=rep1&type=pdf

Sarigiannis, D. A., & Gotti, A. (2008). Biology-based dose-response models for health risk assessment of chemical mixtures. *Fresenius Environmental Bulletin, 17*(9 B), 1439-1451.

Sarigiannis, D. A., & Karakitsios, S. P. (2012, October 28 - November 2). A dynamic physiology based pharmacokinetic model for assessing lifelong internal dose. *Paper presented at the AICHE '12*, Pittsburgh, PA.

Sarigiannis, D., Karakitsios, S., Handakas, E., Simou, K., Solomou, E., & Gotti, A. (2016). Integrated exposure and risk characterization of bisphenol-A in Europe. *Food and Chemical Toxicology, 98*(Part B), 134-147. doi:10.1016/j.fct.2016.10.017

Sarigiannis, D. A., & Gotti, A. (2014). New methods for personal monitoring of air pollution through the use of passive sensors during childhood. *Pneumologia Pediatrica*, *54*, 37–43.

Sarigiannis, D. A., Karakitsios, S. P., Gotti, A., Liakos, I. L., & Katsoyiannis, A. (2011). Exposure to major volatile organic compounds and carbonyls in European indoor environments and associated health risk. *Environment International*, *37*(4), 743–765. doi:10.1016/j.envint.2011.01.005 PMID:21354626

Sarigiannis, D. A., Karakitsios, S. P., Gotti, A., Papaloukas, C. L., Kassomenos, P. A., & Pilidis, G. A. (2009). Bayesian algorithm implementation in a real time exposure assessment model on benzene with calculation of associated cancer risks. *Sensors (Basel, Switzerland)*, *9*(2), 731–755. doi:10.3390/s90200731 PMID:22399936

Sarigiannis, D., Gotti, A., Cimino Reale, G., & Marafante, E. (2009). Reflections on new directions for risk assessment of environmental chemical mixtures. *International Journal of Risk Assessment and Management*, *13*(3-4), 216–241. doi:10.1504/IJRAM.2009.030697

Sarigiannis, D., Gotti, A., & Karakitsios, S. (2011). A Computational Framework for Aggregate and Cumulative Exposure Assessment. *Epidemiology (Cambridge, Mass.)*, *22*(1), S96–S97. doi:10.1097/01.ede.0000391962.03834.66

Sarigiannis, D., & Karakitsios, S. (2011). Perinatal Exposure to Bisphenol A: The Route of Administration Makes the Dose. *Epidemiology (Cambridge, Mass.)*, *22*(1), S172. doi:10.1097/01.ede.0000392202.15822.bf

Sasso, A. F., Isukapalli, S. S., & Georgopoulos, P. G. (2010). A generalized physiologically-based toxicokinetic modeling system for chemical mixtures containing metals. *Theoretical Biology & Medical Modelling*, *7*(1), 17. doi:10.1186/1742-4682-7-17 PMID:20525215

Sayle, R., & Bissell, A. (1992). RasMol: A program for fast, realistic rendering of molecular structures with shadows. *Proceedings of the 10th Eurographics UK*. Retrieved from http://mail.ccl.net/cca/software/X-WINDOW/rasmol2.5/paper.ps

Schapire, R., Freund, Y., Bartlett, P., Lee, WS.,. (1998). Boosting the margin: A new explanation for the effectiveness of voting methods. *the Annals of Statistics, 26*(5), 1651–1686.

Schena, M., Shalon, D., Davis, R. W., & Brown, P. O. (1995). Quantitative Monitoring of Gene Expression Patterns with a Complementary DNA Microarray. *Science*, *270*(5235), 467–470. doi:10.1126/science.270.5235.467 PMID:7569999

Schlosshauer, M., & Ohlsson, M. (2002). A novel approach to local reliability of sequence alignments. *Bioinformatics (Oxford, England)*, *18*(6), 847–854. doi:10.1093/bioinformatics/18.6.847 PMID:12075020

Schneider, G., & Fechner, U. (2005). Computer-based de novo design of drug-like molecules. *Nature Reviews. Drug Discovery*, *4*(8), 649–663. doi:10.1038/nrd1799 PMID:16056391

Schneidman-Duhovny, D., Inbar, Y., Nussinov, R., & Wolfson, H. J. (2005). PatchDock and SymmDock: servers for rigid and symmetric docking. *Nucleic Acids Research, 33*(Web Server issue), W363-7. http://doi.org/<ALIGNMENT. qj></ALIGNMENT>10.1093/nar/gki481

Scholthof, K. B. G. (2007). The disease triangle: Pathogens, the environment and society. *Nature Reviews. Microbiology*, *5*(2), 152–156.

Schultz, T. (2013). Turning healthcare challenges into Big Data opportunities: A use-case review across the pharmaceutical development lifecycle. Bulletin of the Association for Information Science and Technology, *39*(5), 34–40. doi:10.1002/bult.2013.1720390508

Schulz, M. H., Zerbino, D. R., Vingron, M., & Birney, E. (2012). Oases: Robust de Novo RNA-Seq Assembly across the Dynamic Range of Expression Levels. *Bioinformatics (Oxford, England)*, *28*(8), 1086–1092. doi:10.1093/bioinformatics/bts094 PMID:22368243

Schumacher, A., Pireddu, L., Niemenmaa, M., Kallio, A., Korpelainen, E., Zanetti, G., & Heljanko, K. (2014). SeqPig: Simple and scalable scripting for large sequencing data sets in Hadoop. *Bioinformatics (Oxford, England), 30*(1), 119–120. doi:10.1093/bioinformatics/btt601 PMID:24149054

Schuster, S. C. (2007). Next-generation sequencing transforms today's biology. *Nature, 200*(8), 16–18. PMID:18165802

Schwikowski, B., Uetz, P., & Fields, S. (2000). A Network of Protein-Protein Interactions in Yeast. *Nature Biotechnology, 18*(12), 1257–1261. doi:10.1038/82360 PMID:11101803

Segura, J., Marín-López, M. A., Jones, P. F., Oliva, B., Fernandez-Fuentes, N., Ewing, R., & Chikova, A. et al. (2015). VORFFIP-Driven Dock: V-D2OCK, a Fast and Accurate Protein Docking Strategy. *PLoS ONE, 10*(3), e0118107. doi:10.1371/journal.pone.0118107 PMID:25763838

Sengupta, S., Peterson, T. R., & Sabatini, D. M. (2010). Regulation of the mTOR complex 1 pathway by nutrients, growth factors, and stress. *Molecular Cell, 40*(2), 310–322. doi:10.1016/j.molcel.2010.09.026 PMID:20965424

Seno, M., & Karypis, G. (2001). LPMiner: An Algorithm for Finding Frequent Itemsets Using Length-Decreasing Support Constraint. *Paper presented at the 1st IEEE Conference on Data Mining.* doi:10.1109/ICDM.2001.989558

Seyednasrollah, F., Laiho, A., & Elo, L. L. (2015). Comparison of Software Packages for Detecting Differential Expression in RNA-Seq Studies. *Briefings in Bioinformatics, 16*(1), 59–70. doi:10.1093/bib/bbt086 PMID:24300110

Shachak, A. (2006). Diffusion pattern of the use of genomic databases and analysis of biological sequences from 1970–2003: Bibliographic record analysis of 12 journals. *Journal of the American Society for Information Science and Technology, 57*(1), 44–50. doi:10.1002/asi.20251

Shachak, A., & Fine, S. (2008). The effect of training on biologists acceptance of bioinformatics tools: A field experiment. *Journal of the American Society for Information Science and Technology, 59*(5), 719–730. doi:10.1002/asi.20772

Shah, R., Lu, Y., Hinkle, C. C., McGillicuddy, F. C., Kim, R., Hannenhalli, S., & Reilly, M. P. et al. (2009). Gene profiling of human adipose tissue during evoked inflammation in vivo. *Diabetes, 58*(10), 2211–2219. doi:10.2337/db09-0256 PMID:19581417

Shamir, R., & Sharan, R. (2000). Click: A clustering algorithm for gene expression analysis. *Paper presented at the 8th International Conference on Intelligent Systems for Molecular Biology (ISMB '00).*

Shao, L., Goronzy, J. J., & Weyand, C. M. (2010). DNA-dependent protein kinase catalytic sub-unit mediates T-cell loss in rheumatoid arthritis. *EMBO Molecular Medicine, 2*(10), 415–427. doi:10.1002/emmm.201000096 PMID:20878914

Sharp, A.J., Locke, D.P., Mcgrath, S.D., Cheng, Z., Bailey, J.A., …, Segraves, R. (2005). Segmental Duplications and Copy-Number Variation in the Human Genome. *The American Journal of Human Genetics, 77*(1), 78–88. doi:10.1086/431652

Shatkay, H., Edwards, S., Wilbur, W.J., & Boguski, M. (2000). Genes, themes, microarrays: using information retrieval for large-scale gene analysis. *Paper presented at the Int. Conf. Intell. Syst. Mol. Biol.*

Sheng, C., Dong, G., Miao, Z., Zhang, W., Wang, W., Arkin, M. R., & Sperandio, O. et al. (2015). State-of-the-art strategies for targeting protein–protein interactions by small-molecule inhibitors. *Chemical Society Reviews, 44*(22), 8238–8259. doi:10.1039/C5CS00252D PMID:26248294

Shen, Y., Maupetit, J., Derreumaux, P., & Tufféry, P. (2014). Improved PEP-FOLD Approach for Peptide and Miniprotein Structure Prediction. *Journal of Chemical Theory and Computation, 10*(10), 4745–4758. doi:10.1021/ct500592m PMID:26588162

Sherlock, G. (2000). Analysis of large-scale gene expression data. *Current Opinion in Immunology*, *12*(2), 201–205. doi:10.1016/S0952-7915(99)00074-6 PMID:10712947

Sheskin, D. J. (2007). Handbook of Parametric and Nonparametric Statistical Procedures (4th ed.). Chapman & Hall/CRC.

Shoichet, B. K., McGovern, S. L., Wei, B., & Irwin, J. J. (2002). Lead discovery using molecular docking. *Current Opinion in Chemical Biology*, *6*(4), 439–446. doi:10.1016/S1367-5931(02)00339-3 PMID:12133718

Signorini, A., Segre, A. M., & Polgreen, P. M. (2011). The use of Twitter to track levels of disease activity and public concern in the U.S. during the Influenza A H1N1 pandemic. *PLoS ONE*, *6*(5), e19467. doi:10.1371/journal.pone.0019467 PMID:21573238

Silva, A., Cortez, P., Santos, M. F., Gomes, L., & Neves, J. (2008). Rating organ failure via adverse events using data mining in the intensive care unit. *Artificial Intelligence in Medicine*, *43*(3), 179–193. doi:10.1016/j.artmed.2008.03.010 PMID:18486459

Simon, S. R., McCarthy, M. L., Kaushal, R., Jenther, C. A., Volk, L. A., Poon, E. G., & Bates, D. W. et al. (2006). Electronic health records: Which practices have them, and how are clinicians using them? *Journal of Evaluation in Clinical Practice*, *14*(1), 43–47. doi:10.1111/j.1365-2753.2007.00787.x PMID:18211642

Singh, A., Kaushik, R., Mishra, A., Shanker, A., & Jayaram, B. (2016). ProTSAV: A protein tertiary structure analysis and validation server. *Biochimica et Biophysica Acta (BBA) - Proteins and Proteomics*, *1864*(1), 11–19. doi:10.1016/j.bbapap.2015.10.004

Singh, D., Febbo, P. G., Ross, K., Jackson, D. G., Manola, J., Ladd, C., & Lander, E. S. (2002). Gene expression correlates of clinical prostate cancer behavior. *Cancer Cell*, *1*(2), 203–209. doi:10.1016/S1535-6108(02)00030-2 PMID:12086878

Singh, N., Srivastava, S., & Sharma, A. (2016). Identification and analysis of miRNAs and their targets in ginger using bioinformatics approach. *Gene*, *575*(2), 570–576. doi:10.1016/j.gene.2015.09.036 PMID:26392033

Sirikulviriya, N., & Sinthupinyo, S. (2011). Integration of rules from a random forest. *International Conference on Information and Electronics Engineering IPCSIT*, 6.

Sivasubramanian, A., Sircar, A., Chaudhury, S., & Gray, J. J. (2009). Toward high-resolution homology modeling of antibody Fv regions and application to antibody-antigen docking. *Proteins: Structure, Function, and Bioinformatics*, *74*(2), 497–514. doi:10.1002/prot.22309

Skalak, D. B. (1994, February). Prototype and feature selection by sampling and random mutation hill climbing algorithms. *Proceedings of the eleventh international conference on machine learning*, 293-301. doi:10.1016/B978-1-55860-335-6.50043-X

Smith, A. E., Nugent, C. D., & McClean, S. I. (2003). Evaluation of inherent performance of intelligent medical decision support systems: Utilising neural networks as an example. *Artificial Intelligence in Medicine*, *27*(1), 1–27. doi:10.1016/S0933-3657(02)00088-X PMID:12473389

Smith, R. A., M'ikanatha, N. M., & Read, A. F. (2015). Antibiotic resistance: A primer and call to action. *Health Communication*, *30*(3), 309–314. doi:10.1080/10410236.2014.943634 PMID:25121990

Snyder, E. G., Watkins, T. H., Solomon, P. A., Thoma, E. D., Williams, R. W., Hagler, G. S., & Preuss, P. W. et al. (2013). The changing paradigm of air pollution monitoring. *Environmental Science & Technology*, *47*(20), 11369–11377. doi:10.1021/es4022602 PMID:23980922

Soding, J. (2005). Protein homology detection by HMM-HMM comparison. *Bioinformatics (Oxford, England)*, *21*(7), 951–960. doi:10.1093/bioinformatics/bti125 PMID:15531603

Song, G., Zeng, H., Li, J., Xiao, L., He, Y., Tang, Y., & Li, Y. (2010). miR-199a regulates the tumor suppressor mitogen-activated protein kinase kinase kinase11in gastric cancer. *Biological & Pharmaceutical Bulletin, 33*(11), 1822–1827. doi:10.1248/bpb.33.1822 PMID:21048306

Song, M., Kim, S., Zhang, G., Ding, Y., & Chambers, T. (2014). Productivity and influence in bioinformatics: A bibliometric analysis using PubMed central. *Journal of the Association for Information Science and Technology, 65*(2), 352–371. doi:10.1002/asi.22970

Spirtes, P., Glymour, C., & Scheines, R. (1993). *Causation, prediction, and search.*

Spruit, M., Vroon, R., & Batenburg, R. (2014). Towards healthcare business intelligence in long-term care: an explorative case study in the Netherlands. *Computers in Human Behavior, 30*, 698–707.

Srihari, S., Yong, C. H., Patil, A., & Wong, L. (2015). Methods for protein complex prediction and their contributions towards understanding the organisation, function and dynamics of complexes. *FEBS Letters, 589*(19 Part A), 2590–2602. doi:10.1016/j.febslet.2015.04.026 PMID:25913176

Stanford Sentiment 140. (2014). Retrieved from http://www.sentiment140.com/

Statnikov, A., Aliferis, C. F., Tsamardinos, I., Hardin, D., & Levy, S. (2005). A comprehensive evaluation of multicategory classification methods for microarray gene expression cancer diagnosis. *Bioinformatics (Oxford, England), 21*(5), 631–643. doi:10.1093/bioinformatics/bti033 PMID:15374862

Stein, L. D. (2010). The case for cloud computing in genome informatics. *Genome Biology, 11*(5), 207. doi:10.1186/gb-2010-11-5-207 PMID:20441614

Stenzel, L. M. (2006). A influência da imagem corporal no desenvolvimento e manutenção dos transtornos alimentares. In *Transtornos alimentares e obesidade* (pp. 73–81). Porto Alegre: Artmed.

Stief, A., Altmann, S., Hoffmann, K., Pant, B. D., Scheible, W. R., & Baurle, I. (2014). Arabidopsis miR156 regulates tolerance to recurring environmental stress through SPL transcription factors. *The Plant Cell, 26*(4), 1792–1807. doi:10.1105/tpc.114.123851 PMID:24769482

Story, E. N., Kopec, R. E., Schwartz, S. J., & Harris, G. K. (2010). An update on the health effects of tomato lycopene. *Ann. Rev. Food Sci. Technol., 1*(1), 189–210. doi:10.1146/annurev.food.102308.124120 PMID:22129335

Strizh, I. G. (2006). Ontologies for data and knowledge sharing in biology: Plant ROS signaling as a case study. *BioEssays, 28*(2), 199–210. doi:10.1002/bies.20368 PMID:16435295

Su, J., Yoon, B. J., & Dougherty, E. R. (2009). Accurate and reliable cancer classification based on probabilistic inference of pathway activity. *PLoS ONE, 4*(12), 155–161. doi:10.1371/journal.pone.0008161 PMID:19997592

Suji Pramila, R., Shajin Nargunam, A., & Affairs, A. (2010). A study on data confidentiality in early detection of Alzheimer's disease. Proceedings of the 2012 International Conference on Computing, Electronics and Electrical Technologies (ICCEET) (pp. 1004-1008).

Suplatov, D., Voevodin, V., & Švedas, V. (2015). Robust enzyme design: Bioinformatic tools for improved protein stability. *Biotechnology Journal, 10*(3), 344–355. doi:10.1002/biot.201400150 PMID:25524647

Svantesson, D., & Clarke, R. (2010). Privacy and consumer risks in cloud computing. *Computer Law & Security Report, 26*(4), 391–397. doi:10.1016/j.clsr.2010.05.005

Szilagyi, A., & Zhang, Y. (2014). Template-based structure modeling of protein–protein interactions. *Current Opinion in Structural Biology, 24*, 10–23. doi:10.1016/j.sbi.2013.11.005 PMID:24721449

Taberlet, P., Coissac, E., Pompanon, F., Gielly, L., Miquel, C., Valentini, A., & Willerslev, E. et al. (2007, January 26). Power and limitations of the chloroplast trnL (UAA) intron for plant DNA barcoding. *Nucleic Acids Research*, *35*(3), e14–e14. doi:10.1093/nar/gkl938 PMID:17169982

Tamanini, I., Castro, A. K. A., Pinheiro, P. R., & Pinheiro, M. C. D. (2011). Verbal Decision Analysis Applied on the Optimization of Alzheimers Disease Diagnosis: A Study Case Based on Neuroimaging. *Advances in Experimental Medicine and Biology*, *696*, 555–564. doi:10.1007/978-1-4419-7046-6_56 PMID:21431596

Tamayo, P., Solni, D., Mesirov, J., Zhu, Q., Kitareewan, S., Dmitrovsky, E., . . . Golub, T. R. I. (1999). Interpreting patterns of gene expression with self-organizing maps: Methods and application to hematopoietic differentiation. *Paper presented at the Natl. Acad. Sci.* doi:10.1073/pnas.96.6.2907

Tan, F., Fu, X., Zhang, Y., & Bourgeois, A. G. (2006, July). Improving feature subset selection using a genetic algorithm for microarray gene expression data. In *2006 IEEE International Conference on Evolutionary Computation* (pp. 2529-2534). IEEE.

Tange, H. (2008). Electronic patient records in the Netherlands. *Health Policy Monitor*. Retrieved from http://hpm.org/en/Surveys/BEOZ_Maastricht_-_Netherlands/12/Electronic_patient_records_in_the_Netherlands.html

Taniguchi, Y., Choi, P. J., Li, J. W., Chen, H., Babu, M., Hearn, J., & Xie, X. S. et al. (2010). Quantifying E. coli Proteome and Transcriptome with Single-Molecule Sensitivity in Single Cells. *Science*, *329*(5991), 533–538. doi:10.1126/science.1188308 PMID:20671182

Tan, Y. M., Liao, K., Conolly, R., Blount, B., Mason, A., & Clewell, H. (2006). Use of a physiologically based pharmacokinetic model to identify exposures consistent with human biomonitoring data for chloroform. *Journal of Toxicology and Environmental Health - Part A: Current Issues*, *69*(18), 1727–1756. doi:10.1080/15287390600631367 PMID:16864423

Tarazona, S., Furió-Tarí, P., Turrà, D., Di Pietro, A., Nueda, M. J., Ferrer, A., & Conesa, A. (2015). Data Quality Aware Analysis of Differential Expression in RNA-Seq with NOISeq R/Bioc Package. *Nucleic Acids Research*, *43*(21), e140. doi:10.1093/nar/gkv711 PMID:26184878

Tarini, M., Cignoni, P., & Montani, C. (2006). Ambient Occlusion and Edge Cueing for Enhancing Real Time Molecular Visualization. *IEEE Transactions on Visualization and Computer Graphics*, *12*(5), 1237–1244. doi:10.1109/TVCG.2006.115 PMID:17080857

Tehseen, Z., Shehbaz, M. S., Nawaz, M. S., Shahzad, B., Abdullatif, A., Mustafa, R. U., & Lali, M. I. (2016). Identification of Hatred Speeches on Twitter. *Proceedings of 52nd The IRES International Conference* (pp. 27-32).

Teichmann, S. A., & Madan Babu, M. (2004). Gene Regulatory Network Growth by Duplication. *Nature Genetics*, *36*(5), 492–496. doi:10.1038/ng1340 PMID:15107850

Tenenbaum, J. D. (2016). Translational Bioinformatics: Past, Present, and Future. *Genomics, Proteomics & Bioinformatics*, *14*(1), 31–41. doi:10.1016/j.gpb.2016.01.003 PMID:26876718

Teotico, D. G., Babaoglu, K., Rocklin, G. J., Ferreira, R. S., Giannetti, A. M., & Shoichet, B. K. (2009). Docking for fragment inhibitors of AmpC beta-lactamase. *Proceedings of the National Academy of Sciences of the United States of America*, *106*(18), 7455–7460. doi:10.1073/pnas.0813029106 PMID:19416920

The International Medical Informatics Association (IMIA). (2016). Retrieved from http://imia-medinfo.org/wp/welcome-to-imia-2/

The International Medical Informatics Association (IMIA). (2016). Retrieved November 21, 2016, from http://imia-medinfo.org/wp/welcome-to-imia-2/

The Phenotype-Genotype Integrator (PheGenI). (2016). Retrieved from https://www.ncbi.nlm.nih.gov/gap/phegeni

The Phenotype-Genotype Integrator (PheGenI). (2016). Retrieved November 21, 2016, from https://www.ncbi.nlm.nih.gov/gap/phegeni

The Precision Medicine Initiative® (PMI) Cohort Program. (2016). Retrieved November 21, 2016, from https://www.nih.gov/precision-medicine-initiative-cohort-program

Thompson, L. A., Black, E., Duff, W. P., Black, N. P., Salibi, H., & Dawson, K. (2011). Protected Health Information on Social Networking Sites: Ethical and Legal Considerations. *Journal of Medical Internet Research, 13*(1), e8. doi:10.2196/jmir.1590 PMID:21247862

Thuraisingham, D. B. (2015). Big data security and privacy. *Proceedings of the 5th ACM Conference on Data and Application Security and Privacy CODASPY '15* (pp. 279-280).

Thuraisingham, D. B. (2015). *Big Data Security and Privacy. National Science Foundation.*

Tijssen, R., Spruit, M., van de Ridder, M., & van Raaij, B. (2011). BI-FIT: Aligning Business Intelligence end-users, tasks and technologies. In M. Cruz-Cunha & J. Varajão (Eds.), *Enterprise Information Systems Design, Implementation and Management: Organizational Applications* (pp. 162–177). doi:10.4018/978-1-61692-020-3.ch011

Todorović, D. (2008). Gestalt principles. *Scholarpedia, 3*(12), 5345. doi:10.4249/scholarpedia.5345

Tomida, S., Hanai, T., Honda, H., & Kobayashi, T. (2002). Analysis of expression profile using fuzzy adaptive resonance theory. *Bioinformatics (Oxford, England), 18*(8), 1073–1083. doi:10.1093/bioinformatics/18.8.1073 PMID:12176830

Torchala, M., Moal, I. H., Chaleil, R. A. G., Fernandez-Recio, J., & Bates, P. A. (2013). SwarmDock: A server for flexible protein-protein docking. *Bioinformatics (Oxford, England), 29*(6), 807–809. doi:10.1093/bioinformatics/btt038 PMID:23343604

Toro, J., Gomez, G., Sentis, J., & Rodriguez, R. (2006). Eating disorders and body image in Spanish and Mexican female adolescents. *Social Psychiatry and Psychiatric Epidemiology, 41*(7), 556–565. doi:10.1007/s00127-006-0067-x PMID:16685478

Toronen, P., Kolehmainen, M., Wong, G., & Castren, E. (1999). Analysis of gene expression data using self-organizing maps. *FEBS Letters, 451*(2), 142–146. doi:10.1016/S0014-5793(99)00524-4 PMID:10371154

Torres, A., & Nieto, J. J. (2003). The fuzzy polynucleotide space: Basic properties. *Bioinformatics (Oxford, England), 19*(5), 587–592. doi:10.1093/bioinformatics/btg032 PMID:12651716

Tovchigrechko, A., & Vakser, I. A. (2006). GRAMM-X public web server for protein-protein docking. *Nucleic Acids Research, 34*(Web Server issue), W310-4. Doi:<ALIGNMENT.qj></ALIGNMENT>10.1093/nar/gkl206

Tran, B. Q., Goodlett, D. R., & Goo, Y. A. (2016). Advances in protein complex analysis by chemical cross-linking coupled with mass spectrometry (CXMS) and bioinformatics. *Biochimica et Biophysica Acta (BBA). Proteins and Proteomics, 1864*(1), 123–129. doi:10.1016/j.bbapap.2015.05.015

Trapnell, C., Pachter, L., & Salzberg, S. L. (2009). TopHat: Discovering Splice Junctions with RNA-Seq. *Bioinformatics (Oxford, England), 25*(9), 1105–1111. doi:10.1093/bioinformatics/btp120 PMID:19289445

Trapnell, C., Williams, B. A., Pertea, G., Mortazavi, A., Kwan, G., van Baren, M. J., & Pachter, L. et al. (2010). Transcript Assembly and Quantification by RNA-Seq Reveals Unannotated Transcripts and Isoform Switching during Cell Differentiation. *Nature Biotechnology, 28*(5), 511–515. doi:10.1038/nbt.1621 PMID:20436464

Triguero, I., del Rio, S., Lopez, V., Bacardit, J., Benitez, J. M., & Herrera, F. (2015). ROSEFW-RF: The winner algorithm for the ECBDL'14 big data competition: An extremely imbalanced big data bioinformatics problem. *Knowledge-Based Systems*, *87*, 69–79. doi:10.1016/j.knosys.2015.05.027

Trott, O., & Olson, A. J. (2010). AutoDock Vina. *Journal of Computational Chemistry*, *31*, 445–461. doi:10.1002/jcc.21334 PMID:19499576

Trott, O., & Olson, A. J. (2010). AutoDock Vina: Improving the Speed and Accuracy of Docking with a New Scoring Function, EfficientOptimization, and Multithreading. *Journal of Computational Chemistry*, *31*(2), 455–461. doi:10.1002/jcc PMID:19499576

Tufte, E., & Roger, J. (2007). *The Visual Display of Quantitative Information*. Cheshire, Connecticut: Graphics Press LLC.

Tumasjan, A., Sprenger, T. O., Sandner, P. G., & Welpe, I. M. (2010). Predicting elections with Twitter: what 140 characters reveal about political sentiment. *Proceedings of Fourth International AAAI Conference on Weblogs and Social Media* (pp. 178-185).

Tungtur, S., Parente, D. J., & Swint-Kruse, L. (2011). Functionally important positions can comprise the majority of a protein's architecture. *Proteins: Structure, Function, and Bioinformatics*, *79*(5), 1589–1608. doi:10.1002/prot.22985 PMID:21374721

Tung, W. L., Quek, C., & Cheng, P. (2004). GenSo-EWS: A novel neural-fuzzy based early warning system for predicting bank failures. *Neural Networks*, *17*(4), 567–587. doi:10.1016/j.neunet.2003.11.006 PMID:15109685

Tusnády, G. E., & Simon, I. (2001). The HMMTOP transmembrane topology prediction server. *Bioinformatics (Oxford, England)*, *17*(9), 849–850. Retrieved from http://www.ncbi.nlm.nih.gov/pubmed/11590105 doi:10.1093/bioinformatics/17.9.849 PMID:11590105

Tuszynska, I., Bujnicki, J. M., Chen, Y., Varani, G., Lukong, K., Chang, K., & Bujnicki, J. et al. (2011). DARS-RNP and QUASI-RNP: New statistical potentials for protein-RNA docking. *BMC Bioinformatics*, *12*(1), 348. doi:10.1186/1471-2105-12-348 PMID:21851628

Tuszynska, I., Magnus, M., Jonak, K., Dawson, W., & Bujnicki, J. M. (2015). NPDock: A web server for protein-nucleic acid docking. *Nucleic Acids Research*, *43*(W1), W425-30. doi:10.1093/nar/gkv493 PMID:25977296

Twitter Search, A. P. I. (2015, November 12). Retrieved from https://dev.Twitter.com/rest/public/search

Twitter Study. (2009, August 12). Retrieved from http://pearanalytics.com/wp-content/uploads/2009/08/Twitter-Study-August-2009.pdf

Uetz, P., & Hughes, R. E. (2000). Systematic and Large-Scale Two-Hybrid Screens. *Current Opinion in Microbiology*, *3*(3), 303–308. doi:10.1016/S1369-5274(00)00094-1 PMID:10851163

Ullman, S., Poggio, T., Harari, D., Zysman, D., & Seibert, D. (2014). *Unsupervised Learning: Clustering. In Center for Brains, Minds & Machines. Document 9.54 used in Class 13*. Massachusetts Institute of Technology.

United Nations (UN). (2016). *Sustainable Development Goals. 17 Goals to Transform the World*. Retrieved from http://www.un.org/sustainabledevelopment/sustainable-development-goals/

United Nations (UN). (2016). *Sustainable Development Goals. 17 Goals to Transform the World*. Retrieved November 21, 2016, from http://www.un.org/sustainabledevelopment/sustainable-development-goals/

United Nations (UN). (2016). *Vast majority of world – 6.76 billion people – living with excessive air pollution – UN report*. Retrieved from http://www.un.org/apps/news/story.asp?NewsID=55138#.WDNFVH2K_NI

Vaithianathan, R., Jiang, N., & Ashton, T. (2012). *A Model for Predicting Readmission Risk in New Zealand. Faculty of Business and Law*. AUT University.

Vajda, S., & Kozakov, D. (2009). Convergence and combination of methods in protein-protein docking. *Current Opinion in Structural Biology*, *19*(2), 164–170. doi:10.1016/j.sbi.2009.02.008 PMID:19327983,

Valcke, M., & Krishnan, K. (2011). Evaluation of the impact of the exposure route on the human kinetic adjustment factor. *Regulatory Toxicology and Pharmacology*, *59*(2), 258–269. doi:10.1016/j.yrtph.2010.10.008 PMID:20969910

Valencia, A., & Pazos, F. (2002). Computational methods for the prediction of protein interactions. *Current Opinion in Structural Biology*, *12*(3), 368–373. doi:10.1016/S0959-440X(02)00333-0 PMID:12127457

Väli, U., Brandström, M., Johansson, M., & Ellegren, H. (2008). Insertion-deletion polymorphisms (indels) as genetic markers in natural populations. *BMC Genetic*, *9*(8). doi:10.1186/1471-2156-9-8

Valiant, L. G. (1984). A theory of the learnable. *Communications of the ACM*, *27*(11), 1134–1142. doi:10.1145/1968.1972

Valverde, J., Tejada, J., & Cuadros, E. (2015). *Comparing Supervised Learning Methods for Classifying Spanish Tweets*(Vol. 1397). Universidad Católica San Pablo.

van der Linden, F. J., Schmid, K., & Rommes, E. (2007). *Software product lines in action: The best industrial practice in product line engineering*. Berlin, Germany: Springer–Verlag. doi:10.1007/978-3-540-71437-8

Van Dijk, A. D. J., Boelens, R., & Bonvin, A. M. J. J. (2005). Data-driven docking for the study of biomolecular complexes. *The FEBS Journal*, *272*(2), 293–312. doi:10.1111/j.1742-4658.2004.04473.x PMID:15654870

Vázquez, A., & Moreno, Y. (2003). Resilience to Damage of Graphs with Degree Correlations. *Physical Review E: Statistical, Nonlinear, and Soft Matter Physics*, *67*(1 Pt 2), 15101. doi:10.1103/PhysRevE.67.015101 PMID:12636544

Ventola, C. L. (2014). Social media ad health care professionals: Benefits, risks and best practices. *Pharmacy & Therapeutics*, *39*(7), 491–500. PMID:25083128

Verdino, P., Witherden, D. A., Havran, W. L., & Wilson, I. A. (2010). The molecular interaction of CAR and JAML recruits the central cell signal transducer PI3K. *Science*, *329*(5996), 1210–1214. doi:10.1126/science.1187996 PMID:20813955

Verkooij, K., & Spruit, M. (2013). Mobile Business Intelligence: Key considerations for implementation projects. *Journal of Computer Information Systems*, *54*(1), 23–33. doi:10.1080/08874417.2013.11645668

Verner, M. A., Charbonneau, M., Lopez-Carrillo, L., & Haddad, S. (2008). Physiologically based pharmacokinetic modeling of persistent organic pollutants for lifetime exposure assessment: A new tool in breast cancer epidemiologic studies. *Environmental Health Perspectives*, *116*(7), 886–892. doi:10.1289/ehp.10917 PMID:18629310

Vidal, M., Cusick, M. E., & Barabási, A.-L. (2011). Interactome Networks and Human Disease. *Cell*, *144*(6), 986–998. doi:10.1016/j.cell.2011.02.016 PMID:21414488

Villas-Bôas, S. G., Roessner, U., Hansen, M., Smedsgaard, J., & Nielsen, J. (2007). *Metabolome Analysis: An Introduction*. Hoboken, NJ: John Wiley & Sons, Inc. doi:10.1002/0470105518

Vleugel, A., Spruit, M., & van Daal, A. (2010). Historical data analysis through data mining from an outsourcing perspective: The three-phases method. *International Journal of Business Intelligence Research*, *1*(3), 42–65. doi:10.4018/jbir.2010070104

von Heijne, G. (1985). Signal sequences: The limits of variation. *Journal of Molecular Biology*, *184*(1), 99–105. doi:10.1016/0022-2836(85)90046-4 PMID:4032478

W3Schools (2012). Browser Display Statistics. *W3Schools*. Retrieved from http://www.w3schools.com/browsers/browsers_display.asp

Wagner, A., & Fell, D. A. (2001). The Small World inside Large Metabolic Networks. *Proceedings. Biological Sciences, 268*(1478), 1803–1810. doi:10.1098/rspb.2001.1711 PMID:11522199

Wallner, B., & Elofsson, A. (2003). Can correct protein models be identified? *Protein Science : A Publication of the Protein Society, 12*(5), 1073–86. doi:10.1110/ps.0236803

Wall, R., Cunningham, P., Walsh, P., & Byrne, S. (2003). Explaining the output of ensembles in medical decision support on a case by case basis. *Artificial Intelligence in Medicine, 28*(2), 191–206. doi:10.1016/S0933-3657(03)00056-3 PMID:12893119

Walsh, K. (2009). Adipokines, myokines and cardiovascular disease. *Circulation Journal, 73*(1), 13–18. doi:10.1253/circj.CJ-08-0961 PMID:19043226

Walter, R. P. Scott, Philippe H. Hünenberger, Ilario G. Tironi, Alan E. Mark, Salomon R. Billeter, Jens Fennen, … Gunsteren. (1999). The GROMOS Biomolecular Simulation Program Package. doi:10.1021/JP984217F

Wang, C., Zhang, H., Zheng, W.-M., Xu, D., Zhu, J., & Wang, B. … Bu, D. (2016). FALCON@home: a high-throughput protein structure prediction server based on remote homologue recognition. *Bioinformatics (Oxford, England), 32*(3), 462–4. doi;10.1093/bioinformatics/btv581

Wang, E. T., Sandberg, R., Luo, S., Khrebtukova, I., Zhang, L., Mayr, C., & Burge, C. B. et al. (2008). Alternative Isoform Regulation in Human Tissue Transcriptomes. *Nature, 456*(7221), 470–476. doi:10.1038/nature07509 PMID:18978772

Wang, J. (2008). Computational biology of genome expression and regulation - A review of microarray bioinformatics. *Journal of Environmental Pathology, Toxicology and Oncology, 27*(3), 157–179. doi:10.1615/JEnvironPatholToxicolOncol.v27.i3.10 PMID:18652564

Wang, J. W., Wang, L. J., Mao, Y. B., Cai, W. J., Xue, H. W., & Chen, X. Y. (2005). Control of root cap formation by microRNA-targeted auxin response factors in Arabidopsis. *The Plant Cell, 17*(8), 2204–2216. doi:10.1105/tpc.105.033076 PMID:16006581

Wang, J., Luo, S., & Zeng, X. (2008). A random subspace method for co-training. In *IJCNN* (pp. 195–200). IEEE.

Wang, K., Singh, D., Zeng, Z., Coleman, S. J., Huang, Y., Savich, G. L., & Liu, J. et al. (2010). MapSplice: Accurate Mapping of RNA-Seq Reads for Splice Junction Discovery. *Nucleic Acids Research, 38*(18), e178. doi:10.1093/nar/gkq622 PMID:20802226

Wang, L. J. Z. (2014). *BigData Bench: a Big Data Benchmark Suite from Internet Services. State Key Laboratory of Computer Architecture*. Institute of Computing Technology, Chinese Academy of Sciences.

Wang, L., & Sauer, U. H. (2008). OnD-CRF: Predicting order and disorder in proteins using [corrected] conditional random fields. *Bioinformatics (Oxford, England), 24*(11), 1401–1402. doi:10.1093/bioinformatics/btn132 PMID:18430742

Wang, L., Wang, S., & Li, W. (2012). RSeQC: Quality Control of RNA-Seq Experiments. *Bioinformatics (Oxford, England), 28*(16), 2184–2185. doi:10.1093/bioinformatics/bts356 PMID:22743226

Wang, Q. C. W. (2009). *Enabling Public Verifiability and Data Dynamics for Storage Security in Cloud Computing*. ESORICS. doi:10.1007/978-3-642-04444-1_22

Wang, S., Ma, J., & Xu, J. (2016). AUCpreD: Proteome-level protein disorder prediction by AUC-maximized deep convolutional neural fields. *Bioinformatics (Oxford, England)*, *32*(17), i672–i679. doi:10.1093/bioinformatics/btw446 PMID:27587688

Wang, T., Wu, M.-B., Chen, Z.-J., Chen, H., Lin, J.-P., & Yang, L.-R. (2015). Fragment-based drug discovery and molecular docking in drug design. *Current Pharmaceutical Biotechnology*, *16*(1), 11–25. Retrieved from http://www.ncbi.nlm.nih.gov/pubmed/25420726 doi:10.2174/1389201015666141122204532 PMID:25420726

Wang, W., & Krishnan, E. (2014). Big Data and clinicians: A review on the state of the science. *JMIR Med Inform.*, *2*(1), e1. doi:10.2196/medinform.2913 PMID:25600256

Wan, Y., Wang, M., Ye, Z., & Lai, X. (2016). A feature selection method based on modified binary coded ant colony optimization algorithm. *Applied Soft Computing*, *49*, 248–258. doi:10.1016/j.asoc.2016.08.011

Waseem, M., Lakhan, A., & Jamali, I. (2016). Data Security of Mobile Cloud Computing on Cloud Server. *OALib*, *3*(4), 1–11. doi:10.4236/oalib.1102377

Watts, D. J., & Strogatz, S. H. (1998). Collective Dynamics of small-World Networks. *Nature*, *393*(6684), 440–442. doi:10.1038/30918 PMID:9623998

Webb, B., Sali, A., Webb, B., & Sali, A. (2014). Comparative Protein Structure Modeling Using MODELLER. In *Current Protocols in Bioinformatics* (p. 5.6.1-5.6.32). Hoboken, NJ, USA: John Wiley & Sons, Inc. doi:10.1002/0471250953.bi0506s47

Webb, G., & Zheng, Z. (2004). Multistrategy ensemble learning: Reducing error by combining ensemble learning techniques. *Paper presented at the IEEE Transactions on Knowledge and Data Engineering*. doi:10.1109/TKDE.2004.29

Weichenberger, C. X., & Sippl, M. J. (2006). NQ-Flipper: Validation and correction of asparagine/glutamine amide rotamers in protein crystal structures. *Bioinformatics (Oxford, England)*, *22*(11), 1397–1398. doi:10.1093/bioinformatics/btl128 PMID:16595557

Wellons. W. C. (2015, January). 11 Predictions on the Future of Social Media. Retrieved from www.cnbc.com/id/102029041

Wells, J. A., & McClendon, C. L. (2007). Reaching for high-hanging fruit in drug discovery at protein-protein interfaces. *Nature*, *450*(7172), 1001–1009. doi:10.1038/nature06526 PMID:18075579

Wetterstrand, K. A. (2016). DNA Sequencing Costs: Data from the NHGRI Genome Sequencing Program (GSP). Retrieved from www.genome.gov/sequencingcostsdata

WHA 57.13: Genomics and World Health, Fifty Seventh World Health Assembly Resolution. (2004, May 22).

White, S. H. (2004). The progress of membrane protein structure determination. *Protein Science : A Publication of the Protein Society*, *13*(7), 1948–9. doi:10.1110/ps.04712004

WHO Infectious Disease Fact Sheet. (2015, December 8). Retrieved from http://www.who.int/topics/infectious_diseases/factsheets/en/

WHO. (2002). Genomics and World Health: Report of the Advisory Committee on Health research.

Wiederstein, M., & Sippl, M. J. (2007). ProSA-web: interactive web service for the recognition of errors in three-dimensional structures of proteins. *Nucleic Acids Research*, *35*(Web Server issue), W407-10. doi:10.1093/nar/gkm290

Wiewiórka, M. S., Messina, A., Pacholewska, A., Maffioletti, S., Gawrysiak, P., & Okoniewski, M. J. (2014). SparkSeq: Fast, scalable, cloud-ready tool for the interactive genomic data analysis with nucleotide precision. *Bioinformatics (Oxford, England)*, *30*(18), 2652–2653. doi:10.1093/bioinformatics/btu343 PMID:24845651

Wijaya, S., Spruit, M., & Scheper, W. (2008). Webstrategy Formulation: benefiting from web 2.0 concepts to deliver business values. In M. Lytras, E. Damiani, & P. Ordóñez de Pablos (Eds.), *Web 2.0: The Business Model* (pp. 103–132). Springer. doi:10.1007/978-3-540-87781-3_41

Wikipedia. (2016). Gestalt psychology. Retrieved from https://en.wikipedia.org/wiki/Gestalt_psychology

Wild, C. P. (2005). Complementing the genome with an exposome: The outstanding challenge of environmental exposure measurement in molecular epidemiology. *Cancer Epidemiology, Biomarkers & Prevention, 14*(8), 1847–1850. doi:10.1158/1055-9965.EPI-05-0456 PMID:16103423

Willard, L., Ranjan, A., Zhang, H., Monzavi, H., Boyko, R. F., Sykes, B. D., & Wishart, D. S. (2003). VADAR: A web server for quantitative evaluation of protein structure quality. *Nucleic Acids Research, 31*(13), 3316–3319. doi:10.1093/nar/gkg565 PMID:12824316

Willmann, S., Lippert, J., Sevestre, M., Solodenko, J., Fois, F., & Schmitt, W. (2003). PK-Sim: A physiologically based pharmacokinetic 'whole-body' model. *Drug Discovery Today: BIOSILICO, 1*(4), 121–124.

Witkos, T. M., Koscianska, E., & Krzyzosiak, W. J. (2011). Practical aspects of microRNA target prediction. *Current Molecular Medicine, 11*(2), 93–109. doi:10.2174/156652411794859250 PMID:21342132

Wolf, E., Kim, P. S., & Berger, B. (1997). MultiCoil: A program for predicting two-and three-stranded coiled coils. *Protein Science, 6*(6), 1179–1189. doi:10.1002/pro.5560060606 PMID:9194178

Wong, B. (2011). Points of view: Color blindness. *Nature Methods, 8*(6), 441. doi:10.1038/nmeth.1618 PMID:21774112

Wong, J. W. H., Cagney, G., & Cartwright, H. M. (2005). SpecAlign - Processing and alignment of mass spectra datasets. *Bioinformatics (Oxford, England), 21*(9), 2088–2090. doi:10.1093/bioinformatics/bti300 PMID:15691857

Wong, J. W. H., Durante, C., & Cartwright, H. M. (2005). Application of fast Fourier transform cross-correlation for the alignment of large chromatographic and spectral datasets. *Analytical Chemistry, 77*(17), 5655–5661. doi:10.1021/ac050619p PMID:16131078

Woo, H., Cho, Y., Shim, E., Lee, J. K., Lee, C. G., & Kim, S. H. (2016). Estimating Influenza Outbreaks Using Both Search Engine Query Data and Social Media Data in South Korea. *Journal of Medical Internet Research, 18*(7), e177. doi:10.2196/jmir.4955 PMID:27377323

Woolf, P., & Wang, Y. (2000). A fuzzy logic approach to analyzing gene expression data. *Physiological Genomics, 3*(1), 9–15. PMID:11015595

Workman, C. T., Mak, H. C., McCuine, S., Tagne, J. B., Agarwal, M., Ozier, O., … Ideker, T. (2006). A systems approach to mapping DNA damage response pathways. *Science, 312*(5776), 1054-1059.

World Health Organization (WHO). (2016) Retrieved from http://www.who.int/en/

World Health Organization (WHO). (2016) Retrieved November 21, 2016, from http://www.who.int/en/

Wu, S., & Zhang, Y. (2007). LOMETS: a local meta-threading-server for protein structure prediction. *Nucleic Acids Research*. Retrieved from http://nar.oxfordjournals.org/content/35/10/3375.short

Wu, S., & Zhang, Y. (2008). MUSTER: improving protein sequence profile–profile alignments by using multiple sources of structure information. *Proteins: Structure, Function, and*. Retrieved from http://onlinelibrary.wiley.com/doi/10.1002/prot.21945/full

Wu, S., Zhang, Y., Neal, S., Berjanskii, M., Zhang, H., & Wishart, D. … Zhang, Y. (2008). ANGLOR: A Composite Machine-Learning Algorithm for Protein Backbone Torsion Angle Prediction. *PLoS ONE, 3*(10), e3400. doi:10.1371/journal.pone.0003400

Wu, S., & Zhang, Y. (2010). Recognizing Protein Substructure Similarity Using Segmental Threading. *Structure (London, England), 18*(7), 858–867. doi:10.1016/j.str.2010.04.007 PMID:20637422

Wu, T. D., & Nacu, S. (2010). Fast and SNP-Tolerant Detection of Complex Variants and Splicing in Short Reads. *Bioinformatics (Oxford, England), 26*(7), 873–881. doi:10.1093/bioinformatics/btq057 PMID:20147302

Xing, E. P., & Karp, R. M. (2001). Cliff: Clustering of high-dimensional microarray data via iterative feature filtering using normalized cuts. *Bioinformatics (Oxford, England), 17*(Suppl. 1), 306–315. doi:10.1093/bioinformatics/17.suppl_1.S306 PMID:11473022

Xu, D., & Liu, Y., hang, M., Ma, S., Cui, A., & Ru, L. (2011). Predicting Epidemic tendency through search behaviour analysis. *Proceedings of 22th International Joint Conference on Artificial Intelligence* (pp. 2361-2366).

Xu, D., & Zhang, Y. (2012). Ab initio protein structure assembly using continuous structure fragments and optimized knowledge-based force field. *Proteins: Structure, Function, and.* Retrieved from http://onlinelibrary.wiley.com/doi/10.1002/prot.24065/full

Xu, D., Jaroszewski, L., Li, Z., & Godzik, A. (2014). FFAS-3D: Improving fold recognition by including optimized structural features and template re-ranking. *Bioinformatics (Oxford, England), 30*(5), 660–667. doi:10.1093/bioinformatics/btt578 PMID:24130308

Xu, D., & Zhang, Y. (2011). Improving the Physical Realism and Structural Accuracy of Protein Models by a Two-Step Atomic-Level Energy Minimization. *Biophysical Journal, 101*(10), 2525–2534. doi:10.1016/j.bpj.2011.10.024 PMID:22098752

Xue, Z., Xu, D., Wang, Y., & Zhang, Y. (2013). ThreaDom: Extracting protein domain boundary information from multiple threading alignments. *Bioinformatics (Oxford, England), 29*(13), i247–i256. doi:10.1093/bioinformatics/btt209 PMID:23812990

Xu, M., Unzue, A., Dong, J., Spiliotopoulos, D., Nevado, C., & Caflisch, A. (2016). Discovery of CREBBP Bromodomain Inhibitors by High-Throughput Docking and Hit Optimization Guided by Molecular Dynamics. *Journal of Medicinal Chemistry, 59*(4), 1340–1349. doi:10.1021/acs.jmedchem.5b00171 PMID:26125948

Xu, Y., & Xu, D. (2000). Protein threading using PROSPECT: Design and evaluation. *Proteins, 40*(3), 343–354. doi:10.1002/1097-0134(20000815)40:3<343::AID-PROT10>3.0.CO;2-S PMID:10861926

Yachdav, G., Kloppmann, E., Kajan, L., Hecht, M., Goldberg, T., & Hamp, T. … Rost, B. (2014). PredictProtein--an open resource for online prediction of protein structural and functional features. *Nucleic Acids Research, 42*(W1), W337–W343. doi:10.1093/nar/gku366

Yan, R.-X., Si, J.-N., Wang, C., Zhang, Z., Petrey, D., & Honig, B. … Bourne, P. (2009). DescFold: A web server for protein fold recognition. *BMC Bioinformatics, 10*(1), 416. doi:10.1186/1471-2105-10-416

Yang, D., Parrish, R. S., & Brock, G. N. (2014). Empirical evaluation of consistency and accuracy of methods to detect differentially expressed genes based on microarray data. *Computers in Biology and Medicine, 46*, 1–10. doi:10.1016/j.compbiomed.2013.12.002 PMID:24529200

Yang, J., He, B.-J., Jang, R., Zhang, Y., & Shen, H.-B. (2015). Accurate disulfide-bonding network predictions improve ab initio structure prediction of cysteine-rich proteins. *Bioinformatics (Oxford, England), 31*(23), 3773–3781. doi:10.1093/bioinformatics/btv459 PMID:26254435

Yang, J., Yan, R., Roy, A., Xu, D., Poisson, J., & Zhang, Y. (2015). The I-TASSER Suite: Protein structure and function prediction. *Nature Methods, 12*(1), 7–8. doi:10.1038/nmeth.3213 PMID:25549265

Yang, X., Di Liu, F. L., Wu, J., Zou, J., Xiao, X., Zhao, F., & Zhu, B. (2013). HTQC: A Fast Quality Control Toolkit for Illumina Sequencing Data. *BMC Bioinformatics, 14*(January), 33. doi:10.1186/1471-2105-14-33 PMID:23363224

Yang, Y., Faraggi, E., Zhao, H., & Zhou, Y. (2011). Improving protein fold recognition and template-based modeling by employing probabilistic-based matching between predicted one-dimensional structural properties of query and corresponding native properties of templates. *Bioinformatics (Oxford, England), 27*(15), 2076–2082. doi:10.1093/bioinformatics/btr350 PMID:21666270

Yang, Y., Xu, X., & Georgopoulos, P. G. (2010). A Bayesian population PBPK model for multiroute chloroform exposure. *Journal of Exposure Science & Environmental Epidemiology, 20*(4), 326–341. doi:10.1038/jes.2009.29 PMID:19471319

Yaseen, A., & Li, Y. (2013). Dinosolve: A protein disulfide bonding prediction server using context-based features to enhance prediction accuracy. *BMC Bioinformatics, S9*(Suppl. 13). https://doi.org/10.1186/1471-2105-14-S13-S9 PMID:24267383

Yaslan, Y., & Cataltepe, Z. (2010). Co-training with relevant random sub-spaces. *Neurocomput., 73*(10-12), 1652–1661. doi:10.1016/j.neucom.2010.01.018

Ye, J., Li, T., Xiong, T., & Janardan, R. (2004). Using uncorrelated discriminant analysis for tissue classification with gene expression data. *IEEE/ACM Transactions on Computational Biology and Bioinformatics, 1*(4), 181–190. doi:10.1109/TCBB.2004.45 PMID:17051700

Yeow, W. L., Mahmud, R., & Raj, R. G. (2014). An application of case-based reasoning with machine learning for forensic autopsy. *Expert Systems with Applications, 41*(7), 3497–3505. doi:10.1016/j.eswa.2013.10.054

Yin, Y., Shen, C., Xie, P., Cheng, Z., & Zhu, Q. (2016). Construction of an initial microRNA regulation network in breast invasive carcinoma by bioinformatics analysis. *The Breast, 26*, 1–10. doi:10.1016/j.breast.2015.11.008 PMID:27017236

Yom-Tov, E., & Gabrilovich, E. (2013). Postmarket drug surveillance without trial costs: Discovery of adverse drug reactions through large-scale analysis of web search queries. *Journal of Medical Internet Research, 15*(6), e124. doi:10.2196/jmir.2614 PMID:23778053

Yu, W., & Smith, S. (2009). *Reusability of FEA software: A program family approach.* Paper presented at the 2nd International Workshop on Software Engineering for Computational Science and Engineering (SE–CSE 2009), Vancouver, Canada. doi:10.1109/SECSE.2009.5069161

Yuan, Z., Mattick, J. S., & Teasdale, R. D. (2004). SVMtm: Support vector machines to predict transmembrane segments. *Journal of Computational Chemistry, 25*(5), 632–636. doi:10.1002/jcc.10411 PMID:14978706

Yu, J., Vavrusa, M., Andreani, J., Rey, J., Tufféry, P., & Guerois, R. (2016). InterEvDock: A docking server to predict the structure of protein–protein interactions using evolutionary information. *Nucleic Acids Research, 44*(W1), W542–W549. doi:10.1093/nar/gkw340 PMID:27131368

Zadeh, L. A. (1965). Fuzzy Sets. *Information and Control, 8*(3), 338–353. doi:10.1016/S0019-9958(65)90241-X

Zafarani, R., & Liu, H. (1998). *Asu repository of social computing databases.* Academic Press.

Zarrei, M., Macdonald, J. R., Merico, D., & Scherer, S. W. (2015). A copy number variation map of the human genome. *Nature Reviews. Genetics*, *16*(3), 172–183. doi:10.1038/nrg3871 PMID:25645873

Zeng, J., Zhu, S., & Yan, H. (2009). Towards accurate human promoter recognition: A review of currently used sequence features and classification methods. *Briefings in Bioinformatics*, *10*(5), 498–508. doi:10.1093/bib/bbp027 PMID:19531545

Zhang, H. (2004). A new nonlinear equation for the tissue/blood partition coefficients of neutral compounds. *Journal of Pharmaceutical Sciences*, *93*(6), 1595–1604. doi:10.1002/jps.20084 PMID:15124216

Zhang, J., Chiodini, R., Badr, A., & Zhang, G. (2011). The impact of next-generation sequencing on genomics. *Journal of Genetics and Genomics = Yi Chuan Xue Bao*, *38*(3), 95–109. doi:10.1016/j.jgg.2011.02.003 PMID:21477781

Zhang, J., Liang, Y., & Zhang, Y. (2011). Atomic-Level Protein Structure Refinement Using Fragment-Guided Molecular Dynamics Conformation Sampling. *Structure (London, England)*, *19*(12), 1784–1795. doi:10.1016/j.str.2011.09.022 PMID:22153501

Zhang, J., Yang, J., Jang, R., & Zhang, Y. (2015). GPCR-I-TASSER: A Hybrid Approach to G Protein-Coupled Receptor Structure Modeling and the Application to the Human Genome. *Structure (London, England)*, *23*(8), 1538–1549. doi:10.1016/j.str.2015.06.007 PMID:26190572

Zhang, L., Kuljis, J., & Liu, X. (2008). Information visualization for DNA microarray data analysis: A critical review. *IEEE Transactions on Systems, Man and Cybernetics. Part C, Applications and Reviews*, *38*(1), 42–54. doi:10.1109/TSMCC.2007.906065

Zhang, S., Jin, G., Zhang, X. S., & Chen, L. (2007). Discovering functions and revealing mechanisms at molecular level from biological networks. *Proteomics*, *7*(16), 2856–2869. doi:10.1002/pmic.200700095 PMID:17703505

Zhang, S., Kumar, K., Jiang, X., Wallqvist, A., Reifman, J., Ghosh, S., & Holbeck, S. et al. (2008). DOVIS: An implementation for high-throughput virtual screening using AutoDock. *BMC Bioinformatics*, *9*(1), 126. doi:10.1186/1471-2105-9-126 PMID:18304355

Zhang, T. (2010). The design of information security protection framework to support Smart Grid. *Proceedings of the 2010 International Conference on Power System Technology (POWERCON)* (pp. 1-5).

Zhang, W., Han, S., He, H., & Chen, H. (2016). Network-aware virtual machine migration in an overcommitted cloud. *Future Generation Computer Systems*. doi:10.1016/j.future.2016.03.009

Zhang, X., Dou, W., Pei, J., Nepal, S., Yang, C., Liu, C., & Chen, J. (2015). *Proximity-Aware Local-Recoding Anonymization with MapReduce for Scalable Big Data Privacy Preservation in Cloud. IEEE transactions on computers*, *64*(8), 2293–2307.

Zheng, C. H., Yang, W., Chong, Y. W., & Xia, J. F. (2016). Identification of mutated driver pathways in cancer using a multi-objective optimization model. *Computers in Biology and Medicine*, *72*, 22–29. doi:10.1016/j.compbiomed.2016.03.002 PMID:26995027

Zheng, J., Kundrotas, P. J., Vakser, I. A., Liu, S., Kozomara, A., Griffiths-Jones, S., & Lapointe, J. et al. (2016). Template-Based Modeling of Protein-RNA Interactions. *PLoS Computational Biology*, *12*(9), e1005120. doi:10.1371/journal.pcbi.1005120 PMID:27662342

Zhou, S., Liao, R., & Guan, J. (2013). When cloud computing meets bioinformatics: A review. *Journal of Bioinformatics and Computational Biology*, *11*(5), 1330002. doi:10.1142/S0219720013300025 PMID:24131049

Zhou, X., & Rokas, A. (2014). Prevention, diagnosis and treatment of high-throughput sequencing data pathologies. *Molecular Ecology*, *23*(7), 1679–1700. doi:10.1111/mec.12680 PMID:24471475

Zhou, X., Ye, J., & Feng, Y. (2011). Tuberculosis surveillance by analyzing Google trends. *IEEE Transactions on Bio-Medical Engineering, 58*(3), 2247–2254. doi:10.1109/TBME.2011.2132132 PMID:21435969

Zhou, Y., & Goldman, S. (2004). Democratic co-learning. *Proceedings of the 16th IEEE International Conference on Tools with Artificial Intelligence, ICTAI '04*, 594–202. doi:10.1109/ICTAI.2004.48

Zhou, Z.-H., & Li, M. (2005). Tri-training: Exploiting unlabeled data using three classifiers. *IEEE Transactions on Knowledge and Data Engineering, 17*(11), 1529–1541. doi:10.1109/TKDE.2005.186

Zhou, Z.-H., Wu, J., & Tang, W. (2002). Ensembling neural networks: Many could be better than all. *Artificial Intelligence, 137*(1-2), 239–263. doi:10.1016/S0004-3702(02)00190-X

Zhu, M., Deng, X., Joshi, T., Xu, D., Stacey, G., & Cheng, J. (2012). Reconstructing Differentially Co-Expressed Gene Modules and Regulatory Networks of Soybean Cells. *BMC Genomics, 13*(1), 437. doi:10.1186/1471-2164-13-437 PMID:22938179

Zhu, X. (2005). *Semi-Supervised learning literature survey. Technical report, Computer Sciences.* University of Wisconsin-Madison.

Zia, T., Akhter, M. P., & Abbas, Q. (2015). Comparative study of feature selection approaches for Urdu text Categorization. *Malaysian Journal of Computer Science, 28*(2), 93–109.

Zibakhsh, A., & Abadeh, M. S. (2013). Gene selection for cancer tumor detection using a novel memetic algorithm with a multi-view fitness function. *Engineering Applications of Artificial Intelligence, 26*(4), 1274–1281. doi:10.1016/j.engappai.2012.12.009

About the Contributors

Miltiadis D. Lytras is Associate Professor at Deree- The American College of Greece with a research focus on semantic web, knowledge management and e-learning, with more than 100 publications. He has co-edited more than 45 special issues in International Journals (IEEE Transaction on Knowledge and Data Engineering, IEEE Internet Computing, IEEE Transactions on Education, Computers in Human Behaviour, Interactive Learning Environments, Journal of Knowledge Management, Journal of Computer Assisted Learning) and has authored/(co-)edited 42 books (e.g. Open Source for Knowledge and Learning Management, Ubiquitous and Pervasive Knowledge Management, Intelligent Learning Infrastructures for Knowledge Intensive Organizations, Semantic Web Based Information Systems, China Information Technology Handbook, Real World Applications of Semantic Web and Ontologies, Web 2.0: The Business Model, etc.). He (has) serves(ed) as the (Co) Editor in Chief of 8 international journals (e.g. International Journal on Semantic Web and Information Systems, International Journal of Knowledge Society Research, International Journal of Knowledge and Learning, International Journal of Technology Enhanced Learning).

Paraskevi Papadopoulou is Professor of Biology at Deree-The American College of Greece. She holds Biology degrees from the University of California, Los Angeles and from the University of Athens and a PhD in Biophysics and Cell Biology from the University of Athens. Her research interests are focused in the fields of Structural Biology/Molecular Biophysics and Computational Biology/Bioinformatics, on structural and self-assembly studies of fibrous proteins, which form extracellular, proteinaceous structures of physiological importance like lepidopteran, dipteran and fish chorions. Model structures of chorion proteins and their interactions have been proposed. Her current engagement includes the development of genetic testing protocols for genetic diseases such as Tuberous Sclerosis and of Neurofibromatosis type 1. She is also interested in Higher Education research and innovative ways of teaching. In addition to teaching biology and environmental studies courses she has served as Head of the department of Science, Technology and Mathematics at Deree-The American University of Greece for 6 years.

* * *

Prativa Agarwalla received the Bachelor and Master Degree, both from Calcutta University in Radio Physics and Electronics in 2010 and 2012 respectively. She is currently an Assistant Professor with the Heritage Institute of Technology, India. Her main research interests include optimization, soft computing, evolutionary computation and computational biology.

Raquel Souza Bino Araújo earned the Nursing (2016) degrees from the University of Fortaleza.

Ankush Bansal worked as Associate Scientist in Cellworks Research India Pvt Ltd, Bangalore, India and later he joined Complex Systems Lab, Indian Institute of Technology, (IIT) Indore. Currently, he is pursuing Ph.D in Bioinformatics from Jaypee University of Information Technology.

Mohammed El Amine Bechar got his Master Degree in Biomedical Engineering with the option of medical image processing in 2013, from the University of Tlemcen, Algeria. Currently, he is a third-year Ph.D. student of characterization and recognition of medical data in Biomedical engineering laboratory at the University of Tlemcen, Algeria. His research interests include the areas of computer-assisted medical, decision support systems, artificial intelligence and image processing.

Layane Mayara Gomes Castelo Branco earned the Nursing (2008) degrees from the Faculdade Integral Diferencial; Specialization Urgency and Emergency by the Institution of Higher Education in Teresina (2010) and Master Business Administration in Health Services Audit by the Integrated Units of Postgraduate, Research and Extension (2011).

Hirak Jyoti Chakraborty received his MSc. (Tech.) in Bioinformatics from the West Bengal University of Technology. He is presently pursuing his doctoral degree in the structural characterisation of peptide antibiotics. His research interests include structural bioinformatics, protein modelling, metagenomics and antibiotic resistance.

Dimitris Chapizanis is a PhD candidate at the Environmental Engineering Laboratory (EnvE Lab) of the Department of Chemical Engineering, Aristotle University of Thessaloniki, Greece. He holds a diploma in Chemical Engineering. His research activities focus on atmospheric pollution, exposure assessment and environmental risk. His current work involves the development of an Agent Based Model that determines personal exposure based on time-geography information and pollutants concentration data derived by sensor technologies. He has been involved in research projects URGENCHE, TRANSPHORM, CROME, HEALS and ICARUS.

Mohammed Amine Chikh is a Professor at the Tlemcen University. He is graduated from The Electrical Engineering Institut (INELEC) of Boumerdes –Algeria in 1985 with engineering degree in Computer science and in 1992 with a Magister of Electronic from Tlemcen University. He also received a Ph.D in electrical engineering from the University of Tlemcen (Algeria) and INSA of Rennes (France) in 2005. Actually, he is currently Professor at Tlemcen University, Algeria, and head of CREDOM research team at Biomedical Engineering Laboratory. He conducted post-doctoral teaching and research at the University of Tlemcen. Pr Chikh has published over 120 journal and conference papers to date and is involved in a variety of funded research projects related to biomedical engineering. His is a member of several scientific conferences. His research interests have been in artificial intelligence, machine learning, and medical data.

Victor Damasceno Camera earned the B.Sc (2016) degrees in Science Computation from the University of Fortaleza.

Abhijit Datta is working in the field of Molecular Biology and Bioinformatics since 1989 and has more than fifty publications.

Mostafa El Habib Daho received his Master degree in 2011 and Ph.D. degree in 2015, both in Computer Sciences from the University of Tlemcen (Algeria). Shortly after completing his Ph.D, he joined the same University as assistant professor / research fellow. His research focuses on Machine Learning, Data Mining, Ensemble Methods, Medical and Biologic Data Classification, Intelligent Decision Systems and Deep Learning.

Aditi Gangopadhyay received her post-graduation in Molecular Biology and Genetics from Presidency College, Kolkata in 2010. She is a doctoral student in the department of Biophysics, Molecular Biology and Bioinformatics at the University of Calcutta. Her research interests include computational drug design, Natural Product chemistry and structural bioinformatics.

Srijan Goswami is the Honorary Director and one of the co-founder of Indian School of Complementary Medicine & Allied Sciences (ISCMAS), a non-profit, non-government organization for promoting quality Education, Training, Treatment and social awareness about the various complementary medical sciences. He is currently associated as the Honorary Professor, Department of Biochemistry, Shree Krishna Biochemic College, India. And also associated as Lecturer, Department of Biotechnology, Institute of Genetic Engineering, India. He received his training in Medical Microbiology and Biochemistry from R.G.Kar Medical College and Calcutta National Medical College, Kolkata, India respectively. He is currently pursuing his post graduate medical training in the field of Biochemic System of Medicine from Indian Council of Biochemic Medicine and Yoga Therapy, India. He completed M.Sc in Medical Biotechnology with specialization in human genetics from The West Bengal University of Health Sciences, India in the year 2012. His research area of interest is medical informatics and medical sciences, biochemistry and complementary medical sciences. He has teaching and clinical research experience of around four years.

Alberto Gotti is a physicist of the University of Milan with over 20 years of experience in environment and health impact assessment, data assimilation and exposure modelling. In the last ten years he has worked for the European Commission's Joint Research Centre (EC-DG-JRC), for Aristotle University of Thessaloniki (AUTH), for the European Centre for Training and Research in Earthquake Engineering (EUCENTRE) and for the Centre for Research and Technology Hellas (CERTH). Dr. Gotti has an extensive experience on environment and health impact assessment, exposure modelling including biologically-based toxicokinetics/dynamic models (PBTK/PD), development of dose-response relationships based on both mechanistic Biology-Based Dose Response (BBDR) modelling and epidemiological approach through statistical modeling. Climate change processes and policies, use of GIS for environment and health impact assessment, data fusion comprising the assimilation and integration of data from different information sources, advanced statistical data analysis and techniques (Markov Chain Monte Carlo) to assess and reduce uncertainty in human health risk assessment, air quality assessment using satellite data. He was involved in the EU-funded projects ICAROS-NET, SMAQ, HEIMTSA, 2-FUN, HEREPLUS, TAGS, INTERA, URGENCHE, INTEGRA, CROME-LIFE, CHERRIE and in the ongoing ones HEALS, ICARUS, PEC, BLUEHEALTH and HBM4EU.

Malka N. Halgamuge is a Research Fellow / Scientist in the Department of Electrical and Electronic Engineering of University of Melbourne. She obtained her PhD from the same department. She is the Founder and Director at the SenseRadiation Pty Ltd (www.senseradiation.com), since July 2015. SenseRadiation Pty Ltd provides electromagnetic radiation risk assessment and prediction services for community, industry and the government including councils. She also works as Electro Magnetic Radiation (EMR) Consultant since January 2014 (radiation hazards (RADHAZ) safety measurement and assessment). She also a member of the Electromagnetic Radiation Safety Committee, The University of Melbourne, since Sep 2013. Publications: She has published more than 55 articles attracting over 566 Citations. Her Research Gate: RG Score = 26.60. One of her papers has been selected as a highly cited paper by ISI's Essential Science Indicators (May 2014). She currently co-supervises a group of 2 PhD students and she has co-supervised 3 PhD student to completion (2013 & 2015) at the University of Melbourne. Awards: Awarded the Incoming Leaders Fellowship from Australia India Institute @ Delhi (2016), Next Step Initiative Fellowship (2015), Australia-China Young Scientist Fellowship (2014), Dyason Fellowship to undertake research at Department of Epidemiology, University of California (UCLA), Los Angeles, USA (2013). Early Career Researcher (ECR) Award (2013) from Alexander von Humboldt Foundation. Two of the papers she has co-authored with her PhD students received the Best Paper Award (2012) and Best Student Paper Award (2011). Awarded the Vice-Chancellor's Engagement Award (2010) and Vice-Chancellor's Knowledge Transfer Award (2008) for her research at the University of Melbourne. She also was awarded the Solander Fellowship (2007 and 2008) for research collaboration with the Departments of Neurosurgery and Radiation Physics, Lund University. She was among the short listed applicants for both 2009 and 2010 LOreal Australia for Women in Science Fellowship, out of over 200 female scientists applied in Australia. Professional Developments: She is the Associate Editor for International Journal of Wearable Device and International Journal of Biosensors & Bioelectronics, Editorial Board Member, an IEEE Senior Member and was the Program Co-Chair, Track Co-Chair, Publication Chair, Advisory Chair, Publicity Co-Chair, Track Chair, Track Co-chair, Session Chair and a Member of the Technical Program Committee (TPC) for 61 international conferences, Guest Editor for 3 Special Issues. In addition to publications, these works have acquired significant attention, resulting in an invitation to present 32 invited/guest lectures including Oxford University, Ohio State University and 7 IEEE talks. She has also conducted 14 journalists/media interviews and articles (Science Alert, Melbourne Voice, Moreland Leader and GradNews etc.) as well as two video interviews (ABC News, Australia-TV interview, 2014).

Evangelos Handakas is a scientific researcher in the Environmental Engineering Laboratory of the Department of Chemical Engineering of the Aristotle University of Thessaloniki (AUTH). He has a diploma in Chemical Engineering (AUTH) and M.Sc. in "Statistics and Modeling" (AUTH). His main research interests are in the field of computational modeling with an emphasis on biology and environmental systems and in computation, big-data analysis and bio-informatics science. Moreover, he advances computational methods and algorithms for exposure assessment and exposure reconstruction as well as for innovative statistical methods for the interpretation of environmental and biomonitoring data. He has contributed to several large-scale European scientific projects such as TRANSPHORM, CROME, HEALS, CheRRIE, PEC, ICARUS and the CEFIC LRI project INTEGRA.

Spyros Karakitsios is an environmental health scientist, with studies in physics (degree), environmental and computational chemistry (M.Sc.) and applied biology (PhD) of the University of Ioannina. He has worked 3 years at the European Commission Joint Research Centre (Institute for Health and Consumer Protection) with an overall 10 years of experience in environmental modelling and 4 years of experience in advanced human exposure science, health impact assessment of environmental stressors and neural computation. He is also breaking new ground in biologically-based models for human risk assessment. He has contributed to the large-scale European integrated projects HEIMTSA, 2-FUN, HEREPLUS, TRANSPHORM, URGENCHE, TAGS, INTERA, INTEGRA, HEALS. Since early 2011, he is scientific collaborator in EnvE-Lab.

Kijpokin Kasemsap received his BEng degree in Mechanical Engineering from King Mongkut's University of Technology, Thonburi, his MBA degree from Ramkhamhaeng University, and his DBA degree in Human Resource Management from Suan Sunandha Rajabhat University. Dr. Kasemsap is a Special Lecturer in the Faculty of Management Sciences, Suan Sunandha Rajabhat University, based in Bangkok, Thailand. Dr. Kasemsap is a Member of the International Economics Development and Research Center (IEDRC), the International Foundation for Research and Development (IFRD), and the International Innovative Scientific and Research Organization (IISRO). Dr. Kasemsap also serves on the International Advisory Committee (IAC) for the International Association of Academicians and Researchers (INAAR). Dr. Kasemsap is the sole author of over 250 peer-reviewed international publications and book chapters on business, education, and information technology. Dr. Kasemsap is included in the TOP 100 Professionals–2016 and in the 10th edition of 2000 Outstanding Intellectuals of the 21st Century by the International Biographical Centre, Cambridge, England.

M Ikram Ullah Lali received his master in software engineering degree from COMSATS Institute of Information Technology (CIIT), Islamabad, Pakistan in 2002. Later, after spending a few years in industry, he did his PhD from the same university. Currently, he is working as assistant professor in the department of CS & IT, University of Sargodha, Pakistan. His areas of interests includes formal methods, machine learning and social network data analysis. He is author of more than 30 research articles published in reputed national and internal journals. He has supervised more then 20 MS computer science students at university of Sargodha. He has worked at University of Groningen, Netherlands for some time for his research.

Max Lammertink is an Information Science graduate. Now working as a consultant on different cloud and CX solutions with a focus on the Oracle Sales Cloud. Certified Oracle Sales Cloud 2016 Implementation Specialist.

Christina Marouli studied biochemistry (B.A.), Urban and environmental policy (M.A.) and sociology (M.A and PhD) in the USA – with a specialisation in environment and social inequalities. Her doctoral research focused on urban environment, gender and class in Athens, Greece. Her present research interests include experiential learning, higher education and sustainability, sustainable cities, environmental behaviours and social change. She is teaching at the Environmental Studies Program of Deree – American College of Greece (ACG) mainly on environmental management, environmental justice, sustainable cities, research methods, education for sustainability. She has created a "Greening the Campus" course, an example of experiential learning. She is also the Director of the Center of Excellence for Sustainability at ACG. She has also taught at the Greek public university system in Greece on environmental protection, environmental education, occupational safety and health, sociology and environmental management. She has experience on environmental education - creating modules, training and doing research. She was also awarded a Fulbright award in the context of which she did research on multicultural environmental education programmes in the USA in collaboration with a Turkish professor. In addition, she has extensive consulting experience on environmental and occupational safety health issues in the private sector. In the context of her NGO work, she has worked on women's and children's issues and she was a co-founder of the Emergency Research Center.

Marley Costa Marques earned the Nursing (2016) degrees from the University of Fortaleza.

Sumitra Mukhopadhyay received the Master Degree and Ph.D degree, both from Jadavpur University in electronics and communication engineering in 2004 and 2009 respectively. She is currently an Assistant Professor with the University of Calcutta. Her main research interests include embedded system, field programmable gate array based prototype design, optimization, soft computing, evolutionary computation.

Raza Ul Mustafa completed his Bachelor in Computer Science in 2012. Then he received his MS degree in Computer Science in 2014. Currently, he is working as a Lecturer in Department of Computer Science COMSATS Institute of Information Technology (CIIT) Sahiwal. His research area includes Machine Learning, SEO, Software Defined Networking and Web Mining.

M. Saqib Nawaz is currently pursuing his PhD in Information Science from Peking University, China. He did his MS (Computer Science) from Sargodha University, Pakistan in 2014 and BS (Computer Engineering) from Engineering University, Peshawar, Pakistan in 2011. His areas of interest include Big Data Analytics, Formal Methods and Machine Learning.

Krystalia Papadaki holds a diploma in Chemical Engineering and is now pursuing her PhD at the Environmental Engineering Laboratory of the Department of Chemical Engineering, Aristotle University of Thessaloniki, Greece. Her research activities focus on the development and application of Quantitative Structure – Activity Relationships (QSARs) for the prediction of physicochemical and biochemical determinants of Absorption, Distribution, Metabolism and Excretion (ADME) processes of environmental chemical compounds. She has been involved in the European research projects INTEGRA, TRANSPHORM, CROME, HEALS, CheRRIE and PEC.

Mirian Caliope Dantas Pinheiro earned the Nursing (1984) and Licentiate in Nursing (1986) degrees from the University of Fortaleza; Specialization in Surgical Medical Nursing from the University of Fortaleza (1988); Specialization in Pediatric and Neonatal Nursing from the State University of Ceará (1992); M.Sc (1994) degree in Nursing from the Federal University of the State of Rio de Janeiro; Doctor in Nursing from the Federal University of Rio de Janeiro (1999). Full Professor at the University of Fortaleza, allocated in the Nursing Undergraduate and Professional Master's Degree Program in Technology and Innovation in Nursing. Coordinator of the Study Group Technologies in Child and Adolescent Health Care. She has experience in Nursing, with the emphasis in Pediatric Nursing, working mainly in the following subjects: Primary Health Care, Pediatric nursing, adolescent health education, community health and Public Health, Family Health Strategy. He has published in national and international periodicals with highlights for his citations.

Plácido Rogerio Pinheiro earned the B.Sc(1979) and Licentiate(1984) degrees in Mathematics by the Federal University of Ceará, Electrical Engineering (1983) by the University of Fortaleza, and the M.Sc(1990) degree in Mathematics by the Federal University of Ceará and Ph.D.(1998) in Systems Engineering and Computing degree by the Federal University of Rio de Janeiro. Currently, he is a Titular Professor of University of Fortaleza and Associate Professor of the State University of Ceará. He has experience in industrial processes modelling applying mathematical programming and multicriteria. His academic formation allows publishing in Applied Mathematics area, with an emphasis on Discrete and Combinatorics Mathematics, working mainly in Mathematical Programming and Multicriteria.

Suganya Ramamoorthy currently serves as an Assistant Professor at the Department of Information Technology at Thiagarajar College of Engineering, Madurai. Her areas of interest include Medical imaging, Big data Computing, Software Engineering, Video processing, Wireless Sensor Networks and Automation. Dr. R.Suganya completed her B.E. (Computer Science and Engineering) from R.V.S College of Engineering in 2003. She then completed her M.E (Computer Science and Engineering) from P.S.N.A College of Engineering. She completed her PhD in Information and Communication Engineering from Anna University, Chennai. She has published in 11 International Conference, 12 International Journal and One Edited Book Chapter. She has publication in eight Scopus indexed journals. He has published a Book on Classification of US liver images using Machine Learning techniques. She is a reviewer for many Journals. She is working with Thiagarajar College of Engineering, Madurai since 2006.

Salvador Sanchez-Alonso is a senior member of the Information Engineering group, a research unit dependent of the Computer Science Department of the University of Alcalá, Spain. He previously worked as an assistant professor at the Pontifical University of Salamanca, and also as a software engineer at a software solutions company in the UK. He earned a Ph.D. in Computer Science at the Polytechnic University of Madrid in 2005 with a research on learning object metadata design for better machine "understandability", and finished a degree on Library Science on 2011. He has participated or coordinated in several EU-funded projects in the last 10 years on the topics of learning object repositories and metadata, remarkably LUISA, Organic.Edunet, VOA3R, OPen Discovery Space, Organic.Lingua and agInfra just to name a few. His current research interests include Technology enhanced Learning, Learning object repositories, Web Science and Computer science education.

Denis Sarigiannis is Associate Professor of Environmental Engineering at the Aristotle University of Thessaloniki in Greece, Associate Professor of Environmental Health Engineering at the Institute for Advanced Study (IUSS) in Pavia, Italy and Professor and member of the Board of Directors at the graduate program on Environmental Chemical Risk at the Institute of Advanced Studies of the University of Pavia in Italy. Dr. Sarigiannis received his MSc in Energy and Resources and PhD in Engineering at the University of California, Berkeley under Prof. John P. Holdren, the Director of the White House Office of Science and Technology Policy. He is the President of the Mediterranean Scientific Association for Environmental Protection, Vice-President of the Hellenic Society of Toxicology and member of the Expert Committee on Air Pollution of the Greek Ministry of Health for the period 2013-2016. Since 2013 he is an advisor to the WHO European Centre for Environment and Health on combined exposure to multiple stressors in the indoor environment, human biomonitoring and endocrine disrupting chemicals. In 2015 he received the Bo Holmstedt award from EUROTOX and the Bo Holmstedt Foundation for toxicology contributions to drugs and chemicals.

Nesma Settouti is an Assistant professor at Tlemcen University, Algeria. She received her Engineer degree in Electrical Biomedical from the Tlemcen University in 2009. In 2011, she obtains a Magisterial degree in the same option. She also received a Ph.D in Biomedical Engineering from the University of Tlemcen (Algeria) in co-direction with LIMOS of Aubière (France) in 2016. Her research interests are in computer assisted medical decision support systems, ensemble methods, neural networks, clustering methods, optimization, classification and artificial intelligence. She had published a great deal of research studies published at national and international journals, conference proceedings as well as chapter book in computer assisted medical decision support systems.

Miguel-Angel Sicilia is full professor at the Computer Science Department of the University of Alcalá. He obtained a University degree in Computer Science from the Pontifical University of Salamanca in Madrid, Spain (1996) and a PhD from Carlos III University in Madrid, Spain (2002). He is currently director of a PhD program in applied IT and coordinates a MSc program on the same topics. He has been involved in the last ten years in different research projects, and coordinated the agINFRA and SEMAGROW FP7 projects on research infrastructures and Big Data in agricultural sciences. His current research interests include metadata and ontologies, and in general applied computational techniques and machine learning. He has published more than sixty papers in international journals and served on the editorial boards or scientific committees of numerous international journals and conferences.

Rajaram Sivasubramaniam works as an Associate Professor, Department of Electronics and Communication Engineering, Thiagarajar College of Engineering, Madurai, India. He completed his B.E (Electronics and Communication Engineering), M.E., (Microwave & Optical Engineering) and Ph.D in Madurai Kamaraj University. He received Post Doctoral Fellowship from Georgia Institute of Technology. He has received the Young Scientist Fellowship award from TNSCST during 2001-2002 and BOYSCAST Fellowship from DST during 2010-2011.He has guided 10 PhD Scholars. He has published research articles more than 150 International conferences and 80 reputed journals. He is a reviewer for IEEE transaction and many reputed Journals. He is the co-coordinator of DST project on TIFAC Core in Wireless Technologies –Phase II, and Co-investigator for FIST, DST project and AICTE, New Delhi. In addition to, he did many Consultancy projects.

Marco Spruit is a researcher at the Information and Computing Sciences department of Utrecht University in the Netherlands. Marco's research theme centres around Analytic Systems for Applied Data Science, with special attention to Health Analytic Systems. Marco serves on the editorial boards of the international journals on Decision Analytics, Business Intelligence Research, Autonomic Computing, and Computer Information Systems. Before 2007 Marco worked in industry as a software developer for fourteen years in the fields of Business Intelligence and Text Analytics.

Pulkit Anupam Srivastava is pursuing B.Tech in Bioinformatics from Jaypee University of Information Technology, Solan, Himachal Pradesh, India.

Index

F

Feature Selection 278, 296, 302-303, 306, 315, 318, 341-342, 362, 387-388

Fold Recognition 50, 56, 60-61, 66, 79

Fragment 61, 131, 156, 207, 212, 228, 241

Fragment Docking 212

G

Gene 2-4, 9, 19-20, 27-28, 33-35, 47, 81-82, 85, 90-91, 93-94, 116, 146-147, 149-152, 154, 160, 162, 174-179, 188-190, 192-194, 197-198, 200, 337-342, 344-353, 356-357, 361, 363

Genomic Medicine 7-8, 10, 91

Genomics 1-2, 6, 8-9, 17, 21, 26-27, 29-31, 34-35, 47, 82-83, 91, 94-95, 150, 188, 200, 357

Gestalt Theory 243, 262, 268

Google 6, 272-278, 282, 285-286, 292-293

Graph Theory 10, 190, 372

H

Health 1-11, 13-22, 27, 29-30, 80-81, 84, 86, 89-92, 99-101, 103, 111, 115-118, 124, 128, 132-133, 137, 145-146, 165-166, 172-175, 178, 180, 243-244, 252, 255, 269, 272-276, 286, 292-293, 323, 364-367, 371-372, 374-375, 381-382

Health Informatics 1-4, 7, 10-11, 15-16, 18-21

Healthcare Institution 292

Healthcare Professionals 244, 274, 286

Healthcare Providers 244, 255, 284-286, 292

high dimensional dataset 314, 316, 318

High-Throughput Docking 228, 230

High-throughput Screening Data 1-2

Homology Modelling 50, 55-56, 59-60, 79, 217

I

Individualized Medicine 19

Influenza 272-278, 280, 282-286, 292-293

Internal Dosimetry 129, 137

L

Library 5, 56, 60, 79, 189-190, 217, 228, 241

Ligand 63, 212, 214-215, 241

Long-term Healthcare 264, 268

M

Machine Learning 2-3, 7, 10, 30-31, 47, 115, 146, 148-149, 156, 158-159, 187, 217, 219, 278, 294, 322-324, 326, 332, 334-335, 362, 381, 387, 389-390, 392

Machine learning algorithms 3, 10, 149, 156, 278, 324, 335, 381, 389, 392

medical diagnosis 333-334, 338, 344, 367, 380-381

Medical Genetics 80, 84, 92-93

Medical Image processing 380-381, 384, 387

Metabolomics 17, 20, 88-89, 95, 116-117, 128, 162-163, 165, 178, 187-188, 190, 194

MicroRNAs 26, 28, 33, 47, 357

Minimisation 59, 63, 79, 210

Molecular Dynamics 63-65, 228

N

NANDA 367, 369-370, 373-376

NB 279

Netica-J 371-372

Network Model 135, 190, 196-197

Next Generation Medicine 1

Next Generation Sequencing 189

O

Omics 6, 13, 17, 20, 28, 80, 87, 116-117, 128, 146-147, 162, 172-175, 188, 199

Opinion Mining 273, 292

Optim Co-Forest 294-296, 299, 302-303, 306-309, 311-316, 318

P

Pathway Analysis 163-165, 177, 187

Pattern Recognition 3, 10, 146, 187, 326

Patterns 21, 30, 32, 47, 86, 90, 100, 106, 109, 118, 120-121, 124-125, 127-128, 135, 147-150, 153, 155-156, 158, 160, 162-163, 165, 168, 170, 175, 177, 187, 189, 193, 247-248, 274-275, 322, 325-326, 330, 333-335, 368-369, 387

Personal Sensor 118, 135, 144

Pharmacogenetics 82-83, 92

Pharmacogenomics 82, 92

Pharmacoproteomics 92-93, 95

Physiology Based Biokinetic Models 144

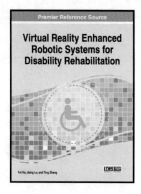
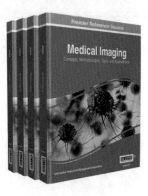

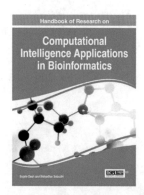

 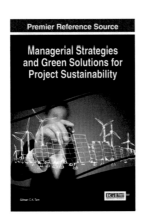  

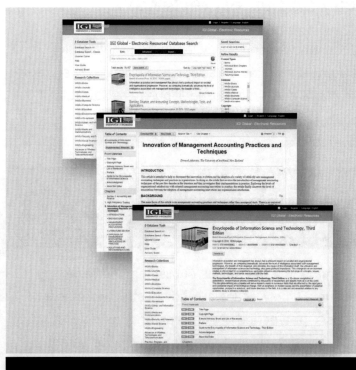

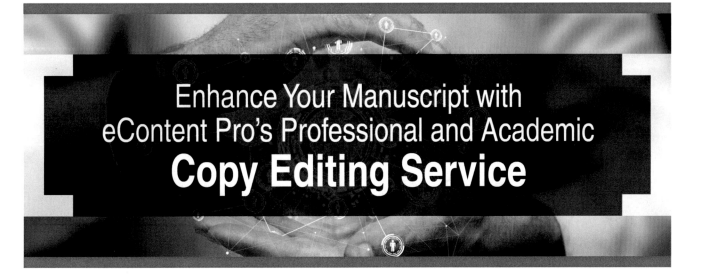

Information Resources Management Association

Become an IRMA Member

Members of the **Information Resources Management Association (IRMA)** understand the importance of community within their field of study. The Information Resources Management Association is an ideal venue through which professionals, students, and academicians can convene and share the latest industry innovations and scholarly research that is changing the field of information science and technology. Become a member today and enjoy the benefits of membership as well as the opportunity to collaborate and network with fellow experts in the field.

IRMA Membership Benefits:

- **One FREE Journal Subscription**

- **30% Off Additional Journal Subscriptions**

- **20% Off Book Purchases**

- Updates on the latest events and research on Information Resources Management through the IRMA-L listserv.

- Updates on new open access and downloadable content added to Research IRM.

- A copy of the Information Technology Management Newsletter twice a year.

- A certificate of membership.

IRMA Membership $195

Scan code or visit **irma-international.org** and begin by selecting your free journal subscription.

Membership is good for one full year.

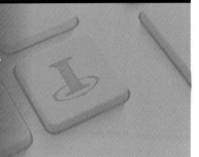